2.49
0/17
M.C

DICKENS'S
DICTIONARY
OF
LONDON
1888

An *Unconventional* Handbook

"Mr Weller's knowledge of London was extensive and peculiar" - Pickwick

Old House Books
Moretonhampstead
Devon
www.OldHouseBooks.co.uk

Old House Books produce facsimile copies of long out of print maps and books that we believe deserve a second innings. Our reprints of Victorian and Edwardian maps and guide books are of interest to genealogists and local historians. Other titles have been chosen to explore the character of life in years gone by and are helpful to anyone who wishes to know a bit more about the lives of their ancestors, whether they were respectable gentlewomen or cunning poachers.

For details of other Old House Books titles please see the final pages of this book and, for the most up to date illustrated information, please visit our website www.OldHouseBooks.co.uk or request a catalogue.

The first edition of this book was compiled and published by Charles Dickens, son of the famous author, in 1888. See also Dickens's Dictionary of The Thames 1887 also published by Old House Books.

This edition was published in 1993 by
© Old House Books
Reprinted 1997, 2001, 2003, 2006 and 2007
The Old Police Station, Pound Street, Moretonhampstead,
Devon TQ13 8PA UK
Tel: 01647 440707   Fax: 01647 440202
info@OldHouseBooks.co.uk   www.OldHouseBooks.co.uk
ISBN 978 1 873590 04 1

Jacket illustration: The New Law Courts, London by George Stein
The new law courts were completed in 1888 a few years before this book was first published.

PREFACE.

IN issuing the revised, and, I venture to hope, much improved edition of the "Dictionary of London" for 1888, I am happy to take this opportunity of expressing my grateful thanks to the public for the very large measure of favour which has been accorded to the book, as well as to the ladies and gentlemen who have so kindly responded to my appeal for corrections and advice.

Although considerations of space have made it impossible for me to adopt all the valuable suggestions which have reached me, I have endeavoured to make such a selection of subjects as should be of most practical value and interest, and every care has been taken to render the information contained in the book accurate and trustworthy. I shall be greatly obliged to any correspondents who may aid me still further in carrying out these objects in future issues.

Charles Dickens.

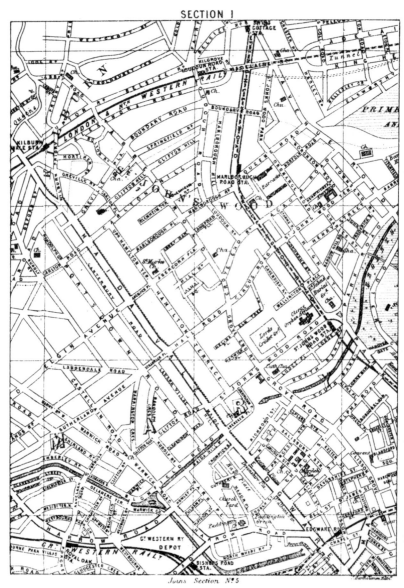

See also *A coloured street Map of London 1843*. Published by Old House Books

SECTION 2

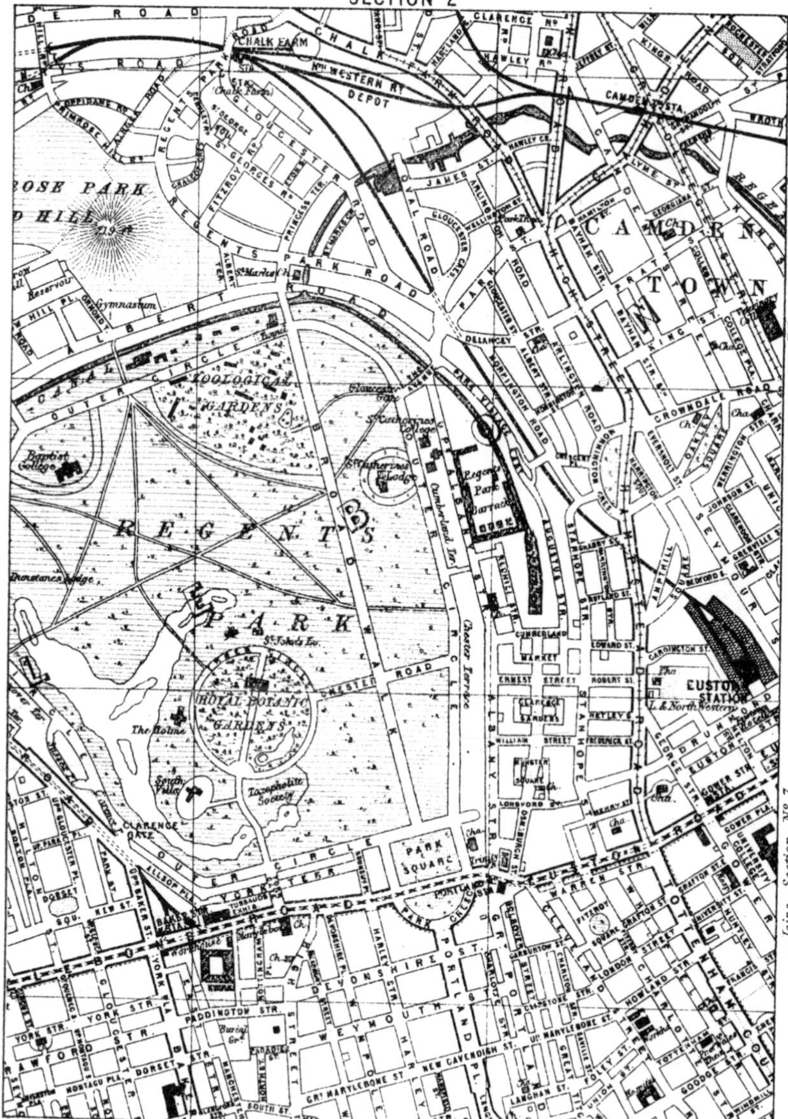

Joins Section No. 8

Joins Section No. 7

Joins Section No. 6

J. Bartholomew Edin.

Continued on Nos 7 & 8

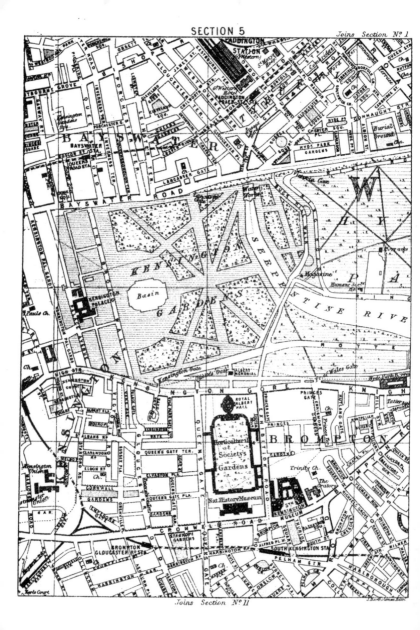

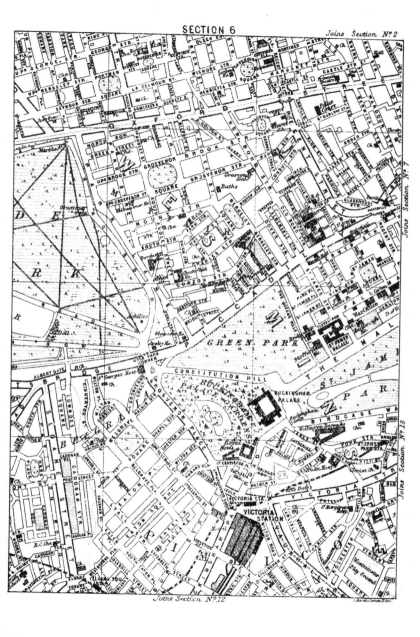

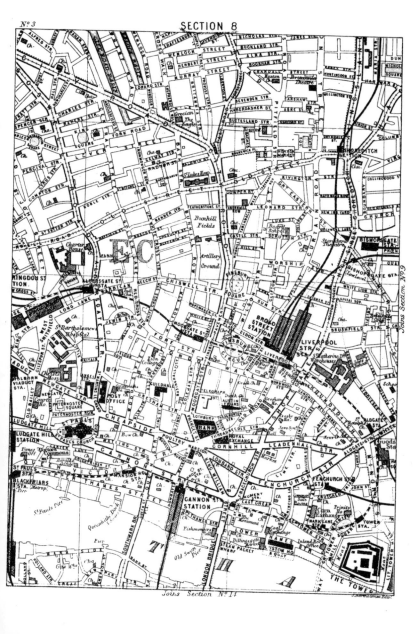

No⁴

REGENT'S CANAL

EASTERN RAILWAY

LICHFIELD RD

RAYNARD ST

RALEIGH SQUARE

BOW ROAD

BOW ROAD STA

Drapers Alms Ho.

High St

Board School

Mile End Workhouse

Jew's Burial Ground

Bancroft's Alms Ho.

Mile End

Tower Hamlets & City of London Cemetery

Board Sch.

Gt Central Gas Wks

FRIENDLY ST

Wheler Cemetery

Commercial Gas Works

STEPNEY GREEN STA

Ben Johnson Rd

STEPNEY

Ch.

HAYFIELD

CATHERINE

CAYLEY ST

COMMERCIAL ROAD EAST

CREPTON ST

HENRY ST

RHODES ST

NIXON ST

LIMEHOUSE CUT

Gt CENTRAL ST

BURDETT RD

GUILFORD RD

STEPNEY

YORK SQ

YORK RD

CLIFF

LIMEHOUSE

MEDLAND ST

LIMEHOUSE BASIN

LIMEHOUSE STA

WEST INDIA DOCK ROAD

EAST INDIA DOCK ROAD

PIGOTT ST

CANTON STREET

PENNY FIELDS

GRUNDY

WEST INDIA DOCKS STA

KING

Regents Canal Ent.

Limehouse Cut End

ROPEMAKERS FIELDS

NARROW ST

Limehouse Pier

Limehouse

Globe Stairs Pier

Cuckolds Pt

Limehouse Ent.

Limehouse Basin

Upper Dock

WEST INDIA DOCK (Import)

Globe Pond

Lavender Pond

Nelsons Dk

Ch.

Queens Wf

WEST INDIA DOCK (Export)

Acorn Pond

Limehouse Ent.

SOUTH WEST IN

SOUT

Continued on No 15

J. Bartholomew, Edin.

CHELSEA

OLD BROMPTON

SW

NEW BROMPTON

Cancer Hosp.

COLLEGE PL.

LITTLE CHELSEA

CHELSEA

WEST LONDON CEMETERY

Cha.

St Marks College

CHELSEA STA.

Ch.

Cheyne Walk

Pier

Lindsey Row

Pier

Pier

EXTENSION RAILWAY

Gas Works

Bd Sch.

Battersea Ch.

BATTERSEA

Chelsea Basin

Eagley Lane

Sands End

BRIDGE

SURREY ROAD

The Town Meadows

Battersea Reach

Nat. Societys Training Col.

Green Lane

BATTERSEA STA.

Battersea Creek

Price's Candle Ws.

FALCON ROAD

J. Bartholomew Edin.

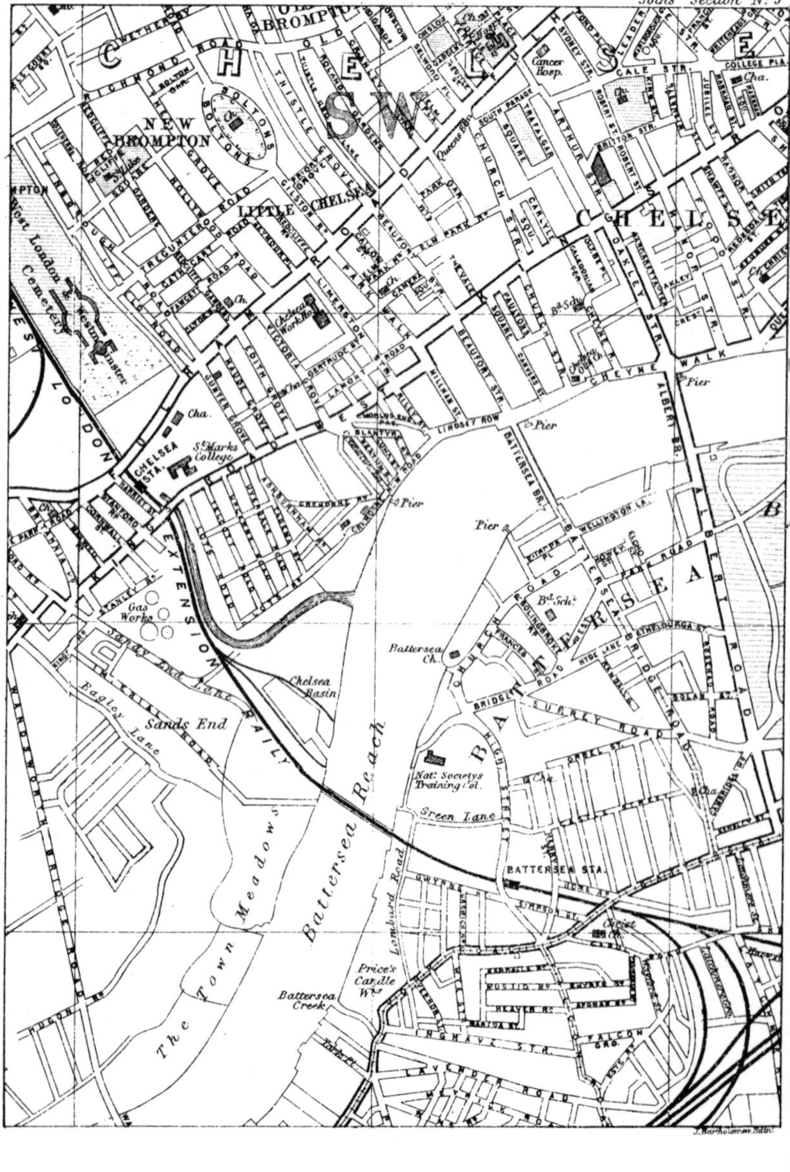

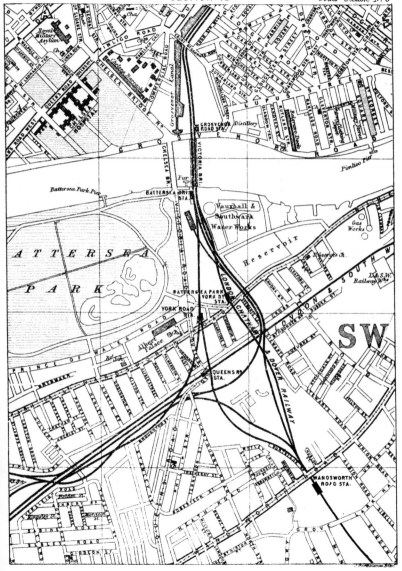

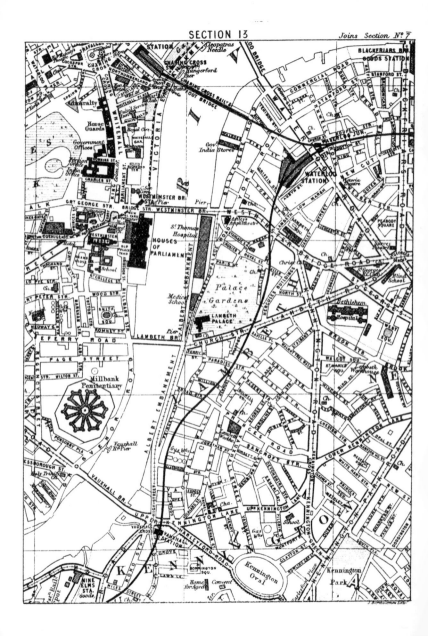

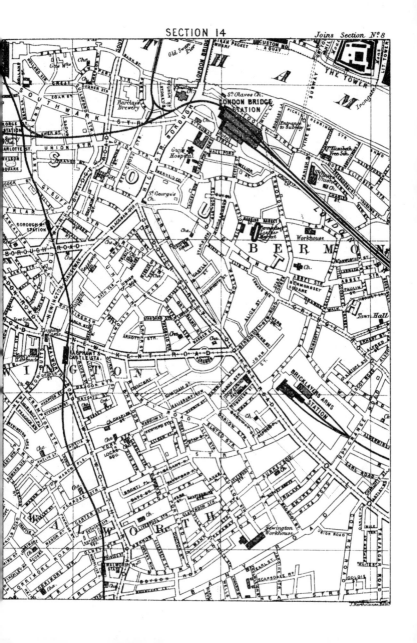

Continued on Nº.10

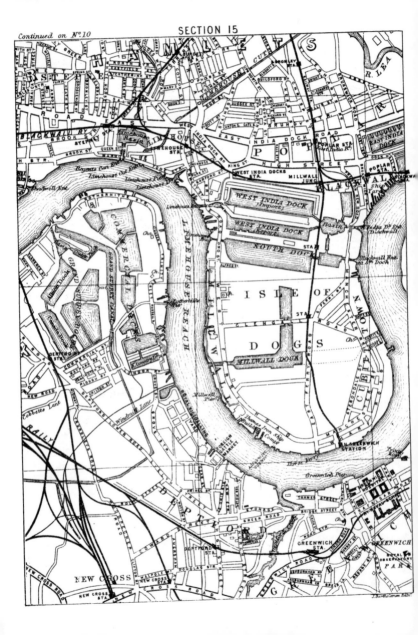

J. Bartholomew Edin.

DICKENS'S
DICTIONARY OF LONDON.

Hospitals, Hotels, Householders (Hints to), Houses, Houses of Parliament, Humane Society Royal), Hungary, Hurlingham Club, Hyde Park.

ILLUMINATIONS, Imperial Theatre, India, Indian Section of South Kensington Museum, Inland Revenue, Inns of Court (The), Insurance Companies, International Club, Invalid Carriages and Chairs, Irish Exhibition in London, Irish Office, Ironmongers' Company (The), Isle of Dogs, Isthmian Club, Italian Exhibition, Italy.

JAPAN, Jews, Judge Advocate-General's Office, Junior Army and Navy Club, Junior Athenæum Club, Junior Carlton, Junior Constitutional Club, Junior Garrick Club, Junior Travellers' Club, Junior United Service Club.

KENNEL Club, Kennington Park, Kensington Gardens, Kensington Palace, Kew Gardens, King's College, King's College School, King's Cross.

LADIES Shopping, Ladies' Victoria Club, Lady Artists (Soc. of), Lambeth Bridge, Lambeth Palace, Lancaster Club, La Plata, Law Courts, Lawn Tennis, Law Society (Incorporated) of the United Kingdom, Leicester Square, Liberia (Republic of), Libraries (Circulating), Libraries (Public), Lincoln's Inn, Liverpool Street Station, Lloyd's, Local Government Board, Local Marine Board, Lodging Houses (Common), Lodgings, Lodging Houses (Model), London Bridge, London Bridge Station, London Crystal Palace, London Stone, Lord Advocate's Office, Lord Chamberlain's Department, Lord Great Chamberlain's Office, Lord Mayor's Show, Lost Property, Lowther Arcade, Ludgate Hill, Lunacy Commissioners, Lyceum Theatre, Lyric Club.

MADAGASCAR, Magistrates, Mansion House, Mansion House Street, Maps, Marble Arch, Markets, Marlborough Club, Marlborough House, Marylebone Theatre, Medical Education and Registration, Mendicity Society, Mercers' Company (The), Merchant Taylors (The), Merchant Taylors' School, Meteorological Office, Metropolitan Board of Works, Mexico, Middle-class Hospital, Middlesex County Officers, Middlesex Magistrates, Middlesex Sessions House, Military and Royal Naval Club, Military Home District, Milk, Millbank Prison, Mines (Royal School of), Mint

(Royal), Missionary Museum, Model Lodging Houses, Monte Video, Monument, Moving, Museums, Music, Music Halls, Music (Royal Academy of).

NATIONAL Church Club, National Club, National Conservative Club, National Gallery, National Liberal Club, National Portrait Gallery, National Union Club, Natural History Museum, Naval and Military Club, Naval School, Needlework (Art), Royal School of, Netherlands, New Club, Newgate, Newgate Street, New Granada, New Jerusalem Church, New Law Courts, New Oxford and Cambridge Club, New River, New Road, New Sadler's Wells Theatre, New Salisbury Club, New South Wales, Newspapers, New Thames Yacht Club, New University Club, New Zealand, Nicaragua (Republic of), Northbrook Indian Club, North London Collegiate School for Girls, North London Collegiate School, Novelty Theatre, Nuisances, Nurses.

OIL Colours, Institute of Painters in, Old Bailey, Old Paulines' Club, Olympia, Olympic Theatre, Omnibuses, Opera Comique, Orange Free State, Oriental Club, Orleans Club, Oxford and Cambridge Club, Oxford Street, Oysters.

PACKING, Paddington Station, Paintings and Sculpture, Pall Mall, Pall Mall Club, Paraguay, Parcels, Parcels Post, Parkes Museum of Hygiene, Parliamentary Constituencies, Parliamentary Papers, Parochial District Establishments, Parochial School Districts, Parochial Sick Asylum Districts, Patent Museum, Patent Office, Paternoster Row, Paulatim Club, Pavilion Theatre, Pentonville Prison, People's Palace (The), Persia, Peru, Petty Sessional Divisions in the Metropolitan Police District, Piccadilly, Picture Galleries, Pigeon Clubs, Pigeons, Police, Police Courts, Police Force (City), Police Force (Metropolitan), Police Office (City), Police Office (Metropolitan), Police Orphanage (Metropolitan and City), Portland Club, Portugal, Postage and Inland Revenue Stamps, Postal Regulations, Poste Restante, Post Office, Post Office Savings Bank Department, Poultry and Fancy Fowls, Pratt's Club, Presbyterian Church of England, Press Club, Primitive Methodist Connexion, Primrose

Club, Primrose Hill, Prince of Wales's Theatre, Princess's Theatre, Prisons, Private Letter Boxes, Private Theatricals, Private Wires, Privy Council Office, Prussia, Public Halls, Public Offices, Public Schools' Club, Public Works Loan Board, Putney Embankment.

QUEEN Anne's Bounty and First Fruits and Tenths Office, Queensland.

RACING, Railway Commissioners, Railways, Railway Stations, Railway Ticket Offices, Raleigh Club, Ranelagh Club, Ratcliff Highway, Reading Rooms, Record Office, Reform Club, Regent Circus, Regent's Park, Regent Street, Registers of Births, Marriages, and Deaths, Restaurants, Riding Horses and Schools, Roumania, Rowing, Royal Academy of Arts, Royal Academy of Music, Royal Botanic Society, Royal College of Surgeons, Royal Colonial Institute, Royal Courts of Justice, Royal Exchange, Royal Horticultural Society, Royal Institution, Royal London Yacht Club, Royal Naval School, Royal Palace of Justice, Royal Society of British Artists, Royal Society, Royal Thames Yacht Club, Royalty Theatre, Russia.

SADLER'S Wells Theatre, St. George's Club, St. George's Hall, St. James's Club, St. James's Hall, St. James's Palace, St. James's Park, St. James's Street, St. James's Theatre, St. John of Jerusalem in England (Order of), St. Pancras, St. Paul's Cathedral, St. Paul's Churchyard, St. Paul's School, St. Stephen's Club, Salisbury Club, Salisbury Club (New), Salters' Company (The), Salvation Army, San Domingo, San Salvador (Republic of), Sanger's Amphitheatre, Sanitary Assurance Association, Savage Club, Savile Club, Savoy Theatre, Scandinavian Club, School Board, School Board Committees, School Board Constituencies, School Board (Members of), Scotland Yard (Great), Scottish Club, Sea-water Baths, Servants, Servia, Sessions of the Peace, Seven Dials, Sharpers, Shoeblacks, Siam, Sight-Seeing, Sion College, Skating Club, Skinners' Hall (The), Smithfield Club, Soane Museum, Society of Arts, Society of British Artists (The), Soho Bazaar, Somerset House, South African Republic, South Australia, South Kensington Museum, Southwark

Bridge, Southwark Park, Spain, Standard Theatre, Stationery Office, Statues, Steamboats, Stock Exchange, Strand, Strand Theatre, Stratford Market, Streets, Sunday, Suppers, Surgical Aid Society, Surrey County Officers, Surrey Magistrates, Surrey Theatre, Surveyors, Sweden and Norway, Swedenborgians, Switzerland.

TELEGRAPH Department, Telegraph Offices, Telephones, Temperance Restaurants, Temple, Terry's Theatre, Thames (The), Thatched House Club, Theatres, Toole's Theatre, Tourist Agencies, Tower of London, Tower Subway, Trafalgar Square, Tramways, Travellers' Club, Treasury, Tricycling, Trinity College, Trinity House, Trotting, Turf Club, Turkey, Tussaud's Exhibition of Waxworks and Napoleonic Relics, Tyburn Gate.

UNION Club, Unionist Club, United Club, United Service Club, United Service Institution(Royal), United States, United Telephone Company (Limited), United University Club, University College, University College School, University of London, Uruguay (Republic of Monte Video), Uxbridge-road.

VAUDEVILLE Theatre, Vauxhall Bridge, Vegetarian Restaurants, Venezuela (United States of), Vernon Town and River Club, Vestries and District Boards of Works, Veterinary College Museum, Victoria, Victoria Club, Victoria Coffee Music Hall, Victoria Embankment, Victoria Park, Victoria Stations, Vine Club, Vintners' Company (The), Volunteers.

WAR Office, Water, Water-Colours, Royal Institute of Painters in, Water-Colours, Royal Society of Painters in, Waterloo Bridge, Waterloo Station, Weights and Measures, Wellington Club, Wesleyan Methodists, and Places of Worship, Western Australia, Westminster Abbey, Westminster Bridge, Westminster Hall, Westminster School, White Friars Club, Whitehall, Whitehall Club, White's Club, Wimbledon Common, Windham Club, Woods, Forests, and Land Revenues.

YACHTING, York Club, Young Men's Christian Association Young Men's Christian Institute.

ZOOLOGICAL Society of London.

Academy of Arts (Royal).
—(See ROYAL ACADEMY.)

Adelphi (The)
(Map 7).—Comprises three or four streets on the south side of the Strand and the handsome Adelphi-ter facing the river, and was built about the middle of the last century by four brothers of the name of Adam, whose names were given to the streets, such as Adam-st, Robert-st, &c. The Adelphi-ter has recently been entirely renovated, and now that the Embankment has concealed the muddy foreshore of the river, is a most desirable place of residence. At his house on Adelphi-ter David Garrick died in 1779. In John-st, Adelphi, is the house of the Society of Arts, which will be found described under its proper heading. The greater part of the Adelphi is built upon arches, which at one time were the chosen resort of thieves and bad characters of every kind. The alterations which were made when the Adelphi arches were put into thorough repair some few years ago, finally closed this modern Alsatia.

Adelphi Theatre,
411, Strand, built 1858 (Map 7); the old house, the least convenient and the most popular in London, having been pulled down. The present building is handsome and roomy, with a large balcony in lieu of dress-circle. The old Adelphi was for years the recognised home of melodrama and screaming farce, and this speciality is fairly preserved in the productions of the modern house. There is only one entrance—from the Strand—to all parts of the house, except the gallery, the door of which is in Bull-inn-ct, Maiden-la, but there are additional exits at the right-hand side into Bull Inn-ct, which can be opened in case of fire. The lessees having recently acquired additional house property adjoining the theatre, great improvements have been and are being made in the principal entrances. NEAREST *Ry. Stns.*, Charing + (Dis. & S.E.); *Omnibus Rtes.*, Strand, St. Martin's-la, Chancery-la, Waterloo-br; *Cab Rank*, Bedford-st.

Admiralty.
—The Admiralty, by which all the affairs of the navy and cognate services are administered, is divided into two great departments—the naval and the civil. The naval department, which is in Whitehall (NEAREST *Ry. Stns.*, Charing + (Dis. & S.E.); *Omnibus Rtes.*, Strand and Whitehall; *Cab Rank*, Horse Guards), is sub-divided into the following branches: The Secretary's Department, the Contract and Purchase Department, the Department of the Controller of the Navy, the Naval Store Department, the Victualling Department, the Department of the Director of Transports with a special sub-division for India, the Hydrographic Department, the Coast Guard Compassionate Fund, the Coast Guard Life Insurance Fund, and the Commissioner for Property and Income-tax for the Naval Department. The office hours in these departments are 10 to 5. The hours in the Civil Department are also from 10 to 5, and the branches of the department, with their addresses, are as follows: The Department of the Accountant-General of the Navy and Controller of Navy Pay, 57, Spring-gdns (NEAREST *Ry. Stns.*, Charing + (S.E. and Dis.); *Omnibus Rte.* and *Cab Rank*, Trafalgar-sq); the Director-General of the Medical Department of the Navy, Whitehall, S.W.; the Department of the Director of Works, 21, Craven-st, W.C.; and the Nautical Almanac Office, 3, Verulam-buildings, Gray's-inn (NEAREST *Railway Station*, King's + (Metropolitan); *Omnibus Routes*, Gray's-inn-rd and Holborn; *Cab Rank*, Holborn). The Royal Schools of Naval Architecture and Marine Engineering form part of the Royal Naval College, Greenwich. The building itself was constructed about 1726 by Ripley, satirised by Pope in the Dunciad; the screen, with its characteristic ornaments, being designed by the brothers Adam, 1776. The remains of Lord Nelson lay in state here. Adjoining the Admiralty is a house for the first lord, and formerly junior lords had residences in the northern wing. There is here a portrait of Lord Nelson, painted at Palermo in 1799 by Guzzardi, wearing the Sultan's diamond plume, and in the secretary's house are portraits of the persons who have filled that office. The Admiralty has direct telegraphic communication with Portsmouth and the other royal naval yards.

Advertising appears a very simple affair, but it is really a difficult art, and is becoming yearly more difficult. It is still possible, with a comparatively small sum judiciously expended, to produce an almost startling result. On the other hand, there are few things more easy than to fool away £1,000 in advertisements without producing any result at all. A man who could spend say £50,000 a year in advertising anything would probably make his fortune. But such need not be catered for here. The ordinary advertiser must be careful so to lay out every shilling that it shall ensure at the least a fair twelve-pennyworth of publicity. To this end he has three points to consider : First, the nature of the things advertised; second, the special public to which the advertisement may be advantageously addressed ; and third, the particular organs best calculated to reach that special public. The subject is too large to be exhaustively discussed here, and indeed would require a volume to itself. But a glance at the list of London newspapers will give as good an idea of the organs to choose in each case as can be given by anything but actual experience. One especial desideratum of the skilful advertiser is what is termed "display," and against this most of the daily papers strongly set their faces, the *Times* being especially fastidious on this head, and having elaborated its restrictions to a refinement which renders evasion almost impossible. Those who do not care to be at the trouble of going to the newspaper office can forward their advertisements through one of the agents. Among the best of these may be mentioned— Adams and Francis, 59, Fleet-st ; Browne, 125, Queen Victoria-st ; Clark, Son, and Platt, 85, Gracechurch-st ; F. L. May and Co., 159, Piccadilly ; C. Mitchell and Co., 12 and 13, Red Lion-ct, Fleet-st ; Sell, 167, Fleet-st ; Street, 30, Cornhill ; Watson, 150, Fleet-st ; Willing, 125, Strand.

Agricultural Hall, Royal (Map 3).—A building of the railway-station order, close by the Angel at Islington. The Christmas cattle show of the Smithfield Club is held here, as are also sundry horse and other shows. The building is now commonly opened during the winter holidays with a variety show in the nature of an old-fashioned fair, with menageries, fat ladies, merry-go-rounds, swings, and all the rest of the queer entertainments which never seem to lose their popularity. The Mohawk Minstrels generally occupy the smaller hall with a negro minstrelsy entertainment. NEAREST *Ry. Stns.*, King's ✠ (G.N. and Met.), Highbury (N.L.) ; *Omnibus Rtes.*, Islington High-st, Pentonville-rd, and City-rd ; *Cab Rank*, Upper-st.

Albany (The) (Map 6) is, although not intended for such by the owners or occupiers, a very convenient thoroughfare for those who have the audacity so to use it, from Burlington-gdns to Piccadilly. The Albany is a collection of queer houses, let as chambers. At present it has but little significance, but when George IV. was old, and when Queen Victoria was young, the "Bachelor of the Albany" was a recognised variety of the "man about town." Many literary celebrities have lived in the Albany ; and in the days when the uncomfortable fashion of early breakfast parties obtained—when Sydney Smith jested, and when Rogers prosed—the old houses were a favourite resort of the wits and beaux of the time. The names of "Monk" Lewis, Macaulay, Bulwer, and Byron, are inseparably connected with these chambers.

Albemarle Club, 25, Albemarle-st, W. — For ladies and gentlemen : above 21 years old, if gentlemen, or 18 years, if ladies. Entrance fee, £8 8s. ; sub., £5 5s.

Albert Embankment (Map 13).—The Albert Embankment, on the right bank, from a point a little below Vauxhall-br to Westminster-br. The carriage way diverges to the right after leaving Lambeth Palace, and enters Westminster-br-rd at the corner of Stangate ; St. Thomas's Hospital, and a walk for foot passengers only, occupying the river frontage at this point. With the exception of Lambeth Palace, the fine specimens of modern architectural boldness recently erected by Messrs. Doulton, and the carefully designed new St. Thomas's Hospital, the Albert Embankment presents along its length of rather more than half a mile but little to attract attention. NEAREST *Ry. Stns.*, Vauxhall and Westminster-br ; *Omnibus Rte.*, Westminster-br-rd ; *Steamboat Pier*, Lambeth.

Albert Exhibition Palace (The), Battersea-pk (Map 12).— Opened in May, 1885 This is the elegant glass and iron structure well-known in Dublin, where it was re-opened by H.R.H. the Duke of Edinburgh in 1872, and now re-erected, with substantial additions and improvements. The main portion of the edifice consists of a nave 60 ft. high, 473 ft. long, and 84 ft. wide, with a gallery all round. At the back of this are various offices, refreshment, smoking, billiard, and reading rooms, and over them, for the entire length of the building, a very fine picture-gallery. At the end of the nave is the great "Connaught Hall," specially adapted for musical entertainments of a high class, and in it there is one of the largest and finest organs ever constructed. The original Albert Palace Company having collapsed, the building and grounds passed last year into the hands of the enterprising Mr. William Holland, but were closed at the time of our going to press, and without announcement that they are to be re-opened this season.

Albert Hall, Kensington-rd (Map 5), was opened in May, 1871, and is a huge building of elliptical form in the style of the Italian Renaissance, the materials of the façade being entirely red brick and terra-cotta. The larger exterior diameter is 272 ft., interior 219 ft. ; the smaller exterior 238 ft., interior 185 ft. The frieze above the balcony was executed by Messrs. Minton, Hollins & Co., and is divided into compartments containing allegorical designs by Messrs. Armitage, Armstead, Horsley, Marks, Pickersgill, Poynter, and Yeames. There are two box entrances—on the east and west—with a private doorway from the Horticultural Society's Gardens on the south side, and separate entrances on either side for the balcony, the gallery, and the area, and for the platforms on either side of the great organ. The interior, which is amphitheatrical in construction—like, for example, the Coliseum at Rome— is not very appropriate to any purpose for which it is ever likely to be required except musical performances on a large scale. For gladiatorial exhibitions of any kind, the central area, measuring 102 ft. by 68 ft., would, of course, though rather small, be capitally adapted. A bull-fight, even, on a very small scale, might be managed here. As a matter of fact, it is used almost exclusively for concerts, when the area is filled up with seats, and the surrounding tiers, specially constructed with a view to commanding the centre of the building, are filled with an audience whose entire attention is specially directed to the extremity, where a space has been chipped out for the orchestra. However, it is a "big thing," at all events. At the top of the hall is the picture gallery, capable of accommodating 2,000 persons, and used on ordinary occasions as a promenade. There are hydraulic lifts to the upper floors. The hall is 135 ft. in height, and is crowned by a domed skylight of painted glass, having a central opening or lantern, with a star of gas-burners. Altogether the hall is calculated to hold an audience of about 8,000. The organ was built by Mr. Henry Willis. There are five rows of keys — belonging to the choir, great, solo, swell, and pedal organs — 130 stops, and 10,000 pipes, the range being ten octaves. The orchestra accommodates 1,000 performers. Large tanks are provided in case of fire on the roof of the picture gallery, and supplied with water from the artesian well of the Rl. Horticultural Society, 430 ft. deep. NEAREST *Ry. Stns.*, High-st, Kensington, and S. Kensington ; *Omnibus Rte.*, Kensington-rd ; *Cab Rank*, Queen's-gate.

Albert Memorial, Hyde-pk (Map 5). — Erected to the memory of the late Prince Consort at a cost of £120,000. The memorial was designed by Sir Gilbert Scott, and consists of a bronze gilt statue of the Prince Consort by Foley, under a Gothic canopy, and surrounded by four groups of statuary—America by John Bell, Africa by Theed, Asia by Foley, and Europe by Macdowell. There are several smaller groups of statues by Weekes, Calder, Marshall, Thorneycroft, &c. Around the basement are a large number of life-sized figures by Birnie Phillip and Armstead. NEAREST *Ry. Stns.,&c.,see*ALBERTHALL *above.*

Alexandra Club, 12, Grosvenor-street, W.—For ladies only. Proprietary. Members are elected by the Committee. No one is eligible who has been, or who probably would be, precluded from attending Her Majesty's Drawing Rooms. The entrance fee is £3 3s., and the annual subscription is for town members, £3 3s., and country members, £2 2s. Any further information may be obtained on application to the Secretary.

Alexandra Palace and Park, Muswell-hill, six miles N. of London.—The building, after having been for some time closed, was open for short seasons in 1885 and 1887 ; and another season has been announced to commence in May, 1888. The races take place as usual. Reached by rail from Moorgate-st and King's ✠ (G.N.).

Alhambra Theatre, Leicester-sq (Map 7), originally the Panopticon, a rival institution to the Polytechnic, then altered into a music-hall, then into a theatre, and now again a music-hall. The building was—except as to the outer walls — entirely destroyed by fire on the night of Thursday, December 7th, 1882, and was reopened on Monday, December 3rd, 1883. NEAREST *Ry. Stns.*, Charing ✠ (Dis. & S.E.); *Omnibus Rtes.*, Regent-st, Piccadilly, St. Martin's-la, and Strand ; *Cab Rank*, Leicester-sq.

All England Lawn Tennis Club, Wimbledon ; Secretary, Julian Marshall, Esq., 13, Belsize-av, N.W.—Ladies and gentlemen are eligible. Election by ballot, in committee, one black ball in five excluding. The subscription and entrance fees are as follows :—For playing members,subscription, lady or gentleman, £2 2s. ; husband and wife, or parent and daughter, £3 3s.; for non-playing members, subscription, lady or gentleman, £1 1s. ; husband and wife, or parent and daughter, £1 11s. 6d. Entrance fee, lady or gentleman, £3 3s. The number of members is limited to 250. The Lawn Tennis Championship of the World is competed for annually on this Club's ground early in July.

Alpine Club, 8, St. Martin's-pl, Trafalgar-sq, W.C.—This club was founded, in 1857, with the object of encouraging Alpine exploration and travel, and of providing head-quarters for those who are interested in all subjects connected therewith, including the formation of a library of Alpine literature, and a collection of maps. *The Alpine Journal*—the club publication—is published once a quarter by Longman & Co. The mountaineering qualification of the club is a severe one, the object being to secure that only thoroughly experienced and qualified mountaineers should become members. The name of every candidate, together with a list of mountain expeditions, or a statement of the contributions to Alpine literature, science, or art, upon which he founds his claim for membership, must be first submitted to the committee, who will decide upon the sufficiency of his qualification. The election is by ballot of the whole club, one black ball in ten excluding. Entrance, £1 1s. ; subscription, £1 1s.

America.—(*See* UNITED STATES *and* CANADA, DOMINION OF.)

Amusements.—In a general way, and especially during the nine months from July to April inclusive, London cannot be said to be well supplied with amusements. During the season the West End is gay enough, especially for anyone with influential introductions ; most London gaieties being of a private character. The early morning begins with an exercise ride in Rotten-row. In the afternoon, grand parade in the same place, with splendid show of carriages in the Drive. It is here that a stranger will get his best view of the London "world." About the middle of the season come the Derby, Oaks, and Ascot (*see* RACING). This is the time for excursions to Richmond, Hampton Court, Kew, the Crystal Palace, &c. (*and see* EXCURSIONS), and for "whitebait dinners" at Greenwich (*see* FISH DINNERS). In the evening, except the ALEXANDRA and CRYSTAL PALACES, where occasional displays of fireworks are given, there are no open-air amusements—Cremorne, like the Surrey Gardens and Vauxhall, having been long closed and built upon, and the only thing of the kind within reach being the gardens at Rosherville, Gravesend (*see* DICKENS'S DICTIONARY OF THE THAMES), which are worth a visit. Almost all the theatres, however, are open, some of them giving one or more afternoon performances per week, and there is sometimes Italian opera at Covent Garden, and occasionally French plays at the Gaiety or Royalty. On Sundays bands play in the afternoon in some of the parks, and the Zoological Gardens (*which see*) are open to Fellows and those to whom they give tickets. The great Annual Flower Shows, formerly held at Chiswick, will take place in 1888 in the Drill Hall, James-st, Victoria-st, S.W. (*see* HORTICULTURAL SOCIETY.) There are also flower shows at the Botanical Gardens, Regent's-pk (*see* BOTANIC SOCIETY)—a very much prettier site. Polo, cricket, and other outdoor games, noted under their respective heads, are in full swing; extra "excursion" boats are run upon the river and to Margate, Southend, Ipswich, &c.; and four-horse coaches (*see* COACHING) run to various country towns. During August and September London is "empty," and amusement, except for half-a-dozen theatres and such places as the Crystal Palace, almost at an end. Most music-halls (*see* MUSIC HALLS), indeed, keep open throughout the year, but the programme is during this time reduced to its narrowest dimensions. The Agricultural Hall (*which see*) provides something to be looked at at almost every season; the horse, dog, dairy, and cattle shows being all of the first class. In the summer there is usually a very important horse show at the Alexandra Palace Park; and the managers of the Crystal Palace provide shows in great variety and at all periods of the year; the flower, rose, fruit, cat, bird, poultry, and pigeon shows being all excellent. Another exhibition, viz., the Anglo-Danish, will be opened by the Princess of Wales in the Exhibition Grounds, South Kensington, on the 14th of May, and continue open during the summer months. A recent addition to the great halls of London is Olympia, at Kensington, which is designed for the exhibition of all sorts of shows (*and which see*). In 1888, "The Irish Exhibition in London" will occupy the greater part of this vast building (for particulars of which *see* Appendix, under OLYMPIA.) A still more recent and attractive exhibition has been opened in Westminster, near St. James's Park Station, where a really marvellous and realistic panorama of the Falls of Niagara, by the celebrated French painter, Phillip-

poteaux, is on view. With October the theatres begin to re-open. With Lent town dulls again, the chief excitement of this period being the Oxford and Cambridge Boat Race (*see* DICKENS'S DICTIONARY OF THE THAMES.)

Analysts. — Public analysts are under the Metropolitan Board of Works. Among private analysts may be mentioned A. Dupré, Westminster Hospital; A. Voelcker, 11, Salisbury-sq; T. Redwood, Pharmaceutical Society, 17, Bloomsbury-sq; Dr. Wright, St. Mary's Hospital; Dr. Stephenson, Guy's Hospital; J. A. Wanklyn, 7, Westminster-chambers; W. J. Cooper, 7, Westminster-chambers. Some of the above analysts undertake the analysis of gas, as well as that of food, water, and milk.— (*And see* VESTRIES.)

Anglo - Danish Exhibition (The), South Kensington. —(*See* APPENDIX.)

Apothecaries' Hall, Waterla, Blackfriars, is occupied by the Society of Apothecaries of London, incorporated by charter of James I., dated 6th December, 1617. The original charter and subsequent Acts of Parliament conferred on the society the powers and privileges of making all persons desirous of becoming apothecaries throughout England and Wales liable to examination by the court of examiners of the society, and rendered everyone subject to considerable penalties who should practise as an apothecary without the licence or certificate of the society. The powers possessed by the society were considerably enlarged by the Medical Act of 1858, and by the "Apothecaries Act Amendment Act, 1874," and are now as extensive as those possessed by any other licensing body, the former Act enabling the society to combine with any other licensing bodies in the formation of a conjoint board for the examination of candidates for the medical profession throughout England and Wales.

The BOTANIC GARDEN of the Society at Chelsea is well worthy a visit, the public being admitted by tickets, which can be readily obtained on application to the beadle at the hall. It is mostly used by medical students and by students of botany, the society annually offering several prizes for proficiency in pharmaceutical chemistry, botany, &c. NEAREST

Ry. Stn. to the garden, Grosvenord (L.C. & D.), and it can be easily reached by steamboat to Chelsea.

Aquarium (Royal), Westminster (Map 13).—In addition to the objects of interest peculiar to an aquarium, every kind of music-hall entertainment is presented, as well as various shows. The price of admission is one shilling. There is an excellent restaurant on the premises. NEAREST *Ry. Stn.*, St. James's-pk (Dis.); *Omnibus Rtes.*, Victoria-st and Parliament-st; *Cab Rank*, Palace-yard and Tothill-st.

Aquatics.—Full information on all matters connected with London yachting, rowing, &c., will be found in DICKENS'S DICTIONARY OF THE THAMES.

Archery.—The members of the Royal Toxophilite Society may be considered the representative supporters of this ancient national sport in London. The society, which is under the patronage of the Prince of Wales, and numbers over a hundred members, has occupied since 1834 pretty grounds near the Inner Circle of the Regent's-pk, in which stands Archer's Hall, where the hon. secretary may be addressed. The society was founded so far back as 1781 by Sir Ashton Lever, and represents the ancient society of Finsbury Archers, and the Archers' Company of the Honourable Artillery Company. Members are elected by ballot. There are no lady members, but ladies may use the ground under certain conditions; and the annual meeting in July, known as the Ladies' Day, always brings together about 90 of the best shots in the kingdom. The subscription is £5 5s., and there is no entrance fee. The annual general meeting takes place on the first Thurs. in May. The Skating Club established a rink in the gardens in 1869. The rink is flooded between the 15th Nov. and the 1st March. Members of the society have the privilege of skating on the rink, and of inviting their friends to look on. They may also, on certain conditions, become members of the Skating Club without entrance fee.

Architectural Museum (Royal).—And also SCHOOL OF ART, in connection with the Science and Art Department, 18, Tufton-st, Dean's-yd, Westminster. Founded, in 1851, for the purpose of helping the Gothic movement by giving carvers in wood and stone examples of old carvings to study from. The original intention has been much extended, and the museum now contains examples of classic and renaissance as well as of Gothic carvings, amounting in number to some 4,500. The hours are every day from 10 to 4 ; Saturday from 10 to 6. Admission free, Monday, Wednesday, and Friday evenings from 6 to 9, 0, when the evening classe. of the School of Art attached to the Museum are held from 7 to 9.30. Fees, 2s. 6d. to 5s. a month. A life class is held on Saturdays from 2 to 5, and a ladies' class on the same day from 2 to 4. Other day classes are open, and are about opening. NEAREST *Ry. Stn.*, St. James's-pk (Dis.); *Omnibus Rte.*, Victoria-st ; *Cab Rank*, Tothill-st, Westminster.

Argentine Republic, La Plata.—MINISTRY, 16, Kensington Palace Gdns, W. NEAREST *Ry. Stn.*, High-st, Kensington, **and** Notting Hill-gate ; *Omnibus Rtes.*, Kensington-rd & Uxbridge-rd ; *Cab Rank*, Kensington-rd. CONSULATE, 16, Bishopsgate-st Without, E.C. NEAREST *Ry Stn.*, *Omnibus Rte.*, and *Cab Rank*, Bishopsgate-st.

Armourers' Company (The), Coleman-st.— The hall, which is of recent date, is not particularly interesting in itself, but is of good proportions, and decorated in extremely good taste. The Armourers possess a remarkably fine collection of mazers and hanaps and cups, and some curious pieces of armour—the latter, however, not so numerous as might reasonably be expected. In the hall and other rooms are some fair pictures, and the whole of one end of the hall is occupied by a gigantic Shakespearian picture by Northcote, R.A., one of the worst of the many bad pictures engraved in Boydell's Shakespeare.

Army and Navy Club, 36 to 39, Pall Mall.—For the association of commissioned officers of all ranks in Her Majesty's Regular Army, Rl. Navy, Rl. Marines, and Rl. Marine Artillery. Election by ballot in club meeting. Fifty members must actually vote, and one black ball in ten excludes. Entrance fee, £40 ; subscription, £7 7s. for old members ; and for new members, £10 10s., but these, after five years, revert to the old members list, and pay only £7 7s.

Army and Navy Pensioners Employment Society, 44, Charing ✠, S.W.—All men discharged from Her Majesty's military or naval forces with permanent pensions are eligible to be registered for employment through the aid of this society, on complying with certain rules which may be obtained from the Sec. at the office. The society's register contains the names of pensioners of good character, and well qualified for all kinds of indoor and outdoor employments. Employers can be supplied with men on application, either personally or by letter to the Sec., at the office, 44, Charing ✠, S.W. "No Fees." Donations and subscriptions are invited.

Arthur's Club, 69 and 70, St. James's-st, W.—Non-political. Entrance fee, £31 10s. ; subscription, £10 10s.

Artillery Company.—The Honourable Artillery Company of the City of London dates from as far back as 1537. All the officers of the old City Trained Bands were selected from members of the Company. The Artillery Ground, near Finsbury-sq, contains a good drill-hall, armoury, and the like. The Honourable Artillery Company is noticeable as being the only volunteer corps which includes horse artillery, and is distinguished by wearing the bearskin head-dress otherwise peculiar to the Guards. The history of the regiment has been graphically and exhaustively written by Captain G. A. Raikes, F.S.A., and the book should be referred to by any one desirous of complete information on the subject.

Arts.—(*See* SOCIETY OF ARTS.)

Arts Club, 17, Hanover-sq, W.—For the purpose of facilitating the social intercourse of those connected with, or interested in, art, literature, or science. Entrance fee, £15 15s. ; subscription, £6 6s. Travelling members pay a subscription of £1 1s.

Art Students' Home 4 and 5, Brunswick-sq, W.C. President, The Baroness Burdett-Coutts.— This institution was the outcome of a want which had been much felt by students attending the Female School of Art in Queen-sq, whose homes were in the country. The leases of the two houses were purchased, and furniture, &c., provided through the liberality of the president. The home was opened

early in 1879, and has met with complete success. It may be noted that "Art Student" is understood to include ladies studying for music, or for special training in other kindred work. The charges range from 21s. to 30s. per week (with reductions in a few special cases). All applications for residence must be made to the Lady Resident, who can be seen at the Home on Thurs. from 12 to 4.

Art Training School (National), SOUTH KENSINGTON (Map 5).—*Principal* J. C. L. Sparkes ; *Visitor*, Edward J. Poynter, R.A. (1) The courses of instruction pursued in the school have for their object the training of teachers, male and female, in the practice of art, and in the knowledge of its scientific principles, with a view to qualifying them as teachers of schools of art, competent to develop the application of art to the common uses of life, and to the requirements of trade and manufactures. The instruction comprehends the following subjects : Freehand, architectural, and mechanical drawing ; practical geometry and perspective ; painting in oil, tempera, and water-colours ; modelling, moulding, and casting. The classes for drawing, painting, and modelling include architectural and other ornament, flowers, objects of still-life, &c., the figure from the antique and the life, and the study of anatomy as applicable to art. (2) These courses of instruction are open to the public on the payment of fees ; the classes for male and female students meeting separately. The fees are as follows : Fees for classes studying five whole days, including evenings, £5 for five months, and an entrance fee of 10s. Evening classes : male school, £2 per term ; female school £1 per term ; three evenings a week. Schoolmasters, school-mistresses, and pupil teachers of public elementary schools may attend on any two evenings in each week ; fee, 5s. for the term. Students may attend special architectural and designing classes on Mondays or Tuesdays. Fees, £1 1s. per term, and 10s. entrance. Governesses in private schools or families may attend the day classes for not more than three months on payment of £1 per month, without payment of the entrance fee. An evening artisan class is held in the elementary room; fees, 10s. per term or 3s. per month. Students of this class may pass into the general classrooms at the same fee, when they have passed examinations in the four subjects of the 2nd grade. (3) No students can be admitted to these classes until they have passed an examination in freehand drawing of the 2nd grade, except under special conditions which relate only to students in the class of architecture. Examinations of candidates for admission will be held weekly, on Tuesdays, at the commencement of each session, and at frequent intervals throughout the year. The examination fee is 2s. 6d. for day students, and 6d. for evening students, to be paid at the time of examination. Candidates should bring their own lead-pencils and india-rubber. Candidates who have already passed examination in 2nd grade freehand drawing are admitted, on application to the registrar, without further examination. (4) The annual session consists of two terms, each lasting five months, and commencing on the 1st of March and the 1st Wednesday of October. Students who have passed the examination may join the school at any time, on payment of fees for not less than five months, but those who have already paid fees for five months may remain until the end of the session on payment of a proportional fee for each month unexpired up to the 31st of July. The months of August and September are not counted as part of the five months paid for. Those months, one week at Christmas, and one week at Easter and Whitsuntide, are vacations. The school is open every day, except Sat. Hours of study: Day, 9 to 3.30; evening, 7 to 9, except during May, June, and July, when they are open from 6 to 8. Evening classes for women on Tues., Thurs., and Friday. All day-students are expected to attend at 9 a.m., and to remain in the school until the bell rings at 3.30 p.m., except during the half-hour for lunch from 1 to 1.30 p.m., or when permission has been specially obtained. (5) Students properly qualified have full access to the collections of the museum and library, either for consultation or copying, as well as to all the school lectures of the de-

partment. (6) A register of the students' attendance is kept, and may be consulted by parents and guardians. (7) Masters and students in the National Art Training School and other schools of art under the department who are desirous of studying in the galleries in foreign countries, and who have obtained one or more certificates of the 3rd grade, may receive, on application to the secretary, a form of recommendation as to their competence, which may be presented, with their certificate, to the British Consul, or to the directors of the galleries in question.

Further information may be obtained on personal application to the Registrar at the schools, or by letter addressed to the secretary, Science and Art Department.

A course of twelve lectures on anatomy, as applicable to the arts, is given in each session. The spring course may be attended by ladies. Fee for the course, 6s.; for a single lecture, 1s. Other lectures will be delivered occasionally, and duly announced. A distinct series of rooms has been provided for male and female students. In each series separate rooms are assigned to drawing, painting, modelling, &c., and there is a lecture-room in common for the male and female classes. Entrances in Exhibition-rd.

Metropolitan District Schools of Art are now established at the following places: The Female School of Art, 43, Queen-sq, Bloomsbury; Bayswater, 22, Delamere-ter, W.; Blackheath, Lee, and Lewisham, Bennett-pk; Blackheath-hill, 13, Lansdowne-pl; Chancery-la, Birkbeck Inst.; Chelsea, Onslow College; Chiswick, Bath-rd, Bedford-pk; Clapham, Verison-rd; Clapton, 37, Clapton-common; Croydon, George-st; Holloway, Camden School; Hornsey; Islington, Barnsbury Hall; Lambeth, Miller's-la, Upper Kennington-la; North London, Sandringham-rd, Kingsland; Putney, S.W.; Richmond; Saffron-hill, Board School; St. Martin's-in-the-Fields, Castle-st, Long Acre; St. Thomas Charterhouse, Goswell-rd; Stoke Newington; Stratford, Maryland Point; West London, 155, Gt. Titchfield-st; Westminster, Royal Architectural Museum. There are female and evening classes at most of these schools. Applications for information should be made at the schools.

THE ART LIBRARY at South

Kensington is open during the same hours as the Museum. It contains about 62,000 volumes and pamphlets on all subjects bearing on art; a collection of about 31,000 drawings, designs, and illuminations; about 117,000 engravings, chiefly of ornament; and about 61,000 photographs of architecture, objects of art, original drawings, &c. All its contents are rendered, as far as possible, available to students of the schools of art and general readers.

THE MUSEUM lends books and objects to all schools of art.

The Collections comprise: Objects of Ornamental Art as applied to Manufactures; the National Art Library; British Pictures, Sculptures, and Engravings; the Educational Library and Collections, including appliances and models for scholastic education, scientific apparatus, &c.; Materials and Models for Building and Construction; Substances used for Food; Reproductions, by means of Casting, Electrotype, and Photography, of objects displaying the Art-Manufactures of all nations; Naval Models. NEAREST *Ry. Stn.*, South Kensington; *Omnibus Rtes.*, Brompton-rd and Fulham-rd; *Cab Rank*, Opposite.

Art Union of London, 112, Strand, near the Savoy.—This institution is announced as having been "established to promote the knowledge and love of the fine arts, and their general advancement in the British Empire, by a wide diffusion of the works of native artists; and to elevate art, and to encourage its professors, by creating an increased demand for their works, and an improved taste on the part of the public." The means by which it is sought to further these important aims take the form of an annual lottery. Every member for each guinea subscribed is entitled to: 1. One chance in the distribution of prizes at the annual meeting on the last Tu. in April. 2. An impression of one or more plates produced exclusively for the society; admission for himself and friends to the general meeting, and the exhibition of prizes; and, on application, the annual report with list and almanack. Winners of the principal prizes have the right to select works of art from the public exhibitions of the year, and the less fortunate members become entitled to bas-reliefs, statuettes, medals, and other minor gifts. All further particulars may be had at the office of the society, which, it may be added, is now in its fifty-first year.

Arundel Club, 12, Salisbury-st, Strand.—Instituted to promote the association of gentlemen of literary, scientific, and artistic pursuits and tastes. Election by Committee; ten members must vote, and no candidate can be elected unless at least seven members vote in his favour; one adverse vote in seven, or five in any case, exclude. Entrance fee, £5 5s.; subscription, £3 3s.

Ashes, with all other refuse, are cleared away from time to time, as required, by the carts of the regular dust contractors. If the carts do not pass often enough, or you have any difficulty with them, write to the Vestry Clerk (*see* VESTRIES). If still unsuccessful, apply at the police-court. No vegetable or animal refuse ought, under any circumstances, to be thrown into the dust-bin. It should all be first dried under the kitchen fire and then burned. N.B.—Dust contractors are not bound to remove trade refuse, for which a special arrangement must be made.

Astley's Theatre. — (*See* SANGER'S AMPHITHEATRE.)

Asylums (Metropolitan District).— The following list includes the whole of the Metropolitan parishes and unions: Caterham, for imbeciles; Leavesden, for imbeciles; Homerton, for fever; Stockwell, for fever; Homerton, for small-pox; Stockwell, for small-pox; Darenth, near Dartford, schools for imbecile children; *Exmouth*, training-ship, for pauper boys.

Athenæum Club, 107, Pall Mall.—Eminence in, or patronage of, science, literature, or any branch of the fine arts, as also distinction in the public service, are the qualifications for membership of this club. The Athenæum possesses one of the best club houses, and the finest club library, in England. Election is by ballot, also by choice of the committee to the number of nine yearly, the candidate being of distinction in the above - mentioned categories, and also, under another rule, in virtue of being a cabinet minister, a bishop, or a judge, &c.

At the ballot one black ball in ten excludes. Entrance fee, £31 10s.; subscription, £8 8s.

Athletics. — Clubs for the practice of athletic sports of all kinds exist in London in great numbers, and it is only possible here to mention three of the principal and most representative associations; the Amateur Athletic Club, the London Athletic Club, and the German Gymnastic Soc. The Amateur Athletic Club has for its objects the promotion and supervision of athletic sports and pastimes, and the ensuring "as far as practicable that they are legitimately and honourably conducted." It has now resigned the management of its Challenge Cups into the hands of the Amateur Athletic Association, a body of younger men elected by the principal Athletic Clubs. Members are divided into three classes, life, honorary, and active; the first paying one sum of £12 12s., and the others an annual subscription of £2 2s. and £1 1s. The election is by committee, and one black ball excludes. The grounds of the club are at Stamford Bridge, Fulham, where the secretary may be addressed.

The London Athletic Club is by far the most important of all the clubs with similar objects in London. Founded as the Mincing Lane Club in 1863, it was re-named in 1866, now contains upwards of 700 members, and takes the lead in almost all matters connected with amateur pedestrianism. Its object is declared to be the cultivation of athletic sports, and it consists of active and non-active members. The former pay £2 2s. annually, and the latter £1 1s. A member can, by paying a sum of £10 10s., become free of the club. Active members are admitted to all the advantages of the club; non-active members are not permitted to compete in the sports. The election, after the candidate has been duly proposed and seconded, is by committee, one black ball in five excluding. Meetings for prizes given by the club take place frequently, and one of the most important rules is that "no member may enter for any sports which are not confined to amateurs, nor compete with professional runners for either prize or money." The definition of an amateur is that adopted by the Amateur Athletic Association, the

entries (to the open competitions) of all strangers being subject to the ballot of the committee, the club always reserving the right of refusing the entry of anyone not a member of the club. The London Athletic Club possesses thirteen handsome challenge cups (100 yards, quarter of a mile, 600 yards, half a mile, 1 mile, 3 miles walking, 7 miles walking, 10 miles, 120 yards hurdle, 2 miles bicycle, 2 miles steeplechase, Ladies' Lawn Tennis London Championship, Gentlemen's ditto), which (with the exception of the two last mentioned, which are open to non-members, and may be won outright) are considered as its absolute property. The club has an excellent ground at Stamford Bridge, Fulham, opposite the Chelsea Stn. of the West London Extension Ry. (cab fare from Charing +., 2s.; from the Bank of England, 3s.), with a first-rate path of four laps to the mile, and a straight run of 280 yards. There are convenient dressing-rooms with shower baths, and all the usual pavilion accommodation. Lawn-tennis is provided, for active members only, there being twenty-six courts. Boxing and fencing classes are held in the Iron House at the Grounds twice a week during the winter months. That the London Athletic Club is in a very "live" state will be seen at once when it is stated that in 1886 there were 76 competitions for 200 prizes, for which over 1,000 starters came to the post, and that 110 new members were elected during the year. The hon. secretary is Mr. S. K. Holman, Stamford Bridge Grounds, Fulham, S.W

As the London Athletic Club takes the lead among the clubs formed for the practice of athletics in general, so the German Gymnastic Society, which was founded in 1861, stands at the head of all institutions of its class. Whether "the art of gymnastics will restore the lost equilibrium of human education," as appears to be the opinion of the leaders of the society, may be an open question. It is, at all events, certain that the G.G.S. does not neglect any means by which this desirable end may be obtained. The seven hundred and thirty - four members (about half of whom were English) who were on the roll in 1887 not only had the opportunity of thoroughly earning all that the German and English system of gymnastics has to teach, combined with fencing and boxing, but the privilege of joining a singing-class, a literary club, a chess club, and an English dramatic club; an extensive library being also at their disposal. A ladies' class is held twice a week. The entrance-fee is 5s., and the yearly subscription £1 10s. A half-yearly subscription of 15s. is optional, should the subscriber only desire to avail himself of the advantages of the society for that period. The gymnasium is situated at 26, Pancras-rd, King's ✠, N.W., where the secretary may be addressed. The nearest railway stations are the King's ✠ terminus of the Great Northern, the St. Pancras terminus of the Midland, and the King's ✠ Junction of the Metropolitan. It is also convenient for all omnibuses passing King's ✠.

During the winter there is plenty of cross-country sport promoted by the paper-chasing clubs, of which there are a dozen or more in various parts of London. The oldest of these is the Thames Hare and Hounds, with headquarters at the "King's Head," Roehampton; and next in importance come the South London Harriers, running from the "Greyhound," Streatham; and the Spartan Harriers, hailing from the "Angel" at Edmonton. *And see* Archery, All England Lawn Tennis Club, Bicycling, Boxing, Cricket, *and* Rowing.

Auctions, of all kinds, are institutions which those who have not their London at their fingerends would do well to avoid. The "Mock Auction" is a swindle pure and simple. It is commonly carried on in a small shop, carefully darkened by filling the window with all kinds of ostensible merchandise, and tenanted chiefly by the proprietor and his confederates, who keep up a lively bidding till some unwary passer-by is seduced into entering, and speedily "stuck" with some perfectly worthless article at a fabulous price. Should the victim find that he is called upon to pay too dearly for his folly, he may, by stoutly denying having made any bid, calling in the police, and, if necessary, showing fight, make his way out again scot free. But he will possibly be roughly

handled, probably have his pockets picked, and certainly pass an extremely "*mauvais quart d'heure.*" There is also a kind of sale of a less distinctly fraudulent description, but still anything but *bonâ fide*. It takes place at auction rooms of more or less legitimate position, usually in the evening, and is known to the initiated as a "rigged sale," consisting chiefly of articles vamped up or originally manufactured for the purpose. It is, indeed, a too frequent custom among the less responsible auctioneers to introduce a number of such articles into sales, and the purchaser will do well to bear this in mind. But the "rigged sale" is practically a mart for such articles only, and for anyone in search of value for his money there are few better places to avoid. The legitimate auction is, of course, a different affair. But the casual patron of the smaller auction sales will not find himself very much better off. As a buyer he will be opposed by a mob of "brokers," all in league with each other to either crush him altogether, or run him up to the highest price that can be screwed out of him. As a seller he will find the same combination exerting all their skill to secure the knocking down of each lot to one of their own gang; the article being afterwards again put up privately amongst themselves, and the profits of the transaction divided among the confederates in the "knock out." The only chance for a novice is, when selling, either to get an experienced friend to watch the sale, or to put a reserve price upon the article; when buying, to make up his mind as to the highest price he is prepared to pay, and put himself in the hands of a broker. It is not advisable to purchase safes at public auction, at all events until all possibly existent keys shall have been satisfactorily accounted for. It is a by no means unknown thing for a purchaser to receive a few days after the installation of his purchase a nocturnal visit from a gentleman of the burgling persuasion, who has taken the precaution to possess himself of one of them, and has watched the "safe" home to its new abode. The principal auction-rooms are: Christie's, King-st, St. James's, and Foster's, Pall Mall, for pictures, china, and valuables generally; Phillips', 73, New Bond-st, for works of art, furniture,

&c.; Hodgson's, 115, Chancery-la, Puttick and Simpson's, 47, Leicester-sq, and Sotheby, Wilkinson, and Hodge, 13, Wellington-st, Strand, for books, &c.; Oxenham's, 187, Oxford-st, and Bonham's, 65, etc., Oxford-st, and 6, Wardour-st, for household furniture, &c.; Debenham, Storr, and Sons, 26, King-st, Covent-garden, for plate, books, wearing apparel, wines, jewellery, and all kinds of miscellaneous property; Johnson and Dymond, Gracechurch-st, also for miscellaneous property; and Stevens's, 38, King-st, Covent-gdn, with a specialty for poultry and pigeons, plants and bulbs. The principal sales, by the leading auctioneers, of valuable property, such as land, houses, reversions, &c., are held at the Auction Mart, Tokenhouse-yard, E.C. Horses, carriages, &c., are sold at Tattersall's, Knightsbridge; at Aldridge's, St. Martin's-lane; and Rymill's, Barbican. The principal sales of foreign and colonial produce are held by the brokers concerned at the Commercial Sale Rooms, Mincing-lane. The wool sales take place at the Wool Exchange, in Coleman-st. Timber is largely sold at the "Baltic."

Austria and Hungary.—
Embassy, 18, Belgrave-sq, S.W. Nearest *Ry. Stn.*, Victoria; *Omnibus Rtes.*, Knightsbridge, Grosvenor-pl, Buckingham Palace-rd, and Sloane-st. Consulate, 11, Queen Victoria-st, E.C. Nearest *Ry. Stns.*, Mansion House (Dis.) and Cannon-st (S.E.); *Omnibus Rtes.*, King William-st, Cannon-st, and Queen Victoria-st; *Cab Rank*, King William-st.

Avenue Theatre, Charing ✠ (Map 13).—This commodious theatre, intended for the performance of comic opera, etc., was opened under the management of M. Marius, on the 11th of March, 1882. It is situated at the South end of Northumberland-avenue. Nearest *Ry. Stns.*, Charing ✠ (Dis. & S.E.); *Omnibus Rte.*, Strand; *Cab Rank*, Opposite

Bachelors' Club, 8, Hamilton-pl, W.—Established in 1881 under the Presidency of his late R.H., the Duke of Albany. Limited to 600 members, exclusive of supernumerary and honorary members. Members may continue to belong to the club after marriage, as hon. members, on payment of £25, and the usual annual subscription; the president, however, for the time being not being required to resign on ceasing to be a bachelor. Management by the committee, in whom is also vested the election of members, which is determined by ballot, two black balls excluding in a quorum of nine. Members have the privilege of introducing their friends (ladies or gentlemen) as visitors, special rooms being set aside for their reception. Entrance fee, £11 10s.; annual subscription, £10 10s.

Badminton Club, 100, Piccadilly.—A sporting club, of which the entrance is £10 10s., and the subscription, £6 6s.—(*See* COACHING.)

Baker-street Bazaar, 28, Baker-st, Oxford-st.—Specially noticeable for carriages, and Chinese and Japanese goods. Open daily from 10 a.m. till 6 p.m. NEAREST *Ry. Stn.*, Baker-st; *Omnibus Rtes.*, Baker - st, Edgware - rd, Marylebone-rd, and Oxford-st; *Cab Rank*, Dorset-st.

Bankers' Clearing House, near the Post-office, Lombard-street, is the medium through which bankers obtain the amount of cheques and bills in their hands for collection from other bankers. NEAREST *Ry. Stns.*, Cannon-st (S.E.) and Moorgate-st (Met.); *Omnibus Rtes.*, King William-st and Cornhill; *Cab Rank*, King William-st.

Bank of England, Threadneedle - st (Map 8), is divided into the following departments: The Accountant's, the Cashier's, and the Secretary's, all of which have a vast number of smaller subdivisions which are rendered necessary by the great and intricate business transacted by the Bank. NEAREST *Ry Stns.*, Broad - st (N.L.), Moorgate - st (Met.), and Cannon-st (S.E.); *Omnibus Rtes.*, Moorgate-st and Cornhill; *Cab Rank*, Bartholomew-la. The office hours are 9 to 4, and the Bank has branches at Burlington-gdns. W., and the New Law Courts, E.C.

DIVIDENDS are now payable at the Bank the day after they fall due, and need no longer be received personally or by power of attorney, and are paid in one of the following modes:

I. To the Stockholders personally, or to their authorised representatives at the Bank of England. [Stockholders may arrange for the receipt of their dividends, free of charge, at any of the country branches, on application to the agent.]

II. By transmission of dividend-warrants by post at the risk of the stockholder, under the following regulations:

1. Any stockholder residing within the United Kingdom who desires to have his dividend-warrant sent to his address by post, must fill up a form of application to be obtained at the Bank, or at any of its country branches.

2. In the case of joint accounts, the application must be signed by all the members of the account, directing the warrant to be sent to one of them at a given address.

3. Post dividend-warrants will be crossed "& Co.," and will only be payable through a banker. They will be drawn to the order of the stockholder, and must be endorsed.

The following are the dividend days:

Stock.	Dividends due.
New 3½ per Cent.	Jan. 5 & July 5
New 2½ per Cent.	,, ,,
India 3½ per Cent.	Jan. 5, April 5, July 5, Oct. 5.
Bank Stock ..	April 5 & Oct. 5
Annuities for 30 years	,, ,,
India 4 per Cent. Stock ..	,, ,,
3 per Cent. Reduced ..	,, ,,
New 3 per Cent.	,, ,,
India Bonds ..	Mar. 31 & Sept. 30
India 4 per Cent. Transfer Loan Stock ..	Apl. 25 & Oct. 25
Red Sea & India Telegraph Annuities.. ..	Feb. 4 & Aug. 4

New 2¾ per Cent. and Consols. —The dividends on the converted stock will be paid *quarterly*, the first being due on July 5, 1888.

TRANSFER DAYS, Mondays, Tuesdays, Wednesdays, Thursdays, and Fridays, from 11 to 3; for buying and selling, 10 to 1; for accepting and payment of dividends, 9.30 a.m. to 4 p.m. Transfer-books are closed at 1 o'clock on Saturdays. Dividends on India

Bonds payable 9.30 a.m. to 4 p.m. Private transfers may be made at other times, *the books not being shut*, by paying an extra fee of 2s. 6d.

HOLIDAYS.—Good Friday, Easter Monday, Whit Monday, First Monday in August, Christmas Day, and 26th or 27th Dec., as the case may be ; and in the Stock-offices, 1st May and 1st Nov.

The business of the Bank was originally carried on in the Mercers' Hall. Thence it was removed to the Grocers' Hall, and thence again to the buildings at the back of the present court towards Threadneedle-st ; the existing not very satisfactory pile being the work of Sir John Soane half a century later. There is much to be seen in the Bank of England of interest to the visitor. The bullion office, the printing department, and other of the more private offices, may be seen by an order to be obtained through a director.

At a General Court held at the Bank of England, on the 10th and 11th of April, 1888, the following gentlemen were elected Governors and Directors of the Bank for the year ensuing, viz :

Governor.—Mark Wilks Collet, Esq.

Deputy - Governor. — William Lidderdale, Esq.

Directors.—The Rt. Hon. Lord Addington, Charles George Arbuthnot, Esq., Henry Wollaston B'ake, Esq., John William Birch, Esq., Herbert Brooks, Esq., Robert Wigram Crawford, Esq., James Pattison Currie, Esq., Samuel Steuart Gladstone, Esq., Benjamin Buck Greene, Esq., Henry Riversdale Grenfell, Esq., Henry Hucks Gibbs, Esq., John Saunders Gilliat, Esq., M.P., Charles Hermann Goschen, Esq., Everard Alexander Hambro, Esq., Thomas Hankey, Esq., Henry Lancelot Holland, Esq., The Hon. Ronald Ruthven Leslie Melville, Samuel Hope Morley, Esq., Edward Howley Palmer, Esq., David Powell, Esq., The Rt. Hon. Lord Revelstoke, Alfred Charles de Rothschild, Esq., Hugh Colin Smith, Esq., Alexander Falconer Wallace, Esq.

Bankruptcy Court.— (*See* LAW COURTS.)

Banks.—The following are the principal London banks. List A—bankers keeping current accounts n London, members of Clearing House being marked (*). List B—Colonial, Provincial, Foreign, and Discount, &c., Banks. In both lists Joint Stock Banks, with unlimited liability, are in capitals; Joint Stock Banks (limited), in italics; and Private Banks in ordinary type.

A.

Alexanders & Co., 24, Lombard-st.

*Alliance Bank, Bartholomew-la; 88, Kensington High-st; 239, Regent-st; 176, High-st, Camden Town; 74, High-rd, Kilburn; 30, Victoria-rd, Battersea; 201, Earl's-ct-rd; Holloway-road; and 14, Sloane-sq, S.W.

*Bank of England, Threadneedle-st; 1, Burlington-gdns; the New Law Courts, E.C.

BANK OF SCOTLAND, 43, Lothbury

*Barclay, Bevan, Tritton, Twells, & Co., 54, Lombard-st

Barker, Geo., & Co., 35, Mark-la

Biggerstaff, W. and J., 18, West Smithfield; 6, Bank - bdgs; Metropolitan Cattle Market; and Foreign Cattle Market, Deptford

BRITISH LINEN COMPANY BANK, 41, Lombard-st.

Brooks & Co., 81, Lombard-st

*Brown, Janson & Co., 32, Abchurch-la

Brown, J., & Co., 25, Abchurch-la

Capital and Counties Bank, 39, Threadneedle-st; 25, Ludgate-hill; 68, Oxford-st; 195, Edgware-rd; 35, King-st, W.C.

Carlton Bank, 38, Finsbury-pavement, E.C.

*Central Bank of London, 52, Cornhill; 488, Bethnal Green-rd; 91, Newgate-st; 1, Stamford-st, S.E.; Charterhouse - bdgs, Goswell-rd; 31, High-st, Shoreditch; 110, High - st, Whitechapel; 26, Tooley-st; and 237, Tottenham-ct-rd

Child & Co., 1, Fleet-st

*City Bank, 5, Threadneedle-st; 61, Ludgate-hill; 34, Old Bond-st; 159, Tottenham-ct-rd; 221, Edgware - rd; Lowndes - ter; Aldgate-bdgs; Great Eastern-st; 34, Holborn Viaduct; Queen Victoria-st; and 100, Fore-st, E.C.

Clydesdale Banking Company, 30, Lombard-st

Cocks, Biddulph & Co., 43, Charing ✠

Commercial Bank of Scotland, 123, Bishopsgate-st, E.C.

*Consolidated Bank, 52, Threadneedle-st; 450, West Strand

Coutts & Co., 57, 58, & 59, Strand

*Dimsdale, Fowler & Co., 50, Cornhill

Drummond & Co., 49, Charing ✠

*Fuller, Banbury & Co., 77, Lombard-st

*GLYN, MILLS, CURRIE & CO., 67, Lombard-st

Goslings & Sharpe, 19, Fleet-st

Herries, Farquhar & Co., 16, St. James's-st

Hill, Chas. & Son, 17, West Smithfield; Metro. Cattle Market; and Cattle Market, Deptford

Hoares & Co., 37, Fleet-st

*Hopkinson, Charles, & Sons, 3, Regent-st

*Imperial Bank, 6, Lothbury; 10, Victoria Mansions, Westminster; 1, Sydney-pl, Onslow-sq; 107, High-st, Marylebone; 49, High-st, Peckham; and E. Dulwich

Lacy, Hartland & Co., 60, West Smithfield; 8 & 9, Bank-bdgs; Islington Cattle Market; Deptford Dockyard; and 98, Jamaica-rd, S.E.

*Lloyds, Barnetts, & Bosanquets' Bank, 60, Lombard-st, E.C.; 54, St. James's-st, S.W.; and at Hampstead, Pimlico, and West Kensington.

*London and County Banking Company, 21, Lombard-st; 21, Hanover - sq; 3, Albert - ga; Upper-st, Islington; 134, Aldersgate-st; 369, Brixton-rd, S.W.; 1, Connaught-st, Edgware-rd; 111, New Oxford-st; 34, Borough High - st; Sussex-pl, Queen's-ga; 67, Kensington High-st; 87, High-st, Kingsland, E.; 181, Shoreditch High-st; 74, Westbourne gr; 6, Henrietta-st, W.C.; 165, Westminster - br-rd; Deptford Broadway; Stratford Broadway; 324, High Holborn; 1, Amherst-rd, Hackney; 18, Newington Butts; 3, Victoria-st; 266, Pentonville-rd; 490, Holloway-rd; and at Blackheath, Greenwich, Norwood, Hammersmith, and Woolwich

London and General Bank, 20, Budge-row, E.C.

*London Joint - Stock Bank, 5, Princes-st, Bank; 69, Pall Mall; 123, Chancery-la; Charterhouse-st; Cattle Market, Islington; Cattle Market, Deptford; 2, Craven-rd, W.; 28, Borough High-st; and 87, Great Tower-st

London and Provincial Bank, 7, Bank-bdgs; 163, Edgware-rd; South Kensington; 1, High-st, Kingsland; Canning Town; Hackney; Leytonstone; Stoke Newington; Stratford; Walham Gn; Wood Gn; and Woolwich

*London and South Western Bank, Head Office: 7, Fenchurch-st, E.C.; 27, Regent-st, S.W.; Battersea Park-rd, S.W.; 159, Old Kent-rd, S.E.; 90, Bow rd, E.; 275 and 465, Brixton-rd, S.W.; 324, High Holborn; Camberwell-gn, S.E.; 67, Park-st, N.W.; 3, Garfield-ter, S.W.; Clapham-com, S.W.; Clapton, E.; 82, Finsbury - pavement, E.C.; Finsbury - pk - bdgs, N.; Forest - gate, E.; Forest - hill, S.E.; Hammersmith, W.; 6, Sutherland - gdns, Harrow - rd, W.; 403, Holloway-rd, N.; 228, Kentish Town-rd, N.W.; Kilburn, N.W.; 137, Ladbroke-gr, W.; 451, Oxford-st, W.; High-st, Peckham, S.E.; 193, East India Dock-rd, E.; Wellington-rd, N.W.; Uxbridge-rd, W.; 48, Finchley New-rd, N.W.; 368, Commercial-rd-east, E.; Streatham, S.W.; 202, Fulham-rd, S.W.; Chiswick, W.; Turnham Gn, W.; and Wimbledon

*London and Westminster Bank, 41, Lothbury; 1, St. James's-sq; 214, High Holborn; 6, Borough High-st; 130, High-st, Whitechapel; 4, Stratford-pl, W.; 217, Strand; 91, Westminster-br-rd; 1, Brompton-sq; 269, Upper-st, N.; 44, Hampstead-rd; 114, Holborn; Victoria-st, S.W.; and Westbourne-grove

*McGrigor, Sir C. R., & Co., 25, Charles-st, St. James's

*Martin & Co., 68, Lombard-st

Merchant Banking Company, 112, Cannon-st

*NATIONAL BANK, 13, Old Broad st; 9, Charing ✠; 68, Gloucester-gdns, W.; 189, High-st, Camden Tn.; 21, Grosvenor-gdns, S.W.; Elgin-villas, Harrow-rd, W.; 361, Goswell-rd; 276, Oxford - st; 286, Pentonville-rd; 158, High-st, Notting Hill; and Harlesden, N.W.

NATIONAL BANK OF SCOTLAND, 37, Nicholas-la

*National Provincial Bank of England, 112, Bishopsgate-st; 212, Piccadilly; 53, Baker-st; 218, Upper-st, Islington; 88, Cromwell - rd, S.W.; Carey-st.

Lincoln s-inn; South Audley-st, W.; and 185, Aldersgate-st

Praeds & Co., 189, Fleet-st

*Prescott & Co., 62, Threadneedle-st

PROVINCIAL BANK OF IRELAND, 8, Throgmorton-av, E.C.

Ransom, Bouverie & Co., 1, Pall Mall East

*Robarts, Lubbock & Co., 15, Lombard-st

ROYAL BANK OF SCOTLAND, 123, Bishopsgate-st-within

Royal Exchange Bank, 126, Cannon-st

Scott, Sir Samuel, Bart., & Co., 1, Cavendish-sq

Shank, J., Met. Cattle Market

*Smith, Payne, Smiths, 1, Lombard-st

Twining, R., & Co., 215, Strand

*Union Bank of London, 2, Princes-st; 66, Charing ✠; 14, Argyll-pl; 95, Chancery-la; Holborn-cir; 67, Bishop's-rd, W.; 89, Aldgate High-st; and 97, Tottenham-ct-rd

Union Bank of Scotland, 62, Cornhill

*Williams, Deacon & Co., 20, Birchin-la.

B.

Agra Bank, 35, Nicholas-la, E.C.

ANGLO - AUSTRIAN BANK, 31, Lombard-st

Anglo-Californian, 3, Angel-ct

Anglo-Egyptian, 27, Clement's-la

Anglo-Foreign Banking Company, 2, Bishopsgate-st

Anglo-Italian, 9, St. Helen's-pl

AUSTRALIAN JOINT - STOCK, 2, King William-st

BANK OF AUSTRALASIA, 4, Threadneedle-st

BANK OF BRITISH COLUMBIA, 28, Cornhill

BANK OF BRIT. N. AMERICA, 3, Clement's-la, Lombard-st

Bank of Constantinople, 19, Great Winchester-st, E.C.

BANK OF EGYPT, 26, Old Broad-st

BANK OF MONTREAL, 22, Abchurch-la, E.C.

BANK OF NEW SOUTH WALES, 64, Old Broad-st

BANK OF NEW ZEALAND, 1, Queen Victoria-st

BANK OF ROUMANIA, 15, Moorgate-st

Bank of South Australia, 31, Lombard-st

BANK OF VICTORIA, Australia, 28, Clement's-la, E.C.

BIRKBECK, 29, Southampton-bdgs, Holborn

Blydenstein, B. W. & Co., 55 and 56, Threadneedle-st

Burt, F., & Co., 71 and 72, Cornhill

CHARTERED BANK OF INDIA, AUSTRALIA, & CHINA, Hatton-ct, Threadneedle-st

CHARTERED MERCANTILE BANK OF INDIA, LONDON, AND CHINA, 65, Old Broad-st

Cheque Bank, 20, King William-st; 20, Cockspur-st, S.W.

COLONIAL BANK, 13, Bishopsgate-st-within

COLONIAL BANK OF NEW ZEALAND, 13, Moorgate-st

Commercial Bank of Australia, 1, Bishopsgate-st-within, E.C.

COMMERCIAL BANK OF SOUTH AUSTRALIA, 24, Lombard-st.

COMMERCIAL BANK OF SYDNEY, 18, Birchin-la

COMPTOIR D'ESCOMPTE DE PARIS, 52, Threadneedle-st

CREDIT LYONNAIS, 40, Lombard-st

Cunliffe, Roger, & Co., 6, Princes-st, Mansion House

Delhi and London Bank, 123, Bishopsgate-st

DEUTSCHE BANK, 1, Draper's-gdns, E.C.

English Bank of Rio Janeiro, 2A, Moorgate-st, E.C.

ENGLISH, SCOTTISH, & AUSTRALIAN BANK, 73, Cornhill

German Bank of London, 34, Old Broad-st, E.C.

Gillett Bros. & Co., 9, Birchin-la, E.C.

Green, Tomkinson & Lloyd, 32, Nicholas-la

Grindlay & Co., 55, Parliament-st.

Harwood, Knight, and Allen, 18, Cornhill

HONG KONG AND SHANGHAI BANK, 31, Lombard-st

Imperial Ottoman Bank (limited by shares to bearer), 26, Throgmorton-st

International Bank of London, 50, Old Broad-st

IONIAN BANK, 33, Lombard-st

King, Henry S., & Co., 45, Pall Mall; and 65, Cornhill

Land Mortgage Bank of India, 4, East India-avenue

Land Mortgage Bank of Victoria, 17, King's Arms-yard, E.C.

London and Hanseatic Bank, 27, Lombard-st

London and River Plate Bank, 52, Moorgate-st

London and San Francisco Bank, 22, Old Broad-st

London and Yorkshire Bank, Draper's-gdns, E.C.

London Bk. of Mexico & South America, 144, Leadenhall-st

LONDON CHARTERED BANK OF AUSTRALIA, 2, Old Broad-st

MERCANTILE BANK OF SYDNEY, 158, Leadenhall-st

Mercantile International Bank, 5, Copthall-bdgs, E.C.

NATIONAL BANK OF AUSTRALASIA, 149, Leadenhall-st

National Bank of India, 39A, Threadneedle-st

National Bank of New Zealand, 71, Old Broad-st

National Dis. Co., 35, Cornhill

New London and Brazilian Bank, 8, Tokenhouse-yd

New Oriental Bank Corporation, 40, Threadneedle-st

Queensland National Bank, 29, Lombard-st

Richardson & Co., 13, Pall Mall

RUSSIAN BANK, 32, Lombard-st

Samuel Montagu & Co., 60, Old Broad-st

Seyd & Co., 38, Lombard-st

SOCIÉTÉ GÉNÉRALE DE PARIS, 38, Lombard-st

Standard Bk. of Brit. S. Africa, 10, Clement's-la, Lombard-st

Town and Country Bank of South Australia, 18, King William-st

Union Bank of Australia, 1, Bank-bdgs, E.C.

Union Bank of Spain and England, 21, Old Broad-st, E.C.

Baptists.—The Baptist Union of Great Britain and Ireland comprises all the churches contained in the revised list appended to the annual report of 1873, together with such other churches, &c., as have since been admitted in conformity with its rules. Its declaration of principle is thus stated: "In this Union it is fully recognised that every separate church has liberty to interpret and administer the laws of Christ, and that the immersion of believers is the only Christian baptism." The objects of the Union include, besides the general advancement and well doing of Baptists, both socially and from the special points of view of their religious faith, conference and co-operation with other Christian communities, as occasion may require, and the maintenance of the right of all men everywhere to freedom from disadvantage, restraint, and taxation in matters purely religious. The Union acts by its assembly and through its officers and council. The assembly consists of representative, personal, and honorary members. Representative members comprise ministers of churches, heads and tutors of colleges, and delegates from churches, associations, and societies. Personal members are members of Baptist churches, who have been duly accredited in writing by at least three members of the assembly, and accepted by the council. Honorary members are chosen by a resolution of the assembly on the nomination of the council. The assembly meets in London in the spring to receive the report of the council and the audited accounts, to elect officers, council, &c., and for other business; and in the autumn at such place, if possible in the provinces, as the council may arrange. The offices of the Union are at 19, Furnival-st, Holborn, and the secretary is the Rev. S. H. Booth, D.D. Full particulars respecting the Baptist community throughout the United Kingdom will be found in the Baptist Handbook, published under the direction of the Union by Messrs. Alexander and Shepheard, 21, Furnival-st, Holborn. *The Freeman*, weekly, price 1d., the *Baptist Magazine*, monthly, price 6d. (both published at 21, Furnival-st) and *The Baptist*, weekly, 1d. (published at 61, Paternoster-row), are the organs of the denomination.

THE LONDON BAPTIST ASSOCIATION is the main organisation of the denomination in London. Its objects are stated to be "The co-operation of the associated churches in efforts to advance the Kingdom of Christ in connection with the Baptist denomination in London and its suburbs; the promotion of Christian union amongst their officers and members; the erection, or purchase, of at least one chapel in each year in the metropolis or its suburbs; and the adoption of such

measures as shall from time to time be deemed conducive to the prosperity and consolidation of the associated churches."

The secretary to the London Baptist Association is Rev. F. A. Jones; 23, Douglas-rd, Canonbury.

Amongst the institutions connected with the denomination is the Pastors' College (under the entirely gratuitous management of the Rev. C. H. Spurgeon), which, commenced upon a very small scale in the year 1856, has since that date educated and sent forth a small army of men into the ministry, besides giving gratuitous evening education to an even larger number.

Also under the presidency of the Rev. C. H. Spurgeon is the Stockwell Orphanage, which is purely undenominational in its character, and was founded, about fifteen years ago, for the maintenance and education of destitute fatherless boys between the ages of six and ten. The boys are selected by the committee, and are located in separate houses, under the care of matrons. The committee add, in their report, that the lads "are not distinguished by a uniform, which in many cases becomes a degrading badge of poverty."

THE METROPOLITAN ASSOCIATION OF STRICT BAPTIST CHURCHES represents a smaller body, and has for its objects: "To promote the unity, edification, and prosperity of these churches, and to devise and employ means for extending the cause of God in London and its suburbs." Secretary, Rev. J. Box, 80, Grove-la, Camberwell, S.E.

The following is a list of those Baptist churches in the metropolitan district which have seats for 400 persons and upwards, with the dates of their foundation :—
(L., London Baptist Association. M., Metropolitan. G.B., General Baptist Association. E., Essex. S.M., Surrey and Middlesex. Churches marked * are not connected with the Union. Places in italics are subordinate stations, mostly with chapels.)

Acton. 1865. L.
Balham, Ramsden-rd. 1874. L.
Barking-rd Tabernacle. 1871. L.
Battersea Chapel. 1797. L.
Battersea, Lammas Hall, Surrey-la. 1868. L.
Battersea-pk Chapel. 1870. L.

Belle Isle. 1877. L.
Bermondsey :—
   Drummond-rd. 1866. L.
   *Lynton-rd. 1813.
   Abbey-st. 1878.
Blackheath, Shooter's-hill-rd. 1866.
Bloomsbury Chapel. 1849. L.
   *Moor-st, St. Giles's. 1867.
Bow, High-st. 1785. L.
Bow-com, Blackthorn-st. 1867. L.
Brentford, N., Park Chapel. 1819. S.M.
Brixton-hill :—
   Cornwall-rd. 1868. L.
   Barrington-rd. 1868. L.
   New Park-rd. 1840. L.
Brockley. 1867. L.
   „   Creek-rd. 1877.
Brompton, Onslow Chapel. 1852. L.
Bromley & Poplar Taber. 1856. L.
Brondesbury. 1879.
Camberwell :—
   Denmark-pl. 1823. L.
   Cottage-gn. 1854. L.
   Charles-st. 1835. L.
Camberwell-gate. 1833. L.
Camden-rd. 1857. L.
Castle-st, Oxford-st. 1859. L.
Chalk Farm, Berkley-rd. 1866. L.
Chelsea, Lower Sloane-st. 1814. L.
Child's-hill. 1877. L.
Clapham-com. 1787. L.
Clapton, Downs Chapel. 1869. L.
Clerkenwell :—
   *Chadwell-st. 1851. M.
   *Wilderness-row. 1865.
Commercial-rd. 1653. G.B. and L.
*Dalston, Queen's-rd. 1852.
Dalston Junction. 1871. L.
Deptford :—
   Octavius-st. 1863. L.
   *New ⊥-rd. 1842. M.
Dulwich, East. 1871. L.
Ealing Dean. 1866. L.
East London Tabernacle. 1858. L.
Edgware-rd :—
   Church-st. 1831. G.B. & L.
   John-st. 1800. L.
   Shouldham-st. 1870. M.
*Enfield Highway, Totteridge-rd. 1868. L.
Finchley, North. 1868. L.
*Finsbury, Eldon-st. 1823.
Golden-la and Hoxton. 1864. L.
Gower-st, Euston-sq. 1820.
Greenwich :—
   Lewisham-rd. 1838. L.
   South-st. 1859. L.
*Gunnersbury, Trinity. 1874.
Hackney, Mare-st. 1798. L.
   „   Lauriston-rd. 1825.
Hampstead, Heath-st. 1862. L.
Hatcham, Lausanne-rd. 1871. L.
Henrietta-st, Brunswick-sq. 1817. L.
Highgate-rd. 1878. L.
Highbury-hill. 1871. L.
*Hill-st, Dorset-sq. 1827. M.

Holloway, Upper. 1868. L.

Hornsey Rise, Sunnyside-rd. 1871. L.

Ilford, High-st. 1801.

Islington :—
Cross-st. 1840. L.
Salters' Hall, Baxter-rd. 1821. L.

John-st, Bedford-row. 1818. L.

Kennington-la, Upper. 1864. L.

*Kensington Tabernacle. 1870. L.

Kensington, Addison-pk. 1848. M.

Keppel-st. 1795. M.

*Kilburn.Canterbury-rd. 1865. L.

King's ✛ rd :—
Arthur-st. 1646. L.
Vernon Chapel. 1860. L.

Kingsgate-st, Holborn. 1735. L.
Lambeth :—
Regent-st. 1819.
Upton Chapel. 1783. L.

Lee, High-rd. 1855. L.

Leyton. 1876. L.

Leytonstone. 1878. L.

Leytonstone-rd. 1875. L.

Little Wild-st, W.C. 1691. L.

Metropolitan Tabernacle. 1719. L.

*New North-rd, Wilton-sq. 1857.

Norwood, Lower :—
Chatsworth-rd. 1878. L.
Gipsy-rd. 1882. L.

Norwood, Upper. 1852. L.

Notting-hill :—
Cornwall-rd. 1865. L.
West London Tab. 1864.

Old Kent-rd :—
*Maze Pond Chapel. 1692.

Oxford-st, Soho Chapel. 1825. M.

Paddington :—
Westbrne-pk. 1877. G.B. and L.
Praed-st. 1834. G.B. and L.
Bosworth-rd. 1878.

Peckham :—
Park-rd. 1854. L.
Rye-la. 1819. L.

Penge, Maple-rd. 1866. L.

Pimlico :—
*Westbourne-st. 1830. M.

Poplar, Cotton-st. 1811. L.

*Putney, Ravenna-rd. 1859.

Regent's-pk Chapel. 1855. L.

*Shepherd's Bush. 1868.

Shoreditch Tabernacle. 1835. L.

Southwark :—
Borough-rd. 1674. L.
*Trinity-st, Borough. 1877.

Spencer-pl, Goswell-rd. 1815. L.

*Stepney, Whitehorse-st. 1824.

Stockwell Chapel. 1866. L.

Stoke Newington-rd. 1638.

St. John's Wd, Abbey-rd. 1863. L.

Stratford :—
Carpenter's-rd. 1877. L.
The Grove. 1854. L.

Surrey Tabernacle.

Sydenham. 1858. L.

Tottenham :—
High-rd. 1827. L.
West-gn. 1869. L.

*Victoria Docks. 1871. L.

Victoria-pk :—
Grove-rd. 1868. L.
Parnell-rd. 1858. L.

Waltham Abbey, Paradise - row. 1729. L. & E.

Walthamstow :—
Boundary-rd. 1876. L. & E.
Wood-st. 1851. L.

Walworth, East-st. 1791. M.

Walworth-rd. 1805. L.

Wandsworth, East-hill. 1859. L.

Wandsworth-rd. 1873. L.

Westbourne-gr. 1823. L.

Westminster, Romney-st. 1866. L

Whitechapel :—
Commercial-st. 1633. L.
*Little Alie-st. 1753.
Zoar Chapel. 1865.

Woodberry Down, Finsbury pk. 1883.

Barber's Hall,

Monkwell-st, Cripplegate, E.C.—This fine old building, designed by Inigo Jones, was one of the few old City halls which escaped the Great Fire. It contains amongst other curious objects, the shell of an immense turtle presented by Her Majesty Queen Anne, and a pair of antlers, the gift of Charles II. But the principal objects of interest are the pictures, which comprise amongst others, a portrait of the Countess of Richmond by Sir Peter Lely, a portrait of Inigo Jones by Van Dyke, and the celebrated painting by Holbein of King Henry VIII. granting the charter to the Barber-Surgeons. There are other good pictures of less interest, and the hall is on the whole worthy a visit. NEAREST *Ry. Stn.*, Aldersgate-st ; *Omnibus Rte.*, Aldersgate-st ; *Cab Rank*, Aldersgate-st (Jewin-st).

Bargains

are to be had in London, of course, but only by those who know very well what they are about. The numerous "bankrupt's stocks," "tremendous sacrifices," and so forth, are simply traps for the unwary. Avoid, especially, shops where the windows are packed so full that there is no light inside to examine articles by. One of the commonest tricks of all is that of putting in the window, say a handsome mantle worth eight or ten guineas, and labelled say, "£3 15s.," and keeping inside for sale others made up in precisely the same style, but of utterly worthless material. If they decline to sell you the actual thing out of the window, be sure

that the whole affair is a swindle. See, too, that in taking it from the window they do not drop it behind the counter and substitute one of the others, an ingenious little bit of juggling not very difficult of performance. Another very taking device is the attaching to each article a price-label in black ink, elaborately altered in red to one twenty or five-and-twenty per cent. less. This has a very ingenuous air. But when the price has been —as it commonly has—raised 30 or 40 per cent. before the first black-ink marking, the practical economy is not large. Of course, if you do buy anything out of one of these shops, you will take it with you. If you have it sent, be particularly careful not to pay for it until it arrives, and not then until you have thoroughly examined it. When a shop of this kind sends you "patterns," you will usually find a request attached not to cut them. Always carefully disregard this, keeping a small piece for comparison. There are, however, some houses where, if you at all understand your business, real bargains are at times to be had. The only safe guide to these is the advice of some London friend personally acquainted with the particular shop recommended.

Barracks.

— Compared with any Continental capital, the permanent accommodation for troops in London is almost inappreciably small. The following is a list of the various barracks :

CHELSEA, Chelsea-br-rd *(Infantry).*— NEAREST *Ry. Stns.*, Sloane-sq and Grosvenor-rd ; *Omnibus Rte.*, Pimlico-rd ; *Cab Rank*, Sloane-sq.

HYDE-PK, Knightsbridge *(Cavalry).*— NEAREST *Ry. Stn.*, High-st, Kensington ; *Omnibus Rte.*, Knightsbridge ; *Cab Rank*, Ennismore-gdns.

KENSINGTON, Church-st *(Cavalry and Infantry).*— NEAREST *Ry. Stn.*, High-st, Kensington ; *Omnibus Rte.*, Kensington-rd ; *Cab Ranks*, Edwardes-sq and Albert-hall.

REGENT'S-PK, Albany-st *(Cavalry).*— NEAREST *Ry. Stn.*, Portland-rd ; *Omnibus Rte.*, Albany-st ; *Cab Rank*, Great Portland-st.

ST. GEORGE'S, Trafalgar-sq *(Infantry & Recruiting).*— NEAREST *Ry. Stns.*, Charing ✛ (Dis.

S.E.); *Omnibus Rtes.*, Trafalgar-sq, St. Martin's-la, and Strand; *Cab Rank*, Trafalgar - sq (E. side).

ST. JOHN'S WOOD, Ordnance-rd *(Horse Artillery)*.—NEAREST*Ry. Stn.*, Marlborough-rd; *Omnibus Rte.*, Wellington-rd; *Cab Rank*, Queen's-rd.

TOWER *(Infantry, Artillery, & Royal Engineers)*.—NEAREST *Ry. Stns.*, Tower of London (Met.) and Fenchurch-st(G.E.); *Omnibus Rte.*, Fenchurch - st; *Cab Rank*, Gt. Tower-hill.

WELLINGTON, Birdcage - walk *(Infantry)*.—NEAREST *Ry. Stn.*, St. James's-pk; *Omnibus Rtes.* Grosvenor-pl and Victoria-st; *Cab Ranks*, James-st and Buckingham gate.

Baths.—The following are the principal, from which returns have been received *(and see* SEA WATER BATHS) :

ALBANY BATHS, 83, York-rd, Westminster-br-rd.— Open daily from 6 a.m. till 10 p.m. Sunday mornings from 6 till 10. Swimming, tepid, 6d.; Hot, 1st class, 1s., 2nd, 6d.; Cold, 1st class, 1s., 2nd, 6d.; Shower, cold, 6d. Swimming taught by Prof. Parker. Special arrangements with schools and clubs.

ARGYLL BATHS, 10, Argyll-pl, Regent-st, W., open from 7 a.m till 9 p.m. Terms : Warm bath, 1s. ; Bran or Saltwater do. (Tidman's sea salt), 2s. ; Russian vapour or Harrogate do., 3s. 6d. ; Turkish hot-air do. (private), 4s.; "The Sultan's Bath," 5s. ; Sulphur - vapour, medicated, and mineral, 4s. Subscriptions: Twelve transferable warm bath tickets, 10s. ; 26 do., 20s. ; 6 sultan's or hot-air do., 21s.; 8 sulphur, medicated, or mineral do., 20s. ; 12 bran or sea-salt (Tidman's) do., 21s. ; 8 Russian vapour or Harrogate do., 21s. Douche baths, ascending, descending, or spinal, under the bather's control, 1s. 6d. ; 21 transferable tickets, 21s.

BELL'S BATHS, 119, Buckingham Palace-rd.—Swimming, cold, 1s. ; Plunge, 1s. ; Shower, hot or cold, 1s. ; Vapour, 3s. 6d. ; Turkish Bath open from 8 a.m. to 6 p.m ; Sundays from 9 a.m. to 1 p.m., 2s. 6d. ; 12 tickets £1 5s.

BURTON'S BATHS, 182 and 184, Euston - rd, N.W.—Turkish or Roman baths for ladies and gentlemen. For ladies : From 8 a.m. to 5 p.m., 2s. 6d. ; from 5 p.m. to 8 p.m., 1s. 6d. A course of ten Baths, from 8 a.m. to 5 p.m., £1 ; ditto, from 5 p.m. to 8 p.m., 12s. 6d. For gentlemen : From 7 a.m. to 5 p.m., 2s. 6d. ; from 5 p.m. to 9 p.m., 1s. 6d.

CAMDEN TURKISH BATHS, 11A, Kentish Tn.-rd, and 176, High-st, Camden Tn.—Turkish bath, 8 a.m. to 5 p.m. 2s. 6d., 5 p.m. to 10 p.m. 1s. 6d. ; 3 transferable tickets 7s. and 4s., 7 tickets 15s. and 9s.; Sulphur bath, 5s. ; Electric bath, 3s. ; Warm, Cold, and other baths in great variety. Particulars on application.

CROWN BATHS, Kennington Oval.—One of the largest swimming baths in London. Facing the Surrey Cricket Ground. Swimming, 6d.; Hot or Cold, 6d.; ditto, ladies, 6d.

DALSTON JUNCTION BATHS, Ashwin-st, Dalston, facing station.—Open 8 a.m. to 10 p.m. every day except Sun. Turkish, 1s. 6d. Ladies' days, Mon. and Fri., 8 a.m. to 5 p.m., and Wed., till 9 p.m. Hot, cold, shower, and plunge, ladies and gentlemen, daily, from 6d. to 1s. Reductions on transferable tickets taken in series, and on tickets available between 8 a.m. and 4 p.m. only.

FAULKNER'S, G.E. Ry. Station, Fenchurch-st.—Hot or cold, 1s.; Shower, hot or cold, 1s. The shower if taken with other baths is 6d.

FAULKNER'S, 26 and 27, Villiers-st.—Sulphur, vapour, medicated, mineral, 4s., 6 tickets for £1 ; Russian vapour baths, 3s., 8 tickets for £1 ; Hot or Cold, 1s. ; Shower, hot or cold, 1s. If the shower is taken with ordinary bath only 6d. is charged.

FAULKNER'S, 50, Newgate-st.— Hot or cold, 1s. ; Plunge, 9d. ; Shower, hot or cold, 1s. ; Turkish, 2s. ; after 5 p.m. 1s. 6d. ; Douche, 1s. The shower, if taken with another bath, 6d.

GOUDY'S TURKISH, 8, Harrow-rd.—7 a.m. to 9 a.m., and 4 p.m.

to 9 p.m., Saturdays from 2 p.m., 1s. 6d. ; 9 a.m. to 4 p.m., and 9 p.m. to 10 p.m., 2s. 6d.

GROSVENOR TURKISH BATH, 119, Buckingham Palace-rd, S.W. —The bath is heated and ventilated on the new principle. For gentlemen only. Open daily, from 8 a.m. until 9.30 p.m. ; Sun., 8 a.m. until 1 p.m. From 8 a.m. to 9.30 p.m., single ticket, 3s.

HAMMAM TURKISH BATH, 76, Jermyn-st. — From 7 a.m. to 9 p.m. ; 12 tickets, 36s. (3s. each); after 7 p.m., 2s., 12 tickets, 20s. ; members of the medical profession at reduced rates. Chiropodist in attendance at the bath.

KING'S ✠ TURKISH BATHS, 9, Caledonian-rd, King's ✠.—Gentlemen only ; open from 8 a.m. to 10 p.m. ; Sundays, 8 a.m. to 1 p.m. Turkish bath, 2s. 6d.; 10 tickets, transferable, £1.

LAMBETH BATHS, 156, Westminster-br-rd. — The swimming baths are open during the summer only. Swimming, 1st class, 6d., 2nd, 2d.; Hot or Cold, 1st class, 6d., 2nd, 3d.; superior ditto, with fire, &c., 1s.

MARLBOROUGH BATHS, 100, Walworth-rd, Newington. — Prepared with sea-salt. Female attendants for ladies. Hot or Cold, 1s.; Shower, hot or cold, 1s.

NEVILL'S BATHS (The Aldgate), Gentlemen's entrance, 44, High-st, E. ; Ladies', 7, Commercial-rd, E —Two distinct baths in the same building, one for ladies and one for gentlemen. Open from 9 a.m. till 10 p.m. Turkish, 2s. 6d.; after 6 in the evening, 1s. 6d. Their Turkish Baths, 7 and 8, Railway Approach, London-bridge, S.E., are open from 9 a.m. to 10 p.m., and their Charing Cross Turkish Bath, Northumberland - avenue, from 7 a.m. t 10 p.m.

PADDINGTON PUBLIC BATHS and WASHHOUSES, Queen's-rd, Bayswater, close to the Queen's-rd and Rl. Oak Stations.—Swimming, 1st class, 8d., or 10 for 5s. ; 2nd, 4d. ; 3rd, 2d. ; Hot, 1st class, 6d., 2nd, 2d.; Cold, 1st class, 3d.; 2nd, 1d. ; Shower, hot, 1st class, 6d., 2nd, 2d.; cold, 1st class, 3d., 2nd, 1d. There is besides a first class swimming bath for ladies, 8d., or 10 for 5s. ; and private baths the same as for men. There is also a public laundry, where persons may have the use of tubs, hot and cold water, steam wringers, drying chambers, irons, and mangles, at a charge of 1½d. per hour.

PUBLIC BATHS AND WASHHOUSES, St. Giles-in-the-Fields and St. George's, Bloomsbury, Endell-st, Bloomsbury. — Swimming, 1st class, 4d.; 2nd, 2d.; Warm, 1st class, 6d., 2nd, 2d.; Cold, 1st class, 3d., 2nd, 1d.; Shower, warm, 1st class, 6d, 2nd, 4d.; Shower, cold, 1st class, 3d., 2nd, 2d. Washing places, with wringing machine, drying closets, mangles, and iron, for each hour, 1½d. During the months of April, May, June, July, August, and September the baths are open from 6 a.m. till 9 p.m.; on Fri. and Sat till 10.30 p.m. On Sun. men's baths only are open from 6 till 8.30 a.m. During the other six months the baths are open from 8 a.m. till 9 p.m., except Sat., when the baths are open till 10 p.m. The washhouses are open from 8 a.m. till 8 p.m.

ROMAN BATH, 5, Strand-la, Strand (near Somerset House).— A cold plunging bath, built by the Earl of Essex in 1588, open all the year round, from 7 a.m. to 8 p.m. on week-days, and on Sundays from 8 a.m. to 1 p.m. Subscription: yearly, £2; half-yearly, £1 5s.; quarterly, 18s.; monthly, 10s.; twelve tickets, 8s. 6d.; six tickets, 4s. 6d.; three tickets, 2s. 6d.; single ticket, 1s. From 1st October to 30th April, a single ticket is 6d. The bath is constantly supplied from the spring, and discharges at the rate of ten tons each day.

ROYAL YORK BATHS, 54, Yorker, York - gate, Regent's - pk.— Hot or cold, 1st class, 1s., 2nd, 6d.; Shower, hot, 1s., cold, 6d.; Vapour, 2s. 6d.; with electricity, 3s.; Turkish, until 5 p.m., 2s. 6d., after, 1s. 6d.; with electricity, double; Douche, 1s. 6d. Dr. Caplin's electro-chemical, Turkish, and medicated baths.

ST. GEORGE'S BATHS AND WASHHOUSES, 8, Davies-st, Berkeley-sq.—Swimming bath, 66ft. by 30ft. Tepid, 1st class, 4d., 2nd, 2d.; Hot, 1st class, 6d., 2nd, 2d.; Cold, 1st class, 3d., 2nd, 1d.; Shower, hot, 1st class, 6d., 2nd, 2d.; cold, 1st class, 3d., 2nd, 1d.

There is only one swimming bath: open Mon., Wed., and Fridays, for 1st class, and Tu., Th., and Sat. for 2nd class. This establishment is closed on Sundays. The laundry is open from 8 a.m. till 8 p.m. Each person is furnished with separate washing and drying compartments, with the use of tables, ironing stove, &c., at a charge of 1½d. per hour for the first three hours, and 2d. per hour afterwards.

ST. GEORGE'S BATHS AND WASHHOUSES, Buckingham Palace-rd, are at present being rebuilt.

ST. MARTIN-IN-THE-FIELDS BATHS AND LAUNDRIES, Orange-st, Leicester-sq. — Estab. 1849. Hot, 6d. and 2d.; Cold, 3d. and 1d.; Shower, hot, 6d., cold, 3d.

ST. MARYLEBONE PUBLIC BATHS AND WASHHOUSES, 181, Marylebone-rd, N.W.—Swimming (four baths), 2d., 4d., 6d., and 8d.; Hot, 1st class, 6d., 2nd, 2d.; Cold, 1st class, 3d., 2nd, 1d.; Shower, hot, 1st class, 6d., 2nd, 3d.; cold, 1st class, 3d., 2nd, 1d.; Vapour, 6d. The baths are open as follows: Men's baths, May, June, July, and August, from 5 a.m. till 10 p.m.; Sun., from 6 till 9 a.m. September, October, March, and April, from 7 a.m. till 9 p.m.; Sun., from 7 till 9 a.m. November, December, January, and February, from 8 a.m. till 8 p.m. Sat. nights till 10 throughout the year. Women's baths, open at 7 a.m. from June 1st to September 30th, and at 8 the remaining months; closing at 9 p.m. from March 1st to October 31st, and at 8 the rest of the year. Sat. nights till 10 throughout the year. The women's baths are not open on Sun. The tepid swimming baths are open from April 1st to October 31st. The washhouses are open throughout the year from 8 a.m. till 8 p.m. Each person is furnished with separate washing and drying rooms, the use of tables, irons, and ironing blankets, at the charge of 1½d. per hour. The entrance to the washhouses and 2nd class women's baths is in Seymour-pl.

ST. PANCRAS PUBLIC BATHS AND WASHHOUSES, 70, King-st, Camden Tn., and Tottenham-ct-rd, near Euston-rd. — 1st class, Warm, 6d.; Cold, or cold shower, 3d.; Swimming, 6d.; Warm, includ-

ing shower, 9d.; Warm, Vapour, or Needle, 1s. 2nd class, Warm, 2d.; Cold, 1d.; Swimming, 2d. The baths are open from May to August inclusive, from 6 a.m. till 10 p.m.; during September, October, March, and April, from 7 a.m. till 9 p.m. From November to February inclusive, from 8 a.m. to 8.30 p.m. On Sun. from the time of opening until 9 a.m. The washhouses are open from 8 a.m. to 8 p.m., at 1½d. per hour. The swimming baths are open for the use of ladies on the following days: Sat. at the King-st baths, and Wed. at the Tottenham-ct-rd baths, from the time of opening until noon.

SMITH'S BATHS, 275, City-rd.— Hot, 6d., cold, 3d.; Shower, 6d.; Turkish, 1s.; Douche, 6d.; Plunge, 6d. Ladies' day every Wed.

TURKISH BATH, 29, Church-st, Islington, near the Agricultural Hall.—Open for gentlemen: Sun., 9 a.m. till noon; Mon., 5 p.m. till 9 p.m.; Tu., Wed., Fri., and Sat., 9 a.m. till 9 p.m.; Th. is a ladies' day only. Ladies: Mon., 9 a.m. till 2 p.m.; Th., 9 a.m. till 8 p.m. A single bath, day or night, 1s.6d.; a book of 8 tickets, 10s. 6d. Closed on Bank Holidays and Christmas Day.

Battersea Park (Maps 11 and 12) is on the Surrey side of the river, in the S.W. dis. One of the youngest of London parks, it is certainly one of the prettiest. No park or garden in London can compare with the sub-tropical garden, which is emphatically one of the sights which no visitor should fail to see, especially in the latter part of the summer. The park contains excellent drives, and is encircled by a superior Rotten Row, or prepared ride. There is every accommodation for cricketers, and boating may be indulged in on the lake, which adds greatly to the picturesqueness of the ingeniously planned grounds. The park gates are in Albert-rd, Prince of Wales's-rd, and Victoria-rd, and the fine terrace-walk facing the river is directly approached from the steamboat pier. Light refreshments may be had at nearly all the lodges, and in the neighbourhood of the park there is good accommodation. The best way of approaching Battersea from the west is along the Grosvenor-rd and over Chelsea Suspension-bridge. NEAREST *Bridges,*

Chelsea and Albert; *Steamboat Pier* and *Ry. Stn.*, Battersea-pk.

Bedford College for Ladies, 8 & 9, York-pl, Baker-st, is under the management of a council, and gives a good education to young women. Students are not admitted under 16 years of age, and may either pursue a systematic course of study, or select any number of separate classes. The work is suitable for ladies desirous of matriculating and graduating at the University of London. There are lectures in biology, chemistry, and physics, and there are biological, chemical, and physic laboratories for the use of students. All information may be obtained of the hon. sec. at the college.

Beefsteak Club, 24, King William-st, Strand.—"There is no particular object in this club, nor is there any particular qualification." Entrance fee, £10 10s.; subscription,£5 5s. The accommodation being limited, visitors are not admitted.

Beggars. — Visitors should bear in mind—what residents should know already—that the impostorship of street beggars is the one rule to which, as yet, there has been no known exception. London beggardom is a close corporation, and allows of no nonprofessional interlopers. If you wish to relieve "distress" of any deserving—or undeserving—object enquire, according to your personal predilections, of the parish clergyman, the Little Sisters of the Poor, or the relieving officer, and you may find plenty. In the streets you will find none but professional toll-takers levying *ad valorem* dues on personal weakness. To get rid of your beggar, when wearisome, if he be English, take no notice of him at all. He will follow you till you meet a more likely-looking person, but no farther. If he has anything to sell, reply simply, "Got one," and pass on. If your tormentor be an Italian, lift your forefinger, knuckle upwards, to the level of your wrist, as it hangs by your side, and wag it twice or thrice from side to side. Your Italian, who will take no other negative, accepts that instantly. Charitably disposed persons, especially residents in London, who, by reason of their public position, or even from the fact of their names being in the *Court Guide*, or in any of the charity subscription lists, are objects of interest to the great army of begging - letter writers, cannot do better than become members of the society for the Suppression of Mendicity. This institution, which has been established upwards of 60 years, has its office in Red Lion-sq, Holborn, where the secretary may be addressed. The plan of the society is stated in its report to be the issue of printed tickets to be given to street beggars instead of money; which tickets refer them to the society's office, where their cases are investigated and disposed of according to circumstances. Relief in money, blankets, clothing, &c., is afforded to applicants who, upon investigation, are proved to be deserving. The society is in constant communication with the several metropolitan parishes, hospitals, dispensaries, &c., with a view to provide for necessitous and afflicted persons: whilst the managers also have it in their power to offer suitable employment at the Society's labour premises to every able-bodied mendicant referred to the office. Governors may obtain tickets for distribution at any time on applying by letter, or personally, at the society's office. The annual payment of £1 1s. constitutes the donor a governor, and the payment of £10 10s. at one time, or within a year, a governor for life. A system of enquiry into the merits of persons who are in the habit of begging by letter is incorporated with the society's proceedings. The following persons are entitled to refer such letters to the office for investigation—it being understood that the eventual relief rests with the subscriber sending the case: all contributors to the general funds of the society to the amount of £21; all contributors to the general funds of the society to the amount of £10 10s., and who also subscribe £1 1s. annually; all subscribers of £2 2s. and upwards per annum. The Charity Organisation Society, 15, Buckingham-st, W.C., also undertakes the investigation of the cases of persons soliciting relief from the benevolent, and also obtains and furnishes confidentially accurate information as to the *bona fides* of the numerous charitable societies which appeal for public support. The Society also procures and gives a large amount of charitable relief.

Belgium. — MINISTRY, 36, Grosvenor-gdns. NEAREST *Ry. Stn.*, Victoria; *Omnibus Rtes.*, Buckingham Palace-rd, Grosvenor-pl, and Victoria-st; *Cab Rank*, Victoria Station. CONSULATE, 118, Bishopsgate-st, E.C. NEAREST *Ry. Stn.*, *Omnibus Rte.*, and *Cab Rank*, Bishopsgate-st.

Bermondsey Leather Market.—This great leather, or rather hide market, lies in Weston-st, ten minutes' walk from the Surrey side of London-br. The neighbourhood in which it stands is devoted entirely to skinners and tanners, and the air reeks with evil smells. The population is peculiar, and it is a sight at 12 o'clock to see the men pouring out from all the works. Their clothes are marked with many stains their trousers are discoloured by tan; some have apron and gaiters of raw hide; and about them all seems to hang a scent of blood. The market itself stands in the centre of a quiet block of buildings on the left-hand side of Weston-st the entry being through a gateway. Through this, a hundred yards down, a small square is reached. Most of it is roofed but there is an open space in the centre. Under the roofing are huge piles of fresh hides and sheepskins. There is no noise or bustle, and but few people about. There are no retail purchasers, the sales being almost entirely made to the great tanners in the neighbourhood. The warehouses round are all full of tanned hides; the yards behind the high walls are all tanneries, with their tens of thousands of hides soaking in the pits. Any visitor going down to look at the Bermondsey hide-market should, if possible, procure beforehand an order to visit one of the great tanning establishments Unless this be done the visit to the market itself will hardly repay the trouble of the journey, or make up for the unpleasantness of the compound of horrible smells which pervade the whole neighbourhood. NEAREST *Ry. Stns.*, London-br *Omnibus Rtes.*, Tooley-st, Boro High-st, and Gt. Dover-st; *Cab Rank*, Bermondsey-sq.

Bethnal Green Branch of the South Kensington Museum (Map 4).—The Bethna

Green Museum stands on a plot of ground purchased by contributions of residents in that district, and transferred in February, 1869, by the subscribers, to the Lords of the Committee of Council on Education, as a site for a local museum. The building is externally of brick; the interior consists in part of the materials of the temporary structure originally erected at South Kensington. It was opened on the 24th June, 1872, by their Royal Highnesses the Prince and Princess of Wales, and was for nearly three years mainly occupied by the magnificent collections of paintings and other works of art belonging to Sir Richard Wallace, Bart. On the withdrawal of these collections they were replaced by various contributions on loan. The collection of National Portraits has been temporarily transferred from South Kensington by consent of the trustees, and now occupies the entire range of the picture gallery; and the central floor of the building is filled with paintings and art objects, many on loan from various owners. The rest of the space is chiefly occupied by the permanent collections of the Museum illustrating food, animal products, the utilisation of waste products, and paintings and other art objects on loan from various owners. THE FOOD COLLECTION was first established and became part of the South Kensington Museum in 1857; it is arranged with the express object of teaching the nature and sources of food, representing the chemical composition of the various substances used as food, and the natural sources from which they have been obtained. In a separate room is the Doubleday collection of British butterflies and moths, on loan from the trustees. As a branch of the South Kensington Museum, this institution is managed by the same staff, and the regulations as to admission, reception of objects, &c., are in most respects the same as in the parent museum. Omnibuses from the Mansion House pass close to the Museum; and trains run from Liverpool-st to Cambridge Heath station (within five minutes of the Museum) every ten minutes. Admission free from 10 a.m. to 10 p.m. on Mon., Th., and Sat., and from 10 a.m. to 4, 5, or 6 p.m. on Tu. and Fri. On Wed., 6d.,

from 10 a.m. till 4, 5, or 6 p.m. NEAREST *Ry. Stn.*, Cambridge-heath (G.E.); *Omnibus Rtes.*, Hackney-rd and Bethnal Gn.-rd; *Cab Rank*, Bethnal Gn.-rd.

Bicycling; or rather cycling, which signifies the art of riding the bicycle, the tricycle, and all of their kind; although of comparatively recent introduction, is already very prominent among athletic exercises. Not only are there over 300,000 machines in constant use, in every grade of society, but the visitor to London or any other large city cannot fail to see upon all sides tangible evidence of the manifold uses to which the cycle is put for carrying messages, mails, newspapers, parcels, etc. It is probable that, in spite of the crowded condition of the streets, this branch of the art will be illimitably extended, to the saving of a vast amount of money, to say nothing of cruelty to horseflesh. Nor is the social aspect of the sport is the metropolis in the background, for a great number of cycling clubs exist within the City and suburban limits. The oldest of these is the Pickwick, the largest of the London, each of which, in conjunction with kindred clubs, in years gone by demonstrated to the British public, by an annual meet and parade at Hampton Court, the importance of the pastime. The toleration for which the growing army of wheelmen then prayed, has long since been granted; their *locus standi* is established in the courts beyond dispute; and conflicts with the remainder of the road-using community are happily conspicuous by their absence. Races upon the road are now wisely discountenanced by the majority of clubs, but a highly satisfactory alternative is provided in contests held on specially constructed tracks, which in the metropolitan area are located at the Crystal and Alexandra Palaces, Stamford Bridge, and Surbiton; at one or the other of which every Saturday afternoon during the summer season an attractive programme is offered to the general public. The legal rights of the cyclists are ably looked after by the National Cyclists' Union, established in 1878, whose head-quarters are at 57, Basinghall-st, E.C. It consists of affiliated clubs and unattached riders, numbering in the aggregate close upon 10,000. The

Union occupies, in relation to cycling, a position identical with that of the Jockey Club in connection with the turf. It framed and upholds the tenets of Amateurism, by which the sport is governed; it inaugurated and still promotes the Bicycling and Tricycling Championships annually competed for under its auspices; and, while on the one hand it protects to the full the rights of subscriber and non-subscriber alike, it discourages all infractions of even the spirit of the law. The Cyclists' Touring Club, whose chief offices are at 139 and 140, Fleet-street, like its coadjutor, the Union, was formed some ten years since. It provides at greatly reduced rates excellent hotel accommodation, not only in Great Britain, but also in the Colonies, the United States, and upon the Continent; gives information as to the best routes; appoints consuls, who, in provincial towns, guide their visiting fellows to the local "lions"; and in countless other ways encourages and simplifies the prosecution of the pastime. The subscriptions to both these bodies are only nominal.

Cycling has long had a literature of its own. *The Cycling Times* (East Temple Chambers, Whitefriars-st), and the *Monthly Gazette* of the Cyclists' Touring Club before referred to, are the chief publications.

Billiards.—Amateurs of this game should remember that "billiard sharps," as well as billiard tables, abound in every quarter of London. As these gentry get their living by infesting public tables, the unskilled amateur should avoid playing or betting with strangers, whose "form" is apt to improve at critical moments in the most unlooked-for fashion. "Championship" and other important matches, as well as the popular "American Tournaments," have, during the last year or two, been extremely popular. These matches take place at the Royal Aquarium, the Billiard Hall in Argyll-st, and elsewhere, and comfortable accommodation will be found for spectators at varying charges. Occasionally an afternoon is set apart for ladies, when smoking is not allowed. Full particulars will always be found advertised in the principal sporting papers. Tables are to be found in most of the chief thoroughfares, and all hotels and the larger public-houses possess at least one. The usual charges are 1s. an hour for daylight play, or 1s. 6d. by gaslight. If by the game, 6d. for 50 up.

Billingsgate (Map 8), so called, according to Geoffrey of Monmouth, after Belin, King of the Britons, who built the first water-gate here in 400 B.C.—is styled by Fuller "the Esculine gate of London," and is a stone building, completed in 1874. It stands on the left bank of the river, a little below London-br. For full description see DICKENS'S DICTIONARY OF THE THAMES. The market opens at 5 a.m. throughout the year, its business being practically completed by 10 a.m. Until very recently it was the only fish-market in London, the magnificent Columbia Market presented to the metropolis by the liberality of the Baroness Burdett-Coutts having hopelessly failed to establish any hold upon the trade. But for the last three years an experimental fish market has been opened in Farringdon-rd, which has proved anything but a success. NEAREST *Ry. Stns.*, Mansion House (Dis.), Cannon - st (S.E.), and Fenchurch - st (G.E.) ; *Omnibus Rtes.*, Cannon-st, King William-st, Gracechurch-st, Fenchurch-st, and London-br ; *Cab Rank*, Fish-st-hill.

Bill-posting.—The ordinary charge for exhibiting bills on hoardings is from a penny to twopence per sheet of "double crown" or "double demy," but very great judgment is required both in selecting stations and composing the bill itself. One chief point to bear in mind is to have as little in your bill as possible. Another is to have something novel and striking to the eye. All the best stations are in private hands, and must be treated for in detail. Be careful in all cases to have a written agreement.

Births.—(See REGISTERS.)

Blackfriars Bridge (Map 7) one of the handsomest in London, and would have a still better effect were not its appearance marred by the proximity of its neighbour, the Alexandra (London Chatham and Dover Ry.) Bridge. It was built in 1864-9, at a cost of £265,000, from the designs of Mr. J. Cubitt, although those of

Mr. Page, the architect of Westminster-br, had been selected in the first instance. It crosses the river in five spans, the centre span being 185 feet. The piers are of granite, surmounted by recesses resting on short pillars of polished red Aberdeen granite, and with ornamental stone parapets. The parapet of the bridge itself is very low, which, with the extreme shortness of the ornamental pillars at the pier ends, gives the whole structure rather a dwarfed and stunted look ; but the general outline is bold and the *ensemble* rich, if perhaps a trifle gaudy, especially when the gilding, of which there is an unusual proportion, has been freshly renewed. NEAREST *Ry. Stns.*, St. Paul's (L. C. & D. R.), and Blackfriars (Dis.), north side ; *Omnibus Rtes.*, Blackfriars-rd (south) and Ludgate-hill and Fleet-st (north) ; *Cab Rank*, Bridge-st.

Blackwall (Map 9). — Here are the East India Docks, where the principal sailing ships trading from London load and discharge. The visitor may in these docks inspect long tiers of China tea-clippers—now almost run off the line by fast steamers—and the fine passenger ships trading to the Australasian ports. Adjoining the docks is the spacious ship-building yard of Messrs. Green, and farther down the river are the Trinity House head-quarters, beyond which again are the Royal Victoria and Albert Docks. There is a railway-station on the steamboat-pier. Fares from Fenchurch-st (17 min.) 1st, -/6, -/10 ; 2nd, -/4, -/6 ; trains running each way every 15 min. Steamers from Westminster, Charing +, Temple, and London-bridge, every half-hour. Fares : aft, -/6 ; forward, -/4. Omnibus from Bank of England.

Blue Coat School.—(See CHRIST'S HOSPITAL.)

Board of Green Cloth, Buckingham Palace, is a branch of the Lord Steward's Department. Hours 11 to 4. NEAREST *Ry. Stns.*, Victoria ; *Omnibus Rtes.*, Victoria-st and Grosvenor-pl ; *Cab Rank*, James-st.

Bolivia. — CONSULATE, 14, Austin Friars, E.C. NEAREST *Ry. Stns.*, Broad-st and Cannon-st ; *Omnibus Rtes.*, Old Broad-st and Bishopsgate-st ; *Cab Rank*, Liverpool-st Stn.

Bond Street (Map 6) is, next only to Regent-st, the main artery between Oxford-st and Piccadilly. It was once, *par excellence*, the fashionable street of London. Here the "beaux" of one period and the "bucks" of another strolled up and down, criticising the exterior of others, and showing off their own. In those days a man was made or marred by the fold of his neck-cloth or the set of his coat, and men spent as much thought on their attire as did women. In this respect Bond-st is entirely changed, it is no longer a lounge, and those who would see the "lounger" of the present day must look for him in the "Row." Except, indeed, in Pall Mall, there is too much traffic and bustle for the languid walk which appears to be one of the marked characteristics of "beaux" of all times and of all nations ; and the ghost of Brummell would sigh over a Bond-st occupied by a busy throng of foot-passengers, and invaded by omnibuses. As a fashionable street it has been eclipsed by Regent-st, but in point of high-class shops it can still hold its own against its younger rival, and it is strong in exhibitions and art galleries. In this respect a great addition was made by the erection by Sir Coutts Lindsay of the Grosvenor Gallery, a handsome building on the western side of the street. On the eastern side is the Doré Gallery, devoted solely to the pictures of the great French artist, and there are almost invariably many other picture shows in Bond-st, Old and New.

Boodle's Club, 28, St. James's-st.—Proprietary. No particular qualification. Number of members limited to 600. Entrance fee, £31 10s. ; subscription, £11 11s.

Books of Reference. — The first and most universally useful of London books of reference is, of course, Messrs. Kelly's POST OFFICE DIRECTORY. In this gigantic annual will be found every kind of information as to the local habitation of Londoners of every class. Collingridge's CITY DIRECTORY does the same service with regard to the more limited area with which it deals, giving at the same time a large amount of very interesting information with regard to other matters affecting the City and its Corporation

Webster's Royal Red Book deals in similar fashion, as does also the Court Guide, with the West End of the town, and is a much more manageable volume in point of size; whilst Dean & Sons' Export Merchant Shippers of London, &c., gives in comparatively small compass a vast amount of information as to the commercial operations of the great metropolitan market; and Lieut-Col. Ivey's Club Directory contains a good deal of information concerning, not only most of the London, but a large number of foreign and colonial clubs. Of Railway Guides, we have the London and Provincial Bradshaw, and the handy A B C Alphabetical Guide, for the especial behoof of travellers from and to London. As a companion to the picture galleries of London, nothing better could be desired than Miss Thompson's compact little Handbook to the Picture Galleries of Europe (Macmillan & Co.), which gives catalogues of all the principal galleries, with critical notices both of paintings and masters. To those more particularly interested in the ecclesiological aspect of London may be recommended Mackeson's Guide to the London Churches and Chapels; the Rev. J. H. Sperling's Church Walks in Middlesex (Masters); the very compact little Tourist's Church Guide, issued by the English Church Union, with detailed information as to every church where Holy Communion is celebrated weekly; the (Roman) Catholic Directory, Ecclesiastical Register, and Almanac (Burns and Oates); The Baptist Handbook (Alexander and Shepheard), published under the direction of the Baptist Union; and The Congregational Year-Book (Hodder and Stoughton), which contains the proceedings of the Congregational Union, and the general statistics of the denomination. Mitchell's Newspaper Directory gives a comprehensive list of the newspapers—daily, weekly, fortnightly, monthly, and others —not only of London, but of the entire kingdom, with particulars of their politics, circulation, &c., in the *ipsissima verba* of the several proprietors. The same may be said in respect of the charities of the metropolis with regard to Mr. Herbert Fry's admirable little

work, the Royal Guide to the London Charities, wherein will be found at full length the nature and object of each institution dealt with, the names of its various officers, the mode in which application for assistance from it is to be made, the amount collected by it in the preceding year, and the purposes to which that amount has been applied. Haunted London (Chatto and Windus) is a cheap reprint of Mr. Thornbury's interesting work, edited by Mr. E. Walford, and an invaluable companion for those who care for something beyond the mere practical workaday view of our somewhat prosaic London streets. The Tower and the Scaffold (C. Kegan Paul & Co.) is a brief historical sketch, a little one-sided here and there, but interesting and pleasantly written, and Mr. Timbs's History of Clubs and Club Life (Chatto and Windus), a bulky little volume of 530 solid pages, thickly interspersed with capital woodcuts, gives a mass of entertaining information on one of the most characteristic features of London life. Of guide books proper we have the usual three—Murray, Black, and Baedeker—each in his own peculiar style doing for strangers in London the useful work he has so often done for Londoners elsewhere. Mr. Murray, in particular, has issued a new edition of his handbook, bearing date 1879, the revision of which, however, has hardly been so thorough as might have been anticipated or desired. Messrs. Cook provide a small sixpenny pamphlet for the special benefit of their tourists; and Messrs. Bacon another at the same price for the public at large, with two capital large maps, and about a hundred little illustrations of various features of interest scattered here and there throughout the book; and, finally, Mr. Herbert Fry addresses himself to the general public with a thick volume entitled London in 1884, and presenting the novel feature of a series of bird's-eye views from various central points, such as London-br, looking S., the Poultry, looking E., the Criterion, looking W., and so forth. Messrs. Nelson and Co., on the other hand, provide us with a number of little volumes of the descriptive and pictorial class, one devoted to lithographic illustrations of the principal places of

interest at the West End, with brief historical and descriptive paragraphs; another with effectively executed coloured illustrations of picturesque and interesting localities near London, and so forth. Dickens's Dictionary of the Thames does for the river " From Its Source to the Nore " what Dickens's Dictionary of London has done for the metropolis. Its object is " To give practical information to oarsmen, anglers, yachtsmen, and others directly interested in the river; to serve as a guide to the numerous strangers who annually visit the principal places on its banks; to furnish a book of reference for residents; as well as to provide in a concise form a useful handbook for those conected with the port of London and its trade." Racing men, boating men, naturalists, scientists, anglers, and idlers, will all alike find their tastes and interests specially consulted, whilst the collector of curiosities of literature will be agreeably surprised by the space devoted to the epitaphs of more or less eccentricity, culled from the numerous churchyards along the river bank, which forms one of the most prominent features of the work. Messrs. Taunt & Co. also publish a capital little Pocket Guide to the Thames. The Tourist's Guide Round About London (Edward Stanford, Charing ┼) deals generally with the historical, architectural, archæological, and picturesque aspect of the environs within a circle of 12 miles. It does not, however, confine itself strictly within those limits, outlines of a few walking excursions being given to places such as Hatfield, Windsor, &c. The book is arranged alphabetically and divided into two sections; one dealing with the places within, the other with those beyond, the four-mile circle. As might be anticipated, a prominent feature in the book is its map, which extends from Southall to Crayford, and from Potter's Bar to Caterham Junction, and is one of the clearest we have seen. Messrs. Bemrose and Sons send us a whole series of handbooks, one for each of the railways, and printed uniform with the time-books issued by the companies. They are compiled on the panoramic plan, each page being vertically bisected by a little railway, with two little trains running, one up to, the other down from town, and with all the stations, tunnels, river-crossings, &c., duly marked. On either side is a brief description of the various places lying on that side of the road, and the whole forms a handy companion on any of those country excursions which are probably never so thoroughly enjoyed as after a long spell of London. Messrs. Marlborough's POPULAR GUIDE UP THE THAMES TO KEW, RICHMOND, AND HAMPTON COURT is a useful little sixpenny pamphlet, full of neat little woodcuts; and Messrs. Waterlow's UP THE RIVER FROM WESTMINSTER TO WINDSOR AND OXFORD, is a large work on a similar plan, and with two capital folding maps. Weldon's GUIDE TO THE RIVER LEA is not illustrated, but contains a great deal of useful information, and has a map of the river; and Weldon's GUIDE TO EPPING FOREST, with a coloured map, is a capital little handbook, which all who propose indulging in summer rambles, through as wild and picturesque a bit of country as may well be found within an easy half-hour of the "great metropolis," will do well to get.

Borough (The) (Map 14).—Lies on the Surrey side of London-br, and is one of the busiest parts of London. In the Borough will be found the headquarters of the hop trade, merchants' and factors' offices clustering thickly about the north end of the High-st. The Borough Market, at the foot of St. Saviour's Church, is one of the largest fruit and vegetable markets in London. The beautiful church of St. Saviour's, close to the western corner of the southern approach to the bridge, although externally spoilt and dwarfed by the high-level line of railway which runs by its side, is one of the ecclesiastical gems of London.

Botanic Garden, Chelsea, S.W. (*See* APOTHECARIES' HALL.)

Botanic Society (Royal) of London, Regent's-pk (Map 2).—Candidates for admission to the society must be proposed by 3 Fellows of the society, and elected by ballot. Persons elected Fellows pay an admission fee of £5 5s., and an annual contribution of £2 2s., or one sum of £26 5s., which payment includes the admission fee,

and exempts from all further contributions. Fellows are entitled to vote at general meetings, to personal admission to the gardens, &c., whenever they are open, and to the personal admission of two friends to the gardens, &c., on ordinary occasions. Persons elected members pay a sum of £10 10s. for life, without entrance fee. Members have personal admission to the gardens, &c., whenever they are open, but not the privilege of admitting friends to the gardens. A payment of £15 15s. by a Fellow of the Society (in addition to his or her subscription) will entitle him or her to the possession of one ivory transferable ticket, admitting two persons daily to the gardens on all occasions, including exhibitions, fêtes, &c. The ivory tickets are only available during the natural or legal life of the Fellow of the Society to whom they are issued. These tickets can be had, either in the form of one white ticket admitting two persons, or two red, each admitting one person. Annual transferable tickets, admitting two visitors to the gardens daily, including all exhibitions and fêtes, are issued to Fellows of the Society at the price of £3 3s. in addition to the subscription. This society was incorporated in 1839 by a royal charter granted to several noblemen and gentlemen for the "Promotion of Botany in all its branches, and its application to Medicine, Arts, and Manufactures, and also for the formation of extensive Botanical and Ornamental Gardens within the immediate vicinity of the Metropolis." The gardens of the society (nearly 20 acres in extent) comprise the whole of the inner circle of the Regent's-pk, held under a Crown lease, terminating in the year 1901; and comprise an ornamental park, a piece of water, a winter garden, hothouses, and a tank for tropical plants, collections of medico-botanical, economic, and other plants and trees, arranged in the order of their natural affinities in the open ground, a library of botanical works, and a museum. Botanical lectures, free to visitors to the gardens, are given at 4 o'clock on Fridays in May and June. Free tickets for three months' study are issued to artists and students, and specimens given to students and teachers.

Exhibitions of plants and fruits for prizes take place at stated periods during the spring and summer; provision is also made for extensive displays of special plants during the season.—*(For dates for* 1888, *see* CALENDAR.) There are musical promenades on the Wednesdays in May, June, and July not occupied by exhibitions. Admission by the special promenade orders only. On promenade, exhibition, and fête days, bands of music are engaged. NEAREST *Ry. Stns.,* Baker-st and Portland-rd (Met.); *Omnibus Rtes.,* Marylebone-rd, Baker-st, and Albany-st; *Cab Ranks,* Portland-rd Stn and Baker-st.

Boxing.—Professional pugilism has died out, as much choked by the malpractices of its followers as strangled by public opinion; and the public-houses kept by such men as Ben Caunt, Nat Langham, or Jem Ward, are no longer among the attractions London life has to offer to the Corinthian Toms or Jerry Hawthorns of the day, whose manner of enjoying themselves would indeed somewhat astonish their prototypes. The "noble art of self-defence" is not, however, altogether neglected, but finds its place among the athletic sports, and the clubs by which it is encouraged may be congratulated on keeping alive one of the oldest institutions, in the way of manly exercise, on record. Perhaps the two most important of these clubs are the Cestus Boxing Club, and the West London Boxing Club, the latter being an offshoot of the West London Rowing Club, Boxing, it may be noted, has always been popular with rowing men as a capital exercise for keeping up some sort of condition during the winter months. The Cestus Boxing Club requires an entrance fee of 5s., and an annual subscription of 5s.; the election is by ballot at a general meeting, one black ball in five to exclude. The season is from October to March, and the practice-night is Wednesday, when a professional instructor attends. Valuable prizes are from time to time offered for competition among gentleman amateurs. The head-quarters of the club are at the Surrey Cricket Ground, where the hon. sec. may be addressed. With a, perhaps unconscious, touch of humour, the club has adopted red and black as its distinctive colours—delicately suggestive of the "claret" which is occasionally "tapped" at its meetings, and the black eyes sometimes "worn" by the members. The members of the West London Boxing Club meet at Wafte's Rooms, 19, Brewer-st, Regen -st. Some few years ago the Marquis of Queensberry presented three handsome challenge cups for the encouragement of amateur boxers, and the light, middle, and heavy weights compete for these once a year. The entrance fee is 10s. for each candidate, and the winners receive silver medals. There is the further inducement that if the prize be won three years in succession the holder will receive a handsome silver cup. The judging is in the hands of the committee of the Amateur Athletic Club, the secretary of which may be applied to for further information, and there is an important clause in the rules that the committee reserve the right of requiring a reference or of refusing an entry. Other London boxing clubs are the "Belsize," Swiss Cottage, Finchley-rd ; "German Gymnastic," St. Pancras - rd ; "London Athletic," Stamford-br; "St. James's," Albert - viaduct, Peckham ; the "Mid-London," Champion Hotel, Aldersgate-st ; the "Myddleton," Bricklayers' Arms, New North-rd ; and the "Royal Victor," Royal Victor Hotel, Old Ford-rd. The Amateur Boxing Association is composed of the clubs before mentioned and of several other important clubs, mostly having their head-quarters in the metropolis, and was founded in 1880 with the following objects : (a) The association of all recognised amateur boxing and athletic clubs, who shall abide by, and conduct all open competitions under the rules and regulations of the Boxing Association. (b) The encouragement and development of boxing, the holding of boxing matches or competitions, and assaults-at-arms, and the giving of prizes at such matches or competitions. (c) The institution (where necessary) of championship prizes ; the governing of championship meetings ; the acceptance of money given or subscribed ; the distribution thereof ; and the granting of sums of money, in order to establish prizes in connection with boxing matches or competitions, on such terms as may be prescribed by the committee. The subscrip-

tion for boxing or other clubs joining the association is £1 1s. per annum ; its management is vested in the committee, which is to be annually elected by ballot, and the secretary is Mr. Eugene Cox, 2, Angel-ct, Throgmorton-st, from whom any information regarding the association may be obtained.

Brazil.—MINISTRY, 32, Grosvenor-gdns. NEAREST Ry. Stn., Victoria ; Omnibus Rtes., Buckingham Palace-rd, Grosvenor-pl, and Victoria-st ; Cab Rank, Victoria Stn. CONSULATE, 5, Great Winchester-st. NEAREST Ry. Stns., Broad-st (N.L.), and Bishopsgate (Met.); Omnibus Rte., Old Broad-st ; Cab Rank, New Broad-st.

Bricabrac.—In London, as everywhere else, the bricabrac hunter and collector of works of art must very carefully bear in mind the old maxim, caveat emptor. While among the London dealers in such goods there are many most respectable and trustworthy men, there are many of quite a different class ; and, unfortunately, as a rule, the power of discriminating between them is only to be obtained by, possibly disastrous, experience. Let the buyer, to begin with, bear in mind that there are only three courses open to him, if he would buy with satisfaction to himself and credit to his collection. The first and simplest, as well as the rarest, is that he shall go to market thoroughly understanding what he is about ; the second, which is occasionally dangerous, is to trust to a well-informed friend ; and the third, is to know where to find a straightforward dealer in what he wants who will treat him well and openly. In the last case it is well not to pretend to any more knowledge than you may actually possess. The expert will infallibly find you out, and the temptation to take advantage of you will be immeasurably increased.

The following list includes most of the leading houses in this trade in London :

BOORE, W., 54, Strand. Gold and silver.

DURLACHER BROS., 23A, Old Bond-st. Oriental china and every description of decorative objects.

JOSEPH, E., 158, New Bond-st. Dresden china.

PHILLIPS, S. J., 113, New Bond st. Gold and silver.

RADLEY, EDWARD, 16, Old Bond-st. Furniture.

RATHBONE, F., 20, Alfred-pl-west, South Kensington. Old Wedgwood.

WAREHAM, W., 14 & 15, Charing ✠ road, W.C. Oriental china and enamels.

WERTHEIMER, S., 154, New Bond-st. Ormolu, furniture, Sèvres.

WHITEHEAD, T., 8, Duke-st, St. James's. Bronzes, silver, prints, enamels, majolica, &c.

Bridges.—After a long struggle the metropolitan bridges are now all free. There are 18 bridges in all, from London Bridge to Hammersmith inclusive, viz. : 13 for carriage and foot-passenger traffic ; one for railway traffic, with side-walk for foot-passengers only ; and four exclusively for railway purposes. Commencing with the highest up-stream they run as follows : Hammersmith, Putney, Wandsworth, Battersea (railway), Battersea, Albert, Victoria (Chelsea), Grosvenor (railway), Vauxhall, Lambeth, Westminster, Charing ✠ (railway and foot), Waterloo, Blackfriars, Alexandra (railway), Southwark, Cannon-st (railway), and London. All, together with the Tower Subway, will be found under their proper alphabetical headings.

Britannia Theatre, Hoxton (Map 4).—An unusually well-built theatre, and, apart from any critical estimate of the performances, one of the sights which a visitor should on no account miss seeing. There is very little attempt at decoration, the brick walls being left bare. But the shape of the building is perfect, there not being a single seat from pit to gallery which does not command a good view of the stage. This latter, too, is one of the most commodious in London. The performances are, of course, not of the West End type, not being intended for a West End audience. But they are almost always good of their kind. The great point of interest for the visitor is the audience itself ; and the general arrangements in front, all intended for the accommodation of those accustomed to the penny rather than the pound as the basis of their calculations, are well worth noting. NEAREST Ry.

Stn., Shoreditch (N.L.); *Omnibus Rtes.*, Kingsland-rd, Pitfield-st, and Old-st, St. Luke's.

British Artists, Society of.—(*See* SOCIETY OF BRITISH ARTISTS.)

British Museum, Great Russell-st, Bloomsbury (Map 3).— Free. With the year 1879 this institution commenced a new era. For a century it was scarcely anything else than a storehouse of the treasures of the ancient world, and the curiosities of science, literature, and art; but to-day its invaluable accumulations are being brought out and adapted to the uses of the age, and the public are invited to profit by the many beautiful lessons they can silently but surely teach. The British Museum is now open every day, and the baby in arms is no longer excluded. Lectures are frequently delivered. On Mon. and Sat. all the galleries are thrown open; on Tu. and Th. all except the British and Mediæval Antiquities and Ethnography; on Wed. and Fri. all except the antiquities on the upper floor and the rest of the department of Greek and Roman antiquities (set apart on those days for fine-art students). The hours of admission are from 10 all the year round, in January, February, November, December, till 4; March, April, September, October, till 5; and May to August till 6. On Mon. and Sat. from May 1st till the middle of July till 8, and onwards till the end of August till 7. This variety in the hours of opening is due to the necessity of closing at dusk. The galleries are not artificially lighted: experiments have, however, been tried in the Reading-room with the electric light, which will be continued in the winter months. Admission to the Reading-room (for study and copying), to the department of prints and drawings (for the same), to the sculpture galleries (to draw from statues and busts), and to the coin and medal room (for study), is granted on application to the principal librarian, supported by the recommendation of a householder or someone of known position. To save trouble, the recommendation of a person whose name can be found in the ordinary directories should be sent. The British Museum was first opened on the 15th January, 1759. Its principal components were then the Museum of Sir Hans Sloane of Chelsea (bought for £20,000), the Cottonian library (presented by Sir J. Cotton, 1700), and the Harleian manuscripts (acquired for £10,000). By Act of Parliament, passed in 1753, the institution was vested in trustees for the nation; the £30,000 required for the Sloane and Harley collections, with a further sum to fund for salaries and expenses, having been raised by a lottery sanctioned by the same Act. These tributaries to the stream of knowledge were deposited in Montagu House, a mansion standing in its own grounds, now occupied by the present building. The Museum may be roughly described as a square formed of four wings, the central space covered by a separate structure—the Reading-room. It is an imposing fabric of the Grecian Ionic order, designed by Sir Robert Smirke. Passing into the hall from the stately portico, you have on the staircase the Amravati sculptures recently transferred from the India Museum; on the right hand are books and manuscripts: The GRENVILLE LIBRARY (rarest editions and finest examples of typography, with block books, valued at £54,000, bequeathed); the MANUSCRIPT DEPARTMENT (50,000 volumes, 45,000 charters and rolls. 7,000 seals, and 100 ancient papyri, including the Cotton, Harley, Lansdowne, Egerton, and additional collections); the MANUSCRIPT SALOON (autograph letters of eminent persons, illuminated manuscripts, rich bindings, and great seals); the KING'S LIBRARY (65,000 volumes, presented by George IV., remarkable productions of the printing-presses of Europe and Asia). In the same library an EXHIBITION OF DRAWINGS AND ENGRAVINGS. On the left you have the ROMAN GALLERY (Busts of Emperors, Roman antiquities found in England); three GRÆCO-ROMAN GALLERIES (sculptures of the Greek school, found chiefly in Italy, including the Townley, £20,000, Payne-Knight, valued with other antiquities at £60,000, bequeathed; Farnese, Cyrene, and Priene marbles, including the Venus from Ostia, the Discobolos, Giustiniani Apollo, Clytiè, Muses, Mercury, Satyrs; and in the basement, mosaics, tessellated pavements); the ARCHAIC GREEK ROOM (Harpy Tomb from Xanthus, seated figures from Branchidæ, Etruscan sepulchral monument); the new EPHESUS ROOM (remains of the celebrated Temple of Diana of the Ephesians, recovered by J. Turtle Wood); the ELGIN ROOM (grandest remains of Greek sculpture, the Parthenon marbles and procession-frieze, works of Pheidias, greatest of Greek sculptors; purchased in 1816 of Lord Elgin for £35,000, now priceless; also colossal Lion from Cnidus); the HELLENIC ROOM (frieze, &c., of Temple of Apollo, erected at Phigalia by Iktinos, excavated by C. R. Cockerell, purchased for £19,000; the Diadumenos, athletes); the new MAUSOLEUM ROOM (one of the Seven Wonders of the ancient world, the colossal chariot-tomb erected to Mausolos by his sister-wife Artemisia, discovered by C. T. Newton). ASSYRIAN GALLERIES: Sculptured slabs from Nineveh, now Kouyunjik, and Babylon, acquired during the Layard, Loftus, George Smith (*Daily Telegraph*), and Rassam explorations; illustrating most completely the daily life, religion, warfare, art, literature, and customs of the Assyrians and Babylonians, and bearing strong testimony to the accuracy of portions of biblical history. The clusters of Assyrian ivories, bronzes, seals, and glass are unrivalled, and the cuneiform tablets are a library in themselves; the Creation, Fall of Man, Tower of Babel, and Deluge tablets, Seals of Ilgi, B.C. 2050, Sennacherib, Darius, Assyrian accounts of Sennacherib's expedition against Hezekiah. In Basement: the Siege of Lachish, Lion hunts by Assurbanipal III., Sardanapalus, very finely wrought, also processions, dogs, &c.; Sculptures from the ancient city of Karchemish, showing the undeciphered picture writing of the Hamathites, excavated by Consul P. Henderson in 1880. EGYPTIAN GALLERIES: Colossal statues of divinities and Pharaohs, "the Vocal Memnon," sarcophagi, graveyard tablets, obelisks, fresco paintings, hieroglyphics, the Rosetta stone, key to Egyptian language; from Memphis, Abydos, Thebes, Karnac, and Luxor; dating from before Abraham to the Ptolemies, in beautiful state of preservation. On Staircase: Papyri, the pictured Ritual of the dead. Most of the larger sculptures were surrendered to the English on the capitulation of Alexandria in 1801. Antiquities from Cyprus: small statues, busts, and miscellaneous ornaments. Before you in the hall is the new LYCIAN ROOM: Sculptures from Lycia, obtained by Sir C. Fellows, lofty tombs, friezes, statues of Nereids, graceful and expressive of motion. On the floor above are the galleries containing the smaller objects of antiquity: Etruscan sarcophagi, and other relics of the remarkable people of Etruria: Egyptian mummies, embalmed animals, coffins, sepulchral ornaments, representations of divinities in gold, silver, and porcelain; furniture, ivories, bronzes, vases, dresses, weapons, and tools. Smaller Assyrian objects (bronze gates from Balawat, recording in five reliefs campaigns of Shalmaneser II.). The Refreshment-room. The second northern gallery contains the magnificent collections of coins and medals; the specimens of Nielli (from which the art of engraving was derived); exhibition of engravings, etc. VASE ROOMS: Painted fictile vases, Hamilton, Canino, Payne-Knight, and other collections, from tombs, principally Etruscan and Greek; illustrating by paintings the divine and heroic legends of the Greeks; mural paintings, terra-cotta statuettes, drinking-cups, toys, &c. BRONZE ROOMS: Greek, Etruscan, and Roman bronzes, deities, heroes, mirrors, candelabra, lamps, vases; head of Artemis (finest period of Greek art), Venus, Bacchus, Apollo, Hercules, seated philosopher, Meleager, Mercury. The GLASS COLLECTIONS: Slade and Temple cabinets; Egyptian, Phœnician, Roman, Anglo-Saxon, Venetian, French, German, Dutch, and Spanish examples; "Chri-tian glass." TEUTONIC AND ANGLO-SAXON Antiquities. PREHISTORIC SALOON, (vestiges of early Man). MEDIÆVAL GALLERY (ivories, armour, etc.). ORIENTAL SALOON. These are in process of arrangement, and cannot now be described. They take the place of the Natural History collections. ETHNOGRAPHICAL GALLERY: Idols, fetishes, dresses, ornaments, implements, and weapons of the savage races of the world, including the articles gathered by Captain Cook in the South Sea Islands. ORNAMENT AND GEM ROOM: Payne-Knight, Strozzi

(Blacas) (purchased in 1866 with other antiquities for £40,000), Castellani, and other collections; the Portland Vase; ancient gold, silver, and amber ornaments; fine illustrations of the goldsmith's art among the Etruscans, Greeks, and Romans; intaglios and cameos unsurpassed for delicacy and beauty; Byzantine, Teutonic, Anglo-Saxon, and later ornaments; Keltic gold breastplate and rings. Beyond the new Lycian Room is the READING-ROOM: Tickets to view are given by the messenger in the hall; a circular structure; original suggestion of Thomas Watts, improved by A. (Sir A.) Panizzi, carried out by Mr. Sidney Smirke; dome 140 feet in diameter, height 106 feet; 60,000 books in the three tiers inside; space for 1,500,000 inside and out; in the basement are also the Map and Chart Departments, newspaper and music libraries. There are over 1,500,000 volumes in the department of printed books at the present date. The Reading-room is open daily from Jan. to Apl., and Sept. to Dec., from 9 a.m. till 8 p.m., and from May to Aug. till 7, and is lighted after dusk by the electric light. Beyond, in the north wing, is the old library, in a part of which, once the reading-room, Thomas Carlyle and Lord Macaulay worked; it is now part of the cataloguing department. It may be noted here that, under the new regulations, tickets for the reading-room are not renewed; once on the register, always a reader, and there is no need to show the ticket if the reader is known to the doorkeeper. Persons under twenty-one are not admitted except for purely literary work—not for study for examinations. The Department of PRINTS AND DRAWINGS: Entrance by staircase at the end of the Egyptian Gallery; the richest assemblage of etchings and engravings in Europe; open to students every day in the week at 10; closes at 4 all the year round except from the beginning of April to the end of July, when it is shut at 5. Contains the collections of Sloane (including the Albrecht Dürer drawings), Payne-Knight, Cracherode, Cunningham, early Italian and German prints; Lawrence drawings; Hamilton, Townley, Moll, Sheepshanks, Rembrandt etchings, Harding, Morghen, Gell, Craven, Ed. Hawkins (caricatures), Slade

and Henderson. The Department of COINS AND MEDALS has the choicest and most extensive numismatic collections in the world scientifically arranged; and includes the Roberts, Payne-Knight, Marsden, Temple, De Salis, Wigan, Blacas, Woodhouse, and Bank of England cabinets.

THE NATURAL HISTORY COLLECTIONS are now removed to the elegant terra-cotta building in the Cromwell-rd, near the South Kensington Museum, designed by Mr. Alfred Waterhouse. Open daily at 10. The ZOOLOGICAL DEPARTMENT contains the finest specimens in Europe of birds (British birds and their nests; Gould collection of humming-birds), mammalia, shells, corals, osteology (see collection of skulls), fishes, and other members of the animal creation. The GEOLOGICAL DEPARTMENT comprises fossil plants, fishes, reptiles (South African, &c.), saurians, wingless birds, gigantic eggs, sponges, corals, shells, insects, the mammoth, megatherium, pigmy elephant, human remains, principally formed from the collections of Dr. Solander, Hawkins, Mantell, Dr. Croizet, Bain, &c., and extensive purchases. The MINERAL DEPARTMENT includes a splendid collection of meteorites, aërolites, siderolites, portions of other planets and aerial formations; the Melbourne meteorite, three and a half tons; the collections of Greville, Greg, Kokscharoff, &c.; a well-arranged series of minerals, including diamonds, gold nuggets, crystals, and gems of every variety and degree of purity and splendour. In the BOTANICAL DEPARTMENT are flowerless plants, fungi, sea-weed, lichens, mosses, ferns, flowering plants, grasses and sedges, palms, cycads, conifers, parasitical plants, fruits and stems, fossil plants, polished sections of woods, cones, &c., from the herbaria of Sir Hans Sloane, 1753, Sir Joseph Banks, 1827, Robert Brown, Rev. R. Blight, and others. Admission to study the collections scientifically is granted on application to the Director of the Natural History Museum, Cromwell-rd, S.W. The PORTRAITS, until lately hung in the Zoological Gallery, have been for the most part handed over to the National Portrait Gallery. NEAREST *Ry. Stns.*, Gower-st (Met.) and Temple (Dis.); *Omnibus Rtes.*, Oxford-st, Tottenham-court-rd, and Euston rd; *Cab Ranks*, Bury-st and Southampton-row.

Brooks's Club, St. James's-st.—(Formerly " Almacks.") Entrance fee, £15 15s.; annual subscription, £11 11s.

Buckingham Palace (Map 6) is the only palace in London used by the Queen as a residence, and at one period was confined exclusively to that purpose, both drawing-rooms and levees being held at St. James's. Several years since, however, the crush at the former was found unendurable, and they were, therefore, transferred to the larger rooms of Buckingham Palace. There are some few good pictures, but no regular collection. As the Lord Chamberlain is inundated with applications to view the Palace it is well to state that orders to view are never given, except so far as regards the Royal Stables, for which an order must be obtained from the department of the Master of the Horse. There are fine gardens occupying the space on the north front—where are Her Majesty's private apartments —between Constitution-hill and Grosvenor-place. NEAREST *Ry. Stns.*, Victoria and St. James's-pk; *Omnibus Rtes.*, Grosvenor-pl, Victoria-st, Whitehall, and Piccadilly; *Cab Rank*, James-st.

Buenos Ayres.—(*See* ARGENTINE REPUBLIC.)

Building Societies.—These are societies established for the purpose of raising by subscription a fund for making advances to their members by way of mortgage upon security of freehold, copyhold, or leasehold property, repayable by periodical instalments. The first society on record was the Greenwich Building Society, founded in the year 1809. From that time until 1836 several existed. In the latter year the Act of 6 & 7 William IV. c. 32, was passed for the purpose of affording these societies encouragement and protection, and this Act continues to regulate all societies established previous to 1874, and not registered under the Act passed in that year. In 1874 the Act of 37 & 38 Vict. c. 42, was passed, which not only governs those established after the passing of the Act, but also all the then existing societies which should register

themselves under its provisions. This statute confers various powers upon building societies, treats them as bodies corporate having a common seal, and declares the liability of members to be limited in respect of any share upon which no advance has been made to the amount already paid or in arrear on such share, and in respect of any share upon which an advance has been made, to the amount payable under any mortgage to the society. Since 1836, it is estimated that building societies have enabled more than 100,000 persons to become proprietors of houses or land. They are especially advantageous in the case of members purchasing the houses of which they are tenants, such members applying the rents in repayment of the advance, and thus converting rent into capital. Very little liability attaches to the society on account of any depreciation in the value of any property, as the mortgage securities are constantly improving as every instalment is paid. Members have the advantage of knowing before they commence negotiations the exact amount they will have to pay for legal and survey charges, for which a moderate scale is always provided and set forth in the rules.

Building societies may be divided into three classes, viz.: (*a*) Permanent; (*b*) Terminating; and (*c*) Bowkett and Starr-Bowkett societies.

(*a*) Permanent societies consist of two classes of members, viz.: investing and borrowing. Investing members take shares, which can either be paid up in full or by periodical payments, interest being allowed in the meantime. Borrowing members secure the amount borrowed by way of mortgage, the same being repayable by periodical instalments extending over a fixed period of years.

Amongst the principal societies of this class may be mentioned the following, viz.: Birkbeck, Carlton, Liberator, Monarch, Planet, Reliance, Standard, Sun, and Temperance.

(*b*) Terminating societies consist of members making a periodical subscription during the existence of the society, the object being to continue the society until every member shall have had an advance. When the subscriptions amount to

a sufficient sum to be advanced, the amount is lent to one of the members upon mortgage, who then pays an increased subscription so long as the society lasts. The chief difference between these and permanent societies is that in these societies all the members must join at the same time, or on joining afterwards will be required to make a back payment equal to the subscriptions from the commencement of the society. No member can with certainty calculate how long the society will last, or how long he will have to subscribe; but in permanent societies, membership may commence and cease at any time,

(*c*) Bowkett and Starr-Bowkett societies are also terminating societies, and differ but little from those last mentioned. They were originated by Dr. Bowkett, and have been improved upon by Mr. Starr. Each of the members of these societies subscribes a weekly sum, and when an amount sufficient for an appropriation has been received a ballot or sale takes place, and the member obtaining the appropriation secures the repayment of the amount without interest, by way of mortgage, by periodical instalments extended over 10 or 12½ years. The instalments so repaid increase the funds out of which, together with the other members' subscriptions, future appropriations are made. The member continues the weekly subscription on his shares till he has paid the sum mentioned in the rules, and this is returned to him on the termination of the society, less a small deduction for working expenses. The principle of these societies is, that the member lends the society annually a small sum, to be repaid at its termination, in return for which the society lends him a large sum without interest for a certain period.

The following are the principal Building Societies, according to the official returns furnished by their respective secretaries:

BIRKBECK BUILDING SOC., 29 and 30, Southampton-bdgs, Chancery-lane.—*Subscription:* Amount varies according to the term for which money is borrowed. *Object:* To advance money to its members to purchase their own houses, the advances being repaid by monthly or other instalments extending over any period not exceeding 21 years,

BOROUGH OF LAMBETH NO. 3 PERMANENT BUILDING SOC., 128, Westminster-br-rd.—*Subscription:* 5s. per month per share to investors of £30 shares. Entrance fee, 2s. per share to investors; 2s. 6d. per share to borrowers. *Object:* To enable persons to purchase house property by making advances repayable by monthly instalments.

CARLTON PERMANENT BENEFIT BUILDING SOC., 28, Goldensq.—Shares £20 each, bearing 5 per cent. interest, and payable in full or by monthly instalments; surplus profits divided annually. *Object:* To enable its members to invest large or small sums with perfect security, and to make them advances to enable them to purchase freehold, copyhold, or leasehold property (especially houses of which they are tenants), or to pay off outstanding mortgages, &c.

COMMERCIAL PERMANENT BENEFIT BUILDING SOC., 32, East India Dock-rd, Limehouse.—*Subscription:* Deposit shares, £1 each. May be paid in full or by instalments of 1s. and upwards weekly or otherwise. No fines. *Object:* To enable provident persons to invest large or small sums at a remunerative interest. To lend the funds so invested upon mortgages of freehold and leasehold property to members possessing or purchasing such property.

COMMERCIAL UNION LAND, BUILDING, AND INVESTMENT SOC., 45, Fish-st-hill. Established 19 years.—*Subscription:* Shares, £25 each, payable in one sum or by subscription of 2s. 6d. per share per month; 5 per cent. allowed on deposits, and 3 per cent. on drawing accounts, modified according to notice. *Object:* To enable its members to purchase freehold or leasehold house property or land.

EFFRA MUTUAL BENEFIT BUILDING SOC., 22, Chancery-la (Block C). Established 1859.—*Subscription:* Investing shares, £60, payable by monthly subscriptions of 10s.; borrowing shares, £10 each. *Object:* To enable its members profitably to invest their savings, or to erect or purchase their own dwellings or other leasehold or freehold property.

GENERAL MUTUAL INVESTMENT BUILDING SOC., 44, Bedfordrow.—*Subscription:* 2s. 6d., 5s., and 10s. monthly. *Object:* To make advances towards the purchase of houses for occupation, and generally to assist all classes to acquire real and leasehold estate.

HATHERLEY PERMANENT BUILDING SOC., 30, Great Smith-st, S.W.—*Subscription:* 5s. per month upon each share until £15 shall have been paid, which is the price of a completed share. *Object:* To make advances to its members upon security of freehold or leasehold property.

HOUSE AND LAND INVESTMENT TRUST LIM., Savoy-hill House, W.C. Subscribed Capital, £75,000. —*Subscription:* Any sums from 5s. and upwards, received on deposit. Interest 4, 5, and 6 per cent. *Object:* The purchase and development of approved freehold, leasehold, and copyhold properties, and generally for the buying, selling, and holding of lands and houses.

HOUSE PROPERTY AND INVESTMENT COMP. LIM., 92, Cannon-st. —*Subscription:* Shares, £25 each. *Object:* Purchase and sale of productive and progressive house property, and improving the dwellings of the working classes on the self-supporting principle.

LAND LOAN AND ENFRANCHISEMENT CO. (Incorporated by special Act of Parliament), 22, Gt. George-st, Westminster. — *Subscription:* Not stated. *Object:* The general improvement of landed estates.

LONDON AND GENERAL PERMANENT BUILDING SOC., 337, Strand. *Subscription:* Shares of £40 each, payable either in full or by sums of not less than 5s. monthly. Entrance fee, 1s. per share. *Object:* To enable the members to become possessors of residential or other house property upon easy terms.

LONDON CONGREGATIONAL UNION, Memorial Hall, Farringdon-st, E.C.—The objects of this society are (1) to promote the spiritual intercommunion of the Congregational Churches of the metropolis, to aid such of them as may be weak, to facilitate the expression of their opinions upon social and religious questions, and,

in general, to advance their common interests: (2) To promote the erection or enlargement of Congregational chapels and mission halls, and to secure sites for chapels and halls. The area of its operations includes the whole of Middlesex, and such portions of Surrey, Kent, Essex, and Herts, as are within the twelve mile radius. An annual average of £3,500 is expended in aiding Churches to support their ministers, and in extending and consolidating missionwork. A loan fund of about £11,000 is used for advances for chapel-building purposes without interest. The membership of the Union consists of the representatives of affiliated Churches, and of ministerial, personal, and honorary members. The council consists of sixty members. Sec., Rev. Andrew Mearns.

LONDON PROVIDENT BUILDING SOC. AND BANK (THE), 51, Moorgate-st.—*Subscription:* £10 paid-up shares can always be obtained. Dividend and bonus have averaged 5 per cent. over twenty-four years. *Object:* To provide a good and safe investment for money, and to enable persons to buy houses for their own occupation by instalments; also to assist persons generally to buy freehold and leasehold properties. In the deposit department cheque books are issued, and accounts may be drawn upon subject to fixed regulations, and interest is allowed on customers' balances at 3 per cent. per annum, and other rates.

MONARCH INVESTMENT BUILDING SOC., William H. Mayers, Secretary, 23, Finsbury-circus.—*Subscription:* Shares, £50, fully paid, or by subscription 5s. per month. *Object:* To raise by the subscriptions of its members a fund for making advances to members on security of freehold, leasehold, or copyhold estates by way of mortgage. The society also receives money on deposit at rates generally exceeding those allowed by the banks. This society has already advanced a sum of nearly one million and a half sterling.

MORNINGTON PERMANENT BUILDING SOC., 158, Kentish

Town-rd.—*Subscription :* 5s. per month until £10 share completed. Entrance fee, 2s. per share ; or shares can be fully paid up at once; entrance fee in latter case, 7s. 6d. per share. *Object :* To enable its members to become owners of real or leasehold property, either for occupation or investment, for which purpose repayment of principal and interest can be spread at discretion over any term from 2 to 15 years. This society has also a savings bank department, where money can be paid and withdrawn at any time.

NATIONAL CONTRACT CO. LIM., AND ORDERS OF TEMPERANCE, FIRE-PROOF, AND GENERAL BUILDING SOC. (Established 1866), 156, St. John-st-rd.—*Subscription :* £5 and £10 shares respectively. *Object :* Both societies established for the purpose of advancing money or procuring the same at moderate rates of interest, and so enable the middle and working classes to purchase their own dwellings by easy repayments.

NATIONAL FREEHOLD LAND Soc. (Established 1849), 25, Moorgate-st.—*Subscription :* £30 shares ; entrance fee, 1s. per share of £30. *Object :* To receive money on shares from members ; shares may be paid in full or by any sums at any time at option of member. Interest allowed, 3 per cent. on uncompleted shares, 3¼ per cent. on completed shares.

OCEAN PERMANENT BUILDING Soc., 727, Commercial-rd-east.— Shares, £25 each. Entrance fee, 1s. per share. *Subscription :* 2s. 6d. per month. *Object :* To raise and maintain by the subscription of members and loan, a stock or fund for making advances to members upon the security of freehold, copyhold, or leasehold property by way of mortgage, pursuant to the Building Societies Act, 1874.

OFFICAL AND GENERAL PERMANENT BENEFIT BUILDING Soc., 8, Duke-st, Adelphi.—*Subscription :* Shares £50 each ; entrance fee, 1s. per share. *Object :* To afford its members means of investing capital, and of procuring funds for the purchase of houses for their own occupation or of other kinds of freehold and leasehold property.

PADDINGTON LAND AND BUILDING SOC. LIM., 55, Edgware-rd. —*Subscription :* Shares, £10 each. *Object :* To advance money upon mortgage of freehold, leasehold, or copyhold property, and to receive cash on deposit from shareholders and the general public.

PERPETUAL INVESTMENT BUILDING SOC., 16, New Bridge-st, Blackfriars. — Established 1851. *Object :* To enable persons to invest money in large or small sums at a fair rate of interest, and to assist persons to secure houses for their own occupation or investment, the society advancing the amount required, repayable by instalments spread at discretion over a number of years.

ROCK PERMANENT BUILDING Soc., 52, Chancery-la.— Deposits, 4 per cent. *Object :* For making advances to members on freehold, leasehold, and copyhold estates.

SOCIETIES OF EQUALITY (Nos. 9, 10, 11, 12, & 13. No. 1 established 1845), 341, Yaxwell-rd, E.C.—*Subscription :* 5s. per month per share. *Object :* To make advances (£100 advanced per share at low premium or interest) to its members for the purpose of purchasing houses for residence or otherwise, and as a means of investment.

STEPNEY AND SUBURBAN PERMANENT BUILDING SOC., 527, Commercial-rd-east. — *Subscription :* 5s. per share per month. Completed shares, £25. *Object :* To raise a stock or fund by monthly subscriptions for making advances to members out of the funds of the society upon the security of freehold, copyhold, or leasehold estates by way of mortgage.

SUN PERMANENT BENEFIT BUILDING SOC., 12, Holborn, E.C. —*Subscription :* Realised shares, £10 each ; subscription shares, 5s per month. *Object :* To offer a channel for the investment of savings at a higher rate of interest than is obtained at ordinary savings banks, and to advance money by way of mortgage on freehold and leasehold property.

TEMPERANCE PERMANENT BUILDING SOC., 4, Ludgate-hill, E.C.—*Object :* To make advances to enable members to purchase their houses, &c.

Bunhill Fields.—The great burial-ground of Dissenters. Originally a "chapel of ease" for the City charnel-houses, and later a common burial-ground for the victims of the Great Plague, Bunhillfields came into the possession of the Dissenters about two hundred years ago. The prohibition of intramural interments closed Bunhill-fields, as it closed many other places of burial, and the ground is now planted and open to the public as a place of recreation. Here lie the bodies of John Bunyan and of Daniel Defoe. NEAREST *Ry. Stn.,* Moorgate-st ; *Omnibus Rte.,* City-rd ; *Cab Rank,* Old-st.

Burlington Arcade, Piccadilly (Map 6).—A double row of shops, like a Parisian *passage.* Open on week days, Christmas Day, Good Friday, and Bank Holidays. NEAREST *Ry. Stn.,* St. James's-pk (Dis.); *Omnibus Rtes.,* Regent-st, Oxford-st, and Piccadilly ; *Cab Rank,* Piccadilly.

Burlington Fine Arts Club, 17, Savile-row, W. — Is intended to bring together amateurs, collectors, and others interested in art ; to afford ready means for consultation between persons of special knowledge and experience in matters relating to the fine arts ; and to provide accommodation for showing and comparing rare works in the possession of the members and their friends. To provide in the reading-room periodicals, books, and catalogues, foreign as well as English, having reference to art. To make arrangements in the gallery and rooms of the club for the exhibition of pictures, original drawings, engravings, and rare books, enamels, ceramic wares, coins, plate, and other valuable works. To hold, in addition to the above, once in the year or oftener, special exhibitions which shall have for their object the elucidation of some school, master, or specific art, and to which members have the privilege of introducing strangers. To render the club a centre, where occasionally conversazioni may be held of an art character. To provide, in addition to the above art objects, the ordinary accommodation and advantages of a London club. The club possesses a valuable library of books of reference on art. The entrance fee is £5 5s., and the annual subscription £5 5s. The ower of election of members is vested in the committee, and is by ballot.

Burlington House, Piccadilly (Map 6).—Below is a list of the societies, which, in addition to the Royal Academy of Arts, and the University of London (*both of which see*), are comfortably lodged in these handsome buildings, which form the sides of a quadrangle approached from Piccadilly by a fine archway. The entrance to the building of the University of London is in Burlington-gdns; the rooms of the Royal Academy are immediately facing the entrance from Piccadilly.

CHEMICAL SOCIETY, east side (under the gateway).

GEOLOGICAL SOCIETY, in Piccadilly.

LINNÆAN SOCIETY, west side (under the gateway).

ROYAL SOCIETY (*which see*) east side.

ROYAL ASTRONOMICAL SOCIETY, west side.

SOCIETY OF ANTIQUARIES OF LONDON, west side.

Bushy Park leads from the Teddington-rd to Hampton Court Palace. One of the most favourite resorts of picnic parties, its great attraction being the mile-long avenue of horse-chestnuts.—NEAREST *Ry. Stn.,* Hampton Court. From Waterloo (42 min.), 1st, 2/-, 2/9 ; 2nd, 1/6, 2/- ; 3rd, 1/3, 1/10.

Cabmen's Shelters.—Office: 13, Victoria-bdgs, Victoria Stn.

Archer-st, Westbourne-gr, day and night

Baker-st Stn., noon to 2 a.m.

Clapham-com, 10 a.m. to 10 p.m.

Collingham-br, Cromwell-rd, 10 a.m. to 10 p.m.

Duncannon-st, Charing ✠, day and night.

Eaton-sq, 10 a.m. to 10 p.m.

Eccleston-bridge, Belgrave-rd, 11 a.m. to 3 a.m.

Gloucester-gate, Regent's-pk, 10 a.m. to 11 p.m.

Guilford-st (Foundling), 9 a.m. to 3 a.m.

G. W. Ry., Paddington, 10 a.m. to 10 p.m.

Hampstead, 9 a.m. to 9 p.m.

Harrow-rd (opposite Blomfield-ter), 10 a.m. to 10 p.m.

Holborn-hill, 10 a.m. to 11 p.m.

Holland-pk, Kensington, 11 a.m. to 11 p.m.

Hyde-pk-cor, 10 a.m. to 11 p.m.

Kennington Ch., 3 p.m. to 3 a.m.

Kensington-pk-rd, 11 a.m. to 11 p.m.

Kensington (opposite De Vere-gdns), day and night.

Knightsbridge, day and night.

Langham-pl, 10 a.m. to 10 p.m.

Lewisham-hill, S.E., 10 a.m. to 10 p.m.

Lincoln's-inn-fields, 10 a.m. to 11 p.m.

Maida-vale, 11 a.m. to 5 a.m.

Marble Arch, 10 a.m. to 11 p.m.

Northumberland-av, Charing ✠, day and night.

Palace-yd, Westminster, 10 a.m. to 10 p.m., and day and night during sessions of Parliament.

Park-rd, Regent's-pk, day and night.

Piccadilly, day and night.

Pickering-pl, Bayswater, 9 a.m. to 10 p.m.

Pont-st, Belgrave-sq, day & night

Portland-rd Stn.,11 a.m. to 3 a.m.

Putney Stn., 10 a.m. to 10 p.m.

Royal-cres, Notting-hill, noon to 9 p.m.

Skinner-st (by Midland Hotel), day and night.

S. Kensington, 10 a.m. to 10 p.m.

St. Clement Danes, Strand, day and night.

St. James's-sq, Pall Mall, day and night.

Vauxhall Stn., 9 a.m. to 10 p.m.

Waterloo Stn., 9 a.m. to 9 p.m.

Cabs.—The cab laws of London are now, except with regard to the distinctions drawn somewhat arbitrarily here and there between four-

wheelers and hansoms, very simple and easy to be remembered. The main points to bear in mind are : that luggage carried outside is always to be paid for ; that hansoms, though charged at the same rate as "growlers" when hired by distance—which is almost the only time when there is any particular gain in hiring them—cost 6d. an hour more when hired by time, and 8d. an hour more when standing still ; that if you intend to hire a cab by the hour, you must state your intention to the driver at the time of hiring ; and that you cannot make a man drive you about by the hour for more than one hour at a time. One very important point to bear in mind is the rule which fixes the fare of a cab hired outside the four-mile circle at 1s. per mile wherever discharged. Under this rule, while the fare from the cabstand at the top of Shepherd's Bush-gn to Victoria would be 2s., that from the middle of the green—say 50 yards farther on—would be 4s. The best plan, in most cases, is to agree with the man as to his fare beforehand. Failing this, exchange cabs when you have crossed the magic circle ; or discharge and re-hire your own cab. As for calculating fares, that must depend entirely on your own power of judging distance. Some people when in doubt take the driver's ticket, and tell him to name his own fare ; and when he is satisfied that he will be summoned if he be found to have overcharged, the plan is no doubt efficacious. A better plan is to judge by the time occupied, and it will be found that about 1d. per minute is fair to both parties. For 15 minutes 1s. 6d. should be paid, but 14 minutes may be taken to be within the 1s. This is not an official rate, but it will save trouble and generally prove right. A hirer should always observe the number of a cab. If he leave any property in a cab he will possibly find it next day at the Lost Property Office, Great Scotland-yd, when, on payment of a per centage on the estimated value as a reward to the cabman for his honesty, he can obtain it back again. The following are the fares and general regulations as laid down by the Commissioners of Police, the four-mile circle being measured from Charing ✠ :

FARES BY DISTANCE. — If hired and discharged *within* the four-mile circle, measured from

Charing ✠, for any distance *s. d.*
not exceeding two miles .. 1 0

And for every additional
mile or part of a mile 0 6

If hired *outside* the four-
mile - circle, wherever discharged, for the first and each
succeeding mile or part of a
mile 1 0

If hired *within*, but discharged *outside*, the four-
mile circle, not exceeding one
mile, 1s.; exceeding one mile,
then for each mile within the
circle, 6d. ; and for each mile
or part of a mile outside .. 1 0

FARES BY TIME.—*Inside*
the four-mile circle: Four-
wheeled cabs, for one hour
or less 2s. Two-wheeled cabs 2 6

For every additional quarter
of an hour or part of a quarter,
four-wheeled cab, 6d. ; if a
two-wheeled cab 0 8

If hired *outside* the circle
wherever discharged, for one
hour or less 2 6

If above one hour, then for
every quarter of an hour or
less 0 8

If hired *within*, but discharged *outside*, the four-
mile circle, the same.

EXTRA PAYMENTS.—*Hirers of
Cabs should be particular in noti-
cing these regulations, as disputes
generally arise from their not
being clearly understood.*

Whether hired by distance
or by time :

LUGGAGE.—For each pack- *s. a.*
age carried outside the carriage 0 2

EXTRA PERSONS.—For each
above two 0 6

For each child under 10
years old 0 3

By distance—WAITING :

For every 15 minutes com-
pleted, whether in one stoppage or in several stoppages:

If hired within the four
mile circle, four-wheels, 6d. ;
two-wheels 0 8

If hired without circle, two
or four wheels 0 8

GENERAL REGULATIONS.—
Fares are according to distance or
time at the option of the hirer,
*expressed at the commencement
of the hiring*; if not otherwise
expressed, the fare to be paid
according to distance.

Driver, if hired by distance,
is not compelled to drive more
than six miles ; nor, if hired by
time, to drive for more than one
hour.

Agreement to pay more than
legal fare is not binding ; any sum
paid beyond the fare may be recovered back.

Driver not to charge more than
the sum agreed on for driving a
distance, although such distance
be exceeded by the driver.

If the driver agree beforehand
to take any sum less than the proper fare, the penalty for exacting
or demanding more than the sum
agreed upon is 40s.

The proprietor of every hackney
carriage shall keep distinctly
painted, both on the inside and
outside, a table of fares ; and the
driver shall have with him, and
when required produce, the Authorised Book of Fares.

In case of any dispute between
the hirer and driver, the hirer may
require the driver to drive to the
nearest metropolitan police-court
or justice-room, when the complaint may be determined by the
sitting magistrate without summons ; or if no police-court or
justice-room be open at the time,
then to the nearest police-station,
where the complaint shall be
entered, and tried by the magistrate at his next sitting.

Every driver of any hackney
carriage shall, when hired, deliver
to the hirer a card printed according to the directions of the Commissioner of Police.

All property left in any hackney
carriage shall be deposited by the
driver at the nearest police-station
within twenty-four hours, if not
sooner claimed by the owner ; such
property to be returned to the
person who shall prove to the
satisfaction of the Commissioner of
Police that the same belonged to
him, on payment of all expenses
incurred, and of such reasonable
sum to the driver as the Commissioner shall award.

Tables of Cab Fares will be found
at the end of the DICTIONARY.

Camden School for Girls.
—(*See* NORTH LONDON COLL.
SCHOOL.)

Canada, Dominion of.—
AGENCY - GENERAL, 9, Victoria-
chambers, S.W. NEAREST *Ry.
Stn.*, St. James's Park ; *Omnibus
Rtes.*, Victoria-st and Parliament-
st ; *Cab Rank*, Victoria-st.

Cannon Street (Map 8) is
one of the greatest of the very
numerous improvements in modern
London. It is a thoroughfare
of great width, leading from St
Paul's Churchyard to the end
of King William-st. Its construction has relieved Cheapside of the
greater part of the heavy traffic
Indeed, were Cannon-st now
closed Cheapside would become
impassable. Cannon-st is a street
of wholesale warehouses, and a
few sample goods in each window
alone tell the passer-by the nature
of the immense stock contained in
them. Here are representatives
of many of the largest foreign
as well as English firms ; and
there are large stores of goods
from Manchester, Leeds, Birmingham, Sheffield, Belfast, and, indeed, from every large manufacturing town in the kingdom. In
Cannon-st are the station of the
S.E. Ry., and the Mansion House
Stn. of the District Ry. situated at
the point where Qn. Victoria-st runs
diagonally across Cannon-st. In
the wall of St. Swithin's Church,
opposite the S.E. Ry. Stn., will be
found that curious relic of old
London, called London Stone.
In the Roman days distances
were measured from this point.
The various narrow streets running
between Cannon-st and Cheapside
contain many of the most important warehouses and firms of
the City. The locality is specially
affected by firms connected with
the trades in cotton and other
textile fabrics.

Cannon Street Bridge
(Map 8) belongs to the S.E. Ry.
Co., and was built to carry their
line from London-br. It is a plain,
matter-of-fact structure, with no
very special features about it
either of comparative beauty or
positive ugliness, being built in
five girder spans of iron, the
three central of 167 ft., the two
outer of 135 ft., resting on cylinder
piers. There is a side walk outside the eastern parapet for foot-
passengers, but it is not at present
in use.

Cannon Street Station
(Map 8), the City terminus of the
S.E. Ry., similar in general
arrangements to that at Charing ✠,
with which it is in communication
every few minutes by trains which
run constantly backwards and
forwards. The upper part is
occupied by a huge hotel, a

noticeable feature in which is a fine hall, which can be hired for meetings, &c. The Continental and main line booking - offices are on the west, the North Kent on the east side. The Charing ✠ platform is on the right - hand side on entering. NEAREST *Ry. Stn.*, Mansion House (Dis.); *Omnibus Rtes.*, Cannon-st and Cheapside ; *Cab Fare* to Bank 1/-; to Charing ✠ 1/-.

Carlton Club, 94, Pall Mall. —No special qualification is mentioned in the rules, but the club is the recognised head-quarters of the Conservative party. The entrance fee is £30, and the subscription £10 10s. The election of members is made by the committee and by ballot, twelve being a quorum at each ballot, and two black balls excluding. The names of candidates are taken in the order in which they are inserted in the book, with the exception of peers, heirs apparent to any peerage, and members of the House of Commons, who may be balloted for immediately ; and ten candidates annually selected by the committee from those whose names may be in the book on the 1st of March in each year. In the case of this selection, the rule of the club, that the election of members shall be by ballot, is dispensed with. No candidate, however, is to be deemed elected a member in whose favour less than two-thirds of the committee shall have given their vote.

Carriage Thieves.—Among the many thieves who infest the London streets none are more artful or more active than the carriage thieves. No vehicle should ever be left with open windows ; and valuable rugs in victorias, &c., should always be secured to the carriage by a strap or other fastening. Ladies should be especially careful of officious persons volunteering to open or close carriagedoors. In nine cases out of ten these men and boys are expert pickpockets.

Catholic (Roman) Churches.—The following is a list of the principal Roman Catholic Churches in London. Full particulars in connection with these churches, and other Catholic religious institutions in the metropolis, will be found in the "Catholic Directory," published by Messrs.

Burns & Oates, London, price 1s. 6d. :—

BAYSWATER, W. *St. Mary of the Angels,* Westmoreland - rd. Very Rev. Francis J. Kirk, *Superior.*

BOW-ROAD, E. *Our Lady and St. Catherine of Sienna* (1870). Revs. T. P. Thacker, D.D., and John F. O'Connor.

BUNHILL-ROW, E.C. *St. Joseph's,* Lamb's - bdgs. Revs. T. H. Burnett and Patrick Luttrell.

CHELSEA, S.W. *St. Mary,* Cadogan - st, Sloane - st. Right Rev. J. L. Patterson, Bishop of Emmaus.

CLAPHAM, S.W. *Our Immaculate Lady of Victories.* Very Rev. Hugh Macdonald, *Provincial,* and Very Rev. Edward O'Laverty, *Rector.*

CLAPTON, E. *St. Scholastica,* Kenninghall-rd. Rev. Robert Swift.

CLERKENWELL, E.C. *SS. Peter and Paul,* Rosoman - st. Rev. Joseph L. Biemans.

COMMERCIAL-RD-EAST, E. *SS. Mary and Michael.* Rev. Patrick O'Callaghan.

COVENT-GARDEN, W.C. *Corpus Christi Church,* Maiden - lane, Southampton-st, Strand. Revs. F. Skrimpshire and William Purcell.

FARM-ST, Berkeley-sq, W. *The Immaculate Conception.* Jesuit Fathers. Very Rev. Edward Purbrick, S.J., *Provincial.*

FRENCH CHAPEL. *The Annunciation,* Little George - st, Portman-sq. Rev. Louis Toursel.

FULHAM-RD, S.W. *St. Mary's Priory,* 264, Fulham-rd. Sacred and Sorrowing Hearts of Jesus and Mary. Servite Fathers. Very Rev. Antonino Appolloni, *Prior.*

GERMAN CHURCH. *St. Boniface,* Union-st, Whitechapel - rd, E.C. Rev. H. W. E. Schmitz.

GREAT ORMOND-ST, W.C. *St. John of Jerusalem.* Rev. Robert F. Clarke.

HACKNEY, E. *St. John the Baptist,* The Triangle. Rev. Wm. Fleming.

HAMMERSMITH, W. *The Holy Trinity,* Brook Green. Rev. Alfred White.

HAMPSTEAD, N.W. *St. Mary,* Holly-place, Church-row. Very Rev. Canon A. Dillon Purcell.

HAVERSTOCK-HILL, N.W. *St. Dominic's Priory,* Southampton-rd, Maitland Park. Dominican Fathers. Very Rev. Albert Buckler, D.D., *Prior.*

HIGHGATE, N. *St. Joseph's Retreat,* Highgate Hill. Passionists. Very Rev. Vincent Grogan, *Provincial,* and Rev. Gerald Woollet.

HOLBORN, E.C. *St. Ethelreda,* Ely-place. Fathers of Charity. Rev. W. Lockhart, *Rector.*

HOLLOWAY, N. *Sacred Heart of Jesus,* Eden Grove, Holloway-rd. Rev. W. Ignatius Dolan.

HOMERTON, E. *Immaculate Heart of Mary and St. Dominic,* Ballance-rd. Rev. Thomas W. Hogan.

HOXTON, N. *St. Monica's Priory,* Hoxton-sq. Augustinian Fathers. Very Rev. Michael Kelly, D.D., *Prior.*

ISLINGTON, N. *St. John the Evangelist,* Duncan-ter, City-rd. Rev. L. Pycke.

ITALIAN CHURCH. *St. Peter,* Hatton Garden, E.C. Pious Society of the Missions. Rev. Joseph P. Bannin, *Rector.*

KENSAL NEW TOWN, W. *Our Lady of the Holy Souls,* Bosworth-rd. Revs. Joseph J. Greene and Arnold S. Baker.

KENSINGTON, I. *Pro Cathedral* (which see). II. *Our Lady of Mount Carmel and St. Simon Stock,* Church - st. Very Rev. Alphonsus Liguori Malax Echevarria, *Prior.*

KENTISH TOWN, N.W. *Our Lady the Help of Christians,* 41, Fortess-rd. Rev. James Connolly.

KILBURN, N.W. *Sacred Heart of Jesus,* Quex-rd. Rev. C. Cox, *Superior.*

LEICESTER - SQ, W.C. *Notre Dame de France,* 5, Leicester-pl. Marist Fathers. Rev. Leo Thomas, *Superior.*

LINCOLN'S - INN - FIELDS, W.C. *St. Anselm and St. Cecilia,* Sardinia-st. Rev. George S. Delaney.

MARYLEBONE-RD, N.W. *Our Lady of the Rosary.* Rev. J. J. Brenan.

MOORFIELDS, E.C. *St. Mary,* Blomfield-st. Right Rev. Mgr. Canon Gilbert, D.D.

NOTTING HILL, W. *St. Francis of Assisi,* Pottery-la, Portland-pl, Portland-rd. Rev. C. Robinson.

ORATORY (THE), S.W. *Immaculate Heart of Mary*, Brompton-rd. Fathers of the Oratory of St. Philip Neri. Very Rev. William T. Gordon, *Superior*.

PRO CATHEDRAL, Newland-ter, Kensington, W. *Our Lady of Victories*. Revs. C. Moore, M. Fanning, C. A. Cox, J. Bloomfield, and D. Skrimshire.

ST. GEORGE'S CATHEDRAL, Westminster - br - rd, S.E. Very Rev. William Canon Murnane.

ST. JOHN'S WOOD, N.W. *Church of Our Lady*, Grove-rd. Rev. Philip Cavanagh.

SOHO, W. *St. Patrick*, Sutton-st. Rev. Langton George Vere.

SOMERS TOWN, N.W. *St. Aloysius*, Clarendon - sq. Rev. A. W. Dolman.

SOUTH KENSINGTON. *St.Mary's Priory*, Fulham-rd.—(*See* ORATORY and FULHAM-RD.)

SPANISH-PLACE, W. *St. James*, Manchester - sq. Rev. M. Barry and others.

SPITALFIELDS, E. *St. Anne*, Underwood-st, Buxton-st. Marist Fathers. Rev. Anatole Police, *Superior*.

TOWER-HILL, E. *The English Martyrs*, 23, Great Prescot-st. Very Rev. Matthew Caughran, *Provincial*.

WARWICK - STREET, W. *The Assumption*. Hon. and Right Rev. Mgr. Gilbert Canon Talbot, D.D.

Cattle Market (Copenhagen Fields) (Map 3).—

This great cattle-market lies up the Caledonian-rd, King's ✝. At a mile and a quarter from King's ✝ Market-st is reached, and then turning to the left, in a hundred yards or so the visitor finds himself at the great gates of the cattle market. The market is of immense size, and fully equal to its present requirements. In the centre is a clock tower, round which are the offices of the market clerk and other officials. On one side are the stands for beasts, and on the other the sheep-pens. Portions of the ground are roofed in and fitted for pigs and calves, although few of either now find their way to town in a live state. The market days are Monday and Thursday. The number of beasts exhibited on Monday is about 3,500, and of sheep 12,000, with

250 calves. These figures will give an idea of an average market, but of necessity vary much from numerous causes—such as the outbreak of foot-and-mouth disease in grazing districts, &c. Thursday's market is of a supplemental nature, about 600 beasts and 5,000 sheep being the average number that passes the gate. In the lairs surrounding the market-place, there is excellent provision for housing the animals as they arrive from all parts of the kingdom. NEAREST *Ry. Stns.*, King's ✝ and Holloway (G.N.); *Omnibus Rtes.*, Camden, Caledonian, and Holloway Roads; *Cab Rank*, Camden-rd (Brecknock).

Cemeteries.—

Since the prohibition of intramural interments and the consequent closing of the old graveyards, an immense number of parochial burial-grounds, some open to all, others set apart for the use of special denominations, have been opened in various suburban districts all round London. A full list of these would not only occupy too much space, but would be manifestly beyond the purpose of the present work. The following are the principal London cemeteries with the means of access to each. The official charges and conditions of each can be obtained by application to the various Secretaries :

ABNEY-PARK, Office, 23, Moorgate-st, E.C. — NEAREST *Ry. Stn.*, Stoke Newington (G. E.). From Liverpool-st (18 min.), 1st, -/7, -/9 ; 2nd, -/5, -/7 ; 3rd, -/4, -/5. *Omnibus Rtes.*, Stoke Newington-rd and Albion-rd.

CAMBERWELL. — NEAREST *Ry. Stn.*, Honor Oak (L. C. & D. R.). From Ludgate-hill (27 min.), 1st, -/10, 1/3 ; 2nd, -/8, 1/- ; 3rd, -/6, -/9.

CRYSTAL PALACE DISTRICT, Office, 107A, Fenchurch-st, E.C.— NEAREST *Ry. Stn.*, Elmer's End (S. E. R.), from London-br (45 min.), 1st, 1/4, 2/- ; 2nd, 1/-, 1/6 ; 3rd, -/10, 1/2.

GREAT NORTHERN, Office, 22, Great Winchester - st, E.C.— NEAREST *Ry. Stn.*, New Southgate (G.N.). From King's ✝ (21 min.), 1st, -/11, 1/6 ; 2nd, -/9, 1/3 ; 3rd, -/6.

HAMPSTEAD. — NEAREST *Ry. Stn.*, Child's Hill (Midland). From St. Pancras (23 min.), 1st, -/9, 1/2 ; 3rd, -/5, -/8. *Omnibus*

Rtes., Finchley-rd and Edgware-rd.

HANWELL.— NEAREST *Ry. Stn.*, Hanwell (G.W.). From Paddington (25 min.), 1st, 1/4, 2/- ; 2nd, 1/-, 1/6 ; 3rd, 8d.

HIGHGATE, Office, 29, New Bridge-st, E.C. — NEAREST *Ry. Stns.*, Upper Holloway and Highgate-rd (Tottenham and Hampstead Junc.). From St. Pancras (12 min.), 1st, -/6, -/9 ; 3rd, -/3, -/6. *Omnibus Rtes.*, Highgate-hill and Highgate-rise.

JEWS' BURIAL GROUND, Mile End-rd, N.—NEAREST *Ry. Stn.* Whitechapel (E.L.) ; From Liverpool-st (4 min.), 1st -/4, -/6 ; 2nd, -/3, -/5 ; 3rd, -/2, -/4. Old Ford (G.E.); From Liverpool-st (10 min.), 1st, -/6, -/9 ; 2nd, -/4, -/6 ; 3rd, -/3, -/5. Bethnal Gn. Junc. (G.E.) ; From Liverpool-st (5 min.), 1st, -/4, -/5 ; 2nd, -/3, -/4 ; 3rd, -/2, -/3. *Omnibus Rte.*, Mile End-rd.

KENSAL GREEN, Office, 95, Gt. Russell-st, W.C.—NEAREST *Ry. Stn.*, Kensal Gn. (L. & N.W.) From Broad-st (33 min.), 1st, -/9, 1/2 ; 2nd, -/8, 1/- ; 3rd, -/5, -/8. *Omnibus Rte.*, Harrow-rd.

NORWOOD.—NEAREST *Ry. Stn.*, Lower Norwood (L. B. & S.C.). From London-br (34 min.), 1st, 1/3, 2/- ; 2nd, 1/-, 1/6 ; 3rd, -/7, 1/-.

NUNHEAD, Peckham-rye, Office, 29, New Bridge-st, E.C.—NEAREST *Ry. Stn.*, Nunhead (L.C.& D.). From Ludgate - hill (26 min.), 1st, -/8, 1/- ; 2nd, /6, -/10 ; 3rd, -/4, -/6. *Omnibus Rte.*, Peckham-rye.

PADDINGTON.—NEAREST *Ry. Stns.*, Kilburn (L. & N.W.). From Broad - st (45 min.), 1st, -/9 1/- ; 2nd, -/6, -/9. Edgware-rd (Met.) ; From Aldgate (24 min.), 1st, -/9, 1/2 ; 2nd -/7, -/11 ; 3rd, -/5, -/8. *Omnibus Rte.*, Edgware-rd.

ST. MARYLEBONE, East End, Finchley ; Office, Court House, Marylebone-la. — NEAREST *Ry. Stn.*, East End. From King's ✝ (21 min.) 1st, -/10, 1/3 ; 2nd, -/8, 1/1 ; £rd, -/5½, -/11.

WEST OF LONDON AND WESTMINSTER, Fulham-rd; Office, 12, Haymarket, S.W.—NEAREST *Ry. Stns.*, West Brompton (19 min.) and Chelsea (15 min.). From Waterloo, 1st, -/8, 1/- ; 2nd, -/6, -/9 ; 3rd, -/4, -/6. Both on West London Extension. Earl's Court (Met.);

From Mansion House (23 min.), 1st, -/8, 1/-; 2nd, -/5, -/7½; 3rd, -/4, -/6. *Omnibus Rte.*, Fulham-rd.

WOKING, Offices, 2, Lancaster-pl, W.C., and Westminster - br - rd, S.E.—NEAREST *Ry. Stn.*, Brookwood (S.W.). From Waterloo (about 1 h.), 1st, 5/8, 8/- ; 2nd, 4/-, 6/- ; 3rd, 2/3½, 4/-.

Central Criminal Court.

—*See* LAW COURTS *and* SESSIONS. NEAREST *Ry. Stns.*, Blackfriars (Dis.), Holborn-viaduct (L. C. & D.) ; *Omnibus Rtes.*, Newgate-st and Ludgate-hill ; *Cab Rank*, Old Bailey.

Chancery Pay Office,

Royal Courts of Justice, W.C.— Office hours, 10 to 4. For payment of cheques, 10.30 to 3.30. NEAREST *Ry. Stn.*, Temple (Dis.); *Omnibus Rtes.*, Strand, Fleet-st, and Chancery-la ; *Cab Rank*, St. Clement's Danes Church, Strand.

Change Ringing is exten-

sively practised in London, where the Ancient Society of College Youths has its head-quarters. The Society of College Youths was founded, in 1637, by Lord Brereton and Sir Cliff Clifton, for the purpose of promoting the art of change ringing ; and the society, having outlived its first youth, prefixed the "Ancient" to their original title. For many years the headquarters of the society were at St. Martin's-in-the-Fields. They are now at St. Saviour's, Southwark. There is another society of change ringers in London, called the Cumberland, and practising at St. Martin's-in-the-Fields, which probably sprang from the internal dissensions which at one time agitated the elder society. The London Scholars, who are frequently mentioned in the records of the Ancient College Youths, have become extinct as a change-ringing society. The rules of the College Youths are few and simple, and the subscription and expenses low ; and for this reason, no doubt, the society has gradually attracted more and more members from the working classes. The early list of members contains the names of many Lord Mayors and of more than one member for the City ; and Sir Watkin Wynne, Lord Dacre, and the Marquis of Salisbury also figure in the roll. The principal peals of bells in London, besides that newly hung in the belfry of St. Paul's Cathedral,

are to be found in the following churches: St. Mary-le-Bow, Cheapside ; St. Michael's, Cornhill ; St. Magnus the Martyr, Lower Thames-st ; St. Matthew, Bethnal Gn. ; St. Saviour's, Southwark ; St. Bride's, Fleet-st ; St. Martin's-in-the-Fields.

Chapels Royal.

ST. JAMES'S (Map 6).—Many visitors to London think it necessary to attend service at the Chapel Royal. The building itself is in no way remarkable, and the service in no way peculiar ; but as it is the fashion amongst courtiers in the season to put in an appearance here, it naturally follows that all the people who like to be thought "somebodies" eagerly compete for admission. The chapel is small, and tickets are not easily obtained without the assistance of "a friend at court." They are in the gift of the Lord Chamberlain. NEAREST *Ry. Stns.*, St. James's-pk (Dis.) and Charing ✠ (S.E.) ; *Omnibus Rtes.*, Piccadilly and Waterloo-pl ; *Cab Rank*, St. James's-st.

SAVOY (Map 7).—Still a Chapel Royal, belonging to the Crown in connection with the Duchy of Lancaster. There are many quaint brasses and monuments in the chapel, but the days of embankments, of new streets, and great buildings have robbed the Savoy of its chief charm. An old brass, long missing from the chapel, was brought to light some time ago, and is now placed in the chancel, embedded in a block of marble. A curious and interesting picture—a third part of "a Triptych "— is now placed in the chapel by the side of the font. It is known that three pictures belonged to the Savoy at its dissolution, and this picture has every appearance of being of the period of Henry VII. Much interesting matter referring to the Savoy is published in the "Savoy Annual." The old "precinct," of not many years since, was like a bit of an old cathedral town dropped in some strange way between the Strand and the river, and it was difficult even for an imaginative Londoner to suppose, as he paced the calm solitudes of the Savoy, that he was only some fifty yards from the rush and strife of the busiest London life. (For hours of Services *see* CHURCHES.) NEAREST *Ry. Stns.*, Temple (Dis.) and Charing ✠(S.E.); *Omnibus Rte.*,

Strand ; *Cab Rank*, Burleigh-st Strand.

WHITEHALL (Map 13).—This Chapel Royal is all that remains of the old Palace, and was adapted from the Banqueting House designed by Inigo Jones. Service is performed here on Sundays, but, except on one day in the year, there is nothing peculiar to note in connection with the chapel. On the Thursday preceding Good Friday the distribution of the Royal Bounty, or "Maundy Money," to a number of old men and women corresponding to the age of the Sovereign, takes place here. The procession on the occasion is one of the quaintest relics of old-fashioned Court ceremonial to be seen in London. The royal gifts are brought into the chapel by the Yeomen of the Guard on a William and Mary salver, and are then deposited in front of the Royal Closet, which is usually occupied by some of the Royal Family. A special service is held on the occasion, and at certain intervals the gifts are distributed. They consist of sums of money, shoes and stockings, woollen and linen clothes, purses, &c. (For hours of Services *see* CHURCHES.) NEAREST *Ry. Stns.*, Charing ✠ (S.E.) and Westminster-br (Dis.) ; *Omnibus Rtes.*, Whitehall and Charing ✠ ; *Cab Rank*, Whitehall.

Charing Cross (Map 13) is a

position rather than a place, and is, in fact, the triangular piece of roadway where Parliament-st runs into the S. side of Trafalgar-sq. It is the titular centre of London, the point from which distances are measured. A line drawn N. and S. through it may be said to separate the London of pleasure and fashion from that of work and business. Of the original cross no vestige remains, not even a stone to mark where it stood. It stands reproduced in front of the Charing ✠ Hotel, and one cannot but regret that so beautiful an object should be placed there, instead of in the centre of the wide roadway looking down Parliament-st.—(*See also* TRAFALGAR SQUARE.)

Charing Cross Bridge

(Map 13) stands on the site of the old Hungerford Suspension-bridge, which was removed in 1863. The lower parts of the two brick piers, on which were built the supporting towers of the old bridge, still remain, and have been utilised for the new work. They are supplemented by two intermediate sets of iron piers, a large number of which also support the fan-shaped extension of the bridge towards the station. Along either side of the bridge runs a footpath ; that on the E. side being open to passengers, and affording the shortest route from all the Charing ✠ district to the Waterloo Stn. These footpaths, however, are not an integral portion of the structure, but are carried on small supplementary cantilevers bolted on to the bridge proper. NEAREST *Ry. Stn.*, &c., North side as

Charing ✠ Station. South side *Ry. Stn.*, Waterloo (S.W.) ; *Omnibus Rte.*, Waterloo-br-rd. ; *Cab Rank*, Waterloo Stn.

Charing Cross Station
(Map 13).—The terminus of the S.E. Ry., the upper portion occupied by a large hotel (*See* HOTELS) belonging to the company. The ground floor is given up to the booking offices ; that for Continent and main line being on the W., and that for North Kent, &c., on the E. side. The custom-house, where registered luggage from the Continent is examined, is at the farther end of the main line arrival platform. The Cannon-st trains run from

the platform on the E. side of the station, where also there is a staircase leading down to the foot of Villiers-st, the Embankment, and the Charing ✠ Stn. of the District Line. It is worth bearing in mind that trains for Dover and elsewhere, starting from Charing ✠, reverse themselves on leaving Cannon-st, so that those who leave the former station with their backs to the engine will have to travel the rest of the way with their faces to it, and *vice versâ*. NEAREST *Ry. Stn.*, Charing ✠ (Dis.); *Omnibus Rtes.*, Strand, St. Martin's-la, and Whitehall; *Cab Fare* to Bank 1/.

Charities.—The following is a list of the principal London Charities, with their objects. For complete information regarding all the London charities, reference should be made to Mr. Herbert Fry's excellent and careful " Guide," published by Chatto and Windus, Piccadilly, price 1s. 6d.

ABORIGINES PROTECTION SOC., Sec., 3, Broadway-cham, Westminster	Especially of British colonies
ACTORS' BENEVOLENT FUND, 8, Adam-st, Adelphi, W.C.	
AFTER CARE ASSOCIATION, Sec., Emblewood, Osbaldeston-rd, Stoke Newington	Jasylums for the insane Female Convalescents leaving
AMERICANS IN DISTRESS, SOC. FOR RELIEF OF, Angel-ct, E.C.	
ARCHBISHOP TENISON'S SCHOOLS, Head Master, Leicester-sq	Boys St. Martin's & St. James's
ARCHITECTS' BENEVOLENT SOC., Sec., 9, Conduit-st, W...	Professional
ARMOURERS AND BRAZIERS' CO.'S ALMSHOUSES, Clerk, 81, Coleman-st..	
ARMY & NAVY PENSIONERS' EMPLOYMENT SOC., Sec., 44, Charing ✠..	*See special article*
ARNEWAY'S CHARITY, daily, betw. 10 and 3, 9, Victoria-cham, S.W.	To lend to poor occupiers, &c.
ARTISTS' BENEVOLENT FUND, Sec., 23, Garrick-st, W.C.	Professional
,, GENERAL BENEVOLENT INST., Sec., 24, Old Bond-st, W.	Professional
,, ORPHAN FUND, Sec., 24, Old Bond-st	Education of artists' orphans
ASYLUM FOR FATHERLESS CHILDREN, Sec., 26, Finsbury-pavement, E.C.	
BAKERS' CO.'S ALMSHOUSES, Clerk, 16, Harp-la, Tower-st	
BAPTIST ANNUITY FUND, Sec., 19, Castle-st, Holborn	
,, COLLEGE, Sec., near North-gate, Regent's-pk	Students for Baptist ministry
,, FUND (PARTICULAR), Sec., 19, Castle-st, Holborn	For ministers, and churches
,, HOME AND IRISH MISSIONS, Sec., 19, Castle-st, Holborn	
,, MISSIONARY, Sec., 19, Castle-st, Holborn	
,, PASTORS' COLLEGE, Pres., Metropolitan Tabernacle, Newington	
BARRISTERS' BENEVOLENT ASSOCIATION, Hon. Sec., 7, Figtree-ct, Temple	Professional
BARTHOLOMEW (ST.) HOSPITAL SAMARITAN FUND, Smithfield..	Patients leaving hospitals
BATTERSEA TRAINING COLLEGE, Principal, Terrace House, Battersea..	Masters for Church schools
BENEVOLENT BLUES, Sec., 3, Crown-ct, Cheapside..	Christ's Hospital
,, OR STRANGERS' FRIEND SOC., 52, Finsbury-pavement	Poor of London
BETHLEM ROYAL HOSPITAL, St. George's-rd, Southwark	Lunatics not fit for County Asy.
BLIND, ASSOC. FOR WELFARE OF THE, Manager, 28, Berners-st..	Employment and teaching trades
,, BRITISH AND FOREIGN ASSOC., Hon. Sec., 33, Cambridge-sq, W.	Education and employment
,, CHILDREN'S COLLEGE, Avenue, Hackney, E.	Industrial education for blind children
,, CHRISTIAN RELIEF, Hon. Sec., 59, Burdett-rd, E.	Pensions 5s. per mth., 2s. 6d. wk.
,, FEMALE ANNUITY SOC., Hon. Sec., 25, Fairfax-rd, South Hampstead	Pensions for blind women
,, HETHERINGTON'S CHARITY TO AGED, Christ's Hospital ..	Pensions of £10 a year
,, HOME FOR CHILDREN, Miss Newbury, 127, Portsdown-rd, W.	Train blind children
,, HOME TEACHING FOR THE, Sec., 31, New Bridge-st, Blackfriars	Teaching blind at own homes
,, HUMSTON'S CHARITY, Clerk, Vestry Office, St. Botolph, E.	Parochial
,, INDIGENT VISITING, Sec., 27, Red Lion-sq, W.C.	Visits, relieves, and educates
,, LONDON SOCIETY FOR TEACHING, Sec., 13, Upper Avenue-rd, Regent's-pk	On Lucas's system
,, MAN'S FRIEND, Treasurer, 34, Savile-row ..	Pensions of £12, £16, or £20

BLIND, PROTESTANT PENSION, Hon. Sec., 235, Southwark-br-rd	Pensions
,, ROYAL NORMAL COLLEGE & ACADEMY OF MUSIC, Principal, Upper Norwood	Educational, general and musical
,, SCHOOL FOR THE INDIGENT, Hon. Sec., St. George's Fields, Obelisk, S.E.	
,, SURREY ASSOCIATION FOR GENERAL WELFARE OF, Sup., 3, Pelican-bdgs, Peckham-rd	Indust. school for children and [adults
BOOKBINDERS' PENSION AND ASYLUM SOCIETY, Sec., 3, River-st, Myddelton-sq, N.	
BOOKSELLERS' PROVIDENT INST. ASSOC., Sec., 6, Amen-corner, E.C.	Trade
,, ,, RETREAT, Sec., 6, Amen-corner, E.C.	Trade
BOWYERS' CO.'S EXHIBITION, C. B. Arding, Esq., 22, Surrey-st, Strand.	Exhibitions £10 Oxf. and Cam.
BOYS' HOME, Treasurer, Regent's-pk-rd, N.W.	Destitute, not convicted
,, AND REFORMATORY, FRIENDLESS, Sup., Spanish-rd, Wandsworth-com..	Whether convicted or not
BOYS' ORPHANAGE, Hon. Sec., The Old Vicarage, Greenwich	Industrial training for Boys, £20 a year
,, REFUGE, 28, Commercial-st, Whitechapel	Between 11 and 14 years old
,, ST. ANDREW'S HOME AND CLUB FOR WORKING, Superintendent, 71, Dean-st, Soho	Working boys
BRASS & COPPER TRADES PEN. INST., Sec., 32, Frederick-st, Gray's-inn-rd	Trade
BREWERS' CO.'S CHARITIES, Clerk, 18, Addle-st, Wood-st, E.C. :	
BILLOWE'S CHARITY ..	Small sums to poor members of Co
GRAMMAR SCHOOL ..	Allhallows, Barking, and St. John's, Wapping, free
HICKSON'S CHARITY..	Almshouses and schools
HUNT'S CHARITY	For teaching the poor
JEMMITT'S ,,	Freemen of Co. or widows
JOHN BAKER'S ALMSHOUSES	8 poor women of Christ Ch. parish
OWEN'S ,,	Homes, &c., for widows & schools
PLATT'S ,,	Boys of Aldenham, and of Co.
POTTER'S ,,	£6 yearly amongst 6 mems. of Co.
ROCHDALE'S ,,	£3 ditto
CLARKE'S ,,	£3 ditto
WHITBREAD'S ,,	Trade
BRITISH HAIRDRESSERS' BENEVOLENT & PROVIDENT INST., Sec., 32, Sackville-st, S.W.	Trade
BRITISH HOME FOR INCURABLES, Sec., 73, Cheapside	Homes or pensions.
,, LADIES', FOR REFORMING FEMALE PRIS., Sec., 195, Mare-st, N.	[prosperity
,, ORPHAN ASYLUM, Sec., 47, Cannon-st, E.C.	For orphans of those once in
BROCKHAM HOME, near Reigate, Sec., Holmewood, Dorking	Trains orphan girls for service
BUILDERS' BENEFIT INST., Sec., 4, Vernon-place, Bloomsbury-sq	Trade
,, CLERKS' BENEVOLENT INST., Sec., 27, Farringdon-st	Trade
,, FOREMEN, &c., INST., Sec., 9, Conduit-st, Regent-st	Trade
BURLINGTON CHARITY SCHOOL, Treasurer, Boyle-st, Savile-row	Girls of St. James's, Westminster
BUTCHERS' CHARITABLE INST., Sec., 4, Guildhall-chambers, E.C.	Trade
BUTLERS' ALMSHOUSES, Clerk, Rochester-row, Westminster	Two poor men and their wives
CABDRIVERS' BENEVOLENT ASSOC., Hon. Sec., 15, Soho-sq	Trade
CABMEN'S MISSION, Minister, King's-‡-circus	
,, SHELTER FUND, 68, Buckingham Palace-rd, S.W.	See special article
CAMBRIDGE.—ROYAL ASYLUM, Sec., 40, Charing ✠, any day but Sat...	Widows of N.C.O. and privates
CAMDEN & KENTISH TN. ALMSHO., Trust., Lit. Randolph-st, Camden Tn.	For old women
CARON'S ALMSHOUSES, Rev. Canon Jennings, Smith-sq, Westminster	For poor old women of Lambeth
CARPENTERS' CO., Clerk, 68, London-wall, E.C.	Exhibition to Cambridge
CATHOLIC (ROMAN) CHARITIES	
AGED POOR SOC., Sec., 31, Queen-sq, W.C.	Pensions to men and women
CATHOLIC POOR SCHOOL COMMITTEE, Sec., 82, Gloucester-pl, Portman-sq, W.	Training and primary schools
CONVENT OF FAITHFUL VIRGIN, Mother Superioress, Norwood	Orphanage for girls
CRECHE, THE B. BENEDICT JOSEPH'S, Mother Sup., 4, Bulstrode-st	Infants from 3 weeks to 3 years
LITTLE SISTERS OF THE POOR, Suprs., Portobello-rd, Notting-hill	To assist the poor of both sexes
LONDON SEC. CLERGY FUND, Adminis., 49, Clarendon-sq, Somers Tn.	Westminster and Southwark
LONDON SEC. CLERGY, NEW FUND, Sec., 54, Lincoln's-inn-fields ..	Ditto
NAZARETH HOUSE, Gen. Supt., Hammersmith	Hospice for aged men & women
NIGHT HOME, Superioress, 9, Lower Seymour-st	For girls of good character
,, REFUGE, Crispin-st, Bishopsgate-st	For men, women, & children, &c.
ORPHANAGE OF THE SISTERS OF PROV.., Bartrams, Hampstead-gn	
ST. AGNES'S ORPHANAGE, Man., Archbishop's House, Westminster	Workh. boys under 7 years of age

CATHOLIC (ROMAN) CHARITIES (*continued*):

ST. ANN'S CATHOLIC ORPHANAGE, 8, Alpha-rd, Regent's-pk	For poor girls
INDUS. SCHOOL & ORPH., St. Wilfred's Convent, Cale-st, Chelsea	For poor girls
ST. EDWARD'S REFORMATORY, Manager, East Ham	For boys
ST. ELIZABETH'S HOME, Mother Abbess, 59, Mortimer-st, W.	Train girls for service
ST. HELEN'S ORPHANAGE, the Very Rev. Canon Kyne, Brentwood	To train poor boys
ST. JOHN'S INDUS. SCHOOL., Supt., Shern Hall-st, Walthamstow, E.	For boys
ST. JOSEPH'S ALMSHOUSES, Sec., 31, Queen-sq, Bloomsbury	Homes with pensions
" & POOR SCH. FOR GIRLS, Sec., Ingatestone Hall	
" HO. ASY. FOR AGED POOR, Rev. Moth., Portobello-rd, W.	All denominations
ST. MARGARET'S INDUS.SCH., Man., HolcombeHo., Mill-hill, Hendon	Destitute girls from 8 to 16
ST. MARY'S INDUSTRIAL SCHOOL, Lady Superior, Eltham	For girls
" ORPHANAGE, Manager, Archbp.'s House, Westminster	Pauper boys
" " Hon. Sec., 17, Portman-st..	Sons of respectable Rom. Cath.
" " near Walthamstow	Girls for service partly at expense of friends.
" TRAINING COLLEGE, the Principal, Hammersmith	Train pupil-teachers as masters
ST. NICHOLAS'S INDUS.SCHOOL, Director, Manor Hse., Little Ilford	Dest. boys not convicted of crime
ST. PATRICK'S SCH.& ASY. FOR FEM.ORP., Tudor-pl, Tottenham-ct-rd	
ST. SCHOLASTICA'S RETREAT, Warden, Kenninghall-rd, Clapton	For superior classes
ST. STEPHEN'S INDUS. SCH., Man., Archbishop's Hse., Westminster	For poor Catholic boys
ST.VINCENT DE PAUL SOCIETY, Pres., 31, Queen's-sq, Bloomsbury	To visit families, assist boys, &c.
ST. VINCENT'S HOME, Harrow-rd	For destitute boys
WESTMINSTER DIOC. EDUCATION FUND, Sec., Archbp.'s Hse., Wstm.	Poor of Westminster diocese
"	*See* BEGGARS.
CHARITY ORGANISATION SOCIETY, 15, Buckingham-st, W.C.	
CHARTERHOUSE, Registrar personally, Hospital, Charterhouse-sq, E.C.	Homes for old men, scholarships
"CHICHESTER" & "ARETHUSA" TRAINING SHIPS, Sec., 25, Gt.Queen-st	Train destitute boys for sea
CHILDREN, HOME FOR INCURABLE, Sec., 33, Maida-vale, W.	
" St. MONICA'S HOME FOR, Lady Sup., Quex-rd, N.W.	Sick and incurable
CHILDREN'S DINNERS.—"GOOD SHEP." MISSION, Wagner-st, Hatcham	Teach, clothe, & feed little chi!.
" HOME, Miss Cotton, Leytonstone, E.	To rescue young girls
" HOME, Rev. T. B. Stephenson, Bonner-rd, Victoria-pk	For orphan & destitute children
" (SICK) DINNER-TABLE, Lady Sup., 47, Earl-st, Lisson-gr..	Hot meat dinners, milk, &c.
CHOIR BENEVOLENT FUND, Sec., 1, Berners-st, W.	Organists and lay clerks
CHRISTIAN UNION ALMSHOUSES, 233 and 235, Marylebone-rd	Prot. with at least 4s. 6d. per wk.
" WITNESS FUND, Sec., 13, Blomfield-st, London Wall	Aged Congregational ministers
CHURCH MISSION CHILDREN'S HOME, Director, Highbury-gr, N.	Children of Church Mission
" PENITENTIARY ASSOC., Sec., 14, York-bdgs, Adelphi.	Houses of mercy and refuges
CITY MESSENGER BRIGADE, Hon. Director, 18, Stepney-causeway: E..	Boys
" OF LONDON FREEMEN'S ORPHAN SCHOOL, Town Clerk, Guildhall	*See* CITY OF LONDON
" " GENERAL PENSION, Sec., 44, Finsbury-pavement	Permt. pensions to artisans, &c.
" " TRUSS SOC., Sec., 35, Finsbury-sq	Bandages, instruments, &c.
" WAITERS' PROV. & PEN. SOC., Sec., 28, Martin's-la, Cannon-st, E.C.	

CLERGY :

ARNOLD FUND, Trustees, 57, Coleman-st	To assist wid. and orph. of clergy
ASHTON'S CHARITY, Receiver, Gresham House, 25, Old Broad-st	Relieve poor clergymen and wid.
BISHOP PORTEUS'S FUND for, Trea., Archd. of Midd., 41, Leinster-gdn	Poor clergy of diocese
BOYCE'S CHARITY TO, Rector, Christ Church, Blackfriars-rd	
BROMLEY COLLEGE FOR WIDOWS OF, Clk. to Trustees, Bromley, Kent	Grants & annu. Also schools, &c.
CHOLMONDELEY FUND FOR, Treas., 1, Middle Scotland-yd, Whitehall	
CLERGY LADIES' HOMES, Miss T. J. Matthews, 55, Sussex-gardens, Hyde-pk.	Homes for widows & unmarried daughters.
CURATES' AUGMENTATION FUND, Sec., 2, Dean's-yd, Westminster..	Curates of 15 years' standing
"EVANGELICAL MAGAZINE" FUND, Sec., 62, Paternoster-row	Grants to 150 widows
FRIEND OF CLERGY CORPORATION, Sec., 4, St. Martin's-pl, W.C...	Pensions and temporary aid
LONDON CLERGY, SOC. FOR RELIEF OF, Trea., Sion Coll., Lond.Wall	Clerg., their wid. & chil. (Midd.)
RICHARDS'S, REV. DR., CHARITY, Sec.,7,Godliman-st, Doctors' Com.	Superannuated & infirm clergy
ST. JOHN'S FOUND. SCH., SONS OF POOR CLER., Sec., 1A, St. Helen's-pl	Sons of living clergymen
SMITH'S CHARITY TO, Solicitors, 99, Great Russell-st, Bloomsbury..	£20 each to 23 preachers
STRETCHLEY'S CHARITY TO, Trea., Christ's Hospital, Newgate-st ..	Gratuities of £1 triennially
THOMSON HANKEY, CHARITY OF, Trustees, 7, Mincing-la	Donations to widows & orphans
CLERGY ORPHAN CORPORATION, Sec., 63, Lincoln's-inn-fields	Clothe,educate, & maintain orph.
CLOCK AND WATCH MAKERS' ASYLUM, Sec., 33, Northampton-sq, E.C.	Homes and pensions

CLOTHWORKERS' CO.'S CHARITIES, Clerk, 41, Mincing-la :

ACTON'S CHARITIES	Pensions for poor blind
BURNELL'S CHARITY..	Exhibition to Oxford
CORNELL'S CHARITIES	Pensions for poor blind

CLOTHWORKERS' CO.'S CHARITIES (*continued*):

HEATH'S ALMSHOUSES	Homes for poor members
HEATHER'S CHARITY	Grants to housekeepers'widows
HEWETT'S CHARITY	Exhibition to Oxford
KENT'S ALMSHOUSES AND CHARITY	Homes for wid. of decayed mem.
NEWNAM'S CHARITY	Pensions to blind
PILSWORTH'S CHARITY	Exhibition to Mag. Col., Oxford
THWAYTE'S CHARITIES	Pensions to blind
WEST'S CHARITIES FOR THE BLIND	Pensions to blind
COACHBUILDERS' (MASTER) BEN. INST., Hon. Sec., 5, King-st, Baker-st	Trade
COACHMAKERS' OPERATIVE BEN. SOC., Sec., 469, Oxford-st	Trade
COBURG HOME, Hon. Sec., 66, Thistle-gr, S.W.	Orphan or deserving girls
COFFEE & EATING HOUSE KEEPERS' BEN. ASS., Trea., Anderton's Hotel, Fleet-st, E.C.	Trade
COLUMBIA MES. & SHOEBLACK BRIGADE, Man., 11, Wood-st, Spitalfields	Training destitute boys
COMMERCIAL TRAVELLERS' BEN. INST., Sec., 47, Finsbury-circus, E.C.	Trade
,, ,, SCHOOLS, Sec., 37, Milk-st, E.C.	Children of decd & poor com.trav
COMMISSIONAIRES, CORPS OF, 419A, Strand	*See special article*
CONGREGATIONAL FUND BOARD, Sec., 5, Warwick-la, Paternoster-row	Poor ministers
,, PASTORS' RETIRING FUND, Sec., Memorial Hall, E.C.	Annuities for disabled pastors
,, PASTORS' WIDOWS' FUND, ditto ..	Annuities for pastors' widows
,, SCHOOL, Sec., Lewisham, S.E.	Sons of ministers
CONSUMPTIVE FEMALES, HOME FOR, Sec., 57-8, Glo'ster-pl, Portman-sq	One guinea entrance, 5s. a week
COOK'S, CAPTAIN, ALMSHOUSES, Vestry Clerk, Bancroft-rd, E. ..	Wid. of seamen Mile End Old Tn.
COOKS' CO.'S CHARITIES:	
CORBETT'S & KENNEDY'S GIFT, Clerk, 24, Laurence Pountney-la ..	Clergymen's widows, £5 each
DAVIS'S GIFT, ditto	Apprentice 1 child
PHILLIPS'S GIFT, 24, Laurence Pountney-la	Apprentice 2 children
COOPERS' CO.'S CHARITIES:	
GIBSON'S ALMSHOUSES, Clerk, 71, Basinghall-st	Homes for women,schls.for boys
SHAW'S CHARITY, ditto	Exhibs. to Oxford or Cam.
STRODE'S SCHOOL AND ALMSHOUSES, ditto	Poor of Egham parish
WOOD'S ALMSHOUSES AND SCHOOL, ditto	Freemen and school for boys
CORDWAINERS' CO.'S CHARITIES:	
BLIND, CAMES'S CHARITY TO, Clerk, 7, Cannon-st	Pensions to blind men & women
CLERGYMEN'S WIDOWS, CAMES'S CHARITY TO, ditto ..	Pensions
CAMES'S CHARITY TO DEAF AND DUMB, ditto..	Pensions
CORN EXCHANGE BENEVOLENT SOC., Sec., Mark-lane, E.C	Trade
CORPORATION OF LONDON BENEVOLENT FUND, Sec., Guildhall	Mems. of the Corp.,widows, &c.
,, SONS OF CLERGY, Regis., 2, Bloomsbury-pl, W.C. ..	Clergymen,their widows & chil.
COUTTS'S, BARONESS BURDETT, SEWING SCH., Man., 16, Hanbury-st, E.	
COVENT GARDEN THEATRICAL FUND,Sec.,Beaufort House, Beaufort-bdgs	Annuities, members and widows
COW-CROSS MISS., Supt.,Gloucester Hall,Upr.Gloucester-st, Clerkenwell	Breakfasts, dinners, & visitation
CRECHE, INFIRMARY AND HOME, Manager, 14, Stepney-causeway, E.	*See special article*
,, ST. ANDREW'S, Manager, 37, Mortimer-st, W. ..	Receive infants by day
CRIPPLED BOYS,NAT.IND. HOME&RELIEF,Man.,Wright's-la,Kensington	To teach a trade
CRIPPLES' HOME AND INDUSTRIAL SCHOOL, Sec., 17A, Marylebone-rd ..	For girls
,, HOME FOR ORPHANS AND DESTITUTE, Queen-st, Edgware-rd ..	For boys
,, NURSERY, Sec., 15, Park-pl, Regent's-park	Boys and girls
CUMBERLAND BENEVOLENT INST., Sec., 33, Cheapside ..	Pensions
CURRIERS' CO., Clerk to Co., 6, London Wall	Members, wids., & journeymen
CUSTOMS ORPHANAGE, Sec., H.M. Customs, Port of London	Children of deceased officers
CUTLERS' CO.'S CHARITIES, Clerk of Court, 23, Lincoln's-inn-fields ..	Homes for poor persons
BUCKE'S CHARITY, ditto	Exhibitions to University
CRAYTHORNE'S CHARITY, ditto	Two Exhibitions to University
DAIRYMEN'S BENEVOLENT INST., Sec., 191, Fleet-st, E.C.	Trade
	[education
DATCHELOR'S CHARITY AND SCHOOLS FOR GIRLS, Clerk, 1, Fenchurch-buildings, E.C. ..	Pensions and partly gratuitous
DAVIS'S ALMSHOUSES, Trea., 3, Highbury-pl, N. ..	Homes and pensions
DEACONESS INST., LONDON DIOC., Hon. Chap., 12, Tavistock-cres, W.	To visit, nurse, and teach
DEAF & DUMB CHILDREN, ASYLUM FOR, Sec., 93, Cannon-st	Support and education
,, ,, ,, LADIES' CHR. HOMES, Sec., 80, Pentonville-rd	4 years of age (oral system)
,, ,, CHARITABLE & PROVIDENT SOC., Sec., 46, Craven-st	Pensions for aged and infirm
,, ,, FEMALES, BRITISH ASYLUM FOR, Sec., 27, Red Lion-sq	Education
,, ,, ROYAL ASSOC. IN AID OF, Sec., 419, Oxford-st ..	Relig. services and employment
DESTITUTE SAILORS' ASYLUM, Sec., Well-st, nr. London Docks	
DISCHARGED CRIMINALS, MIDDLESEX SOC. FOR REFORMATION OF, Sec., Sessions House, Clerkenwell ..	To assist convicts on discharge

DISCHARGED PRIS. AID SOC., Sec., Nine Elms House, Wandsworth-rd..	For females
" PRISONERS' (MET.) RELIEF COM., Sec., 27, Chancery-la..	Short-term male prisoners
" " ROYAL SOC. FOR ASS. OF, Sec., 39, Charing ✝	
" " SURREY SOC. FOR EMPLOYMENT OF, Sec., H.M.'s Prison, Wandsworth	County prisoners
DISSENTING MINISTERS, SOCIETY FOR ASSISTING TO APPRENTICE CHILDREN OF, Sec., Memorial Hall, Farringdon-st	
DISSENTING MINISTERS, Soc. FOR REL. OF, Sec., 2, Villas, S. Norwood-hill	Aged and infirm
" " WIDOWS' FUND, Sec., Park-villas, Bromar-rd, Denmark-hill, S.E.	Yearly grants and donations
DISTRESS, SOC. FOR RELIEF OF, Secs., 28, King-st, St. James's-sq	No distinction of creed or race
DOGS, TEMPORARY HOME FOR LOST, Man., Battersea-pk-rd, S. Lambeth	Lost and starving dogs
DRAMATIC AND MUSICAL SICK FUND ASSOC., Sec., 9, Adam-st, Adelphi	Dramatic, and musical
DRAPERS' CO.'S CHARITIES:	
BANCROFT'S ALMSHOUSES, Clerk of Co., 27, Throgmorton-st, E.C..	Home for 30 members
" HOSPITAL SCHOOL, ditto	100 poor boys
BLIND, GRAINGER'S CHARITY TO, ditto ..	£10 pension
CAMES'S ALMSHOUSES, ditto	
CORNEY'S SCHOOL, ditto	Female orph. of respect. parents
EDMONSON'S ALMSHOUSES, ditto	12 persons
HARMAR'S ALMSHOUSES, ditto	12 single men and women
HOWELL'S CHARITY, ditto	Marriage portions
JOLLE'S, SIR J., SCHOOL, ditto	Boys of Bow and Bromley
MELBOURNE'S CHARITY, ditto	For poor widows of Co.
QN. ELIZABETH'S COLLEGE, ditto..	Maintain 20 poor persons
RUSSELL'S CHARITY, ditto	Exhibits. Oxford or Cambridge
STOCKER'S CHARITY, ditto	Bread to various London prisons
WALTER'S ALMSHOUSES, ditto	Widows appointed by Company
DRESSMAKERS AND MILLINERS' ASSOC., Matron, 72, Gower-st, W.C.	Home for those engd. in business
DROVERS' BENEVOLENT INST., Sec., 5, Adelaide-pl, S.E...	Almshouses, &c., for drovers
DRURY LANE THEATRICAL FUND, Sec., 27, Great Queen-st, W.C.	Members of H.M. company
DUDLEY STUART HOME, Lady Sup., 77, Market-st, Edgware-rd	For training girls in difficulty or danger, 3s. 6d. a week, except in special cases
DUKE OF YORK'S SCHOOL, Sec., Royal Military Asylum, Chelsea	Sons of British soldiers
DULWICH COLLEGE	*See special article*
DUTCH ALMSHOUSES, Trustees of Dutch Church, Austin Friars..	Aged members of Church
DYERS' CO.'S CHARITIES:	
BALLS'-POND ALMSHOUSES, Clerk, Dyers' Hall, 10, Dowgate-hill ..	Freemen and Widows
CHAMBERS'S CHARITY, ditto	Pensions
GOLDSMITH'S CHARITY, ditto	To lend to young freemen
TREVILLIAN'S CHARITY, ditto	To assist poor debtors
EAST END JUVENILE MISS., Hon. Direc., 18 & 20, Stepney-causeway..	Adults & chil. of poorest classes
EAST LONDON GEN. PENSION SOC., Sec., 164, Bethnal Green-rd.	Weekly pensions
EMIGRATION HOME FOR DES. LITTLE GIRLS, Trea., High-st, Peckham	To assist emigration of orphan and destitute girls
EVANG. PROT. DEACONESSES' INST., Treas., The Green, Tottenham	Training for nursing
FALLEN WOMEN, REFUGE FOR, Mrs. Wilkes, The Elms, Copper Mill, Walthamstow	
FELTMAKERS' CO.'S CHARITIES:	
KING'S GIFT CHARITY, Clerk of the Company, 17, Salisbury-sq	Mem. of Co. and their widows
MACHAM'S CHARITY, ditto ..	For members of the Company
FEMALE EMIGRANT SOC., BRIT. LADIES', Sec., 43, Fitzroy-st, Fitzroy-sq	Provide matrons, books, &c.
" MISS. TO FALLEN WOM. OF LONDON, Sec., 435, West Strand..	
" ORPHAN ASYLUM, Sec., 32, Essex-st, Strand	For fatherless girls
" ORPHANS' HOME, Sec., 85, Queen-st, Cheapside	
" ORPHANS, HOME FOR, Sec., Grove-rd, St. John's Wood	Fem. who have lost both parents
" PREV. & REFORM. INST., Sec., Central Home, 200, Euston-rd	Friendless and penitent women
" SERVANTS' HOME SOCIETY, Sec., 85, Queen-st, Cheapside	
" WELFARE, SOCIETY FOR PROMOTING, Sec., 47, Weymouth-st	A centre for Institutions
FIELD-LANE RAGGED SCHOOLS, Sec., Vine-st, Clerkenwell-rd ..	The destitute poor
FISHMONGERS' CO.'S CHARITIES:	
CARTER'S CHARITY, Clerk, Fishmongers' Hall, E.C...	Exhib., St. John's, Cambridge
GRESHAM'S GRAMMAR SCHOOL, ditto	50 free scholars of Holt, Norfolk
JESUS HOSPITAL, ditto	40 persons, 6 free of Company
QUESTED'S CHARITY, ditto..	8 exhibs. students and M.A.
" " ditto..	Chil. of freemen in Christ's Hos
" HOSPITAL, ditto	12 persons, 6 free of Company

HMONGERS' CO.'S CHARITIES (*Continued*):

RANDOLPH'S CHARITY, Clerk, Fishmongers' Hall, E.C.	.. ..	Exhibition at Cambridge
ST. PETER'S HOSPITAL, ditto	.. ..	Members over 50, 5 years free
THE COMPANY'S EXHIBITION' CHARITY, ditto	.. ..	Exhibitions to Students
HMONGERS AND POULTERERS' INST., Sec., 3, Ship Tavern-pas, E.C.		Trade
OOD'S CHARITY, Churchwardens of St. Luke's, Chelsea	.. ..	Local
REIGNERS, SOC. OF FRIENDS OF, Sec., 27, New Broad-st, E.C.	..	Temporary relief and pensions
UNDLING HOSPITAL, Sec., Guildford-st, Russell-sq, W.C. ..	..	*See special article*
,, BENEVOLENT FUND, ditto..	.. ..	Aged foundlings
K COURT RAGGED SCHOOL, Hon. Sec., Fox-ct, Gray's-inn-rd	..	
AMEWORK KNITTERS' CO.'S ALMSHOUSES, Clerk, 93, Finsbury-pavmt		Freemen and widows
ENCH MAISON DES ETRANGERS, Treasurer, 6, Frith-st, Soho		French poor
,, PROTESTANT HOSPITAL, Sec., Victoria-pk-rd, E.	..	A home for French Protestants
ENDLY FEMALE SOC., Sec., East View, Church-rd, Up. Norwood..		Wom. who have seen better days
W, ELIZABETH, REFUGE, Secs., 195, Mare-st, Hackney	..	For criminal women on release
LLER'S ALMSHOUSES, Clerk of Trustees, 36, Newnham-st, W.	..	Homes and pens. for old women
,, HOSPITAL, Clerk, Town Hall, Shoreditch	..	Homes for women of Shoreditch
RNITURE BROKERS' BENEVOLENT INST., Treasurer, 108, New Oxford-st		Trade
RDENERS' ROYAL BENEVOLENT INST., Sec., 14, Tavistock-row, W.C.		Trade
NERAL BENEVOLENT ASSOCIATION, Sec., 22, Berners-st, W. ..		Assistance for business purposes
,, DOMESTIC SERVANTS' BENEV. INST., Sec., 32, Sackville-st, W.		
NTLEWOMEN, ESTAB. FOR, IN ILLNESS, Lady Sup., 90, Harley-st		Wives and dau. of prof. men, &c.
NTLEWOMEN'S SELF-HELP INST., Sec., 15, Baker st, W. ..		To dispose of needlework, provide employment, &c.
RDLERS' CO.'S ALMSHOUSES, Clerk, 39, Basinghall-st ..	..	Members of Co. or widows
RLS' HOME, Hon. Sec., 22 & 41, Charlotte-st, Portland-pl ..		Girls not convicted of crime
, INDUSTRIAL HOME, Sec., 57, Stockwell-rd, S.W. ..	..	For domestic service
,, ORPHAN HOME, Sec., High-rd, Tottenham..	..	Domestic service
, MISS LEE'S HOME FOR, Miss Lee, Upperton-rd, Eastbourne		Train for service destitute girls of London
, ORPH. HOMES, MOUNT HERMON, Cambridge-rd, Kilburn, N.W.		Train for domestic service
, PRINCESS MARY VILLAGE HOMES FOR LITTLE, Nine Elms House, Wandsworth-rd		Train for domestic service
, VILL. HOMES FOR NEGLECTED, Hon. Direc., 18, Stepney-causeway		
ADSTONE'S (MRS.) FREE CONVAL. HOME, Sec., London Hospital ..		Convalescents, non-contagious
LDEN-LANE COSTERS' MISSION, Sec., 81, Old-st, E.C. ..	..	
LDSMITHS' & JEW. ANNUITY & ASY. INST., Sec., 65, Northampton-rd		Trade
,, BENEVOLENT INST., Sec., 15, Hanover-sq, W. ..	..	Trade
LDSMITHS' CO.'S CHARITIES:		
ASH'S CHARITY, Clerk to Co., Goldsmiths' Hall, Foster-lane, E.C..		£20 annually (Derby)
BARRATT'S CHARITY, ditto	.. ..	Coals
BOWES'S ALMSHOUSES, ditto	.. ..	Homes for Widows (Woolwich)
CHENEY'S CHARITY, ditto	.. ..	£4 annually to members
CURETON'S CHARITY, ditto..	.. ..	Pensions to freemen
DAVY'S CHARITY, ditto	.. ..	Weekly to members
FOWLER'S CHARITY, ditto	.. ..	40s. annually to widows
FOX'S CHARITY, ditto	.. ..	£10 annually to Dean's School, and £9 9s. ann. to almsman
HILLE'S CHARITY, ditto	.. ..	Clothing and coals
JENNER'S CHARITY, ditto	.. ..	St. John Zach., & St. Leonard
MIDDLETON'S (SIR H.) CHARITY, ditto	.. ..	Small money to members
MORRELL'S CHARITY, ditto..	.. ..	For almsmen of Co. [of Co.
PERRYN'S CHARITY, ditto	.. ..	Poor at Bromyard, Hereford, and
REED'S (SIR B.) CHARITY, ditto	.. ..	£10 ann. to Cromer Gram. Sch.
SHAW'S CHARITY, ditto	.. ..	£10 ann. to Stockport Gram. Sch
STRELLEY'S CHARITY, ditto	.. ..	Apprentices and poor soldiers
,, ditto..	.. ..	Exhibitions at University
WOLLASTON'S CHARITY, ditto	.. ..	Lunatics, almsmen, &c.
VERNESSES' BENEVOLENT INST., Sec., 32, Sackville-st, W. ..		Professional
,, HOME FOR UNEMPLOYED, Sec., 9, St. Stephen's-sq, Bayswater		
EENWICH, RL. HOSPITAL SCHOOL, Sec. of the Admiralty, Whitehall		Sons of sailors and marines
OCERS' CO.'S CHARITIES:		
BACKHOUSE'S CHARITY, Clerk, Grocers' Hall, Poultry, E.C.	..	2 Exhib. for scholars at Univ.
GRAMMAR SCHOOL, Master, Hackney Downs, Clapton, E. ..		Boys at £6 per annum
ROBINSON'S CHARITY, Clerk, Grocers' Hall, Poultry, E.C. ..		Exhibitions
OCERS AND TEA DEALERS' BENEVOLENT SOC., Sec., 30, Moorgate-st		Trade
OTTO PASSAGE REFUGE, Sup., 55, Paddington-st, Marylebone		Boys from 15 to 17
ARDIAN SOCIETY, Matron, 21, Old Ford-rd, E.		Penitent women

HABERDASHERS' Co.'s CHARITIES :,
APPRENTICING, GIFTS TOWARDS, Clerk, 31, Gresham-st, E.C.	Poor of Co.
ARNOLD'S, ditto	Pensions for freemen, & schools
ASKE'S CHARITY AND GRAMMAR SCHOOL, ditto	Pensions
BANKS'S CHARITY, ditto	Poor of Co.
BARNES'S „ ditto	Prisoners in Newgate
BLUNDELL'S „ ditto	Clothes and pensions
BOND'S „ ditto	Lothbury and St. Bartholomew
BRAMLEY'S „ ditto	Romf'd, Hoddesdon, Cheshunt
BURGHLEY'S (LADY) CHARITY, ditto	Loans to poor (Rolleston)
CALDWELL'S CHARITY, ditto	Exhibitions
CLARKE'S „ ditto	Exhibitions
CULVERWELL'S GIFT, ditto	
EXHIBITIONS AND EDUCATIONAL GRANTS, ditto	
GOURNEY'S „ „ ditto	Poor of Co.
HAMMOND'S GIFT, ditto	Poor of Co., hos., and prisons
HAZLEFOOT'S „ ditto	Poor of Co., &c.
JESTON'S GIFT, ditto	Metropolitan
JONES s PREACHERSHIPS, ditto	School (Monmouth)
MONMOUTH „ ditto	Poor of Oswestry
MORGAN'S CHARITY, ditto	Exhibitions to University, &c
NEWPORT FREE SCHOOL, ditto	Poor and poor debtors
PEACOCK'S CHARITY, ditto	Poor men and wid., small gifts
RAINTON'S CHARITY, ditto	12 poor men
SOMERS'S CHARITY, ditto	Various
SCHOLARS (POOR) CHARITY FOR, ditto	School and lectures
TROTMAN'S CHARITY, ditto	Church livings. Clothing
WELD'S „ ditto	Parish of St. Edmund the King
WHITMORE'S „ ditto	Shoreditch
HACKNEY ROAD ALMSHOUSES, Clerk of Trust, Town Hall, Shoreditch..	
HAMMERSMITH GODOLPHIN SCHOOL, Head Master, Hammersmith	Decayed Jewish tradesmen
HAND-IN-HAND ASYLUM, Sec., 23, Wells-st, Hackney	Young girls for servants
HANS TOWN SCHOOL OF INDUSTRY, Matron, 103, Sloane-st, Chelsea	Aged widows
HEDGER'S ALMSHOUSES, Sec., 40, Webber-row, Blackfriars-rd	Sons of Herefordshire parents
HEREFORDSHIRE SOCIETY, Hon. Sec., 2, Temple Gardens	Food, clothing, and silver money
HER MAJESTY'S ALMONRY CHARITIES, Sec. & Treas., Middle Scotland-yd	
HIGHGATE FREE GRAMMAR SCHOOL, Head Master, Highgate	
HILL'S ALMSHOUSES, Clerk, 31, Abingdon-st, S.W.	Six married couples, and six widows or single women
HOME AND COLONIAL SCH. SOCIETY, Prin., 344 to 354, Gray's-inn-rd	Train female teachers
„ FOR CONFIRMED INVALIDS, Sec., 22, Leigh-rd, Highbury-pk-south	For women. Chronic, except cancer and consumption
„ „ DESERTED DESTITUTE CHILDREN, Clayton House, Epsom..	Destitute young girls
„ „ DESERTED MOTHERS AND INFANTS, Sec., 3, Cumberland-st, Pimlico	Servants fallen for first time
„ „ INVALID CHILDREN, 70, Montpellier-rd, Brighton	For homeless boys under 10 ; by
„ „ LITTLE BOYS, Sec., corner of St. Bride-st, E.C.	election free, or 6s. weekly
„ „ WORKING AND DEST. LADS, Director, 18, Stepney-causeway	Boys of the Arab class
„ „ THE AGED POOR, Miss Harrison, 5, Grandacre-ter, Anerley	Six houses, seventy-two inmates
„ „ WORKING GIRLS, Hon. Director, 38, Lincoln's-inn-fields,W.C.	For girls in business
„ „ OF HOPE, Secretary, 4, 5, & 6, Regent-sq, Gray's-inn-rd, W.C.	Fallen & friendless young women
HOPTON'S ALMSHOUSES, Clerk to the Charity, 9, Newcomen-st, Borough	Christchurch parish, Blackfrs-rd.
HOTEL & TAVERN KEEPERS' PROV. INST.,Sec.,Caledonian Hotel,Adelphi	Trade
HOUSEBOY BRIGADE SOCIETY, Hon. Sec., 153, Ebury-st, Pimlico	Train boys for service & printing
HOUSE OF CHARITY FOR DIST. PERSONS, Warden, 1, Greek-st, W.C.	Temporary residence for those of good character
HOUSELESS POOR ASYLUM, Sec., Asylum, Banner-st, St. Luke's..	Widows of nav. and mil. officers
HOWARD INSTITUTON, Trustees, 74, Belgrave-rd, S.W.	Ladies and gent. in reduced cir.
HUGGENS'S COLLEGE, Sec., 25, Austin Friars, E.C.	Austro-Hung. in Unit. Kingdom
HUNGARIAN.—LONDON ASSO., Hon. Sec., 66A, Great Russell-st, W.C.	Grants of books
HUSSEY'S BOOK CHARITY, Clerk, 21, Great George-st, Westminster	Juvenile idiots and imbeciles
IDIOTS, ASYLUM FOR, Sec., 36, King William-st, London-br	Female teachers for India
INDIAN FEMALE NORMAL SCHOOL, &c., Sec., 2, Adelphi-terrace, W.C	For sufferers by the Mutiny
„ MUTINY RELIEF FUND, Sec., 2, East India-av, Leadenhall-st ..	Girls from 8 to 14
INDUSTRIAL HOME FOR GIRLS, Hon. Sec., 125, Sloane-st, Chelsea	Girls from 12 to 16 [respectable
„ SCHOOL FOR GIRLS, Hon. Lady Sec., 3, Church-st, Kensington	Unmarried mothers previously
INFANT HOME & REF. DESERTED MOTH., Lady Sup., 35, Gt. Ccram-st	

INFANT NURSERY, 23, Church-pl, Paddington-gn	Paying 2d. or 3d. daily
,, ,, 34, North-bank, Regent's-pk	Infants and orphans
,, ORPHAN ASYLUM, Wanstead, Essex; Sec., 100, Fleet-st	Orphans of formerly prosperous
INVALID ASYLUM, Matron, High-st, Stoke Newington	Respectable women
INVALIDS' DINNER-TABLE, Lady Sup., 47, Earl-st, Lisson-gr	Hot meat dinners, &c.
IRON, HARDWARE, METAL TRADES' PEN. SOC., Sec., 67A, Up. Thames-st	Trade
IRONMONGERS' CO.'s CHARITIES:	
BETTON'S CHARITY, Trustees, Ironmongers' Hall, Fenchurch-st	Church of England schools
,, ,, ditto	Widows and children of freemen
CHAPMAN'S ,, Clerk to Company, Ironmongers' Hall..	Exhibitions
DANE'S ,, ditto	Exhibitions
GEFFEREY'S ALMSHOUSES AND CHARITY, ditto..	Homes and pensions
HALLWOOD'S CHARITY, ditto	Exhibitions
LEWEN'S ALMSHOUSES, Gt. Mitchell-st, St. Luke's, ditto	Poor of Company
,, CHARITY, ditto	Exhibitions
ISLINGTON INDUSTRIAL HOME FOR BOYS, Sec., 119, Copenhagen-st, N.	
,, YOUNG MEN'S CHRIST. BENEV. SOC., Sec., 198, Upper-st, N.	Relieve sick at own dwellings
ITALIAN BENEVOLENT SOC., Sec., 9, Greville-st, Hatton-gdn, E.C.	Poor Italians
JEWISH CONVALESCENT HOME, Hon. Sec., Portland-rd, S. Norwood	
,, FAITH, SOC. FOR SUP.AGED NEEDY OF, Sec., 13, Devonshire-sq, E.	5s. a week
,, HAND-IN-HAND ASYLUM, Sec., 23, Wells-st, Hackney	Jewish tradesmen
,, INST. FOR RELIEVING THE INDIGENT BLIND, 5, Duke-st, E.C.	Jews only
,, LADIES' BENEVOLENT LOAN SOC., Sec., 5, Duke-st, Aldgate	Money lent free
,, POOR, BOARD OF GUARDIANS FOR, Sec., 13, Devonshire-sq, E.	
,, WIDOWS' HOME ASY., Sec., 15, Newcastle-st, Whitechapel	
JEWS' DEAF AND DUMB HOME, Hon. Sec., Walmer-rd, Notting-hil	
,, EMIGRATION SOC., Hon. Sec., 5, Duke-st, Aldgate, E.C...	
,, FOOD FOR POOR, MESHEBAT NAPHESH SOC., Sec., 5, Duke-st, E.C.	
,, FREE SCHOOL, Sec., Bell-la, Spitalfields	
,, HOSPITAL AND ORPHAN ASYLUM, Sec., 13, Spital-sq, E...	
,, INFANT SCHOOLS, Sec., Commercial-st, Spitalfields, E.	
,, ORPHAN ASYLUM, Master, St. Mark's-st, E...	
,, PHILANTHROPIC SOC. FOR RELIEVING WIDOWS OF, Sec., St. Mark's-st, Goodman's-fields, E.	
,, WESTMINSTER FREE SCHOOL, Sec., 60, Greek-st, Soho	
JOB AND POSTMASTERS' PROVIDENT FUND, Sec., 36, King-st, E.C.	Trade
KENSINGTON FEMALE SERV. HOME, Mat.,7, Up. Phillimore-pl, Kensington	Servants out of place
KING EDWARD GIRLS' REFUGE & INDUSTRIAL SCHOOL, Albert-st, Mile End New Town, E.	Girls from 6 to 16.
KING EDWARD'S SCHOOLS, Steward, St. George's-rd, S.E.	Boys & girls between 12 and 15
LABOURING CLASSES, SOC. FOR IMPROV. COND. OF, Sec., Bloomsbury Mansion, Hart-st, W.C..	Plans for model buildings
LADIES' CHARITY SCHOOL, Sec., Powis-gardens, Notting-hill	Training for service
,, HOME, Hon. Sec., 53, Abbey-rd, St. John's Wood, N.W.	Ladies in reduced circumstances
,, SAMARITAN SOCIETY, Hon. Sec., 23, Queen's-sq, Bloomsbury..	Paralysed and epileptic
,, SCHOOL OF TECHNICAL NEEDLEWORK AND DRESSMAKING, Hon. Sec., 15, Dorset-st, Portman-sq	Instruction to ladies in dress making
,, WORK SOC., Hon. Sec., 31, Sloane-st, S.W.	Remun. employment for ladies
LAMBETH PENSION SOCIETY, Sec., 246, KenningtonPark-rd, S.E.	Householders of parish
LAW ASSOCIATION, Devereux-ct, Temple	Professional
LAW CLERKS' SOCIETY, Sec., 3, Serjeants'-inn, Chancery-la	Professional
LEATHERSELLERS' CO.'s CHARITIES:	
AYRE'S ALMSHOUSES, Clk., Hall of Leathersellers' Co., St. Helen's-pl	Housekeepers of parish
ELLIOTT'S CHARITY, ditto ..	One exhibition
HOLMDEN'S ,, ditto ..	One exhibition
HUMBLE'S ,, ditto ..	Two exhibitions
LEATHERSELLERS' ASYLUM, ditto..	Men and women of Co.
MOSELEY'S CHARITY, ditto..	One exhibition
ROGER'S ,, ditto..	Four exhibitions
,, ALMSHOUSES, ditto	Poor freemen and wives
LEATHER TRADES PROV. AND BENEV INST., Sec., 30, Moorgate-st, E.C.	Trade
LEICESTER-SQ SOUP KITCH. & HOSPICE, Sup., Ham-yd, Gt. Windmill-st	Food and shelter
LICENSED VICTUALLERS' ASYLUM, Sec., 67, Fleet-st	Trade
,, ,, PERM. FUND & SCHOOL, Sec., 127, Fleet-st ..	Trade
LIMEHOUSE PHILANTHROPIC SOC., Hon. Sec., Copenhagen-wf, Limehouse	Limehouse and its vicinity
LINEN AND WOOLLEN DRAPERS', &c., INST., Sec., 43, Finsbury-sq	Trade
LITERARY ASSOC. OF FRIENDS OF POLAND, Sec., 10, Duke-st, St. James's	Polish refugees

LITERATURE AND ART, GUILD OF, Sec., 26, Wellington-st, Strand	Grants to members and widows
LITTLE SISTERS OF POOR, Superioress, Fentiman-rd, S. Lambeth	Old and needy of both sexes
LLOYDS' PATRIOTIC FUND, Sec., 14, Cornhill	Soldiers, seamen, and marines
LOCK ASYLUM, Sec., Westbourne-gn, Harrow-rd, W.	*See* HOSPITALS
,, ,, SERVANTS' HOME, ditto	Former inmates of Lock Asylum
LONDON AGED CHRISTIAN SOC., Sec., 32, Sackville-st, Piccadilly	Pensions [daughters
,, ALMSHOUSES, INST. OF THE, Town Clerk, Guildhall	Freemen, their wid. & unmarried
,, AUXIL. OF PENITENTIARY, Warden, Park House, Highgate	Fallen and penitent women
,, ,, SCOTTISH EPISCOPAL CHURCH SOC., Sec., Homeleigh, Lower Richmond-rd, Putney	Aid for clergy and congregations
,, FEMALE PENITENTIARY, Matron, 166, Pentonville-rd, N.	To train for service
,, HIBERNIAN SOC., Sec., 13, Henrietta-st, Strand	Schools for Irish children
,, MASTER BAKERS' ALMSHOUSES AND PENSION SOC., Sec., Lea Bridge-rd, N.E.	Trade
,, HOSPITAL SAMARITAN SOC., Sec., London Hospital	To assist convalescents
,, MARITIME INST., Sec., South Sea House Asylum, Bow-com	Members, their wid. and child.
,, ORPHAN ASYLUM, Sec., 1, St. Helen's-pl, E.C.	Either sex
,, PHILANTHROPIC SOC., Sec., 17, Ironmonger-la, Cheapside	Bread and coal
LUMLEY'S ALMSHOUSES, Trustees, Shepherdess-walk, City-rd	Women of Aldgate&Bishopsgate
LYCEUM THEATRE FUND, Sec., at the Theatre	Members of Lyceum Co.
MAGDALEN HOSPITAL, Chaplain, Streatham, S.W...	For penitent women
MAIDA-HILL INDUSTRIAL SCHOOL & HOME FOR WORKING BOYS, 95, North-st, N.W.	Destitute and orphan boys
MARINE SOC., Sec., 54½, Bishopsgate-st-within	Training destitute boys for sea
MARSHALL'S CHARITY, Clerk, 9, Newcomen-st, Southwark	Augmentation of poor livings, University Scholarships, &c.
MASTER MARINERS' BENEVOLENT SOC., Sec., 12, Borough High-st	Professional
MAYFAIR PAROCHIAL ASSOC., Hon. Sec., 5, Derby-st, Mayfair	Relief of poor
MAY FEAST SOC., Sec., 6, St. Thomas's-ter, Maze-pond	For apprenticing boys
MEDICAL.—BRITISH MED. BENEV. FUND, Sec., 34, Seymour-st, W.	Med.men, their wids. & orphans
MERCERS' CO.'S CHARITIES :	
APPRENTICES, SEVERAL GIFTS FOR BINDING, Clerk, Mercers' Hall, Ironmonger-la, E.C.	Paying apprentice fees
BANCK'S CHARITY, ditto	Loans to young men of Co.
BARRETT'S ,, ditto	Exhibition
BENNETT'S ,, ditto	Poor of Wallingford, &c.
BLUNDELL'S ,, ditto	Poor in Bethlem Hospital
BRADBURY'S ,, ditto	Coals
CHERTSEY'S ,, ditto	Poor freemen of Company
DAUNTSEY'S ALMSHOUSES, ditto	Poor of West Lavington
DEBTORS' CHARITIES, POOR, ditto	Poor debtors
FISHBORNE'S CHARITY, ditto	Loans, clothing, &c.
GRESHAM COLLEGE LECTURES, ditto	Lectures, almshouses, &c.
HORSHAM FREE SCHOOL, ditto	Boys of Horsham, Sussex
LOANS TO YOUNG MEN, ditto	Assist in commencing business
MERCERS' GRAMMAR SCHOOL, ditto	Free instruction
MICO'S (LADY) ALMSHOUSES, ditto	10 widows of freemen of City
MORLEY'S CHARITY, ditto	Poor persons
NORTH'S (LADY) CHARITY, ditto	Exhibitions
ROBINSON'S CHARITY, ditto	Exhibitions
ST. PAUL'S SCHOOL, ditto	*See special article*
TRINITY ALMSHOUSES, ditto	Decayed seafaring men&widows
,, HOSPITAL, ditto	Greenwich & Shottesham, Norf.
WALTHALE'S CHARITY, ditto	Exhibitions
WHITTINGHAM'S COLLEGE ALMSHOUSES	Pensioners appointed by Co.
MERCHANT SEAMEN'S ORPHAN ASYLUM, Sec., 132, Leadenhall-st.	Orphns.of Brit.Merchnt.Seamen
MERCHANT TAYLORS' CO.'S CHARITIES :	
ALMSHOUSES, Clerk, 30, Threadneedle-st	Poor widows of Company
SCHOOL, ditto	*See special article*
MET. ASS. FOR BEFRIENDING YOUNG SERVTS., Sec., 14, Grosvenor-rd	Friendless girls
METROPOLITAN DISPENSARY AND CHARITABLE FUND, Fore-st, E.C.	Medical attendance, &c.
,, DRINKING FOUNTAIN ASSOC., Man., 111, Victoria-st, S.W.	Fountains and cattle troughs
,, HOSPITAL SUNDAY FUND, Sec., 1, Q. Victoria-st, E.C.	Church collections for hospitals
,, TABERNACLE (*see* RIPPON'S)	
,, TYPOGRAPHICAL FUND, Sec., 3, Raquet-ct, E.C.	Trade
,, VISITING AND RELIEF ASSOC., Sec., 46, Pall Mall, S.W.	Grants to poor parishes
MIDDLE-CLASS EDUCATION, LONDON COR. FOR, Sec., Cowper-st, City-rd	Child. of clerks in City or suburbs
MIDNIGHT MEETING MOVEMENT, Sec., 8A, Red Lion-sq, W.C.	To rescue fallen women

MILDMAY MED. MISS. HOS., Lady Sup., Conference Hall, Mildmay-pk	
MILITARY BENEV. FUND, Hon. Sec., Mrs. Ellis Williams, 40, Bedford-sq	Various charitable objects
MILLINERS AND DRESSMAKERS' PROV. INST., Sec., 32, Sackville-st	Wid. or dau. officers H.M. Army
MILTON'S-YARD RAGGED SCHOOLS AND MISSION, Master, Milton's-yd, Liverpool-rd, Islington ..	Trade
MINISTERS' FRIEND OR ASSO. FUND, Sec., Memorial Hall, Farringdon-st.	For working boys and girls
MISSIONARIES, HOME & SCH. FOR SONS & ORP. OF, Hon. Sec., Blackheath	Congregational
,, INST. FOR EDUCATION OF DAUGHTERS OF, Sec., St. Katharine's, Seven Oaks	Partly gratuitous education
MODEL SOUP KITCHEN, Sec., 257, Euston-rd	Partly gratuitous education
MONOX'S ALMSHOUSES, Churchwardens, Walthamstow, Essex	Food during the winter
MORDEN COLLEGE, Treasurer, Blackheath, Kent	Homes and schools
MUSIC HALL SICK FUND PROV. SOC., Sec., York Hotel, Waterloo-rd, S.E.	Decayed merchants above 50 yrs.
NATIONAL BENEVOLENT INST., Sec., 65, Southampton-row, W.C.	Professional
,, ORPHAN HOME, Ham Common, Surrey, Sec., 9, West Strand	Members of the up. & mid. classes
,, TRUSS SOCIETY, Sec., 28, King William-st, E.C.	Train for service of all denom.
NETHERLANDS BENEVOLENT SOC., 5, Austin Friars, E.	Provide poor with trusses, &c.
NEWCOMEN'S CHARITY, Master, Newcomen-st, St. Saviour's, Southwark	Dutch in London
NEWPORT-MARKET REF. & INDUST. SCH., Sup., 48, Long-acre..	Parochial
NEWSPAPER PRESS FUND, 55, Strand ..	Shelter seven nights, and food
NEWSVENDORS' BENEV. AND PROVIDENT INST., Sec., Hercules-bdgs, Lambeth, S.E.	Professional
NIGHT REFUGE, 37, Manchester-st, King's ✝	Trade
NURSES.—METROPOLITAN AND NATIONAL NURSING ASSOC., Sec., 23, Bloomsbury-sq	Shelters homeless females
NURSES, NIGHTINGALE FUND FOR TRAINING, Sec., 91, Gloucester-ter, W.	Trained nurses for sick poor
,, ST. JOHN'S HOUSE AND SISTERHOOD, 6, 7, 8, Norfolk-st, Strand	Hospital and infirmary nurses
,, TRAINED, ANN. FUND, Hon. Sec., F. W. Macan, Esq., 3, Fenchurch-avenue, E.C.	
,, WESTMINSTER TRAINING SCH., Lady Sup., 8, Broad Sanctuary	Trained hos. & surgical nurses
NURSING HOME, Head Sister, 12, Tavistock-cres, Westbourne-pk..	School and home
,, SISTERS' INST., Lady Sup., 4, Devonshire-sq, Bishopsgate	Respectable women in illness
OPERATIVE JEWISH CONVERTS' INST., Prin., Palestine-pl, Cambridge Hth.	Train nurses for private families
ORPHANAGE OF THE INFANT SAVIOUR, Matron, Percy-rd, Kilburn, N.W.	A temporary home
ORPHAN INST., ADULT (Princess Helena College), Sec., 11, St. Andrew's-pl, Regent's-pk ..	Payment of 3s. to 5s. per week
ORPHANS' HOMES, Lady Sup., 21, West-sq, Southwark	Daughters of clergy and officers
ORPHAN WORKING SCHOOL, Sec., 73, Cheapside	Train for service
OVERMAN'S ALMSHOUSES, Clerk, Fishmongers' Hall, E.C.	Orphan and necessitous children
PAINTERS' CO.'S CHARITIES :	Widows & sing. wom. Ch. of Eng
STOCK'S AND OTHER CHAR. TO THE BLIND, Clerk, Painters' Hall, Little Trinity-lane, E.C. ..	
PAINTERS' CHARITY TO LAME PAINTERS, &c., ditto ..	Respectable English poor
,, ,, FOR DECAYED LIVERYMEN, ditto	£10 annually
PALMER'S ALMSHOUSES, Clerk, Palmer's-passage, W. M. Trollope, Esq., 31, Abingdon-street, S.W.	
PARISH CLERKS' WIDOWS' ALMSHOUSE INST., 24, Silver-st, E.C.	12 poor persons
PAROCHIAL MISSION WOMEN FUND, Hon. Sec., 11, Buckingham-st, Strand	
PATRIOTIC FUND, ROYAL COM. OF, Sec., St. Martin's-pl, Trafalgar-sq..	Promotes self-help among poor
	Relief of widows and orphans of soldiers, sailors, and marines, fallen in wars
PAWNBROKERS' CHARITABLE INST., Sec., Almshouses, West Ham, Essex	Trade
PEABODY DONATION FUND, Sec., 64, Queen-st, Cheapside	Dwellings of London poor
PEOPLE'S ENTERTAINMENT SOC., Hon. Sec., 180, Brompton-rd, S.W.	Rational entertainments, Saturday evenings (winter)
PHARMACEUTICAL SOC.'S BENEV. FUND, Sec., 17, Bloomsbury-sq, W.C.	Trade
PHILANTHROPIC SOCIETY, Sec., Farm School, Redhill, Surrey ..	Reformation of criminal boys
PIMLICO ORPHANAGE, Matron, 36, Bessborough-gdns, Pimlico	On paym. of 10 or 12 gs. per ann.
POLICE-COURTS' POOR BOX, Personally, at the several Police-courts	For distribution by magistrate
POLICE.—METRO. & CITY POLICE ORPHANAGE, Sec., 4, Whitehall-pl, S.W	
POOR CLERGY RELIEF CORPORATION, Sec., 36, Southampton-st, Strand	Immediate relief
POPLAR HOSPITAL FOR ACCIDENTS, 303, East India Dock-rd	
PORTER'S ALMSHOUSES, Clerk, Town Hall, Shoreditch	Eight women of Shoreditch par
PORTERS', LONDON GENERAL, BENEV. ASSOC., Sec., 33, Cheapside	Trade
PORTUGUESE AND SPANISH JEWS' HOSPITAL, 251-5, Mile End-rd, E.	
POST OFFICE CLERKS' BENEVOLENT FUND, General Post Office	
,, ORPHAN FUND, ditto	

Princess Louise Home,&c. for Young Girls, Sec., 54, New Broad-st, E.C.	Young girls (not thieves)
Printers' Pension, Almshouses, &c., Corp., Sec., 20, High Holborn	Trade. Almshouses & orph. asy.
" Westminster Abbey Pension Fund for Aged Daughters of, Sec., 20, High Holborn	Trade
Protection of Women & Children, Soc. for, Sec., 85, Strand, W.C.	
" " Associate Inst. for Improving and Enforcing the Laws for the, 30, Cockspur-street, W.C.	
Providence Row Night Refuge & Home, Hon. Sec., 21, City-rd	Shelter and food
Provident Clerks' Benevolent Fund, 27, Moorgate-st, E.C.	Trade
" Medical Institute and Lying-in Charity, Dispensary, 20, Pimlico-rd, S.W.	Advice, home, attendance, &c.
Quebec Chapel Temp. Home for Young Wom., Mat., 115, Crawford-st	Before enter. Q. Charlotte's Hosp
Queen Adelaide Naval Fund, Hon. Sec., Admiralty, 57, Spring-gdns	Orp. dau. of R. Nav. & R.M. offi.
" Anne's Bounty, Sec., 3, Dean's-yd, Westminster..	Augmentation of small benefices
Ragged School Union, Sec., 12 and 13, Exeter Hall, W.C.	To promote free education
Railway Benevolent Inst., Sec., 57, Drummond-st, N.W.	Trade
" Guards' Soc., 29, Southampton-bdgs, W.C.	Trade
" Officers' and Servants' Assoc., Sec., 21, Moorgate Stn-bdgs	Trade
" Signalmen, &c., Soc., 37, Landor-rd, Clapham Rise	
Raine's Asylum and Schools, Master, Cannon-st-rd, E.	
Reformatory and Refuge Union, Sec., 32, Charing ✝	Destitute & neglect. wom. & chil.
" " Provident Fund, ditto	Offi. of inst. connected with union
Refuge for the Destitute, Manor House, Dalston-la, E.	Female criminals or service
Refuges for Homeless & Destitute Children, Sec., 25, Gt. Queen-st	Train for service
Relief of Poor, Assoc. for, Sec., 24, Knightrider-st, Doctors'-commons	Coals
Rescue of Young Wom. & Chil., Soc. for, Sec., 85, Queen-st, Cheapside	
Rippon's, now Metropolitan Tabernacle Almshouses, Walworth	Female worships. at Tabernacle
Robinson's Relief Fund, Treasurer, Upgang, Upper Norwood	Grants to aged Diss. ministers
" Retreat, ditto	Widows of Dissenting ministers
Royal Albert Orphan Asylum, Sec., 18, Newgate-st	Thoroughly destitute orphans
" Alfred Aged Merch. Seamen's Inst., Sec., 58, Fenchurch-st	Home and out pensions
" Asylum of St. Anne's Society, Sec., 58, Gracechurch-st	Chil. of per. formerly in sup. sta.
" Caledonian Asylum, Sec., Caledonian-rd, Holloway	Chil. of Scotch sol., sail., & mar.
" Female Philanthropic Society, Sec., 23, Lincoln's-inn-fields	Young female prisoners & others
" Gardeners' Benev. Inst., 14, Tavistock-row, Covent-gdn	
" " Dispensary, 25, Bartholomew-close, E.C.	Medical and surgical relief
" " Theatrical Fund, Sec., 8, Catherine-st, W.C.	Professional
" Homes for Ladies of Limited Income, 31, Park-rd, Wandsworth-com	[with less than £50 income Homes for ladies over 50 years
" Humane Society, Sec., 4, Trafalgar-sq	Recovering apparently drowned, and rewards for saving life
" Jennerian Inst., 37, Worship-st, E.C.	Gratuitous vaccination
" Literary Fund, Sec., 7, Adelphi-ter, Strand	Professional
" Masonic Benev. Inst., Sec., 4, Freemasons' Hall, Gt. Queen-st	Aged Freemasons & their wids.
" " Inst. for Boys, Sec., 6, ditto	From 8 to 16 years
" " Girls, Sec., 5, ditto	From 8 to 16 years
" Maternity Charity, Sec., 31, Finsbury-sq, E.C..	Poor married wom. at own homes
" Medical Benevolent College, Sec., 37, Soho-sq, W.	Poor med. men, widows, & sons
" National Lifeboat Inst., Sec., 14, John-st, Adelphi, W.C.	Lifeboats, and rewards
" Naval Benevolent Soc., Sec., 18, Adam-st, Adelphi, W.C.	Naval offi., their wid., orph., &c.
" " Female School, Sec., 32, Sackville-st	Dau. of Nav. & Royal Mar. offi.
" Sea-bathing Infirmary, Sec., 30, Charing ✝	Scrofulous patients only, on payment of 5s. or 6s. per week
" School for Dau. of Officers of Army, Sec., Cockspur-st, S.W.	Dau. of offi. of Army & Marines.
" Society of Musicians, 84, New Bond-st	Professional
" Victoria Patriotic Asy., Sec., 5, St. Martin's-pl, Trafalgar-sq	Sons and dau. of soldiers, sailors, and marines fallen in war
Rupture Society, The, Sec., 27, Great James-st, Bedford-row	To provide trusses gratuitously
Sabbath Meal Soc., 49, Mansell-st, Aldgate	
Saddlers' Co.'s Charity : Honnor's Home, Clerk, 141, Cheapside	Members of the Company
Sailors' Orphan Girls, Sec., 50, Bishopsgate-st-within	School and Home
St. Andrew's Sick Kitchen, 37, Mortimer-st, W.	Dinners
St. Clement Danes' Holb. Estate Char., Clk., 16, Houghton-st, W.C.	
Almshouses, Garrett-la, Lower Tooting, ditto	Householders in parish
Grammar School, ditto	A middle-class school for boys
Infant Schools, ditto	Children up to seven years
Middle Class Girls' School, ditto	
St. George, Hanover-sq, Visiting Ass., Sec., 18, Grosvenor-mews, W.	The poor of the district

ST. JAMES'S DIOCESAN HOME, Sister Superior, Fulham	Female penitents of an up. class
ST. JUDE'S INDUSTRIAL HOME, 9, Franklin's row, Queen's-rd, Chelsea	Girls for service
ST. KATHARINE ROYAL HOSPITAL, The Master, Regent's-pk	Residences, allowances, &c.
ST. MARTIN'S-IN-THE-FIELDS' ALMSHOUSES, Clk., Bayham-st, CamdenTn.	Resident householders in parish
ST. MARYLEBONE ALMSHOUSES INST., Sec., 65, Marylebone-rd, W	Householders of St. Marylebone
,, CHARITY SCHOOL, Sec., Devonshire-pl-north, Marylebone-rd.	Poor girls of parish
,, FEMALE PROTECTION SOC., 157-9, Marylebone-rd.	Fallen women not dissipated
ST. MARY MAGDALENE CONV. HOME, Sec., 14, Ranelagh-rd, Paddington	Before & aft. Q. Charlotte's Hos.
ST. MATTHEW'S HOME FOR FEM. ORPH., Hon. Sec., 37, Ossington-st, W.	Born in wedlock
ST. PANCRAS ALMSHOUSES, Sec., 48, Camden-rd, N.W.	Parishioners
,, FEMALE CHARITY SCHOOL, Trea., 108, Hampstead-rd	Children of parishioners
ST. PATRICK BENEVOLENT SOC., Sec., 61, Stamford-st, Blackfriars-rd.	Chil. born in London, Irish par.
ST. PETER'S HOME & SISTERHOOD, Lady Supt., Mortimer-rd, Kilburn.	Convalescent poor women, &c.
,, ORPHANAGE, Lady Superin., Upper Kennington-la, S.E.	Orphan dau. of professional men
ST. STEPHEN'S INFANT NURSERY, 101, Tabard-st, late Kent-st, Boro', S.E.	1d. each a day
ST. THOMAS CHARTERHOUSE INSTITUTION, Master, 44, Goswell-rd	Children of working classes
SALTERS' CO.'S ALMSHOUSES, Clerk, Salters' Hall, St. Swithin's-la.	Men and women of company
,, SCHOOL (RAINEY'S FOUNDATION), ditto	English, French, Latin, music
SAMARITAN FREE HOSPITAL FOR WOMEN & CHILDREN, 13, Lower Seymour-st, W.	
SCHOOL OF DISCIPLINE, GIRLS', Hon. Sec., 2, Queen's-rd-west, Chelsea	Vagrant children
SCIENTIFIC RELIEF FUND, Sec., Burlington House	Scientific men and their families
SCOTTISH CORPORATION, Sec., 7, Crane-ct, Fleet-st.	Scots resident in London
SHERIFF'S FUND SOC., Hon. Sec., Newgate	Fam. of pris. or discharged pris.
SHIP-BROKERS', &c., BENEVOLENT SOC., Sec., 17, Gracechurch-st.	Ship-brokers, &c.
SHIPWRECKED FISHERMEN AND MARINERS' ROYAL BENEVOLENT SOC., Sec., Hibernia-chambers, London-br	Shipwrecked fishermen and mariners, & their widows & orphs.
SHOEBLACK SOCIETIES' HOMES:	
CENTRAL, Superintendent, Great Saffron-hill, E.C.	For homeless and friendless boys
EAST LONDON, Superintendent, 96, Mansell-st, Whitechapel	Ditto
ISLINGTON AND NORTH LONDON, Sup., 30, York-rd, King's ✠	Ditto
NORTH-WEST LONDON, Superintendent, 33, John-st, N.W.	Ditto
NOTTING HILL, Superintendent, St. James's-pl, W.	Ditto
SOUTH LONDON, Superintendent, 223, Borough High-st.	Ditto
TOWER HAMLETS, Superintendent, Mile End-rd, E.	Ditto
UNION JACK SHOE BRIGADE, Hon. Director, Limehouse, E.	Ditto
WEST LONDON, Superintendent, Bessborough-pl, Pimlico	Ditto
SHOEMAKERS: MASTER BOOTMAKERS' INST., Sec., 17, Great George-st, S.W.	Trade
SILVER TRADE PENSION SOC., Sec., 32, Frederick-st, Gray's-inn-rd	Ditto
SION HOSPITAL, 66, Gresham House, Old Broad-st	Pensions to poor men and women
SISTERS OF CHARITY, Sisters in Charge, 123, Bethnal Green-rd	To visit, relieve, and nurse, &c.
SKINNERS' CO.'S ALMSHOUSES, Clerk, 8, Dowgate-hill	Widows
HOLLER'S TRUST, ditto	Men and women
JUDD'S ALMSHOUSES, ditto	Members of Company
LANCASTER'S CHARITY, ditto	Exhibitions
LEWIS'S CHARITY, ditto	Exhibition
LOANS TRUST, ditto	Not exc. £200, without interest
SMALL POX & VACCINATION HOSPITAL, Whittington Place, Highgate-hill	
SMITH'S CHARITY, Solicitors, 99, Great Russell-st, Bloomsbury, W.C.	Poor relations of Ald. Smith
SOANE'S, SIR JOHN, FUND, Hon. Sec., 13, Lincoln's-inn-fields	Distressed architects wid. & chil.
SOCIETE BELGE DE BIENFAISANCE, Hon. Sec., 10, London-st, E.C.	For distressed Belgians in London
,, FRANCAISE DE BIENFAISANCE, Sec., 10, Poland-st, Oxford-st.	Poor French persons
SOCIETY FOR ORGANISING CHARITABLE RELIEF AND REPRESSING MENDICITY, 15, Buckingham-st, W.C.	
SOCIETY FOR RELIEF OF WIDOWS & ORPHANS OF MEDICAL MEN, Sec., 53, Berners-st, W.	
SOCIETY OF SCHOOLMASTERS, Sec., 7, Adelphi-ter, Strand	Distressed schoolmasters
SOLDIERS' DAUGHTERS' HOME, Sec., 7, Whitehall	Train for domestic service
SOLDIERS, FUND FOR OLD AND DISABLED, Chairman, at Coutts & Co., Strand	
SOLICITORS' BENEVOLENT ASSOC., Sec., 9, Clifford's-inn, E.C.	For indigent solicitors & families
SOMERSETSHIRE SOCIETY, Sec., 13, Featherstone-bdgs, W.C.	Apprent. chil. of Somersetsh. par.
SOUTHWARK FEMALE SOC., Sec., 72, Gt. Guildford-st, Southwark	To relieve sickness and want
SPANISH & PORTUGUESE JEWS' BOARD OF GUARDIANS, 12, Bevis Marks	

SPANISH & PORTUGUESE JEWS' ORPHAN SOCIETY, 10, Bevis Marks, E.	[Queen's-sq
„ „ „ HOSPITAL, 12, Bevis Marks, E.	S. Andrew, Holborn, or S. Geo.,
STAFFORD'S ALMSHOUSES AND CHARITY, Sec., 8, Gray's-inn-sq	
STATIONERS' CO.'S CHARITIES :	
BALDWIN'S GIFT, Clerk, Hall, Stationers' Hall-ct, E.C	Great-coat to liverym. or freem.
BLACKWELL'S GIFT, ditto	Journeyman printers
BOWYER'S „ ditto	Journeyman comps. or pressmen
CATER'S „ ditto	St. Martin's, Lud., and Christch.
CLARKE'S „ ditto	Widow of liverym. or freeman
COMPTON'S „ ditto	Compositors
DAVIS'S „ ditto	Compositors
DILLY'S „ ditto	Widows of liverymen
GUY'S „ ditto	Widows of freemen
HAMBLIN'S „ ditto	Widows of liverymen or freemen
HANSARD'S „ ditto	Compositors, pressmen, &c.
JOHNSON'S „ ditto	Widows of liverymen, 60 yrs. old
NICHOL'S „ ditto	To compositors or pressmen
STRAHAN'S (A.) „ ditto	Compositors or pressmen
DITTO „ ditto	To printers
STRAHAN'S (W.) ditto	10 journeymen printers
WHITTINGHAM'S ditto	Widows of comps. or pressmen
WRIGHT'S (ALD.) ditto	24 freemen
STATIONERS' CO.'S SCHOOL, ditto	Sons of liverymen and freemen
STATIONER AND PAPER MANUFAC. PROV. SOC., Sec., 66, Cannon-st	Members, their wid. & children
STEPNEY MEETING ALMSHOUSES, Deacons, White Horse-ter, Stepney.	Poor of the Chapel
STOCK EXCHANGE BENEVOLENT FUND, Sec., Stock Exchange, E.C.	Trade
STOCKWELL ORPHANAGE, Rev. Pres., Metro. Tabernacle, Newington.	Fatherless boys
STRANGERS' HOME FOR ASIATICS, Hon. Sec., W. India Dock-rd, E.	Asiatic seamen, &c.
SUNDAY SOCIETY, Hon. Sec., 9, Conduit-st, W.	Rational Sunday entertainments
SURGICAL AID SOCIETY, Sec., Salisbury-sq, E.C.	See special article.
SURREY CHAPEL ALMSHOUSES, Trustees, Hill-st, Blackfriars-rd, S.E.	Christian women, especially members of Surrey Chapel
„ ORPHANAGE AND HOME, GIRLS', Sup., New Thornton-hth, Surrey	£12 per annum
TAILORS, BENEV. INST. FOR RELIEF OF, Sec., 8, Warwick-st, W.	Trade
TALLOW CHANDLERS' BENEV. SOC., Sec., 65, Blackman-st, S.E.	Trade
„ CO.—MONK'S CHAR., Clerk, Dowgate-hill	Members of Co.
TANCRED'S CHARITIES, Clerk, 28, Lincoln's-inn-fields	£100 studentships, and 12 pensions of £80 to aged gentlemen
TINPLATE WORKERS' CO., 6, London Wall, E.C.	Pensions
TOBACCO TRADE BENEVOLENT ASSO., Sec., 31, Moorgate-st, E.C.	Trade
TOWER HAMLETS MISSION, 31, Mile End-rd, and Branches	
TREWINT INDUST. FEMALE HOME, Matron, Philip-la, Tottenham	Girls over 14
TYLERS AND BRICKLAYERS' ALMSHOUSES, Clerk, 6, Bedford-row, W.C.	Freemen and liverymen of Co. and their widows
UNITED COOKS' PENSION SOCIETY, Sec., 16, Sherborne-la, E.C.	Trade
„ KINGDOM BENEFICENT ASSOC., Sec., 4, Berners-st, W.	Annus. to persons of better class
„ ST. SAVIOUR'S ALMSHOUSES, Clerk, Norwood, S.E.	Men and women
UNIVERSAL BENEFICENT SOCIETY, Sec., 15, Soho-sq, W.	Pensions, and general relief
VAUGHAN'S (MRS.) CHARITY, Sec., 43, Charlotte-st, Blackfriars-rd	Women of parish of Christchurch
VELLUM BINDERS' PENSION SOCIETY, Sec., 114, Beresford-st, Walworth	Trade
VINTNERS' CO.'S ALMSHOUSES, Clerk, 68½, Upper Thames-st, E.C.	Widows of members of Co.
WANDERERS' HOME, Sec., 6, Cambridge-lodge-villas, Mare-st, Hackney	Jews and Jewesses in distress
WAREHOUSEMEN AND CLERKS' SCHOOLS, Sec., 97, Cheapside	Trade
WATCH & CLOCK MAKERS' BENEV. INST., Hon. Sec., 8, Northampton-sq, E.C.	Trade
WATERMEN AND LIGHTERMEN'S ASYLUM, Committee, 18, St. Mary-at-Hill	Trade
WEAVERS' CO.'S CHARITIES, Clerk, 70, Basinghall-st, E.C.	Pensions
„ ALMSHOUSES, ditto	Freemen of Co. or weavers by trade
WELSH CHARITY SCHOOLS, Sec., The Ferns, Balham, S.W.	Children of Welsh parentage
WESLEYAN TRAINING COLL., 130, Horseferry-rd, Westminster	To train male & female teachers
WESTBY'S TRUST, Treasurer, 52, Threadneedle-st	Ten poor women of Independent denominations
WESTMINSTER FEMALE REFUGE, Lady Sup., 14, Gt. College-st, S.W.	Penitent women
„ FRENCH PROTESTANT SCHOOL, Bloomsbury-st, W.C.	Daughters of descendants of Huguenot refugees
„ JEWS' FREE SCHOOL, Sec., Hanway-pl, W.	Both sexes
„ MEMORIAL REFUGE, Sec., 39, Charing ✠	Female prisoners on release

WESTMINSTER SCHOOLS :

GREYCOAT HOSPITAL (ENDOWED) SCHOOL FOR GIRLS—	
The Day School, Sec., Alexandra-st, Victoria-st, S.W.	300, includ. 100 free exhibitioners
UNITED WESTMINSTER (ENDOWED) SCHOOLS FOR BOYS—	
The Day School, Sec., Alexandra-st, Victoria-st, S.W.	600, includ. 160 free exhibitioners
EMANUEL (BOARDING) SCHOOL, ditto	60, will be 300, includ. 75 free do.
WESTMORELAND SOCIETY SCHOOL, Sec., 14, Bedford-row, W.C. ..	Chil.of Westmoreland parentage
WHITELANDS TRAINING COLLEGE, Principal, 33, King's-rd, Chelsea	Training for schoolmistresses
WHITWORTH'S SCHOLARSHIPS, Sec., South Kensington Museum	Mechan. science and handicrafts
WIDOWS AND ORPHANS OF MEDICAL MEN, SOC. FOR RELIEF OF, Sec.,	
53, Berners-st, W.	Professional
WIDOWS' FRIEND SOC., 11, Lawrence Pountney-la, E.C...	To help widows who can help themselves
" SOC. FOR RELIEF OF DISTRESSED, Sec., 32, Sackville-st, W. ...	Applying by letter from a subscriber within the first month after widowhood
WILSON'S LOAN FUND, City Chamberlain, Guildhall, E.C.	Trade loans at low interest
WOMEN, SOC. FOR PROMOTING EMPLOYMENT OF, Sec., 22, Berners-st, W.	
WOOD-CHOPPING BRIGADE, Sec., 18, Stepney-causeway, E. ..	Employment to honest boys
WORCESTERSHIRE SOCIETY, Hon. Sec., 41, Finsbury-pavement, E.C. ..	Children of natives
WORK GIRLS' PROTECTION SOCIETY, 138, New Kent-rd, S.E.	
WORKING BOYS' HOME, 23, Tollet-st, Mile End	Homeless and destitute boys from 13 to 18
" LADS' INSTITUTES, SOCIETY FOR PROMOTING, Whitechapel	
" MEN'S COLLEGE, 45, Gt. Ormond-st, W.C.	Education at the lowest possible cost
YORKSHIRE SOCIETY'S SCHOOL, Sec., Westminster-br-rd, S.E.	Boys born in Yorkshire or of Yorkshire parentage

Charity Commissioners for England and Wales,

Gwydyr House, Whitehall, S.W. Hours 10 to 4. NEAREST *Ry. Stn.*, Westminster - br ; *Omnibus Rtes.*, Parliament-st, Victoria-st, Westminster-br, and Strand ; *Cab Rank*, Palace-yd.

Charity Organisation Society.—(*See* BEGGARS.)

Charterhouse. — Originally founded in 1371 by Sir Walter de Manny as a Carthusian convent, the London Charterhouse rapidly grew in wealth and importance, until the Dissolution brought about the end of all such institutions, and the monks had to seek such shelter as they could find elsewhere, Henry preventing their money from troubling their minds by kindly taking charge of it himself. The Priory of the Charterhouse after this passed through various hands, more or less unworthy, until it came into the possession of the family of the Dukes of Norfolk, from whom it was bought by that Thomas Sutton with whose name it is imperishably connected. Of an ancient Lincolnshire family, and educated at Eton and Cambridge, Sutton became in course of time a great coal owner, and naturally amassed considerable wealth. Childless and a widower in his old age, he determined to devote his fortune to the foundation of a hospital for the maintenance of old

men, and for the education of poor children, and, after buying the Charterhouse, obtained letters patent for his foundation in 1611. Shortly afterwards Sutton died, and the usual edifying wrangling and robbery over the pious founder's will set in. The heir-at-law, Lord Bacon, and King James, all had their turn, and it is difficult to understand how the hospital ever came to do any good at all. The history of the hospital is the history of most largely endowed almshouses. A good deal was done for the officers as the property improved in value, and not much for the poor brethren, and the usual scandals went on until they could be tolerated no longer. Then came reform, and the condition of the old gentlemen was much ameliorated. The poor brothers are eighty in number, and receive, each, £36 a year with rooms rent free, and are somewhat mournfully clad in black cloaks. There is a good deal of chapel-going, with a system of fines of a rather objectionable sort, and it may be doubted whether the pensioners are always of the class intended to be benefited under Sutton's will. Colonel Newcome was a poor brother, as all the world knows, and his memory sheds imperishable lustre on the aged eighty. The buildings of the Charterhouse, more especially the chapel which contains the superb tomb of the founder, are well worth inspection.

Charterhouse School. — One of the old London foundations which has been wise enough to move into the country. The buildings formerly occupied by the school are now in the occupation of the Merchant Taylors' School, and Charterhouse School itself is located at Godalming.

Cheapside (Map 8).—Cheapside is what it was five centuries ago, the greatest thoroughfare in the City of London. Here the two great arteries of Oxford-st and Holborn and of the Strand and Fleet-st from the west, and of Bishopsgate and Leadenhall from the east, together with a mighty stream of traffic from Moorgate on the north and King William-st on the south, are all united, and the great flow of traffic is constantly blocked and arrested by the cross tide setting in from Southwark-br up Queen-st. In its importance as a place of trade it has decayed. The great wholesale houses are in Cannon-st, or in the narrow lanes which run right and left from Cheapside, and the bright displays made by the Flemish merchants, the great traders of Genoa, and the cunning artificers of Milan, are gone. Sir John Bennett stands at the head of the watchmakers of Cheapside, and his clock, with moveable figures which strike the chimes and hours, is one of the sights of the place. Bow Church, with its

C

projecting clock looking up and down the street, is one of the few relics of the Cheapside of the past. Until lately the Poultry contained many houses of considerable antiquity, but it was at last felt that the narrow gut of this lane was an intolerable nuisance in the face of the enormously increasing traffic, and the whole of the northern side of Cheapside, from King-st to the corner of Princes-st, has now been thrown back, to the immense convenience of traffic, and to the advantage of Cheapside in general by the open view now given of the Royal Exchange and adjoining buildings. From Cheapside, King-st leads up to the Guildhall. Cheapside is always crowded, always a wonder to strangers and foreigners, but the best time to see it is either at 9 a.m., when the great tide of traffic is flowing into the City, or between 5 and 7 p.m., when the offices and warehouses are closing, and the tens of thousands of business men are off again to their homes. The stranger will be particularly struck with the absence of women from the moving crowd in Cheapside, and indeed generally in the City.

Chelsea Hospital (Map 12), one of the most interesting sights of London, was built by Charles II. from designs of Sir Christopher Wren. The foundation stone was laid in 1682 by the king himself, and the building was completed in 1690. It is generally supposed that it was Nell Gwynne's influence with the king which caused him to establish this splendid hospital for old soldiers. It is built of deep red brick with stone facings, and consists of two quadrangles and a grand central court open on the side facing the river. In the dining hall and chapel are battle-flags taken by the British Army in all parts of the world. The public are admitted to see these halls, and can also be shown over the wards. The hospital is of great interest from its tradition and history, and still more so from its quiet and old-world appearance. Walking among its silent courts it is difficult to believe that one is in the heart of London. NEAREST *Ry Stn.*, Grosvenor-rd (L. B. & S. C.); *Omnibus Rtes.*, King's-rd and Pimlico-rd; *Cab Rank*, Oakley-st.

Chelsea Suspension

Bridge (Map 12), otherwise known as Victoria-br, is another work by the designer of West-minster-br, and has something of the same thin appearance. It was made in Edinburgh, and set up in its present position in 1858 at a cost of £80,000. NEAREST *Ry. Stn.*, &c., North, same as Chelsea Hospital; South, Battersea-pk (S. Lon.).

Chess Clubs.—What may be termed the coffee-house epoch in the history of Chess in England ended in the year 1810 with the establishment of the London Chess Club, where members met for play in a private room in Cornhill. For some sixteen years afterwards it was the only association of the kind in London, and being supported chiefly by City merchants and members of the Stock Exchange, who played chess in the middle of the day, it was practically closed to amateurs whose occupations or pursuits were not "of the City," or whose only leisure was to be found in the evenings. It had other disadvantages from the ordinary amateur's point of view, not the least of which was that the members comprised a host of experts in the science of chess, giants in whose company the tyro of the period was much more likely to be awed than edified. There was no chess club at the west end of the town at this period, but accommodation for players was provided in numerous coffee-houses where "Monsieur" and "Herr," who since the first French Revolution have been always with us, dispensed instruction at such charges as their modest requirements suggested. In 1823 a West End chess club was established, with special rooms, &c., at the Percy Coffee House in Rathbone-pl. The members met for play at seven in the evening, sat down to a hot supper at ten—it was sixty years ago—and broke up at half-past eleven. Murphy, a miniature painter of note at that time, became a member of this club soon after its foundation, and introduced to the members the greatest player of the period—William Lewis. Lewis was then a merchant's clerk, and, after the death of Sarratt, the strongest chess-player in England. He won the admiration of the Percy Chess Club by beating their best player at the odds of a rook. In 1825 the Percy Chess Club was closed, and Lewis opened subscrip-

tion rooms in St. Martin's-la, where he was patronised by nearly all the best players in London: Alexander Macdonnell, subsequently the famous rival of La Bourdonnais; John Cochrane, the most brilliant player that ever appeared in the chess arena; Richard Penn, the author of the quaintest book in the language, "Maxims and Hints for Chess Players and Anglers" (illustrated by Stanfield); Bohn, the bookseller; and Pratt, of Lincoln's-inn, the author of a book on chess, which was described by Professor Allen, of Philadelphia, as a marvellous mixture of "Schoolmaster's English and Johnsonese." These rooms were closed in 1827, through the failure of Lewis. The London Chess Club still prospered; and it was not until the year 1832 that a rival association appeared upon the scene. Early in that year the famous Westminster Chess Club was opened in a room upon the first floor of a coffee-house in Bedford-st, Covent-gdn, kept by one Huttman. The new club was immediately successful, and under its auspices was played the celebrated match between Westminster and Paris in 1834. The club was temporarily dissolved in 1835, and was reorganised in the same year, the members meeting in Mr. Ries's drawing-room and joining the Divan in the Strand, of which establishment that gentleman was the proprietor. Here Howard Staunton, for many years the champion chess-player of England, made his first appearance and here were played the games in his match with Popert. In 1840 the Westminster Chess Club was again dissolved—the City Club still prospering—but it was once more revived by Staunton, and the meetings were held in Charles-st off the Haymarket. Its career was brief, however, and it was finally closed in 1843. In the same year a new chess club at the West End was formed, at Beattie's Hotel George-st, Cavendish-sq, and was called after the name of the street in which its first meeting were held, the St. George's Chess Club. Beattie's Hotel was closed in the following year, and the St. George's removed to new quarters at the Polytechnic. Here was played the first International Chess Tournament in 1851, and here the club remained until the end of 1854, when it became associated with the Cavendish, a newly-formed club in Regent-st, and soon afterwards moved to the house formerly Crockford's, in St. James's-st, then called the Wellington. In the year 1857 the St. George's removed to Palace-chambers, King-st, St. James's, and has since located itself at 47, Albemarle-st. Meanwhile, in 1852, a club was formed in the City, under the title of the City of London Chess Club, by a few amateurs of little note at the time. This association is now, in point of numbers, and the chess force and public repute of its members, the strongest chess club in the world. In 1866, a chess club reviving the name of the "Westminster," whose history we have recounted, was formed by a number of influential amateurs, but it ceased to exist as a chess club in 1875, when it was dissolved and reconstituted under the name of the Junior Portland as a whist club.

St. George's Chess Club, 47, Albemarle-st. — Annual subscription, town members, £2 2s.; country members, £1 1s. Hon. Sec., J. I. Minchin. Open daily from 12 noon. Established in 1843. The play is almost entirely limited to the afternoons—12 noon to 7 p.m.

City of London Chess Club, Mouffet's Hotel, 24, Newgate-st, E.C.—Annual subscription, 10s.6d. Election by ballot in committee. Open on the evenings of Mon., Wed., and Fri. in each week throughout the year. The meetings of this club are attended by most of the best English chess-players. Established in 1852.

The British Chess Club, 37, King-st, Covent-garden. Established in 1887. Is also a great resort for players of the first rank.

The foregoing are the principal chess clubs in London, but there are, besides, several local (or parochial) associations meeting during the months of the spring and winter.

The College Chess Club, Ladies' College, Little Queen-st, Holborn, is the only Chess Club to which lady players are admitted.

At the Birkbeck Literary and Scientific Institution, Southampton-bdgs, Chancery-la, there is an evening Chess Class. Charges for members 1s., and for the public 3s.

Public Chess Rooms. — The Divan, 101, Strand. Open from 12 noon to 11 p.m. Subscription, £2 2s. Single admission, including coffee and cigar, 1s.; and free to all persons dining at Simpson's Restaurant. The Divan is a favourite resort of the professional chess-players resident in London, and is visited by every foreign player of eminence whom business or pleasure leads to London. Pursell's Restaurant, Cornhill. — Open from noon to 9 p.m. Admission free. An afternoon resort for professional players, and much patronised by City clerks, warehousemen, &c. Gatti's, Adelaide-st, Strand.—Open from noon to midnight. Admission free. Another favourite resort of the professional chess-players.

Chess Journals in London. — *The Chess Monthly*. First number appeared Sept., 1879. —*Illustrated London News*. A chess column every week. First article on chess appeared June 25, 1842.—*The Field*. A chess column every week. First article appeared Jan. 1, 1853.—*Land and Water*. A chess column every week. First article appeared Jan., 1870.—*Illustrated Sporting and Dramatic News*. A chess column every week. First article appeared Jan., 1874.

Besides the foregoing, the following (among other) periodicals devote some portion of their space to chess: *English Mechanic*, *Society*, and *Knowledge*.

Cheyne Walk, Chelsea (Map 11), is a bit of old London, with its quaint houses, and its row of noble trees. The picturesque aspect has not been much destroyed by the Thames Embankment, which now runs in front of it. Cheyne-row is still picturesque and quiet, and is the abode of many artists and literary men. East of Cheyne-walk are the gardens of the Apothecaries' Company, with their famous cedars, which are considered as among the oldest and finest in the country. The admirably - designed red brick houses in the Queen Anne style, lately erected on the Cadogan estate, are thoroughly in accordance with Old Chelsea traditions and associations.

Chili.—Ministry, 88, Harley-st, W. Nearest *Ry. Stns.*, Portland rd and Baker-st (Met.); *Omnibus Rte.*, Marylebone-rd. Consulate, Winchester House, Old Broad-st. Nearest *Ry. Stns.*, Broad-st (N. Lon.) and Cannon-st (S.E.); *Omnibus Rtes.*, Old Broad-st, Bishopsgate-st, Cheapside, and Moorgate-st; *Cab Rank*, New Broad-st.

Chimney on Fire.—Newcomers from the country will do well to bear in mind that it is not safe in London to clean a kitchen chimney by "burning out." Apart from all question of danger and damage, the (maximum) penalty for a "chimney on fire" in London is 20s.

China.—Ministry, 49, Portland-pl, W. Nearest *Ry. Stn.*, Portland-rd (Met.); *Omnibus Rtes.*, Marylebone-rd, Oxford-st, and Regent-st; *Cab Rank*, Portland-pl.

Chops and Steaks.—It is only recently that a great superstition as to chops and steaks has been exploded. It was for very many years a popular delusion that west of Fleet-st chops and steaks could not be had—or, at all events, could only be had in a very inferior style. The West End chop or steak, it is true, was for a long time difficult to come at; and, as a rule, exceedingly bad when you got it, although the grill-loving Londoner was even then able to go to Stone's in Panton-st with a tolerable certainty of finding what he wanted. This house, which dates from the beginning of the century, and has long been well known to literary London, still holds its own, although grills have of late years grown up round it in all directions. The Inns of Court, Grand, and First Avenue Hotels, the Criterion, the Gaiety, the Royal Aquarium, the Café Royal in Regent-st, the St. James's Hall, the "Holborn," and the "Horse-shoe" restaurants, and many of Spiers and Pond's railway refreshment-rooms make a specialty of their grills, and the foreign reader of the Dictionary who wishes to try this form of meal can be recommended to any of these places. The City itself absolutely swarms with chop-houses, and it is only possible here to say that anywhere about Finch-la and Cornhill the grill business is thoroughly well understood and well done. Between the City proper and the West End is the "Cheshire Cheese," Wine Office-ct, Fleet-st, one of the old-fashioned chop-houses, specially famous for a rump-steak pudding on Saturday afternoons. The "Cock," at 201, Fleet-st, immortalised many years ago by the Poet Laureate, has gone the way of many other London institutions, having been closed in April, 1886.

Christ's Hospital, Newgate-street(Map 8).—Presentations to this school, which maintains and educates about 1,100 children, can only be obtained (except in connection with certain local and other special trusts) from governors under certain regulations. It is generally understood that the principal requirements are, briefly, that the children must be presented when between eight and ten years of age, and must be free from active disease, as well as from any physical defect which would render them unable to take care of themselves ; that their parents (if one or both be living) have not adequate means of educating and maintaining them ; and that the children have not such means of their own. A written statement, showing the amount, or average amount, of the parental income, with particulars of its source or sources, the total number of children in the family, and how many of these are still young and dependent, and any other relevant circumstances, is in each case required to be made in the petition on the form of presentation for the consideration of the court or committee of governors, who have the power to reject any case which they may not deem a proper one for admission to the charitable advantages of the institution. The form of presentation is to be obtained from the individual governor presenting ; and the child's name in full is to be inscribed therein in the handwriting of such governor, with a statement of his conscientious belief that the child so presented is a proper object for admission into this hospital. It is particularly requested that persons who are in no real need of assistance from a charitable foundation like this hospital will refrain from importuning the governors for presentations, or seeking the admission of their children into the hospital. Boys on admission are sent to the hospital's preparatory school at Hertford, and from thence drafts are made three times a year to the London school. The girls' school of the hospital, for about 90, is at the Hertford establishment. A printed list of the governors, and all necessary information in regard to the school, may be obtained on application (and payment) to the clerk, at the Counting House, Christ's Hospital. NEAREST *Ry. Stns.,* Holborn-viaduct (L.C. & D.) and Aldersgate-st (Met.); *Omnibus Rte.,* Newgate-st ; *Cab Rank,* Old Bailey.

Christy Collection of antiquities and ethnography has been lately removed from Victoria-st to the British Museum.

Churches.—The following is a list of the principal London Churches, with their Hymnals and hours of Service. Where no indication is given as to the nature of the Services, they must be understood to be those ordinarily appointed for the Morning and Evening. The figures in brackets denote the Hymnals in use in the various churches, according to the following list :

[1] Ancient and Modern	[5] S. P. C. K.	[9] People's	[13] Irons's
[2] Anc. and Mod. Revised	[6] Hymnal Companion	[10] New Mitre	[14] Barry's
[3] Hymnal Noted	[7] Songs Gr. and Gl.	[11] Mercer's	[15] Windle's
[4] Hymnary	[8] Kemble's	[12] Church Hymns	[16] Chope's.

AGATHA, ST., Finsbury-avenue, Sun-st, Finsbury-sq, E.C. [1.] Sun., 11 a.m. (Matins), 4 p.m. (Lit.) and 7 p.m. Holy Days, 8 p.m. Holy Com., Sun., 8 a.m. and 11.30 a.m.

AGNES, ST., Kennington-pk, S.E. [2.] Sun., 10.15 a.m. (Matins), 4 p m. (Lit.), and 7 p.m. Week Days, 8 a.m. (Matins) and 8 p.m. Holy Com., Sun., 7 a.m., 8 a.m., and 11 a.m. (Choral) ; Holy Days, 6.45 a.m., 7.30 a.m., and 11 a.m. (Choral).

ALBAN, ST., Wood-st, E.C. [6.] Sun., 11 a.m. and 7 p.m. Holy Com., 1st Sun., 11 a.m.

ALBAN THE MARTYR, ST., Brooke-st, Holborn, E.C. [3.] Sun., 10.15 a.m. (Matins), 2.15 p.m. (Lit.), 3.15 p.m. (Special), 4 p.m. (Special), and 7 p.m. Holy and Week Days, 8.30 a.m. (Matins), and 8 p.m. Wed. and Fri., noon (Lit.). Holy Com., Sun., 7 a.m., 8 a.m., and 11 a.m. (Choral) ; Holy and Week Days, 7 a.m. and 8 a.m.; Holy Days, 6.45, 7.30, and 11 a.m.

ALL HALLOWS BARKING, Great Tower-st, E.C. [5.] Sun., 11 a.m. and 6.30 p.m. Wed., 7 p.m. Holy Com., 1st Sun., after mng., 3rd Sun., after evg. serv.

ALL HALLOWS, Bow Common, E. [6.] Sun., 11 a.m. and 6.30 p.m. Wed., 7.30 p.m. Holy Com., 1st Sun., after mng. and evg. servs.

ALL HALLOWS, Southwark, S.E. [2.] Sun., 11.30 a.m. (Matins), 3.30 p.m. (Special), and 7 p.m. Holy and Week Days, 8 a.m. (Matins). Daily, 8 a.m. and 8 p.m. Holy Com., Sun., 8 a.m., 10.15 a.m., and 11.15 a.m.; Holy and Week Days, 7.30 a.m.

ALL HALLOWS, GREAT AND LESS, Upper Thames-st, E.C. [6.] Sun., 11 a.m. and 7 p.m. Holy Com., 1st Sun., after mng. serv.

ALL SAINTS, Colville-gdns, Kensington-pk, W. [1.] (Services fully Choral.) Sun., 11 a.m. (Matins), 3.15, 4.15, 5.30, and 7 p.m. Week Days, 10 a.m. (Matins) and 5 p.m. Holy Com., 7 and 8 a.m., and 12.30 p.m. ; Holy Days, 8 and 10.30 a.m. ; Mon., 10.30 a.m. ; Thurs., 8 a.m.

ALL SAINTS, Ennismore-gdns, Knightsbridge, S.W. [6.] Sun., 11 a.m., 3.30 p.m., and 7 p.m. Week Days in Lent, 5 p.m. Holy Days, 11 a.m. (Matins). Wed., 8 p.m. (Special), and Fri., 11 a.m. (Lit.). Holy Com., 2nd and last Sun., 8.30 a.m.; 1st and 3rd Sun., after mng. serv.; 4th Sun., after evg. serv.; Holy Days, 8.30 a.m.

ALL SAINTS, Gordon-sq, W.C. [1.] Sun., 11 a.m., 3.30 p.m., and 7 p.m. Holy Days, 11 a.m. Wed. and Fri., 11 a.m. (Matins) ; Wed., 7 p.m. Holy Com., 1st Sun., 8.30 and 11 a.m. ; 2nd Sun., after mng. serv. and 7 p.m.

ALL SAINTS, Hatcham Park, New Cross-rd., S.E. [6.] Sun., 11 a.m. and 6.30 p.m. Wed., 7.30 p.m. Holy Com., 1st Sun. after mng. and 3rd after evg. serv.

ALL SAINTS, Lambeth, S.E. [3.] Sun., 11 a.m. (Matins), 3.30 p.m. (Special), and 7 p.m. Wed., Fri., and Holy Days, 8 p.m. Holy Com., Sun., 8 a.m. and 11.45 a.m. (Choral); Tues., Thurs., and Holy Days, 8 a.m. Special Services in Lent, Advent, and Easter.

ALL SAINTS, Margaret-st, W [1.] Sun., 10.30 a.m. (Matins), 3.30 p.m. (Lit.), 4 p.m., and 7 p.m. Week and Holy Days, 7.45 a.m. (Matins) and 5 p.m. Wed. and Fri., noon (Lit.). Holy Com., Sun., 7 a.m., 8 a.m., 9 a.m., and 11.45 a.m. (Choral); Week and Holy Days, 7 a.m.; Holy Days, 8 a.m.; Week Days, 8.15 a.m.; Thurs., 11 a.m.

ALL SAINTS, Norfolk-sq, Paddington, W. [2.] Sun., 11 a.m. (Matins), 3.30 p.m. (Lit.), and 6 p.m. Week Days, 10 a.m. (Matins). Holy Days, 5.30 p.m. Holy Com., Sun., 8.30 a.m., 1st Sun. after Matins; Holy Days, 11 a.m.

ALL SAINTS, Poplar, E. [2.] Sun., 11 a.m. (Matins and Lit.) 3 p.m. and 7 p.m. Week Days, 8 a.m. (Matins), except Wed. and Fri., when 11 a.m. (Matins and Lit.). Daily, except Wed., 4.30 p.m.; Wed., 7 p.m. Holy Com., Sun., and Greater Festivals, 8 a.m., and 11.45 a.m.; other Holy Days, 8 a.m.

ALL SAINTS, St. John's Wood, N.W. [2.] Sun., 11 a.m. (Matins), 3.30 p.m. (Lit.), and 7 p.m. Holy Com., Sun., 11 a.m., 2nd Sun., 8.30. a.m., 4th Sun. (Choral), and daily at 10.30 a.m.

ALL SAINTS, Stepney, E. [5.] Sun., 11 a.m. and 6.30 p.m. Thurs., 7.30 p.m. Holy Com., 1st Sun 11 a.m.; and every Sun. at 8.30 a.m.; 3rd and 5th, 8 p.m.

ALL SOULS, Langham-pl. [5.] Sun., 11 a.m., 4 and 7 p.m. Holy Com., 1st Sun., 8 a.m. and after mng] serv.; 2nd, 4 p.m.; 3rd, at mng. serv.; 4th, after evg. serv.; 5th, 8 a.m.

ALL SOULS, Loudoun-rd, St. John's Wood, N.W. [1.] Sun., 11 a.m. (Matins) and 7 p.m. Wed. and Fri., 11 a.m. Holy Com., Sun., 8.30 a.m. and after Matins; Holy Days, 7.30 a.m. and 11 a.m.

ALPHAGE, ST., London Wall, E.C. [1.] Sun., 11 a.m. and 7 p.m. Friday, evg. serv. in Advent and Lent (Choral). Holy Com., 1st and 3rd Sun. after mng. serv., and on Great Festivals.

ALPHEGE, ST., Southwark, S.E. [1.] Sun., 11.30 a.m. (Matins), 2.45 p.m., 3.45 p.m. (Special), 7 p.m., and 8.30 p.m. (Special). Holy and Week Days, 8 p.m. Holy Com., Sun., 6.30 a.m. and 7.30 a.m.; Holy Days, 6.30 and 7.30 a.m., 8 p.m.; Week Days, 7.30 a.m.

ANDREW, ST., Ashley-rd, Victoria-st, Westminster, S.W. [1.] Sun., 11 a.m., 3.30 p.m. (Special), and 7 p.m. Week-days, daily; summer, noon; winter, 5.30 p.m.; Saint Days, noon; Thurs., 8 p.m. High Festivals, 11 a.m. and 7 p.m. Holy Com., 1st Sun., after mng. serv.; 2nd Sun., after evg. serv.; 3rd Sun., 8 a.m.

ANDREW, ST., Hoxton, N. [2.] Sun., 11 a.m. and 7 p.m.; Last Sun., 3 p.m. (Special). Daily, 8.30 a.m. in Advent and Lent; Wed., Fri., and Holy Days, 8 p.m. Holy Com., 2nd and 4th Sun., 8 a.m. 1st, 3rd, and 5th, after Matins.

ANDREW, ST., Stamford-st, S.E. [6.] Sun., 11 a.m., 3.15, and 6.30 p.m. Wed., 8 p.m. Holy Com., 1st Sun., after mng. serv.; 3rd Sun., after evg. serv.

ANDREW, ST., Thornhill-sq, Islington, N. [6.] Sun., 11 a.m., 3.30 p.m., and 6.30 p.m. Wed., 7.30 p.m. Holy Com., 1st Sun. after mng. serv.; 3rd Sun. after evg. serv.

ANDREW, ST., Undershaft, St. Mary Axe, E.C. [2.] Sun., 11 a.m. and 6.30 p.m.; 1st Sun., 3.30 p.m. (Special). Wed., Fri., and Holy Days, 1.15 p.m. (Lit.). Holy Com., 1st and 3rd after mng. serv.; other Suns., 8 a.m.

ANDREW, ST., Wells-st, W. [4.] Sun., 9.15 a.m., 11.15 a.m. (Matins), 3.30 p.m. (Lit.), 4 p.m., and 7 p.m. Week Days, 10 a.m. (Matins), and 5 p.m. Holy Days, 11 a.m. (Matins) and 5 p.m. Wed., 10 a.m. and 5 p.m. Holy Com., Sun. and High Festivals, 7 a.m. and 8 a.m., 9.45 a.m. (Choral) and 11.45 a.m. (Choral); Holy Days, 8 a.m. and 11.45 a.m.; Wed., 11 a.m.

ANN, ST., South Lambeth-rd, S.W. [1.] Sun., 11 a.m., 3.15 p.m. (Special), and 6.30 p.m. Holy Days, 11 a.m. and 7 p.m. Holy Com., 1st and 3rd Sun., 8 a.m.; 2nd and last Sun., and Holy Days, after mng. serv.

ANNE, ST., Dean-st, Soho, W. [4.] Sun., 11 a.m., 4 p.m. (Lit.), and 7 p.m. Holy and Week Days, 11 a.m. (Matins), 5.30 p.m., except Wed., when there is no afternoon serv. Holy Com., Sun., 8 a.m. and after mng. serv.

AUGUSTINE, ST., Haggerston, York-st, Hackney-rd., E. [2.] Sun., 10.30 a.m. (Matins), 4 p.m. (Lit.), and 7 p.m. Holy and Week Days, 9 a.m., and 8 p.m. Wed. and Fri., noon (Lit.). Holy Com., Sun., 7.15 a.m. and 8 a.m., and 11.15 a.m. (Choral); Holy and Week Days, 7.15 a.m.; Holy Days, 6.30 a.m.

AUGUSTINE, ST., Kilburn, Park-rd, N.W. [1 & 3.] Sun. 10.30 a.m. (Matins), 3.15 p.m. (Lit.), 4 p.m. (Children), and 7 p.m. Holy Days, 10.30 a.m. (Matins) and 8 p.m. Week Days, 8 a.m. and 8 p.m. Wed. and Fri., noon (Lit.). Holy Com., Sun., 7, 8, and 11.45 a.m.; Holy Days and Thurs., 7 and 8.30 a.m.; Week Days, 7 a.m., and on Great Festivals at 6, 7, 8, and 9 a.m.

AUGUSTINE, ST., Lynton-rd, Bermondsey, S.E. [2.] Sun., 11 a.m. and 7 p.m. Holy Com., 8 a.m. except 3rd Sun., when after mng. serv.; Holy Days, 7 a.m.

AUGUSTINE, ST., AND ST. FAITH, Old Change, E.C. [4.] Sun., 10.40 a.m. (Lit.), 11 a.m. (Matins), and 7 p.m. Holy Days, 7.15 p.m. Holy Com., 11.45 a.m. (Choral); 1st Sun., 8.30 a.m.; Holy Days, 7.45 a.m.

AUGUSTINE, ST., Queen's-gate, S.W. [16.] Sun., 11 a.m. (Matins), 3 p.m. (Children), 4 p.m., and 7 p.m. Week Days, 11 a.m. (Matins) and 5 p.m. Holy Com., Sun., 8 a.m. and after Matins (the latter Choral); Week Days, 8 a.m.; Holy Days, 11 a.m.

BARNABAS, ST., Addison-rd, Kensington, W. [5.] Sun., 11 a.m., 3.30 p.m., and 7 p.m. Wed. and Fri., 11.30 a.m. Holy Com., 11.30 a.m. Holy Com., Sun., 8 a.m. and noon; Holy Days, 8 a.m.

BARNABAS, ST., Bell-st, W. [2.] Sun., 11 a.m., 3.30 p.m., and 7 p.m. Wed. 8 p.m. Holy Com., Sun., 8.30 a.m.; Thurs. and Holy Days, 7.30 p.m.

BARNABAS, ST., Bethnal Green, E. [2.] Sun., 11 a.m. (Matins), 3 p.m. (Lit.), and 7 p.m.; Daily, 8 p.m. Holy Com., Sun., 8 a.m., and after Matins on last Sun.; Holy Days, 7.30 a.m.

BARNABAS, ST., Plough-rd, Rotherhithe, S.E. [1.] Sun., 11 a.m. (Matins) and 6.30 p.m. Last Sun., 10 a.m. (Lit.) and 3.30 p.m. (Special). Week Days, 8 a.m. (Matins) and Wed., 7.30 a.m. Holy Com., Sun., 8 a.m., and on last Sun. after Matins; Holy Days, 7.30 a.m.

BARTHOLOMEW, ST., Shepperton-rd, Islington, N. [6.] Sun., 11 a.m., 6.30 p.m., and 8.30 p.m. (Special). Wed., 7.30 p.m. Holy Com., 1st Sun., after mng. serv.; 3rd Sun., after evg. serv.

BARTHOLOMEW THE LESS, ST., St. Bartholomew's Hospital, E.C. [2.] Sun., 11 a.m. and 7 p.m. Holy Com., Sun. and Holy Days, 8.30 a.m. Special Services in Lent and Advent.

BEDFORDBURY MISSION CHURCH, St. Martin's-in-the-Fields, W.C. [2.] Sun., 11 a.m. (Matins) and 7 p.m. Week Days, 7.30 p.m. Holy Com., Sun., 8 a.m.; 1st Sun., 11.45 a.m.; Holy Days, 7.30 a.m.

BELGRAVE CHAPEL, Belgrave-sq, S.W. [12.] Sun., 11 a.m., 3.30 and 7 p.m. Thurs., 11.30 a.m. Holy Com., 1st Sun., at mng. serv.; 3rd Sun., at aftern. serv.

BENET, ST., Mile End-rd, Stepney, E. [6.] Sun., 11 a.m. and 6.30 p.m. Wed., 8 p.m. Holy Com., 1st Sun., after mng. serv.; 3rd Sun., after evg. serv.

BISHOP SUMNER CHURCH, Amelia-rd, Spa-rd, Bermondsey, S.E. [6.] Sun., 11 a.m. and 6.30 p.m. Tues. and Fri., 8 p.m. Holy Com., 1st Sun., after mng. serv.; 3rd Sun., after evg. serv.

BRIDE, ST., Fleet-st, E.C. Sun., 11 a.m., 3.30 and 7 p.m. Wed., 7 p.m. Holy Com., Sun., mng. serv.

BRUNSWICK CHAPEL, Upper Berkeley-st, W. [6.] Sun., 11 a.m. and 7 p.m. Wed., 7.30 p.m. Holy Com., 1st Sun., noon ; 3rd Sun., 8.30 p.m.; 1st Wed., noon.

CAMDEN TOWN PARISH CHURCH, Camden-st, N.W. [1.] Sun., 8 a.m. and 11 a.m. (Matins), 3.15 p.m. (Lit.), and 7 p.m. Holy and Week Days, 8 a.m., except in winter when the hour is 11 a.m. Wed. and Fri., 11 a.m. (Matins and Lit.) Holy Com., Sun., 8 and 11 a.m.

CARLTON HILL CHURCH, St. John's Wood, N.W. [6.] Sun., 11 a.m. and 7 p.m. Holy Com., 1st Sun., noon ; 3rd Sun., 7 p.m.

CHAD, ST., Nichols'-sq, Hackney-rd, E. [9.] Sun., 10.45 a.m. (Matins and Lit.), 3.45 (Children), and 7 p.m. Week Days, 9.30 a.m. (Matins) and 8 p.m.; Wed. and Fri., noon (Lit.) Holy Com., Sun., 8 a.m., 9.45 and 11.30 a.m. (both Choral); Holy and Week Days, 7.30 a.m.; Holy Days only, 9.30 a.m.

CHRIST CHURCH, Albany-st, N.W. [1.] Sun., 11 a.m. (Matins), 3.30 p.m. (Special), 4 p.m. (Lit.), and 7 p.m. Holy and Week Days, 7.45 a.m. (Matins). Holy Days, 11 a.m. (Matins). Wed. and Fri., noon (Lit.) and 8 p.m.; Mon., Tues., Thurs., and Sat., 5 p.m. Holy Com., 7.45 a.m. and after Matins, and 1st Sun., 7 a.m.; Holy Days, 7 and 11.30 a.m.; Thurs., 7 a.m.

CHRIST CHURCH, Chalton-st, Somers Town, N.W. [5.] Sun., 11 a.m. and 7 p.m.; Wed., 7.30 p.m.; Fri., 11 a.m. Holy Com., 1st Sun., after mng. serv.; 2nd Sun., 8 a.m.; and 3rd Sun., 7 p.m.

CHRIST CHURCH, Church-st, Spitalfields, E. [6.] Sunday, 11 a.m., 3.15 p.m. (Lit.), and 7 p.m. Daily, 10.30 a.m. Holy Com., 2nd Sun. after mng. serv.; 4th Sun., after evg. serv.; and every Sun. at 8.30 a.m.; Holy Days after Matins.

CHRIST CHURCH, Clapham, Union-gr, Wandsworth-rd, S.W. [7.] Sun., 10.30 a.m. (Matins.), 3.30 p.m. (Children), and 7 p.m. Holy Days and Week Days, 7 a.m. (Matins) and 8 p.m. Holy Com., Sun., 8 a.m. and 11 a.m.; Holy and Week Days, 7.30 a.m.; Holy Days, 7 a.m.; Thurs., 9 a.m.; Wed. and Fri., noon.

CHRIST CHURCH, Endell-st, W.C. [2.] Sun., 11 a.m. and 7 p.m. Holy Days, 11 a.m. Wed., 7.30 p.m. Holy Com., Sun., noon ; except 3rd Sun. after evg. serv.

CHRIST CHURCH, Highbury Grove, N. [6.] Sun. 11 a.m., 3.30 p.m., and 7 p.m. Wed., 7.30 p.m. Holy Com., 1st Sun after mng. serv. ; 2nd Sun., 8.30 a.m. ; 3rd Sun., at evg. ser.

CHRIST CHURCH, Hoxton, New North-rd, N. [2.] Sun., 11 a.m. and 6.30 p.m.; 1st Sun., 3 p.m. (Lit. and Special). Fri., 7.30 p.m. Holy Com., 2nd Sun., 8 a.m.; Last Sun., after mng. serv.

CHRIST CHURCH, Jamaica-st, Stepney, E. [12.] Sun., 11 a.m. and 6.30 p.m. Wed., 7.30 p.m. Holy Com., 1st Sun. after mng. serv., and 3rd Sun. after evg. serv.

CHRIST CHURCH, Lancaster-ga, W. [1.] Sun., 11 a.m., 4 p.m., and 7 p.m. Daily, 8 a.m.; Wed. and Fri., noon; Fri., 5.30 p.m. Holy Com., Sun., 8 a.m., 1st and 3rd Sun., after mng. serv., last Sun., 4 p.m.; Holy Days, noon.

CHRIST CHURCH, Mayfair, W. [5.] Sun., 11 a.m., 3.30 p.m. (Lit., and Sermon), 6.30 p.m. Wed., Fri., and Holy Days, 11 a.m. (Matins). Holy Com., Sun., 8.30 a.m.; and 1st and 3rd, after mng. serv.

CHRIST CHURCH, Newgate-st, E.C. [12 & 2.] Sun., 11 a.m. and 7 p.m. Holy Com., 1st Sun. after mng. serv.; 3rd Sun., 9 a.m.

CHRIST CHURCH, Camberwell, Old Kent-rd, S.E. [6.] Sun., 11 a.m. (3rd Sun., 3.15 p.m.), and 7 p.m. Thurs., 7 p.m. Holy Com., 1st Sun., after mng. serv.; 3rd, after evg. serv.; 5th, 9 a.m.

CHRIST CHURCH, St. George's East, Watney-st, E. [2.] Sun., 11 a.m., 3.15 p.m., and 6.30 p.m. Wed. and Fri., 11 a.m. (Lit.); Thurs., 8 p.m. Holy Com., Sun., 8 a.m., and on 1st and 3rd, 12.30 p.m. Holy Days, 7.30 a.m.

CHRIST CHURCH, Southwark, Blackfriars-rd, S.E. [2.] Sun. 11 a.m. (Matins), 3 p.m. (Special), 4 p.m. (Lit.), and 7 p.m. Holy Days 11 a.m. (Matins). Wed. and Fri., 11 a.m. (Lit.) Holy and Week Days 8 p.m. (Choral). Holy Com., Sun., 8 a.m., and on 1st Sun., after Matins; Holy Days, 8 a.m.

CHRIST CHURCH, Victoria-st, Westminster, S.W. [2.] Sun., 11 a.m. (Matins), 3.30 p.m., and 7 p.m. Holy Days, 9 a.m. (Matins); Wed. 11.30 a.m.; Thurs., 7.30 p.m. Holy Com., 1st and 3rd Sun., after Matins; 2nd, 4th, and last Sun., 8 a.m.; Holy Days, 8 a.m.

CHRIST CHURCH, Woburn-sq, W.C. Sun., 11 a.m., 3.30 p.m. (Lit.), and 7 p.m. Daily, 8.30 a.m. and 5 p.m.; Wed. and Fri., noon (Lit.) Holy Com., Sun., 8 a.m., and after mng. serv.; Thurs. and Holy Days, 8.30 a.m. and 11 a.m., and thrice on Greater Festivals.

CLEMENT, ST., Arundel-sq, Barnsbury, N. [6.] Sun., 11 a.m. and 6.30 p.m. (Partly Choral). Wed., 11.30 a.m. during Lent; Thurs., 7 p.m. Holy Com., 2nd Sun., 11 a.m. and 6.30 p.m.; Festivals, after mng. serv.

CLEMENT DANES, ST., Strand. [12.] Sun., 11 a.m. and 7 p.m. Daily, 12.15 p.m. Wed., 7 p.m. Holy Com., 8.30 a.m. Saint Days, 8.30 a.m. and 7 p.m.

CLEMENT, ST., Clement's-la, E.C. Sun. 11 a.m. and 7 p.m. Saint Days, 1.15 p.m. Wed., from Michaelmas to Lady Day, 1.15 p.m.; Fri., 1.15 p.m. Holy Com., Sun., at mng. serv.

CLEMENT, ST., Lever-st, City-rd, E.C. [1.] Sun., 10.30 a.m. (Matins), 4 p.m. (Lit.), 7 p.m. Holy Days, 10.30 a.m., 8 p.m. Week Days, 8 p.m. Wed. and Fri., 2 p.m. (Lit.). Holy Com., Sun., 8 a.m., and 11.30 a.m. (Choral).

COLUMBA, ST., Kingsland-rd, E. [3.] Sun., 10.15 a.m. (Matins) and 7 p.m. Holy and Week Days, 8.30 a.m. (Matins) and 7.30 p.m. Holy Com., Sun., 7 a.m. and 8 a.m., and 11.15 a.m. (Choral); Holy and Week Days, 7.30 and 8 a.m.; Holy Days 7.30, 8, and 9 a.m.

CYPRIAN, ST., Dorset-sq, N.W. [1.] Sun., 9.30 a.m. (Children), 10.30 a.m. (Matins), 3.30 p.m. (Lit.), and 7 p.m. Holy and Week Days, 8 a.m. (Matins), 5 p.m., and 8 p.m.; Wed. and Fri. noon (Lit.). Holy Com., Sun., 7 a.m. and 8 a.m., and after mng. serv. (Choral); Holy and Week Days, 7.30 a.m.; Holy Days, 10.30 a.m.

DAVID, ST., Westbourne-rd, Islington, N. [8.] Sun., 11 a.m. and 6.30 p.m. Wed., 7.30 p.m. Holy Com., 1st Sun., after mng. serv.; 3rd Sun., after evg. serv.

DUNSTAN, ST., Idol-la, Eastcheap, E.C. [5.] Sun., 11 a.m. and 3 p.m. Holy Com., every Sun. after mng. serv.

DUNSTAN-IN-THE-WEST, ST., Fleet-st, E.C. Sun., 11 a.m. and 7 p.m. Thurs., 8 p.m. Holy Com., 1st Sun., after matins; 3rd, after evg prayer.

EDMUND, ST., Lombard-st, E.C. [2.] Sun., 11 a.m., and 4 and 7 p.m. Week Days, 1.15 p.m. Holy Com., Sun., 8.30 and 11.45 a.m.; Holy Days, midday.

EMMANUEL, Camberwell-rd, S.E. [1.] Sun., 11 a.m. and 7 p.m. Wed., 7 p.m. Holy Com., 1st Sun.

FAITH, ST., Londesborough-rd, Stoke Newington, N. [9.] Sun., 7, 8, 10.30, and 11.30 a.m., 4 and 7 p.m Holy Days, 7 and 8.15 a.m., and 8 p.m. Week Days, 7.30 a.m. and 8 p.m. Holy Com., Sun., 7, 8 and 10.30 a.m.; Week Days, 7.30 a.m.; Holy Days, 7 and 8.15 a.m.

GABRIEL, ST., Clifton-st, W. [2.] Sun., 11 a.m. (Matins and Lit.) and 7 p.m. Holy Days, 8 p.m. Wed., 8 p.m. Holy Com., Sun., 8 a.m.; and 2nd and 4th, 12.30 p.m.; Holy Days, 8 a.m.

GABRIEL, ST., Chrisp-st, Bromley, E. [1.] Sun., 10 a.m. (Matins) and 7 p.m. Holy Days, 7.30 p.m. Wed., 7.30 p.m. Holy Com., Sun., 8 a.m. and 11 a.m.; Holy Days, 7.30 a.m.

GABRIEL, ST., Newington. Sun., 11 a.m., 3.30 p.m. (Special) and 6.30 p.m. Wed., 8 p.m. Holy Days, 8 a.m. Holy Com., 1st, 3rd, and 5th Sun., 7 a.m.; 2nd and 4th, after mng. serv.

GABRIEL, ST., Warwick-sq, Pimlico, S.W. [1.] Sun., 11 a.m., 3 p.m., and 7 p.m. Week Days, 8.30 a.m. and 5.30 p.m. Holy Days, 8.30 a.m., 11 a.m., and 5.30 p.m. Wed. and Fri., noon. (Lit.). Holy Com., Sun., 8.30 a.m. and noon; Holy Days, 7.45 and 11 a.m.

GEORGE'S, ST., George-st, Hanover-sq, W. [5.] Sun., 11 a.m., 3.30 and 7 p.m. Week Days, 10 a.m., except Wed. and Fri., when noon, and 5 p.m. from Advent to Lent. Holy Days, noon. Holy Com., Sun., 8 a.m., and 1st and 3rd, noon; Holy Days, noon.

GEORGE-IN-THE-EAST, ST., Cannon-st-rd, E. [1.] Sun., 11 a.m., 3 p.m., and 7 p.m. Holy and Week Days, 11 a.m. Holy Com., Sun., noon; and occasionally at 8 a.m.

GEORGE'S, ST., HOSPITAL CHAPEL, Grosvenor-pl, S.W. [5.] Sun., 10 a.m. (Matins) and 2.45 p.m. Wed., 10 a.m. (Matins); Tues., Evensong, 7 p.m. Holy Com., Sun., after mng. serv.; Alternate Suns., 6.30 a.m.

GEORGE, ST., THE MARTYR, Queen-sq, W.C. [12.] Sun., 11 a.m. (Matins), 3.30 p.m., and 7 p.m. Daily, 8 a.m.; Wed., Fri., and Holy Days, 11 a.m., and Wed., 8 p.m. Holy Com., Sun., 8 a.m. and after mng. serv.

GRAY'S INN CHAPEL, W.C. [1.] Sun., 11.30 a.m. and 3.30 p.m. High Festivals, 11.30 a.m. Holy Com., 1st Sun. after mng. serv.

GROSVENOR CHAPEL, South Audley-st, W. [2.] Sun., 11.30 a.m., 3.30 p.m., and 7 p.m. Wed., Fri., and Holy Days, 11 a.m. (Matins); Fri., 7.30 p.m. Holy Com., 1st and 3rd Sun., after mng. serv., other Sun., 8.30 a.m.

HANOVER CHURCH, Regent-st, W. [1.] Sun., 11 a.m. (Matins), and 7 p.m. (Lit.) Holy Com., Sun., noon; 1st and 3rd Sun., 8 a.m.; Holy Days, after Matins.

HELEN, ST., Bishopsgate-st, E.C. [1.] Sun., 11 a.m. Holy Com. (Choral), 1st Sun. and Festivals.

HOUSE OF CHARITY CHAPEL, Greek-st, Soho, W. Sun., 10.30 a.m. (Matins) and 3.30 p.m. Daily, 7.45 a.m. and 5 p.m. Holy Com., Sun., 7.30 a.m.; Daily, 7 a.m.

INNOCENTS', HOLY, Dalling-rd, Hammersmith, W. Sun., 11 a.m. (Children) and 7 p.m.

JAMES, ST., Clerkenwell, E.C. [6.] Sun., 8 and 11 a.m., 3.30 and 6 p.m. Tues., 8 p.m. Holy Com., Sun., 8 a.m. and at noon. serv.

JAMES, ST., Curtain-rd, Shoreditch, E. [2.] Sun., 11 a.m. (Matins), 3.30 p.m., and 7 p.m. Wed. and Fri., 11 a.m. and 8 p.m.; Holy Days, 8 p.m. Holy Com., 1st and 3rd Sun., noon (Choral); others, 8 a.m.

JAMES, ST., Garlickhithe, E.C. [1.] Sun., 11 a.m. (Matins), 3.30 p.m. (Special), and 7 p.m. Week Days, except Holy Days, 1 p.m.; Holy Days, 7.30 p.m. Holy Com., Sun., after mng. serv.

JAMES, ST., Kennington-pk-rd, S.E. [12.] Sun., 11 a.m. and 7 p.m.; 1st Sun. 3.30 p.m. (Special). Wed. and Holy Days, 8 p.m. Holy Com., 1st and 3rd Sun., after mng. serv.; every Sun., 8 a.m.; High Festivals, 8 a.m. and noon.

JAMES, ST., Marylebone, Westmoreland-st, W. Sun., 11 a.m., 3, and 7 p.m. Holy Com., 1st Sun., noon.

JAMES, ST., Prebend-sq, Islington, N. [6.] Sun., 11 a.m. and 6.30 p.m.; last Sun., 3.15 p.m. (Special). Fri. 11 a.m.; Thurs., 8 p.m. Holy Com., 1st Sun., after mng. serv.; 3rd Sun., after evg. serv.

JAMES, ST., Ratcliff, Butcher-row, E. [2.] Sun., 11 a.m. and 7 p.m.; 1st Sun., 3.15 p.m. (Special); Fri., 8 p.m. Holy Days, 11 a.m. Holy Com., Sun., 8 a.m. (except 1st and 3rd, when after mng. serv.).

JAMES, ST., Spa-rd, Bermondsey, S.E. [8.] Sun., 11 a.m., 3 p.m., and 6.30 p.m. Wed., 8 p.m. Holy Com., 1st Sun., after mng. serv.; 3rd and 5th Sun., after evg. serv.; 2nd and 4th, 8 a.m.

JAMES, ST., THE LESS, Upper Garden-st, Westminster, S.W. [2.] Sun., 11 a.m. (Matins), 3.30 p.m. (Children), and 7 p.m. Wed. and Fri., noon (Lit.) and 7 p.m. Holy Com., 8 a.m. and after mng. serv.; Daily at 12, Lent, Advent, and on Saint Days.

JAMES, ST., Westminster, Piccadilly, W. [5.] Sun., 11 a.m., 3 p.m., and 7 p.m. Holy Days (Nov. to Lent), 10 a.m., (Lent to Nov.) 8 a.m. (Matins). Week Days, 8 a.m. (Matins); Wed. and Fri., noon (Lit.); Thursday, 8 p.m. Holy Com., Sun., 8 a.m., and 1st and 3rd Sun., after mng. serv.; Holy Days, 8 a.m.

JOHN, ST., Cambridge-rd, Bethnal Green, E. [2.] Sun., 11 a.m., 3.30 p.m. (Lit.), and 6.30 p.m. Thurs. and Holy Days, 9 p.m. Holy Com., 1st and 3rd Sun., after mng. serv.; others, 8 a.m.; Holy Days, 7.30 a.m.

JOHN, ST., Church-st, Wapping, E. [2.] Sun., 11 a.m. (Matins) and 6.30 p m. Wed., 11 a.m.; Fri., 7 p.m. Holy Com., 1st Sun. after mng. serv.; 3rd Sun., 8 a.m.; and on the Great Festivals.

JOHN, ST., Hackney, E. [2.] Sun., 11 a.m., 3, 4, and 7 p.m. Daily, 8 a.m. and 5 p.m., or 7.30 p.m.; Wed and Fri., 11 a.m. Holy Com., Sun., 8 a.m.; 1st and 3rd Sun. at noon.

JOHN, ST., Larcom-st, Walworth, S.E. [2.] Sun., 11 a.m. (Matins), 3.30 p.m. (Lit.), and 6.30 p.m. Holy Com., Sun., 8.30 a.m., and after mng. serv.; Holy Days, 8 a.m. and 11 a.m.; Week Days, 7.30 a.m.

JOHN, ST., Notting Hill, Ladbroke-gr, W. [5.] Sun., 11 a.m., 3.30 p.m., and 7 p.m. Mon., Tues., Thurs., and Sat., 9 a.m. (Matins); Wed. and Fri., 11 a.m. (Matins and Lit.). Holy Days, 11 a.m. Holy Com., Sun. and Festivals, 8 a.m.; 3rd Sun., 9 a.m.; and 1st Sun., after mng. serv.

JOHN, ST., Roserton-st, Cubitt Town, E. [12.] Sun., 11 a.m. and 6.30 p.m. Holy Com., Sun., 8 a.m.; 1st and 3rd Sun., noon; Daily, 7.45 a.m.

JOHN, ST., Marylebone, Park-rd, N.W. Sun., 11 a.m., and 3 and 7 p.m. Holy Days, 11 a.m. Holy Com., Sun., 8.30 a.m. and after mng. serv.; Holy Days, after mng. serv.

JOHN, ST., Upper Holloway, N. [6.] Sun., 11 a.m., 3.30, 6.30, and 9 p.m. Fri. and Saint Days, 11 a.m. (Matins); Wed., noon (Matins) and 7.30 p.m. Holy Com., 1st Sun., noon; 2nd Sun., 8 a.m.; 3rd and 4th Sun., 8 p.m.

JOHN, ST., Waterloo-rd, S.E. [6.] Sun., 11 a.m. and 6.30 p.m. Wed., Fri., and Holy Days, 10 a.m.; Thurs., 8 p.m. Holy Com., 1st Sun. after mng. serv.; 2nd and 4th, 9.30 a.m.; 3rd, 8 p.m.; 5th, 8 a.m.

JOHN BAPTIST, ST., Clerkenwell, St. John's-sq, E.C. [2.] Sun., 11 a.m. (Matins) and 6.30 p.m. Holy Days, 8 p.m.; Daily, 7.45 p.m., except Wed., 8 p.m. Holy Com., Sun. and Holy Days, 8.30 a.m.; 1st Sun., 11 a.m.

JOHN BAPTIST, ST., Holland-rd, Kensington, W. [2.] Sun., 11 a.m. (Matins), 3.30 p.m. (Special), 4.15 p.m., and 7 p.m. Holy and Week Days, 7.30 a.m. (Matins). Daily, except Wed., 5 p.m.; Wed. and Holy Days, 7.30 p.m. Holy Com., Sun., 8 a.m. and after Matins (Choral); Holy and Week Days, 7.30 a.m., except Wed., 8 a.m.

JOHN BAPTIST, ST., Gt. Marlborough-st, W. [2.] Sun., 11 a.m. (Matins) and 7 p.m. Holy Days, 11.45 a.m. (Matins) and 8 p.m. Holy Com., Sun., 11 a.m. (Choral); Great Festivals, 9 a.m., and after mng. serv.

JOHN BAPTIST, ST., New North-rd, Hoxton, N. [12.] Sun., 8 a.m., 11 a.m., and 6.30 p.m. Wed. and Fri., 11 a.m.; Wed., 8 p.m. Holy Com., Sun., 8 a.m.; 1st Sun., 11 a.m.; 3rd Sun., 6.30 p.m.

JOHN THE DIVINE, ST., Vassall-rd, Kennington, S.W. [2.] Sun., 11.45 a.m. (Lit. and Matins), 4 p.m. (Children), and 7 p.m. Holy and Week Days, 8 a.m. (Matins) and 7 p.m. Holy Com., 7 a.m. and 8 a.m., and 10 a.m. (Choral); Holy and Week Days, 7 a.m.; Tues., Thurs., and Holy Days, 8.30 a.m.

JOHN, THE EVANGELIST, ST., Fair-st, Horselydown, S.E. [1.] Sun., 10 and 11 a.m., 3.15, 4 (Children), and 6.30 p.m. Daily, 7.30 a.m., and 7 p.m. Holy Com., Sun., 8 and 11 a.m. (Choral), and on Holy Days, 7.30 a.m.

JOHN THE EVANGELIST, ST., Glenthorne-rd, Hammersmith, W. [2.] Sun., 11 a.m. (Matins), 3.15 p.m. (Lit.), and 7 p.m. Week Days, 8 a.m. (Matins); Wed. and Fri., 12 p.m.; Wed., Fri., and Holy Days, 7 p.m.; other Week Days, 5 p.m. Holy Com., Sun., 7 a.m., 8 a.m., and 11 a.m. (Choral); Thurs. and Holy Days, 7 a.m.; Tues. and Holy Days, 11 a.m.

JOHN THE EVANGELIST, ST., Oxford-sq, Paddington, W. [2.] Sun., 11 a.m., 3.30 p.m. and 7 p.m. Holy and Week Days, noon (Matins). Holy Com., 1st and 3rd Sun., after mng. serv.; 2nd and 4th Sun., 8 a.m.; last Sun., 7 p.m.; Holy Days, after mng. serv.; High Festivals, 8 a.m., and after mng. serv.

JOHN THE EVANGELIST, ST., Queen's-crescent, Haverstock-hill, N.W. [2.] Sun., 11 a.m. (Matins), and 7 p.m. Holy Com., noon; 1st and 3rd Sun., 8 a.m.; High Festivals, 8 a.m. and noon (Choral).

JOHN THE EVANGELIST, ST., Red Lion-sq. [1.] Sun., 9.45 a.m. (Children), 11 a.m. (Matins), 3.30 p.m. (Children), and 7 p.m. Week Days, 7.30 a.m. (Matins), and 8 p.m. Holy Com., Sun., 7 and 8 a.m., and after Matins (Choral on 1st and 3rd Sun.); Thurs. and Holy Days, 7 a.m.

JUDE, ST., Commercial-st, Whitechapel, E. [1.] Sun., 11.15 a.m., 6.30 p.m., and 8.30 p.m. "Worship Hour." Holy Com., 1st Sun., after mng. serv.; 3rd Sun., after evg. serv.

JUDE, ST., Gray's-inn-rd, W.C. [1.] Sun., 11 a.m. (Matins), 3.30 p.m., and 7 p.m. Week Days, 9 a.m. (Matins) and 5 p.m.; Wed. and Fri., noon; Wed., 8 p.m. Holy Com., Sun., 8 a.m.; Holy Days, 7.30 and 11 a.m.

JUDE, ST., St. George's-rd, Southwark, S.E. [6.] Sun., 11 a.m. and 6.45 p.m. Holy Days, 11 a.m (Matins), and 8 p.m. Wed., 7.45 p.m. Holy Com., 1st Sun., after mng. serv.; 3rd Sun., after evg. serv.

KATHARINE, ST., Regent's-pk, N.W. [5.] Sun., 11 a.m. and 3 p.m. Holy Days, 11 a.m. (Matins). Holy Com., 1st, 3rd, and 5th Sun., 8.30 a.m.; 2nd and 4th Sun., after mng. serv.

KATHERINE CREE, ST., Leadenhall-st, E.C. Sun., 11 a.m. and 6.30 p.m. Holy Com., 1st Sun. after mng. serv., and on Great Festivals.

KENTISH TOWN PARISH CHURCH, Highgate-rd, N.W. [1.] Sun., 11 a.m., 3.30 and 7 p.m.; Wed. Fri., and Holy Days, 11 a.m.; Thur., 8 p.m. Holy Com., Sun., 8 a.m.; on 1st and 3rd Sun., also 12.30 p.m.

KING'S COLLEGE CHAPEL, Strand, W.C. [2.] Sun., 11 a.m. (Matins). Evg. Serv. (Occasional), 7 p.m. Week Days, 10 a.m. (Matins). Holy Com., Sun., after mng. serv.; Holy Days, 10 a.m. Services only during Term.

LAWRENCE JEWRY, ST., Gresham-st, E.C. Sun., 8 a.m., 10.45 a.m., and 7 p.m. Holy Days, 8 p.m. Daily (except Sat.), 1.15 p.m. Holy Com., Sun., after mng. serv., alternate Plain and Choral.

LEONARD, ST., Shoreditch, E. [2.] Sun., 11 a.m., 3.30 p.m., and 6.30 p.m. Week Days, 9.30 a.m. and 6.30 p.m., and Fri., 8 p.m. Holy Com., Sun., 8 a.m. and noon; Holy Days, 7 or 8 a.m.

LOCK HOSPITAL CHAPEL, Harrow-rd, W. [6.] Sun., 11 a.m. and 7 p.m.; 5th Sun., 3.30 p.m. (Special). Wed., 7.30 p.m.

LONDON HOSPITAL CHAPEL, Whitechapel-rd, E. [5.] Sun., 10 a.m., 11 a.m., and 6.30 p.m. Tues. and Sat., 10 a.m. (Special). Holy Com., 9 a.m. every Sun. except 2nd, when it is 11.30 a.m.

LUKE, ST., Berwick-st, Soho, W. [2.] Sun., 11 a.m. (Matins), 3.20 p.m. (Children), and 7 p.m. Holy and Week Days, 5.30 p.m., except Wed., when service is 8.30 p.m. Holy Com., Sun., 8 a.m. and after mng. serv. (Choral); Holy Days, 8 a.m.

LUKE, ST., Burdett-rd, Stepney, E. [2.] Sun., 11 a.m., 3.15 p.m. (Special), and 7 p.m. Week Days, 8 p.m. Holy Com., Sun., 8 a.m., and after mng. serv. (Choral); Holy Days, 7.30 a.m.

LUKE, ST., CONSUMPTION HOSPITAL CHAPEL, Fulham-rd, S.W. [1.] Sun., 11 a.m. and 7 p.m. Week Days, 9.30 a.m. (Matins). Holy Com., alternate Sun., after mng. serv.; Holy Days, 9.30 a.m.

LUKE, ST., Evelyn-st, Deptford, S.E. [5.] Sun., 11 a.m. and 6.30 p.m. Holy Com., 1st Sun., after mng. serv.; 3rd Sun., after evg. serv.; Thursdays and Festivals, 7.30 a.m.

LUKE, ST., Nutford-pl, Edgware-rd, W. [12.] Sun., 11 a.m. (Matins), and 7 p.m.; 3rd Sun., 3.15 p.m. Holy Com., 1st and 3rd Sun., after mng. serv., and 2nd and 4th Sun., after evg. serv.

LUKE, ST., Oseney-cres, Kentish Town, N.W. Sun., 11 a.m. (Matins), 3.30 p.m. (Children), 7 p.m., and in Lent and Advent only, 5 p.m. Week days, 10 a.m. and 8 p.m.; Wed., Fri., and Holy Days, 8 p.m. Holy Com., Sun., 8 a.m., and after mng. serv. (Choral); Thurs., 7.30 a.m. and 10.30 a.m.

LUKE, ST., Redcliffe-gdns, S.W. [1.] Sun., 11 a.m., 3.30 p.m. (Lit.), and 7 p.m. Wed. and Fri., 11 a.m. (Matins). Holy Com., 1st Sun. and High Festivals, after mng. serv.; 3rd Sun., 8.30 a.m.; last Sun., 7 p.m.

LUKE, ST., Robert-st, Chelsea, S.W. [12.] Sun., 11 a.m., 3 p.m., and 7 p.m. Wed. and Fri. and Holy Days, noon. Holy Com., 1st Sun., 9 a.m.; 3rd Sun., after mng. serv.; 5th Sun., after evg. serv.

LUKE, ST., West Holloway, Hillmarten-rd, N. [6.] Sun., 11 a.m. and 7 p.m. Wed., 11 a.m. (Lit.), and 7 p.m. Holy Com., 1st Sun., after mng. serv.; 2nd, and 8.30 a.m.; and 3rd Sun., after evg. serv.

MARGARET PATTENS, ST., Rood-la, E.C. [1.] Sun., 10.30 a.m. (Matins) and 7 p.m. Wed. and Fri. 1.15 p.m.; Fri., 7.30 p.m. Holy Com., Sun., 8.30 a.m. and 11.30 a.m. (Choral); Holy Days, noon.

MARGARET, ST., Westminster, S.W. [I.] Sun., 11 a.m. (Matins), 3.30 p.m., and 7 p.m.; Holy Days, 11 a.m. (Matins). Wed., noon (Lit.) and 7.30 p.m. Holy Com., Sun., 8 a.m.; also on 1st Sun., after mng. serv.; 5th Sun., after evg. serv.

MARK, ST., COLLEGE CHAPEL, Stamford-br, Fulham-rd, S.W. [I.] Sun., 8 a.m., 11 a.m. and 4 p.m. Week Days, 7.45 a.m. and 9.15 p.m. Holy Com., 1st, 3rd, and 5th Sun., 8 a.m.; 2nd and 4th Sun., after mng. serv.

MARK, ST., East-st, Walworth, S.E. [6.] Sun., 11 a.m., and 6.30 p.m.; 2nd Sun., 3.30 p.m. Holy Days, 8 p.m. Wed. and Fri., 8 p.m. Holy Com., Sun., 8 a.m., except 1st, after mng., and 3rd, after evg. serv.

MARK, ST., Gloucester Gate, N.W. [12.] Sun., 11 a.m. (Matins), 3.30 p.m., and 7 p.m. Wed., Fri. and Holy Days, 11 a.m. Holy Com., Sun., after mng. serv.; Holy Days, 8 a.m.

MARK, ST., Kennington, S.E. [I.] Sun., 11 a.m., 6.30 p.m., and 2nd Sun., 3.30 p.m. Holy Com., Sun., 8.30 a.m., and 1st and 3rd Sun., after mng. serv.; 2nd Sun., after evg. serv.; Holy Days, 8 a.m.

MARK, ST., Marylebone-rd, N.W. [12.] Sun., 11 a.m. and 7 p.m. Holy and Week Days 11 a.m. (Matins). Holy Com., 1st Sun., after mng. serv.; 3rd Sun, 7 p.m.

MARK, ST., Myddelton-sq, E.C. [2.] Sun., 11 a.m. (Matins), 4 p.m. (Lit.), and 7 p.m. Daily 8 a.m. (Matins), and 5 p.m., except Wed. and Fri., at 11 a.m.; Wed., 8 p.m. Holy Com., Sun., 8 a.m., and after mng. serv.; Holy Days, 7.30 a.m.

MARK, ST., North Audley-st, W. [2.] Sun., 11 a.m., 3.30 p.m., and 7 p.m. Week Days 8 a.m. and 5 p.m.; Wed. and Holy Days, 8.30 p.m. Holy Com., Sun., 8 and 11.45 a.m.; Thurs., 8 a.m.; Holy Days, 8 and 11.45 a.m.

MARK, ST., St. Mark's-rd, Notting-hill, W. [I.] Sun., 11 a.m., 3.30 p.m., and 7 p.m. Holy and Week Days, 11.30 a.m. (Matins). Holy Com., 8 a.m. and after mng. serv. on all Suns. and Holy Days.

MARTIN-IN-THE-FIELDS, ST., Trafalgar-sq, W.C. [5.] Sun., 8.30 a.m., 11 a.m., and 3 p.m. and 7 p.m. Daily, 8 a.m. and 11 a.m.; Wed., 8 p.m. Holy Com., Sun., 8.30 a.m.; 1st and 3rd Sun., at noon; Holy Days, 8 a.m. and 11 a.m.; Wed., 8 p.m.

MARTIN, ST., Ludgate-hill, E.C. [15.] Sun., 11 a.m. and 3 p.m. Holy Com., last Sun. after mng. serv.

MARY, ST., Aldermanbury, E.C. [I.] Sun., 11 a.m. and 6.30 p.m. Holy Com., 1st Sun. and Great Festivals, after mng. serv.

MARY, ST., Brunswick-st, Haggerston, E. [2.] Sun., 11 a.m (Matins) (Lit., 2nd and 4th), 7 p.m. Holy Days, 8 p.m. Wed. and Fri., 11 a.m. (Lit.); Thurs., 8 p.m. Holy Com., Sun., 8 a.m., and after Matins (Choral); Holy Days, 7 a.m.; Thurs., 7 a.m. and 8.30 p.m.

MARY, ST., Cable-st, St. George's-in-the-East, E. [5.] Sun., 11 a.m., 3 and 6.30 p.m.; Wed., 7.30 p.m. Holy Com. twice a month.

MARY, ST., Hornsey Rise, N. [6.] Sun., 11 a.m. and 6.30 p.m. Holy Com., 1st Sun., after mng. serv.; 3rd Sun., 3 p.m. and after evg. serv.; Great Festivals, after evg. serv.

MARY, ST., Hoxton, Britannia-st, N. [5.] Sun., 11 a.m. (Matins) and 7 p.m. Holy Com., Sun., 8 a.m., and after mng. serv.; Holy Days, 8 a.m.

MARY, ST., Islington, Upper-st, N. [6.] Sun., 11 a.m., 3.30 p.m., and 6.30 p.m. Wed. and Fri., 11.30 a.m.; Thurs., 8 p.m. Holy Com., 1st Sun. after mng. serv.; 2nd Sun., 8 a.m.; 3rd Sun., 6.30 p.m.

MARY, ST., Newington, Kennington-pk-rd, S.E. [I.] Sun., 11 a.m. (Matins), noon, and 6.30 p.m. Week Days, 9 a.m. and 8 p.m. Holy Com., Sun., 8 a.m., and 1st, 3rd, and 5th Sun., after Matins; Holy Days, 3.30 p.m.

MARY, ST., Rotherhithe, Church-st, S.E. [I.] Sun., 11 a.m., 3.30 p.m., and 6.30 p.m. Week Days, 6 p.m. Holy Com., Sun., 8 a.m.; 1st Sun. and High Festivals, after mng. serv.; Holy Days, 8 a.m.

MARY, ST., Somers Town, Seymour-st, N.W. [II.] Sun., 11 a.m. and 7 p.m. Thurs., 7.30 p.m. Holy Com., 1st Sun., after mng. serv., and 3rd Sun., after evg. serv.

MARY, ST., Wyndha.n-pl, Bryanston-sq, W. [5] Sun., 11 a.m., 3.30 p.m., and 7 p.m. Holy and Week Days, noon. Thurs., 7.30 p.m. Holy Com., 8 a.m., 1st and 3rd Sun. after mng. serv.

MARY ALDERMARY, ST., Bow-la, Queen Victoria-st, E.C. [6.] Sun., 11 a.m., (1st Sun., Special), 3.30 p.m.; and 7 p.m. Week Days (except Sat.), 1.15 p.m. (Lit.). Holy Com., 1st Sun. and on Great Festivals after mng. serv.

MARY-AT-HILL, ST.. Eastcheap, E.C. [I.] Sun., 11 a.m. (Matins and Lit.), 7 p.m. Week Days, 8 a.m. (Matins) and 7 p.m. Holy Com., Sun. (except 1st), 8 a.m.

MARY CHARTERHOUSE, ST., Golden-la, E.C. [2.] Sun., 11 a.m. (Matins), 3.30 p.m. (Special), and 7 p.m. Holy and Week Days, 8 a.m. (Matins) and 8 p.m., except Mon. and Thurs. 3.45 p.m. Holy Com., Sun., 8 a.m. and 11.45 a.m.; 1st Sun., 9 a.m. also; Holy and Week Days, 7.30 a.m.

MARY-LE-BOW, ST., Cheapside, E.C. Sun., 11 a.m. and 6.30 p.m. Thurs., 1 p.m. Holy Com., 1st Sun. after mng. serv., and on Great Festivals.

MARY-LE-STRAND, ST. Sun., 11 a.m. and 7 p.m.; Wed., 7 p.m. Holy Com., 1st Sun., after mng. serv.; 3rd Sun., after evg. serv.

MARYLEBONE, ST., Marylebone-rd, N.W. [2.] Sun., 11 a.m., 3.30 p.m., and 7 p.m. Week Days, 8 a.m. (Matins), and 5 p.m. (Evensong). Holy Days, 11 a.m. and 5 p.m. Wed. and Fri., noon (Lit.) Holy Com., Sun., 8 a.m. and mid-day; Holy Days, 8 a.m.

MARY MAGDALEN, ST., Bermondsey, Bermondsey-st, S.E. [12.] Sun., 11 a.m., 3.30 p.m., and 6.30 p.m. Wed., 7 p.m. Holy Com., 1st Sun., after mng. serv.; 2nd, 4th, and 5th Sun., 8.30 a.m.; 3rd Sun. 8 p.m.

MARY MAGDALEN, ST., Munster-sq., N.W. [I.] Sun., 10.30 a.m. (Matins), 4 p.m. (Lit.), and 7 p.m. Week Days, 9 a.m. and 7 p.m. Holy Days, 7 p.m. Holy Com., Sun., 7.30 a.m. and 9 a.m., and after Matins (Choral) ; Holy Days, 7.30 a.m. and 9 a.m.; Week Days, 7.30 a.m.

MARY MAGDALEN, ST., Old Kent-rd. [5.] Sun., 11 a.m., 3.15 p.m. (Lit.), and 6.30 p.m. Wed., 7.30 p.m. Holy Com., 1st Sun., after mng. serv.; 3rd and 5th Sun., after evg. serv.

MARY MAGDALEN, ST., Woodchester-st, Paddington, W. [2.] Sun., 10.30 a.m. (Matins), 2.45 p.m. (Lit.), 3.15 p.m. (Special), 4 p.m., and 7 p.m. Week Days, 8 a.m., 5 p.m., and 8 p.m. Holy Days, 5 p.m. and 8 p.m. Holy Com., Sun., 7 a.m., 8 a.m., 8.15 a.m. (in St. Ambrose Chapel), and 11.45 a.m. (Choral) ; Holy Days, 7 a.m. and 8 a.m.; Week Days, 7 a.m.; Wed., 12.30 p.m.; Thurs., 7.30 a.m.

MARY MATFELON, ST., Whitechapel, E. [5.] Sun., 11 a.m., 6.30 and 8.15 p.m. Wed. and Fri., 10.30 a.m.; Thurs., 8 p.m. Holy Com., 1st and 3rd Sun., at mng. serv.; 2nd Sun., 9 a.m.; last, at evg. serv.

MARY THE VIRGIN, Crown-st, Soho, W.C. [2.] Sun., 11 a.m. (Matins), 4 p.m. (Children), and 7 p.m. Holy and Week Days, 8 p.m. Holy Com., Sun., 8 a.m., and 11.30 a.m.; Holy and Week Days, 7 a.m

MARY THE VIRGIN, ST., Lambeth, near the Pier, S.E. [6.] Sun., 11 a.m. and 6.30 p.m. Holy Days, 11 a.m. Wed., 7 p.m. Holy Com., Sun., 8 a.m.; also 1st Sun., after mng. serv.; last Sun., after evg. serv.

MARY THE VIRGIN, ST., Primrose Hill, N.W. [2.] Sun., 11.15 a.m. (Matins), 3 p.m. (Special). 3.30 p.m (Lit.), and 7 p.m. Holy Days, 10 a.m. (Matins). Wed. and Fri., 10 a.m. (Lit.), and 8 p.m.; Mon., Tues., and Thurs., 5 p.m. Holy Com., Sun., 8 and 9.45 a.m. ; Holy and Week Days, 7.30 a.m.

MARY WOOLNOTH, ST., Lombard-st, E.C. [I.] Sun., 11 a.m. and 6 p.m. Holy Com., 1st and 3rd Sun. after mng. serv., and on all Great Festivals.

MATTHEW, ST., Bayswater, St. Petersburgh-pl., W. [II.] Sun., 11 a.m., 3.30 p.m., and 7 p.m. Wed and Fri. 11.30 a.m. Holy Com., 1st Sun., after mng. serv.; 3rd Sun., after evg. serv.; last Sun. 8.30 a.m.; and on last Fri., after mng. serv.

MATTHEW, ST., Church-row, Bethnal Green, E. [12.] Sun., 11 a.m. (Matins), 3 p.m. (Lit.), and 6.30 p.m Wed., 8 p.m. Holy Com., Sun., 8.30 a.m., and 1st Sun. after Matins ; Holy Days, 8 a.m.

MATTHEW, ST., Maida Hill, W. [8.] Sun., 11 a.m. and 7 p.m. Holy Com., 1st Sun. after mng., and 3rd Sun. after evg. serv.

MATTHEW, ST., New Kent-rd, S.E. [12.] Sun., 11 a.m. and 6.30 p.m., and 3rd Sun., 3 p.m. Wed., 7.30 p.m. Holy Com., 1st Sun., after mng. serv. ; 3rd Sun., after evg. serv. ; other Suns. and Festivals, 8 a.m.

MATTHEW, ST., Pell-st, St. George's-in-the-East, E. [2.] Sun., 11 a.m. and 6.30 p.m. Wed., 7 p.m. Holy Com., 1st Sun., after mng. serv., and on Great Festivals.

MATTHEW, ST., Mission Hall, Walton-st, Chelsea, S.W. Sun, 11 a.m. and 7 p.m. Holy Com., on 2nd and last Sun.

MATTHEW, ST., Westminster, Great Peter-st, S.W. [I.] Sun., 11 a.m. (Matins), 3 and 7 p.m. Holy and Week Days, 7.45 a.m.; Wed., 7 p.m. Holy Com., Sun., after Matins, and 8 a.m.

MATTHIAS, ST., Caledonian-rd, N. [6.] Sun., 11 a.m. and 6.30 p.m.; 3rd Sun., 3 p.m. (Special). Thurs., 7.30 p.m. Holy Com., 2nd Sun. after mng. serv.; 4th, after evg. serv.

MATTHIAS, ST., Chilton-st, Bethnal Green, E. [6.] Sun., 11 a.m., and 6.30 p.m. Wed., 8 p.m. Holy Com., 1st Sun. after evg. serv.; 3rd Sun. after mng. serv.; 4th Sun., 8 a.m.

MATTHIAS, ST., Earl's Court, S.W. [I.] Sun., 10.45 a.m. (Matins), 3.30 p.m. (Lit.), and 7 p.m. Wed- and Fri , noon (Lit.); Wed. 8 p.m. Holy Com. 7 a.m. and 8 a.m., and after Matins (Choral) . Holy Days, 7, 8, and 11 a.m. (Choral) ; Week Days, 8 a.m.; Thurs., 7 and 8 a.m.

MERCERS' CHAPEL (St. Thomas of Acon), Ironmonger Lane, Cheapside, E.C. [2.] Sun., 7 p.m. (Choral). During Lent, Thurs., 8 p.m., and other occasional services.

MICHAEL, ST., Chester-sq., S.W. [I.] Sun., 11 a.m., and 3.30 and 7 p.m. Wed., noon ; Thurs., 7.30 p.m.; Fri., 11 a.m. Holy Com., Sun. 8.30 a.m.; also noon, 1st and 3rd Suns.: alter evg. serv. on last Sun. and on Great Festivals.

MICHAEL, ST., AND ALL ANGELS, Ladbroke-gr-rd, W. [I.] Sun., 11 a.m. (Matins), 4 p.m. (Lit.), and 7 p.m. Holy Days, 10 a.m. Wed., noon ; Fri., 5 p.m. Holy Com., Sun., 8.30 a.m., after mng. serv., and after the 7 p.m. serv.; Holy Days, 11 a.m.

MICHAEL, ST., AND ALL ANGELS, Market-st, Paddington, W. [2.] Sun., 10.15 a.m. (Children), 11.30 a.m. (Matins), 3.30 p.m. (Lit.), and 7.30 p.m. Holy Days, 11.30 a.m. Week Days, 8 a.m. and 5 p.m.; Wed. 12.30 p.m. and 8 p.m.; Fri., 12.30 p.m. Holy Com., Sun., 8 a.m.; 1st Sun., also at 7 a.m.; Holy Days, 8 and 11.30 a.m.

MICHAEL, ST., Cornhill, E.C. [5.] Sun., 11 a.m. and 6.45 p.m. Wed. and Fri. in Advent and Lent, and on Saint Days, 12.15 p.m. Holy Com., 1st and 3rd Sun. after mng. serv., and on Great Festivals ; Saint Days, 12.15 p.m.

MICHAEL, ST., Shoreditch, Mark-st, Finsbury, E.C. [9.] Sun., 9 a.m., noon (Lit.), 3 p.m. (Children), and 8 p.m. Week Days, 9 a.m., and 7.30 and 8.50 p.m. Holy Com, Sun., 8 a.m., and 9.30 a.m. (Choral); Week Days, 7 a.m,

NICHOLAS, ST., Deptford, Deptford-gn, S.E. [I.] Sun., 11 a.m., 3.30 and 6.30 p.m. Thurs., 7 p.m Holy Com., Sun., 8.30 a.m., and 1st and 3rd Sun., after mng. serv.

OLAVE, ST., Hart-st E.C. [I.] Sun., 11 a.m. and 6.30 p.m. Daily, 1 p.m. (Lit.) Holy Com., 1st Sun and Great Festivals, after mng. serv.

PANCRAS, ST., Euston-rd, N.W. [6.] Sun., 11 a.m., and 3 and 7 p.m. Week Days, 5 p.m.; an Thurs., 8 p.m. Holy Com., Sun., 8 a.m.; and 1st and 3rd after mng. serv.; Holy Days, noon an 5 p.m.

PAUL, ST. Avenue-rd N.W. [2.] Sun., 11 a.m., 3.30 p.m. (Lit.), and 7 p.m. Holy and Week Day 9 a.m and 5 p.m., and Wed. and Fri., noon (Lit.). Holy Com., Sun., 8 a.m.; 1st and 3rd Sun., afte mng.serv.; Holy Days, 8 a.m.; 3rd Sun.,and all Great Festivals, Choral Celebration after mng. serv.

PAUL, ST., Bermondsey, Nelson-st, S.E. [I.] Sun., 11 a.m., 3.15 and 6.30 p.m. Wed., 7.45 p.m. Ho Com., 2nd Sun., after mng. serv., and 4th Sun., after evg. serv. Baptisms every Wed. at 11.30, an 3rd Sun., 3.30 p.m.

PAUL, ST., Bow Common, E. [2.] Sun. 11 a.m. (Matins) and 7 p.m.; 1st and 3rd Sun., 3.30 p.m (Special). Holy and Week days, 10 a.m. (Matins), and 5 p.m.; Wed. and Fri., 11.30 a.m. (Lit and 8 p m. Holy Com., Sun.,8 a.m.,and after Matins (Choral); Tues.,Thurs.,and Holy Days, 7.30 a.m

PAUL, ST., Bunhill-row, E.C. [2.] Sun., 11 a.m., 4 p.m. (Lit.), and 7 p.m. Holy and Week Days 9.30 a.m. and 8 p.m. Holy Com., Sun., 8 a.m., and 1st Sun. after mng. serv. (Choral); Holy Days 8 a.m.

PAUL, ST., Covent Garden, W.C. [12.] Sun., 11 a.m. (Matins) and 7 p.m. Holy Com., 1st Sun., afte mng. serv., and 3rd Sun., after evg. serv.

PAUL, ST Dock-st E. [6.] Sun., 11 a.m. (Matins), 3 p.m. (Special), and 6.30 p.m. Holy Com. 1st Sun., after mng. serv., and 3rd Sun., after evg. serv. ; Thurs., 7 p.m.

PAUL, ST., Essex-rd, N. [6.] Sun., 11 a.m., 3.30 p.m., and 7 p.m. Wed., 11 a.m. (Matins); Thurs. 7.30 p.m. Holy Com., 1st and 3rd Sun., at mng. serv.; 2nd, 8.30 p.m.; 4th, 3.30 p.m.; 5th, 8 a.m.

PAUL, ST., Globe-st, Rotherhithe, S.E. [I.] Sun., 11 a.m. and 6.30 p.m. Holy Com., 2nd Sun., afte mng. serv.

PAUL, ST., Lorrimore-sq, S.E. [I.] Sun., 11 a.m. and 7 p.m. Week Days, 8 a.m. and 9 p.m. Holy Com., Sun., 8 and 11 a.m.; Holy Days, 7.30 a.m.

PAUL, ST., Marlborough-pl, Harrow-rd, W. [12.] Sun., 11 a.m., 3.30 and 7 p.m. Wed., and on Holy and Saint Days 8 p.m.; High Festivals, 11 a.m. (Matins). Holy Com., Sun., 8 a.m.; 1st and 3rd 11 a.m., and 3rd, 7 p.m.

PAUL, ST., Old Ford, E. [6.] Sun., 11 a.m., 3 p.m., and 6.30 p.m. Wed. and Fri., 11 a.m. (Lit.) Thurs., 7.30 p.m. Holy Com., 2nd and last Sun.

PAUL, ST., Onslow-sq, S.W. [6.] Sun., 11 a.m., 3.30 p.m., and 7 p.m.; 2nd Sun., 3.30 p.m. (Children) Wed., 7.30 p.m. Holy Com., 1st Sun. after mng. serv.; 2nd Sun., 8.30 a.m.; 3rd Sun., after evg serv.; 4th Sun. after mng serv. ; 5th Sun. after afternoon serv.

PAUL, ST., Wilton-pl, Knightsbridge, S.W. Sun., 11 a.m. (Matins), 3 p.m. (Lit.), 3.30 p.m., 4.15 p.m. (Children), and 7 p.m. Holy and Week Days, 8 a.m. (Matins) and 5 p.m. Holy Com., 7 a.m. 8 a.m., and 12.15 p.m. (all Choral); Holy and Week Days, 7, 8.30, and 11 a.m.; Thurs., 7 a.m.

PETER, ST. Bayswater Kensington-pk-rd, W. [2.] Sun., 11 a.m. (Matins and Lit.), 4 p.m., and 7 p.m. Week Days, 8.30 a.m. and 5 p.m.; Wed. and Fri., noon (Lit.), and 8 p.m. Holy Com., Sun. 8 a.m.; after mng. serv. (Choral); Holy Days, 7 a.m. and 11 a.m.; Thurs., 7 a.m.

PETER, ST. Clerkenwell, St. John-st-rd, E.C. [5.] Sun., 11 a.m., 3, 6.30, and 8 p.m. Wed., 11 a.m. and 8 p.m.; Fri., 8 p.m. Holy Com., 1st Sun., 12.30 p.m.; 2nd Sun., 10 a.m.; 3rd Sun., 8 p.m.; 4th Wed., 8 p.m.

PETER, ST., Cornhill, E.C. [2.] Sun., 11 a.m. and 6.45 p.m. Holy Days, 11 a.m. Thurs., noon. Holy Com., 1st and 3rd Sun., after mng. serv., and on Great Festivals.

PETER, ST., Eaton-sq, S.W. [I.] Sun., 11 a.m. (Matins and Lit.), 3.30 and 7 p.m. Holy Days, 8 and 11 a.m. 3.30 and 5 p.m. Wed., 8 a.m., 11 a.m., and 5 p.m.; Fri., 8.30 a.m. and 11 a.m.; other Days, 8.30 a.m. and 5 p.m. Holy Com., Sun., 7 and 8.30 a.m. and 12.45 p.m.; Holy Days, 8.30 and 11 a.m.; Wed., 8.30 and 11.15 a.m.; Fri., 7.30 a.m; other Days, 7.30 a.m.

PETER, ST., Gt. Saffron-hill, E.C. [6.] Sun., 11 a.m. and 7 p.m. Thurs., 8 p.m. Holy Com., 1st Sun., after mng. serv.; 3rd Sun., after evg. serv.; last Sun., 8.30 a.m.

PETER, ST., Hoxton-sq, N. [6.] Sun., 11 a.m.; 2nd Sun., 3.30 p.m. (Special), and 7 p.m. Wed. and Fri., 8 p.m Holy Com., 1st Sun. after mng. serv.; 3rd Sun., 8.30 p.m.; 2nd,4th, and 5th Sun., 8 a.m.

PETER, ST., Liverpool-st, Walworth-rd, S.E. [I.] Sun., 11 a.m., 4 p.m (Special), and 6.30 p.m. Holy Days, 11.30 a.m. Wed. and Fri., 11.30 a.m. (Matins and Lit.). Holy Com., 2nd and last Sun., after mng. serv ; 1st Sun., 8 p.m.

PETER, ST., London Docks, Old Gravel-la, E. [3.] Sun., 10.15 a.m. (Matins), 2.30 p.m., 3.30 p.m., and 7 p.m. Holy and Week Days, 7.30 a.m. (Matins) and 8 p.m. Holy Com., Sun., 7 a.m., 8 a.m., and 9 a.m., and after Matins (Choral); Holy and Week Days, 6.45 a.m. and 8 a.m.; Holy Days. 10 a.m. (Choral).

PETER, ST., Regent-sq, W.C. [2.] Sun., 11 a.m., 4 p.m. (Lit.), and 7 p.m. Holy and Week Days, 8 a.m. (Matins) and 7.30 p.m. Holy Days only, 11 a.m. Week Days only, 5 p.m., except Wed. and Fri., noon (Lit.), and 8 p.m. Holy Com., Sun., 8 a.m., and after mng. serv. (Choral); Thurs. and Holy Days, 8 a.m.

PETER, ST., Southwark, Sumner-st, S.E. Sun., 11 a.m. and 6.30 p.m. Thurs., 7.30 p.m. Holy Com., 1st Sun. and High Festivals, after mng. serv. ; 3rd Sun., after evg. serv.

PETER, ST., Stepney, St. Peter's-rd, Mile End-rd, E. [2.] Sun., 11 a.m. and 6.30 p.m. Holy Days, 11 a.m. Wed., 7 p.m. Holy Com., 1st and 3rd Sun., after mng. serv.; 2nd and 4th Sun. and Festivals, 8.30 a.m.

PETER, ST., Streatham, Leigham-ct-rd, S.W. [2.] Sun., 11 a.m. (Matins), 4 p.m. (Lit.), and 7 p.m. Holy Days, 11 a.m. (Matins) and 8 p.m. Week Days, 8 a.m. (Matins) and 5 p.m. (except Fri.). Wed. and Fri., 11 a.m. (Lit.), and Fri., 8 p.m. Holy Com., Sun., 8 a.m. and noon ; Holy Days, 7.30 and 11.30 a.m.; Thurs, 7.30 a.m.

PETER, ST., Vauxhall, Upper Kennington-la, S.E. [2.] Sun., 11 a.m., alternate Sun., 9 a.m. (Matins); Sun., 3.30 p.m. (Lit.), and 6.30 p.m. Holy and Week Days, 7.45 a.m ; Wed. and Fri., noon (Special) ; Wed., 6.30 p.m.; other Week Days, 8 p.m. Holy Com., 1st and 3rd Sun., 7 and 8 a.m., 2nd and 4th Sun., 6.30 and 7.30 a.m.; Holy Days, 7 a.m. ; Week Days, 7 a.m.

PETER, ST., Vere-st, W. [2.] Sun., 11 a.m. and 7 p.m. Holy Days, 11 a.m. (Matins). Holy Com., Sun., after mng. serv.

PHILIP, ST., Avondale-sq, Old Kent-rd, S.E. [6.] Sun., 11 a.m., 3 p.m., and 7 p.m. Wed. 7.30 p.m. Holy Com., 1st Sun., after mng. serv., and 3rd after evg. serv.

PHILIP, ST., Granville-sq, King's Cross-rd, W.C. Sun., 10.30 a.m. and 7 p.m. Week Days, Mon., Tues., and Thurs., 5 p.m. ; Wed., Fri., Sat., and Holy Days, 8 p.m. Holy Com., Sun., 8 a.m., and 11.45 a.m. (Choral) ; Mon., Wed., and Fri., 7 a.m. ; Tues. and Sat., 8 a.m., and Thurs., 11 a.m.

PHILIP, ST., Kennington-rd, S.E. [5.] Sun., 11 a.m., 3 p.m., and 6.30 p.m. Wed., 7 p.m. Holy Com., 1st Sun., at mng. serv., 3rd, at evg. serv.

PHILIP, ST., Manor-place, Cuthbert-st, W. Sun., 10 a.m. and 6.30 p.m. Holy Com., Sun., 8.15 a.m., if the day of the month is an uneven number; others, 10.45 a.m.

PHILIP, ST., Sydenham, Wells-rd, S.E. [1.] Sun., 10.45 a.m. (Matins), 3.45 p.m. (Children), 4.30 and 7 p.m. Week Days, 10 a.m. and 5 p.m. Holy Days, 11 a.m., 5 p.m., and 8 p.m. Fri., 8 p.m. Holy Com., Sun., 7 and 8 a.m. and noon (Choral) ; Holy Days, 7 a.m. and 8 a.m. ; Thurs., 7 a.m. ; other days, 7.30 a.m.

PHILIP, ST., Waterloo-pl. [I.] Sun., 11.15 a.m. and 7 p.m. Holy Days, 11 a.m. and 8 p.m. Wed., 8 p.m. Holy Com., 1st, 3rd, and 5th Sun., 8.30 a.m., and 2nd and 4th after mng. serv.

QUEBEC CHAPEL, Old Quebec-st, W. [I.] Sun., 10 a.m. (Special), 11.30 a.m. (Matins), 3.30 p.m., and 7 p.m. Week Days, 8 a.m. and 4.30 p.m. Holy Days, noon (Matins). Wed. and Fri., 12.30 p.m. (Lit.); Wed., 8.30 p.m. Holy Com., Sun., 8.30 a.m. ; 1st Sun., 8 a.m., and after Matins ; 2nd Sun., 8 and 6 a.m.; Holy Days, 8 a.m.

SAVIOUR, ST., Fitzroy-sq, N.W. [5.] Sun., 11 a.m. and 7 p.m. Holy Days, 11 a.m. (Matins), and 8 p.m. Wed., 8 p.m. Holy Com., 1st Sun. and High Festivals, after mng. serv. ; 3rd Sun., 7 p.m. ; others, 8 a.m.

SAVIOUR, ST., High-st, Southwark, S.E. [6.] Sun., 11 a.m., 3.30 p.m., and 6.30 p.m. Wed. and Fri., 4.30 p.m

SAVIOUR, ST., Hoxton, Penn-st, N. [2.] Sun., 10.45 a.m. (Matins), 6.30 p.m. (Lit.), and 7 p.m. Holy and Week Days, 10 a.m. (Matins) and 8 p.m. Holy Com., Sun., 8 a.m. and after Matins ; 1st Sun., 7 a.m.; Week days, 7.30 a.m.

SAVIOUR, ST., Northumberland-st, Poplar, E. [I.] Sun., 11 a.m. (Matins) and 7 p.m. Wed., Fri., noon and 8.30 p.m. and Saint Days, 8 p.m. Holy Com., every Sun., 8 a.m. ; 1st and 3rd Sun., after Matins (Choral) ; Holy Days, 8 a.m. ; Wed. 8 p.m.

SAVIOUR, ST. (for Deaf and Dumb), 419, Oxford-st, W. [5.] Sun., 11 a.m. and 7 p.m. Thurs., 8.15 p.m.

SAVIOUR, ST., St. George's-sq, Pimlico, S.W. [I.] Sun., 8 a.m., 11 a.m. (Mat. and Lit.), 3.30, and 7 p.m. Holy and Week Days, 8 a.m. (Matins), 5.30 p.m. Holy Com., Sun., 8 a.m., and after Matins ; Thurs. and Holy Days, 8 a.m.

SAVIOUR, ST., Warwick-rd, Paddington, W. [2.] Sun., 11 a.m., 3.30 p.m. and 7 p.m. Daily, 5.30 p.m. Holy Com., Sun. and Holy Days, 8 a.m. ; 1st and 3rd Sun., after Matins.

SAVOY CHAPEL ROYAL, Savoy, Strand, W.C. [2.] Sun., 11.30 a.m. (Matins), 4 p.m. (Lit.), and 7 p.m. Holy Com., 1st Sun. (Choral) ; 3rd Sun., 10.15 a.m. (Choral) ; others, 8.30 a.m. ; Saint Days and Festivals, 11.30 a.m.

STEPHEN, ST., Avenue-rd, N.W. [I.] Sun., 11 a.m., 3.30 p.m. (Children), and 7 p.m. Holy Days, 11 a.m. (Matins). Holy Com., 1st Sun. after mng. serv., and 3rd Sun. 8.30 a.m.

STEPHEN, ST., Camberwell-gate, S.E. [14.] Sun., 11 a.m. and 6.30 p.m. Thurs., 7.30 p.m. Holy Com., 1st Sun. after mng. serv., 3rd after evg. serv.

STEPHEN, ST., Coleman-st, E.C. [6.] Sun., 11 a.m. and 6.45 p.m. Wed., 8.15 p.m. Holy Com., 1st Sun. and chief Holy Days, after mng. serv., and occasionally after evg. serv.

STEPHEN, ST., Gloucester-rd, S.W. [12.] Sun., 11 a.m., 4 p.m., and 7 p.m. Week Days, 10 a.m. (Matins), 5.30 p.m., except Wed. and Fri.; and, on Wed. only, 8 p.m. Wed., Fri., and Holy Days, 11 a.m. (Matins, Choral). Holy Com., Sun., 8.30 a.m. and 12.30 p.m. (Choral); Thurs. and Holy Days, 8 a.m., and 11 a.m (Choral); High Festivals, 7, 8, and 9 a.m., and 12.30 p.m.

STEPHEN, ST., Haggerston, Goldsmith's-row, Hackney-rd, E. [1.] Sun., 10.45 a.m. (Matins), 3.45 p.m. (Lit.), and 7 p.m. Holy and Week Days, 8.30 a.m. (Matins), and 8 p.m. Fri., 7.30 p.m. Holy Com., 8 a.m. and after Matins (Choral); Thurs. and Holy Days, 8 a.m.; Wed., 7.30 p.m.; Fri., 8 p.m.

STEPHEN, ST., Islington, Canonbury-rd, N. [6.] Sun., 11 a.m., 3.30 and 7 p.m. Wed., 7.30 p.m. Holy Com., 1st Sun. after mng. serv., and 3rd Sun. after evg. serv.

STEPHEN, ST., Lewisham. [2.] Sun., 10.30 a.m. (Matins), 4 p.m. (Lit.), and 7 p.m. Week Days, 8 a.m. (Matins) and 5.30 p.m. Holy Days, 10.30 a.m. (Matins), and 8 p.m. Wed. and Fri., noon and 8 p.m.(Lit.) Holy Com., Sun, 7 a.m, 8 a.m., 9 a.m., and after Matins; Holy Days, 7 a.m., 8 a.m., and 11.15 a.m.; Thurs., 8.30 a.m.; other Week Days, 7.15 a.m.

STEPHEN, ST., North Bow, E. [6.] Sun., 11 a.m., 6.30 and 8.15 p.m. Thurs., 7 p.m. Holy Com., last Sun., after mng. serv.; 1st Sun., 8.30 a.m.; 2nd Sun., after evg. serv.

STEPHEN, ST., Spitalfields, Commercial-st, E. [6.] Sun., 11 a.m., and 3 and 7 p.m. Wed., 8 p.m. Holy Com., 1st Sun., 8.30 a.m.; 2nd, after mng. serv.; 3rd, after evg. serv.

STEPHEN, ST., Walbrook, E.C. [15.] Sun., 11 a.m. and 6.45 p.m. Holy Com., 1st Sun., after mng. and also after evg. serv.

STEPHEN, ST., Westminster, Rochester-row, S.W. [5.] Sun., 11 a.m., 3.30 p.m. (Special), and 7 p.m. Holy and Week Days, except Fri., 10 a.m. (Matins) and 6 p.m.; Fri., 9 a.m.; Wed. and Thurs., 8 p.m. Holy Com., Sun., 8.30 a.m., also on 1st, 3rd, and 5th, after mng. serv. (Choral); Holy Days, 10 a.m. and 6 p.m.

THOMAS, ST., King-st, Regent-st, W. [1.] Sun., 11 a.m. (Matins), 3.30 p.m. (Lit.), and 7 p.m.; Wed. and Fri., noon (Lit.) Holy Com., Sun., 8 a.m., 9.30 a.m., and noon (Choral); Holy and Week Days 8 a.m.; Thurs. and Holy Days, 7 a.m.

THOMAS, ST., Newton-rd, Westbourne-gr, W. [2.] Sun., 11 a.m. and 7 p.m. Wed. and Fri., noon. Holy Com., 1st Sun., evg.; 2nd and 4th, 11 a.m.; 3rd and 5th, 8.45 a.m.

THOMAS, ST., Orchard-st, W. [5.] Sun., 11 a.m., 3.30 p.m., and 7 p.m. Daily, 8 a.m. and 5.30 p.m.; Wed. and Fri., noon (Lit.); and Wed., 7.45 p.m. Holy Com., 2nd Sun., 9 a.m.; 1st and 3rd Sun., after mng. serv.; 4th Sun., 7 p.m.; every Sun. except 2nd, 8 a.m.

THOMAS, ST., Stepney, Arbour-st-west, E. [6.] Sun., 11 a.m. (Matins and Lit.), 4 p.m., and 6.30 p.m. Thurs., 7.30 p.m. Holy Com., 1st and 3rd Sun., 8 a.m. and 8 p.m.; 2nd, 4th, and 5th Sun., after mng. serv.

TRANSFIGURATION, Algernon-rd, Lewisham. [2.] Sun., 11 a.m., 4 p.m. (Children), and 7 p.m. Tues. and Thurs., 8 p.m. Holy Com., Sun., 8 a.m.; Wed. and Holy Days, 7 a.m.

TRINITY, HOLY, Bishop's-rd, Paddington, W. [1.] Sun., 11 a.m. (Matins), 3.30 p.m., and 7 p.m. Holy and Week Days, 8.15 a.m. (Matins). Wed., 11 a.m. (Matins); Fri., noon (Lit.). Holy Com. Sun., 8 a.m.; 1st and 3rd Sun., after Matins; last Sun., after evg. serv.

TRINITY, HOLY, Carlisle-st, Lambeth, S.E. [6.] Sun., 11 a.m. and 7.30 p.m. Wed., 7.30 p.m. Holy Com., Sun., 8 a.m.; 1st Sun., after mng. serv.; 3rd Sun., after evg. serv.

TRINITY, HOLY, Church-st, Shoreditch, E. [1.] Sun., 11 a.m. (Matins), 4 p.m. (Lit.), and 7 p.m. Holy and Week Days, 10 a.m. (Matins) and 8 p.m. Week Days, 8 p.m. Holy Com., Sun., 8 a.m., 9 a.m., and 11 a.m. (Choral); Holy Days, 8 a.m.; Week Days, 8 a.m.

TRINITY, HOLY, Great New-st, E.C. [5.] Sun., 11 a.m. and 7 p.m. Holy Com., 2nd and last Sun. after mng. serv. Special Services in Advent and Lent.

TRINITY, HOLY, Marylebone-rd, N.W. [12.] Sun., 11 a.m., 3.30, 7, and 9 p.m. Holy and Week Days, 8 a.m. (Matins) and 8 p.m. Wed. and Fri., 11 a.m. Holy Com., Sun., 8 a.m.; Holy Days, 11 a.m.

TRINITY, HOLY, Westminster, Vauxhall-br-rd, S.W. [2.] Sun., 11 a.m. (Matins), 3.30 p.m. (Lit.), and 7 p.m. Week Days, 10 a.m. and 5.30 p.m., except Wed. and Fri., when the services are at 10 a.m. and 8 p.m. Holy Days, 11.15 a.m. and 8 p.m. Holy Com., Sun., 8 a.m., and after Matins (Choral); Holy Days, 8 a.m.

VEDAST, ST., Foster-lane, E.C. [2.] Sun., 11 a.m. and 7 p.m. (Choral). Holy Com., Sun., 11 a.m.; Holy Days, 8 a.m.

WHITEHALL CHAPEL ROYAL, S.W. [2.] Sun., 11 a.m. and 3 p.m. Holy Com., 1st Sun. after mng. serv.

St. Paul's Cathedral. [2.] Sun., 8 and 10.30 a.m., 3.15 p.m., and 7 p.m. Holy and Week Days, 8 a.m., 10 a.m., 1.15, 4, and 8 p.m. Also on Week Days (short service), 1.15 p.m. Holy Com., Sun. and Holy Days, 8 a.m. and after mng. serv. (Choral); High Festivals, 7.15 and 8 a.m.; Week Days, 8 a.m.

Westminster Abbey. Sun., 10 a.m., 3 p.m., and during Advent and Lent, and from Easter to end of July, 7 p.m. Week Days, 8.30 and 10 a.m., and 3 p.m. Holy Com., Sun., 8 a.m., and after mng. serv.; Holy Days, after mng. serv.; and occasionally at 8 a.m. only, or 8 a.m. and noon.

Cisterns.—The water supplied to London householders is so bad in itself, even when it is first turned on, that it is a pity to run any risk of having it made even worse than it is. All cisterns should be thoroughly cleaned out about once a month, and the careful housekeeper will not only order the job to be done, but will himself see that his orders are executed. The family medical man and the family medical man and the family medical man would make much smaller incomes than they do now, if all cisterns were regularly seen to.—(*See* ANALYSTS *and* VESTRIES.)

City and Guilds of London Institute, for the advancement of technical education. This association, as its name imports, is supported by the Corporation and Livery Companies of the City of London, some of which latter have subscribed large sums towards its establishment and building fund.

The four great divisions of its work are : (1) The maintenance of a Central Institution of a Technical College at Finsbury ; (2) the organisation of technical classes, and the encouragement of technical instruction by the payment of grants to teachers on the results of technological examinations ; (3) the establishment and maintenance of local technical colleges, of which the Finsbury Technical College is the most important ; (4) the subvention of technical colleges in some of the principal manufacturing centres.

The Central Institution, Exhibition-rd, provides technical instruction for persons desiring to qualify as (1) technical teachers ; (2) mechanical, civil, electrical, and chemical engineers ; (3) principals, superintendents, and managers of manufacturing works.

Technological examinations are held annually, in May, in fifty trade subjects. Money prizes. medals, and certificates are awarded on the results of the examinations.

The Finsbury Technical College in Tabernacle-row is in thorough working order, and in 1887 numbered over 1000 students, and has for its objects the education of : (1) persons wishing to receive a scientific and technical training for intermediate posts in industrial works ; (2) apprentices, journeymen, and foremen who desire to receive evening instruction in the theory and principles of science underlying their trades ; (3) pupils from higher elementary and middle schools preparing for higher technical instruction at the Central Institution or elsewhere.

The South London Technical Art School provides instruction in drawing, painting, and modelling applied to all kinds of decorative art-work.

Full particulars of the work of the Institute may be obtained from the offices of the respective schools, or from the Assistant Secretary, Mr. R. Harrison.

City Carlton Club, St. Swithin's-la, E.C.—In connection with the Conservative party, and designed to promote its objects. Number of members, 1,000. The election of members is vested solely in the committee, and is by ballot. Entrance fees and subs.: for town members, £15 15s. and £8 8s. ; and for country members, £10 10s. and £5 5s. respectively.

City Companies. — There are upwards of eighty City Companies, few of which have at the present time much to do with the trade which they are supposed to represent. Indeed, it may be said that the most onerous duties which fall to the lot of many of the governing bodies of these institutions consist in the management of wealthy charities, and in the exercise of a profuse hospitality. To this, as to all other rules, there are, of course, honourable exceptions.

The most interesting of the halls will be found described under their proper alphabetical headings, and a list of the companies themselves is here appended. Elaborate information in regard to fees payable upon taking up the freedom of any of the companies, by patrimony, servitude, purchase, or otherwise ; upon admission to the livery, and upon election to the courts, together with much interesting matter respecting the charities under the control of the several companies, will be found set forth in Messrs. Collingridge's CITY DIRECTORY. The following is a list of the livery companies and their halls. A supplementary list is added of the companies who are without halls :

Apothecaries, Water - la ; Armourers & Braziers, Coleman-st.

Bakers, Harp-la, E.C. ; Barbers, Monkwell-st ; Brewers, Addle-st ; Butchers, Eastcheap.

Carpenters, Throgmorton - av ; Clothworkers, Mincing-la ; Coach and Coach Harness Makers, Noble-st ; Coopers, Basinghall-st ; Cordwainers, Cannon - st ; Curriers, London-wall ; Cutlers, Cloak-la.

Drapers, 27, Throgmorton - st ; Dyers, 10, Dowgate-hill.

Fishmongers, Adelaide-pl, London-br ; Fletchers, St. Mary Axe ; Founders, 13, St. Swithin's-la.

Girdlers, Basinghall-st ; Goldsmiths, Foster-la ; Grocers, Grocers' Hall-ct ; Gunmakers, Commercial-rd.

Haberdashers, 31, Gresham-st.

Innholders, 6, College-st, Dowgate - hill ; Ironmongers, Fenchurch-st.

Joiners, Joiners' Hall-bdgs.

Leathersellers, St. Helen's-pl.

Mercers, 4, Ironmonger-la ; Merchant Taylors, 30, Threadneedle-st.

Painters (otherwise Painter Stainers), 9, Little Trinity - la ; Pewterers, 15, Lime-st.

Saddlers, 141, Cheapside ; Salters, St. Swithin's-la ; Skinners, 8, Dowgate-hill ; Stationers, Stationers' Hall-ct.

Tallow Chandlers, Dowgate-hl.

Vintners, 68½, Upper Thames-st.

Watermen and Lightermen, 18, St. Mary-at-hill ; Wax Chandlers, Gresham-st.

Basket Makers, Blacksmiths, Bowyers, Borderers (Embroiderers), Clockmakers, Cooks, Distillers, Fanmakers, Farriers, Feltmakers. Framework Knitters, Fruiterers, Glass-sellers, Glaziers, Glovers, Gold and Silver Wire Drawers, Horners, Loriners, Masons, Musicians, Needle Makers, Patten Makers, Plasterers, Playing Card Makers, Plumbers, Poulters, Scriveners, Shipwrights, Spectacle Makers, Tilers and Bricklayers, Tinplate Workers, Turners, Upholders, Weavers, Wheelwrights, Woolmen.

City Liberal Club, Walbrook, E.C.—Was instituted shortly after the General Election of 1874, for the purpose of promoting intercourse between Liberals, and to afford means for remedying the disorganisation into which the Liberal party had fallen in the City. Election by committee. Candidates are put up for election in the order in which they appear in the book, excepting those of members of either House of Parliament, and of others who, in the opinion of the committee, have rendered special services to the Liberal cause, to whom precedence shall be given. The political business of the club is conducted by a council, elected at general meetings of the club. Life members, £126; ordinary members, entrance £21, subscription £10 10s. Country members, with no residence or office within twenty miles, entrance, £10 10s.; subscription, £6 6s.

City of London (The).—The Municipality of the City originally exercised jurisdiction over London proper, but the town has so outgrown its original limits that the Corporation is now entirely surrounded by rival powers, and may be called in truth an *imperium in imperio.* The City is divided into wards, each of which returns a member of the Upper House or Aldermen, and in certain proportions the members of the Common Council or House of Commons. The Lord Mayor, who during his year of office is the constitutional king of the City, is elected by the Livery from the members of the Court of Aldermen below the chair. Two Aldermen are returned by the Livery for the Court to choose which of the two shall be Lord Mayor. Occasionally an extremely popular Lord Mayor is re-elected for a second term of office, and instances have been known where a still longer lease of power has been granted; on the other hand, the alderman first below the chair has been passed over and a junior preferred. The Lord Mayor exercises high judicial functions as chief magistrate of the City. The City has from time immemorial enjoyed the great privilege of appointing its own judicial functionaries, and many highly distinguished lawyers have figured on the roll of the Recorders of the City of London. The Sheriffs of London are also conjointly Sheriff of the county of Middlesex, and are elected by the Livery. The City has its own police,

and the Livery possesses many privileges conferred and confirmed by a series of royal charters, of which they are properly tenacious. Within the boundaries of the City the Corporation has taxing powers, notably in the case of coal and wine dues. It is difficult to attain to any exact knowledge of the manner in which the civic revenues are expended, but, although it is quite possible that a more economical system of expenditure might be adopted, the vast sums of money disbursed of late years in improvements of great public advantage, such as the Holborn Viaduct, the great markets in Smithfield, Billingsgate, Islington, and Deptford, &c., speak volumes in favour of the public spirit of the Corporation. The official palace of the Lord Mayor is the Mansion House, the head-quarters of the Corporation are at the Guildhall. In the Guildhall also is the magnificent library, which is open free and without restriction daily from 10 till 9. It contains some 60,000 volumes of books of all sorts, except on theology, and, as a specialty, of books on London, science, and the arts, and in the Free Reading Room will be found a dictionary of every language, as well as directories for every English county, besides foreign and colonial. The numbers in 1887 were 380,315, giving an average daily attendance of 1,344 persons. There is also a Local Museum containing Roman, Saxon, and Mediæval Antiquities found in the City, and a Fine Art Gallery has been lately opened. Amongst the noteworthy institutions which are supported by the Corporation may be mentioned the Freemen's Orphan School, in which 150 children of both sexes, admitted on the nomination of members of the Common Council, are maintained, educated, and clothed free of cost. A sum of £4,000 is anually appropriated to this object. The City of London School and the School of Music are also assisted by the Corporation. Several City livings are in the gift of the Court of Common Council, namely, St. Peter's, Cornhill, St. Margaret Pattens (alternate with the Crown, by whom the present rector was presented), and St. James's, Duke's-pl, and St. Catherine Cree (alternate with Magdalene College, Cambridge, which has the next pre-

sentation).—(*Ana see* FREEDOM OF THE CITY.) For the Courts of Law within the City, *see* LAW COURTS.

The following list shows the principal officers of the Corporation. It may be noted that the Chamberlain is the Treasurer; that the Town Clerk transacts all the municipal business, is the City Secretary and Recording Officer, and attends meetings of the various courts and committees; that the Comptroller is the Conveyancing Officer; that the Remembrancer is the Ceremonial and Parliamentary Officer of the Corporation; and that the Secondary is permanent agent of the Undersheriffs.

(A In the appointment of the Court of Aldermen. B In the appointment of the Court of Common Council. C In the approval of the Court of Common Council. D In the appointment of the Livery. E In the appointment of the Library Committee.)

A Recorder, Sir T. Chambers, Knt., Q.C. (1878.)

D Chamberlain, Benj. Scott, Esq., F.R.A.S. (1858).

B Town-Clerk, Sir John Braddick Monckton, F.S.A. (1873).

B Common Serjeant, Sir William Thos. Charley, Q.C., D.C.L. (1878).

B Judge of the City of London Court, R. Malcolm Kerr, LL.D. (1859).

C Assistant Judge of the Mayor's Court, F. Roxburgh Esq. (1887).

B Commissioner of the City Police, Colonel Sir James Fraser, K.C.B. (1863).

B Comptroller of the Chamber and of the Bridge House Estates, John Alexander Brand, Esq. (1879).

B Remembrancer, Gabriel Peter Goldney, Esq. (1882).

B Solicitor, Henry Homewood Crawford, Esq. (1885).

B Secondary, Thomas Roderick, Esq. (1885).

B Coroner for London & Southwark, Sam. F. Langham, Esq., 10, Bartlett's-bdgs, Holborn (1884)

A Steward of Southwark, Sir T. Chambers, Q.C. (1884).

B Clerk of the Peace, Edward James Read, Esq. (1865).

B Architect and Surveyor, A. M. Peebles, Esq. (1887).

B Head Master of the City of London School, Rev. Edwin Abbott Abbott, D.D. (1865).

B Head Master of the Freemen's Orphan School, Marcus Tulloch Cormack, Esq., M.A. (1867).

B High Bailiff of Southwark, Thomas Roderick, Esq. (1885).

B Registrar of the Mayor's Court, Richard Jas. Pawley, Esq. (1875).

B Sword Bearer, George James White Winzar, Esq. (1874).

B Common Crier and Serjeant-at-Arms, W. R. Baggallay, Esq. (1885).

E Librarian, W. H. Overall, Esq., F.S.A. (1865).

B City Marshal, Major E. B. Burnaby (1886).

Election Days.—Lord Mayor, Sept. 29; if Sunday, then 28th. Sheriffs, June 24; if Sunday, then 25th. Common Council, Dec. 21; if Sunday, then 22nd.

John Watney, Esq., Mercers' Hall, Cheapside, for all information *re* Gresham Lectures.

City of London Club, 19, Old Broad-st, E.C.—For merchants, bankers, and shipowners, principals in wholesale mercantile, manufacturing, or trading establishments. Entrance, £31 10s.; subscription, £10 10s.

City of London College (The) (EVENING CLASSES FOR YOUNG MEN AND WOMEN), White-st, Moorgate-street Station (Map 8).—This useful institution had its origin in the Metropolitan Evening Classes for Young Men which were founded at Crosby Hall in 1848. In 1860 a move was made to Sussex Hall, Leadenhall-street, where the classes were carried on under the name of the City of London College, and where, in little more than twenty years, the number of students increased from 750 to 1,500. The lease of the premises in Leadenhall-st expired in 1882, and the council then took the piece of land in White-st on which they erected, at a cost of about £15,000, their present building, which is capable of accommodating 4,000 students for evening instruction. The classes are very numerous and afford instruction in very many branches of knowledge, and there is no lack of prizes and scholarships to stimulate

the energies of the students. Reading and coffee rooms, and a library, are also provided.

The principal examinations are the College "Annual," when certificates and prizes are awarded, the most important of which are the "Lubbock Testimonial Scholarship," founded in honour of the passing of the Bank Holidays Act, and of the value of £10; the Saddlers' Guild Jubilee Prize of £10 10s.; the Society of Arts' examination; and those of the Science and Art Department, South Kensington; the City and Guilds of London Institute; and the London University. For full particulars of class-work, prizes, fees, &c., which are too voluminous to be given here, application should be made to the secretary and registrar at the college. The government of the institution is in the hands of the council, consisting of the President and Principal, ten vice-presidents and twenty other members, the election of whom, as to the ten vice-presidents and ten of the twenty members, is in the hands of members and registered students, the remaining ten members on the council being elected by members only; this judicious arrangement securing to students a voice in the government of the institution. Donors to the funds of the college have, in proportion to the amount subscribed, certain privileges in regard to sending students to the college free of expense. Since the number of students has been upwards of 1,000 the institution has been self-supporting. NEAREST *Ry. Stn.,* Moorgate-st (Met.); *Omnibus Rte.,* Moorgate-st; *Cab Rank,* Finsbury-pav.

City of London School, Thames Embankment, near Blackfriars-br (Map 7).—Established by the Corporation under Act of Parliament in 1834, and endowed with an annual sum derived from estates bequeathed in 1442 by John Carpenter, once town clerk. The object of the school is to furnish a liberal and useful education to the sons of persons engaged in professions or trades, without the necessity of removing them from the personal care and control of their parents. Boys are admissible between the ages of 7 and 15. Forms for admission, with all other information, may be obtained

of the secretary. The charge for each pupil is £12 12s. a year, payable £4 4s. each term in advance, up to the age of twelve, and after that £15 15s. a year, payable £5 5s. each term in advance, the only extras being drawing and shorthand. Certain masters receive boys as boarders, and dinner is supplied to day boarders at a moderate charge. The prizes and scholarships at the school are unusually numerous and valuable, as are also the scholarships tenable at the universities. It is satisfactory to be able to add that these rewards of merit have produced most gratifying results. The history of the City of London School is writ large on the honour lists of both universities. NEAREST *Ry. Stns.,* Blackfriars - br (Dis.) and Ludgate (L. C. & D.); *Omnibus Rtes.,* New Bridge-st and Fleet-st; *Cab Rank,* New Bridge-st.

City of London Society of Artists, formed for the purpose of holding periodical exhibitions of works in oil and water-colours, and sculpture, and for promoting the technical education of art in the City of London. The inaugural exhibition took place in the spring of 1880, in the hall of the Skinners' Company. The annual subscription is £5 5s. The liability of each member is limited to £10, exclusive of annual subscription. Fellows are also admitted by election of the Council, and pay an annual subscription of £2 2s. Fellows are entitled to free admission for self and friend to all opening ceremonies, private views, exhibitions, lectures, and two conversazioni. Commission on sales of pictures by members, 5 per cent., and 10 per cent. for non-members. For rules, applications for membership, and regulations for exhibitions, apply to W. J. Ferguson, Hon. Sec., 7, Garfield-villas, Woronzow-rd, St. John's Wood.

City Prison (Map 3), situated at Holloway, covers, with its appurtenances, about ten acres, and cost about £100,000. It will hold 436 prisoners, and is constructed on the "panopticon principle, with six wings. It is a good specimen of the style, and may be inspected by order from the Home Secretary. NEAREST *Ry. Stn.,* Camden-rd (Midland), a long half-mile; *Omnibus Rte.,* Camden-rd; *Tramway* Holloway-rd.

Civil Service Commissioners, Cannon-row, Westminster. Hours 10 to 5.—NEAREST *Ry. Stn.*, Westminster-br ; *Omnibus Rtes.*, Parliament-st, Victoria-st, Westminster-br, and Strand ; *Cab Rank*, Palace-yard.

Clare Market, or what is left of it, lies at the western side of Lincoln's-inn, on ground once occupied by the monastery of St. Clare. It is a market without a market-house ; a collection of streets and lanes, where the shops are tenanted by butchers, greengrocers, &c., and where the roadways are crowded with costermongers' carts, and the kerbs and kennels with stalls where nearly everything is vended. Here herrings or mackerel, as the season may be, are sold at marvellously low prices; while the vegetables, equally cheap, are fresh and excellent in quality. The din and bustle last till midnight, and it is a strange phase of life to study the faces and listen to the conversation of people bargain-hunting in this market.

Cleopatra's Needle (Map 7), on the Victoria Embankment. This famous monolith of granite, from Alexandria, originally stood at Heliopolis, and was presented to this country by Mehemet Ali in 1819. No ministry was bold enough to face the difficulty and expense of transporting it across the Bay of Biscay, and for many years it lay half buried by sand at Alexandria, at the foot of its still erect sister, which, according to some people, is the real original Cleopatra's Needle. In the Alexandrian sand the English obelisk would probably have remained until the end of time, but for the untiring exertions of the late General Sir James Alexander, who ried hard to induce the Government to bring it over, and the public spirit of the late Sir (then Mr.) Erasmus Wilson. Mr. Wilson put down £10,000 for the expenses of transport, and Mr. John Dixon, contractor, undertook to deliver the monument in the Thames for that sum on the principle of "no cure, no pay"—no obelisk, no £10,000. A special cylinder boat was designed, in which the needle was encased, and justified Mr. Dixon's expectations by making good weather of it until it became unmanageable and untenantable in a heavy gale in the Bay of Biscay. Abandoned by

the steamer which had it in tow, after the sacrifice of six lives in a last gallant attempt to save the Cleopatra, few people doubted that the Needle would find its last resting-place at the bottom of the sea. Fortunately a passing steamer succeeded in securing it, and towed it into Ferrol. Much ingenuity was shown in the machinery designed for its erection, the obelisk being over 68 feet in height, and weighing 180 tons. NEAREST *Steamboat Piers* and *Bridges*, Waterloo and Charing ✠ ; *Ry. Stns.*, Charing ✠ (Dis. and S.E.) ; *Omnibus Rtes.*, Waterloo-br and Strand.

Clergy Club, 135, New Bond-st, W. (now called NATIONAL CHURCH CLUB).—Established as a proprietary club in 1883, on a social and non-political basis, for members of the Church of England (clerical and lay), or of Churches in communion therewith. A drawing-room has been provided for the exclusive use of ladies introduced by members, and there is also a dining and refreshment-room for ladies accompanied by members. Election by committee. Entrance fee, £5 5s. ; subscription : town members, £4 4s. ; country members, £2 2s.

Clothworkers' Company (The), an offshoot of the Drapers and Merchant Taylors, was originally incorporated by Edward IV. as "The Fraternity of the Assumption of the Blessed Virgin Mary of the Shearmen of London." In Queen Elizabeth's reign the company was reincorporated as the Clothworkers. The present hall, which stands in Mincing-lane, was completed in 1870, and is about as gorgeous a building as its admirers could wish. The effects produced by the judicious blending of various-coloured marble, and the ingenious designs of the decorator illustrating the wealth and commerce of the nation, are the most conspicuous ornaments. Two gilded statues of deceased monarchs, which stand in the hall, could well be spared ; but to these relics of a bygone art the company, we are informed, is singularly attached. In one of the reception rooms is a cartoon by Mr. Wm. Beverley, representing a young apprentice saving a maiden from drowning in the river Thames. The lad's name was Osborne. His gallantry

brought him the favour of his master, who took him into partnership, and gave him the rescued daughter for a wife. Osborne was the ancestor of the present Duke of Leeds. Samuel Pepys was a member of the Clothworkers' Company, and gave it a silver loving-cup. The free schools belonging to the company are in the Isle of Man, and at Sutton Valence.

Clubs.—The following are the principal London Clubs, particulars being given under their respective heads. Those marked * are for ladies and gentlemen ; to those marked † ladies are admitted as visitors ; while ladies only are eligible for the Alexandra and Ladies' Victoria Clubs.

*Albemarle, Alexandra, Alpine, Army and Navy, Arthur's, Arts, Arundel, Athenæum.

†Bachelors', Badminton, Beefsteak, Boodle's, Brooks's, Burlington Fine Arts.

Carlton, City Carlton, City Liberal, City of London, †Clergy, Cobden, Cocoa Tree, Conservative, Constitutional, Crichton.

Devonshire.

East India United Service Farmers'.

Garrick, Grafton, Green Room, Gresham, Guards'.

Hogarth, †Hurlingham.

International, Isthmian.

Junior Army and Navy, Junior Athenæum, Junior Carlton, Junior Constitutional, Junior Garrick, Travellers', Junior United Service.

Kennel.

Ladies' Victoria, Lancaster, Law Society, †Lyric.

Marlborough, Military.

National, National Conservative, National Church, National Liberal, National Union, Naval and Military, New, New Oxford and Cambridge, New Salisbury, New Thames Yacht, New University, Northbrook.

Old Paulines, Oriental, Orleans, Oxford and Cambridge.

Pall Mall, Paulatim, Portland, Pratt's, Press, Primrose.

Raleigh, Ranelagh, Reform, Royal London Yacht, Royal Thames Yacht.

St. George's, St. James's, St. Stephen's, Savage, Savile, Scandinavian, Scottish, *Skating, Smithfield.

Thatched House, Travellers, Turf.

Union, Unionist, United, United Service, United University.

Vernon Town and River, Victoria.

Wellington, White Friars, Whitehall, White's, Windham.

† York.

Coaching Clubs and Road Coaches.

The Benson Driving Club, established in 1807 and broken up in 1854, consisting of twenty-five members, was the last of the old coaching clubs known to the past generation; as the Four Horse Club, which was organised a year later, expired in 1826, and the Richmond Driving Club did not last long. In 1856, however, the late Mr. Morritt succeeded in getting thirty good men together, and established the present Four-in-hand Driving Club, which soon was found to be too exclusive for the growing taste for the road, and in 1870 Mr. George Goddard and a few other gentlemen laid the foundation of the Coaching Club, which on its first appearance in Hyde-pk, turned out twenty-two drags, and last year the list of members (confined to 100) was full, with many aspirants on the books. Both clubs meet twice a year, generally at the Magazine in Hyde-pk: the Four-in-hand Club's first meet being mostly the Wednesday before the Derby, and the other gathering later on, full notice of which is always given in the sporting and daily papers. These clubs have no habitation or abode, but drive from their meets to dine or lunch at Greenwich, Richmond, the Crystal Palace, or elsewhere; and the want of some congenial rendezvous was felt so much that in 1875 Mr. Hurman opened a Club at 100, Piccadilly, where "The Badminton" is now established, with every luxury for its *habitués*, and capital stabling for fifty horses. The Club has always one or two teams with a coach, break, &c., in the yard, and the Coaching Club hold their annual and committee meetings there. The Duke of Beaufort is president, as he also is of the Four-in-hand and Coaching Clubs. The "Brighton Age" being taken off the road in 1862, there were no stage coaches running out of London until the spring of 1866, from which date the present revival of road coaching must date, when "The Old Times" commenced the new era

on the same road; and each year since there has been a steady increase, until in 1875 there were eleven coaches starting from the "White Horse Cellars," in Piccadilly. The Virginia Water, the "Old Times," Mr. Selby, proprietor and coachman, leaves during the summer months at 10.45 a.m., and gets back at 6.30 p.m., giving the passengers plenty of time for luncheon and inspection of the beautiful lake, &c.; this season the coach will run *viâ* Oatlands-pk, thus giving a much more extended drive, and river scenery; in the winter the times are changed, and it only goes as far as Oatlands Park Hotel, but the coach goes on all the year round, and has not been off the road a day since Nov. 4, 1878. Capt. Knatchbull, Messrs. Beckett, Wilson, and Blackwood, are the most frequent drivers of this coach. The Guildford coach, the "New Times," Mr. Walter Shoolbred, sole proprietor, with Tom Thorogood for his professional, leaves Hatchett's at 11 a.m., and gets back to Piccadilly at 7 p.m. The Dorking "Perseverance" (Perrin, guard), route *viâ* South Kensington, Barnes, Surbiton, Worcester-pk, Ewell, Epsom, and Boxhill, leaves the "White Horse Cellars" at 11.10 a.m., arriving back at 6.40 p.m. The "Wonder" runs between Piccadilly and St. Alban's every day (Sundays excepted), starting at 10.45 a.m., and arriving back at 6.15 p.m. There will also be a coach daily from Piccadilly to Bentley Priory and back, leaving town at 11.40 a.m., and being due on the return journey at 6 p.m. Intending passengers by any of the above London coaches can secure their places, and pay their fares, which average between 3d. and 4d. per mile, at the "White Horse Cellars," Piccadilly, where Messrs. Banks Bros. are always ready to give every information. The Provincial coaches book from the chief hotels in the towns from which they start.

Coal Exchange (Map 8).

This building, situate at the corner of St. Mary-at-Hill and Thames-st, facing the Custom House, was opened in 1849 by the Prince Consort, accompanied by the Prince of Wales and the Princess Royal, in the mayoralty of Alderman Duke, who was made a baronet in honour of the occasion. The building was designed by

Mr. J. B. Bunning, F.S.A., the late City architect. It is in shape a rotunda, 60 ft. in diameter; it has three galleries, and is crowned by a dome 74 ft. high, which rests on eight piers. The walls of the interior are decorated with views of the Wallsend, Percy, and other celebrated collieries, some of the principal ports from whence coal is shipped, and inside the dome are paintings of specimens of the flowers and fossil plants found in the coal measures. On the galleries are a few cases containing specimens of coral and fossil plants found in different parts of the world. The floor is made with 4,000 pieces of inlaid wood, and represents the face of a mariner's compass. In the centre are the City shield, anchor, &c.: the dagger blade in the arms being a piece of a mulberry-tree planted by Peter the Great when he worked as a shipwright in Deptford dockyard. In excavating for the foundation of the present building, the remains of an old Roman bath were brought to light, which have now been enclosed, and can be seen upon application to one of the beadles. The offices in the building are occupied by coal factors, and others connected with the trade; the three trade societies; and the Corporation officers, who enter all ships bringing coal into the port of London, and collect the City dues on all coal brought within certain limits. The money collected is afterwards employed for metropolitan improvements. The exchange is the property of the Corporation, and a market is held there three days a week, on Mon., Wed., and Fri. NEAREST *Ry. Stns.*, Monument (or Mark-la) (Dis. and Met.), and Cannon-st (S.E.); *Omnibus Rte.*, K. William-st; *Cab Rank*, Great Tower-hill.

Cobden Club.

The Cobden Club has for its object the diffusion in all parts of the world of the economic and political principles with which Richard Cobden's name is associated. Election by committee. Subscription, £3 3s. There is no club house. Secretary's address, 6, Upper Park-rd, Hampstead, N.W.

Cocoa-Tree Club, 64, St.

James's-st.—Was the Tory Chocolate House of Queen Anne's reign, the Whig Coffee House being the St. James's, lower down in the same street. There is no special qualification; the elections are now vested in the members of the club, two black balls excluding when 20 members or less shall vote. If more than 20 vote, one black ball in every ten shall exclude, but no election shall take place unless 10 votes are recorded. Entrance fee, £5 5s.; subscription, £4 4s.

Coffee Public Houses.— In 1879 a company, of which Lord Shaftesbury was president, made the first attempt on a large scale to give the lower section of the inhabitants of London a chance of escape from the public-house. The object of this company was to establish attractive places of refreshment in the "more densely peopled parts of London, and elsewhere, to serve as a counter-attraction to the public-house and gin palace." It would appear, from the interesting *brochure* by Mr. Hepple Hall, that the enterprise for some reason or another did not succeed so well as its promoters expected, and the houses opened under the auspices of the company were afterwards leased to a private individual, but the results attained could not be called altogether satisfactory. In 1877 the Coffee Public House Asso. was organised under the presidency of the Duke of Westminster, for the purpose of helping forward the movement generally, but the association was dissolved in March, 1881. Again to quote Mr. Hall: "Adequate provision for the wants of the population of London alone requires that coffee public-houses should be numbered, not by tens or scores, but by hundreds. It was the business of the association: 1. To ascertain the localities in which Coffee Publics can be most aptly planted, and the character of the structure and fittings best suited to each locality. 2. To investigate the schemes submitted to it by those who desire its help, and the claim which each scheme has upon it. 3. To make the necessary advances upon the most expedient terms, and whenever the conditions of success are sufficiently assured." It will be seen that the last-mentioned clause distinguished this society from any other of its class. It was a promoter of coffee taverns, not a trader in them.

Some of the northern towns contain finer examples of the modern coffee public-house or coffee-tavern than are yet to be seen in London. The movement, however, has made rapid progress in the metropolis since 1876, the date of the formation of the People's Café Co., which took the lead in the establishment of these houses on a strictly commercial basis. Some few coffee public-houses of the modern type were opened at about the same time by private individuals or local committees, the most notable being the "Rose and Crown Coffee Palace," opposite the barracks at Knightsbridge. The success of this house has led to the opening of others on a somewhat similar plan, but the general tendency has been more and more to lift the movement out of the sphere of mere philanthropy by the formation of companies with limited liability, which for the most part adopt ordinary business methods and endeavour to secure such profits as shall be fairly remunerative to the shareholders. Circumstances, into which it is needless to enter here, have tended to retard the development of the People's Café Co., which nevertheless has done very useful work, and appears to have a prosperous future before it. Its establishments are at 61, St. Paul's-churchyard, 1, Ludgate Circus Buildings, and 61, Gracechurch-st, and are arranged for a middle-class trade. The Coffee Tavern Co., which was next in the field, has adhered closely to its original design of catering strictly for the working classes, though some of its more recently opened houses contain "first-class bars" or rooms where refreshments are served at increased rates. At several of their houses lodgings may be obtained by working men.

The following are the names of companies, with the number of establishments in London belonging to each, in December, 1887:—People's Café Co., 3; Coffee Tavern Co., 8; Lockhart's Cocoa Rooms, 43; Kiosk and Coffee Stall Co., Bow-st, W.C. The last-named company was formed by members of the Coffee Public House Asso. for the purpose of opening "kiosks" for the supply of refreshments in the parks and other public places, and also with the view of introducing improvements in the quality of the non-intoxicating beverages sold to the public. The kiosk near the Broad Walk in the Regent's-pk

is the property of this company. Some idea of the progress made during the years 1878-80 may be gathered from the fact that the association in a recent report recorded the existence of 200 coffee-tavern companies in the United Kingdom, many of which have paid satisfactory dividends; and of 717 coffee public-houses, while no doubt many more of the latter have been opened of which the association had no information.

Messrs. R. Etzensberger and Co., already well-known for their machines and appliances for brewing good tea and coffee, started at the end of 1884 a large coffee restaurant in Tottenham-court-rd, opposite Messrs. Shoolbred and Maple's, with the object of proving that a good cup of coffee and tea, with milk and sugar, can profitably be supplied at a penny a cup. For this purpose a large portion of the premises, comfortably fitted, is specially devoted to the working classes. There is also a separate first-class room, as well as on the first floor, lavatories and waiting-rooms for ladies and gentlemen. This establishment distinctly supplies a want, and probably will be the precursor of many similar coffee-houses.

Coldbath Fields (Map 8) was the great prison of Middlesex, and though covering a somewhat smaller space than the City Prison, contained considerably more than three times as many prisoners. Most of its inmates were removed in November, 1885, and it was closed in the spring of 1886, and handed over to the vestry of Clerkenwell. Artisans' dwellings are, it is stated, to be erected on the site of the old prison.

College of Arms (Royal). —(*See* HERALD'S COLLEGE.)

College of Surgeons (Royal), Lincoln's-inn-fields (Map 7), has a fine museum, library, and lecture theatre. In the council-room are portraits and busts of eminent surgeons, including Reynolds's portrait of John Hunter. The museum, generally known as the "Hunterian Museum," is open on the first four days of the week (except in Sept.), from 11 to 5 (Sat. 11 to 1) o'clock, to fellows and members of the college and of all learned societies, and to other visitors on giving their names and addresses. It originated in the purchase by Parliament of John

Hunter's museum in 1799. It contains one of the largest and best arranged collections in the world of specimens illustrating human and comparative anatomy, and also numerous preparations of morbid anatomy and of malformations. The series of skeletons and skulls of people of all races is very extensive, and includes that of the celebrated Irish giant, O'Brien, nearly eight feet high. There are also skeletons of gigantic whales, and of other animals of almost every kind. The osteological specimens are on the ground floor of the three large rooms ; the other parts, preserved in spirits, and interesting chiefly to professional visitors, are arranged in two galleries. The conservator is Prof. C. Stewart NEAREST *Ry. Stn.,* Temple (Dis.) ; *Omnibus Rtes.,* High Holborn and Strand ; *Cab Rank,* Lincoln's-inn-fields, Serle-st.

College Hall. — Residence or female University Students.— (*See* UNIVERSITY COLLEGE.)

Colombia. — No Ministry. VICE - CONSULATE, Ethelburga House, Bishopsgate-street, E.C. NEAREST *Ry. Stn.,* *Omnibus Rte.,* and *Cab Rank,* Bishopsgate-st.

Colonial Institute (The Royal), Northumberland-avenue, W.C., was established in 1868 with the object of "providing a place of meeting for all gentlemen connected with the Colonies and British India, and others taking an interest in Colonial and Indian affairs." It is under the presidency of H.R.H. the Prince of Wales. *Membership :* There are two classes of fellows, resident and non - resident, both elected by the council on the nomination of any two fellows. The former pay an entrance fee of £3, and an annual subscription of £2 ; the latter an entrance fee of £1 1s., and an annual subscription of £1 1s., increased to £2 when temporarily visiting the United Kingdom. Resident fellows can become life members on payment of £20, and non-resident fellows on payment of £10, in addition to the entrance fee. *Privileges of Fellows :* Use of house, papers, and library. All fellows, whether residing in England or the Colonies, have the annual volume of the proceedings of the institute forwarded to them.

Fellows are also privileged to be present at the evening meetings and to introduce one visitor, and to be present at the annual conversazione and to introduce a lady. Contributions to the library will be thankfully received. For further information application should be made to the Sec., at the Institute.

Colonial Office, Downing-st. Hours 10 to half-past 6. Open to the public from 11 to 6. NEAREST *Ry. Stns.,* Westminster-br and Charing ✠ (S.E. and Dis.) ; *Omnibus Rtes.,* Whitehall and Parliament-st ; *Cab Rank,* Palace-yard.

Columbia, British.— AGENCY-GENERAL, 33, Finsbury-cir, E.C. NEAREST *Ry. Stns.,* Mansion House (Dis.) and Moorgate-st (Met) ; *Omnibus Rtes.,* Moorgate-st and Old Broad-st ; *Cab Rank,* Finsbury-pavement.

Comedy Theatre (Royal), Panton-st (Map 7).—Opened on the 15th of October, 1881. The specialty of this so far very successful theatre is comic opera. A medium-sized theatre, sufficiently convenient, but not specially remarkable architecturally or decoratively. NEAREST *Ry. Stns.,* Charing ✠ (S.E. and Dis.) ; *Omnibus Rtes.,* Haymarket and Charing ✠ ; *Cab Rank,* Haymarket.

Commissionaires.— Office, 419, Strand, about 200 yards east of Charing ✠ Station, on opposite side of the way. The corps is formed of retired soldiers and sailors, of first-class character only, and is strictly disciplined. TARIFF FOR COMMISSIONAIRES ON PUBLIC POSTS.—*By Distance :* Half a mile or under, 2d. ; one mile, or over half, 3d. *By Time :* 6d. per hour, or 2d. per quarter ditto. When taken by time, the commissionaire is to do 2½ miles per hour if walking. Should the employer pay the fare of a commissionaire by rail, boat, or omnibus he may require him to execute his duty by the time tariff. This will be calculated according to the time actually consumed in his going from and returning to his post. The corps also undertakes an immense variety of work, including almost everything for which an "odd man" can well be utilised, and many branches of employment of a permanent character. The tariff and conditions of these numerous services are too extensive and complicated for insertion here, but can be obtained on application to the Secretary.

Commissioners of Sewers, Guildhall.—Hours 10 to 4, Saturdays 10 to 2. NEAREST *Ry. Stns.,* Mansion House and Moorgate-st ; *Omnibus Rtes.,* Cheapside and Moorgate-st ; *Cab Rank,* Lothbury.

Commissioners of Works, Hours 10 to 4, Saturdays, 10 to 1 (the office is closed on Christmas Day, the day following, Good Friday, and the Queen's Birthday), 12, Whitehall-place, S.W., with subdivision Royal Parks and Gardens.—NEAREST *Ry. Stn.,* Charing ✠ ; *Omnibus Rtes.,* Whitehall and Parliament-st ; *Cab Rank,* Horse Guards.

Committee of Council on Education, Whitehall, S.W., with subdivisions, Scotch Education Department and In spectors of Schools (hours 11 to 5) The Science and Art Department is at South Kensington. —NEAREST *Ry. Stn.,* Westminster-br ; *Omnibus Rtes.,* Whitehall and Parliament-st ; *Cab Rank,* Horse Guards.

Committee of County Court Judges, Treasury Chambers, Whitehall. Hours 11 to 4, Saturdays 10 to 1 ("holidays —Christmas Day, Good Friday, Sat. following, Easter Monday and Tuesday, Whit Monday, Bank-holiday in August, and any other day on which the offices may be closed by order of the Lord Chancellor ").—NEAREST *Ry. Stn.,* Westminster-br ; *Omnibus Rtes.,* Whitehall and Parliament-st ; *Cab Rank,* Horse Guards.

Committee of Privy Council for Trade, Whitehall Gardens, S.W., hours 11 to 5. —NEAREST *Ry. Stn.,* Westminster-br ; *Omnibus Rtes.,* Whitehall and Strand ; *Cab Rank,* Horse Guards. Commonly known as the Board of Trade. Sub-departments: Standard Weights and Measures, 7, Old Palace-yd, S.W. (Hours 11 to 5.) NEAREST *Ry. Stn.,* Westminster-br; *Omnibus Rtes.,* Parliament-st and Westminster-br ; *Cab Rank,* Palace-yd. Corn Return Inspector's Office, Mark-la, E.C. (Hours 10 to 4.) NEAREST *Ry. Stn.,* Fenchurch-st ; *Omnibus Rte.,* Fenchurch-st ; *Cab Rank,* Fenchurch-st. General Register and Record Office of Shipping and Seamen, 82, Basinghall-st, E.C. (Hours 10 to 4.) NEAREST *Ry. Stn.*, Moorgate-st (Met.); *Omnibus Rtes.*, Moorgate - st and Cheapside; *Cab Rank*, King-st, Guildhall. Consultation Branch of the Marine Department, 13, Downing - st. (Hours 10 to 4.) NEAREST *Ry. Stns.*, Westminster-br and St. James's-pk ; *Omnibus Rte.*, Parliament-st ; *Cab Rank*, Palace-yd. Office for Survey and Measurement of Steam Ships. (Hours 10 to 4.) Examination of Engineers and Superintendence of Emigration, St. Katharine Dock House, Towerhill. NEAREST *Ry. Stns.*, Aldgate (Met.) and Fenchurch-st (G.E.); *Omnibus Rte.*, Aldgate ; *Cab Ranks*, Minories and Great Tower Hill.

Common Lodging Houses.
—(*See* LODGING HOUSES.)

Concerts.—Years ago it was a favourite byword with foreigners that England was not a musical country. Without staying to enquire into the accuracy of the original statement, we may take it now as an accepted fact that in few other countries does music enter more universally into the lives of the people, or receive more liberal acknowledgment. Far earlier than the commencement of the present century no form of amusement was more in favour than concerts, and now London boasts permanently established series of musical performances — sufficient to satisfy the most eager and insatiable amateur. The conversion of the Hanover Square Rooms, some few years back, has removed the centre of attraction from a locality so long associated with the progress of the art to the newer and more commodious St. James's Hall. Willis's Rooms, once so fashionable, have fallen into disuse for regular concert purposes, and Exeter Hall has now retired from the field ; the only other places available for concerts on a really large scale being now the Crystal Palace and the Royal Albert Hall. The oldest musical society in London is the Philharmonic, which has seen seventy - four seasons ; the performances are given on a complete scale, and consist of orchestral and other instrumental compositions, relieved by vocal excerpts. The maintenance of classical art has always been the avowed object of the Philharmonic Society. Held at St. James's Hall, the annual series of concerts

usually consists of six or eight, which commence early in the year, and end about the period when the London season is at its height. The musical institution next in order in respect of longevity was the Sacred Harmonic Society, now, after fifty years' good work, defunct. A younger society (incorporated with limited liability under the Companies Acts), under the same name, and with similar objects, was founded in 1882, and oratorios are given by a full band and chorus in St. James's Hall on Friday evenings. The season comprises about ten concerts, and extends over the winter months. Of the highest musical importance are the Popular Concerts, held at St. James's Hall on Saturday afternoons and Monday evenings during the winter season. These justly celebrated entertainments of chamber classical music have reached their twenty-fifth year, and the manner in which the quartetts, trios, &c., are rendered by the first living artists, affords a theme for eulogistic comment throughout the world of art. The concerts were instituted by Mr. S. Arthur Chappell, who continues to hold the direction. The New Philharmonic Concerts were founded some thirty years ago by Dr. H. Wylde, in imitation of the Old Philharmonic Concerts. Amongst other entertainments which have stood the test of years, we may cite Mr. John Boosey's London Ballad Concerts. Their *locale* is St. James's Hall, and they are held on successive Wednesday evenings during the autumn and spring months. For four-and-twenty years Mr. Henry Leslie gave subscription concerts, with the aid of the choir which owns him for its founder. The excellent singing of this choir, in respect of delicacy and refinement, has long been universally acknowledged, and at the Paris Exhibition of 1878 they carried off the prize offered for competition. Mr. Leslie confined his season to a few performances, given on those Thursday evenings when a "date" could be obtained at St. James's Hall. Unfortunately Mr. Leslie's choir, as such, no longer exists. The Crystal Palace has played so important a part for many years in music that its claims to be classed to rank amidst London musical attractions cannot be ignored. The Saturday

winter classical concerts have done more to foster the appreciation of high art in all its branches than any similar institution in the same space of time. Mr. August Manns, the conductor, has shown true eclecticism in the works produced at Sydenham, and not one of the least interesting features of the entertainments have been the analytical notes supplied to the programmes by [G.]. There is an important Choral Society in connection with the Albert Hall, its conductor being Mr. Barnby, and the organist Dr. Stainer of St. Paul's Cathedral, and the great size of the building lends itself better to the performance of oratorio on a large scale than to most other purposes. Benefit and other concerts are given in the Langham Hall, the Royal Academy of Music, the "Horns" at Kennington, the "Eyre Arms," &c., as well as in the halls already mentioned.

Congregational Church (The), frequently called "Independent."—The declaration of faith, Church order, and discipline adopted at the annual meeting of the Congregational Union, May, 1833, begins by saying : " Disallowing the utility of creeds and articles of religion as a bond of union, and protesting against subscription to any human formularies as a term of communion, Congregationalists are yet willing to declare, for general information, what is commonly believed among them, reserving to every one the most perfect liberty of conscience. Upon some minor points of doctrine and practice, they, differing among themselves, allow to each other the right to form an unbiassed judgment of the Word of God." The principles of religion thus alluded to are twenty in number, of which it is not necessary in this place to quote more than the first, which runs as follows : "The Scriptures of the Old Testament, as received by the Jews, and the book of the New Testament as received by the Primitive Christians from the Evangelists and Apostles, Congregational Churches believe to be Divinely inspired, and of supreme authority. These writings, in the languages in which they were originally composed, are to be consulted, with the aids of sound criticism, as a final appeal to all controversies ; but the common version they consider to be adequate to the ordinary purposes of

Christian instruction and edification." The government is founded upon "the principles of Church order and discipline," thirteen n number, according to No. 5 of which "The only officers, placed by the apostles over individual Churches, are the bishops or pastors and the deacons; the number of these being dependent upon the number of the Church; and that to these, as the officers of the Church, is committed respectively the administration of its spiritual and temporal concerns—subject, however, to the approbation of the Church." The same principle of freedom from external control is displayed in the constitution and laws of the Congregational Union of England and Wales, which recognise the right of every individual Church to administer its own affairs, and affirm that the Union shall not in any case assume legislative authority or become a court of appeal. The Union consists of representative members, honorary members, and associates. Two general meetings are held in each year, called respectively the annual and autumnal meetings, the former in London in May, the latter in the autumn, and generally at some other city or town in England or Wales. The head-quarters are at the Memorial Hall, Farringdon-st, E.C. The Secretary is the Rev. Alexander Hannay, D.D., to whom all communications on the business of the Union are to be addressed. The London Congregational Union (Rev. A. Mearns, Sec.) also has its head-quarters at the Memorial Hall. "The Congregational Year Book," published by the Congregational Union, price 2s., by post, 2s. 7d., gives all information in regard to the Congregational Churches.

The following is a list of the principal Congregational Churches in London, with the dates of their original foundations:—

Balham. 1879.
Barking. 1662.
Battersea. 1865.
Bayswater, Craven-hill. 1854.
Bermondsey, Jamaica-rd. 1662.
    „   Rouel-rd. 1864.
Bethnal Gn.-rd. 1704.
    „   Mansford-st. 1868.
    „   Sydney-st. 1844.
Blackheath. 1854.
Borough-rd. 1866.
Bow, Harley-st. 1836.
    „   North. 1857.

Brixton, Loughboro -pk. 1860.
    „   Trinity, Church-rd. 1828.
    „   Independent Ch. 1870.
Bromley-by-Bow, Bruce-rd. 1866.
Brompton, Trevor Ch. 1816.
    „   West, Edith-gr. 1859.
Buckhurst - hill, Palmerston - rd. 1866.
Buckhurst-hill, King's-pl. 1871.
Camberwell-gn. 1780.
    „   New-rd. 1853.
    „   Albany-rd. 1830.
Camden Town, Bedford Ch., Charrington-st. 1851.
Camden Tn., Park Ch. 1843.
Canning Tn., 1855.
Chelsea, Ashburnham. 1879.
    „   Markham-sq. 1856.
    „   Radnor-st (Welsh). 1859.
Chigwell Row. 1784.
City-rd. 1848.
City of London :
    Bishopsgate-st. 1700.
    City Temple. 1642.
    Falcon-sq. 1660.
    Fetter-la. 1660.
        „   (Welsh). 1850.
    Finsbury. 1826.
    New Tabernacle, Old-st. 1832.
    Weigh House. 1662.
    Whitefield Tabernacle. 1753.
Clapham, Grafton-sq. 1645.
    „   Lavender-hill. 1879.
    „   Park-cres. 1819.
    „   -rd (Claylands). 1835.
    „   -rise (Augustine). 1875.
Clapton, Lower. 1850.
    „   -pk. 1804.
    „   Upper. 1815.
    „   Collier's Rents. 1720.
Craven, Marshall-st, Foubert's-pl, Regent-st. 1822.
Crouch End, Park Church. 1853.
Dalston Church, Middleton - rd. 1809.
Dalston, Shrubland-rd. 1870.
    „   Pownall-rd. 1864.
Deptford, High-st. 1660.
Dulwich, East. 1877.
    „   West. 1854.
    „   -gr. 1879.
Finchley, East. 1815.
    „   North. 1864.
Finsbury-park, Seven Sisters'-rd. 1864.
Forest-gate. 1856.
Forest-hill, Queen's-rd. 1864
Greenwich, Maze-hill. 1786.
    „   -rd. 1750.
Hackney, Cambridge-heath. 1861.
    „   Old Gravel Pit. 1716.
    „   -rd, Adelphi. 1790.
    „   South. 1871.
Hammersmith Broadway. 1662.
    „   Albion, Dalling-rd. 1784.
Hampstead, Rosslyn-hill. 1876.
Haverstock-hill. 1849.
Highbury-quadrant. 1878.

Highgate, South-gr. 1862.
Holloway, Camden-rd. 1802.
    „   Upper, Junction-rd. 1866.
Horselydown, Parish-st. 1822.
Hoxton (Academy). 1796.
Islington, Arundel-sq. 1858.
    „   Barnsbury. 1835.
    „   Britannia-row. 1865.
    „   Caledonian-rd.
    „   Hare Court, Canonbury 1660.
    „   Offord-rd. 1855.
    „   River-st. 1743.
    „   Union Church. 1802.
    „   Upper-st. 1815.
Kennington, Carlisle. 1856.
    „   Esher-st. 1832.
Kensington, Allen-st. 1793.
    „   North, Golborn-rd. 1871
Kent-rd, Old, Marlboro'. 1833.
Kentish Tn. 1807.
    „   New Tn., St.Paul's, Hawley-rd. 1851.
Kilburn. 1864.
    „   Greville-pl. 1858.
Kingsland. 1790.
    „   Maberly. 1825.
    „   -rd, Ware-st (W.). 1846.
Lambeth, York-rd. 1839.
Lewisham. 1797.
    „   High-rd. 1854.
Limehouse, Coverdale. 1838.
Mile End New Town, Trinity. 1780
    „   -rd. 1640.
Mill Hill, N.W. 1728.
Millwall, West Ferry-rd. 1817.
Mitcham, Upper, Sion. 1818.
New North-rd (Barbican). 1854.
Norwood, West. 1820.
    „   New Town, Union. 1870
    „   Selhurst-rd. 1862.
    „   South. 1870.
    „   Upper. 1864.
Notting Dale, Horbury Mission. 1876.
    „   Hill, Horbury. 1849.
    „   „ Lancaster-rd. 1866.
    „   „ Norland, Union. 1872
Orange-st. 1686.
Paddington, Marylebone-rd. 1813.
Peckham, Asylum-rd. 1852.
    „   Hanover. 1657.
    „   Rye, Linden-gr. 1858.
Pentonville, Claremont. 1819.
    „   -rd, King s ✠. 1857.
Pimlico, Buckingham. 1801.
    „   Eccleston-sq. 1848.
    „   St. Leonard-st. 1856.
Ponder's End. 1745.
Poplar, Trinity. 1842.
Putney, Oxford-rd. 1799.
    „   Ravenna-rd, Union. 1860
Richmond, Vineyard Ch. 1830.
Robert-st, Grosvenor-sq. 1814.
Rotherhithe, Maynard-rd. 1863.
St. George's-in-the-East, Ebenezer 1785.

St. George's - in - the - East, Old Gravel-la. 1680.
St. John's Wood-ter. 1841.
St. John's Wood. New Coll. 1853.
Sheen Vale, Mortlake. 1662.
Shepherd's Bush, Oaklands. 1858.
Southgate. 1805.
  ,,   -rd. 1662.
Southwark-br-rd (Welsh). 1806.
  ,,   Earl - st, London - rd. 1881.
  ,,   -park. 1863.
  ,,   (Pilgrim Fathers), New Kent-rd. 1592.
Stamford-hill. 1871.
Stepney Meeting-house. 1644.
  ,,   Burdett-rd. 1866.
  ,,   Latimer. 1750.
  ,,   Wycliffe, Philpot - st. 1642.
Stockwell-rd. 1800.
Stoke Newington, Abney. 1662.
  ,,   ,,   Raleigh Memorial. 1865.
  ,,   ,,   Rectory - rd. 1865.
Stratford. 1866.
  ,,   Brickfields. 1680.
Streatham-hill. 1832.
Sydenham, Ch.-in-Grove. 1850.
Tollington-pk. 1662.
Tolmers-sq, Hampstead-rd. 1839.
Tonbridge Ch., Euston-rd. 1810.
Tooting. 1688.
Tottenham-ct-rd, Whitefield Tabernacle. 1756.
Tottenham High ✠. 1867.
Tufnell-pk. 1875.
Turnham-gn. 1873.
Victoria-st, Approach-rd. 1862.
Victoria Docks, Union. 1871.
Walthamstow, Marsh-st. 1672.
  ,,   Trinity. 1862.
  ,,   Wood - st, Union. 1852.
Walworth, Sutherland. 1818.
  ,,   York-st. 1793.
Wandsworth, East-hill. 1573.
  ,,   -rd, Priory. 1865.
Wardour-st, Soho. 1665.
Westminster-br-rd, Christchurch, late Surrey Chapel. 1783.
Westminster, James-st. 1840.
Whitechapel-rd, Sion. 1790.
Willesden. 1815.
Wimbledon. 1872.
Winchmore-hill. 1810.
Woodford. 1815.
  ,,   George-la. 1875.
Wood Green, Lordship-la. 1862.

Conservative Club, 74, St. James's-st.—To carry out Conservative principles. Every candidate must be a Conservative. Entrance fee, £31 10s.; subscription, £10 10s. Towards the library fund, the first year only, £2 2s. Solicitors can only be elected on a vacancy of 6 per cent. on 1,200 members.

Constituencies, Parliamentary.—The following is a list of the Metropolitan Boroughs, with the names of the sitting Members, the number of registered Electors in each Borough, and the number of votes polled by the successful Candidates.

Battersea, 10,018
  O. V. Morgan, *L* .. 3,683
Bethnal Gn (Nth. East), 7,102
  George Howell, *L* .. 2,278
Bethnal Gn (Sth. West), 8,265
  E. H. Pickersgill, *L* .. 2,551
Camberwell (North), 8,603
  J. R. Kelly, *C* ..   2,717
Camberwell (Dulwich), 8,963
  J. Blundell Maple, *C* .. 4,021
Camberwell (Peckham), 9,713
  A. A. Baumann, *C* .. 3,439
Chelsea, 11,104
  C. A. Whitmore, *C* .. 4,304
City of London, 29,152
  Sir Robert Fowler, *C* .. ⎫
  Thos. Chas. Baring, *C* .. ⎬ *unopposed*
    ⎭
Clapham, 9,454
  J. S. Gilliat, *C* ..   3,816
Deptford, 9,371
  Charles John Darling, Q.C., *C* .. 4,345
Finsbury (Central), 7,462
  Capt. F. T. Penton, *C* .. 2,245
Finsbury (East), 6,105
  J. Rowlands, *L* .. 1,973
Finsbury (Holborn), 9,802
  Col. F. Duncan, *C* .. 3,651
Fulham, 6,499
  W. Hayes Fisher, *C* .. 2,557
Greenwich, 8,632
  T. W. Boord, *C* .. 3,240
Hackney (Central), 7,381
  Sir W. G. Hunter, *C* .. 3,047
Hackney (North), 8,058
  Major-Gen. Sir Lewis Pelly, *C* .. 3,326
Hackney (South), 8,684
  Sir Chas. Russell, Q.C., *L* 2,800
Hammersmith, 9,611
  Major-General Goldsworthy, *C* .. 3,991
Hampstead, 5,981
  E. Brodie Hoare, *C* *unopposed*
Islington (East), 8,092
  Cowley Lambert, *C* 3,732
Islington (North), 7,774
  G. C. T. Bartley, *C* .. 3,456
Islington (South), 7,024
  Sir A. K. Rollit, *C* .. 2,774
Islington (West), 7,276
  R. Chamberlain, *U L* .. 2,793
Kensington (North), 8,297
  Sir R. Lethbridge, *C* .. 3,394
Kensington (South), 8,859
  Sir A. Borthwick, *C* .. 4,156

Lambeth (Brixton), 7,963
  Marquis of Carmarthen, *C* 3,307
Lambeth (Kennington), 8,313
  Robert Gent-Davis, *C* .. 3,222
Lambeth (North), 7,939
  Major-General Fraser, *C* 2,723
Lambeth (Norwood), 7,501
  T. L. Bristowe, *C* .. 3,334
Lewisham, 9,280
  Lord Lewisham, *C* .. 3,839
London University, 2,579
  Sir John Lubbock, *U L* 1,314
Marylebone (East), 6,884
  Lord Charles Beresford, *C* 3,101
Marylebone (West), 7,566
  F. Seager Hunt, *C* .. 3,064
Newington (Walworth), 5,598
  L. C. Isaacs, *C* ..   1,983
Newington (West), 6,377
  C. W. R. Cooke, *C* .. 2,447
Paddington (North), 5,345
  Lionel L. Cohen, *C* .. 2,300
Paddington (South), 5,193
  Lord Randolph Churchill, *C* .. 2,576
St. George's (Hanover-sq), 10,500
  G. J. Goschen, *C* .. 5,702
St. Pancras (East), 5,913
  R. Grant Webster, *C* .. 2,327
St. Pancras (South), 5,450
  Sir Julian Goldsmid, *U L* 1,915
St. Pancras (North), 5,357
  Hon. W. C. Baillie, *C* 2,074
St. Pancras (West), 7,103
  H. L. W. Lawson, *L* .. 2,563
Shoreditch (Haggerston), 6,737
  W. R. Cremer, *L* .. 2,054
Shoreditch (Hoxton), 8,469
  Prof. J. Stuart, *L* .. 2,324
Southwark (Bermondsey), 9,433
  Alfred Lafone, *C* .. 3,356
Southwark (Rotherhithe), 8,455
  Col. C. E. Hamilton, *C* 3,202
Southwark (West), 7,776
  R. K. Causton, *L* .. 3,638
Strand, 11,264
  Rt. Hon. W. H. Smith, *C* 5,034
Tower Hamlets (Bow and Bromley), 8,887
  Capt. J. R. Colomb, *C* 2,967
Tower Hamlets (Limehouse), 5,954
  E. S. Norris, *C* .. 2,230
Tower Hamlets (Mile End), 5,804
  S. Charrington, *C* .. 2,110
Tower Hamlets (Poplar), 9,041
  Sydney Buxton, *L* .. 2,903
Tower Hamlets (St. George's, E.), 4,317
  C. T. Ritchie, *C* .. 1,546
Tower Hamlets (Stepney), 6,925
  F. W. Isaacson, *C* .. 2,237
Tower Hamlets (Whitechapel), 6,140
  Samuel Montagu, *L* .. 2,179
Wandsworth, 10,088
  Henry Kimber, *C, unopposed*

West Ham (North), 10,026
   Forrest Fulton, *C* ..   3,920
West Ham (South), 8,942
   Major G. E. Banes, *C*   2,878
Westminster, 7,670
   W. Burdett-Coutts, *C*, *unopposed*
Woolwich, 9,769
   Edwin Hughes, *C* ..   4,647

Constituencies, School Board.

—Members of the Board.

City of London. — Henry Spicer, Esq., M.P., Miss Davenport-Hill, Mr. Alderman Savory, Sir Richard Temple, Bart., M.P. (Vice-Chairman).

Chelsea.—George White, Esq., B.A., LL.B., Rev. Prebendary Eyton, M.A., William Bousfield, Esq., Professor Gladstone, F.R.S., Mrs. Webster.

Finsbury.—Mark Wilks. Esq., W. Roston Bourke, Esq., Benj. Lucraft, Esq., James Wilson Sharp, Esq., Thomas Francis Stonelake, Esq., Hon. Conrad A. Dillon.

Greenwich.—Colonel Hughes, M.P., William Phillips, Esq., Henry Gover, Esq., Rev. Richard Rhodes Bristow, M.A.

Hackney. — John Lobb, Esq., F.R.G.S., Charles Deacon, Esq., James Hart, Esq., Rev. Charles George Gull, M.A., Benjamin S. Olding, Esq.

East Lambeth.—Rev. Andrew A.W.Drew, M.A., Rev.Charles E. Brooke, M.A., Thomas E. Heller, Esq., G. Crispe Whiteley, Esq.,

West Lambeth.—Henry Lynn, Esq., Harry Seymour Foster, Esq., F.C.A., Rev. Arthur W. Jephson, M.A., Fredk. William Lucas, Esq., James Thomas Helby, Esq., and Reginald Saunders, Esq.

Marylebone.—Edmund Barnes, Esq., J. Russell Endean, Esq., Rev. John J. Coxhead, M.A., General Moberly, Rev. Joseph R. Diggle, M.A. (Chairman), Rev. Canon Barker, M.A., Mrs. Westlake.

Southwark.—Sir John Bennett, Edric Bayley, Esq., Rev. Charles D. Lawrence, M.A., Rev. Wm. Lees Bell, M.A.

Tower Hamlets. — Rev. W. Parkinson Jay, M.A., Colonel Lenox Prendergast, Rev. John Fletcher Porter, Frederick J. W. Dellow, Esq.

Westminster.—H. N. Bowman Spink, Esq., Rev. Wm. Sinclair, Captain Clifford Probyn, James S. Burroughes, Esq., Sir Guyer Hunter, M.P.

The following is an alphabetical List of Members, with addresses. The letters prefixed to each name indicate the various committees (*which see*) on which the member in question serves.

All committees. CHAIRMAN, Rev. Joseph R. Diggle, M.A. (Marylebone), 19, Cornwall-terrace, Regent's-pk, N.W.

All committees. VICE - CHAIRMAN, Sir Richard Temple, Bart., M.P. (City), Athenæum Club, Pall-Mall.

f.k.l.t.y. Barker, Rev. Canon, M.A. (Marylebone), 38, Devonshire-pl, W.

a.f.h.w.x. Barnes, Edmund, Esq. (Marylebone), 220, Camden-rd, N.W.

a.r.y. Bayley, Edric, Esq. (Southwark), Raydon House, Potter's-flds, Tooley-st, Southwark, S.E.

f.t.w.y. Bell, Rev.Wm.Lees, M.A. (Southwark), Christ Church Vicarage, Spa-rd, S.E.

b.m.o.r.v. Bennett, Sir John, (Southwark), Cheapside, City.

a.f.g.h.t.x.y. Bourke, W. R., Esq. (Finsbury), Holloway College, Spencer-rd, Lorraine-rd, N.

b.c.f.h.j.l. Bousfield, Wm., Esq. (Chelsea), 33, Stanhope - gdns, Queen's-ga, W.

f.k.l.r.t. Bristow, Rev. Richard Rhodes, M.A. (Greenwich), St. Stephen's Vicarage, Lewisham, S.E.

f.k.t. Brooke, Rev.Chas. E., M.A. (East Lambeth), 123, Vassall-rd, Brixton, S.W.

a.b.d.e. Burroughes, James S., Esq. (Westminster), 9, Fitzroy-sq, W.

d.m.o.r.u. Coxhead, Rev. John J., M.A. (Marylebone), St. John's Vicarage, Fitzroy-sq, W.

f.h.j.m.o.w.x.y. Davenport-Hill, Miss (City), 25, Belsize-avenue, N.W.

b.c.d.m.q. Deacon, Charles, Esq. (Hackney), 22, Navarino - rd, Hackney, E.

b.c.e.l.y. Dellow, Frederick J. W., Esq. (Tower Hamlets), 72, St. George-st, E.

t. Dillon, Hon. Conrad A. (Finsbury), 53, Oakley-st, Chelsea.

a.f.t. Drew, Rev. Andrew A. W., M.A. (East Lambeth), St. Antholin's Vicarage, Peckham Rye, S.E.

b.c.d.e.x. Endean, J. Russell, Esq. (Marylebone), National Liberal Club, Victoria Embankment, W.C.

f.h.j.l.t.y. Eyton, Rev. Prebendary, M.A. (Chelsea), 141, Sloane-st, Chelsea, S.W.

a.e.r. Foster, Harry Seymour, Esq., F.C.A. (West Lambeth), 3, Copthall-bdgs, E.C.

a.f.h.t.x. Gladstone, Professor, F.R.S. (Chelsea), 17, Pembridge-sq, W.

f.l.t.w. Gover, Henry, Esq. (Greenwich), 3, Adelaide - pl, London-br, E.C.

a.f.h.k.l.t. Gull, Rev. Charles George, M.A. (Hackney), 41, Downs-rd, Clapton, E.

m.q.y. Hart, James, Esq. (Hackney), 304, Mare-st, Hackney, E.

b.c.d.e.f.h.l.w.x. Helby, James Thos., Esq. (West Lambeth), Elm Lodge, Herne-hill, S.E.

f.h. Heller, Thomas E., Esq. (East Lambeth), 40, Gauden-rd, Clapham, S.W.

a.e.r. Hughes, Col., M.P.(Greenwich), 38, Green's-end, Woolwich, S.E.

a.e.x. Hunter, Sir Guyer, M.P. (Westminster), 21, Norfolk-cres, Hyde-park, W.

a.f.l.t. Jay, Rev. W. Parkinson, M.A. (Tower Hamlets), Christ Church Vicarage, Watney-st, E.

b.c.d.f.k.l.t. Jephson, Rev. Arthur W., M.A. (West Lambeth), 34, Waterloo-rd, S.E.

b.c.r. Lawrence, Rev. Charles D., M.A. (Southwark), The Rectory, Bermondsey, S.E.

e.f.h.k.m.q.w.x. Lobb, John, Esq., F.R.G.S. (Hackney), Dursley-villa, Cawley-rd, Victoria-pk, E.

b.c.d.f.l.r. Lucas, Frederick Wm., Esq.(West Lambeth), 22,Surrey-st, W.C.

b.c.d.y. Lucraft, Benjamin, Esq. (Finsbury), 67, Canonbury-rd, Islington, N.

f.r.w.y. Lynn, Henry, Esq. (West Lambeth), 5, King's Bench-wk, Temple, E.C.

b.f.k.l.t. Moberly, Gen. (Marylebone), 50, Sutherland-gdns,W.

l.x.y. Olding, Benjamin, Esq. (Hackney), Lissant House, St. Mary's-rd, Long Ditton.

b.d.e.m.p. Phillips,William, Esq. (Greenwich), Coal Exchange, E.C.

e.f.h.m.o.t. Porter, Rev. John Fletcher (Tower Hamlets), 59, Driffield-rd, Bow, E.

m.p. Prendergast, Colonel Lenox (Tower Hamlets), 22, Grosvenor-gdns, S.W.

a.l.r.x. Probyn, Captain Clifford (Westminster), 55, Grosvenor-st, W.

Saunders, Reginald, Esq. (West Lambeth), 3, Essex-court, E.C.

e.r.x. Savory, Mr. Alderman (City), Buckhurst-pk, Ascot.

a.b.l. Sharp, James Wilson, Esq. (Finsbury), 49, Highbury-pk, N.

e.f.h.l.t.x. Sinclair, Rev. William (Westminster), St. Stephen's Vicarage, Westminster, S.W.

a.e.m.n.o.p.q. Spicer, Henry, Esq., M.P. (City), 14, Aberdeen-pk, Highbury, N.

m.p.r. Spink, H. N. Bowman, Esq. (Westminster), 3, Marsham-st, Westminster, S.W.

b.c.d.l.r.x. Stonelake, Thomas Francis, Esq. (Finsbury), 55, Packington-st, Islington, N.

f.h.j.r.y. Webster, Mrs. (Chelsea), Temple Lodge, Hammersmith.

c.h.k.m.p.w. Westlake, Mrs. (Marylebone), The River House, 3, Chelsea Embankment, S.W.

b.c.e.f.h.j. White, George, Esq., B.A., LL.B. (Chelsea), 2, Garden-ct, Temple, E.C.

b.e.f.j. Whiteley, G. Crispe, Esq. (East Lambeth), The Chestnuts, Dulwich-com, S.E.

b c.f.k.j. Wilks, Mark, Esq. (Finsbury), 12, St. Bartholomew-rd, Camden-rd, Islington, N.

The following is a list of the Standing Committees with their principal Sub-Committees.

A. STATISTICAL AND LAW AND PARLIAMENTARY COMMITTEE.—Meet every alternate Wednesday at 3 p.m. Lieut-Colonel Hughes, M.P. (Chairman).

B. WORKS AND GENERAL PURPOSES COMMITTEE.—Meet every alternate Monday, at 2.30 p.m. William Bousfield, Esq. (Chairman).

C. SUB-COMMITTEE OF WORKS COMMITTEE ON SITES AND BUILDINGS.—Meet every alternate Monday, at 3 p.m. William Bousfield, Esq. (Chairman).

D. SUB-COMMITTEE OF WORKS COMMITTEE ON FURNITURE AND REPAIRS.—Meet every alternate Monday, at 2 p.m. on the same day as the Sites and Buildings Sub-Committee. Frederick Wm. Lucas, Esq. (Chairman).

E. FINANCE COMMITTEE.—Meet every alternate Tuesday, at 10.30 a.m. Sir Richard Temple, Bart., M.P. (Chairman).

F. SCHOOL MANAGEMENT COMMITTEE.—Meet every Friday, at 2 p.m. Rev. Joseph R. Diggle, M.A. (Chairman).

G. SUB-COMMITTEE OF SCHOOL MANAGEMENT COMMITTEE FOR GENERAL BUSINESS.—Meet every Monday, at 12.30 p.m. W. R. Bourke, Esq. (Chairman). Besides the Chairman of the Sub-Committee, and the Chairman and Vice-Chairman of the Board, four Members of the Committee are summoned to attend in rotation.

H. SUB-COMMITTEE OF SCHOOL MANAGEMENT COMMITTEE ON BOOKS AND APPARATUS. Professor Gladstone, F.R.S. (Chairman).

J. SUB-COMMITTEE OF SCHOOL MANAGEMENT COMMITTEE ON COOKERY.—Meet every alternate Friday at 1.30 p.m. Miss Davenport-Hill (Chair).

K. SUB-COMMITTEE OF THE SCHOOL MANAGEMENT COMMITTEE TO SUPERINTEND THE CLASSES FOR THE INSTRUCTION OF THE BLIND AND THE DEAF AND DUMB.—Meet first Monday of month at 2 p.m. Rev. Charles George Gull, M.A. (Chairman).

L. BYE-LAWS COMMITTEE.—Meet every alternate Wednesday at 3 p.m. Rev. John J. Coxhead, M.A. (Chairman).

M. INDUSTRIAL SCHOOLS COMMITTEE, AND MANAGERS OF BOARD INDUSTRIAL SCHOOLS.—Meet every alternate Tuesday at 3 p.m. Henry Spicer, Esq. (Chairman).

N. SUB-COMMITTEE OF INDUSTRIAL SCHOOLS COMMITTEE FOR INDUSTRIAL SCHOOLS CASES.—Meet on Tuesday immediately after the Industrial Schools Committee, and the alternate Tuesday, at 4 p.m. Besides the Chairman of the Sub-Committee, Henry Spicer, Esq., and the Chairman and Vice-Chairman of the Board, three members of the Committee are summoned to attend.

O. SUB-COMMITTEE ON THE BRENTWOOD SCHOOL. The Chairman of the Board (Chairman).

P. SUB-COMMITTEE ON THE SHIP "SHAFTESBURY." The Chairman of the Board (Chairman).

Q. SUB-COMMITTEE ON UPTON HOUSE SCHOOL. The Chairman of the Board (Chairman).

R. EDUCATIONAL ENDOWMENTS COMMITTEE.—Meet every alternate Monday at 4 p.m. Rev. Charles D. Lawrence, M.A. (Chairman).

S. SPECIAL COMMITTEE ON SALARIES.—Meet as business requires. The Chairman of the Board (Chairman).

T. SUB-COMMITTEE OF THE SCHOOL MANAGEMENT COMMITTEE ON SCRIPTURE INSTRUCTION.—Rev. Canon Barker, M.A. (Chairman).

U. SUB-COMMITTEE OF BYE-LAWS COMMITTEE FOR GENERAL BUSINESS.—Meet every alternate Wednesday at 3.30 p.m. Besides the Chairman of the Sub-Committee, Rev. J. J. Coxhead, M.A., and the Chairman of the Board, four members of the Committee are summoned to attend in rotation.

W. COMMITTEE ON NEEDLEWORK.—Meet every alternate Tuesday at 2 p.m. James Thomas Helby, Esq. (Chairman).

X. STORES COMMITTEE.—Meet on Mondays at 2 p.m. in the alternate week with the Finance Committee. John Lobb, Esq., F.R.G.S. (Chairman).

Y. EVENING CLASSES COMMITTEE.—Meet every alternate Monday at 2.30 p.m. Thomas E. Heller, Esq. (Chairman).

Constitutional Club, Northumberland - avenue. — Established in 1883. "Its objects being to provide a central and convenient club in London for all members of the Conservative party who may be elected in accordance with the rules, and to do all such things as in the opinion of the Committee shall tend to promote the interests of the Conservative party in the United Kingdom of Great Britain and Ireland." Entrance fee, £10 10s. for town members; country members, £6 6s. Subscription, town members, £5 5s.; country members, £3 3s. Election by ballot, and vested in the Committee, of which at least eight members must be present. No candidate shall be elected unless he have the votes of at least three-fourths of those voting at the election.

Consulates. — (*See under their respective heads.*)

Cookery and Cooking Schools.—The National School of Cookery, Exhibition-rd, South Kensington, commenced its work in the year 1873 under the title of the Popular School of Cookery, and was located in the building of the International Exhibition of that year. At the close of the

International Exhibition the commissioners granted to the executive committee of the National School of Cookery the temporary use of that portion of the building already occupied by it, together with some more space for an additional kitchen and offices. Up to the present time it has not been found possible for the school to provide its own premises, and therefore the use of the Exhibition building has been up to now continued to it. But in 1888 it was intimated to the committee that the site would be shortly required for other purposes, and it is therefore proposed to incorporate the school as a company under the Joint Stock Acts, and to raise a fund for a suitable building. Cooks and others are instructed in all branches of cookery, and lessons can be had singly or in a course. The public are admitted to see the school at work every afternoon, except Sat., between three and four o'clock. The dishes cooked are for sale to the public, at cost price, at 4 p.m.

Co-operative Stores.—A good deal of misunderstanding exists on the subject of what are called "Co-operative Stores." The co-operative principle is in itself plain enough, consisting simply in the clubbing together of a number of retail buyers for the purpose of procuring their joint requirements at wholesale prices. A purely co-operative association is one exclusively distributive, and distributive only among its own members, to whom it re-issues the goods it has purchased with their money at just so much advance upon the price it has paid for them as shall cover the actual cost of the double transaction. Practically, however, it soon becomes obvious that this exact balance is not to be obtained, and that in order to insure against loss it is necessary to have at least a "margin" of profit. To carry out the co-operative principle in its integrity, the accumulations accruing from time to time out of this margin should be distributed among the purchasers *pro ratâ* on the amount of their purchases. So much for theory. Practically the co-operative business of London is carried on upon a rather different principle. Even with those which most nearly approach the ideal, a considerable deviation has been made in the admission of

a class of member called a ticket-holder, who, while paying a small fee—2s. 6d. or 5s. per annum—for permission to make his purchases at the stores, is entirely excluded from any participation in the profits, whilst the majority of the associations divide their accumulations simply on the basis of so much per share, without any reference to the amount laid out by the shareholder. Some so-called co-operative associations have neither shareholders nor ticket-holders—or, at all events, do not limit their dealings to them—and are, in point of fact, not co-operative societies at all, but just large ready-money establishments, which, by the diminished expenses and rapid turnover of the "store" system, are enabled to offer their goods at little more than wholesale price.

The principal real co-operative associations are the Civil Service Supply Association, 136, Qn. Victoria-st, E.C., Chandos-st, W.C., Tavistock-st, W.C., and 27, Howley-pl, Belvidere-rd, S.E. ; the Civil Service Co-operative Society, 28, Haymarket, S.W.; the Army and Navy Co-operative Society, 117, Victoria-st, S.W. ; the Port of London Co-operative Society, 16, Camomile-st, E.C. ; the International Exhibition Co - operative Wine Society, 11, Chandos-st, W. ; the London and Westminster Supply Association, 10, 11, & 12, New Bridge-st, E.C. ; the New Civil Service Co-operation (Limited), 122, Qn. Victoria-st, E.C.; the Agricultural and Horticultural Association, 3, Agar-st, Strand, and 3, Creek-rd, Deptford, S.E.; the Coal Co-operative Society, 115, Chancery-lane, W.C. ; and the Ladies' Dress Association, 70 & 71, Jermyn-st, S.W., and 25, Bury-st, S.W.; particulars of each of which may be had from their respective secretaries.

Copyhold Enclosure and Tithe Commission, 3, St. James's-sq, S.W. — Office hours 10 to 4, searches 10 to 3. There is a subdivision "Survey Map Department." NEAREST Ry. Stns., Charing ✠ (S.E. & Dis.) and St. James's-pk ; *Omnibus Rtes.*, Piccadilly and Regent-st ; *Cab Rank*, S. side of square.

Coroners within the Metropolitan Police Districts.—[*See* 6 Vict. c. 12; 6 & 7 Vict. c. 83; 7 & 8 Vict. c. 92;

22 Vict. c. 33; 23 & 24 Vict. c. 116.]

City and Liberties of Westminster.—Charles St. Clare Bedford, Esq., Broad Sanctuary, Westminster, S.W. *Deputy*, John Troutbeck, Esq., 4, Dean's-yard, S.W.

City of London and Borough of Southwark.—Sam. Fred. Langham, Esq., 10, Bartlett's-bdgs, Holborn. *Deputy*, A. Braxton Hicks, Esq., 2, Elm-court, Temple.

County of Essex. — Charles Carne Lewis, Esq., Brentwood. *Deputy*, W. Bindon Blood, Esq., Witham. *East Essex.* — John Harrison, Junr., Esq., Braintree.

County of Kent. — Edward Arundel Carttar, Esq., Greenwich, S.E.; W. J. Harris, Esq., Sittingbourne.

County of Middlesex (Central District). — George Danford Phillips Thomas, Esq., Park Lodge, Park-place-villas, Paddington, W. *Deputy*, W. Wynn Westcott, Esq., M.B., 4, Torriano-avenue, Camden-rd, N.W.

County of Middlesex (Eastern District).—W. E. Baxter, Esq., 9, Lawrence Pountney-hill, E.C. *Deputy*, G. Collier, Esq. *Coroner's Office*, 33, Spital-sq, E.

County of Middlesex (Western District).—T. B. Diplock, Esq., M.D., Arlington House, Gunnersbury, Chiswick. *Deputy*, Fred. James Hand, Esq., Tinwell Lodge, St. Peter's-sq, Hammersmith.

County of Surrey (Lambeth Div.).—William Carter, Esq., Althorp House, Wandsworth-com, S. *(Camberwell Div.).*—G. P. Wyatt, Esq., 33, Wiltshire-rd, Brixton, S.W.

Duchy of Lancaster (in Middlesex and Surrey).—Sam. F. Langham, Esq., 10, Bartlett's-bdgs, Holborn, E.C.

For the Queen's Household and the Verge. — William Thomas Manning, Esq., 2, Westminster Chambers, S.W.

Liberty of the Tower of London. — Thomas Wrake Ratcliff, Esq., District Board Offices, White Horse - st, Commercial-road, E., and 60, New Broad-st, E.C.

Costa Rica, Republic of. —MINISTRY, none. CONSULATE, 19, St. Swithin's-la, E.C. NEAREST Ry. Stns., Mansion House

(Dis.), Cannon-st (S.E.); *Omnibus Routes*, King William-st and Cheapside; *Cab Rank*, Cannon-street.

Costumes, Artists'.—Most of the respectable theatrical costumiers provide correct costumes of almost every period; and in addition to these, Mr. Barthe, of 4, Limerston-st, Fulham-rd, gives special attention to this class of business.

County Courts (Metropolitan).—The hours of business at the offices of the various Registrars are from 10 till 4 daily, except on Sat., when they close at 1. They are closed on Good Friday and following day, Easter Mon. and Tu., first Mon. in Aug., on Christmas and Boxing Days, and on such other days as may be appointed by the Lord Chancellor. The following is a list of these Courts :

BLOOMSBURY, Gt. Portland-st Regent's-pk.

Bow, Bow-rd, E.

BROMPTON, Whitehead's-grove, Chelsea, S.W.

CLERKENWELL, 33, Duncan-ter, Islington, N.

LAMBETH, Camberwell New-rd, S.E.

MARYLEBONE, 179, Marylebone-rd, N.W.

SHOREDITCH, 221, Old-st, E.C.

SOUTHWARK, 50, Swan-st, Boro', S.E.

WESTMINSTER, 82, St. Martin's-la, W.C.

WHITECHAPEL, 16, Gt. Prescot-st, E.

For information as to the dates of sittings of the Courts, application should be made to the respective Registrars at their offices.

Court Theatre, Sloane-sq (Map 6), was pulled down in the autumn of 1887, and not re-opened at the time of our going to press. Next to Toole's and the Royalty, it was the smallest house in London, but from its position just opposite the Sloane-sq Stn. of the District Ry. unusually easy of access. NEAREST *Ry. Stn.*, *Omnibus Rte.*, and *Cab Rank*, Sloane-sq.

Covent Garden Market (Map 7).—No visitor to London should miss paying at least two visits to Covent-garden : one, say at 6 a.m., to see the vegetable

market ; the other, later on, to see the fruits and flowers. All night long on the great main roads the rumble of the heavy waggons seldom ceases, and before daylight the "market" is crowded. The very loading of these waggons is in itself a wonder, and the wall-like regularity with which cabbages, cauliflowers, and turnips are built up to a height of some 12 ft. is nothing short of marvellous. Between 5 and 6 o'clock the light traps of the greengrocers of the metropolis rattle up, and all the streets around the market become thronged with their carts, while the costermongers come in in immense numbers. By 6 o'clock the market is fairly open, and the din and bustle are surprising indeed. After 8 o'clock the market becomes quiet. The great waggons have moved off ; the débris of cabbage-leaves and other vegetable matter has been swept up, and Covent-garden assumes its everyday aspect. And a very pretty aspect it is. The avenue is at all times of the year a sight, the shops competing with each other in a display of flowers and fruit such as can scarcely, if at all, be rivalled in any capital of Europe. On each side of the main avenue are enclosed squares, and here the wholesale fruit market is carried on. Outside the market there is almost always something to see. In winter a score of men are opening orange boxes and sorting their contents ; in autumn dozens of women and girls are extracting walnuts from their juicy green outside cases ; in spring-time the side facing the church is occupied by dealers in spring and bedding flowers, and the pavement is aglow with colour of flower and leaf, and in the early summer hundreds of women and girls are busily occupied in shelling peas. NEAREST *Ry. Stns.*, Charing ✠ (S.E. & Dis.); *Omnibus Rtes.*, Strand, St. Martin's-la, and Holborn ; *Cab Ranks*, Bedford-st and Burleigh-st.

Covent Garden Theatre, Bow-street (Map 7). — One of the largest theatres in Europe, ranking next after San Carlo at Naples, the Scala at Milan, and the Pergola at Florence. Was intended primarily for Italian opera, for which it is still occasionally used, but is now commonly used in the autumn for promenade

concerts, and has been adapted to the purposes of a circus in the winter season. The main front is in Bow-street, where there is a covered entrance for carriages, and the façade of which is decorated with Flaxman's statues of Tragedy and Comedy, rescued from the fire which destroyed the late building. NEAREST *Ry. Stns.*, Charing ✠ (S.E. & Dis.) and Temple ; *Omnibus Rtes.*, Strand, St. Martin's-lane, and Holborn ; *Cab Rank*, Catherine-st and Endell-st.

Creche (Infant Infirmary and Infant Home), 12, 14, and 16, Stepney-causeway, Commercial-rd, E. ; Mrs. Marie Hilton, Hon. Superintendent. — For the care of young children while their mothers are at work ; orphan home ; the care of orphans and the temporary care of children whose mothers are in hospitals or convalescent homes. Children are received at the Crèche every morning at 7 o'clock and remain till 7 o'clock at night. Visitors admitted every day, except Sat., from 12 noon till 5 p.m. Admission for children twopence per day, as many being received as can be accommodated. The institution closes at 2 o'clock on Sat., and is under the medical care of John MacFie, M.D., and Robert Debenham, M.R.C.S., F.S.A. There is also a Training and Convalescent Home at The Limes, Feltham, for training the older girls from the Home, and for giving the younger children change of air.

Crichton Club, 10, Adelphi-ter.—Proprietary and non-political. An artistic, musical, and literary club, one of the largest of its class, and in one of the best situations in London. No entrance fee. Subscription, £3 3s.

Cricket. — The famous grounds of "Lord's" and the "Oval" are the principal cricket grounds of London. "Lord's," the head-quarters of the Marylebone Club, is notoriously a difficult ground, but the Marylebone Club has recently expended a great deal of money in draining and relaying, and a great improvement is observable. A tavern is attached to the ground, and besides racket and tennis courts, there are billiard rooms and a variety of grand stands and pavilions. The Marylebone Club (entrance fee, £1; annual subscription, £3; election by committee) are the present proprietors of Lord's, which is situated in the St. John's Wood-rd, N.W. NEAREST *Ry. Stn.*, St. John's Wood-rd; *Omnibus Rtes.*, Wellington-rd and St. John's Wood-rd. Cab fare from Charing ✠, 2s.; from the Bank of England, 2s. 6d. The Oval at Kennington, S.E., is the head-quarters of the Surrey County Cricket Club, and some of the very best matches of the season are played on the ground. A spacious pavilion, a tavern with billiard-room and a large dining-room, add to the attractions of the Oval. The ground itself is as nearly perfection as can be, and in seasonable weather a wicket can be selected as true as a billiard-table. NEAREST *Ry. Stn.*, Vauxhall (L. & S. W. R.); *Omnibus Rtes.*, Kennington-rd and Clapham-rd; *Cab Rank*, St, Mark's Church, Clapham-rd. The cab fare from Charing ✠ is 1s. 6d., and from the Bank of England 2s. The Surrey County Club (election by ballot by the members generally, ten to make a ballot and two black balls to exclude) requires an entrance fee of one guinea; and a subscription of the same amount entitles a member to every privilege except that of practice from the Club bowlers, of whom there are eight. An annual subscription of £2, and an entrance fee of £1, entitle a member to every privilege the Club affords.

Criterion Theatre, Regent-cir, Piccadilly (Map 6).—Is built entirely underground. The house is small, but handsome, commodious, and at least as well ventilated as any other. There is nothing to suggest to the visitor in the stalls that he is below the level of the sewers, which, in point of fact, are about the height of the gallery. One advantage of this mode of construction is that the way out lies in every case upstairs, which not only modifies any rush, but greatly mitigates the danger of stumbling over the trailing dresses of the ladies. For specialty, this theatre was formerly addicted almost exclusively to translations of rattling pieces of the Palais Royal school, in which it has achieved considerable success, but of late has given plays of more serious interest. NEAREST *Ry. Stns.*, Charing ✠

(S.E. & Dis.); *Omnibus Rtes.*, Piccadilly, Regent-st, and Waterloo-pl; *Cab Rank*, Haymarket.

Croquet.—(*See* ALL-ENGLAND.)

Crosby Hall, 32, Bishopsgate-st (Map 8).— A fine specimen of Gothic domestic architecture, first known as Crosby Place, was built in 1466 on ground leased from the Convent of St. Helen, by Sir John Crosby, grocer and woolstapler, alderman and member of Parliament for London. Sir John died in 1475, as is testified to this day by his tomb in the church of St. Helen. In the following year Crosby House took its place in the History of England, by becoming the residence of Richard Duke of Gloucester, and it was here that the crown was offered to the future king. After this Crosby Hall had a chequered career. For some time it was the residence of the Lord Mayor of London, and later Sir Thomas More became its occupant. By Sir Thomas it was sold to his friend Antonio Bombici, and subsequently passed through the hands of many different owners. For nearly a hundred years after 1672, the great hall was used as a place of meeting for Nonconformists, and the East India Company were lodged in Crosby Hall for a short time in 1700. After it was disused as a meeting-house, the hall fell into private hands and suffered considerable damage, and it was not until about 1836 that it was restored to something like its old appearance. For eighteen years, from 1842, the premises were occupied by a literary and scientific society. To this succeeded a firm of wine merchants, and all that remains of Crosby Hall is now occupied as a great restaurant, the proprietors of which have adapted the requirements of their business to the architectural and historical associations of the building.

Crystal Palace, Sydenham.—About seven miles from London. Erected at a cost of nearly £1,500,000. The Palace and Grounds, which cover about 200 acres, were opened in 1854. Concerts, dramatic entertainments, flower-shows, shows of different kinds of live-stock, &c., are held annually, the charge for admission being usually one shilling, or by guinea season ticket. Fireworks

during the summer season. The Aquarium is well stocked with choice specimens of fish. There is a good picture-gallery, to which the admission is free. The Grounds are tastefully laid out with flowers, cascades, and fountains. Reached by rail from London-br, Victoria, and Kensington (L. B. & S. C. R.), also from Moorgate-st, Holborn, Ludgate-hill, and Victoria (L. C. & D. R.). Fares from Victoria, 1st, 1/3, 2/-; 2nd, 1/-, 1/6; 3rd, -/7, 1/-. King's ✠ to High Level, 1st, 1/6, 2/-; 2nd, 1/-, 1/6; 3rd, -/9, 1/-. Kensington, 1st, 1/9, 2/6; 2nd, 1/4, 2/-; 3rd, -/10, 1/6. Return tickets, including admission, on 1/- days, 3/-, 2/3, 1/9. Liberal arrangements for reduction of fares in the case of large parties of excursionists are made both by the L. B. & S. C. R. and the L. C. & D. R. in connection with the Crystal Palace Co., to the managers of which application should be made at least three days before the intended visit. A reduction in the price of admission is also made in favour of large parties visiting the Palace by road. Application to be made to the Secretary of the Crystal Palace Company at least two days before the excursion.—(*And see* APPENDIX AND CALENDAR.)

Customs.—The Custom House (Map 8) is in Lower Thames-st, and the departments are: the Secretary's, Surveyor - General's, Law Officers', Comptroller of Accounts', Statistical, and Long Room, the office hours being from 10 to 4. The outdoor department comprises surveyors, assistant-surveyors, examining officers, gaugers (with inspectors and assistant-inspectors). On arriving from the Continent by train, unregistered luggage is examined at the port of debarkation; registered luggage at the terminal station of the line in London. By boat, the examination takes place on board on the way up from Gravesend, unless the passenger lands at Gravesend, when his luggage is searched there. NEAREST *Ry. Stns.*, Monument (or Mark-la) (Dis. and Met.) and Cannon-st (S.E.); *Omnibus Rte.*, King William - st; *Cab Rank*, Great Tower-hill.

Cycling.—(*See* BICYCLING.)

Deaths. — (*See* REGISTERS, *and* HEALTH.)

Denmark. — MINISTRY, 18, Grosvenor-sq, W. NEAREST *Ry. Stn.*, Edgware-rd (Met.); *Omnibus Rtes.*, Oxford-st and Park-la; *Cab Rank*, Portman-st, W. CONSULATE, 5, Muscovy-ct, Towerhill. NEAREST *Ry. Stns.*, Tower of London and Aldgate (Met.); *Omnibus Rtes.*, Gracechurch-st and Fenchurch-st; *Cab Rank*, Royal Mint-st.

Devonshire Club, 50, St. James's-st.— Political club, on a broad basis, in strict connection with, and designed to promote the objects of, the Liberal party. Only those entertaining Liberal principles and who recognise individual freedom of political opinion, combined with unity in party action, are eligible as candidates. Entrance fee, £31 10s.; subscription, £10 10s.

Dinners.—The Langham Hotel, the Midland Hotel, the St. James's Hotel, the Burlington Hotel, the Hotels Métropole and Victoria in Northumberland-avenue, the Criterion Restaurant, the Holborn Viaduct Hotel, the "Albion," in Aldersgate-st, the "Ship and Turtle," Leadenhall-st, and the Holborn Restaurant, all have excellent reputations for large dinners in the best style.—(*See also* RESTAURANTS, CHOP-HOUSES, *and* FISH DINNERS.)

Distances from the Bank (in minutes) to the principal stations of the Underground Railway :—

	Viâ District.	Metrop.
Acton	42	—
Addison-rd	38	—
Aldersgate..........	—	11
Aldgate	—	8
Baker-st............	—	25
Bishopsgate	—	6
Bishop's-rd	—	30
Blackfriars	—	5
Brondesbury........	—	39
Charing ✝...........	11	—
Ealing Broadway ..	51	—
,, Common	48	—
Earl's Court	28	—
Edgware-rd	—	27
Farringdon-st	—	12
Finchley-rd	—	34
Gloster-rd	26	—
Gower-st	—	20
Grove-rd	—	46
Gunnersbury	44	56
Hammersmith	34	46
High-st Kensington.	31	—
Kew-gdns	47	59

	District.	Metrop.
King's ✝...........	—	16
Latimer-rd	45	41
Mansion House	5	—
Mark-la	—	7
Marlboro'-rd.......	—	30
Mill Hill-pk	45	—
Moorgate-st	—	7
Notting Hill........	—	38
Notting Hill-gate ..	35	36
Parson's-gn	35	—
Portland-rd	—	22
Praed-st............	—	30
Putney-br	38	—
Queen's-rd	37	34
Richmond	52	64
Royal Oak	—	33
St. James's-pk	15	—
St. John's Wood-rd..	—	28
Shaftesbury.......	37	49
Shepherd's Bush ...	—	43
Sloane-sq	20	—
South Kensington ..	24	—
Swiss Cottage	—	32
Temple	9	—
Turnham-gn	40	52
Uxbridge-rd	39	45
Victoria	17	—
Walham-gn	33	—
Westbourne-pk	—	35
West Brompton	30	—
West Hampstead ..	—	36
West Kensington ..	31	—
Westminster........	13	—
Willesden	—	42

The line of equidistance from the Bank—*i.e.*, that from one side of which the shortest route is by way of the Metropolitan, and the other by way of the District Line—may be taken roughly to extend from St. Botolph's Church, Aldersgate-st, along the north of Christ's Hospital, and through Cock-la and Snow-hill to the Holborn end of Hatton-gdn; thence along Hatton-gdn, Cross-st, Leather-la, &c., to the Foundling Hospital; thence south again along Gt. Ormond-st, Cosmo-pl, Southampton-row, and Gt. Russell-st, to the junction of Tottenham-ct-rd and Oxford-st; along Oxford-st to Poland-st, thence by Gt. Marlboro'-st and Argyll-pl into Hanover-sq, and *viâ* Brook-st, in a straight line across Hyde-pk and Kensington-gdns to the Round Pond and Kensington Palace.

District Boards of Works.—(*See* VESTRIES.)

Docks.—The principal London Docks are :—

EAST AND WEST INDIA DOCKS, Blackwall and Tilbury. NEAREST *Ry. Stns.* for Blackwall, West India Dock, Poplar, or Blackwall

(G.E.); *Omnibus Rte.*, Blackwall. Offices, Billiter-st, E.C. NEAREST *Ry Stns.*, Fenchurch-st (G.E.) & Aldgate (Met.); *Omnibus Rtes.*, Fenchurch-st, Gracechurch-st, and Leadenhall-st.

LONDON DOCKS, E. Smithfield. NEAREST *Ry. Stn.*, Leman-st (G.E.); *Omnibus Rte.*, Commercial-rd, E. Offices, Leadenhall-st. NEAREST *Ry. Stns.*, Fenchurch-st (G.E.) and Mark-la (Dis. and Met.); *Omnibus Rtes.*, Fenchurch-st, Leadenhall-st, and Gracechurch-st.

MILLWALL DOCKS, Isle of Dogs. NEAREST *Ry. Stn.*, Millwall (G.E.); *Omnibus Rte.*, East India-rd, Blackwall. Offices, Railway-pl, Fenchurch-st. NEAREST *Ry. Stns.*, Fenchurch-st (G.E.) and Aldgate (Met.); *Omnibus Rtes.*, Fenchurch-st, Gracechurch-st, and Leadenhall-st.

ST. KATHARINE'S DOCKS, East Smithfield. NEAREST *Ry. Stn.*, Leman-st (G.E.); *Omnibus Rte.*, Commercial-rd, E. Offices, Leadenhall-st. NEAREST *Ry. Stn.*, Fenchurch-st (G.E.); *Omnibus Rtes.*, Aldgate and Fenchurch-st.

SURREY COMMERCIAL DOCKS, Rotherhithe. NEAREST *Ry. Stns.*, Rotherhithe and Deptford-rd (East London); *Omnibus Rtes.*, Deptford Lower-rd (Rotherhithe). Offices, 106, Fenchurch-st. NEAREST *Ry. Stns.*, Fenchurch-st (G.E.) and Aldgate (Met.); *Omnibus Rtes.*, Fenchurch-st, Gracechurch-st, and Leadenhall-st.

REGENT DOCK, Limehouse. NEAREST *Ry. Stn.*, Limehouse (G.E.); *Omnibus Rte.*, Commercial-rd, E. Offices, 85, Gracechurch-st. NEAREST *Ry. Stns.*, Fenchurch-st (G.E.) & Cannon-st (S.E.); *Omnibus Rtes.*, Gracechurch-st, Cannon-st, and Cornhill.

VICTORIA AND ALBERT (ROYAL) DOCKS, Nrth. Woolwich. NEAREST *Ry. Stns.*, Victoria Docks, Connaught-rd, Central, and Gallion's (G.E.); *Omnibus Rte.*, East India-rd. Offices, Leadenhall-st. NEAREST *Ry. Stn.*, Fenchurch-st (G.E.); *Omnibus Rtes.*, Aldgate and Fenchurch-st.

Applications for permission to view the warehouses, &c., should be addressed to the Secretaries at their respective offices.

Doctors.— (*See* HOSPITALS.)

Dog Stealers.—Lost dogs are often found at the Home for

Lost Dogs, Battersea, whither those found straying by the police are sent. Information of the loss of a dog should be given to the nearest police-station, and if, after an advertisement offering reward, overtures be made for the restoration of the animal, a further appointment should be made and the police informed. Even although the dog may not be recovered, it is a public duty to endeavour to punish this class of offence.

Drainage.—Notwithstanding all the boasted advance of sanitary science, the sewage of London, with the exception of a not inconsiderable quantity which leaks through defective pipes and joints into the soil and renders basements damp and unhealthy, is still discharged into the River Thames. The gigantic work of sewerage was undertaken by the Metropolitan Board of Works, and carried into effect at immense cost. As the outfall is now near the mouth of the river, the danger to health of the residents in the metropolis is considerably less than when the sewage was discharged at many points in the upper parts of the stream; but it is still carried by the tide far up the river, and, while that is the case, the sanitary condition of London can never be considered satisfactory. Nor is London water defiled by its own sewage only. The whole valley still drains into the Thames; and as the House of Commons in 1879 refused by a majority of 22 in a house of 314 to allow the discussion in committee of the elaborately prepared scheme of the Lower Thames Valley Main Sewerage Board, there does not seem to be any very immediate prospect of any amendment. In the older London houses cesspools and brick drains are still to be found. These should, in all cases, be removed, and glazed stoneware pipe-drains substituted. Should it be necessary to make a new connection between the house drain and the sewer, application must be made to the parish authorities at the District Board of Works or Vestry, who will cause the connection to be made by their own contractor. The cost of this work varies according to circumstances, and is charged to the applicant. The connection of the house with the sewer, however, is not by any means all that is required. One of the chief dangers

to health in cities is sewage gas; and it is not too much to say that, in the majority of London houses, the general drainage arrangements tend rather to its admission than to its exclusion. Dr. Buchanan, one of the medical officers of the Local Government Board, says: "The air of the sewers is, as it were, 'laid on' to the houses." The larger the house the greater is the danger, as, unless the drainage and plumbers' work has been executed in the most perfect manner, every lavatory, bath, sink, &c., is an additional danger. Authors of books on drainage generally make a point of telling their readers that in no case should drains run under the house. In the majority of London houses, it is impossible that they should run any other way, the sewer generally being under the road in front, and the sink, baths, &c., at the back of the house. The only thing to be done, therefore, is to make the house gas-tight, and to this end both good material and good workmanship are essential. Assuming the glazed stoneware pipes to be properly jointed in cement and laid to regular falls, the next most important operation is the introduction of a water-trap between the house and the sewer, and the construction in the area, or other convenient situation, of a chamber or chambers in which are open channels, through which the whole of the drainage from the house must pass. This chamber, or manhole, should be covered with an iron grating or close lid, according to circumstances. In the latter case, air-flues, or in-lets, must be inserted. The fresh air enters this chamber, traverses the drains, and passes up the soil-pipe, which should be carried well above the roof of the house, and left open at the top. The ventilating pipe should not be less than 4-in. in diameter, and care should be taken that it does not terminate near a window. This system of disconnection and ventilation is considered by the leading authorities to be the best means of preventing sewage-gas from entering dwelling-houses, and no expensive patent cowls or traps are necessary. No waste or overflow pipes should be directly connected with the drain or soil-pipe, but all should discharge in the open air over trapped gullies. Before taking a house in London, a fee to a competent architect or

engineer to inspect the drainage will be money well invested *(see* HOUSES*.*)

Drapers' Company (The) possess a local habitation in Throgmorton-st, which for luxury and magnificence could hardly be surpassed. Architect, decorator, and upholsterer seem to have done their utmost. There has been no attempt to reproduce the aspect of a mansion in the sixteenth or seventeenth century, as everything is new, solid, comfortable, and costly. The hall, court, and reception-rooms are on the first floor of the building, and overlook the quadrangle, which is a handsome square of some forty-five feet. Dispersed through the various apartments are a valuable collection of oil paintings. Of these a portrait of Mary Queen of Scots and her little son, alleged to be the work of Zucchero, and Sir W. Beechey's portrait of Nelson, are the most interesting. A portrait of Mr. John Taber, once master of the company, by Richmond, R.A., is one of the latest works acquired by the company. The principal staircase is conspicuous for its marble baluster and statues of Edward III., who granted a charter to the company, and of his queen. The Drapers believe that their body supplied the first Lord Mayor of London. Schools at Barton, Stratford-le-Bow, Worsborough, Kirkham, Greenwich, &c., are in possession of the company.

Dreadnought Seamen's Hospital.—(*See* HOSPITALS.)

Dress.—If all you care about is not to be stared at, you may now walk about most parts of London in any ordinary English costume. If, however, you wish to go into the park during parade hours in the season, to the "Zoo" on Sunday afternoons, the Horticultural Gardens, or any other fashionable resort, gloves, chimney-pot hat, orthodox morning coat, &c., are still essential. If you have business to transact you will find it also an advantage to be got up in conventional style. Evening dress is not *de rigueur* in any part of any of the theatres, though on the whole it predominates in the stalls, especially in theatres such as the Lyceum, the Gaiety, the Savoy, the Haymarket, the Comedy, the Court, and the Criterion. Don't wear a scarlet opera-cloak, however, if you can help it. It is commonly regarded by the initiated as strong evidence that its owner has come in with an "order." Ladies frequent the stalls as much as any other part of the theatre. At the Italian operas evening dress is indispensable in every part except gallery and amphitheatre stalls. This rule is rigorously enforced to the smallest detail, and it is hopeless to think of evading it. If, however, you have no dress-suit of your own, and do not object to wearing other people's, there are shops in King-st, Covent-gdn, Chandos-st, and elsewhere, where you can hire for the night. The usual prices are, for hire for the day, coat, 5s. ; vest, 2s. ; trousers, 3s. ; overcoat, 5s. Black suits are let for funerals at similar prices, and umbrellas at 2s. 6d. per day. Of course, a deposit of the value of the articles has to be left during the hiring.

Drinking Fountains.—Until the last few years London was ill-provided with public drinking fountains and cattle-troughs. This matter is now well looked after by the Metropolitan Drinking Fountain and Cattle Trough Association, which has erected and is now maintaining more than 1,200 fountains and troughs, at which an enormous quantity of water is consumed daily. It is estimated that 300,000 people take advantage of the fountains on a summer's day, and a single trough has supplied the wants of 1,900 horses in one period of 24 hours. Several ornamental fountains have been provided by private munificence. Amongst these may be instanced the Baroness Burdett Coutts's beautiful fountains in Victoria-pk and Regent's-pk ; the Maharajah of Vizianagram's in Hyde-pk ; Mrs. Wheeler's at the north of Kew-br ; and Mr. Buxton's at Westminster ; nearly all of which were erected by the association.

Drury Lane Theatre, Catherine-st, Strand (Map 7).—The oldest, as it is also one of the largest, of the theatres proper of London. It is the only house about which any historical flavour now lingers, and its stage has been trodden by Elliston, Dowton, Bannister, Wallack, Mrs. Glover, the Kembles, the Keans, Grimaldi, Braham, Young, Mrs. Nisbett,

Storace, Oxberry, Irish Johnstone, Farren, Harley, Keeley, Mdme. Vestris, Helen Faucit, Ellen Tree, Macready, and many others. In the green room, the windows of which look out on Vinegar-yd, are busts of Siddons, Kemble, and Kean, and here on Twelfth Night is rather a curious ceremony, when a cake, provided by a bequest of Baddeley the actor, is cut up and eaten by the company. In the hall are several other busts and statues. The modern taste for flimsy pieces, and the enormous runs to which the public are accustomed at the smaller houses, renders a theatre on the scale of Drury Lane a rather hazardous speculation nowadays. People forget that a three weeks' "run" at Drury Lane is equivalent to a hundred nights at many theatres, and, as at least nine people out of ten go to see a piece simply because it is a success, the big building is apt to be left out in the cold. At the same time there is no stage in London where a play depending in any degree upon broad and massive effects can be presented to anything like the advantage which may be given it at Drury Lane. NEAREST Ry. Stn., Temple ; Omnibus Rte., Strand ; Cab Rank, Opposite.

Duchy of Cornwall, Buckingham-gate, St. James's-pk, S.W. Hours 10 to 4.—NEAREST Ry. Stn., Victoria ; Omnibus Rtes., Victoria-st and Grosvenor-pl ; Cab Rank, James-st.

Duchy of Lancaster, Lancaster-pl, Strand. Hours 10 to 5, Saturdays 10 to 2.—NEAREST Ry. Stn., Temple ; Omnibus Rtes., Wellington-st and Strand ; Cab Rank, Wellington-st.

Dudley Gallery Art Society (The), Egyptian Hall, Piccadilly, W. (Map 6).—There are three Dudley Exhibitions in the year. The spring exhibition of water-colour drawings, from Jan. 7 to April 1, for members of the society ; the summer exhibition of water-colour drawings, open to all, from June to August ; and the exhibition of cabinet pictures in oil, from November to Christmas, for members of the society. The exhibitions are opened at 10 a.m., the hours of closing being regulated according to the season, and the charge for admission is 1s., catalogues 6d. "Sending in"

day this year for the oil pictures is the 6th October. A commission of 7½ per cent. in the case of water colour drawings and oil picture is charged on sale of exhibits. A further particulars as to condition under which works may be exhibited, &c., may be obtained o application to the Secretary Colonel Freeth, at the hall NEAREST Ry. Stns., Charing (S.E. and Dis.); Omnibus Rte. Piccadilly ; Cab Rank, Piccadill

Dulwich College wa founded in the year A.D. 1619 by Edward Alleyn, under Letter Patent of King James I., by which licence was granted t Alleyn to establish a College "t endure and remain for ever ;" an to be called "The College o God's Gift in Dulwich, in the County of Surrey." The Mano of Dulwich—which constitutes the most important part of the en dowment of the college—was pur chased by Alleyn in A.D. 1606 from Sir Francis Carlton, to whose ancestor, Thomas Carlton it had been granted by Henry VIII. on the dissolution of the Monastery of Bermondsey. Al leyn's gift was for many years no exception to the general rule, tha the benevolent intentions of pious founders are pretty certain to be perverted by those to whom it fall to administer them. Until within the last thirty years, the growing wealth of Dulwich College—in creasing year by year, as the great city came nearer and neare to the manor of Dulwich—wa followed by no increase of useful ness. Indeed, Dulwich was rapidly taking its place amongst the scan dals to which the enemies of piou founders are so fond of pointing and reform became absolutely necessary. A vigorous effort wa made by the dramatic profession headed by Mr. Benjamin Webster to obtain a share of Alleyn's gift which seems originally to hav had distinct reference to his own profession—for Alleyn himself hae been, and had made his money as an actor. Indeed, there was n ack of claimants. An arrange ment was arrived at in 1857, when the old Corporation of the "Col lege of God's Gift" was dissolve by Act of Parliament, and a new Governing Body was established consisting of nineteen Governors of whom eleven were to be ap pointed by the Court of Chancery and two by each of the parishes o

Camberwell, Bishopsgate, St. Luke, Finsbury, and St. Saviour, Southwark. A further scheme for the management of the charity was approved by Her Majesty in Council on 18th August, 1882—greatly modifying the arrangement of 1857. By it the Educational Branch is entirely separated from the management of the estates, and a separate Governing Body was constituted for each division. The Upper and Lower Schools are now entirely separate and distinct institutions; the former being now known as Dulwich College, the latter as Alleyn School, and £12,000 capital was provided under the scheme for the erection of new school buildings. The Eleemosynary Branch of the charity is placed under the jurisdiction of the Estate Governors, but remains practically unchanged.

THE PICTURE GALLERY.—Open free every week day from 10 to 5 from April to October; from 10 to 4 from November to March. The easiest access to the Gallery is by the L.C. & D. Ry. from Ludgate, Holborn Viaduct, or Victoria. Distance five miles.

Dust.—(*See* ASHES.)

East India United Service Club, 16, St. James's-sq.—Consists of gentlemen who are or have been commissioned officers in Her Majesty's or the East Indian army or navy; members of the Indian civil, ecclesiastical, or medical services; judges of a high or civil court; members of a legislative council; or law officers of government in India. The members elect, and more than one black ball in ten excludes. The "entrance donation" is £30, and "library donation" £1; subscription, for home members, £8 8s., absentee members, £1.

Ecclesiastical Commissioners, 10, Whitehall - place, S.W.—Hours 10 to 4. NEAREST *Ry. Stns.*, Charing ✠ (Dis. and S.E.); *Omnibus Rtes.*, Whitehall, Strand, and Victoria-st; *Cab Rank*, Horse Guards.

Ecuador, Republic of.—CONSULATE, 9, New Broad-st. NEAREST *Ry. Stn.*, *Omnibus Rte.*, and *Cab Rank*, Bishopsgate-st.

Edgware Road (Map 1), the great north-western road, starts from the west end of Oxford-st, and leads past Maida-vale, St. John's Wood, and Kilburn to Hendon,

and so north. About four miles from the Marble Arch lies the "Welsh Harp," a great place in summer for parties in vans, bean-feasters, and other pleasure-seekers. The nearest railway-station to the Welsh Harp is the Welsh Harp Station on the Midland Railway.

Egyptian Hall, Piccadilly (Map 6).—This building has for some years been successfully occupied by Messrs. Maskelyne & Cooke's Entertainment. NEAREST *Ry. Stn.*, St. James's-pk; *Omnibus Rtes.*, Piccadilly and Regent-st; *Cab Rank*, Albany.

Elephant and Castle Theatre, New Kent-rd, S.E. (Map 14).—A transpontine house of no particular characteristic. NEAREST *Ry. Stn.*, Elephant and Castle; *Omnibus Rtes.*, London-rd, Walworth-rd, New Kent-rd, and Newington-causeway; *Cab Rank*, St. George's-rd.

Embassies.—(*See under their respective heads.*)

Emigration Agents for the Colonies.—
CANADA, 9, Victoria-chambers, S.W.
CAPE OF GOOD HOPE, 7 & 9, Albert Mansions, Victoria - st, S.W.
NATAL, 21, Finsbury-cir, E.C.
NEW SOUTH WALES, 5, Westminster-chambers, S.W.
NEW ZEALAND, 7, Westminster-chambers, S.W.
QUEENSLAND, 1, Westminster-chambers, S.W.
SOUTH AUSTRALIA AND VICTORIA, 8, Victoria-chambers, S.W.
Other Colonies, the Colonial Office, Downing-street, S.W.

Empire Club, 4, Grafton-st, Piccadilly, was closed in 1886, when most of the members joined the St. George's Club, Hanover-sq.

Empire Theatre, Leicester-sq (Map 7).—A large, commodious, and very handsome structure, capable of holding about 1,500 persons, opened as a theatre on the 17th of April, 1884, and licensed as a music hall on the 12th of October, 1887. NEAREST *Ry. Stn.*, Charing ✠ (Dis. and S.E.); *Omnibus Rtes.*, Regent-st, Piccadilly, and St. Martin's-la; *Cab Rank*, Leicester-sq.

Envelope Addressers.—G. S. SMITH & Co., 220, Gresham House, Old Broad-st, 7s. 6d. per 1,000. HORNCASTLE'S CENTRAL

ADVERTISEMENT OFFICES, 61, Cheapside, 7s. 6d. per 1,000. STAFF & Co., 2, Soho-sq, 5s. per 1,000

Epping Forest and neighbourhood.—(*See* EXCURSIONS.)

Euston Station (Map 2).—Terminus of the L. & N.W. Ry., on the north side of Euston-sq, through which a road has been cut, leading directly from the Euston-rd to the station. The station itself is split in two by a huge hall. On either side is a booking office, with a corresponding departure platform. The Euston Hotel is just outside the station gates. NEAREST *Ry. Stn.*, Gower-st (Met.); *Omnibus Rtes.*, Hampstead-rd, Euston-rd, and Old St. Pancras-rd; *Cab Fare* to Bank, 1/6; to Charing ✠, 1/-

Exchequer and Audit Department, Somerset House, Strand, W.C.--Hours 10 to 4, Sat. 10 to 2. The department is subdivided into the Directing Branch and the Examining Branch. There is also a third, the Chancery Audit Branch, in Chancery-la, W.C. NEAREST *Ry. Stn.*, Temple; *Omnibus Rte.*, Strand; *Cab Rank*, Catherine-st.

Excursions.-The Londoner's great excursion districts are the river to the West, Epping Forest to the East, Hampstead and Highgate (*which see*) to the North, and to the South the varied scenery of Surrey, Sussex, and Kent, and the sea. With regard to the first of these the fullest and most detailed information will be found in DICKENS'S DICTIONARY OF THE THAMES. Enough here to note that for what may be termed the home section of the river, including Wandsworth, Fulham, Putney, Castlenau, Hammersmith, Chiswick, Barnes, Mortlake, Kew, Brentford, and Richmond, the best route is by the District Railway. The stranger to London and the beautiful country near it should on no account omit to visit Richmond. There is a branch line (*see* RAILWAYS) from Earl's Court to Fulham and Putney - br, whence a line of special omnibuses connects with the Common, &c. Beyond Richmond is a short stretch of river which can only be reached, railway-wise, by crossing Waterloo-br and travelling by the South-Western line. But at "Royal Windsor" the Great Western takes up the running, and from this point, through Maidenhead, Taplow,

D

Cookham, Great Marlow, Henley, Shiplake, Sonning, Reading, and on to Wallingford, Abingdon, Oxford, and the far-away source itself, the line has the national river to itself. The pick of the river is for the home section about Richmond and Kingston; for the upper portion at Cookham and Henley, this latter district affording not only the best of boating and angling, but some very pretty and thoroughly English country scenery. The extensive and carefully-kept beech-woods in their autumn dress are particularly well worth a visit.

The Eastern District is served exclusively by the Great Eastern Railway, which in the excursion season lays itself out with considerable energy for the accommodation of the Londoner in search of the fresh air and singularly wild and picturesque scenery of Epping Forest and its neighbourhood. The principal points are

Ambresbury Bank, about halfway between the Wake Arms and Epping, and nearly opposite Copt Hall Lane. Supposed to have been the camp of Suetonius the night before his final victory over Boadicea. Nearest station, Theydon Bois.

Buckhurst Hill, the starting-point of the once famous Epping Hunt, originally founded early in the thirteenth century, when the citizens of London received from Henry III. royal permission to hunt deer. The deer themselves were at that time to be found in the wood, and did not require, as in the present century, to be bottled especially for the occasion. Station, Buckhurst Hill.

British Camp (ancient), about two miles north of Loughton.

Chigwell, birthplace of Barnaby Rudge, and still graced by the presence of the "Maypole Inn," known to literal-minded wayfarers of the period as the "King's Head," an old building, "with more gable-ends than a lazy man would care to count on a sunny day; huge zigzag chimneys, out of which it seemed as though even smoke could not choose but come in more than naturally fantastic shapes imparted to it in its tortuous progress." Chigwell stands on the border of Hainault Forest, not far from the famous Fairlop Oak. Stations, by road Chigwell Lane, by footpath, Buckhurst Hill.

Chingford has a quaint old church, entirely shrouded in ivy, and is considered about the best starting-point for walks in the wilder parts of the Forest. Not the least of the recommendations of Chingford is the presence of the Forest Hotel adjoining Queen Elizabeth's Lodge, in the finest part of the Forest. Good residential accommodation, carriages and horses may be hired for excursions. It is close to Chingford Station, and about 35 minutes' journey from Liverpool-st. It is in contemplation to run a coach from the new Grand Hotel, Charing ✝, to Chingford.

Copt (or *Copped*) *Hall*, a fine old place, close to Epping, once the residence of Princess (afterwards Queen) Mary of England. Stations, Theydon Bois or Epping.

Epping, a little old country town, chiefly famous for its sausages, not a pound of which has been manufactured there within the memory of the oldest inhabitants. About three in every four of the houses in the long straggling street of which it solely consists, are inns, which no doubt at one time, say half a century since, did a certain proportion of business. At present they have rather the air of existing chiefly because they would not be worth any one's while to pull down. Station, Epping.

High Beech, a pleasant "objective" for a forest stroll from Loughton station (two miles), returning by Chingford (three miles), or *vice versâ*. Fine view and beautiful woods.

Lea (*The*), a good little river for boating and fishing.

Leyton, the southernmost point of the forest country, possesses no very particular feature of interest, except some quaint old monuments in the very ugly old church. Station, Leyton.

Loughton. One of the best starting-points for the central portion of the Forest, and once, before her accession, the residence of Qn. Anne. A short two miles to the northward is the supposed camp of her more picturesque predecessor, Boadicea. Station, Loughton.

Qn. Elizabeth's Lodge, formerly a hunting-box of that manful monarch, now a favourite headquarter of picnic and pleasure-parties. Close to Chingford Stn., and adjoining the Royal Forest Hotel.

Roding (*The*), a pleasant little stream, skirting the eastern boundary of the forest from Chigwell to Snaresbrook, on its way to Barking Creek.

Snaresbrook. So much of this once picturesque spot has been carried away in the shape of gravel, that it is now chiefly noteworthy for the ponds which, especially in rainy weather, occupy a considerable portion of what was formerly its soil. It is a handy station, however, for the extreme southern district of the Forest.

Theydon Bois—in local parlance, "Theydon Byce"—a good station for the northern end of the Forest, about a mile and a half short of Epping.

Waltham Abbey is hardly a Forest locality, but it is within easy walking distance of the north-western portion, and is handy for the Lea. Harold, last of the Saxon kings, lies buried here. Waltham Abbey itself is on the low, flat ground overlooked by High Beech, distant about a couple of miles. Station, Waltham ✝, on the Cambridge line (G.E.).

Wanstead is the final outlying portion of the Forest in a south-easterly direction, the flats having more the character of common than forest ground, and being much affected by cricketers and devotees of other more or less athletic sports. Stations, Forest Gate and Leytonstone.

Woodford, a good starting point for the southern end of the principal block of unspoiled forest, reaching thence to Epping, distant, by what is known as "the New Road" through the heart of this district, between six and seven miles. Stations, George Lane and Woodford.

Of short seaside trips, that to Brighton occupies, of course, the first place; by far the pleasantest mode of making it being by the excellently appointed four-horse coach which runs daily from the "White Horse Cellar" throughout the season.—(*See* COACHING.) Those who like a milder climate and more countrified surroundings cannot do better than try Hastings, approached by S.E.R., or L.B. & S.C., or through a very pretty and thoroughly English line of country, the road lying through the heart of the Kentish hop grounds. About half-way down is Tunbridge Wells, also quite worthy a visit. Farther east are Ramsgate, Margate, and Broadstairs, attainable by either S.E.R. or L.C. & D., Margate—the Cockney watering-place *par excellence*—having a special interest for the foreign visitor of an enquiring turn. On the same lines, between London and Ramsgate, lies Canterbury. On the L.C. & D., nearer London, is Rochester, with the beautiful country about Cobham; and the country about Orpington, Chislehurst, and St. Mary Cray should also be seen. Guildford, Boxhill, Dorking, and the neighbourhood are well worth a visit, the walks over the downs and hills being especially delightful. Folkestone and Dover are both capital seaside places, the latter accessible either by L.C. & D. or S.E.R., the former, with its quiet little neighbours, Sandgate and Hythe, by S.E. only. The Isle of Wight is perhaps rather too far distant to be included in a list of excursions, but will well repay the tourist for a visit. Westgate-on-Sea, near Margate, and Granville-on-Sea, which is practically the western division of Ramsgate, are pleasant places for a few days' outing. Finally may be mentioned on the Essex coast Southend-on-Sea and Clacton-on-Sea, particularly notable as seaside places of a comparatively unsophisticated type, and with more moderate views as to the relation of cost to accommodation than distinguish their more time-honoured competitors.

Fairs.—The principal fairs in the home counties are:

BRAINTREE, May 8, Oct 2. From Liverpool-st (1 h. 40 min.), 1st 8/6, 12/9; 2nd, 6/6, 10/3; 3rd, 3/10, 7/8.

BRENTFORD, May 17, Sept. 12. From Waterloo (39 min.) and Ludgate-hill (56 min.), 1st, 1/-, 1/6; 2nd, -/10, 1/2; 3rd, -/8, 1/-.

BRENTWOOD, Oct. 15. From Liverpool-st (34 min.), 1st, 3/6, 5/-; 2nd, 2/6, 3/9; 3rd, 1/6, 2/9.

CHELMSFORD, May 12, Nov. 12. From Liverpool-st (47 min.), 1st, 5/9, 8/6; 2nd, 4/4, 6/10; 3rd, 2/6½, 5/1.

CHERTSEY, 1st Mon. in Lent, May 14, Aug. 6, Sep.25. From Waterloo (48 min.), 1st, 4/-, 5/6; 2nd, 3/-, 4/-; 3rd, 1/10, 3/4.

COBHAM, May 1, Dec. 11. From Waterloo (45 min.), 1st, 3/6; 2nd, 2/8; 3rd, 1/7.

CROYDON, Oct. 2 and 3.—From London-br or Victoria to East Croydon, 1st, 2/-, 3/6; 2nd, 1/6, 2/6; 3rd, -/10, 1/6.

DORKING, Ascension Day and previous day. From London-br (1 h. 13 min.), 1st, 4/-, 6/-; 2nd, 3/-, 4/6; 3rd, 2/1, 3/3.

ENFIELD, November 30. From King's ✠ (27 min.), 1st, 1/4, 2/3; 2nd, 1/-, 1/8; 3rd, -/9, 1/3. From Liverpool-st (40 min.), 1st, 1/8, 2/6; 2nd, 1/3, 1/10; 3rd, -/11, 1/4.

EPPING, Nov. 13. From Liverpool-st and Fenchurch-st (1 h. 3 min.), 1st, 2/11, 4/3; 2nd, 2/1, 3/2; 3rd, 1/5½, 2/3.

EWELL, May 12, Oct. 29. From Waterloo (30 min.), 1st, 2/-, 2/6; 2nd, 1/6, 2/3; 3rd, 1/0½, 2/-. From London-br and Victoria (50 min.), 1st, 2/-, 2/6; 2nd, 1/6, 2/3; 3rd, 1/1; 2/-.

FARNHAM, May 10, June 24, Nov. 10. From Waterloo (1 h. 16 min.), 1st, 7/-; 2nd, 5/6; 3rd, 3/1.

FAVERSHAM, Oct. 11. From Victoria or Holborn Viaduct (2 h.), 1st, 12/6; 2nd, 8/6; 3rd, 4/4.

GODALMING, Feb. 13. From Waterloo (1 h. 25 min.), 1st, 6/6, 10/-; 2nd, 5/-, 7/-; 3rd, 2/10.

GREAT DUNMOW, May 6, Nov. 8. From Liverpool-st (1 h. 16 min.), 1st, 7/6, 11/4; 2nd, 5/9, 9/-; 3rd, 3/5, 6/10.

GRAVESEND, Oct. 24.

GUILDFORD, May 4, Nov. 22. From Waterloo (50 min.), 1st, 6/-, 10/-; 2nd, 4/4, 7/-; 3rd, 2/6.

HASLEMERE, May 13, Sept. 26. From Waterloo (1 h. 15 min.), 1st 8/6, 13/6; 2nd, 6/4, 9/6; 3rd, 3/7½.

HOUNSLOW, Trinity Monday, and Monday after Mich. Day. From Waterloo (54 m.), 1st, 1/3, 2/-; 2nd, 1/-, 1/8; 3rd, -/10, 1/6. From Ludgate-hill (1 h. 10 min.), 1st, 1/6, 2/3; 2nd 1/3, 1/9; 3rd, 1/-, 1/6.

KINGSTON, Nov. 1. From Waterloo (33 min.), 1st, 2/-, 2/6; 2nd, 1/6, 2/-; 3rd, 1/-, 1/8.

MAIDSTONE, Feb. 13, May 12, June 20, and Oct. 17. From Victoria or Holborn Viaduct (about 2 h.), 1st, 8/-; 2nd, 5/6; 3rd, 3/3.

MALDON, 1st Thursday in May and Sept. 13. From Liverpool-st (about 1 h. 30 min.), 1st, 8/6; 2nd, 6/6; 3rd, 3/9.

REIGATE, Dec. 9. From Charing ✠, Cannon-st, and London-br (1 h. 15 min.), 1st, 4/-, 6/-; 2nd, 2/6, 4/-; 3rd, 1/10, 2/9.

ROCHESTER, May 30. April 16, Aug. 30, and Dec. 11. From Victoria or Charing ✠ (about 1 h. 15 min.), 1st, 4/6; 2nd, 3/2; 3rd, 2/3.

STAINES, May 11, Sept. 19. From Waterloo (47 min.), 1st, 3/3, 5/-; 2nd, 2/3, 3/6; 3rd, 1/7, 3/-.

Farmers' Club, Salisbury-sq Hotel, Fleet-st, E.C.—Has for its object the discussion of subjects bearing upon agriculture, and to afford a point of union for farmers and others connected with agriculture. Two-thirds of the members must be either directly or indirectly interested in or connected with the cultivation of the soil. Practical farmers and scientific men of all countries are eligible. Entrance fee, £1 1s.; subscription, £1 1s., or £10 10s. for life.

Fetes and Entertainments.—The difficulty of arranging for these will be felt more by the country readers of the DICTIONARY than by the Londoner, although even the latter might possibly find himself in some dilemma on a sudden call for a long afternoon's show; but, as with most things in London, to know where to look for what you want is more than half the battle. The advertising columns of the *Era* will always give the proper clue to matters of this kind. Any of the dramatic agents, whose names may readily be found in the London Directory, can be safely applied to for information, assistance, and prices. A careful contract should always be framed.

Finsbury Park, an open space of about 120 acres, was formed from the old grounds of Hornsey Wood House. It is carefully laid out, and when the trees, &c., have had time to

D 2

grow, will be a very pretty spot. NEAREST *Ry. Stn.*, Finsbury-pk; *Omnibus Rtes.*, Seven Sisters'-rd and Green Lanes.

Fire. — If a fire break out, instant information should be conveyed to the police (*see* FIXED POINTS), and the nearest fire-station (*see* FIRE BRIGADE STATIONS). Windows and doors, admitting the draught, should be kept carefully closed. The women and children should be conveyed away as quickly as possible, and then valuables collected. Strangers should not be admitted until the arrival of the police. When the fire brigade commences operations they should not be hindered in any way in the execution of their duty.

Fire Brigade (Metropolitan), Head-quarters' Station, Southwark-br-rd, S.E. (Map 14).— According to Captain Shaw's report for 1887, the number of calls for fires or supposed fires received during the year has been 3,059. Of these 528 were false alarms, 168 proved to be only chimney alarms, and 2,363 were calls for fires of which 175 resulted in serious damage and 2,188 in slight damage. The fires of 1887, compared with those of 1886, show an increase of 214, and an increase of 408, compared with the average of the last 10 years, but the proportion of serious to slight losses, 175 to 2,188, is still most favourable. The number of fires in the metropolis in which life has been seriously endangered during the year 1887 was 146 ; and the number of those in which life was lost was 55. The number of persons seriously endangered by fire was 198, of whom 143 were saved, while 55 lost their lives. Of the 55 lost, 28 were taken out alive but died afterwards in hospitals or elsewhere, and 27 were suffocated or burned to death. The number of calls for chimneys was 1,655. Of these 517 proved to be false alarms, and 1,138 were for chimneys on fire. The number of journeys made by the fire-engines of the 55 land stations was 33,564, and the total distance run 64,294 miles. The quantity of water used for extinguishing fires in the metropolis during the year was a little more than 26,000,000 of gallons, or about 117,000 tons. Of this quantity about 57,000 tons were taken from the river,

canals, and docks, and the remainder from the street pipes. During the year there were 11 cases of short supply of water, 11 of late attendance of turncocks, and 6 of no attendance, making 28 cases in which the water arrangements were unsatisfactory, as against 29 the previous year. The strength of the Brigade is : 55 land fire-engine stations, 4 floating or river stations, 27 hose cart stations, 127 fire-escape stations, 5 steam fire-engines on barges, 45 land steam fire-engines, 78 6-inch manual fire-engines, 37 under 6-inch manual fire-engines, 74 hose carts, 2 self-propelling fire floats, 5 steam tugs, 9 barges, 146 fire-escapes, 9 long fire ladders, 9 ladder vans, 2 ladder trucks, 1 trolly for ladders, 1 trolly for engines, 11 hose and coal vans, 10 waggons for street duties, 5 street stations for ditto, 102 watch boxes, 591 firemen, including chief officer, second officer, superintendents, and all ranks, 16 pilots, 67 coachmen, 131 horses, 68 telephones between fire stations, 54 alarm circuits round fire stations, with 349 call points, 20 telephones to police stations, 15 telegraphs to public and other buildings, 23 telephones ditto, 17 bell-ringing fire alarms ditto. The number of firemen employed on the several watches kept up throughout the metropolis is at present 115 by day, and 245 by night, making a total of 360 in every 24 hours ; the remaining men being available for general work at fires.

METROPOLITAN FIRE BRIGADE STATIONS.

B DIVISION.

Relton Mews, Brompton-rd.
Westminster, Tothill-fields.

C DIVISION.

53, Great Marlborough-st.

D DIVISION.

Baker-st, 33, King-st, Baker-st

E DIVISION.

Great Scotland Yard.
Holborn, Theobald's-rd.
Portland-rd, 171, Great Portland-st.

G DIVISION.

Clerkenwell, Farringdon-rd.
St. Luke's, 64, Whitecross-st.
Shoreditch, 38, Old-st-rd.

H DIVISION.

Bethnal Gn., 283, Bethnal Gn.-rd.
Whitechapel, Commercial-rd.

K DIVISION.

Bow, Glebe-rd, behind Police Stn.
Mile End, 263, Mile End-rd.
Poplar, West India Dock-rd.
Shadwell, Glamis-rd.
West Ferry-rd, Isle of Dogs.

L DIVISION.

Kennington, Renfrew-rd.
Waterloo, 142, Waterloo-rd.

M DIVISION.

Southwark, Southwark-br-rd.
Tooley-st, cor. of Stony-la.

N DIVISION.

Hackney, Amhurst-rd.
Islington, Essex-rd.
Stoke Newington, Brooke-rd.

P DIVISION.

Camberwell, Peckham-rd.
Lewisham, Rushey-gn.
Old Kent-rd, corner of Thomas-st.
Lower Norwood, High-st, by the Church.
Sydenham, Crystal Palace.

R DIVISION.

Blackheath, Tranquil-vale.
Deptford, Evelyn-st.
Greenwich, South-st, Grove-st.
Rotherhithe, Gomm-rd.
Shooter's-hill, Shooter's-hill-rd.
Woolwich, Sun-st.

S DIVISION.

Hampstead, Heath-st, High-st.
St. John's Wood, Adelaide-rd.

T DIVISION.

Brompton, Trafalgar-sq.
Chelsea, Pavilion-rd.
Fulham, Walham-gn.
Hammersmith, Brook-green-rd.
Kensington, King-st.

V DIVISION.

Battersea-rd, opposite Christ Ch.
Wandsworth, 123, High-st.

W DIVISION.

Brixton, Ferndale-rd.
Clapham, Clapham-com, Old Tn.
Tooting, Balham-hill-rd.

X DIVISION.

North Kensington, Faraday-rd.
Notting Hill, Ladbroke-rd.
Paddington, Hermitage-st.

Y DIVISION.

Camden Tn, King's-rd.
Kentish Tn., Willow-walk.
Seven Sisters-rd, near Nag's Head.

THAMES.

Floating Engines off Bankside, Rotherhithe, Old Pimlico Pier, Limehouse.

CITY DIVISION.

23, Bishopsgate-st-without.
67 to 69, Watling-st, Cheapside.

METROPOLITAN FIRE ESCAPE STATIONS.

B DIVISION.

Broad Sanctuary, Westminster.

Brompton, at Knightsbridge-gn.
Chapel-pl, Brompton-rd.
Eaton-sq, by St. Peter's Ch.
Fulham-rd, Pelham-cres.
Hyde-pk-cor, Marble Arch, movable stn. by night.
Pavilion-rd, at engine-station.
Victoria-st, at the engine-stn.
Warwick-sq, St. Gabriel's Ch.

C Division.

Conduit-st, corner of George-st.
Golden-sq.
Piccadilly, facing St. James's Ch.
Regent-st, Argyll-pl.
South Audley-st, by the Chapel.

D Division.

Baker-st, corner of King-st.
Edgware-rd, near Cambridge-ter.
Oxford-st, corner of Marylebone-la
  ,,   ,,   Connaught-pl.

E Division.

Albany-st, by Trinity Ch.
Bedford-row, South-end.
Endell-st, near Long Acre.
Euston-sq, by St. Pancras Ch.
Great Portland-st, by the Chapel.
Great Scotland Yard.
Guildford-st, Foundling Hospital.
Hart-st, Bloomsbury.
King's ✝, Liverpool-st.
Oxford-st, opposite Dean-st, Soho.
Strand, by St. Clement's Ch., street-stn., and 4 men by night.
Tottenham-ct-rd, by the Chapel, street-stn., day and night.

G Division.

City-rd, street-stn., day and night.
Claremont-sq, Clerkenwell.
Goswell-st, oppo. St. Thomas's Ch.
Old-st, corner Bath-st, St. Luke's.
Old-st-rd, at engine-station.
St. John-st, opp. Corporation-row.

H Division.

Commercial-rd, Whitechapel.
Tower-hill, by the Mint, street-stn., and 4 men by night.

K Division.

Bethnal Gn, opposite St. John's Ch.
Bow, at engine-station.
East & West India Dock-rd.
Mile End-rd, Stepney-gn.
Old Ford, St. Stephen's-rd.
Poplar, opposite All Saints' Ch.
St. George-in-the-East.
St. John's, Wapping, front of Ch.
Stepney, in Commercial-rd, by the "Swan."
Shadwell, at the engine-stn.
Victoria-pk, by Christ Ch., street-station, day and night.
Wapping, Church-st.
West Ferry-rd, Isle of Dogs.

L Division.

Kennington ✝.

Lambeth, junction of Westminster-br and Kennington rds.
Newington-causeway, Elephant & Castle, street-station by night.

M Division.

Bermondsey, St. James's Ch., street-station by night.
Blackfriars-rd, Gt. Charlotte-st.
Southwark, St. George's Ch.
Southwark-br-rd, at engine-stn.
Star-corner, Bermondsey.
Tooley-st, at engine-stn.

N Division.

Hackney, Amhurst-rd.
Hoxton, "Sturt Arms."
Islington, Newington-gn-rd.
  ,,   Richmond-rd, Barnsbury.
  ,,   Green.
Kingsland, Ridley-rd.
Kingsland-rd, by the Workhouse.
Stoke Newington, at engine-stn.

P Division.

Arthur-st, Camberwell-gate.
Camberwell, on the Green
Hill-st, High-st, Peckham.
Lewisham, Avenue-rd.
Lower Norwood, at engine-stn.
Old Kent-rd, "Green Man" Gate.
Penge, Vestry Hall, Anerley-rd.
Sydenham, in the High-st.
Thomas-st, Old Kent-rd, corner of.

R Division.

Blackheath, near the ry.-stn.
Broadway, Deptford.
Deptford, Trinity Ch.
New ✝-rd.
Greenwich, oppo. St. Alphage Ch.
  ,,   at the engine-stn.
Rotherhithe, at the engine-stn.
  ,,   Commercial Docks.
  ,,   the Workhouse.
Spa-rd.
Woolwich, at engine-stn.
Shooter's-hill-rd, at engine-stn.

S Division.

Aberdeen-pl, St. John's Wood-rd.
Camden Tn., front of the "Southampton Arms."
Hampstead, corner of Heath-st.
Marylebone-rd, cor. of Albany-st.
Portsdown-pl, Maida Vale.
St. John's Wood, "Eyre Arms."
St. John's Wood, at the engine-stn.

T Division.

Chelsea, King's-rd, by Carlyle-sq.
Chepstow-pl, N.W. corner of.
Cromwell-rd, south-east side.
Fulham, Walham-gn, Percy ✝.
Hammersmith, engine-stn.
Kensington, King-st, engine-stn.
Lancaster-rd, op. Wesleyan Cha.
Redcliffe-sq, Brompton.
Russell-st, S.W. corner of.
Shepherd's Bush-common.
West Brompton ry.-stn.

V Division.

Battersea, at engine-stn.

Putney, adjoining police-stn.
Wandsworth, at engine-stn.

W Division.

Tooting Old engine-stn.
Brixton, Shepherd's-la.
Clapham Old Town engine-stn.
Orphanage, Clapham-rd.
Vauxhall ✝, street-station, and 4 men by night.

X Division.

Harrow-rd, at Workhouse.
High-st, Camden Tn.
Kentish Tn., Willow-walk.
Kentish Tn.-rd, near N. L. ry.-br.
Kilburn, Bridge-ter.
Lancaster-ga, Bayswater-rd.
Metropolitan Cattle Market.
North Kensington, at engine-stn.
Notting-hill, at engine-stn.
Paddington, Trinity Ch.
Seven Sisters'-rd, at engine-stn.
Victoria-rd, Holloway-rd.

Y Division.

Pond-square, Highgate, street-station by day and night.

City Division.

Aldersgate-st, Carthusian-st.
Aldgate, St. James's-pl, street-station, day and night.
Bishopsgate-st, at the engine-stn.
Eastcheap, corner of Rood-la.
Farringdon-st, street-stn., and 4 men, day and night.
Finsbury-cir, corner of West-st.
Holborn, street-stn., and 4 men by night.
Mansion House-place.
St. Martin's-le-Grand.

Hose Cart Only.

Aldersgate-st.
Fishmongers' Hall.
Fleet-st.
Lothbury.
Moor-lane Police-stn.
Queen Victoria-st.
St. Helen's-churchyard.
Snow-hill, St. Sepulchre's Ch.
Wood-st, St. Alban's-Ch.

The substitution of telephones for telegraphs, which was commenced some years ago, has been completed and proves a great advantage in the working of the establishment. The messages of the Brigade are now transmitted by telephone in considerably less time, and with much greater certainty than by any system of telegraphing.

Fish Dinners. — The typical fish dinner of London is the extraordinary entertainment offered at Greenwich—perhaps the most curious repast ever invented by the ingenuity of the most imaginative hotel-keeper. Many courses of fish prepared in every conceivable way, followed by ducks and peas, beans and bacon, cutlets, and other viands, so arranged as to stimulate a pleasing, if somewhat expensive thirst, are washed down at these Gargantuan feeds by the choicest brands at the highest prices known to civilisation. The effect at the moment is eminently delightful. The sensation experienced when the bill is produced is not so pleasurable, and it has been said that there is no "next morning headache" like that which follows a Greenwich dinner. But there is no doubt that a Greenwich dinner is a very excellent thing in its way—especially if you happen to be invited to dine by a liberal friend, who knows how to order dinner, and pay for it. Only two houses can be recommended for this kind of sport—the "Trafalgar" and the "Ship." It may be noted that when the labours of the session are over, the Ministers of the Crown dine at one of those two houses. A fish dinner of quite a different and more digestible class, although 11 kinds of fish, and a selection of joints, is served twice a day—at 1 and 4—at the "Three Tuns Tavern," Billingsgate, at 2s.—about the price you are expected to give the chambermaid at Greenwich when you wash your hands. But although the price is low, and the accommodation a little rough, the dinner is excellent. The flavour of the old-fashioned tavern dinner and after-dinner entertainment still hangs about Billingsgate. Fish dinners can also be had at almost any restaurant.

Fishing. — Exhaustive information in regard to fishing in the Thames will be found in DICKENS'S DICTIONARY OF THE THAMES, under the heads Angling Clubs, Fishermen, Fishing, &c. There is also good fishing in the Lea, which is looked after by a Preservation Society similar to that on the Thames ; the New River ; the Brent and the "Welsh Harp" reservoir at Hendon ; and other waters to the north of London. A good day's sport may also be had in the Colne, and at Thorney Broad and West Drayton. Every information of value to anglers will be found in the "Angler's Diary," published at the *Field* office at 1s., and in the *Fishing Gazette*,

price 2d., published at 11, Ave Maria-la.

Fishmongers' Company (The) have built their hall appropriately on the north bank of the Thames at London-br. The building is large and imposing, without being able to lay claim to actual beauty. Inside, solid comfort rather than elegance has been realised. The rooms are lofty and spacious, and the great hall is rich in wood-carving and armorial bearings. In one of the rooms is a capacious chair, made out of the first pile that was driven in the construction of Old London-br. The seat of the chair is stone, part of the stone in fact on which the pile rested, and, according to all accounts, these two interesting relics must have been under water for upwards of six hundred and fifty years. Another curiosity on which the Fishmongers set much store is the dagger with which Sir W. Walworth, Lord Mayor, slew Wat Tyler. There is the usual collection of portraits of kings and queens and benevolent liverymen, amongst which may be mentioned Beechey's portrait of Lord St. Vincent ; Mr. Wells's full-length portrait of Lord Chancellor Hatherley in his robes of office ; and an exceedingly fine bust in marble of General Garibaldi, who was a freeman of the company. The bust is the work of Signor Spertini, a Milanese sculptor. The Fishmongers used in olden times to be the object of popular rancour. At one period they had to appeal to the king for protection, and in 1382 Parliament enacted that no Fishmonger should be elected Lord Mayor. Nowadays they are justly popular for their works of charity and excellent dinners. Twelve exhibitions at the Universities are in the hands of the Fishmongers, and six presentations to the Blue Coat School. As a body the Fishmongers profess Liberal opinions.

Fixed Points (Police).— The under-mentioned places are appointed as fixed points where a police constable is to be permanently stationed from 9 p.m. to 1 a.m.

In the event of any person springing a rattle, or persistently ringing a bell in the street or in an area, the police will at once proceed to the spot and render assistance.

A OR WHITEHALL DIVISION.
Bessborough-gdns, nr Vauxhall-br

Bridge-st, at foot crossing Victoria Embankment
Buckingham Palace, The foot crossing opp (4.30 p.m. to 12.30 a.m.)
Buckingham Palace-rd and James-st, corner of
Charing ✠, at National Bank
Horseferry-rd and Regency-pl
Horse Guards, The, Whitehall
Lambeth-br, nr Horseferry-rd
Northumberland - avenue, Charing ✠, centre of crossings
Refuge at junction of Victoria-st and Broad Sanctuary
Smith-sq, near St. John's, Westminster
Victoria-st, junction of, and Vauxhall-br-rd
Victoria-st, Westminster, near Strutton Ground

B OR CHELSEA DIVISION.
Albert Emb, Chelsea, at south end of Oakley-st
Albert-gate, Knightsbridge
Beaufort-st, Chelsea, foot of Battersea-br
Brompton-rd, near Montpelier-st
Buckingham Pal-rd, nr Ebury-br
Cale-st, cor of College-st, Chelsea
Chesham-pl, corner of Pont-st
Cromwell-rd, near Exhibition-rd
Eaton-sq, near St. Peter's Church
Exhibition-rd, corner of, and Kensington-rd
Fulham-rd, St. George's Workhse.
Grosvenor-rd, foot of Chelsea-br
Grosvenor-rd, Thames Bank, near Caledonia-st
Hans-pl, Chelsea
Haven, The, opposite Halkin-st
Keppel-st, Fulham-rd
King's-rd, Chelsea, at north end of Dartrey-st
King's-rd, Chelsea, btwn Manor-st and Vestry Hall
King's-rd, Chelsea, north end of Wellington-sq
Onslow-sq, the end nearest South Kensington ry.-stn.
Pimlico-rd, Chelsea, near Lower Sloane-st
Pont-st, corner Sloane-st
Queen's Elm, Fulham-rd
Redcliffe-sq, by St. Luke's Church
Sloane-sq
Sloane-st, Knightsbridge
St. George's-sq, Lupus-st
Thames Emb., nr Flood-st, Chelsea
Tregunter-rd, Brompton, between The Boltons and Redcliffe-gdns
Victoria ry. - stn., Buckingham Palace-rd
Warwick-sq, Belgrave-rd
Wilton-rd, entrance to Victoria-stn (East Gates)

C OR ST. JAMES'S DIVISION.
Beak-st and Regent-st, corner of

Branch Bank of England, Burlington-gdns

County Fire Office, Regent-st (7 p.m. till 3 a.m.)

Cranbourne - st and Castle - st, junction of*

Cranbourne-st and St. Martin's-la, junction of *

Crown-st and Oxford-st, corner of

Devonshire House, cor Berkeley-st

Greek-st & Shaftesbury-av, cor of *

Hamilton-pl & Piccadilly, corner of

Haven, The, at end of New-rd, Hyde-pk-cor

Haymarket, corner of Pall Mall

John-st & Hill-st, cor of, Mayfair

Mount-st, cor South Audley-st

New Bond-st, corner of Conduit-st

Oxford-st-circus, corner of Swallow-st, south side of Oxford-st, west of Regent-st

Park-la and Oxford-st, corner of

Park-la, opp Stanhope-ga

Piccadilly-cir

Shaftesbury-av, west side of, opp Little Earl-st*

South Molton-st, Oxford-st, cor of

St. James's-st & Piccadilly, cor of

St. James's-st, south end of St. Martin's-pl

Wardour-st, cor Little Pulteney-st

West-st, corner of Lichfield-st*

* A constable is stationed at each of these points from 11 a.m. to 3 a.m. the following day.

D OR MARYLEBONE DIVISION.

Chapel-st, cor of, and Edgware-rd

Duke-st, Manchester-sq, to Duke-st, Grosvenor-sq, crossings

Edgware-rd & Hyde-pk-pl, cor of

Euston-rd, end of Tottenham-ct-rd*

Fitzroy-sq, south-west corner *

High-st, corner of Paradise-st

James-st, corner of Barrett-st

Marylebone-rd, cor Up. Baker-st

Montague-pl & Gloucester-pl, cor of

Museum-st, New Oxford-st

Oxford-st, crossing from Orchard-st to North Audley-st

Oxford-st, crossing from Vere-st to New Bond-st

Portman-sq, corner of Baker-st

Regent-circus, Oxford-st, corner of Princes-st

Regent-cir, north-east corner*

Salisbury-st and Church-st, cor of

Tottenham-ct-rd, Oxford-st

Union-st, corner of Gt. James-st, Lisson-gr

Upper Gloucester-pl, corner of, and Park-rd

Upper Wimpole-st and Devonshire-st, corner of

* A constable is continuously stationed at these points during the whole 24 hours.

E OR HOLBORN DIVISION.

Charing ✠, at Refuge, centre of roadway, opp post-office

Drury-la, at kerb, north-west corner of Long Acre*

Gray's-inn-rd, at Refuge, centre of roadway, Holborn Bars*

King-st, east corner of Garrick-st*

Seven Dials, centre of roadway*

South Eastern Ry., Charing ✠, opp telegraph-office

Southampton - row, at Refuge, centre of roadway, Holborn

Temple Bar, at Refuge, centre of roadway, west side

Wellington-st, at Refuge, centre of roadway, east side

Wellington-st, at Refuge, centre of roadway, west-side

* A constable is continuously stationed at these points during the whole 24 hours.

F OR PADDINGTON DIVISION.

Bathurst-st, cor of Westbourne-st

Bishop's-rd, Paddington, at posts of crossing, opp "Royal Oak"

Christ Ch, Lancaster-ga, front of

Church-st and High-st, Kensington, junction of

Cleveland-sq, corner of, at end of Chilworth-st

Earl's ct-rd, Kensington, at District ry.-stn.

Gloucester-rd, at District ry.-stn.

High-st, Kensington, by District ry.-stn.

High-st, Notting-hill, by Metropolitan ry.-stn.

Holland Villas-rd, Kensington, at junction with Addison-cres and Holland-rd

Kensington-rd, cor of Holland-wlk

London-st, cab - stand at north-west corner of

Norfolk-ter and Pembridge-vils, Westbourne-gr, at pillar letter-box

Old Brompton-rd, crossing from Collingham to Gilston rds

Praed-st and Edgware-rd, cor of

Queen's-rd, west corner of, Bayswater-rd

Southwick-cres, front of St. John's Church

Westbourne-pk-rd, opp Alexander-st, by St. Stephen's Church

G OR FINSBURY DIVISION.

"Angel," Islington

Allerton-st, cor of Nile-st, Hoxton

Brook-st and Beauchamp-st, junction of

Canal-br, City-rd, at the junction of Moreland-st

City-rd, corner of Britannia-st

City-rd, corner of East-rd

Clerkenwell-rd, cor of Eyre-st-hill

Exmouth-st, junction of Tysoe and Rosoman sts

Farringdon-rd, at south-east corner of Baker-st

Farringdon-rd, north-east corner of Charterhouse-st

Finsbury-sq, corner of Chiswell-st

Golden-la, west side, St. Luke's, opp Playhouse-yd

Great Eastern - st, Shoreditch, north-west corner of Curtain-rd

Hatton-gdn, north-east corner of Charles-st

High-st, Shoreditch, corner of French-alley

Holborn Town-hall, at junction of Gray's-inn and Clerkenwell rds

Hoxton-st, corner of Gt. James-st

King's ✠, Metropolitan ry.-stn., Pentonville-rd

Kingsland-rd, corner of Ware-st

New North-st, cor of Bookham-st

Nile-st, north-east corner of, in Britannia-st

Old-st, front of St. Luke's Church

Queen's-rd-br, on the west side of Great Cambridge-st

Rosemary Branch-br, corner of Bridport-pl.

Shepherdess-walk, cor of Sturt-st

St. John-st, junction of Cowcross-st

St. John's-st-rd, junction of Wynyatt, Spencer, and Charles sts

Tabernacle-sq, Shoreditch, at the drinking fountain

York-rd, at cor of Pentonville-rd

H OR WHITECHAPEL DIVISION.

Ben Jonson-rd and White Horse-st, Stepney, junction of

Brick-la and Bethnal-green-rd, junction of

Christian-st and Commercial-rd, end of

Church-st, Wapping

Columbia-rd, Bethnal Gn, corner of Hassard-st

Commercial - rd - east, corner of Bromehead-st

Commercial-st, Spitalfields, corner of Thrawl-st

Flower and Dean-st and Brick-la, Spitalfields, end of

George-yd, High-st, Whitechapel, end of

G.E. Ry., High - st, Shoreditch, front of

Great Garden-st and Whitechapel-rd, opposite end of

Hanbury-st, cor of Deal-st, Mile End New Town

Hare-alley, High-st, Shoreditch, end of

Hermitage-br, Wapping

Leman-st, Commercial-st, and High-st, Whitechapel, junc of.

New Gravel-la-br, London Docks*

Old Gravel-la-br, London Docks*

Ship-alley & St. George's-st-east, south end of

Shoreditch Church

Spencer-st and Watney-st, St. George's East, corner of

Spitalfields Church

Stepney ry.-stn, Commercial-rd-ea.

Upper East Smithfield, principal entrance London Docks.

Warner-pl and Hackney-rd, cor of

Wells-st, Whitechapel, opposite Sailors' Home

Whitechapel Church

White Horse-la and Mile End-rd, junction of

* A constable is stationed at each of these points from 3 p.m. to 7 a.m.

J OR BETHNAL GREEN DIVISION.

Ball's-pond-rd, corner of Southgate-rd

Bridge-st, Water and Morning lanes, Hackney.

Broadway, South Hackney, opposite post-office

Clapton-rd, corner of Lea-br-rd

Gainsborough-rd, Hackney Wick, S.E. corner of Wick-rd

Goldsmith's-row and Pritchard's-rd, junction of

Green-st and Morpeth-st, Bethnal Green, junction of

Hackney and Cambridge rds, junction of

Hackney ry.-stn., Mare-st

High-st, Homerton, corner of Church-rd

Kingsland-rd, corner of Lee-st

Leyton-rd, corner of Grange-pk-rd

Leytonstone-rd, cor of Church-la

Triangle, Mare-st, Hackney.

Whitechapel-rd, in front of East London Ry. stn.

White Post-la and Wick-la, Victoria-pk, corner of

K OR BOW DIVISION.

Armagh and Roman rds, Bow, junction of

Barking-rd ry.-stn.

Blackwall ✠, Blackwall

Burdett and Mile End rds, cor. of

Custom House ry.-stn., Victoria-Docks

Devon's-rd and St. Paul's-rd, Bow-common, junction of

E. & W. India Dock-rds, junctn of

East Ham-gate, East Ham

Forest-gate ry.-stn.

Grove and Roman rds, Bethnal Gn, junction of

High-st and Station-rd, Plaistow, junction of

Manor Park, Ilford, junction of Romford-rd and White Post-rd

Maryland Point-br, Stratford

Poplar Hospital, East India Dk-rd

Rhodeswell-rd and St. Paul's-rd, Bow-common, junction of

Stratford Town Hall

Tidal Basin ry.-stn., at foot-br, Victoria Dock-rd

Upton-pk ry.-stn.

L OR LAMBETH DIVISION.

Broadwall, corner of Roupel-st

Commercial-rd, cor of Princes-st

Delverton-rd and Manor-pl, junction of Surrey Garden Estate

Elephant and Castle, Newington Butts

Kennington and Lambeth rds, corner of

Kennington ✠

Kennington-Pk, cor of Newington-ter

Lambeth Palace

London-rd, south end of

Lower Kennington-la, corner of Kennington-pk-rd

Marsh-gate, Westminster-br-rd

Obelisk, E. end of Kennington-rd

Palace and Westminster-br rds, corner of

Princes-rd, corner of Lambeth-wlk

St. George's Cathedral, in St. George's-rd

Stamford-st and Blackfriars-rd, corner of

Vauxhall ✠

Vauxhall-walk, cor of Leopold-st

Victoria-crossings, Waterloo-rd

Waterloo and Blackfriars rds, junction of

Waterloo ry.-stn.

Waterloo-rd, corner of Gray-st

Waterloo-rd, corner of York-rd

Westminster-br-rd, Tramway Ter.

Westminster-rd, corner of Hercules-bdgs

Wyndham-rd, Camberwell, corner of Toulon-st

At the triangular piece of ground where Kennington-ga once stood

M OR SOUTHWARK DIVISION.

Blackfriars-rd, corner of Friar-st

Black Horse-court, Gt. Dover-st (5 p.m. to 1 a.m.)

Bull-court, Tooley-st

Charlotte-st and Blackfriars-rd, corner of

Derrick-st and Thames-st, Rotherhithe, corner of

Dockhead, Hackney Carriage standing

Findlater's-corner, London-br

Newington-causeway, south end

Plough-rd and Deptford Lower-rd, junction of with several other streets, Rotherhithe

St. James's Church, Jamaica-rd

Southwark-pk-rd and St. James's-rd, crossing at, South side

Southwark-st and Southwark-br-rd, crossing at, S.W. corner

Southwark-br-rd, N.W. corner of Great Suffolk-st

Spa-rd and Grange-rd, corner of

Star - corner, near Bermondsey Church

Upper Grange-rd and Old Kent-rd, corner of, by letter-box

N OR ISLINGTON DIVISION.

Cloudesly-rd, Islington, E. corner of Cloudesly-pl

Essex-rd, corner or Canonbury-rd

Green-lanes, corner of Highbury New-park

Green-lanes, corner of Seven Sisters'-rd.

Highbury-pk, corner of Highbury-gr

Hoe-st ry.-stn (corner of Selborne-rd), Walthamstow

Lordship-rd, corner of Manor-rd, Stoke Newington

St. Andrew's and Chingford rds, corner of

St. Paul's-br, Canonbury. A constable is continuously statione at this point during day & night

St. Peter's-st, Islington, N. corner of Rheidol-ter

Seven Sisters-rd, at junction with St. Ann's-rd, S.E. corner of

Stamford-hill, opposite " Weavers' Arms "

Stamford-hill, north-east corner of High and Upper Clapton rds

Stoke Newington-common, corner of Fountayne & Northwold rds

Upper Clapton, corner of Hill-st

Upper-st, corner of Providence-pl

Upper-st, Islington, junction of St. Paul's-rd, opposite post-office

Walthamstow ry.-stn., St. James-st

Walthamstow, Wood-st, corner of Valentine-rd

P OR CAMBERWELL DIVISION.

Albany-rd, Camberwell, junction with Villa-st

Anerley ry.-br., Anerley (5 p.m. to 1 a.m.)

Bell-gn, near gas works, Lower Sydenham

Canal-br, Old Kent-rd

Catford-br, Catford (2 p.m. to 10 p.m.)

Crescent, Southampton-st, Camberwell, corner of

Elliott-bank and Sydenham-hill-rd, corner of

Forest-hill ry.-stn., Forest-hill

Ivanhoe-rd and Malford-rd, Denmark Park Estate, junction of

Laurie-pk and Kirkdale (junction of), Upper Sydenham

Mount-st, Walworth-rd, north-east corner of

New and Old Kent rds, junction of

New Church-rd, Camberwell, north-west cor. of Addington-sq (5 p.m. to 1 a.m.)

New ✠ and Lewisham rds, junc. of Nunhead ry.-stn.

Peckham, junction of Choumert-rd and Rye-la.

Peckham-rye, S.W. cor. of East Dulwich-rd (5 p.m. to 1 a.m.)

Shield-st, Willowbrook-rd, Peckham.

Station and Anerley rds, junction of, outside Anerley ry.-stn. (9 a.m. to 5 p.m.)

The Palatinate, Rodney-pl, New Kent-rd

Trafalgar-rd, Old Kent-rd, south-west corner of

Tulse-hill ry.-stn., Approach-rd, corner of

Wastdale-rd, Forest-hill

R OR GREENWICH DIVISION.

Bexley Heath, main rd, opp chur.

Bexley High-st, near ry.-stn.

Blackheath-hill, west corner of Gloucester-ter

Blackheath village, centre of, at junction of three roads

Blackwall-la, East Greenwich, near St. Andrew's Church

Charlton village, opp Charlton Hse

Chislehurst, Royal Parade

Crayford-br.

Deptford, Broadway

Deptford, Wellington-st and High-st, corner of

Foot's Cray, High-st and Church-st, junction of

Greenwich Church, opposite

Greenwich-rd, outside ry.-stn.

Grove-pk, Burnt Ash-la and Herbert-rd, corner of

Lee, Burnt Ash-hill and Bromley-rd, corner of

Lee, Love-la, corner of Lee-ter

Lewisham-high-rd, outside St. John's Church

Lewisham-hill, cor of Eliot-pk and Eliot-hill

Lewisham, Lee-rd and High-st, junction of, opposite London & County Bank

Mottingham, corner of Station-rd

New ╪ Gate

New ╪ rd, cor of Amersham-vale, outside South-Eastern ry.-stn.

Nightingale-la and Woolwich-com, corner of

Old Dover-rd, cor of Wickham-la

Old Woolwich-rd and Trafalgar-rd, corner of

Old Woolwich-rd. near Ballast-br.

Orpington, Chelsfield-rd, corner of Orpington-rd

Plumstead, Cage-la and High-st, corner of

Plumstead-common, opp. Slade's Schools

Sand-st and Lower Woolwich-rd, corner of

St. John's-rd and Shooter's-hill-rd, corner of

Sylvan-gr & Old Kent-rd, corner of Vanbrugh-pk, near letter-box

Woolwich, Cross-st, opposite Royal Arsenal ry.-stn.

Woolwich, Market-hill

S OR HAMPSTEAD DIVISION.

Barnet, junction of Station and East Barnet-rds, New Barnet

Camden Tn, Cobden Statue, High-st

Camden Tn, Park-st and High-st, corner of

Cricklewood-la and Edgware-rd, corner of

Euston-rd, corner of Albany-st

Finchley, East End Market-pl

Gower-st ry.-stn., George-st

Hampstead, Belsize-pk, Buckland-cres

Hampstead, High-st

Hampstead, junction of Fleet and Park rds

Hampstead, Southend-rd, junction of Southill-park-rd, near Hampstead-heath ry.-stn.

Hampstead, Upper Heath

Hampstead-rd, cor of Ampthill-sq

Hampstead-rd, cor of Euston-rd.

Hendon, Child's-hill

Kilburn-rise, corner of Palmerston and Edgware rds

North Finchley, Great North-rd, opposite Friern-pk

Primrose-hill-rd, corner of Adelaide-rd

Regent's-pk, North Gate, corner of Avenue-rd

Regent's-pk-rd, The Boys' Home

St. John's Wood, corner of Belsize-rd and Abbey-rd-west

St. John's Wood, cor of Blenheim-ter and Abbey-rd

St. John's Wood, corner of Finchley and Acacia rds

St. John's Wood, corner of Upper Avenue-rd and Finchley-rd

St. John's Wood, corner of Upper Hamilton-ter and Abercorn-pl

West Hampstead, Belsize-rd, Kilburn

West Hampstead, junction of Loudoun and Belsize rds

T OR HAMMERSMITH DIVISION

Blyth-la, Hammersmith, between Masboro-rd-west & Sterndale-rd

Fulham-rd, at north corner of St. John's Schools, Walham-gn

Fulham Tn, Fulham, corner of Church-walk to Putney-br by mission-room

Goldhawk-rd, at north end of the Grove, Shepherd's Bush

Great Western-rd, at junction with Goldhawk-rd, Hammersmith

Hammersmith-br, cor of Rutland-road and Bridge-av

Hampton Court, from Bushy-pk Gates to Hampton-br

Hampton-wick, at junction with Seymour and Upper Teddington rds, opposite Board Schools

Hounslow, at N. end of St. John's-rd at junction with London-rd

Kew-br, by the drinking fountain at tramway-terminus

North-end-rd, Fulham, at south-east corner of Baron's Court-rd

Richmond-rd, Fulham, at junction with Seagrave-rd

Sands-end, Fulham, at corner of King's and Southeron rds

Shepherd's Bush, at east end of Shepherd's-bush-gn., by cab-rank

Sherbrooke-rd, Fulham, at south side of Dawes-rd, between Sherbrooke and Filmer rds

South Acton, cor of Park and Bollo-br rds

Starch-gn, by north side of Pond, between Starch-gn-rd and Ash-church-gr

Star-lane, Fulham, at junction with Field and Greyhound rds

Uxbridge-rd, Shepherd's Bush, at corner of Keith-gr

West Kensington-gdns, Hammersmith, between ry.-br. and North-end-rd

V OR WANDSWORTH DIVISION.

Altenberg-gdns, Battersea-rise

Austin and South rds, Battersea, junc. of

Balham, near ry.-stn.

Clapham Junc., at the entrance of ry.-stn., L. & S.W.R., St. John's-hill, Battersea

Cross-rds, Tibbett's-cor, West-hill, Wandsworth

Culvert-rd, Battersea

East Moulsey, Bridge-rd, near Hampton Court ry.-stn.

Falcon-rd and High-st, Battersea, junction of

Hammersmith-br and Castlenau, approach to

Kew-rd, Richmond, outside ry.-stn.

Kew-green, near residence of the Duchess of Cambridge

Kingston ry.-stn.

Kingston, Market-pl

Malden ry.-stn.

Plough-rd and York-rd, Battersea, corner of

Putney, Roehampton, Upper Richmond, Queen's, and Station rds, junction of

Putney ry.-stn., outside

Red Lion-st and High-st, Wandsworth, corner of

Somerset and Mill rds, Wimbledon Park-side, junction of

Surbiton ry.-stn., outside

Tyneham - road, Lavender - hill, Battersea

Wandsworth, cab - rank outside ry.-stn.

Wandsworth - com, Salcott and Northcote rds corner of

Wandsworth - com, opposite St. Mary's Church, Summer's-town

Wandsworth, Garrett-la, opposite Earlsfield ry.-stn.

Wimbledon, Raynes-pk ry.-stn.

Wimbledon ry.-stn.

W OR CLAPHAM DIVISION.

Clapham, junction of Bedford, Landor, and Clapham rds

Clapham and Dorset rds, junc. of

Clapham-rd, corner Sth. Lambeth and Binfield rds

Coldharbour - la, corner Lough-borough-rd

Croydon, cor of Brighton, Sander-stead, and Croydon rds

Herne-hill, junction of Brandley, Dulwich, and Norwood rds

High-st, Collier's, Water-la, Parch-more-rd, Woodville-rd, Thornton Heath, junction of

London, Elmwood, and Handcroft rds, Croydon, junction of

Nine Elms-la and Wandsworth-rd, Vauxhall, corner of

Pawsons, Whitehorse, and Holmes-dale rds, Thornton Heath, junc of

"Plough," Clapham-com, near the West Croydon ry.-br

Windmill, Whitehorse, Limes, & Nо thcote rds, Croydon, junc. of

X OR KILBURN DIVISION.

Alfred and Harrow rds, Padding-ton, S.W. corner of

Clifton-gdns and Clifton - villas, junc. of, in Warwick-rd, Pad-dington

Ealing, the Feathers ry.-br

Great Western-rd, Paddington, Water Post, E. side of

Hammersmith, outside Uxbridge-rd ry.-stn.

Harrow-rd, E. side of St. John's Church, Kensal-gn

Harrow-rd, Willesden, at junc. of Victor and Harrow rds

Harlesden, junction of Harlesden-gn and Station-rd

Kensington, Hazlewood-crescent (N. E. corner of), Golborne-rd

Kilburn Market-pl, cor of Prince's-rd

Ladbroke-gr-rd and Rackham-st, Notting-hill, junction of

Paddington, junc. of Walterton, Chippenham, and Shirland-rds

Notting-hill, ry.-stn., North Pole-rd

St. Ann's-rd, opposite Crescent-st, Notting-hill

St. Katharine's and Prince's rds, Notting-hill, junction of

St. Luke's and Cornwall rds, Not-ting-hill, S. E. corner of

Silchester and Manchester rds, Notting-hill, junction of

Silchester and Walmer rds, Not-ting-hill, junction of

Uxbridge Market-pl, near

Willesden-la, between Dean-rd and Walm-la

Y OR HIGHGATE DIVISION.

Barnsbury-rd, corner of Copen-hagen-st, Islington

Brecknock-rd, corner of Fortess-rd.

Blenheim and Cottenham rds, Upper Holloway, corner of

Caledonian-rd, nr Copenhagen-st

Charlton-st, junction of Church-way & Chapel-st, Somers Town

Crouch end, at junc. of Crouch-end-hill and Crouch-hill

East Finchley, corner of Fortis-gn and Great North rds.

Freeling-st and Bemerton-st, cor of

Highgate New Town, corner of Dartmouth-pk-hl & Hargrave-rd

Holloway-rd, at Hornsey-rd

Holloway-rd, cor of Tollington-rd

Hornsey Rise, corner of Ashley-rd

Junction-rd, at Holloway-rd

Malden-rd and Prince of Wales'-rd, corner of

Midland-rd, corner of Euston-rd*

Muswell-hill, near entrance to Alexandra Palace

New Southgate, N.E. corner of Station and South rds*

N. London Ry. stn., at corner of Camden-rd and College-st

Pancras-rd, under railway-arch

St. James's-rd, corner of Welling-ton-rd, Barnsbury

Seven Sisters'-rd, near "Nag's Head"

Stroud-gn-rd and Seven Sisters-rd, corner of

Southampton and Circus roads, Haverstock-hill, junction of

Tollington-pk, at Stroud-gn-rd

York-rd, at corner of Brewery-rd

York-rd, at corner of River st

* A constable is stationed at each of these points continuously day and night.

Flats.—In few points does Lon-don, or indeed, English life in gen-eral, differ from that of the Conti-nent more remarkably than in the almost absolute ignoring by the former of all possibility of having more than one house under the same roof. Within the last few years, however, symptoms have appeared of a growing disposition on the part of Londoners to avail themselves of the Continental ex-perience which the increased tra velling facilities of the day have placed within the reach of all, and to adopt the foreign fashion of living in flats. The progress of the new idea has been slow, as is the pro-gress of all new ideas in this most conservative of countries. But progress has been made, and signs are not wanting that it will before long be more rapid. At present many separate *étages* are found in London such as those in the much-talked-of Queen Anne's Mansions; a good number of sets in Victoria-st; a few in Crom-well-rd, just between the rail-way-bridges; seven houses near Clarence-gate, Regent's-pk, known as the Cornwall Residences; the new buildings known as Oxford Mansions, which stand on the site of what was Oxford Market; the Oxford and Cambridge Mansions in the Marylebone-rd; Wynnstay-gdns, Kensington; and others. Not all of these, however, are examples of the real self-con-tained "flat," the inhabitant of which, whilst relieved from all the responsibility and most of the troubles of an isolated house, yet enjoys to the full all the ad-vantages of a separate establish-ment. The houses in Cromwell-rd, nominally divided off into flats, are really mere shapeless buildings, the exigencies of whose site have necessitated a plan of construction incompatible with the dealing with each building in its entirety, and which have there-fore perforce been let off in tene-ments, to which has been given the name of "flats." In the case of the Queen Anne's Mansions the building has been constructed with an especial view to the sepa-ration into tenements, but in this case the self-containing principle has been deliberately set aside, and a kitchen and coffee-room have been built for the use of the entire establishment. One great obstacle to the building of houses laid out in regular flats on the Continental prin-ciple has been in the Building Act; under the provisions of which the expense of construction of houses for such a purpose on any really conve-nient scale is enormously increased in proportion to that of the ordi-nary ten, twelve, or fifteen roomed dwelling house with its 9-inch walls, its five or six narrow storeys piled one above the other, and its domestic treadmill of six or seven dozen weary stairs, the mere bing of which necessitates the keeping of at least one or two xtra servants. Another obstacle found in the fact that most odern London houses are run up y some speculative builder almost atirely without capital, who mort-ages the site to obtain money to uild the ground-floor, the ground-oor for the funds to carry the uilding up a storey higher, the rawing-room floor for the means f building the best bedroom, and on, until by the time the slates re laid it becomes an absolute ecessity to dispose of the build-g *en bloc* for what it will fetch, aat he may close accounts with ae bank, which is the true spe-alator, and realise—if so happy a esult be obtainable—his own profit n the transaction. Such flats, owever, as are to be found, let a spite of all their drawbacks so eadily, and at such enormous ents in comparison with ordinary ouses of an equal area of accom-nodation, that it is not surprising hat the supply is beginning to dapt itself a little more nearly o the demand.

Flaxman Gallery, Univer-sity College, Gower-st (Map 2). –The Hall under the Dome, he adjacent apartments, and he staircase, are adorned with vorks by the late John Flaxman, irst Professor of Sculpture in the Royal Academy. These consist principally of the casts in plaster, rom the original clay models, of groups of figures, statues, and compositions in alto and basso relievo, among which are many of the great artist's noblest produc-tions. They were in his studio at the time of his decease, when they became the property of his execu-trix and adopted daughter, the late Miss Maria Denman, by whom they were presented to University College. The cast of the shield of Achilles was added to the collection by the late C. R. Cockerell, R.A., Professor of Architecture in the Royal Aca-demy, and is placed in a room adjoining the hall. The collection comprises several busts by the great sculptor of some of his eminent contemporaries ; among them are busts of Lord Nelson, Warren Hastings, and John Hunter. For the floor of parquetry, the seats, and other embellishments of the Flaxman Hall, the College is in-debted to the Graphic Society, and to the late Mr. H. Crabb Robinson, whose contribution was given anonymously through the late Mr. Edwin W. Field. A large number of drawings by Flaxman was added to the gallery in 1862. These have been mounted, fixed on screens, and will be found in the same room as the shield of Achilles. In the vesti-bule leading to the hall is a marble statue of Flaxman by Mulgrave L. Watson ; and in the council-room is a portrait in oil of Flaxman, by Henry Howard, R.A., and a small medallion por-trait in plaster of the sculptor, by himself. The public are ad-mitted to the gallery on Saturdays during the months of May, June, July, and August, from 10 to 2, but persons properly introduced to the secretary may obtain ad-mission at any time during the academical year between 11 a.m. and 4 p.m. NEAREST *Ry. Stn.,* Gower-st ; *Omnibus Rtes.,* Euston-rd and Tottenham-court-rd ; *Cab Rank,* Tottenham-court-rd.

Fleet Street (Map 7).— However the tide of life in town may ebb and flow elsewhere, Fleet-st is always busy and its London is always full. The centre of the great newspaper enterprise of England can be marked on a London map very near the middle of Fleet-st ; and within a radius of little more than half a mile from that point some of the greatest newspapers in the world work and think for millions of readers. It is curious to contrast the way in which newspaper work is done now, with that admirable description of the newspaper office of his time that George Warrington gives Penden-nis in one of the most graphic chapters of that wonderful London book. There is no dashing up now of late expresses ; there is none of the pomp and circum-stance of the old press days. Electricity and railways have taken the romance out of that, as out of most things. But although it is not so much on the surface as of yore, good honest hard work is done in and about Fleet-st, and goes forth to the whole English-speaking race. That this is nothing new, every student well knows. Fleet-st may almost be called the nursing mother of English literature. Shakespeare, Ben Jonson, Raleigh, Dryden, Johnson, Goldsmith, and count-less names, brilliant even in brilliant times, are associated with Fleet-st. A tavern-street, as well as a literary centre, Fleet-st was and is. The newest-fashion newspaper and the oldest-style tavern still jostle each other now as they did a century or more ago. It would be rude, perhaps, to compare the "Fleet-streeter" of to-day with the "Grub-streeter" of the olden time ; but as in Grub-st there was no literary work that could not be got for money, so it would be difficult to find any kind of literary work that could not be done in and about Fleet-st.

Fogs are, no doubt, not pecu-liar to London. Even Paris itself can occasionally turn out very respectable work in this way, and the American visitor to England will very probably think, in pass-ing the banks of Newfoundland, that he has very little to learn on the subject of fog. But what Mr. Guppy called "a London particu-lar," and what is more usually known to the natives as "a pea-souper," will very speedily dispel any little hallucination of this sort. As the east wind brings up the exhalations of the Essex and Kentish marshes, and as the damp-laden winter air prevents the dis-persion of the partly consumed carbon from hundreds of thousands of chimneys, the strangest atmo-spheric compound known to science fills the valley of the Thames. At such times almost all the senses have their share of trouble. Not only does a strange and worse than Cimmerian darkness hide familiar landmarks from the sight, but the taste and sense of smell are of-fended by an unhallowed com-pound of flavours, and all things become greasy and clammy to the touch. During the continuance of a real London fog—which may be black, or grey, or more probably orange-coloured—the happiest man is he who can stay at home. But if business—there is no such thing as out-door pleasure during the continuance of a London fog—should compel a sally into the streets, one caution should be carefully observed. Mr. Catlin, well known for his connection with the Indian tribes of North America, once promulgated in print a theory, that a royal road to long life was, sleeping or waking, to keep the mouth as much as possible closed. This advice, whatever its value may be generally, should always be followed when a London fog has to be encountered. Nothing could be more deleterious to the lungs and the air-passages than the wholesale inhalation of the foul air and floating carbon, which, combined, form a London fog. In this connection it may be taken as an axiom that the nose is Nature's respirator. The extraordinary effect which the fogs of the winter of 1879-80 had upon the health of Londoners will be long remembered. It is almost unnecessary to add that the dangers of the streets, great at all times, are immeasurably increased in foggy weather; and that the advantages of being able to dive into the unnatural darkness after successful robbery, are thoroughly appreciated by the predatory classes.

Folly Theatre (*See* TOOLE'S THEATRE).

Football is by far the most popular out-door game of the winter months, and there are few open spaces in or near London where matches may not be seen in progress on any open Saturday afternoon, between the beginning of October and the end of March. The most important scenes of action are Kennington Oval — where the international matches are played in February and March—Battersea-pk, Blackheath, Richmond, Wimbledon, Wormwood Scrubbs, and Woolwich. Both the Rugby Football Union and the Football Association have their head-quarters in London. The Union is the stronger body, and under its laws, which permit the ball being carried, quite five times as many matches are played as under the Association laws, which do not allow of the ball being run with. [To the lay mind it is probable that the Association game would be more likely to answer the idea conveyed by the word *football*. The Rugby game is excellent in its way, but the hand has as much to do with the business as the foot.] The president of the Union is Leonard Stokes; and the honorary secretary, Rowland Hill. Of the Association, Major Marindin, R.E., is president; and C. W. Alcock, 28, Paternoster-row, honorary secretary, of whom all particulars of the two societies can be obtained. The principal matches

played under the auspices of the two societies are — Union : North v. South, played in alternate years in London and Manchester; England v. Scotland, for the Calcutta Challenge Cup, in London and Edinburgh; and England v. Ireland, in London and Dublin. Association : England v. Scotland, played alternately in Glasgow and England; London v. Sheffield; and the matches for the Association Challenge Cup, competed for by Association clubs. The Association matches have 11 players, the Union 15 players on each side. The leading Union clubs in London and the suburbs are Blackheath, head-quarters, Richardson's-field, Blackheath; Richmond, Richmond Old Deer-pk; Royal Military Academy, Woolwich; Royal Naval College, Greenwich-pk; Wimbledon, Wimbledon-com; Clapham Rovers, Wandsworth; West Kent, Chislehurst; Queen's House, and Clevedon, Blackheath; Flamingoes, Battersea-pk; Gipsies, Peckham; Guy's Hospital, Blackheath; King's College, Battersea-pk; Lausanne, Dulwich; Old Cheltonians, Mitcham; Old Marlburians, Blackheath; Walthamstow, Walthamstow; Wasps, Putney. The leading Association clubs are the Wanderers, Old Etonians, and Old Harrovians; the majority of whose matches are played at Kennington Oval, five minutes' walk from the Vauxhall-station on the London and South Western line; Barnes, Barnes; Civil Service, Battersea-pk; Clapham Rovers, Wandsworth; South Norwood, Norwood; Upton Park, Upton; Westminster School, Vincent-sq. The subscriptions to these clubs vary from 2s. 6d. to 10s. per annum, and the number of members from 30 to 200. The dash and pluck necessary to earn distinction at both games render football matches very popular with Londoners, and as many as 7,000 spectators have been seen at the Oval on the occasion of an international match.

Foreign Office, Downing-st, S.W. (Map 13). Hours 12 to 6.—Nearest *Ry. Stns.*, Westminster-br and Charing ✠ (Dis. & S. E.); *Omnibus Rte.*, Parliament-st; *Cab Rank*, Palace-yard.

Foundling Hospital, Guildford-st, W.C. (Map 7).—On a different principle from that of the

Enfans Trouvés in Paris, and from the establishments of a similar nature in St. Petersburg and Vienna, is the admirable institution founded in 1739 by gentle-hearted Capt. Thomas Coram. It is one of the conditions of this thoughtful charity that it aims, not only at educating and maintaining the child, but at reclaiming the mother. No appeal for admission to the hospital is ever entertained except on the personal application. The child who is fortunate enough to be received under the kindly shadow of its good captain is sure to have a fair start in the world, and every possible care is taken to prevent the unfortunate circumstance of the child's birth interfering with its future prospects. Quite apart from its position as one of the most useful and best managed charities in London, the Foundling Hospital claims its place among our most interesting sights. The hospital owes much to Handel, who presented an organ to the chapel, and to Hogarth, whose portrait of Captain Coram is well known, and whose "March to Finchley" is one of the most cherished possessions of the charity. In addition to these, many other pictures by Reynolds, Gainsborough, and Wilson, are to be seen in Guildford-st. The music in the chapel on Sundays has long been a special attraction; and the choir, which is composed of the children themselves, has been assisted at various times by most distinguished singers. Service is at 11 o'clock. After morning service on Sundays visitors may see the children at dinner. The hospital is open to inspection on application to the secretary. NEAREST *Ry. Stns.*, King's ✠ (Met. & G.N.) and Midland; *Omnibus Rte.*, Gray's-inn-rd; *Cab Rank*, at Gates.

France. — EMBASSY, Albert-gate House, Hyde-pk. NEAREST *Ry. Stn.*, Sloane-sq (Met.); *Omnibus Rte.*, Knightsbridge; *Cab Ranks*, Knightsbridge and St. George's-pl. CONSULATE, 38, Finsbury - cir ; NEAREST *Ry. Stn.*, Moorgate - st ; *Omnibus Rte.*, Moorgate-st ; *Cab Rank*, Circus-pl, Finsbury.

SOCIETE FRANCAISE DE BIEN-FAISANCE, 10, Poland-st, Oxford-st, W.—Objects: 1. To distribute temporary relief in money, bread, coals, &c., to the distressed French residing in London. 2, To assist

em in procuring work or employment. 3. To send them back
France when they have no
nance of getting a living here.
To grant pensions to old and
oor French residents who, having
st all their friends abroad, do not
ish to return home.

SOCIETE NATIONALE FRANÇAISE, 1, Adelphi-ter, Strand,
.C.—Objects: 1. To unite all
renchmen residing in England,
aintain and foster amongst them
utual feelings of friendship, love,
d devotedness to their country,
eace and goodwill between all
ations. 2. To provide them with
suitable and convenient place of
eeting for social intercourse, the
udy of all questions relating to
e general progress, the welfare,
d well-being of mankind. 3.
ıch a place of meeting, combining
e necessary arrangements for the
aterial, dietetic, and hygienic
mfort of members, with special
ssembly-rooms for the periodical
eetings of the three sections
stablished within the society,
z : A commercial and industrial
ction, to study political economy;
literary and scientific section, to
udy modern literature and all
ew discoveries in science generally; an artistic section, to study
ıe arts, and organise musical
d dramatic entertainments, for
ıe recreation and enjoyment of
embers and their families. 4.
andidates for admission must
presented by two members.
nglishmen, by statutory exception, can be admitted, as an acnowledgment of the hospitality,
eedom, and protection extended
like to all foreigners residing in
ngland. The fee of admission
£1 1s., and the annual subscription £1 1s. .

Freedom of the City.—

he Freedom of the City may be
btained : 1. *By servitude*—that
to say, by having been bound to
Freeman, according to the cusm of the City, and having served
uly and truly seven years. 2. *By
atrimony*—that is, being the son
r daughter (unmarried or widow)
f a Freeman, born after the adission of the father, and twentyıe years of age. 3. *By Gift of
he City* or *Honorary Freedom*.
. *By redemption or purchase*.
he sons of aliens, born in England, are now admitted under the
ame conditions as natural-born
ubjects,

Freemasonry.—

The headquarters of English Freemasonry
are at the Freemasons' Hall in
Great Queen-street (Map 7),
where are the offices of Grand
Lodge and Grand Chapter, and
where also the meetings of those
two great governing bodies of
Freemasonry take place. Grand
Festival, on which day Grand
Lodge meets for the appointment
and investment of officers, takes
place on the last Wednesday in
April. It is impossible to give
here the very long list of London
lodges and chapters, with their
places of meeting, but information
on these and many other points
will be found in the fullest detail
in the "Freemasons' Calendar
and Pocket Book," published
annually at Spencer's Masonic
Depot, 23A, Great Queen-st, under
the sanction of Grand Lodge.
Among the most popular places of
meeting for metropolitan lodges,
besides the Freemasons' Hall and
Tavern, may be mentioned the
Ship and Turtle, Leadenhall-st ;
Anderton's Hotel, Fleet-st ; the
Café Royal, Regent-st ; the Inns
of Court Hotel ; and the Albion
Tavern in Aldersgate-st. The
three great masonic charities are
as follows : The Royal Masonic
Institution for Girls, St. John'shill, Battersea-rise, S.W. (office, 5,
Freemasons' Hall), for maintaining, clothing, and educating the
daughters of Freemasons. Children are admitted at the age of
8 years, and continue until the
age of 16. The general committee meets on the last Thursday
in every month at Freemasons'
Hall, and the house committee
at the institution on the last
Thursday but one. All particulars
as to mode of application for
admission, &c., may be had at
the office. The Royal Masonic
Institution for Boys is at Wood
Green, N., and the office is at
6 Freemasons' Hall. The same
limits as to age obtain with the
boys as with the girls. The
general committee meets at Freemasons Hall on the first Saturday
in every month, and the house
committee at the institution on the
last Friday but one. All particulars may be had at the office.
Both for the boys' and the girls'
schools the voting privileges of
subscribers are as follows : £1 1s.
gives a vote for each election ;
£5 5s. a vote for life ; £10 10s.
two votes for life, and three votes

if given when serving stewardship,
and four additional votes for every
subsequent stewardship with a
similar donation ; £52 10s. gives
ten votes for life ; and £105 will
buy thirty votes for life. The
arrangements for votes to subscribing lodges are a little different, but are also on a liberal scale.
The Benevolent Institution for
aged Freemasons and Widows of
Freemasons is at Croydon, with
an office at 4, Freemasons' Hall.
No brother is admitted under sixty
years of age, nor unless he has
been a registered Mason for fifteen
years. He must also, unless excused by special circumstances,
have subscribed to a lodge for ten
years. An income of £40 a year
disqualifies for election. A widow
must be 55 years of age before she
is eligible, her husband must have
subscribed for ten years, and she
must have been his wife for five.
An income of £30 a year disqualifies. The general committee meets
at the Freemasons' Hall on the
second Wed. in each month, and
the house committee at Croydon
on the last day of February, May,
August, and November. Here,
as in the case of the schools, the
voting privileges are regulated by
the amount of subscriptions, either
for individuals or lodges. It may
be added that all the Masonic
charities are exceptionally well
administered, and that the educati n given to the children is of
a very superior class. Among
periodicals of special interest to
Freemasons may be mentioned
the *Freemason*, published at 16,
Great Queen-st, W.C.

The best houses in London for
masonic clothing and jewellery,
lodge furniture, &c., whether
craft, royal arch, mark, or any
other variety of the institution,
are Brother Spencer's, 23A, Great
Queen-st, opposite the hall, and
Brother Kenning's, 1, 2, 3, and 4,
Little Britain ; and students of the
various rituals desirous of obtaining
legitimate assistance, can obtain
either in a literary form or otherwise by application to either of
these houses, or at 15A, Cheapside.

Friendly Societies' Registry Office,

28, Abingdon-st, S.W. Hours 10 to 4.—
NEAREST *Ry Stn.*, Westminsterbr ; *Omnibus R tes*, Victoria-st and
Parliament-st ; *Cab Rank*, Palaceyard.

Gaiety Theatre, Strand (Map 7). — A good-sized house, handsomely decorated, and conducted upon very liberal principles. No fees are allowed in any part of the establishment; programmes being supplied gratis. Like the Criterion, this theatre was originally built in connection with a restaurant. The doors of communication, however, were closed by order of the powers that be, and the theatre and the restaurant are now two separate establishments. As at the Criterion, however, a sort of compromise has been effected, and a door just inside the theatre entrance gives admission to the restaurant without actually turning out into the rain. The specialty of the Gaiety has varied from time to time. At present it is elaborate burlesque. NEAREST *Ry Stn*, Temple; *Omnibus Rtes.*, St. Martin's-la, Strand, Chancery-la, and Waterloo-br ; *Cab Rank*, Wellington-st.

Garrick Club, Garrick-st, Covent-gdn. — Instituted for the general patronage of the drama; for the purpose of combining the use of a club, on economical principles, with the advantages of a literary soc. ; for bringing together the supporters of the drama; and for the formation of a theatrical library, with works on costume. The number of member is limited to 650, the election being vested in the general committee. If a less number than twelve voting members of the committee be present, two black balls will exclude ; if twelve or more, three. No candidate to be admitted unless seven of the committee vote. In every case when the minimum amount of black balls is found, the ballot must be taken a second time. Four candidates in each year may be selected by the committee in consideration of their public eminence or distinction. The entrance money is fixed at such amount as the committee may from time to time determine; it being at present £21. The annual subscription is £8 8s.; new members, £10 10s. The committee have power to admit, *pro tem.*, any distinguished foreigner known to the theatrical, musical, or literary world. Visitors are only admitted to the rooms set apart for their reception, except on Wed., when members can take their friends all over the house to inspect the pictures between the hours of 11 a.m. and 3 p.m.

Gas. — The names of the London Gas Companies, with the addresses of their chief offices, are as follows :

THE GAS LIGHT AND COKE COMPANY, Horseferry-rd, S.W.

THE LONDON GAS LIGHT COMPANY, 26, Southampton-st, Strand.

THE SOUTH METROPOLITAN GAS COMPANY, 709A, Old Kent-rd, S.E., and 70, Bankside, S.E.

THE COMMERCIAL, Harford-st, Stepney.

The gas delivered by the various companies is of such an illuminating power, that when consumed at the ordinary pressure, at the rate of 5 cubic feet per hour in a No. 1 Sugg's Standard Argand burner, it gives a light equal to 15 sperm candles. The definition of a candle is the light given by a pure sperm candle, consuming 120 grains of sperm per hour. The price charged for gas varies from 2s. 5d. to 3s. 6d. per 1,000 cubic feet.

THE SERVICE PIPE is the pipe which conducts gas from the company's main in the street to the consumer's meter. It is generally laid to just within the precincts of the consumer's premises, and maintained at the Company's expense. When a new service pipe, or an alteration in the size of an existing one is required, notice must be sent to the gas company's office, stating the number of gas burners for lighting, gas stoves for cooking, and gas fires for heating it is proposed to use. On taking possession of a house the service-pipe is generally found disconnected and capped off in the area. Before making use of it notice must be sent to the gas company, who then send their inspector with a printed form of contract for signature ; and this contract is to the effect that the consumer will hold himself responsible for all gas consumed on the premises, and will permit access to the meter by any one of their authorised servants at all reasonable hours.

When an outgoing tenant quits a house leaving a quarter's gas unpaid, the company cannot make the incoming tenant responsible for such default, or refuse on this account to supply him with gas.

When a stoppage occurs in the service-pipe from the deposit of napthalin, men are sent to remove it on application to the company's office, without any charge being made to the consumer.

THE GAS METER.—In all dwelling houses it is better to employ a "dry" than a "wet" meter, and better to rent it from the gas company, who will be responsible for its proper working and maintenance than to buy one. When a 5-light meter is spoken of, it means a meter of sufficient capacity to supply gas for 5 argand burners, each consuming say from 6 to 8 cubic feet per hour, so that a 5-light meter will be quite sufficient for 8 or 9 ordinary fish-tail burners. The idea that the gas company can force the meter round, or in any way influence its registration in an improper way is absurd. It is however, quite possible for the inspector to make a mistake in the reading ; and as such mistakes are rarely against the company it is as well for the householder to check his readings by personal observation.

Under the "Sale of Gas Acts," gas consumers have the privilege of having their meters tested, should their correctness be doubted, at the offices of the Metropolitan Board of Works. These offices are for the northern and eastern divisions at 56, White Lion-st, Shoreditch. NEAREST *Ry. Stn.*, Liverpool-st (G.E.). ; *Omnibus Rte.*, Norton Folgate ; *Cab Rank*, Bishopsgate st-without. For south-eastern division at 61, Castle-st, Southwark. NEAREST *Ry. Stn.*, London-br *Omnibus Rte.*, Blackfriars-br-rd *Cab Rank*, Southwark-br-rd, Sumner - st. For western division St. Ann-st, Westminster. NEAREST *Ry. Stns.*, St. James's - pk and Westminster-br (Dis.) ; *Omnibus Rte.*, Victoria-st ; *Cab Rank* Victoria-st.

The charge for testing meters is as follows : 1 to 5 light meter inclusive, 6d. each ; 10 to 40 light meter inclusive, 1s. each ; 50 to 60 light meter inclusive, 2s. each ; 80 to 100 light meter inclusive, 3s. each, and so on. Should the Gas Company be proved to be in the wrong they have to pay the expense of testing, which otherwise falls on the consumer.

Gas pipes laid throughout a building should in all cases be of wrought-iron and painted with two coats of oil paint. No pipe less than ½-inch internal bore should be permitted. To burn gas as supplied in London economically, the rule is large pipes and low pressure, The pressure of gas to a house is best regulated by a wet governor, exceedingly simple, durable, and efficient instrument. There are innumerable patent regulators, but one work better than the wet governor.

GAS BURNERS.—The argand and fishtail burners, made by Sugg, of Westminster, and supplied by all respectable gasfitters, are unquestionably the best. It is often supposed that if a good fishtail or flat flame burner is employed, it burns equally well whatever shape of globe be used; this is not the case, the best form of globe is spherical, with a large opening, say 4 in. at the bottom, and 3½ in. at the top. Melon or pine shaped lobes are bad, saucer-shaped are still worse. For reception and bed rooms the opal Christiania shade or globe, with a No. 4 or 5 flat flame steatite burner, gives the best and most agreeable result with the least consumption of gas. The Bronner burner is economical, but must not be used in places exposed to much draught. For basement offices the No. 4 flat flame burner will answer every purpose. The constant complaint of consumers about the "bad gas" either means that the supply of gas is deficient or that it is improperly consumed : with deficient supply the fault rests either with the gas company, whose service-pipe may be stopped, or with the consumer, whose fittings may be choked up or too small ; in the case of bad burners the remedy is an easy one. The comparison on the same chandelier of a No. 5 flat flame burner with a 7½-in. Christiania shade, will at once show whether the old burners and globes are or are not of the right kind. And when a good burner and globe are obtained it is necessary to keep them free from dust by using a soft luster for the former, and by washing the latter twice a week. It should always be remembered that what the consumer wants and pays for is so much light rather than so many cubic feet of gas. And while the quality of the gas supplied in London does not appreciably vary, it is only by using the best burners, fitted in the best and most intelligent manner, that satisfactory results can be obtained.

Most of the Gas Companies now let out gas cooking-stoves at very reasonable rates.

General Post-Office, St. Martin's - le - Grand (Map 8). —

Hours 10 to 4. Subdivided into Secretary's Office ; Medical, Solicitors', Surveyors', Telegraphs, and Engineering Departments ; Receiver and Accountant General's Office ; Money Order Office ; Circulation Department, with further subdivisions : and Returned Letter Office. Admission to view the interior working of the department can be obtained only by permission of the Post-Office authorities, who, on account of the obstruction to public business, are somewhat chary of according it. NEAREST *Ry. Stns.*, Holborn-viaduct (L. C. & D.), Aldersgate (Met.), and Mansion House (Dis.); *Omnibus Rtes.*, Aldersgate-st, Cheapside, and Moorgate-st ; *Cab Rank*, Opposite.

The great establishment of the Savings' Bank Department is now carried on at 144 A, Queen Victoria-street, E.C. (Map 8), in a large and commodious building, open to the public from 10 to 4. NEAREST *Ry. Stns.*, Blackfriars (Dis.) and St. Paul's (L.C.&D.); *Omnibus Rtes.*, Queen Victoria-st and New Bridge-st ; *Cab Rank*, Queen Victoria-st.

Geological Museum, Jermyn-st, Piccadilly (Map 6), contains a superb collection of minerals, metals, and their products. The hall into which the visitor first enters is devoted to stones used in building and for architectural adornments. Here are plinths and columns of an immense variety of marbles, granites, porphyrys, serpentines, elvans, and conglomerate. The building stones of Great Britain are very strongly represented, and in the recesses by the stairs are some cases of British serpentines, granites, limestones, sandstones, &c., which show what an immense variety of useful and ornamental stone our architects have ready at hand. In this hall are busts of eminent geologists. Upstairs on the principal floor are specimens of ore of the chief metals from various parts of the world, as also the manufactured products of the ores. The number and variety of ores of the metals are immense, and the beauty of many of them is very remarkable. There are some lovely specimens of rock crystal, and ladies will be interested in the collection of gems, and in the beautiful examples of agates and amygdaloids. There are many

geological models showing the structure of various localities, and the direction and nature of mineral lodes. Facing the staircase is a model, on a large scale, of the geological structure of the Thames Valley beneath and around London. Just behind this is a gold snuff-box mounted in diamonds, and a magnificent salver in steel and gold. The first was presented by the Emperor of Russia, the second by the Russian Administration of Mines, to the late Sir Roderick Murchison, who bequeathed them to the museum. At the south end of the hall is a very fine collection of glass and British pottery and porcelain. There are also examples of Limoges enamels and other vitreous wares. In the upper galleries is a superb collection of British fossils. In the chambers at the north end of the hall is a collection of models showing the underground and surface workings of mines, pumps, engines, man-ladders, lifts, cages, tools, and, in fact, of all machinery, apparatus, and plant connected with mining. A room in the upper gallery is devoted to the display of rocks. The museum is open free to the public daily, except on Fri. On Mon. and Sat. evenings the museum is illuminated by the electric light until 10 p.m. Mr. W. Whitaker's "Guide to the Geology of London" is sold at the doors of the museum. NEAREST *Ry. Stns.*, Charing ✠ (Dis. & S.E.); *Omnibus Rtes.*, Piccadilly and Regent-st ; *Cab Ranks*, Albany, Piccadilly, and St. James's-sq.

Geological Survey of the United Kingdom, 28, Jermyn-street, S.W. Hours 10 to 4.— NEAREST *Ry. Stns.*, Charing ✠ (Dis. & S.E.); *Omnibus Rtes.*, Piccadilly, Regent-st, and Waterloo-pl ; *Cab Rank*, Piccadilly.

German Empire.—EMBASSY, 9, Carlton House-ter, S.W. NEAREST *Ry. Stns.*, Charing ✠ (Dis. & S.E.); *Omnibus Rte.*, Regent-st ; *Cab Rank*, Waterloo-pl. CONSULATE, 5, Blomfield-st, London Wall. NEAREST *Ry. Stn.*, Bishopsgate (G. E.) ; *Omnibus Rte.*, Bishopsgate-st ; *Cab Rank*, At Station.

GERMAN ATHENÆUM IN LONDON, or "Deutscher Verein für kunst und Wissenschaft," 93, Mortimer-st, W.—A club founded by German artists and literary men in 1869, and numbering many distinguished names among its members. Concerts, conversazioni, exhibitions of pictures and other works of art, and "humoristical evenings" are given from time to time. For further particulars, application should be made to the secretary at the club-house.

German Gymnastic Society.—(*See* ATHLETICS.)

Globe Theatre, Newcastle-st, Strand (Map 7).—A compact little theatre, with a semi-circular *salle* half below ground. It has passed through many vicissitudes, and has been under many different managements, the last of which (Mr. C. H. Hawtrey's) had extraordinary success with "The Private Secretary." NEAREST *Ry. Stn.,* Temple (Dis.); *Omnibus Rtes.,* Strand, Chancery-la, and Waterloo-br ; *Cab Rank,* St. Clement's Church

Gog and Magog—or, to give them their proper titles, Gogmagog and Corinœus, were both born in the year 1707 ; their wicker-work predecessors. formerly carried in procession on grand City occasions, having escaped the Great Fire only to succumb eventually to the combined assaults of old age and the City rats. At what period they agreed to drop the high-sounding name of Corinœus and to divide that of Gogmagog between them, even the "Gigantic Historie of ye two famous giants of ye Guildhall" does not record. But Gog and Magog they have been for more years at all events than the memory of living Cockney runneth to the contrary. The present monsters, who are too substantially built for travelling, were carved by one Richard Saunders, to whom the City paid £70 for the job, and are permanently stationed in the Guildhall.

Goldsmiths' Company (The) possess an immense mansion at the back of the General Post Office, and are famous for their hospitality and their charities. Time was when the Goldsmiths were held to be the most pugnacious of all the guilds. They fought the Fishmongers on a question of precedence, and they constantly met the Merchant Taylors in the streets at night, when much cudgelling ensued. Nowadays the Goldsmiths are as peaceable a body of men as need be. They possess the

right of assaying all articles made of gold and silver. The staircase leading to the hall, made entirely of marble, is well worth a visit ; and Mr. Storey's figures of Cleopatra and the Sibyl are worthy of more than passing attention. Among a valuable collection of plate is a silver-gilt cup, used at the coronation of Queen Elizabeth, and presented by her majesty to Sir Martin Bowes, who was Lord Mayor at the time. This vessel is highly treasured, and is used as a loving-cup at the Goldsmiths' feasts. There is a fair collection of portraits of royal personages, including one of Queen Victoria by Hayter

Government Offices.—(*See under their respective heads.*)

Grafton Club, Grafton-st.— Proprietary. A grill club. Entrance fee, £5 5s. ; subscription, £3 13s. 6d.

Grand Theatre (The), Islington (Map 3), nearly opposite "The Angel," was totally destroyed by fire on the morning of the 29th Dec., 1887, but is in course of re-erection.

Gray's Inn.—(*See* INNS OF COURT.)

Grecian Theatre, City-road. —This old established and popular East End theatre, known long ago as the "Eagle Tavern and Grecian Saloon," has to all appearance finally closed its doors as a place of public amusement. In August, 1882, the lease of the property was acquired, for a considerable sum (raised chiefly by public subscription), by "General Booth," of the Salvation Army, and will be henceforward the principal metropolitan place of meeting of that numerous body. NEAREST *Omnibus Rtes.,* City-rd and New North-rd ; *Cab Rank,* City-rd.

Greece.—MINISTRY, 5, St. James's-sq., S.W. NEAREST *Ry. Stns.,* Charing ✠ (S.E. & Dis.) ; *Omnibus Rte.,* Charing ✠ ; *Cab Rank,* St. James's-sq. CONSULATE, 19, Gt. Winchester-st, E.C. NEAREST *Ry. Stns.,* Broad-st (N.L.) and Moorgate-st (Met.) ; *Omnibus Rtes.,* Bishopsgate-st and Moorgate-st ; *Cab Rank,* Broad-st Station.

Green Park (Map 6).—Lies on the S. side of the W. half of Piccadilly, and is nearly triangular in shape ; its S.W. side being bounded

by Constitution-hill, between which and Grosvenor-pl lie the private gardens of Buckingham Palace. The N.W. corner is just opposite the S.E. corner of Hyde-pk. On the arch at the entrance to Constitution-hill long stood the equestrian statue of the great Duke of Wellington in long cloak and cocked hat ; but the hideous effigy was removed in 1883. Only privileged horsemen and carriages can pass down Constitution-hill. NEAREST *Ry. Stn.,* Victoria (Dis.) ; *Omnibus Rtes.,* Piccadilly and Grosvenor-pl.

Green Room Club, 20, Bedford-st, Covent Garden, instituted to promote the association of members of the dramatic, literary, artistic, and liberal professions. The election of members is vested in the committee. Entrance fee, £5 5s. ; subscription, £3 3s.

Greenwich Hospital and Royal Naval College, Greenwich, S.E. (Map 15), is well worth a visit, although the old pensioners, which constituted perhaps its chief attraction, have been removed since 1871. The Painted Hall contains some fine pictures of sea-fights, and there are some noteworthy statues of celebrated sailors. The most interesting of the Greenwich sights, however, are the relics of Nelson—notably the Trafalgar coat and waistcoat. The public are admitted free. The gates are opened to the public on week-days as follows : At 6 a.m. from 1st April to 30th September 7 a.m. from 1st October to 31st March ; and on Sundays at 1 p.m. And closed : At 6 p.m. from 1st Februaryto 31st March ; 7 p.m. from 1st April to 30th September ; 6 p.m. from 1st to 31st October ; 5 p.m. 1st November to 31st January. The Painted Hall, Chapel, and Naval Museum are open to the public every week-day at 10 a.m. And closed : At 4 p.m. from 1st January to 15th February ; 5 p.m. from 16th February to 31st March ; 6 p.m. from 1st April to 15th September ; 5 p.m. from 16th September to 31st October ; 4 p.m. from 1st November to 31st December. The Painted Hall is open also on Sundays at 2 p.m. The Chapel and Museum are closed on Fridays and Sundays. From Cannon-st (17 min.), 1st, -/10, 1/3 ; 2nd, -/8, 1/- ; 3rd, -/5, -/8. Charing ✠ (27 min.), 1st, 1/-, 1/6 ; 2nd, -/9, 1/2 ; 3rd, -/6, -/9 ; also by steamboat from all piers.

Gresham Club, 1, Gresham-pl, E.C., is composed of merchants, bankers, and other gentlemen of known respectability. No candidate is eligible until he has attained the age of twenty-one years. Election by ballot of the members, of whom thirty must actually vote. One black ball in ten excludes. Entrance fee, £21; subscription, £8 8s.

Grocers' Company (The), that is, dealers *en gros*, were originally called Pepperers, and were incorporated by a charter given by Edward III. They are rich in Church livings, and possess four free grammar schools, besides exhibitions at the universities. Their present abode, close to Cheapside, is not remarkable for beauty, but is spacious and comfortable. The one admirable object in the house is a stained glass window. Portraits of Pitt and Baron Heath are noteworthy ornaments. The Grocers' plate is remarkable, more especially two large silver-gilt loving cups, dated respectively 1668 and 1669. The present hall was finished in 1802.

Grosvenor Bridge is handsomer than most railway bridges, and perhaps wider than any. It forms the connecting link between the Victoria Stn. and the lines on the south side of the river; but there is no accommodation for any other kind of traffic.

Grosvenor Gallery, 136, New Bond-st, W. (Map 6).—This building was erected by Sir Coutts Lindsay, for the purpose of exhibiting the works of such painters, &c., as may receive invitations to contribute to the annual exhibition which is held in the spring. One result of this principle of selection has been that certain schools of art, which are not generally popular elsewhere, have found a congenial home at the Grosvenor, and that its walls display, besides simpler works, many which are only to be appreciated by the amateurs of a peculiar æstheticism. The charge for admission is one shilling, and the price of catalogues is sixpence. There is also a winter exhibition, with the same charge for admission, and somewhat on the plan of that promoted by the Royal Academy of Arts. The Secretary to the Gallery is Mr. J. W. Beck. A convenient restaurant is at-

tached to the premises. (*For the Library, see* LIBRARIES, CIRCULATING.) NEAREST *Ry. Stns.,* Charing✠and Portland-rd; *Omnibus Rtes.,* Bond-st, Regent-st, and Oxford-st; *Cab Rank,* Conduit-st.

Guards' Club, 70, Pall Mall, S.W. — For officers, past and present, of the Grenadier, Coldstream, and Scots Guards only. Entrance fee, £31 10s.; subscription, £11.

Guatemala, Republic of. —MINISTRY, Letters to care of Consul General,22,Gt.Winchester-st. CONSULATE, 22,Gt.Winchester-st. NEAREST *Ry. Stn.,* Bishopsgate; *Omnibus Rtes.,* Old Broad-st and Bishopsgate-st; *Cab Rank,* At Station.

Guildhall (Map 8) dates from the time of Henry IV.,which, however, is not responsible for the mean and miserable jumble of a front stuck on it by Dance in 1789. The old walls, on the other hand, are of so splendid a solidity that they stood triumphant through the Great Fire of 1666, towering amid the flames "in a bright shining coat, as if it had been a palace of gold or a great building of burnished brass." The old crypt, too, of the same date (1411), is a beautiful piece of work, 75 ft. long by 45 ft.wide, and divided into three aisles by six clusters of circular columns in Purbeck marble, supporting a fine groined roof, partly in stone, partly in chalk and bricks, the principal intersections being covered with carved bosses of heads, shields, and flowers. The vaulting, with four-centred arches, is considered to be one of the earliest as well as one of the finest examples of its kind in England. At the eastern end is a fine arched entrance of Early English, and in the south-eastern angle an octagonal recess about 13 ft. in height. The length of the great hall is 150ft., its height 55 ft., and its breadth 50 ft. The side walls, which are 5 ft. in thickness, are divided by clustered columns and mouldings into eight spaces, and at each end of the hall is a splendid Gothic window occupying the whole width, and nearly perfect in all architectural details. Only the upper portions, however, are filled with stained glass, and that chiefly of modern date. In corners, on lofty octagonal pedestals, are the two famous giants. (*See* GOG AND

MAGOG.) The great State Banquets are held here; the hall being capable of-containing between 6,000 and 7,000 persons. It was here that Whittington, entertaining, in his capacity of Lord Mayor, Henry V. and his queen, paid the king after dinner the delicate compliment of burning, on a fire of sandal-wood, his majesty's bonds for £60,000; and it was here also that a successor of equal loyalty, but perhaps hardly equal felicity in its demonstration, seized Charles II. by the arm, as that merry monarch was endeavouring to beat at least a partially sober retreat, and peremptorily insisted upon his brother potentate remaining for "t'other bottle." Even in these moderate times the Lord Mayor's feast is a Gargantuan institution, involving the services of twenty cooks, the slaughter of forty turtles, and the consumption of somewhere about fourteen tons of coal. Around the Guildhall were at one time a cluster of courts, duplicating those at Westminster, and there are also other apartments, such as the Common Council Chamber, the Court of Aldermen, the Chamberlain's Office, the Chamberlain's Parlour, the Library (one of the finest in the kingdom, *see* CITY OF LONDON), &c., with a Court called the Lord Mayor's Court, nominally for the recovery of small debts incurred in the City. NEAREST *Ry. Stn.,* Moorgate-st (Met.); *Omnibus Rtes.,* Moorgate-st and Cheapside; *Cab Rank,* King St.

Guildhall School of Music(Map 8).—This school was established by the Corporation of the City of London for the purpose of providing the highest form of instruction in the art and science of music, at the lowest possible cost. All branches of music are taught by a large body of thoroughly competent professors, under the direction of Mr. H. Weist Hill. In addition to £200 given annually by the Corporation of London, several other exhibitions, ranging in value from £5 to £20, are offered for annual competition. In connection with the school, the Guildhall Orchestral Society has been established for the practice and performance of high-class music. Forms of nomination, which, when filled up, must be signed by a member of the Court of Common Council, may be obtained on application to the Secretary at the School, Victoria Embankment, E.C., where also tables of fees and all other particulars are supplied.

Haberdashers' Company (The) were formed in 1447, and were first known as "Hurrers" and "Millainers" (milliners), from the fact that they supplied goods made in Milan. Their trade was not confined to what is now known as haberdashery, but included swords, knives, spurs, glass, and other articles. The present hall in Gresham-st is not an ancient building, nor is it remarkable in any way, except for its extreme comfort. It contains a couple of portraits of George II. and the wife of Frederick Prince of Wales, around which some mystery gathers. These paintings were missing for about forty years, and it was only in the year 1876 that they were discovered in the collection of a country gentleman by a master of the company, who was enabled to restore them to their original place. The Haberdashers have the patronage of eight livings, and eighteen scholarships, and have five free schools, two of which are in London.

Haiti. — MINISTRY, Vacant. CONSULATE, 101, Leadenhall-st, E.C. NEAREST *Ry Stns.*, Aldgate (Met.) Cannon-st (S.E.), and Mansion House (Dis.); *Omnibus Rtes.*, Cornhill and Leadenhall-st; *Cab Rank*, Leadenhall-st.

Hampstead Heath. — A stretch of real country within easy walk of the heart of London, the only spot within reach ás yet unspoiled by improvement.

Hampstead lies high above the cross of St. Paul's, and though a good deal trenched upon of late years by the builders, still presents a wide expanse of comparatively unsophisticated common, one of the best and healthiest of London's lungs. Its preservation to the public in the future has been assured by its purchase on their behalf, and it is now one of the trusts of the Metropolitan Board of Works.

On summer Saturdays and Sundays its delights are shared by rather more people than a holiday-maker of a retiring turn might care to encounter, nor do the starveling steeds and donkeys so plentifully provided for the delectation of "'Arry" and his young lady add much to the æsthetics of the scene. But even under these trying conditions it is still the most hopeful "draw" in the immediate neighbourhood of London for a breath of comparatively fresh air, and on less popular occasions, especially in the early morning, it is a most enjoyable spot.

The three best places in Hampstead for the refreshment of the inner holiday - maker are the "Spaniards," the "Bull and Bush," and "Jack Straw's Castle." Reached by train, *via* North London; or by omnibus from Victoria by way of Charing ✠, Tottenham-ct-rd, and Hampstead-rd.

Hampton Court.—An old-fashioned village on the Thames, about two miles above Kingston, well known for the old palace of Cardinal Wolsey. Presented by the great Cardinal to Henry VIII. it was for many years a royal residence, and, curiously enough, was a favourite abode of both Charles I. and Oliver Cromwell. At present suites of apartments are granted in the palace to ladies and gentlemen favoured by the Crown. Cavalry barracks are attached to the palace, which are generally occupied by a detachment of the household brigade or some other *corps d'élite.* There are many pictures of great interest, principally in their relation to English History ; the beauties of the court of the second Charles, limned by Sir Peter Lely, being in this respect particularly noticeable. There are also pictures by Holbein, Kneller, Titian, and other masters, but it may be noted that many of the Hampton Court pictures are but of doubtful authenticity. The principal attractions at the Court, however, to the general public are the gardens, with quaint old-world arrangement, and the fish-ponds, which contain patriarchal carp, which might even have competed for crumbs from the hand of William the Silent, as they now do from those of 'Arry the Noisy. The maze is a never-ending source of hilarious enjoyment to crowds of holiday visitors, and the great vine annually attracts its thousands of sightseers. The palace is closed on Fridays. (For a full account of the Hampton Court pictures, &c., *see* DICKENS'S DICTIONARY OF THE THAMES.) From Waterloo (42 min.), 1st 2/-, 2/9 ; 2nd, 1/6, 2/- ; 3rd, 1/3, 1/10.

Hanover Square Club. Incorporated in 1885 with the St. George's Club, Hanover-sq (*which see*).

Hawaiian Islands.— CONSULATE, 3, Gt. Winchester-st. NEAREST *Ry. Stns.*, Broad-st (N.L.) and Moorgate-st (Met.); *Omnibus Rtes.*, Bishopsgate - st, Broad-st, and Moorgate-st; *Cab Rank*, Broad-st Station.

Haymarket Theatre (Map 7), the titular "Home of English Comedy," was for some years in a position by no means correspondent to its pretensions. It then passed into the hands of Mr. and Mrs. Bancroft, by whom it was entirely rebuilt internally from the designs and under the superintendence of Mr. C. J. Phipps, F.S.A. The auditory is arranged in five divisions, all approached from the frontage in the Haymarket, special attention having been paid to the means of ingress and egress. The various staircases are entirely rebuilt of stone, and are of easy ascent with level landings and without winding steps. The auditory still retains the distinguishing feature of the old theatre in having the balcony nearly level with the stage, but it has been advanced considerably nearer to the proscenium, consequently lessening the centre area, which now only admits of the requisite number of stalls being placed in it. Below the entrance vestibule and balcony there is a foyer from which, on either side, a wide corridor leads to the stalls, and adjoining the foyer is a refreshment saloon and cloak rooms. On the levels of the first circle, second circle, and gallery, are refreshment saloons and retiring rooms for both ladies and gentlemen. Mr. and Mrs. Bancroft retired from the management of the Haymarket Theatre, after a very successful career, in 1885, and the theatre was then taken by Messrs. Russell and Bashford. In Sept., 1887, it was opened' by Mr. H. Beerbohm - Tree. NEAREST *Ry. Stns.*, Charing ✠ (S.E. & Dis.); *Omnibus Rtes* , Haymarket, Pall Mall, and Waterloo-pl ; *Cab Rank*, Opposite.

Health.—Since the 1st July, 1837, the statistics of births and deaths, and of the causes of death, have been collected at the Registrar-General's Office at Somerset House. By this means the limits and causes of mortality are determined with much precision, and too high a death-rate leads to a special enquiry as to its causes, and to the more stringent enforcement of the rules of public health. The mean annual mortality (during 10 years, 1877–86) of London was 21·2 per 1,000 of population. In 1887 it was 19.6. In twenty-seven other English towns, the death-rate ranged in 1887 from 16·9 in Brighton to 28·7 in Manchester per 1,000.

Heralds' College, or **College of Arms.**—This is one of the old-fashioned institutions which still survive, although it is difficult to see of what particular service it is to anyone but its officials. In the days when the herald was really an important functionary, not only in state ceremonials, but also in registering the various grants of arms, superintending and chronicling trials by battle and chivalric exercises, it is possible that the thirteen kings-at-arms, heralds, and pursuivants, may have been usefully employed. At present they are mainly occupied in assisting those who desire to trace their descent from the owners of titles, in granting new, and in empowering the adoption of old, armorial bearings on certain conditions.

There are three kings-at-arms—Garter, Norroy, and Clarencieux; six heralds — Somerset, York, Chester, Richmond, Windsor, and Lancaster; and four pursuivants—Rouge Croix, Blue Mantle, Rouge Dragon, and Portcullis.

The College of Arms (Map 8), which was founded by Richard III., occupied, on the destruction of Derby House in Doctors' Commons, new buildings planned by Sir Christopher Wren. The various improvements in that neighbourhood have now brought the frontage of the building into Queen Victoria-st.

There are many objects of interest to antiquaries, especially in the form of curious rolls, pedigrees, MSS., &c., at the college, but to these the general public is not allowed access. Hours 10 to 4. (The Lyon College of Scotland is in the new General Register House, Edinburgh, and the office of Arms for Ireland in the Record Tower, Dublin Castle.) NEAREST *Ry. Stn.*, Mansion House (Dis.) and St. Paul's (L.C. & D.); *Omnibus Rtes.*, Queen Victoria-st, Cheapside, and Cornhill; *Cab Rank*, Opposite.

Her Majesty's Theatre, Haymarket (Map 13).—A handsome theatre, the *salle* built on the lines of the old structure, destroyed by fire in 1867, but not occupying quite the same site. The former stage was one of the shallowest in London, extending almost as much in front of the curtain as behind it. By sacrificing the "crush-room," or *foyer*, which occupied the end of the building farthest from the stage, the *salle* has now been removed a considerable distance to the north of its former position, and the space thus gained has been thrown into the stage, which now occupies its normal relation to the rest of the house. From the point of view of stage effect a great gain has thus been achieved, the actors no longer stepping out of the picture and walking down almost to the middle of the house to sing their solos. Whether the acoustic qualities of the theatre have gained by this improvement is perhaps a question, but they are still very good. The best place for hearing, both here and at the other opera-house, is the amphitheatre stalls; the best for seeing, the middle or back row of the orchestra stalls, or the central portion of the grand tier. Visitors will find a very convenient short exit into the arcade from the lobby on the right-hand side, looking towards the stage. At present the prospects of a resumption of performances of Italian opera at Her Majesty's Theatre appear to be somewhat remote, and, if a forecast of its future may be hazarded, it will probably be as a rival to the Alhambra and the Empire that the theatre will be known in future. The theatre was utilised for Promenade Concerts in 1887. NEAREST *Ry. Stns.*, Charing ✠ (Dis. & S.E.); *Omnibus Rtes.*, Pall Mall, Haymarket, and Waterloo-pl; *Cab Rank*, Opposite.

Highgate lies about N.N.E. of Hampstead, in conjunction with which it occupies the chief of those "Northern Heights of London" celebrated by Howitt. Though by no means free from the universal invasion of brick and mortar, it still preserves here and there a fair specimen or two of the country-lane, a trifle dingy perhaps in country eyes, and with small superfluous hedge-wealth of wild rose or honeysuckle, but quite near

enough to the real thing to make a charming objective for the half-holiday stroll of a smoke-stifled Londoner. The Gate House Tavern, at the top of the hill near the Cemetery, has a well-deserved reputation for its chops and steaks, and, in winter, for its Burton ale. There is a charming walk from here to Hampstead, along Caen Wood. Reached by train *via* Midland or Gt. Northern, or by omnibus from Victoria *via* Charing ✠ and Tottenham-court-rd.

Hogarth Club, 36, Dover-st, W., established to facilitate association amongst artists who wish to enjoy the advantages derived from social intercourse. Candidates are elected at general meetings by ballot; a majority of four-fifths of the members present are required to elect. A limited number of lay members (*i.e.*, not artists) are admitted. Conversazioni are held from time to time, to which the members contribute their paintings prior to their being forwarded to the Academy and other exhibitions. Entrance fee, £5 5s.; subscription, £4 4s. for artists, £10 10s. for lay members.

Holborn (Map 7) is a continuation of Oxford-st, a great link between east and west. Until within the last few years the row of houses which narrowed the street at the Bar formed one of the most curious bits of old London remaining; and the removal of the row, although immensely improving the general aspect of Holborn, has greatly altered its character. The line of houses still remaining at this point on the south side of the street, opposite Furnival's - inn, are well worth seeing, as being by far the most perfect specimens of old street architecture, with its wooden beams and projecting upper storeys, remaining in London. The two chief thoroughfares which run into Holborn are Chancery-la, leading down past Lincoln's-inn to Fleet-st, and Gray's-inn-rd, leading to King's ✠. Gray's-inn, of which only the entrance is visible in Holborn, half-way down on the north side, will be found described elsewhere (*see* INNS OF COURT). Holborn terminates at the circus of the same name, while beyond, the Holborn-viaduct spans the Fleet Valley to St. Sepulchre's Church and Newgate,

With the exception, perhaps, of Queen Victoria-st, this is the finest piece of street architecture in the City of London, and its effect is greatly increased by the fact that it is built in a curve. There is a uniformity in the general architectural design of the houses upon either side, which, although carried to a wearisome extent in many Continental towns, is very rare in London; indeed, of the great thoroughfares, Regent-st and Holborn-viaduct are the sole examples. On the right-hand side, going east, of the Viaduct is the chapel of Dr. Parker, known as the City Temple. The nearest way from Holborn to Blackfriars-br, or the Ludgate-cir at the junction of Fleet-st and Ludgate-hill, is through Shoe-la and Bride-st; Shoe-la runs off diagonally from Holborn-cir. From the same point Charterhouse-st leads down to the Farringdon Stn. of the Metropolitan Ry.

Holborn Viaduct Station (Map 8), the East End terminus of the L.C. & D.R., although one might suppose, from the manner in which people persist in flocking to the dirty, ramshackle, and altogether deplorable Ludgate Station, that the post of honour was held by that most inconvenient of places. The Holborn Viaduct Hotel of Messrs. Spiers and Pond forms part of the buildings of the Viaduct Station, and almost immediately opposite is a station of the Metropolitan Ry. Nearest *Ry. Stn.*, Snow Hill (Met.); *Omnibus Rte.*, Viaduct; *Cab Fare* to Bank or Charing ✠, 1/-.

Home Office, Whitehall (Map 13).—This office undertakes an enormous amount of work in connection with the social government of the country, and contains the following departments: The Factory Department, Whitehall, with a large staff of inspectors, assistant-inspectors, and sub-inspectors; Inspectors of Prisons, under the Act of 1877; Reformatory and Industrial Schools, 3, Delahay-st, S.W. (Nearest *Ry. Stn.*, St. James's-pk (Dis.); *Omnibus Rtes.*, Victoria-st and Parliament-st; *Cab Rank*, Palace-yd); Inspectors of Anatomical Schools, 30, Abingdon-st, S.W. (Nearest *Ry. Stn.*, Westminster-br; *Omnibus Rtes.*, Victoria-st and Parliament-st; *Cab Rank*, Palace-yd); The Prison

Department; The Burial Acts Department; Inspectors of Constabulary; Inspectors of Salmon Fisheries; and Inspectors of Explosives. Hours of attendance at Home Office, 11 to 5. Nearest *Ry. Stns.*, Westminster-br; *Omnibus Rtes.*, Whitehall and Strand; *Cab Rank*, Horse Guards.

Homes for Working Girls in London, founded 1878, accommodating 516. Victoria House, 135 and 137, Queen's-rd, Bayswater, W.; Morley House, 14, Fitzroy-st, Fitzroy-sq, W.; Gordon House, 8, Endsleigh-gdns, N.W.; Woodford House, 28 and 29, Duncan-ter, Islington, N.; Garfield House, 361, Brixton-rd, S.W.; Norfolk House, 50, Well-st, Hackney; Hyde House, 27, Somerset-st, W.; Lincoln House, 12, York-pl, Baker-st, W.; and Domgay House, 11, Fitzroy-st, Fitzroy-sq, W. Office, 38, Lincoln's Inn Fields. Honorary Director, John Shrimpton, Esq. —These homes are intended for girls and young women who are employed in the factories and workrooms of the metropolis. The committee state that it is their endeavour "to help those who help themselves," by providing homes in the various districts of the metropolis for those who are earnestly striving to gain an honest living, but who are "homeless"; at the same time to afford them profitable recreation, and, above all, to surround them with healthful influences and friendly guidance at the most critical period of their lives. Board and lodging are provided at very moderate rates. From the success which has attended the efforts of the committee, it would seem that the homes supply a real want. One of the rules is worth quoting, from the sensible contrast it affords to the practice which too often obtains in institutions of a similar nature. The report says: "No restrictions are imposed upon the occupants of the house to attend daily prayers or meetings of any sort. These meetings are held, also daily prayers; it is quite optional for the residents to be present, but at the same time it is very satisfactory to know that evening prayers are pretty well attended.

Honduras.—Consulate, 13, St. Helen's-pl, E.C. Nearest *Ry. Stn.*, *Omnibus Rte.*, and *Cab Rank*, Bishopsgate-st,

Horse Guards, Whitehall (Map 13).—The offices of the Inspector-General of Artillery and Inspector-General of Fortifications are here. Hours 10 to 5. Nearest *Ry. Stns.*, Charing ✠ (Dis. & S.E.) and Westminster-br; *Omnibus Rtes.*, Whitehall and Strand; *Cab Rank*, Opposite.

Horses and Carriages.—Readers of the Dictionary may possibly find themselves in the position of wanting to hire horses, harness, &c. This is a matter as to which it is most difficult to advise. Prices vary so greatly during the few months of the season and the rest of the year, and in various quarters of the town, that this is emphatically a business in which "circumstances alter cases." But it may roughly be said that at the best West End houses a one-horse carriage (victoria or brougham) will cost about 30 guineas a month; a two-horse carriage, such as a landau, about 45 guineas a month. These prices, of course, include horses, carriage, harness, coachman, stabling, and forage. Horses alone, during the same months, may be hired at about 15 guineas each a month, including forage and stabling (a City firm, in answer to our enquiries, puts this at 8 guineas, exclusive of forage and stabling); but in this case harness will be an extra charge, and the coachman's wages will have to be paid. In ordinary jobbing work a one-horse brougham during the day-time costs about 7s. 6d. for two hours' hiring; theatre and ball work cost from 10s. 6d. to 27s. 6d., according to circumstances and locality. For excursions a one-horse brougham, as a rule, will cost £1 1s.; a two-horse carriage £1 10s.; but for what the job-masters call a "long day" these charges would be increased about 20 per cent. It should be borne in mind that unless the carriage be jobbed for a lengthened period the coachman invariably expects a gratuity. The above prices, be it noted, refer to the best West End establishments. In every district in town there are job-masters who will supply horses and carriages on considerably easier terms. Special charges are everywhere made for races, weddings, Levees, and Drawing Rooms. At most of the termini private broughams can be hired at 3s. 6d. the first hour, and 2s. 6d. per hour afterwards; invalid carriages can also be had from most of the termini, but the charges are very heavy. There is also a very general railway system of private omnibuses for families as in Paris, but they must be ordered beforehand from the station-master. —(*See* RIDING HORSES.)

Horticultural Society (Royal) (Map ᴵ.)—The gardens are at Chiswick, and the offices at 111, Victoria-st, S.W.—The society's fortnightly meetings and shows during 1888 will be held in the Drill Hall of the London Scottish Rifle Volunteers, James-st, Victoria-st, S.W. The privileges of Fellows for 1888 have now been formulated, of which full particulars may be obtained on application to the secretary at the society's offices. Fellows are admitted free, and the public on payment at the door of 1s. on ordinary show days, and 2s. 6d. when larger shows are held. The society's gardens at Chiswick are carried on as usual. (*For Dates of Shows for* 1888, *see* CALENDAR.) For Chiswick from Waterloo (20 min.), 1st, -/11, 1/4 ; 2nd, -/9, 1/- ; 3rd,-/7,-/10. NEAREST *Ry.Stn.* and *Cab Rank* to the Drill Hall, Victoria ; *Omnibus Rtes.*, Grosvenor-pl and Victoria-st.

Hospitals.—The following is a classified list of the principal London Hospitals from returns kindly furnished by their secretaries. Those marked with an asterisk receive paying in-patients ; and those with a dagger treat out-patients on payment.

ACCIDENTS (*and see* GENERAL).
THE POPLAR HOSPITAL FOR ACCIDENTS, 303, East India Dock-rd, Blackwall, E. ; Secretary, Lt.-Col. Feneran. — Out-patients seen daily, except Sundays, at 12 o'clock. Visitors admitted on Tu., 3 p.m., for 2 hours ; Fri., 3 p.m., for 2 hours ; Sun., 2 p.m., for 2 hours. Admission is absolutely free to every case of accident or emergency.
Honorary Surgeons. — F. M. Corner, M. Brownfield, T. E. Bowkett, Dr. A. E. Taylor, P. W. Howse, Dr. C. Dundas Grant.
House Surgeons.—A. C. Waters and F. Bredton.

CANCER.
CANCER HOSPITAL, Brompton (free), founded 1851 ; Secretary, William Henry Hughes.—Out-patients seen daily, Sundays excepted, at 2 p.m. Visitors ad-

mitted on Th. and Sun. from 2 to 4 p.m. Admission free, without letters of recommendation.
Consulting and Senior Surgeon. — Alexander Marsden, M.D., F.R.C.S.
Surgeons.—H. L. Snow, M.D., F. A. Purcell, M.D., F. B. Jessett.
Chloroformists.— G. H. Bailey, N. W. Bourns, M.D.
House Surgeon and Registrar. —C. E. Valpy, M.R.C.S.

*ST. SAVIOUR'S CANCER HOSPITAL, Osnaburg-st, Regent's-pk, N.W. ; Secretary, E. Poitiers. This hospital receives patients who wish to be treated by the medicines of Count Mattei, as well as those who desire homœopathic treatment Out-patients seen every day at 4 p.m. Friends of patients are admitted on Sun., Tu., and Th. from 2 to 4. The hospital can be visited at any time. Admission by governor's letter of recommendation. Private rooms for ladies, at from 2 to 3 guineas per week, attendance of House Physician included. Pay ward, with board, nursing, and attendance, 10s. 6d. per week. Incurables 30s. and £2 2s.
Physician in Charge. — Dr. Pritchard.

CHILDREN (*and see p.* 128.)
* ALEXANDRA HOSPITAL FOR CHILDREN WITH HIP DISEASE, 18, Queen-sq, Bloomsbury, W.C.; Hon. Sec., Mrs. H. Marsh.—There are no out-patients. Visitors are admitted every day, except Sun., from 2 to 5 p.m. Admission by subscriber's letter, and by payment.
Medical Officers. — Howard Marsh, F.R.C.S., Anthony Bowlby, F.R.C.S.

BELGRAVE HOSPITAL FOR CHILDREN, 79, Gloucester-st, Pimlico ; Lady Superintendent, Miss Munro. Hon. Secs., Capt. W. J. Stopford and Rev. John Storrs.— For the treatment of children not suffering from contagious diseases. Out-patients are seen on Mon., Tu., Th., and Fr., at 9 a.m. Visitors admitted daily. Children's friends from 1.15 to 2 p.m., on Tu. and Th. Other visitors from 2 to 4.30 p.m. A letter from a subscriber is necessary. Urgent cases are seen, and sometimes admitted, without a letter.
Physicians.—W. Ewart, M.D., and A. T. Myers, M.D.
Surgeons.—C.T. Dent, F.R.C.S., R. Margerison, F.R.C.S.E.
House Surg.—A. Barry Blacker.
* CHEYNE HOSPITAL FOR SICK

AND INCURABLE CHILDREN, 46, Cheyne-walk, Chelsea, S.W.; Hon. Secretary, Mrs. Wickham Flower ; Secretary, D. M. Evans.— For the alleviation of children suffering incurable complaints, and the treatment of some forms of long and chronic illness. A payment of 4s. per week is required. No out-patients. Visitors admitted from 2 till 4.30 every day, except Sun. Suitable cases received in order of application, subscribers' nominees taking precedence.
Physician.—G. Vivian Poore, M.D.
Surgeons.—J. Macready, J. P. Bartlett.

† EVELINA HOSPITAL FOR SICK CHILDREN, Southwark-br-rd, S.E.; Secretary, Thos. S. Chapman.— For the relief of the sick children of the poor. Out-patients seen every day at 9 a.m. Visitors admitted every day from 2 to 4 p.m Admission free.
Consulting Physician.—W. S. Playfair, M.D.
Consulting Surgeons.— Sir Prescott G. Hewett, Bart., F.R.S., W. Morrant Baker.
Physicians.—James Goodhart, M.D., F. Taylor, M.D.
Surgeons.—H.G. Howse, M.S., R. Clement Lucas, B.S.
Physicians to Out-patients.— Nestor Tirard, M.D., F.Wilcocks, M.D.
Surgeons to Out-patients. — Charters J. Symonds, M.S., G.H. Makins, F.R.C.S.
Ophthalmic Surgeon.—W. A. Brailey, M.D
Dental Surgeon.—R. D. Pedley, M.R.C.S., L.D.S.
House Surgeon.--Albert Martin, M.D.

HOME FOR INCURABLE CHILDREN (*see under* INCURABLES).

HOSPITAL FOR SICK CHILDREN, 49, Gt. Ormond-st, Bloomsbury, W.C. ; Secretary, Adrian Hope.— For the medical and surgical treatment of poor children. Out-patients seen every day, except Sun., from 8.30 to 10 a.m. Visitors admitted every day, except Sun., between the hours of 2 and 4 p.m. Admission : In-patients by a subscriber's letter ; out-patients free.
Consulting Physicians.—W. H. Dickenson, M.D., Samuel Gee, M.D.
Physicians. — W. B. Cheadle, M.D., Octavius Sturges, M.D., Thomas Barlow, M.D,

Assistant Physicians. — David B. Lees, M.D., Montagu Lubbock, M.D., John Abercrombie, M.D., Angel Money, M.D., W. B. Hadden, M.D.

Consulting Surgeon.—Thomas Smith.

Surgeons.—Howard Marsh and Edmund Owen.

Assistant Surgeons. — J. H. Morgan, Bernard Pitts, W. Arbuthnot Lane.

Ophthalmic Surgeon.—Marcus R. Gunn.

Surgeon Dentist.— Alexander Cartwright.

Local Medical Officer for Cromwell House.—A. Henderson, M.D.

House Physician.--C. Batchelor

House Surgeon.—L. M. Gabriel, M.B.

Medical Registrar. — R. C. Priestly, M.B.

Lady Superintendent. — Miss Wood.

* † NORTH EASTERN HOSPITAL FOR CHILDREN, Hackney - rd, E.; City office, 27, Clement's-la, E.C.; Secretary Alfred Nixon.—Out-patients seen daily. Medical cases, Mon., Wed., Thurs., Sat., at 1.30 p.m. Surgical cases, Mon. at 1.30 p.m., and Fri. at 9 a.m. Visitors admitted daily from 2 to 4 p.m. except Sun. Admission for out-patients is by subscriber's free ticket, or by payment of 4d. on admission, and 3d. per week afterwards. For in-patients, by subscriber's free ticket, or by payment of 2s. 6d. per week. All admissions subject to the approval of the medical officers.

Consulting Physicians. — Sir Morell Mackenzie, M.D., A. E. Sansom, M.D., W. Cayley, M.D.

Consulting Surgeons.--Jonathan Hutchinson, F. R. C. S., R. T. Godlee, F.R.C.S.

Physicians. — F. C. Turner, M.D., M.A., C. E. Armand Semple, M.B., W. Pasteur, M.D.

Surgeons. — Waren Tay, F.R.C.S., B. Pollard, F.R.C.S.

House Surgeon. — A. Smith M.R.C.S., L.R.C.P.

Lady Superintendent and Matron.— Miss E. W. Curno.

PADDINGTON GREEN CHILDREN'S HOSPITAL; Sec., W. H. Pearce.—To afford prompt medical relief to poor sick children under 12 years of age. Out-patients seen daily at 9 a.m. Visitors are admitted daily from 2 to 4.30 p.m. No letter required for admission of patients.

Consulting Physician.—Sydney Ringer, M.D., F.R.S.

Consulting Surgeons. — Sir Joseph Lister, Bart., F.R.S., F.R.C.S., Edmd. Owen, F.R.C.S.

Physicians.—T. Lauder Brunton, M.D., F.R.S., Leslie Ogilvie, M.B., G. L. Laycock, M.B., Sidney Phillips, M.D.

Physician to Skin Department. —T. C. Fox, M.B., M.R.C.P.

Surgeons.—W. Watson Cheyne, M.B., F.R.C.S., Stanley Boyd, M.B., F.R.C.S.

Surgeon to Eye Department.— Walter H. Jessop, F.R.C.S.

Dental Surgeon.—C. V. Cotterell, L.D.S.

Pathologist & Chloroformist.-- Alexander Primrose, M.B.

House Surgeon.—G. A. Sutherland, M.B., M.R.C.S.

Matron.—Miss Anderson.

* † THE VICTORIA HOSPITAL FOR CHILDREN, Queen's-rd, S.W., and Convalescent Home, Churchfields, Margate; Secretary, Capt. Blount, R.N.—1. For the treatment, as in-patients, of boys to twelve years, and of girls to sixteen. 2. The attainment and diffusion of knowledge with regard to the diseases of children. 3. The treatment, as out-patients, of children under sixteen years of age. 4. The training of nurses for children. Visitors admitted daily, in summer from 2 to 5 p.m., in winter from 2 to 4 p.m. Admission for in-patients by letter of a subscriber. Accidents or urgent cases admitted at all times.

Consulting Physician.—W. H. Walshe, M.D.

Consulting Surgeons.—J. E. Erichsen, F.R.C.S., and Geo. Cowell, F.R.C.S.

Physicians. — Julian Evans, M.B., Thomas Ridge Jones, M.D.

Surgeons.—T. Pickering Pick, F.R.C.S., H.H.Clutton, F.R.C.S.

Out-patient Department: *Physicians.*—Albert Venn, M.D., T. Colcott Fox, M.D., F. D. Drewitt, M.D., J. H. Philpot, M.D.

Surgeons. — D'Arcey Power, F.R.C.S., Walter Pye, F.R.C.S.

Ophthalmic Surgeon.—W. A. Frost, F.R.C.S.

Surgeon Dentist.—F. Fox, M.R.C.S.

House Physician.—Alex. Harper, M.B.

House Surgeon.--Cameron Kidd M.B.

Convalescent Home: *Attending*

Medical Officers.—Thos. Smith Rowe, M.D., Cecil-st, Margate, and A. W. Rowe, M.B.

CONSUMPTION.

CITY OF LONDON HOSPITAL FOR DISEASES OF THE CHEST, Victoria-park, E.; Office: 24, Finsbury-circus, E.C.; Secretary, Thomas Storrar-Smith. — For the treatment of all the several forms of the diseases of the lungs and heart. Out-patients are seen daily, except Sun., at 1 p.m. Visitors are admitted on Sun. from 2 to 3.30 p.m., and Th. between 3 and 5 p.m. Admission by letter of recommendation from a governor or subscriber.

Consulting Physicians. — Sir J. Risdon Bennett, M.D., F.R.S., James Andrew, M.D., Edmund Lloyd Birkett, M.D.

Consulting Surgeon.—John Eric Erichsen, Esq., F.R.S.

Surgeon.—J.F.C.H.Macready, F.R.C.S.

Physicians.—John C. Thorowgood, M.D., Eustace Smith, M.D., J. Milner Fothergill, M.D., Samuel West, M.D., G. A. Heron, M.D., Vincent D. Harris, M.D.

Assistant Physicians.— J. A. Ormerod, M.D., E. Clifford Beale, M.B., Bedford Fenwick, M.D., Lauriston E.Shaw, M.D., Harrington Sainsbury, M.D., T. Glover Lyon, M.D.

Resident Medical Officer.—Raymond Cousteen, M.B.

HOSPITAL FOR CONSUMPTION AND DISEASES OF THE CHEST, Brompton, which now provides 331 beds in two buildings on opposite sides of the Fulham-rd; Secretary, Henry Dobbin.—For the gratuitous treatment as in and out patients of indigent persons afflicted with consumption and every other disease of the chest (including heart disease). Out-patients are seen every week-day at 11.30. Visitors are admitted any week-day at reasonable hours. Patients may be visited by their friends on Sun. from 2 to 4, and Tu. and Fri. from 2 to 3. Admission by letter from a subscriber; but the secretary is always willing to give any information or assistance.

Consulting Physicians.—C.J.B. Williams, M.D., F.R.S., Physician Extraordinary to the Queen, W. H. Walshe, M.D., Richard Quain, M.D., F.R.S., James E. Pollock, M.D.

Consulting Surgeon. — Prof. John Marshall, F.R.S.

Physicians.—E. Symes Thompson, M.D., C. Theodore Williams, M.D., R. Douglas Powell, M.D., John Tatham, M.D., Reginald E. Thompson, M.D., Frederick T. Roberts, M.D.

Surgeon.— R. J. Godlee, F.R.C.S.

Assistant Physicians.—T. H. Green, M.D., J. Mitchell Bruce, M.D. J. Kingston Fowler, M.D., Percy Kidd, M.D., Cecil T. Biss, M.D., T. Dyke Acland, M.D.

Consulting Surgeon. — Prof. John Marshall, F.R.S.

Dental Surgeon.—C. J. Noble.

Resident Medical Officer — Henry D. Waugh, B.A., M.B.

* HOSPITAL FOR CONSUMPTION (North London), Mount Vernon, Hampstead ; Secretary, L. F. Hill, M.A.—For the relief of persons suffering from diseases of the chest. Out-patients are seen daily at 2 p.m. at 216, Tottenham-ct-rd, and on Tues. and Fri. at 1.30 p.m. at the hospital at Hampstead. Visitors admitted on Sun., Tu., and Th., from 3 to 5 p.m. Admission of patients by subscriber's letter, and by payment.

Consulting Physician.—J. Gardner Dudley, M.A., M.D. Cantab., M.R.C.P.

Physicians — A. Evershed, M.R.C.P., Bernard O'Connor, A.B., M.D., M.R.C.P., G. Douglas Pidcock, B.A., M.B., J. E. Squire, M.D., M.R.C.P., L. Forbes Winslow, M.D., M.R.C.P., D.C.L., Francis Hawkins, M.D., John Gerard, M.D., M.R.C.P.

Consulting Surgeons. — Sir Joseph Lister, Bart., B.A., M.B. F.R.C.S., Henry Smith, F.R.C.S.

INFIRMARY FOR CONSUMPTION AND DISEASES of the CHEST and THROAT, 26, Margaret-st, Cavendish-sq ; Secretary, William Henry Johnson. Out-patients seen daily from 2 to 5. Visitors admitted daily from 2 to 5. Admission by letter.

Physicians. — Dr. J. Cooper Torry, M.R.C.P., Dr. Jagielski, M.R.C.P., Dr. Beckett, M.R.C.P.

Visiting Physicians.— Dr. Marsh, Dr. Tuckey, Dr. Roberson Day.

Surgeon.— Kenneth Millican, Esq., B.A. Cantab., M.R.C.S.

THE ROYAL HOSPITAL FOR DISEASES OF THE CHEST, City-rd, E.C. For all information address The Secretary, John J. Austin.

—For the gratuitous relief of poor persons suffering from diseases of the chest in any of the various forms. Out-patients are seen on Mon. to Fri. at 2 p.m., and on Sat. at 9 a.m. Visitors are admitted on Sun. and Th. from 3 to 4 p.m. Admission by letter signed by a governor.

Consulting Physician. — Dr. Horace Dobell.

Physicians. — Drs. Hensley, Gilbart Smith, Finlay, White, Browne, Davies.

Assistant Physicians. — Drs. Haberston, Steward, Calvert.

Consulting Surgeon. — Mr. Hutchinson.

Surgeon.—A. Pearce Gould.

House Physicians.—Walter S. Strugnell, A. Hill Joseph.

Matron.—Miss M. Leslie Smith.

*THE ROYAL NATIONAL HOSPITAL FOR CONSUMPTION AND DISEASES OF THE CHEST (on the separate or cottage principle). The Institution is at Ventnor, Isle of Wight ; Offices, 34, Craven-st,W.C.; Secretary, Ernest Morgan.—For the reception of patients suffering from consumption in the early stages and other chest diseases. Out-patients are seen daily at Ventnor at 11 a.m. Visitors are admitted daily at all hours. Admission of patients by letter of recommendation from a governor. Each patient pays 10s. a week, the total cost of each being 29s. 1d. per week.

Consulting Physicians.— Dr. Quain, F.R.S., Arthur Hill Hassall, M.D., M.R.C.P., Sir J. Risdon Bennett, F.R.S., F.R.C.P.

Examining Physicians. — Hermann Weber, M.D., F.R.C.P., H. Port, M.D., M.R.C.P., J. C. Thorowgood, M.D., F.R.C.P., Arthur Davies, M.D., M.R.C.P., W. H. Allchin, M.D., F.R.C.P.

Physician.—J. G. Sinclair Coghill, M.D. Edin., F.R.C.P.

Assistant Physicians.—Robert Robertson, M.D., John Whitehead, M.D., M.R.C.S.

Surgeon.—James M. Williamson, M.D., C.M.

Resident Medical Officers.—Dr. W. B. Williams, Dr. Lewis Hawkes. (*And see* THROAT AND CHEST.)

CONVALESCENT.

METROPOLITAN CONVALESCENT INSTITUTION, Walton-on-Thames, Kingston-hill, Surrey, and Bexhill, near Hastings ; Secretary,

Charles Holmes, 32, Sackville-st.— Patients' friends are admitted every Wed. and Sat. afternoon ; subscribers and their friends any time except Sun. Admission by letter of recommendation only. During 1886, 4,725 patients were admitted into the three houses entirely free of charge, and without delay.

Medical Officers.—Dr. Southey, Dr. Samuel West, Dr. Collum, Alfred Willett, Walter Pye, Samuel Osborn, Norman Rushworth, M.R.C.S., L.R.C.P., and F. M. Wallis, M.R.C.S.

DENTAL.

DENTAL HOSPITAL OF LONDON, Leicester - square, W.C. ; Treasurer, R. C. L. Bevan ; Secretary, J. Francis Pink.— To provide the poorer classes with gratuitous advice and surgical aid in diseases and irregularities of the teeth. Patients seen daily from 9 to 11 a.m. Visitors admitted daily. Admission of patients for all ordinary operations and advice, free ; for stoppings and operations under gas, a governor's ticket is necessary.

Consulting Physician.—Sir J. Risdon Bennett, M.D., F.R.S.

Consulting Surgeon. — Christopher Heath, F.R.C.S.

Consulting Dental Surgeons.—Samuel Cartwright, F.R.C.S., Sir John Tomes, F.R.C.S.,F.R.S.

Dental Surgeons.—Storer Bennett, F. Canton, G. Gregson, D. Hepburn, Claude Rogers, R. H. Woodhouse.

Assistant Dental Surgeons.— W. Hern, L. Matheson, G. W. Parkinson, Lawrence Read, C. E. Truman, E. Lloyd Williams.

Administrators of Anæsthetics. —G. H. Bailey, T. Bird, F. W. Brame, J. Mills.

Assistant ditto.—Drs. Dudley Buxton and Frederic Hewitt.

*NATIONAL DENTAL HOSPITAL, 149, Gt. Portland-st, W. ; Secretary Arthur G. Klugh.—For affording to the poorer classes gratuitous advice and surgical aid in diseases and irregularities of the teeth. Out-patients seen from 9 to 11 a.m. daily, except Sun. Visitors admitted from 9 a.m. to 6 p.m. daily, except Sun. Admission free to the necessitous poor and urgent cases ; other persons are required to procure a subscriber's ticket.

Consulting Physicians.—B. W

Richardson, M.D., F.R.S., Wm. Henry Broadbent, M.D.

Consulting Surgeons. — Prof. Erichsen, F.R.S., Prof. Christopher Heath, F.R.C.S., T. Spencer Wells, F.R.C.S.

Consulting Dental Surgeon.— J. Merryweather, M.R.C.S.

Dental Surgeons.—G. A. Williams, L.D.S., Harry Rose, L.D.S., A. F. Canton, L.D.S., F. H. Weiss, L.D.S., T. Gaddes, L.D.S., Alfred Smith, L.D.S.

Assistant Dental Surgeons.— W. G. Weiss, L.D.S., W. R. Humby, L.D.S., G. Bradshaw, L.D.S., Marcus Davis, L.D.S., H. G. Read, L.D.S., W. Scott Thomson.

House Surgeon.—C. Pattinson.

Anaesthetists.—H. F. Winslow, M.D., M.R.C.S., C. W. Glassington, M.R.C.S., Henry Davis, M.R.C.S., James Maughan, M.R.C.S.

EAR.—(*See* THROAT and EAR.)

EYE AND EAR

ST. ANDREW'S EYE AND EAR HOSPITAL, 67, Wells-st, Oxford-st, W.; Secretary, W. Rider.— Established in 1882 as a special hospital for diseases of the eye, ear, throat, and nose, with special department for diseases of the nervous system. Open Monday and Thursday 7 to 9, Tuesday and Saturday 2 to 3. Advice free in all cases, but to those who are able to pay, a charge of one shilling each bottle of medicine is made.

Oculist and Aurist.—A. L. A. Forbes, M.D., F.R.C.S.

Dentist.—Dr. E. Pierrepoint.

For Defects of Speech.— H. W. White.

FEVER.

LONDON FEVER HOSPITAL, Liverpool-rd, Islington; Secretary, Major Christie.— For the prevention and cure of contagious fevers, other than small-pox. No out-patients. Visiting is discouraged, only very near relatives being admitted at all, and then with very strict precautions.

Physicians. — Dr. W. Cayley, Dr. Thomas Barlow.

Assistant Physicians. — Dr. Gulliver, Dr. Sidney Phillips.

Resident Medical Officer.—Dr. Hopwood.

Assistant ditto.—Dr. Goodall.

METROPOLITAN ASYLUM (SOUTH - WESTERN) DISTRICT FEVER ASYLUM, Landor-rd, Stockwell, S.W.; Steward, William

Frost. — For the reception of infectious fevers. No out-patients. Visitors admitted only to patients dangerously ill, from 2 to 4 p.m. daily. Admission by parochial order.

Medical Officer.—P.H. McKellar, M.B.

FISTULA.

ST. MARK'S HOSPITAL FOR FISTULA, AND OTHER DISEASES OF THE RECTUM, City-rd, E.C.; Secretary, Arthur Leared.—Out-patients are seen, men on Wed. at 8.45 a.m., and women on Th. at same time, punctually. Visitors may see patients on Wed. and Sun. from 2.30 to 4 p.m. Visitors to hospital always welcome. Admission of patients free, but governors' letters always have the preference.

Honorary Physician. — Francis de Haviland Hall, M.D.

Honorary Surgeons. — Wm. Allingham, F.R.C.S., Alfred Cooper, F.R.C.S.

Honorary Assistant Surgeons. —David H. Goodsall, F.R.C.S., F. Swinford Edwards, F.R.C.S.

House Surgeon.—A. E. Chilcott, M.R.C.S.

*†GORDON HOSPITAL FOR FISTULA, PILES, AND OTHER DISEASES OF THE RECTUM, 278, Vauxhall bridge-rd, S.W., near Victoria-stn.; Established 1884; Secretary, Captain A. S. Hincks. —Out-patients seen daily at 2 p.m., and on Tuesday evening at 8. Free to the necessitous poor. Special wards for paying patients.

Honorary Consulting Physician.— Francis Henry Laking, M.D., M.R.C.P.

Honorary Surgeons. — Samuel Benton, L.R.C.P. (London), M.R.C.S., W. T. Whitmore, F.R.C.S.Ed.

Honorary Administrator of Anaesthetics.— C. J. Ogle, M.R.C.S.

FRENCH.

FRENCH HOSPITAL AND DISPENSARY, 10, Leicester-pl, Leicester-sq; Hon. Secretary, Ernest Rüffer; Hon. Treasurer, H. Duval; Assist. Sec. and Collector, F. Sorel. — Established to give medical aid to all foreigners speaking the French language. — Out-patients seen every day (Sun. excepted) from 10 to 11 a.m. Visitors admitted on Sun. and Th. from 3 to 4 p.m. Admission without letters of recommendation.

Honorary Physician.—Dr. H. Gueneau de Mussy.

Consulting and Chief Surgeon. —Sir William M'Cormac.

Head Physician.—Dr. Vintras.

Physician and Accoucheur.— Dr. J. Késer.

Surgeon.—H. de Méric.

Oculist.—C. Higgens.

Dental Surgeon.—A. G. Hockley.

GENERAL.

*†BOLINGBROKE HOUSE PAY HOSPITAL, Wandsworth-com, S.W. —This institution was founded as a "home in sickness," and offers to persons, who are able to pay wholly or partially for their support, all the advantages of hospital treatment and nursing, with, as far as possible, the comforts and privacy of home, with the additional advantage that they may be attended by their own doctor if so desired. Adults of both sexes are admitted, and there is a children's ward. Approved patients are admitted on a weekly payment, including charges for medical attendance, nursing, board, and lodging, viz., three guineas for a private room, or from half-a-guinea to two guineas in the general wards. No person is admitted suffering from any infectious malady, insanity, or fits, or whose case is incurable.

Consulting Staff. — Timothy Holmes, M.A., F.R.C.S., Wm. Henry Broadbent, M.D., F.R.C.P. A. L. Galabin, M.D., F.R.C.P., Thos. Bryant, F.R.C.S.

Resident Medical Officer and Secretary.—Cecil R. C. Lyster, M.R.C.S.

Matron—Miss Edith Thompson.

CHARING CROSS HOSPITAL, Agar-st, West Strand, W.C.; Secretary, A. E. Reade.—Out-patients seen daily at 1.30 p.m. Patients may see their friends on Sun. from 3.30 to 4.30 p.m., and on Wed. and Fri. from 4 to 5 p.m. Cases of accident or emergency are at all times immediately admitted as in-patients; other cases are expected to obtain a subscriber's letter. Out-patients are admitted the first time without any subscriber's letter, but are expected to obtain a subscriber's letter if they wish to continue attending, which can be obtained on application to the Secretary.

Consulting Physicians.—Sir J. Fayrer, M.D., K.C.S.I., Sir W. G. Hunter, M.D., K.C.M.G.

Physicians. — Julius Pollock, M.D., T. H. Green, M.D., J. Mitchell Bruce, M.D.

AssistantPhysicians.—A.Abercrombie, M.D., M. Lubbock, M.D., F. Willcocks, M.D., H. Montague Murray, M.D.

Obstetric Physician.—J. Watt Black, M.D.

Assistant Obstetric Physician. —Amand Routh, M.D.

Physician for Diseases of the Skin.—A. Sangster, M.B.

Physician for Diseases of the Throat.—F. Willcocks, M.D.

Consulting Surgeon.—Richard Barwell.

Surgeons. — E. Bellamy, J. Astley Bloxam, John H. Morgan.

Assistant Surgeons. — Stanley Boyd, A. M. Sheild, B. Wainewright.

Aural Surgeon.—A. M. Sheild.

Surgeon-Dentist. — John Fairbank.

*GERMAN HOSPITAL, Dalstonlane and Ritson-rd, Dalston, E.; Sec., Christian Feldmann. — For the reception of natives of Germany, others speaking the German language, and English in cases of accidents. Out-patients admitted, women on Mon., Wed., and Fri. at 2 p.m.; men on Tu. and Th. at 2 p.m. Visitors admitted on Sun. from 2 to 3.15 p.m., and on Th. from 3 to 5 p.m. The patients are admitted without recommendation or letter. Out-patients not conversant with the German language must be provided with a letter of recommendation from a governor.

Consulting Physician. — Sir William Jenner, Bart., M.D., K.C.B.

Consulting Surgeon.—Sir James Paget, Bart., F.R.S., F.L.S.

Physicians.—Hermann Weber, M.D., F.R.C.P., Heinrich Port, M.D., F.R.C.P.

Physician for the Diseases of Women and Children.—Adolphus Rasch, M.D., M.R.C.P.

Surgeons. — George Lichtenberg, M.D., M.R.C.S., Alexander Burger, M.D., M.R.C.S.

Honorary Assistant Surgeon.—Maro Tuchmann, M.D., M.R.C.S.

Honorary Assis. Physician.—Gustav Ludwig, M.D., M.R.C.P.

Resident Medical Officers.—Otto Eugen Keller, M.D., Ernst Michels, M.D.

Dental Surgeon.—Anthony P. Reboul, D.L.R.C.S.Engl.

Assistant Dental Surgeon.—Charles West, D.L.R.C.S. Engl.

Medical Officers of the Dispensaries.—For the East of London, Charles Harrer, M.D., L.R.C.P., sees the out-patients at 49, Mansell-st, Aldgate, E., on Tu. and Fri. between 8 and 10 a.m. For the West of London, Michael Castaneda, M.B., M.R.C.P., sees the out-patients at 239, Oxford-st, W., on Mon. and Th. between 8 and 10 a.m.

GERMAN HOSPITAL CONVALESCENT HOME, 113, Dalstonlane, E.—Contains 17 beds. Visitors admitted Sun. from 2 to 3.15 p.m.

*† GREAT NORTHERN CENTRAL HOSPITAL, Caledonian-rd, N.; Secretary, William T. Grant.—For the relief of the sick and suffering poor, without letters of recommendation. Physicians and Surgeons see out-patients as follows:—Mon., Tu., Th., and Fri. at 2 p.m. Diseases of the eye, Tu. and Fri. at 9.30 a.m., and Sat. at 10 a.m.; diseases of women and children, Wed. at 2 p.m.; dental cases, Wed. at 1.30 p.m.; diseases of the ear, Wed. at 9 a.m.; House Surgeon, daily at 9 a.m. Visitors admitted on Sun., Tu., or Fri., from 2 to 3 p.m.

Consulting Surgeon. — Fred. Le Gros Clark, F.R.S.

Physicians. — Dr. Cholmeley, Dr. Cook, Dr. Burnet, Dr. Beale, Dr. Beevor.

Obsteric Physicians. — Dr. Gustavus C. P. Murray, Dr. F. Barnes.

Ophthalmic Surgeon. — Jonathan Hutchinson, Junr.

Surgeons. — W. Adams, W. Spencer Watson, J. Macready, C. B. Lockwood, H. W. Allingham.

Aural Sugeon.—A. E. Cumberbatch.

Dental Surgeon.—E. Keen.

Chloroformist and Registrar.—Dr. J. F. W. Silk.

House Surgeon.—A. F. Whitwell.

*† GUY'S HOSPITAL, St. Thomas's-st, Southwark; Superintendent, J.C.Steele, M.D.; Clerk to Governors, H. Williams.—Out-patients are seen at 12 daily. Visitors admitted on Wed. from 3 to 4 p.m., and on Sun. from 2 to 4 p.m. Admission free, no recommendations required. Ad-

mission day for medical cases, Wed. at 10 a.m. Accidents at all times.

Medical Officers.—Drs. Pavy, Pye - Smith, Taylor, Goodhart, White, Pitt, Wooldridge, Galabin, and Horrocks.

Surgeons. — Messrs. Bryant, Durham, Howse, Davies-Colley, Lucas, Golding-Bird, Jacobson, Symonds, Moon, Pedley, Laidlaw-Purves, Higgens, and Brailey.

KING'S COLLEGE HOSPITAL, Portugal-st, Lincoln's-inn ; Secretary, T. Mosse Macdonald, B.A. —Out-patients are seen : Men on Tu., Th., and Sat. ; Women on Mon., Wed., and Fri. Visitors are admitted on Sun. and Christmas Day from 2 to 4 p.m., and Wed. from 5 to 6 p.m. Admission by letter of recommendation, but urgent cases are admitted at all times.

Consulting Physicians.—Arthur Farre, M.D., F.R.S., W. O. Priestley, M.D., Alfred B. Garrod, M.D., George Johnson, M.D., F.R.S.

Physicians (with care of in-patients).—Lionel S. Beale, M.B., F.R.S., Alfred B. Duffin, M.D., J. Burney Yeo, M.D.

Assistant Physicians (with care of out-patients).—David Ferrier, M.D., John Curnow, M.D., N. J. C. Tirard, M.D.

Physician - Accoucheur and Physician for the Diseases of Women and Children (with care of in-patients).—Wm. S. Playfair, M.D.

Assist. Physician- Accoucheur, and Assistant Physician for Diseases of Women and Children (with care of out-patients).—T. C. Hayes, B.A., M.D.

Surgeons (with care of in-patients).—John Wood, F.R.S., Sir Joseph Lister, Bart., F.R.S., Henry Smith, F.R.C.S.

Ophthalmic Surgeon (with care of in-patients).—M. M. McHardy, F.R.C.S.

Aural Surgeon.—U. Pritchard, M.D.

Surgeons (with care of out-patients). — H. Royes Bell, F.R.C.S., W. Rose, F.R.C.S.

Assistant Surgeon (with care of out-patients).—W. W. Cheyne, F.R.C.S.

Surgeon Dentist.—S. Hamilton Cartwright, M.R.C.S.

LONDON HOSPITAL, Whitechapel-road, E. ; Secretary, G. Q. Roberts.—For the cure or relief of the sick and injured poor.

Out-patients are seen as follows :— General cases, daily at 1.30. Special cases at 9 a.m. as follows :—Ophthalmic cases, Tues. and Sat.; aural, Sat.; skin, Thurs. Cases of cancer and tumour, distension of bladder, &c., every afternoon from 2 to 3 p.m.; dental cases, daily at 9 a.m. The visiting hours for friends of in-patients are : in General Wards, Tu. and Fri., from 4 to 5 p.m. Sun., from 3 to 5 p.m. ; in Hebrew Wards, Tu. and Fri. from 4 to 5 p.m., and Sat. from 3 to 5 p.m. No more than two visitors can be admitted to any patient at the same time. Exceptions to the above rules are allowed in favour of the friends of patients in a dangerous state ; and of those who come from the country. Admission of patients : accidents and urgent cases without recommendation; general cases, by subscriber's or governor's letter.

Consulting Physicians. — Sir Andrew Clark, Bart, M.D., F.R.S., Jabez Spence Ramskill, M.D.

Consulting Surgeons.—T. B. Curling, F.R.S., Jonathan Hutchinson, F.R.S.

Physicians.—J. Langdon Haydon Down, M.D., J. Hughlings-Jackson, M.D., F.R.S., Henry G. Sutton, M.D., S. Fenwick, M.D., and (with charge of out-patients) Stephen Mackenzie, M.D., A.E. Sansom, M.D., F. Charlewood Turner, M.D., T. Gilbert Smith, M.D., Francis Warner, M.D., Charles Henry Ralfe, M.D.

Surgeons.—John Couper, Walter Rivington, Waren Tay, Jeremiah McCarthy, Frederick Treves.

Assistant Physician. — James Anderson, M.D.

Assistant Surgeons.—Henry A. Reeves, C. W. Mansell-Moullin, E. Hurry Fenwick, F. S. Eve.

Obstetric Physicians.—G. Ernest Herman, M.D., Arthur W. N. Lewers, M.D.

Surgeon Dentist.—A. W. Barrett.

Aural Surgeons. — Edward Woakes, M.D., T. Mark Hovell.

METROPOLITAN FREE HOSPITAL, Kingsland-rd, N.; Offices, 163, Bishopsgate-st-without, E.C.; Secretary, George Croxton.— Out-patients seen every day from 9 to 12 a.m., and 12 to 1 p.m. Visitors admitted on Wed., Sat., and Sun. from 3 to 5 p.m. Admission entirely free.

Physicians. — Dr. C. R. Drys-

dale, Dr. J. G. Dudley, Dr. H. I. Fotherby.

Obstetric Physician.—Dr. Albert Venn.

Assistant Physicians. — Dr. H. H. Tooth, Dr. Alex. Haig.

Surgeons.— E. J. Chance, F.R.C.S., D. H. Goodsall, F.R.C.S., W. J. Walsham, F.R.C.S.

Dentists. — B. E. Manville, M.R.C.S., G. D. Curnock.

MIDDLESEX HOSPITAL, Mortimer-st, W. ; Secretary-Superintendent, F. Clare Melhado.— For sick and lame in and out patients; for cases of cancer, and for supplying lying-in women with medicine and attendance at their own homes. Out-patients are attended (without letters of recommendation) as follows : *Medical:* Every day at 11 a.m. *Surgical:* Men, Mon. and Fri., 1.30 p.m.; and on Wed. and Sat. at 9 a.m.; Women, Tu. and Th., 1.30 p.m.; Wed. and Sat. at 9 a.m.; *Cancer:* Th., 1.30 p.m. *Women, and Children under Three:* Wed. and Sat., 1.30 p.m. *Diseases of the Eye:* Tu. and Fri. at 9 a.m. *Diseases of the Skin:* Fri., 4 p.m. *Diseases of Ear or Throat:* Tu., 9 a.m. *Diseases of the Teeth:* Mon., 9.30 a.m., Wed. and Fri., 9 a.m. Visitors are admitted on Sun. from 3 till 5 p.m., Tu. and Fri. from 4 till 5 p.m. by ticket. Accidents and urgent cases are admitted night and day without letters of recommendation.

Physicians.—Drs. William Cayley, Sidney Coupland, R. Douglas Powell, and David W. Finlay.

Assistant Physicians.—Drs. J. K. Fowler, C. Y. Biss, and J. J. Pringle.

Obstetric Physician. — Dr. Arthur W. Edis.

Assistant Obstetric Physician.—Dr. William Duncan.

Physician, Skin Department.—Dr. Robert Liveing.

Surgeons.—J. W. Hulke, F.R.S. George Lawson, Henry Morris, Andrew Clark.

Assistant Surgeons. — A. Pearce Gould, J. B. Sutton.

Ophthalmic Surg.—W. Lang.

Dental Surgs.—Storer Bennett and W. Hern.

Aural Surgeon.—A. Hensman.

*NORTH LONDON, OR UNIVERSITY COLLEGE HOSPITAL, Gowerst, London, W.C.; Secretary, Newton H. Nixon.—For the

relief of poor sick and maimed persons, and the delivery of poor married women at their own habitations. Admission for out-patients: Physicians and Surgeons daily at 1 o'clock; Obstetric Physicians on Tu. and Fri. at 1.30 ; Dental Surgeon on Wed. at 9 a.m. ; *Skin Department* on Wed. at 1.30, and Sat. at 9 a.m.; *Eye Department* on Mon. and Th. at 2 ; *Ear Department* on Mon. at 9, and Th. at 1.30 ; *Throat Department* on Thurs. at 1. Friends of patients are admitted by card on Tu. and Fri. from 4 to 5 p.m., and on Sun. from 3 to 4 p.m. Admission for cases of casualty and emergency at any time, otherwise by letter.

Consulting Physicians.—Walter Hayle Walshe, M.D., F.R.C.P., Sir W. Jenner, Bart., K.C.B., M.D., F.R.C.P., D.C.L., F.R.S., J. Russell Reynolds, M.D., F.R.C.P., F.R.S., Charles Hare, M.D., F.R.C.P., Graily Hewitt, M.D., F.R.C.P.

Physicians. — Sydney Ringer, M.D., F.R.C.P., F.R.S., Henry Charlton Bastian, M.D., F.R.C.P., F.R.S., F. T. Roberts, M.D., F.R.C.P., William R. Gowers, M.D., F.R.C.P., George Vivian Poore, M.D., F.R.C.P., Thos. Barlow, M.D., F.R.C.P., Angel Money, M.D., M.R.C.P.

Obstetric Physicians. — J. Williams, M.D., F.R.C.P., Herbert Spencer, M.D., M.R.C.P.

Physician for Diseases of the Skin. — H. Radcliffe Crocker, M.D., F.R.C.P.

Consulting Surgeons.—J. Eric Erichsen, F.R.C.S., F.R.S., John Marshall, F.R.C.S., F.R.S., Sir Henry Thompson, M.B., F.R.C.S. T. Wharton Jones, F.R.C.S., F.R.S. (*Ophthalmic*). G. A. Ibbetson, F.R.C.S. (*Dental*).

Surgeons.—M. Berkeley Hill, M.B., F.R.C.S., Christopher Heath, F.R.C.S., M. Beck, M.B., M.S., F.R.C.S., A. E. Barker, F.R.C.S., R. J. Godlee, M.B., M.S., F.R.C.S., Victor Horsley, M.B., F.R.C.S., Bilton Pollard, M.D., F.R.C.S.

Ophthalmic Surgeon. — J. Tweedy, F.R.C.S.

Dental Surgeon.—S. J. Hutchinson, M.R.C.S., L.D.S.

Resident Medical Officer.— Charles J. Arkle, M.D., M.R.C.P.

Surgical Registrar. — Bilton Pollard, M.D., F.R.C.S.

NORTH WEST LONDON HOSPITAL, 18, 20, and 22, Kentish Tn.-

rd, N.W.; Acting Secretary, Alfred Craske; Hon. Sec. and Lady Superintendent, Miss Learmonth. Has forty-five beds. —Out-patients are admitted : Daily (except Sun.) at 2 p.m. The hospital is open daily for inspection from 2 to 5 p.m. Admission of patients by subscriber's free ticket. Accidents at all times without ticket.

Physician. — Donald W. C. Hood, M.D., M.R.C.P.

Surgeon. — Frederic Durham, M.B., F.R.C.S.

Assistant Physicians. —E. J. Edwardes, M.D., M.R.C.P., Harry Campbell, M.D., M.R.C.P., Arthur P. Luff, M.B., M.R.C.S.

Assistant Surgeons. — M. P. Mayo Collier, F.R.C.S., Charles E. Jennings, F.R.C.S., James Black, F.R.C.S.

Ophthalmic Surgeon.—W. J. Collins, M.D., F.R.C.S.

Physician for Skin Diseases.— J. H. Stowers, M.D.

Obstetric Physician. — John Shaw, M.D., M.R.C.P.

Dental Surgeon.-W. A. Maggs, L.R.C.P., M.R.C.S., L.D.S.

Resident Medical Officers. — Cecil Christopherson, M.R.C.S., L. R. C. P., R. H. Wilbe, M. B., M.R.C.S.

ST. BARTHOLOMEW'S HOSPITAL, West Smithfield ; Treasurer, Sir S. H. Waterlow, Bart.; Clerk, W. H. Cross, B.A.—Out-patients are seen every morning except Sun. from 9 to 10 o'clock. Visitors are admitted on Sun. from 2 to 3, and on Tu. and Fri. from 3 to 4. Admission of patients free, without ticket or letter.

Consulting Physician. — Dr. Martin.

Consulting Surgeons.—Sir J. Paget, Bart., D.C.L., F.R.S., L. Holden.

Physicians. — Drs. Andrew, Church, Gee, and Sir Dyce Duckworth.

Surgeons.—W.S.Savory, F.R.S., Thomas Smith, A. Willett, J. Langton, W. Morrant Baker.

Assistant - Physicians. — Drs. Hensley, Brunton, F.R.S., Norman Moore, and S. West.

Assistant Surgeons. — F. H. Marsh, H. T. Butlin, W. J. Walsham, W. H. Cripps, W. Bruce-Clarke.

Physician - Accoucheur. — Dr. Matthews Duncan.

Assist. Physician-Accoucheur. —Dr. Godson.

Aural Surgeon.—A. E. Cumberbatch.

Ophthalmic Surgeons. — H. Power, B. J. Vernon.

Dental Surgeons.—F. Ewbank, W. B. Paterson.

Administrator of Anæsthetics. —J. Mills.

Medical Registrar.—Dr. J. A. Ormerod.

Surgical Registrar. — A. A. Bowlby.

Casualty Physicians. — Drs. Oswald Browne, H. L. Jones, A. E. Garrod.

Electrician.—Dr.W.E. Steavenson.

ST. GEORGE'S HOSPITAL, Hyde Park Corner ; Secretary, C. L. Todd.— For the relief of sick poor. Out-patients are received as follows :—Physicians' and Surgeons' out-patients—Women on Mon. and Tu. at 11 a.m. ; Men on Fri. and Sat. at 11 a.m. Patients with diseases of the throat on Thurs. at 1.30 p.m. ; patients with diseases of the ear on Tues. at 1.30 p.m. ; patients with diseases of the eye on Wed. and Sat. at 1.30 p.m. ; patients with deformities of the spine, limbs, and joints on Wed. at 1.30 p.m. ; patients with diseases of the skin on Wed. at 1.30 p.m. ; patients are seen by the Dental Surgeon on Tu. and Sat. from 9 to 10 a.m., or by his Assistant daily from 9 to 10 a.m., and from 1 to 2 p.m. ; patients desirous of being attended at their homes during their confinement must apply at the hospital on Th. at 11 a.m. ; women with diseases peculiar to their sex are received on Th. at 1.30 p.m. ; vaccination is performed at the hospital every Th. morning at 11 a.m. Visitors to patients are admitted on Tu., Fri., and Sat. from 3 to 4 p.m., and on Sun. from 4.30 to 5.30 p.m. Admission of patients depends on the nature of the case. Accidents and urgent cases received at all hours without letters.

Consulting Physicians. — Drs. Sir Henry Pitman, John Ogle, and Wadham.

Consulting Surgeons.—Sir Prescott Hewett, Bart., F.R.S., George Pollock, Henry Lee, and T. Holmes.

Physicians.—Drs. W. Howship, Dickinson, Whipham, Cavafy, and Ewart.

Assistant Physicians. — Drs. Owen and Gamgee.

Obstetric Physician. — Dr. Champneys.

Surgeons. — James Rouse,

Thomas P. Pick, J. Warrington Haward, and W. H. Bennett.

Assistant Surgeons. — Clinton T. Dent and G. R. Turner.

Ophthalmic Surgeon.—R. Brudenell Carter.

Assistant do.—W. Adams Frost.

Aural Surgeon. — Sir W. B. Dalby.

Dental Surgeon. — Augustus Winterbottom.

Visiting Apothecaries. —Wm. Fuller, T. H. Smith, Francis Laking, F. Morse Evans.

Resident Medical Officer.—F. J. Marshall.

*†ST. MARY'S HOSPITAL, Cambridge-pl, Paddington, W. ; Secretary, Thomas Ryan. — Out-patients are seen daily (Sun. excepted) at 1 p.m. Visitors are admitted on Th. and Sat. from 4 to 5 p.m., and on Sun. from 3 to 4 p.m. Accidents and urgent cases, free ; ordinary cases, by letter from a governor or subscriber.

Physicians. — Drs. Broadbent, Cheadle, Lees, Phillips, Macguire, and Peane.

Surgeons. — Messrs. Norton, Edmund Owen, Page, Pye, Pepper, and Silcock.

Physicians Accoucheur. — Drs. Braxton Hicks and W. Handfield-Jones.

Aural Surgeon.—Mr. Field.

Dental Surgeon.—Mr. Howard Hayward.

Surgeon to the Skin Department.—Mr. Malcolm Morris.

Ophthalmic Surgs. — Messrs. Critchett and Juler.

Physician in Charge of the Electrical Department.—Dr. de Watteville.

ST. THOMAS'S HOSPITAL, Albert Embankment; Steward, Frederick Walker.—Out-patients seen daily at 12 noon. Visitors admitted on Sun. and Wed. from 3 to 4.30 p.m. Admission of patients upon application at 11.30 a.m. Accidents and urgent cases at all hours.

Physicians. — Drs. Bristowe, Stone, Ord, Harley, and Payne.

Assistant ditto.—Drs. Sharkey, Gulliver, Hadden, and Acland.

Obstetric ditto.—Dr. Cullingworth.

Assistant ditto.—Dr. Cory.

Surgeons.—Messrs. Jones, Croft, MacCormac, and McKellar.

Assist. ditto.—Messrs. Clutton, Anderson, Pitts, and Makins.

Ophthalmic Surgeon. — Mr. Nettleship.

Dental Surgeon.—Mr. Truman.

UNIVERSITY COLLEGE HOSPITAL.—(*See* NORTH LONDON HOSPITAL.)

WESTMINSTER HOSPITAL, Broad Sanctuary, S.W; Secretary, Sidney M. Quennell. — For the reception and treatment of the sick and injured poor. Physicians' and Surgeons' out-patients are seen at 1.30 p.m. Patients with diseases of the skin are seen on Wed. at 1.30 p.m.; patients with diseases of the eye are seen on Mon. and Th. at 2 p.m.; patients with diseases of the ear are seen on Mon. at 9 a.m.; women requiring the advice of the Obstetric Physician are seen on Tu. and Fri. at 1.30 p.m.; Surgeon-Dentist's out-patients are seen at 9.15 a.m. on Wed. and Sat. Visitors admitted on Sun. from 2 to 4 p.m., and on Wed. and Fri. from 3 to 4. Admission of patients by letter; but accidents and urgent cases are admitted without recommendation at any hour.

Physicians. — Drs. Sturges, Allchin, and Donkin.

Assistant Physicians. — Drs. De Havilland Hall, A. Hughes Bennett, and W. Murrell.

Obstetric Physician.—Dr. Potter.

Assistant Obstetric Physician. —Dr. Grigg.

Physician for Skin Diseases.— Dr. T. Colcott Fox.

Surgeons.—G. Cowell, Richard Davy, C. N. Macnamara.

Assistant Surgeons.—T. Cooke, T. Bond, C. Stonham, W. G. Spencer.

Surgs. Dentist.—Joseph Walker and Morton Smale.

WESTMINSTER HOSPITAL MEDICAL SCHOOL, Caxton-st, S.W.

WEST LONDON HOSPITAL, Hammersmith-rd, W.; Secretary and Superintendent, R. J. Gilbert. —Out-patients admitted daily at 1.30 p.m. Friends of patients on Sun. and Wed. between 3 and 4 p.m. Visitors daily from 12 till 2 p.m. Patients admitted with and without recommendation. There are now upwards of 100 beds.

Consulting Physicians. — Drs. Henry Maudsley and John C. Thorowgood.

Consulting Physician Accoucheur.—Dr. W. O. Priestley.

Consulting Surgeons.—Samuel Armstrong Lane, William Bird, Alfred Cooper.

Physicians. — Drs. Goddard Rogers, D. W. C. Hood, and Drewitt.

Physician for Diseases of Women.—Dr. Albert Venn.

Assistant ditto—Dr. J. A. M. Moullin.

Surgeons.—C. B. Keetley, F. Swinford Edwards, W. Bruce Clarke; and *for Diseases of the Eye,* B. J. Vernon.

Assistant - Physicians. — Drs. W. P. Herringham, James B. Ball, and Seymour Taylor.

Assistant Surgeons. — C. A. Ballance, H. F. Weiss, B. Wainewright, and *for Diseases of the Eye,* H. P. Dunn.

Surgeon Dentist.—H. L. Albert.

Pathologist.—H. P. Dunn.

Administrators of Anaesthetics. —T. Gunton Alderton, R. W. Lloyd.

Department for Diseases of the Throat and Nose.—Dr. James B. Ball.

HOME.

*HOME HOSPITALS ASSOCIATION (for Paying Patients); Fitzroy House, Fitzroy - square, W.; Honorary Secretary, T. Almond Hind. Provided with every comfort for the reception of medical and surgical cases of both sexes. Patients are attended to by their own medical advisers. Application for admission to be addressed to the Lady Superintendent. No out-patients. The admission of visitors is regulated by the medical attendant of each case.

Medical Board of Reference.— C. A. Aikin, F.R.C.S., Sir J. Risdon Bennett, LL.D., M.D., F.R.S., W. Morrant Baker, F.R.C.S., R. Quain, M.D., F.R.S., J. S. Bristowe, M.D., F.R.S., S. W. Sibley, F.R.C.S., J. Wood, F.R.S.

HOMŒOPATHIC

*†THE LONDON HOMŒOPATHIC HOSPITAL AND MEDICAL SCHOOL, Gt. Ormond-st, Bloomsbury; Secretary, G. A. Cross.—In-patients received every Tues. at 9. Accidents and cases requiring immediate relief received daily. Admission of patients by subscriber's recommendation. In-patients, except the destitute, must be provided with a change of linen, a towel, soap, brush and comb, and some tea, butter, and sugar. In lieu of bringing knives and forks, as formerly, each patient is required, unless destitute, to pay 1s. to cover losses and breakage. The doors for the admission of out-patients are opened at 2.30 p.m., closed precisely at 3.30 p.m., and out-patients will not be admitted after the doors are closed :—Medical Officers are

in attendance in the out-patient department of this hospital daily (Sundays excepted) at 3 p.m., for the treatment of general diseases of men, women, and children, and for the diseases of women on Tues. New out-patients, unless recommended by a subscriber, must obtain from the Lady Dispenser a registration card, for which a payment of 1s. is required. The card is available for one month; and at the end of the time the card may be renewed when a further payment of 1s. will be required. Visitors are admitted on Sun. and Wed. from 2 to 4.

Consulting Physician. — Dr. Hamilton.

Consulting Surgeon. — Dr. Yeldham.

Physicians in charge of In-Patients.—Dr. Carfrae (Diseases of Women), Tues. and Fri. at 3 p.m.: Dr. J. G. Blackley, Mon. and Thurs. at 2.30 p.m.; Dr. Clarke, Wed. and Sat. at 5 p.m.; Mr. Knox Shaw (Diseases of the Eye), Tues. and Fri. at 5 p.m., Dr. Moir, Tues. and Fri. at 5 p.m.

Out - Patients are seen as follows: Diseases of Women—Dr. Carfrae, Tues. at 3 p.m.; Dr. J. G. Blackley, Mon. and Thurs at 3 p.m.; Dr. J. H. Clarke, Wed. and Sat. at 3 p.m.; Dr. W. Epps, Fri. at 3 p.m.; Dr. Moir, Tues. and Fri. at 3 p.m.; Dr. Marsh, Tues. and Thurs. at 3 p.m.; Dr. J. Robertson Day, Mon. and Wed. at 3 p.m. Diseases of the Eye— Mr. Knox Shaw, Fri. at 2.30 p.m. Diseases of the Skin—Dr. Galley Blackley, Thurs. at 3 p.m. Diseases of the Ear—Dr. Cooper, Sat. at 3 p.m.; Dr. Neatby, Wed. and Sat. at 3 p.m.

Dentist.—Mr. Cronin, Mon. at 9 a.m.

Nursing Institute.—A staff of forty-two Nurses has been trained in the wards of the hospital to nurse medical and surgical cases, and several have been specially trained for accouchement cases. These nurses can at all times be obtained for nursing invalids at their residences, at a scale of fees varying from one to three guineas weekly, by application to the Lady Superintendent of Nursing.

INCURABLES.

*BRITISH HOME FOR INCURABLES, 380, Clapham-road, S.W.; Offices, 73, Cheapside, E.C.; Secretary, R. G. Salmond.—To provide for those among the middle classes afflicted with incurable disease, and 35 years old and upwards, either a home, or a pension of £20 per annum for life. The insane, idiotic, blind, imbecile, and those suffering from temporary disease only are not ligible either for pension or admission to the home. The epileptic and those suffering from cancer are eligible for the pension only. Admission by election of subscribers, and under certain conditions by payment. Home open to visitors daily from 2 to 6.

Medical Officer.—Dr. G. Philip Rugg, M.D., attends daily.

HOME FOR INCURABLE CHILDREN, 2, Maida Vale, W.; Acting Secretary, Miss A. Coleman.—For the care, maintenance, and medical treatment of children, from infancy to 16, suffering from chronic or incurable complaints of an aggravated character. A small weekly payment is required. Visitors are admitted on week days from 3 to 5 p.m. Candidates must be recommended by a governor, and patients are admitted according to priority of application, subject to discretion of committee.

Hon. Medical Officer.—F. E. Webb.

THE ROYAL HOSPITAL FOR INCURABLES, West Hill, Putney Heath, S.W., and Seaside House, 5, Marina, St. Leonard's-on-Sea ; Secretary, Frederic Andrew, 106, Queen Victoria-st, E.C.—For the permanent relief by admission to the hospital, or by pension of £20 a year, of persons above the pauper class suffering from incurable maladies, and hereby disqualified for the duties of life. Subscribers and friends admitted every week day from 2 a.m. to 6 p.m. Inmates' relatives on Tu., Th., and Sat. from to 6 p.m. Admission of patients by election.

Hon. Consulting Physicians.—W. Munk, M.D., and W. J. Little, M.D.

Hon. Surgeon.—Bernard E. Brodhurst, F.R.C.S.

Medical Officer to the Establishment.—T. J. Woodhouse, M.D.

Hon. Medical Officer at St. Leonard's.—E. Duke, M.R.C.S.

Surgeon-Dentist.—Francis Fox, M.R.C.S.

LOCK.

LONDON LOCK HOSPITAL AND ASYLUM ; Female Hospital and Asylum, Westbourne-gn, Harrow-

rd, W. ; Male Hospital and Out-patient Department, 91, Dean-st, Soho, W. ; Secretary, D. Harvie ; The asylum affords a home to patients on leaving the Hospital, where they receive an industrial training, and are sent out to respectable service. Out - patients seen : Men on Mon., Tu., and Wed.; women on Fri. and Sat. Both at 12 o'clock, at Dean-st, Soho. In-patients are admitted by the Board on Th., also at 12 o'clock, and at Dean-st, Soho. Urgent cases can be taken in at once by the medical officers. Visitors admitted to female department on Tues., from 2 to 4 p.m.; to male department, on Wed., from 3 to 5 p.m.

Consulting Physician.—T. King Chambers, M.D., F.R.C.P.

Physician. — Edward Henry Sieveking, M.D., F.R.C.P.

Consulting Surgeons.—Samuel Lane, F.R.C.S., James Robert Lane, F.R.C.S.

Surgeons.—Walter J. Coulson, F.R.C.S., Berkeley Hill, F.R.C.S., Buxton Shillitoe, F.R.C.S.

Surgeons to the Out-patients.—Alfred Cooper, F.R.C.S., Edward Milner, M.R.C.S., J. Astley Bloxam, F.R.C.S.

Resident Medical Officer at the Female Hospital.—Sidney Worthington, M.D., F.R.C.S.

Assistant ditto.—E. H. Hicks, M.R.C.S., L.S.A.

Resident Medical Officer at the Male Hospital and Out-patient Department.—G. R. J. Fletcher, M.R.C.S., L.S.A.

Honorary Chloroformist. — G. Bird, M.R.C.S.

NOSE.—*See* EYE AND EAR, THROAT, and THROAT AND EAR.

OPHTHALMIC.

CENTRAL LONDON OPHTHALMIC HOSPITAL, Gray's-inn-rd, W.C.; Secretary, G. H. Leah. —Out-patients seen every day at 1 o'clock, Sun. excepted. Visitors are admitted on Tu., Th., and Sun. between 3 and 5 p.m. No recommendation whatever is required to obtain admission for patients.

Surgeons.—T. Britten Archer, M.R.C.S., W. H. Jessop, M.B., F.R.C.S., Ernest Clarke, M.D., M.R.C.S.

Assistant Surgeons.—John R. Kemp, M. R.C.S., A. P. L. Wells, M. B., M.R.C.S., J. T. James, M.B., F.R.C.S.

ROYAL LONDON OPHTHALMIC

HOSPITAL, Blomfield - st, Moorfields, E.C. ; unendowed. Secretary, R. J. Newstead ; Lady Superintendent, Mrs. Peel.—For the reception of the poor suffering from eye disease. Out-patients seen every morning from 8 to 10. In-patients recommended by yearly subscribers of £1 1s., and contributors of £10 10s. Visitors to in-patients are admitted on Mon. and Th. from 3 to 4. Admission of patients free.

Surgeons.—J. W. Hulke, F.R.S., George Lawson, John Couper, Waren Tay, John Tweedy, E. Nettleship.

Assist.-Surgeons.—R. Marcus Gunn, W. Lang, A. Quarry Silcock.

ROYAL SOUTH LONDON OPHTHALMIC HOSPITAL, 6 and 7, St. George's-circus, Southwark, S.E. ; Secretary, Charles Comyn.—For the relief of the poor suffering from diseases of the eye. Out-patients seen each day at 2 p.m. Visitors are admitted on Sun. from 2 to 4, and on Wed. from 11 to 1. Admission free to necessitous poor.

Medical Officers.—W. S. Watson, M. M. McHardy.

ROYAL WESTMINSTER OPHTHALMIC HOSPITAL, 19, King William-st, Strand. Secretary, T. Beattie Campbell.—For the relief of indigent persons afflicted with diseases of the eye. Out-patients seen every day (Sun. excepted) from 12 noon to 1.30 p.m. Visitors admitted every Tu., Th., and Sun. from 2 to 4 p.m. Admission free to the poor without letter of recommendation, and on their own application.

Medical Officers. — Henry Power, M.B., F.R.C.S., James Rouse, F.R.C.S., George Cowell, F.R.C.S., Charles Macnamara, F.R.C.S.

Assistant Surgeons. — William Adams Frost, F.R.C.S., Gustavus Hartridge, F.R.C.S., Benjamin Wainwright, M.R.C.S.

House Surgeon.—A. S. Percival, M.R.C.S.

*WESTERN OPHTHALMIC HOSPITAL, 153 and 155, Marylebone-rd.; Secretary, E. G. Martin.—Has no endowment. — Requires a small payment, unless it be shown that the applicant is unable to pay. Out-patients seen daily at 1.30 p.m. Visitors are admitted on each week day between 1.30 and 3.30 p.m. Admission of patients by subscriber's letter, or small payment at each attendance.

Consulting Physicians. — J. Russell Reynolds, M.D., F.R.S., F.R.C.P., Sir Andrew Clark, M.D., F.R.C.P.

Consulting Surgeon. — Henry Power, M.B., F.R.C.S.

Surgeons.—R. S. Miller, B.M., B.S. (Lond.), F.R.C.S., W. J. Collins, M.D., B.S., B.Sc. (Lond.), F.R.C.S., T. W. C. Jones, F.R.C.S. (Edin.).

Surgeon Dentist.—W. F. Forsyth.

ORTHOPÆDIC.

CITY ORTHOPÆDIC HOSPITAL, 27, Hatton-gdn, E.C. ; Secretary, Ernest Dereuth.—For the cure of all bodily deformities. New Out-patients seen on Tu. and Fri. at 2 p.m. Visitors are admitted on Wed. and Sun. from 3 to 4 p.m. No letter of recommendation required for admission of patients.

President.—H.R.H. the Duke of Cambridge.

Senior Medical Officer.—E. J. Chance, F.R.C.S.

House Surgeon.—J. Addison.

ROYAL ORTHOPÆDIC HOSPITAL, 297, Oxford-st, W. ; Secretary Benjamin Maskell.—For the treatment of club-foot, spinal, and all other deformities. Out-patients seen daily at 1 p.m. Visitors are admitted on Sun. and Wed. between 2 and 4 p.m. Admission of patients by governor's recommendation ticket.

Medical Officers.—B. E. Brodhurst, H. A. Reeves, Charles Read, W. E. Balkwill, H. F. Baker.

THE NATIONAL ORTHOPÆDIC HOSPITAL (FOR THE DEFORMED), 234, Great Portland-st, Regent's-pk, W. ; for the relief and cure of distortions of the spine ; club-foot ; and all contractions and malformations of the human frame ; Secretary, Herbert Canning. Out-patients seen on every week-day at 2 p.m., except Sat., when there is no attendance. This hospital requires no governor's letter or recommendation with its patients, and any deformed persons (children or adults) of the poor are received free as out-patients. Visitors admitted upon application to the secretary or matron at the hospital.

Consulting Physician.—W. J. Little, M.D., F.R.C.P.

Physician.—Charles E. Beevor, M.D., M.R.C.P.

Surgeons.—Fredk. R. Fisher, F.R.C.S., Waldemar J. Roeckel, F.R.C.S., E. Muirhead Little, F.R.C.S.

Surgeon Dentist. — Hasler Harris, M.R.C.S.

Consulting Surgeon.—William Adams, F.R.C.S.

Surgical Registrar. -- Henry Hoole, M.D., M.R.C.S.

Donations urgently required to enlarge the Hospital. See report.

PARALYSIS.

*† HOSPITAL FOR EPILEPSY AND PARALYSIS, AND OTHER DISEASES OF THE NERVOUS SYSTEM, 32, Portland-ter, Regent's-pk, N.W., near St. John's Wood Station ; Secretary, H. Howgrave Graham. —For the treatment of nervous diseases generally ; and especially epilepsy and paralysis. Out-patients are seen every week day except Sat. at 2 p.m. Visitors are admitted on Sun. and Wed. from 3 to 4 p.m. Special accommodation for private paying patients. Admission or treatment by letter or payment ; but the out-patient department is free to the necessitous poor.

Consulting Physician.—Robert Barnes, M.D., F.R.C.P

Consulting Surgeon. — John Eric Erichsen, F.R.S., F.R.C.S.

Consulting Ophthalmic Surgeon. —G. Lawson, F.R.C.S.

Physicians.—J. Althaus, M.D., M.R.C.P., A. H. Bennett, M.D., F.R.C.P., G. Ogilvie, M.B., B.Sc., G. L. Laycock, M.B.

Surgeons.—J. Astley Bloxam, F.R.C.S., A. Pearce Gould, F.R.C.S.

Ophthalmic Surgeon.—W. Laidlaw-Purves, M.D., M.R.C.S.

NATIONAL HOSPITAL FOR DISEASES OF THE HEART AND PARALYSIS, 32, Soho-sq; Treasurer, the Earl of Glasgow ; Sec., Captain F. Handley.—For paralysis and other nervous diseases arising from affections of the heart. Out-patients are seen daily, except Sat. and Sun., at 2 p.m., and on Mon. and Wed. at 7 p.m. Visitors are admitted on Sun., Mon., and Fri. from 2 to 5 p.m. Admission of in-patients on recommendation of life governors or subscribers.

Medical Officers.—Drs. B. Arcedeckne Duncan, R. Verley, J. Murray, Stretch-Dowse.

Surgeon.—F. Graham-Bennett.

* NATIONAL HOSPITAL for THE PARALYSED AND EPILEPTIC (ALBANY MEMORIAL), Queen-sq, W.C.; Country Branch, East End, Finchley. 180 beds. Secretary and

Gen. Director, B. Burford Rawlings.—To afford medical relief to in and out patients afflicted with paralysis, epilepsy, and kindred nervous diseases, and to grant pensions to incurable sufferers. Out-patients are seen on Mon., Tu., Wed., and Fri. at 1.30 p.m. Friends of patients in the wards are admitted on Th. and Sun. from 2 to 4 p.m. Open to inspection daily from 2 to 5 p.m. Admission of patients by subscriber's recommendation ; patients unprovided with recommendations may apply to the Secretary. There are special wards for persons of the middle class in straitened circumstances who pay 21s. weekly.

Physicians.—J. S. Ramskill, M.D., M.R.C.P., C. B. Radcliffe, M.D., F.R.C.P., J. H. Jackson, M.D., F.R.C.P., F.R.S., T. Buzzard, M.D., F.R.C.P., H. Charlton Bastian, M.D., F.R.C.P., F.R.S.

Physicians for Out-patients.— W. R. Gowers, M.D., F.R.C.P., D. Ferrier, M.D., F.R.C.P., F.R.S. J. A. Ormerod, M.D., F.R.C.P., C. E. Beevor, M.D., M.R.C.P.

Assistant Physicians.— James Anderson, M.D., F.R.C.P., H. Toward Tooth, M.D.

Surgeons.--W. Adams, F.R.C.S., Victor Horsley, F.R.C.S.

Ophthalmic Surgeons.—R. Brudenell Carter, F.R.C.S., Marcus Gunn, F.R.C.S.

Aural Surgeon.—A. E. Cumberbatch, F.R.C.S.

Laryngologist.--Felix Semon, M.D.

House Physicians. — Walter Hull, M.D., R. T. Williamson, M.D., Thomas Wilson, M.D., F. O. Stedman, M.R.C.S.

*† WEST-END HOSPITAL FOR DISEASES OF THE NERVOUS SYSTEM, PARALYSIS, AND EPILEPSY, 73, Welbeck-st; Sec., H. A. Dowell.—For the treatment of the above diseases generally for out-patients, and especially for children as in-patients. Out-patients are seen on Mon., Tues., Wed., and Thurs. at 1.30 p.m., on Wed. at 7 p.m. and on Fri. at 6 p.m. Patients under electrical treatment are galvanised, *men* on Mon., Wed., and Fri., and *women* on Tues., Thurs., and Sat., at 11 o'clock. Visitors are admitted daily, Sat. and Sun. excepted, from 3 to 5 p.m. Admission of patients by letter, which may be obtained on application to the sec. or a sub-

criber. Those in a position to do so are expected to contribute a small weekly sum to their expenses.

Medical Officers.—Dr. Tibbits, Dr. Stretch-Dowse, Dr. S. H Armitage, Dr. Forbes Winslow, Dr. G. Herschell.

PAROCHIAL SICK ASYLUMS (*and see* FEVER *and* SMALL-POX).

CLEVELAND-STREET ASYLUM OF THE CENTRAL LONDON SICK ASYLUM DISTRICT, Cleveland-, Fitzroy-sq, W.; Clerk to the Board, W. Appleton. — For the sick poor of the parishes of St. Giles, and Bloomsbury, and the Strand and Westminster Unions. No out-patients. Visitors admitted on Sun. from 1 to 3 p.m., and Wed. from 2 to 4 p.m. Admission of patients by order of clerk to the guardians of one or other of the parishes above mentioned.

Medical Officer.—John Hopkins, L.R.C.S., L.S.A.

Assistant ditto.—Kenneth A. Matheson, M.B., Ernest E. King, L.R.C.S., L.S.A.

POPLAR AND STEPNEY DISTRICT SICK ASYLUM, Devons-rd, Bromley, Middlesex; Clerk to the Board, Robert Foskett.—For the treatment of the sick poor of the Poplar and Stepney Unions (established under the provisions of the Metropolitan Poor Act, 1867). Visitors admitted to men on Th. from 2 to 4, and to women on Sun. from 3 to 5. Admission of patients by order of guardians.

Medical Superintendent.—R. H. Goldie.

Assistant Medical Officer.—William H. Pearce.

SOUTH EASTERN FEVER HOSPITAL (late DEPTFORD HOSPITAL.) UNDER METROPOLITAN ASYLUM DISTRICT, New ✠-rd, S.E.—For fever patients. Visitors allowed only in cases of dangerous illness. Admission of patients by order of the relieving officer and the district medical officer.

Medical Superintendent.—John McCombie, M.D.

Assistant Medical Officers.— N. Hume, A. B. Brockway.

Steward.—T. C. Monk.

Matron.—Miss Wilcox.

SAILORS.

SEAMEN'S HOSPITAL SOCIETY (late "DREADNOUGHT"), Greenwich; Secretary, P. Michelli. Two hundred and fifty-eight beds. Entirely free to sick seamen from all parts of the world and of every nation, irrespec-

tive of race, colour, or creed. Patients admitted every day ex. Sun. from 9 to 3 p.m., but accidents and urgent cases admitted at all hours. Dispensaries, Well-st, London Docks, and at Gravesend, open each week day from 2 to 2.45 p.m. Patients who attend these dispensaries and need hospital treatment are forwarded to Greenwich. Visitors to patients on Tu., Fri., and Sun. from 2 to 4 p.m. The public are invited to inspect this hospital

Physicians. — Dr. Robert Barnes, F.R.C.P., Dr. Richard Quain, F.R.C.P., Dr. J. Curnow, F.R.C.P., Dr. Herbert J. Griffiths, M.R.C.P.

Surgeons. — J. N. C. Davies-Colley, F.R.C.S., G. R. Turner, F.R.C.S.

Resident Medical Officer. — Wm. Johnson Smith, F.R.C.S.

SKIN DISEASES.

BRITISH HOSPITAL FOR DISEASES OF THE SKIN ; West Branch, 61, Great Marlborough-st, Regent-st, W.; South Branch, 5, Newington-butts, S.E.; Hon. Secretary, E. Morton Daniel.—Days and hours of admission for out-patients: at the West London Branch, on Mon. and Fri. at 2 p.m., and on Wed. at 7 p.m.; and at the South London Branch on Mon. and Fri. at 7 p.m., and on Wed. at 2 p.m. Visitors admitted on Mon. at 2 p.m. Admission to the necessitous on personal application. Those who can afford it are invited to contribute a small weekly sum according to their means.

Medical Officers. — Balmanno Squire, M.B., G. Gaskoin.

*✠HOSPITAL FOR DISEASES OF THE SKIN, 52, Stamford-st, Blackfriars, S.E.; Secretary, Samuel Hayman. — Out - patients seen daily, except Sat. ; at 3 p.m. on Mon. and Wed., and at 2 p.m. other days. New patients to attend one hour earlier Admission free, and on payment.

Medical Officers.—Messrs. Jonathan Hutchinson, Waren Tay, Wyndham Cottle, and J. F. Payne.

†INSTITUTION FOR DISEASES OF THE SKIN, 227, Gray's-inn-rd, King's ✠, W.C. ; Hon. Secretary, J. G. Fisher.—Formerly free, now self-supporting. For the cure of chronic skin disease. Middle-class (out) patients seen by payment on Mon. and Thurs. evenings at 6.

Physician.—Dr. Barr Meadows.

†ST. JOHN'S HOSPITAL FOR DISEASES OF THE SKIN, 49, Leicester-sq, W.C.; Secretary, St. Vincent Mercier. Has 15 beds.— Out-patients seen every week day at 2 p.m., and on week day evenings, except Saturday, at 7. Visitors on Sun. and Wed. from 3 till 5. Friday afternoon is specially for maximum paying patients. In-patients free by letter ; paying patients also received. Out-patients are seen free the first time without a subscriber's letter, but afterwards must obtain one, or pay 3s. to 10s. a month.

Medical Officers.—J. L. Milton, M.R.C.S., H. B. Dow, M.D., T. J. Hitchens, L.R.C.P., Alex. Bowie, M.D., L.R.C.P., M.R.C.S., Morgan Dockrell, M.D.

WESTERN DISPENSARY FOR SKIN DISEASES, 179, Great Portland-st, W. Estab. 1851. Secretary, A. W. Adeney. — Out-patients seen on Tu., Fri.. and Sat. at 2, and on Thurs. evenings at 7.

Physicians.—Drs. F. A. Cox, H. W. Williams.

SMALL-POX.

METROPOLITAN ASYLUM DISTRICT SMALL-POX ASYLUM, Landor-rd, Stockwell ; Steward, Wm. Frost. —*See* METROPOLITAN ASYLUM (SOUTH WESTERN) DISTRICT FEVER ASYLUM.

SMALL-POX AND VACCINATION HOSPITAL, Highgate-hill, Upper Holloway, N.; Secretary, R. H. Wilkins.—Visitors Tu. and Fri. between 12 and 1 if necessary. Admission of patients by payment of £5 5s., or by subscriber's letter.

Resident Surgeon. — Herbert Goude, M.D., F.R.C.S.Edin.

STONE.

*†ST. PETER'S HOSPITAL FOR STONE AND URINARY DISEASES, Henrietta - st, Covent - garden ; Secretary, Walter E. Scott.—The days and hours of admission for out-patients are Mon., Tu., Wed., Th., and Fri. (women only), at 2, Mon., Fri., and Sat. at 5. Visitors admitted on Th., 4 to 5 p.m. and Sundays, 2 to 4 p.m. No letter of recommendation required.

Surgeons. — Walter J. Coulson, F.R.C.S., F. R. Heycock, F.R.C.S.

Surgeons, Out-Patient Department.—F. S. Edwards, F.R.C.S., E. Hurry Fenwick, F.R.C.S.

Resident Medical Officer. — T. H. Norvill, M.B.

TEMPERANCE.

LONDON TEMPERANCE HOSPITAL, Hampstead-rd; Secretary, Tom Mundy. — For treatment without alcohol. Out - patients seen on Mon., Tu., Wed., Th., and Fri. at 1.30 to 2 p.m. Visitors admitted every Sun. and Wed. Admission of patients by subscriber's letter, or payment.

Visiting Physicians. — James Edmunds, M.D., M.R.C.P., R. J. Lee, M.D., F.R.C.P., and James Ridge, M.D.

Visiting Surgeon.—A.P.Gould, F.R.C.S.

House Surgeon.—John Murray, M.B., M.R.C.S.

THROAT.

*†THE HOSPITAL FOR DISEASES OF THE THROAT, 32, Golden-sq; Secretary, W. Thornton Sharp, B.A.—Diseases of the nose, ear, and neck are also treated in this hospital. Out-patients seen every day at 1.30 p.m., and on Tu. and Fri. at 6.30 p.m. Visitors admitted on Wed. and Sun. from 2 to 4 p.m. Admission free to the necessitous, others pay small weekly sums according to means.

Consulting Physician. — Sir Morell Mackenzie, M.D.

Physicians. — Norris Wolfenden, M.D., J. W. Bond, M.D., Greville MacDonald, M.D.

Surgeon.—T. Mark Hovell.

Dental Surgeon. — Leonard Matteson.

Resident Medical Officer.— Procter Hutchinson.

THROAT AND EAR.

*†CENTRAL LONDON THROAT AND EAR HOSPITAL, treating also Diseases of the Nose, Gray's-inn-rd; Secretary, Richard Kershaw. —Out-patients seen on Mon., Wed., Th., and Sat. at 2 p.m. Tu. and Fri. at 5 p.m. Visitors admitted any day, at reasonable hours. No letter necessary; small contributions required from wage-receiving applicants.

Surgeons. — Lennox Browne, F.R.C.S., A. Orwin, M.D., J. Dundas Grant, M.D.

Assistant Surgeons. — Percy Jakins, M.R.C.S., T. W. Carmalt Jones, M.A., F.R.C.S. Edin.

†METROPOLITAN EAR AND THROAT INFIRMARY,25, Howland-st, Tottenham-ct-rd; Hon. Secretary, Colonel A. Samson. — For special treatment of the diseases of the ear and throat. Out-patients admitted daily at 2.30 p.m.,and on Wed. evenings at 7 p.m.; visitors the same. Admission by letter from subscriber, or payment. Free to necessitous poor.

Consulting Surgeons.— Geo. Saunders, C.B., M.D., J. H. Drew, M.R.C.S.

Medical Officers.—J. Pickett, M.D., Dawson Nesbitt, M.D.

† MUNICIPAL THROAT AND EAR INFIRMARY, 266, City-rd, E.C.; Secretary, J. Stock Hanson, —Out-patients and visitors admitted on Mon., Wed., and Fri. from 10 to 12, and on Tu. and Th. from 6 to 8 p.m. No letters required for admission of patients. Partly self-supporting. Entirely free to the necessitous.

Medical Officers.—Drs. Gordon Holmes and J. A. Hatch.

† ROYAL EAR HOSPITAL, Frith-st, Soho-sq; Secretary, M. C. Puddy.—Out-patients seen on Tu. and Fri. from 9 a.m. to 12 noon, and on Mon. and Sat. from 3 p.m. to 5 p.m. In-patients every day. Admission by subscriber's ticket or Charity Organisation Society's ticket, or to the very poor free. Others admitted on provident principles.

Medical Officers.—Urban Pritchard, M.D., F.R.C.S., Farquhar Matheson, M.B., C.M.

WOMEN.

BRITISH LYING-IN HOSPITAL, Endell-st, St. Giles's; Secretary, Fitz-Roy Gardner. — To provide proper nursing, medical attendance, and nourishment for poor married women at the time of childbirth. Out-patients visited at their own homes. Visitors admitted daily from 9 a.m. to 6 p.m. (except on Sundays). Admission of patients by letter of recommendation from governor

Medical Officers.—W. O. Priestley, M.D., Sir T. Spencer Wells, Bart., F.R.C.S., Fancourt Barnes, M.D., John Phillips, M.B., Montagu Handfield-Jones, M.D.

* † CHELSEA HOSPITAL FOR WOMEN, Queen's Elm, Fulham-rd, S.W.; Acting Secretaries, A. C. Davis, John H. Easterbrook.— For the treatment of curable medical and surgical diseases peculiar to women. Out-patients seen on Mon., Tu., Wed., and Fri. at 2. New cases at 1.30. Visitors admitted on Wed. and Sun. from 3 to 4.30. Free admission of patients by subscriber's letter. The paying

department has been a feature of this institution since its foundation.

Consulting Physicians. — Sir Andrew Clark, Bart., M.A., M.D., Robert Barnes, M.D., F.R.C.P., J. H. Aveling, M.D.

Consulting Surgeons.—Sir T. Spencer Wells, Bart., F.R.C.S., Jonathan Hutchinson, F.R.S., F.R.C.S.

Physicians.—Arthur Wellesley Edis, M.D. (Lond.), F.R.C.P., Fancourt Barnes,M.D.,M.R.C.P. Wm. Travers, M.D., L.R.C.P.

Assistant Physicians. — Thos. Vincent Dickinson, M.D., John Mackern, M.D., Gerald Harper, M.D., W. H. Fenton, M.D., H. T. Rutherford, M.D., J. I. Parsons, M.D., F. J. Waldo, M.D.

Anæsthetists.—James Harper, M.D., F. Schacht, M.D.

Surgeon Dentist.—John Hamilton Craigie, F.R.C.S. (Ed.)

Resident Medical Officer.— E. G. Peck, M.A., M.R.C.S.

CITY OF LONDON LYING-IN HOSPITAL, 102, City-rd, E.C. Instituted 1750. Secretary, Robert Arthur Owthwaite.—To afford medical and surgical treatment to poor married women both as in and out patients, and for the training of midwives and monthly nurses. In-patients attend at 10 o'clock, out-patients at 12 o'clock, on Wed. Admission of patients by governor's letter.

Consulting Physician.--Clement Godson, M.D.

Consulting Surgeon. — John Langton, F.R.C.S.

Surgeon - Accoucheur.—George Yarrow, M.D.

GENERAL LYING-IN HOSPITAL, York-rd, Lambeth, S.E.; Secretary, Annie Whyte.—For the reception of respectable married women, whose circumstances compel them to ask the aid of this form of charity. Subscribers' letters changed every Wed. from 11 to 12. Visitors admitted between the hours of 3 and 4 p.m. on Thurs. and Sun. at house-physician's discretion. Admission of patients by governor's or subscriber's letter.

Consulting Physicians.—W. S. Playfair, M.D., F.R.C.P., John Williams, M.D., F.R.C.P., F. H. Champneys, M.D., F.R.C.P.

Consulting Surgeon.-Sir Joseph Lister, Bart., F.R.S.

Visiting Physicians. — G. Ernest Herman, M.D., F.R.C.P., Robert Boyall, M.D., F.R.C.P.

*†Hospital for Women (The), Soho-sq, W.; Secretary, David Cannon.—For diseases peculiar to women. Out-patients seen daily at 10 a.m. Visitors admitted on Sun. from 2 to 4 p.m., and on Wed. from 3 to 5 p.m. Admission for in-patients, by letter of recommenda-tion for free wards. There are wards for paying patients.

Consulting Physician. — Pro-theroe Smith, M.D.

Physicians.—Charles H.Carter, M.D., R. T. Smith, M.D., Ed-mund Holland, M.D., J. A. Man-sell-Moullin, M.B.

Surgeon.—Henry A. Reeves, F.R.C.S. Edin.

Assistant Physicians.— Bedford Fenwick, M.D., James Oliver, M.B.

Assistant Surgeon. — Samuel Osborn, F.R.C.S.

Surgeon - Dentist. — Frederic Canton, M.R.C.S.

Administrators of Anæsthetics. —Dudley W. Buxton, M.D., and Charles J. Ogle, M.R.C.S.

Pathologist and Registrar.— Norman Dalton, M.D.

Hospital of St. John and St. Elizabeth, 50, Gt. Ormond-st, W.C.—For the reception of female patients suffering from incurable or long-standing disease. Doctors meet on Th. at 4 o'clock for the examination of patients; they are admitted as vacancies occur.

Medical Officers.—Sir William W. Gull, Bart., F.R.S., D.C.L., Sir Prescott Hewett, F.R.S., James Rouse, F.R.C.S., Dr. Con-stable, E. Tegart.

*†New Hospital for Women, 222, Marylebone-rd, N.W.; Secre-tary, Miss Bagster—Out-patients are admitted by subscriber's letter, to be renewed every two months. Every patient has to pay sixpence on the first visit, and twopence on each succeeding visit, and again sixpence on the renewal of the letter. Out-patients are seen daily at the following hours: on Mon., Tu., Wed., Th., and Fri from 1 to 3 p.m., and on Sat. from 9 to 10 a.m. Visitors on Sun. and Sat. from 3 to 4. Every patient is required to pay according to means, ranging from 2s. 6d. upwards a week, to be paid in advance on entrance, and on each succeeding Tu.

Visiting Physicians. — Mrs. Garrett Anderson, M.D., Mrs. Atkins, M.D., Mrs. Marshall, M.D., and Mrs. de la Cherois, L.K.Q.C.P.I.

Assistant Physician.—Miss C. Hitchcock, L.R.Q.C.P.I.

Consulting Physicians. — Drs. H. Jackson, F.R.S., Broadbent, Priestley, Elizabeth Blackwell, Routh, Matthews Donkin, F.R.S., Allen Sturge.

Consulting Surgeons.—George Lawson, F.R.C.S., A. T. Norton, F.R.C.S., Thos. Smith, F.R.C.S., W. A. Meredith, M.B.

Dental Surgeon. — Herbert Apperly.

Queen Charlotte's Lying-in Hospital, 191, Marylebone-rd, N.W.; Secretary, G. Owen Ryan.—For in-patients and for the delivery of out-patients at their own homes. Single women admitted, with their first child only. Visi-tors admitted on Sun., Mon., Tu., Wed., Th., and Fri., between 3 and 4 p.m., for half an hour. Ad-mission of patients by letters of recommendation from governors and subscribers. Medical pupils desirous to study practical mid-wifery are admitted, and also women for training as midwives and monthly nurses.

Consulting Physicians.—G. O. Rees, M.D., F.R.S., G. T. Gream, M.D., G. B. Brodie, M.D.

Consulting Surgeons.—Sir W. Mac Cormack, M.A., F.R.C.S., Henry Lee, F.R.C.S.

Physicians to the In-patients.— William Hope, M.D., W. Chap-man Grigg, M.D.

St. Agnes Hospital, 3, Mar-garet-st, Cavendish-sq. Secretary, G. Thurlow. For the nursing of fallen women who are danger-ously ill. No out-patients treated, and no special hours for visitors Admission of patients free.

Medical Officers. — John Wil-ams, M.D., and Andrew Clark, F.R.C.S.

WOMEN AND CHILDREN (*and see p. 117*).

East London Hospital for Children and Dispensary for Women, Glamis-rd, Shadwell, E.; Secretary, Ashton Warner.—To maintain in the east of London a hospital for the medical and surgi-cal treatment of poor children as in-patients, and a dispensary for poor women and children as out-patients. Out - patients are seen daily except Sat. : medical cases— new patients from 1 till 1.30, old patients from 3 to 3.30, daily (ex-cept Sat.); and surgical cases, Tu. and Fri. at 9 a.m. Parents and friends of patients are admitted on

Sun. from 3 to 4 p.m. Visitors are cordially invited to visit the hos-pital, which is open for their in-spection daily from 11 to 5 o'clock. The admission of patients is by governor's letter. Urgent and accident cases are admitted at any time without any recommen-dation.

Consulting Physicians.—Robt. Barnes, M.D., Sir Andrew Clark, Bart., M.D.

Consulting Surgeon.— Buxton Shillitoe.

Consulting Ophthalmic Sur-geon.—George Cowell.

Physicians. — Eustace Smith, M.D., Horatio B. Donkin, M.B. Oxon., H. Radcliffe Crocker, M.D.

Surgeons. — Arthur Cæsar, F.R.C.S., R.W. Parker, M.R.C.S.

Assistant Physicians.— J. A. Coutts, M.D., Dawson Williams, M.D.

Assistant Surgeon.—Louis A. Dunn, M.B., F.R.C.S.

Administrator of Anæsthetics. —Thomas Bird, M.A., M.R.C.S.,

Resident Medical Officer.— J. Scott Battams, M.R.C.S.

† Grosvenor Hospital for Women and Children, Vincent-sq, Westminster, S.W.; Secretary, Hon. F.C. Howard.—The objects of the Institution are the treat-ment, as out-patients, of women and children suffering from any kind of diseases not infectious or contagious. The treatment, as in-patients, of women suffering from diseases peculiar to the sex. Out-patients seen on Tu., Wed., Th., and Sat. from 2 to 3 p.m. Visitors admitted on Wed. and Sun. from 2 to 3.40 p.m. Admission of patients on payment of 10s. weekly, or by subscriber's letter.

Consulting Physicians.—W. H. Broadbent, M.D., H. Gervis, M.D.

Consulting Surgeon.—J. Knows-ley Thornton, M.B., C.M.

Attending Medical and Sur-gical Staff.—A.C. Butler-Smythe, F.R.C.S., M.R.C.P., Robt. W. Parker, M.R.C.S., R. A. Gibbons, M.D., M.R.C.P., W. E. Steaven-son, M.D., M.R.C.P.

* † Royal Hospital for Children and Women, Water-loo-br-rd, S.E. ; Secretary, R. G. Kestin.—To give gratuitous medi-cal and surgical relief to necessitous poor children and women. Out-patients admitted daily from 12 noon to 2 p.m. Visitors daily from

E

11 a.m. to 4 p.m. Admission of patients by letter from subscriber.

Consulting Physicians.—Saml. Wilks, M.D., F.R.C.P., F.R.S., John Williams, M.D., F.R.C.P., George Roper, M.D., M.R.C.P., G. V. Poore, M.D., F.R.C.P., Wm. Park, M.D., M.R.C.P., Alex. Ha gh M.D., M.R.C.P., Septimus Sunderland, M.D., L.R.C.P.

Consulting Surgeon. — Arthur Durham, F.R.C.S.

Physicians.—W. A. Duncan, F.R.C.S., M.D., W. R. Dakin, M.D., M.R.C.P.

Surgeon.—W. H. A. Jacobson, F.R.C.S.

Anæsthetist.— F. W. Hewitt, M.D., M.R.C.S.

Assistant Surgeon.—E. Overman Day, M.R.C.S.

Consulting Surgeon-Dentist.—Walter Whitehouse, L.D.S.

Surgeon - Dentist. — Alfred Barnard, L.D.S.

Resident Medical Officer. — F. M. Johnson, M.B.

SAMARITAN FREE HOSPITAL FOR WOMEN AND CHILDREN, Lower Seymour-st, Portman-sq, W. Branch, 1, Dorset-st, Manchester-sq, W.; Secretary, George Scudamore.—For the treatment of diseases peculiar to women and of diseases of children. Out-patients seen daily (Sunday excepted) from 12 till 2. Visitors admitted to Lower Seymour-st Sun. and Th. from 2 to 4 p.m.; to Dorset House branch, for women, Sun. and Wed. 2 to 4 p.m.; children, on Sundays only. No letter of recommendation for admission of patients needed, poverty and sickness are the only passport required.

Consulting Physicians.—Henry Savage, M.D., F.R.C.S., C.H.F. Routh, M.D., W.R.Rogers, M.D.

Consulting Surgeon. — Sir T. Spencer Wells, Bart., F.R.C.S.

Physicians for In-Patients.—Percy Boulton, M.D., W. H. Day, M.D., Marmaduke Prickett, M.A., M.D., Amand Routh, M.D., B.S.

Physician to Children. — In-Patients.—W. H. Day, M.D.

Surgeons for In-Patients.—G. Granville Bantock, M.D., F.R.C.S. Edin., J. Knowsley-Thornton, M.B., M.C., W. A. Meredith, M.B., M.C.

Surgeon to Children In-Patients. — W. A. Meredith, M.B., M.C.

Physicians for Out-Patients.—Marmaduke Prickett, M.A., M.D., Amand Routh, M.D., B.S., Robert Boxall, M.D.

Surgeons for the Out-Patients —W. A. Meredith, M.B., M.C., Alban H. G. Doran, F.R.C.S., John D. Malcolm, M.B., M.C.

Dental Surgeon.—C. Stoddart.

Hotels.—One of the latest and most remarkable enterprises for providing a large and attractive hotel is that of the Grand Hotel, Trafalgar-sq—a large and sumptuously-fitted building in the very centre of London, and close to most of the chief public resorts. It is very splendidly appointed, and a daily *table-d'hôte* breakfast and dinner is provided, to which non-residents are admitted after the Continental fashion. Still of later date are the large and commodious First Avenue Hotel, Holborn, and the splendid Hotels Métropole and Victoria in Northumberland-avenue. Almost every great railway has now a handsome hotel in connection with its terminus, the most especially noticeable being the Great Western Hotel; the Grosvenor, at the Victoria Stn. of the L. B. & S. C. Ry.; the Charing ✚ Hotel, belonging to the S.E. Ry. Company; the Great Eastern Hotel, Liverpool-st, E.C.; the Holborn Viaduct Hotel; the hotel of the North Western Company in Euston-sq, and the gorgeous Gothic pile which forms the front of the St. Pancras (Midland) terminus. None of these hotels are at all cheap for people who do not understand hotel life, but they are very convenient for the new arrival, especially at night, and will probably prove quite as economical in the end as hunting about in a cab for a cheaper lodging. Indeed, we may go further, and say that it is possible, with judicious management, to live almost as cheaply at one of the large hotels as at any of the ambitious second-class houses. Other handsome establishments are Claridge's in Brook-st, the hotel *par excellence* for foreign ambassadors, princes, and so forth; Westminster Palace, close to the Houses of Parliament; the Alexandra, overlooking the Park at Knightsbridge; the Langham, at the south end of Portland-pl, a special American resort; the Buckingham Palace Hotel, just opposite the great ballroom window of Buckingham Palace; the St. James's Hotel in Piccadilly; the lately re-built Limmer's in Conduit-st, W; the Bristol, Burlington-gardens; and a large number of old-fashioned

family hotels in Brook-st, Bond-st, Clifford-st, Cork-st, North Burlington-st, Albemarle-st, Dover-st, Jermyn-st, &c.; at most of which will be found very first-rate accommodation, for the most part at equally first-rate prices. Next comes a somewhat more moderate class, though still with excellent accommodation, such as the Norfolk, close to the Paddington terminus; Norris's private and family hotel, at the north end of Russell-rd facing the Addison-rd Stn.; De Keyser's Royal Hotel at the corner of Blackfriars-br; and the Inns of Court Hotel, in Holborn, the rear-part of which looks on to Lincoln's-inn-fields. There is also another large class of comfortable hotels, such as Wood's in Furnival's Inn and the Bedford in Covent-gdn for families and gentlemen; and the Tavistock, also in Covent-gdn, for bachelors. Among the cheap hotels, special reference should be made to the Arundel, on the Embankment, at the foot of Arundel-st, Strand, but it is of very little use to look for rooms there, unless bespoken beforehand. Nearly all the streets from the south side of the Strand are full of small private hotels, a sort of compromise between hotel and lodging-house, where the casual visitor will find himself comfortably, if perhaps a little roughly quartered, and where he will be in a thoroughly central position, either for business or pleasure. Hotels on the "Temperance" principle will be found at Shirley's, 37, Queen's-sq, Bloomsbury; Fithian's, 17, Great Coram-st; Devonshire House, 12, Bishopsgate-st-without; Ling's, 11, South-st, Finsbury; Angus's, 22, New Bridge-st, and the West Central, Southampton-row, Russell-sq.

Householders, Hints to. —Never take for granted the report of the house agent or of the landlord's surveyor as to the state of repair of the house. Let the house be examined by your own surveyor, to whom particular instructions should be given to look after flues and drains (*see* DRAINAGE). Be careful to have the receipts for the Queen's and parish taxes last due before signing your lease or agreement. The gas company is very likely to try experiments on your credulity. Full information as to how this matter can be dealt with will be found under the head GAS. The consideration of the terms of a lease or of an agreement, unless the latter be of the very simplest kind, should invariably be referred to a solicitor. Should you elect to deal with tradesmen in a neighbourhood in which you are a stranger, it is as well to be very cautious as to whose advice you take. Personal inspection is in all cases the safest course. Above all things, never trust to the recommendations or importunities of servants.

Too much caution cannot be exercised in regard to the admission of strangers, especially during the absence from home of the master of the house. Every kind of thief is on the watch for a favourable moment to gain admission, and after having induced the servant to leave unprotected the hall or room, into which he contrives to be shown, to lay hands on all the available portable property. A more dangerous class of intruder still is he who comes provided with the card of a friend or acquaintance of the family, and offers for sale lace or other light goods. This is sure to be a fraud of a most dangerous kind. The card which procures the introduction to the house has been stolen, and the object of the visit is invariably plunder. Equally annoying, though perhaps not so ultimately dangerous, is the sham railway porter or messenger. This variety of the predatory race is in the habit of watching the master or mistress clear from the house, and then calls with a bogus parcel, for the carriage of which, and sometimes for the parcel itself, he demands such sums of money as he thinks most likely to be paid without question. In no case should a parcel be taken in under these circumstances. Another well-known parcel dodge is to watch the delivery by some draper's cart of a parcel, and ten minutes afterwards to call and redemand it, on the plea of some mistake having occurred in the delivery. Great care should be taken in the matter of fastenings to doors and windows. Nothing is easier or more common than for a thief to make his entrance into a house by way of the upper windows, or by climbing the portico at a time when the household is engaged at dinner, or when the general attention is otherwise diverted.

If the pattern of your mud-scraper pleases you, or you attach any importance to its possession, it is well not to leave it unsecured out of doors after dusk. It may be taken as a general rule that burglary or thieving on a large scale is never attempted unless the practitioner knows perfectly well that the house contains booty worthy of the risk necessarily involved. It is, therefore, to say the least of it, injudicious to allow servants to make an ostentatious display of plate at area or kitchen windows. Every householder should be careful to make himself acquainted with the nearest "fixed point" (see FIXED POINTS), at which a constable may always be found, the nearest police-station (see POLICE FORCE), and the nearest stations of the fire brigade, both for engines and escapes (see FIRE BRIGADE and FIRE ESCAPES). Nothing is prettier than the custom of decorating window-sills with flowers. It is necessary that the pots or boxes which contain them should be securely fastened. Any accident caused by neglect of this precaution may have unpleasant and expensive consequences for the careless householder. Equal care should be taken in the proper fastening of coal flaps or gratings. Every householder is under obligation to clear snow from the pavement in front of his house. For his own satisfaction he will no doubt clear it away from his roof and gutters. In the latter cases it is necessary to remember that the interests of the passers-by have to be considered, and that broken hats will certainly entail some expense. Among the other winter troubles which may be mentioned here is the supply of coal. If the householder would remember that every coal cart is provided with weights and scales, and would insist on all his coals being weighed on delivery, considerable saving would be effected; the coal merchant is powerless to check the proceedings of his men after the cart is loaded and has left his yard.

Unless under very exceptional circumstances it is unwise to employ peripatetic chair-menders, knife-grinders, tinkers, or the like. A very favourite trick of the "needy knife-grinder" is to undertake the sharpening of scissors for a stated sum, and then having

unscrewed them, to decline to put them together except at a greatly increased charge. But the class of peripatetic workmen who should be most carefully excluded from the house are the glaziers. Their glass is always bad, their work is invariably ill done and in nine cases out of ten their real business is robbery.—(See also POLICE and SERVANTS.)

Houses.—A few general hints upon taking a house may be useful. Having chosen your neighbourhood, and found a house to be let, you will do well to consider if the situation be quiet or noisy; the width of the street; the nature of the paving in front; the outlook at back; whether there are any objectionable businesses or trades carried on in the neighbourhood; any mews, cab-yards, or carriers' premises adjacent, or any public place of resort for folk who like to be merry at midnight; any noisy church or chapel bell to annoy you, or any railway running underneath you; whether near omnibus or tram routes; distance from various railway-stations, and places of public worship and public amusement. The next considerations are the state of repair and sanitary condition of the house, and on these points you will do well to consult some competent practical architect, otherwise you may unexpectedly find a large outlay necessary for a new roof, new floor, new drainage, or other expensive work. Most London houses have basement storeys below the level of the streets, and most basements are damp. Their dampness arises from several causes. The use of porous bricks in the walls, and the absence of damp-proof course to arrest the absorption of moisture from the earth in contact with the lower portions of the wall, are of frequent occurrence. In some parts of London land-springs may give considerable trouble, and in this case land-drains must be laid, care being taken that they are not in direct communication with any soil drain, or with the public sewer. Another source of damp is the absence of air space under the floors, and arrangements for the free admission and passage of air. Air bricks properly distributed, and, perhaps, lowering the level of the ground, will then be necessary. In all cases it is desirable to well drain the subsoil, and to have a good layer of concrete 6 in. thick under all basement floors. The level of the ground externally being higher than the floor internally is frequently the cause of damp, and in this case the construction of a good open area is often practicable, but, if not, a properly constructed dry area will be the best remedy.—(*See* DRAINAGE; *also* GAS.)

One of the greatest dangers to health is the presence of sewage gas in the house.

THE SANITARY ASSURANCE ASSOCIATION, 5, Argyll-pl, Regent-st, undertake to examine houses, and to report what work is required to put them in proper condition, so far as drainage, water supply, and ventilation are concerned. After a house has been reported on, and the necessary work has been done (by the occupant's own builder), to the satisfaction of the officers of the association, certificates are granted, transferable with the property, and thenceforth a yearly inspection is made on very moderate terms. For particulars of charges, etc., application should be made to the secretary at the office.

Houses of Parliament

(Map 13).—A Tudor Gothic building, covering nearly eight acres of ground, and constructed on the design of the late Sir Charles Barry at a cost, up to the present date, of about £3,000,000. The best view at present is from the river —the end next Westminster-br being much injured in effect by the abandonment of the northern façade which formed part of the original design. At the south end of the hall is a flight of steps leading through St. Stephen's porch and hall to the central hall, on the left or north side of which lies the portion of the building allotted to the Commons, and on the right or south side that belonging to the Queen and the Peers. A corridor leads in either direction to the "lobbies" of the respective Houses, where such of the public as have the *entrée* can communicate with the members, and immediately out of which the House itself opens; the Speaker's chair occupying the end opposite the door in the House of Commons, and the Throne a similar position in the House of Lords, the Woolsack being at some little distance in front of it. The various libraries, refreshment-rooms, &c., appertaining to each are grouped around their respective Houses; the libraries occupying the river front, and the Conference Room being placed between them. Beyond the Commons Division are the Speaker's house and the offices, &c., of the Commons; and beyond that of the Peers the royal apartment, the Queen's entrance being through the Victoria Tower. The Committee Rooms are, for the most part, upstairs. The internal arrangement of the Houses proper is entirely different from that which obtains in France and elsewhere. There is no permanent "Right" or "Left," nor any political distinction between the two portions; the right-hand side of the House being always occupied by the party in power and the left by the Opposition, whatever may be their respective principles. Along the right and left sides of the House of Commons run the Division Lobbies—quite distinct from "the" lobby at the farther end—into one or other of which the members walk when a division is called, according as they desire to vote Aye or No, being counted by the "tellers" of the respective sides as they return into the House. Admission to the Strangers' Gallery of the House of Lords to hear debates is by a peer's order. An order from a member, or (preferably) from the Speaker, admits to the Strangers' Galleries of the House of Commons. These galleries are not very convenient, and hold but a small number of persons. It is therefore only the fortunate few who can obtain good places on great occasions, and then only after many weary hours of waiting. When Parliament is not sitting, admission to the Houses may be readily obtained on application at the Lord Great Chamberlain's Office, Royal Court, Palace of Westminster, on Saturdays from 10 till 4. NEAREST *Ry. Stn.*, Westminster-br (Dis.); *Omnibus Rtes.*, Parliament-st, Victoria-st, and Westminster-br; *Cab Rank*, Opposite.

Humane Society (Royal),

Office, 4, Trafalgar-sq. Principal Receiving House on the North Bank of the Serpentine, Hyde-pk. Receiving houses and places appointed for receiving persons apparently drowned or dead, and at which drags and other apparatus are kept:

E

Bethnal Green: Workhouse, "Crown Tavern," Old Ford-rd, Messrs. Tomlin, 281, Green-st, "Queen's Tavern," Acton Lock.
Blackwall: Brunswick Wharf, Collin's Dock, Police-stn.
Bow: The Marsh Gate and Conservancy-cottage.
Bromley: Bromley Locks, "Fishing Boat Tavern."
Cambridge Heath: "Ion Arms."
Clapton, Upper: "Robin Hood," "Prince of Wales Tavern," Trueman's, River Lea.
Cubitt Town: Pier, "Pier Tavern."
Dalston-la: Police-stn.
East Smithfield: London Docks, St. Katharine's Docks.
Haggerston: "Sportsman Tavern."
Hackney: Workhouse.
Hackney-fields: "Duke of Sussex," Haggerston-br. Fire Brigade Stn., "The White Hart," near Temple Mills.
Limehouse Hole: "Royal Oak," West India Docks, "Horns and Chequers," Thames-pl.
Limehouse: "Two Brewers," "Britannia," Regent's Canal Docks and Lock-houses, "Sir J. Franklin," "St. Andrew's Head."
Mile End: "Gunmakers' Arms," Bow Common-la.
Old Ford-rd: "Crown Tavern," "Five Bells Tavern," Messrs. R berts & Co.
Poplar: Police-stn.
Ratcliffe: New England Lighthouse.
Shadwell: "The Ship Tavern," Bell's Wharf-stairs, Bryant's Boat House (Floating).
Sir J. Duckett's Canal: "Three Colts Tavern," two Lock-houses.
Tower Wharf: The Guard-houses.
St. Catherine's and Irongate Wharf.
Victoria-pk: The Lodge, Ornamental Water, "Lea Tavern," White Pond-lane, "Royal Victoria Tavern," Mitford Lock.
Wapping: Hermitage Wharf.
West Ham: "The White Swan."

E.C.

Custom House: The Quay.
London-br (City side): Fresh Wharf, Old Swan Wharf.

N.

Caledonian-rd: Tunnel Cottage.
Finsbury-pk: Keeper's lodge.
Hampstead: "Athenæum Hotel," Vale of Health, Police-stn. "Suburban Hotel."
Highbury: Sluice House.
Highgate: Pond Cottage, Police stn.
Hoxton: "Carver's Arms," Police

stn., "The Block Tavern," Shepherdess Walk.

Kingsland : "Stag's Head," Canal-rd, Police-stn.

N.W.

Camden Tn. : "Devonshire Arms," near the canal bridge, Police-stn., Platt-st, Somers Tn.

Regent's Canal : "Prince Albert," St. George's-rd, near St. Mark's-sq, "York and Albany."

Willesden : "Grand Junction Arms."

S.E.

Bankside : "Waterman's Arms."

Bermondsey Wall : "The Bunch of Grapes Tavern," "Stave Porters," Dockhead.

Blackfriars (Surrey side) : "Bear and Ragged Staff," Upper Ground-st.

Camberwell : "Surrey Canal Tavern," "King's Arms," Wells-st, "Princess Charlotte,"Albany-rd

Deptford : "Black Horse Tavern," Evelyn-st, Mr. Bigsby's, Trundle-la, Surrey Canal.

Greenwich : "Yacht Tavern," the Pier, Police-stn.

Horselydown : Bovill's Wharf.

Nine Elms : "The White Swan Tavern."

Old Kent-rd : "Bridge House Tavern."

Peckham : "Old Barge Tavern" (on the Canal), "Grand Surrey Canal Tavern," "Waterman's Arms," "Surrey View Tavern."

Rotherhithe : "The Horns," Rotherhithe-st, "Ship Tavern," Hanover-stairs, "Globe Tavern," Globe-stairs, Police-stn, "Plough Tavern," Surrey Canal Basin, "Spread Eagle," Church-stairs, "Angel," Cherry Garden-st.

Tooley-st : Wilson's Wharf, Fenning's Wharf, "The Vine Tavern," Vine-st.

Waterloo-br (Surrey side) : Audsley's Boat House.

S.W.

Barnes : "Bull's Head Tavern," Green's Boat House, Railway-br, "White Hart."

Battersea : "Swan and Magpie" (near the bridge), "The Old Swan" (near the Church), Railway-pier, Park-pier, "The White Swan," near Nine Elms.

Chelsea : Johnston's boat-house, Police-stn., New-br, Battersea Steamboat Pier(Middlesex side), "King's Arms," Cheyne-wk.

Chiswick : "Red Lion," Chiswick Improvement Commissioners' Pumping-stn.

Clapham Common : Keeper's lodge.

Fulham : "The Crab Tree Tavern," Phelps's boat-house.

Millbank : "White Hart."

Pimlico : "Spread Eagle Tavern," "William IV. Tavern," Police-stn.

Putney : "The Bells Tavern," The new Railway-pier, U. U. Boat House, East's boat-house.

St. James'-pk : The Lodge, &c.

Wandsworth : "White Horse Tavern," "The Feathers Tavern," Police-stn.

Westminster-br (Surrey side) : "The Coronet Tavern."

W.

Brentford : "Waterman's Arms," Ferry-la, Brentford Gas Works, the Bridge, "Six Bells Tavern," Police-stn.,Thames Lock-house, "Bunch of Grapes," Ferry-la.

Hammersmith : Police-stn., Bridge Pier, Biffen's boat-house, Captain Crispin's (late Sawyer's), "City Arms."

Harrow-rd : "Carleton Arms."

Hyde-pk : Receiving-house, the bridges.

Kensal Green : "Victoria Tavern," Shepherd's hut.

Kensington - gdns : Palace-gate, Bridge-gate.

Paddington : Grand Junc. Canal Office, Warwick-br, Police-stn.

Regent's Canal : The Stop-lock.

Wormwood Scrubs : "The Mitre Tavern."

W.C.

Charing Cross : Railway-pier.

In addition to the above, the Society have iron huts in Regent's and St. James's Parks provided with Apparatus.

Hungary.—(See Austria.)

Hurlingham Club, Fulham.—The club was instituted for the purpose of providing a ground for pigeon-shooting, polo, lawn tennis, &c., surrounded with such accessories and so situated as to render it an agreeable country resort, not alone to those who take part in polo, but also to their families and friends. The club consists, at the time of revising the Dictionary for 1888, of shooting, polo, and non-shooting members. Elected members pay an entrance fee of £15 15s., and an annual subscription of £5 5s. Non-shooting members elected previous to May, 1878, pay £2 2s. annually. They are entitled to all the privileges of the club, and to admit two ladies without payment, and may give orders of admission to as many friends as they please on payment.

Every member is entitled, by the payment of £1 1s. extra per annum, to give one additional order for ladies only for free admission daily. No person is eligible for admission who is not received in general society. The committee elect by ballot, and the candidate balloted for shall be put up not sooner than one week after he is proposed. Five members must be present ; if there be one black ball the candidate shall be considered as not elected.

Hyde Park (Maps 5 and 6)— "the park" *par excellence*—is the great fashionable promenade of London. It stands high, and forms with Kensington-gdns— which are simply a continuation of it, under somewhat different rules in respect of hours of closing, &c.—a vast open space nearly a mile and a half in length, by three - quarters of a mile in width. The park proper, which is crossed in every direction by footpaths, is surrounded by a carriage-drive of about two and a half miles, and has eight gates, viz. : two at the N.W. and N.E. corners, Victoria and Cumberland (Marble Arch) ; two on the E. side, Grosvenor and Stanhope, opposite the respective streets ; two at the S.E. and S.W. corners, Knightsbridge (Hyde-park-corner) and Queen's-gate ; and two on the S. side, Albert-gate and Prince's-gate. A large piece of ornamental water, called by the authorities the Serpentine where it traverses the park, and the Long Water so far as concerns the portion in Kensington-gdns, runs in a sort of irregular quadrant from N. by way of S.W. to E., and is commonly known as the Serpentine throughout. It is a favourite place for skating, and about the most dangerous in London. The Humane Society's establishment stands at about the middle of the N. shore of the Serpentine proper ; and a portion of the S. bank, exactly opposite, and between the water and Rotten-row, is set apart before 8 a.m. and after 7.30 p.m. for bathing. Boats are to be had on hire on the N. shore. Rotten-row is a piece of road set apart for equestrians, extending originally from Hyde-pk-corner to Queen's-gate. A supplementary ride has been laid out on the other side of the Serpentine, and runs from the Magazine by Victoria-gate to Cumberland-gate. From Hyde-pk-

corner to Queen's-gate runs also a carriage-drive, the site of the original Great Exhibition of 1851 lying between. Near the W. end of this drive stands on its N. side the Albert Memorial. For two or three hours every afternoon in the season, except Sunday, the particular section of the drive which happens that year to be "the fashion" is densely thronged with carriages moving round and round at little more than a walking pace, and every now and then coming to a dead-lock. The portion of the road specially affected varies from time to time, but is usually either that along the N. side of the Serpentine or that between Hyde - pk - corner and Queen's-gate. It has become of late fashionable to stroll or to sit by the row on Sundays. The road from Queen's-ga to Victoria-ga is now open to cabs, &c.; the remainder of the park to private carriages only. The park-gates open at 5 a.m. and close at 12 p.m. all the year round. The minor gates are closed at 10 p.m. The great omnibus routes of the Strand and Holborn skirt it on the N. and S. sides, and that from Victoria to Royal Oak on the E. The nearest railway stations are—on the S., Victoria (Dis.), and on the N., Edgware-rd (Met).

Illuminations. — Except in the event of some extraordinary occurrence, such as the proclamation of peace after the Crimean War, or the recovery of the Prince of Wales from his almost fatal illness, the occasions of general illuminations are two a year; the first being the Queen's birthday, which falls on the 24th of May, but is observed on a day specially selected for that purpose in each year; and the second, the Prince of Wales's birthday, on November the 9th. Although a couple of skeleton gas-jet initials, a few Chinese lanterns, or an arrangement in tiny oil lamps, may here and there be dotted at wide intervals N. of Oxford-st, S. of Trafalgar-sq, or E. of where Temple Bar once stood, illumination proper is practically confined to the principal clubs and to tradesmen patronised by members of the Royal Family and their households, whose shops are situated in a few of the chief West End thoroughfares. The most comprehensive route for the sight-

seer is from Cockspur-street, Charing-✝, and Pall Mall-east, up Waterloo-pl and the right-hand side of Regent-st to Oxford-cir; to the right for a short distance up Oxford-st and returning on the reverse side of the way down Regent-st to New Burlington-st; thence through Savile-row and Burlington-gdns into Old Bond-st, down St. James's-st, and along Pall Mall to the original starting point. Strangers must be prepared to encounter an enormous throng of people, many of whom indulge in somewhat rough but usually good-tempered horseplay. Timid and nervous people can avoid a great deal of this by seeing their illuminations from a cab, or, still better, from an open carriage; but, for those who do not object to the annoyances incidental to a multitude, walking is preferable.

Imperial Theatre, Westminster (Map 13), occupied the western end of the Aquarium building, of which it formed part, but for some time was not under the same management. All sorts of performances were given at the Imperial Theatre, which however, did not secure any very firm hold on the favour of the public, and finally lost its separate existence, and became part of the Aquarium.

India.—The office of the Secretary of State for India in Council is in Charles-st, Westminster. The departments are the Council (hours 10 till 4), the Correspondence Department (hours 10 till 4), that for Military Funds (hours 10 till 4), for Registry of Despatches (hours 10 till 4), and the Accounts Branch of the Financial Department (hours 10 till 4). Saturdays, all departments, 10 till 2. There is also a Medical Board and an Audit Office. NEAREST *Ry. Stn.,* Westminster - br (Dis.); *Omnibus Rtes.,* Whitehall and Strand; *Cab Rank,* Palace-yd.

Indian Section of South Kensington Museum, Exhibition-rd, S.W. (Map 5), formerly under control of the India Office, transferred to South Kensington in 1880.—The galleries in which the collections are exhibited are open daily (except Sunday) free, and are under the same regulations as the South Kensington Museum (*which see*). The entrance galleries contain house fronts, carved wood

and stone work, plaster casts, photographs, and drawings, and examples of the various styles of Buddhistic, Hindu, and Mogul architecture, and small painted models of figures and groups, illustrating the trades and industries of India The ground - floor of the main gallery is almost entirely occupied by a large collection of textile fabrics. The first room contains woven fabrics, carpets, Kashmir shawls, etc.; the second, collections of objects from Borneo and Yarkund, and the collection of the Royal Asiatic Society; the third and fourth rooms embroidery in silk, gold, and silver; and the fifth printed cottons. In the first room of the upper gallery are furniture, lacquer and inlay work, carvings in ivory, horn, and various woods, musical instruments, inlaid marbles, and a collection of water-colour paintings by William Carpenter, illustrating life in India; the second room contains pottery and glass; the third is occupied by a collection of arms and armour, models of carriages, etc.; the fourth room jewellery, enamels, carvings in jade, crystal, and agate; among other objects the gold throne of Runjeet Singh. In this room are several reproductions of fine antique carpets. The fifth room contains work in various metals— copper, brass, zinc, etc.; also a large collection of Hindu deities. NEAREST *Ry. Stn.,* South Kensington (Dis.); *Omnibus Rte.,* Kensington-rd and Brompton-rd; *Cab Rank,* "Bell and Horns," Cromwell-rd.

Inland Revenue, Somerset House (Map 7).—Hours 10 to 4. A great department, covering a vast amount of ground. The principal branches are the Receiver-General's; the Accountant and Comptroller-General's; the Chief Inspector's (Excise Branch); the Chief Inspector's (Stamps and Taxes); that for Legacy and Succession Duties; the Companies' Register Office; the Stamp Allowance Office; the Department of the Comptroller of Stamps and Register of Joint Stock Companies; the Stamping Department; Surveyors of Taxes and Special Commissioners of Income Tax (west wing Somerset House). NEAREST *Ry. Stn.,* Temple (Dis.); *Omnibus Rte.,* Strand *Cab Rank,* Catherine-st.

Inns of Court (The) are four in number, viz.; Inner and Middle Temple, Lincoln's-inn, and Gray's-inn. The word inn, like the French *hôtel*, signifies a mansion. Each of these inns is governed by a committee, generally formed of Queen's Counsel, called benchers, who are a self-elected body. The inns consist of a hall, a chapel, a library, a suite of rooms devoted to the benchers, and a number of buildings divided into sets of chambers, occupied, for the most part, by barristers and solicitors. Each inn has the privilege of calling students to the bar, and of disbarring a barrister, subject to an appeal to the judges. Formerly, when a barrister was appointed serjeant or a judge, he forfeited his membership of his original inn and became a member of Serjeants'-inn. As this society has been lately abolished, each of the four inns has re-admitted such of its members as have been raised to the bench.

GRAY'S-INN stands on the north side of Holborn, and was formerly the property of the Grays of Wilton, whence the society derives its name. In the time of Edward III. it began to be an inn of court. Nowadays the society possesses South-sq, Gray's-inn-sq, Field-ct, Gray's-inn-pl, Raymond-bdgs, Verulam-bdgs, and the garden. The chambers are spacious and well adapted for permanent habitation, and are cheaper than those belonging to the Temple and Lincoln's-inn. The hall, which is the smallest of the four, is nevertheless an imposing chamber, and is the oldest but one. The roof is of carved oak, divided into six compartments. The screen is another magnificent specimen of carving, supported by six pillars of the Tuscan order, with caryatides supporting the cornice. Amongst the paintings which decorate the hall are portraits of Charles I., of Charles II. and James II.—both cut down to half their original size—Bishop Gardiner, Lord Coke, Nicholas Bacon, and Lord Bacon. In the windows there is magnificent stained glass; one pane is dated as early as 1552. The name and dignities of the late Lord Chelmsford are emblazoned on a window near, and so are the name and crest of Mr. Justice Lush. The library was rebuilt in 1884, and is both handsome and convenient. The chapel, which is an ancient structure, was completely moder-

nised in the last century; but the east window is gorgeous with the arms of several eminent divines, preachers of the society. There are some eighty students attached to Gray's-inn at the present time, which means that the honourable society is becoming more popular than of yore. Lord Burghley, Sir Philip Sidney, Lord Bacon, and Sir Samuel Romilly were members of the inn.

LINCOLN'S-INN became an inn of court about the year 1310, after the death of Harry Lacy, Earl of Lincoln, from whence the name of the society is derived. The principal entrance in Chancery-la was built in the reign of Henry VII., and over this gateway Oliver Cromwell is said to have lived for some period. In the erection of the wall, Ben Jonson is said to have assisted as a bricklayer. The chapel, altered and enlarged 1882-3, is built upon a cloister of six open arches, under which are buried Thurloe, Cromwell's secretary, Crome, the song-writer, and others. These cloisters served as a promenade in wet weather for the wives and daughters of members of the inn, when barristers used to reside in their chambers in Lincoln's-inn. The chapel would not be particularly remarkable but for the stained glass, on which are represented the arms of deceased worthies and fancy portraits of the saints and biblical heroes. The bell which hangs in the south-west turret was brought by the Earl of Essex from Cadiz after the capture of that town in Elizabeth's reign. The hall, commenced in 1843, and finished in 1845, is the finest in London, with the exception of Westminster Hall, being 120 feet in length, 45 in breadth, and 64 high. The oak roof is a remarkable feature in its construction, divided as it is by trusses into seven compartments. The screen is also a sumptuous piece of work. At the northern end is a fresco painted by Watts, R.A., "The Lawgivers," a magnificent work, which is now unfortunately fading. The artist contributed this important addition to the decoration of the hall gratuitously; but when the fresco was finished, the inn presented him with a gold cup containing eight hundred sovereigns. In the rooms used by the benchers is a fine collection of paintings and old engravings. Hogarth's "Paul

before Felix" occupies here an important position. Two hundred pounds were paid for the picture, and in a frame below the painting is an autograph letter from the artist acknowledging the money. Above the doorway is Gainsborough's portrait of Pitt in excellent preservation. The society also possesses a large work by Giorgione; a portrait of Lord Chief Baron Kelly, which has lately been painted; and a water-colour drawing of Her Majesty and the Prince Consort opening the new hall on the 13th of October, 1845. On that occasion Prince Albert was made a barrister and a bencher of the inn, and the Queen took luncheon in the hall. The Prince wore a field-marshal's uniform, and Her Majesty was attired in a dress of Limerick lace, a blue bonnet and feather, and a scarlet shawl with a broad gold edging. The library which is attached to the hall is a comfortable building, in which space has been economised in many ingenious ways. There are many thousands of books on legal and other subjects. In the gardens close to the entrance of the hall is an iron railing of delicate workmanship; on it are embossed the name Brewster, and the letters I.C.R.V. twice. The work stands as a memorial to Lt.-Col. Brewster, late commandant of the Inns of Court Rifle Volunteers—familiarly called the "Devil's Own."

The TEMPLE, in the reign of Henry II., became the home of the Knights Templars, who built their church in imitation of the temple, near the Holy Sepulchre in Jerusalem. In the reign of Edward II. the order was suppressed, and the Temple subsequently became the property of the Knights Hospitallers of St. John of Jerusalem. These worthies are believed to have let the space to professors of the law for the rent of £10 per annum; at all events, in the reign of Richard II. it is clear that the lawyers were firmly established in the home which they have never since quitted. In Henry VIII.'s reign the two societies became tenants of the Crown, and in the sixth year of James I. received a grant by letters patent of the mansion of the Inner Temple at the sum of £10 yearly. The same amount was exacted for the Middle Temple. The Inner Temple Hall is a modern buildng only a few years old. It is considerably larger than the old one, and better and more spacious as regards its offices and ante-rooms. A luncheon-room for the use of members of the inn is a welcome addition. The principal portraits are William and Mary, QueenAnne, Sir Thomas Littleton, and Lord Chief Justice Coke. The arms and crests of the treasurers of the inn surround the hall, which is replete with all the latest con-trivances in the way of ventilation and illumination. The library consists of a series of apartments leading one into another. It is perhaps the snuggest and quietest of all the four, and contains a number of books on general, besides legal, subjects. Sir Christopher Hatton, Sir Edward Coke, Lord Tenterden, and Wm. Cowper, the poet, were members of the inn. Charles Lamb was born within its precincts, and Dr. Johnson lived there for some time. The gate leading into the Inner Temple from Fleet-street was built in the reign of James I.

MIDDLE TEMPLE HALL was commenced in 1562, and is one of the grandest Elizabethan structures in London. It is about 100ft. long, and is conspicuous for the massive beauty of the dark oak roof. The windows and walls are decorated with the arms of members of the inn, and the screen and the music gallery are of dark oak elaborately carved. Over the dais is a por-trait of Charles I. on horseback, by Vandyke, one of the three original pictures of the monarch painted by that master ; one of the other two being at Windsor, and the other at Warwick Castle. Portraits of Charles II., James II., William III., Queen Anne, and George II. are also to be seen, besides marble busts of Lord Eldon and Lord Stowell. Royal personages have frequently visited Middle Temple Hall ; the Prince of Wales dined there some years ago, and the benchers took the opportunity of calling His Royal Highness to the bar and electing him a bencher within a few minutes' time. Some twenty years ago the new library was opened, a handsome building standing near the river, at the south-west corner of the garden. It is larger than the Inner Temple library, but is perhaps not so well adapted for close study. Besides producing many eminent lawyers, Middle Temple has called to the

bar many celebrated poets and dramatists, amongst them Forde, Rowe, Wm. Congreve, Shadwell, Southerne, Sheridan, and Tom Moore. Sir William Blackstone, who wrote the "Commentaries on the Laws of England," was educated at the Middle Temple. The most interesting object in the Temple is the church, which was dedicated to the Virgin by Heraclius, patriarch of Jerusalem, in 1185. It has been thoroughly restored, new marble columns have been added, and the tombs of the Knights Templars have been renovated. Goldsmith's tomb is in the north-east corner of the churchyard. There are two ser-vices on Sunday (at 11 a.m. and 3 p.m.). Admission to the morning service may be obtained by an order from a bencher of either Temple. Admission to the after-noon service is practically free. The church can be seen daily (ex-cept Sat.) between the hours of 10 and 1, and 2 and 4. Visitors will find a knocker on the door, a judi-cious use of which will produce an attendant *cicerone.*

Insurance Companies.—
FIRE INSURANCE RATES : For merchandise at the principal ports, and for mills and manufactories and other leading industries throughout the United Kingdom, all the offices charge the same, whilst for minor risks each office makes its own estimate, and charges the premium in its judg-ment applicable. The following is a digest of the scale put forward by some of the oldest companies, and the rates and classification are those which are generally adopted. *Common Insurances :* At 1s. 6d. to 2s. per cent. per annum, with certain exceptions. 1. Buildings covered with slates, tiles, or metals, and built on all sides with brick or stone, or separated by party-walls of brick or stone which are carried through the roof, and used for residence, or non-hazardous pur-poses. 2. Goods in buildings, as above, such as household goods, plate, wearing apparel, and printed books, liquors in private use, and personal effects not comprised in the following categories. *Hazard-ous Insurances :* At 2s. 6d. to 3s. per cent. per annum, with certain exceptions. 1. Buildings of timber and plaster, or not separated by partition-walls of brick or stone, or not covered with slates, tiles, or metals and thatched barns and

outhouses, having no chimney, nor adjoining to any building having a chimney ; and buildings falling under the description of common insurances, but in which hazard-ous goods are deposited, or hazardous trades are carried on. 2. Goods. The stock and goods of bread bakers, tallowchandlers (not melters), chemists, inn-holders, grocers, drapers, stationers, etc. *Doubly Hazardous Insurances :* At 4s. 6d. to 5s. per cent. per annum, with certain exceptions. 1. Buildings. All thatched build-ings having chimneys, or com-municating with or adjoining to buildings having one, although no hazardous trade shall be carried on, nor hazardous goods deposited therein, and all hazardous build-ings, in which hazardous goods are deposited, or hazardous trades carried on 2. Goods. All hazard-ous goods deposited in hazardous buildings, and in thatched build-ings having no chimney ; also china, glass, mathematical and musical instruments, pictures, and jewels in private use.

The following are the principal Offices, with the official returns furnished by the secretaries.

ALLIANCE ASSURANCE CO., Bartholomew - la, E.C., 1, St. James's-st, S.W., 34, Chancery-la, and 3, Norfolk - st, Strand. Estab. 1824. Subscribed capital, £500,000.

ANCHOR ("JAKOR") INSURANCE Co. of Moscow, 31, Lombard-st. Founded 1872. Subscribed and paid-up capital, £350,000 ; pre-mium income, £400,000.

ATLAS FIRE AND LIFE AS-SURANCE COMPANY, 92, Cheap-side, and 4, Pall Mall East, S.W. Capital, £1,200,000 ; annual income (premiums and interest) exceeds £338,000. Total assets exceed £1,855,000.

AUSTRALIAN ALLIANCE ASS. Co. (Melbourne), 32, Great St. Helen's, E.C. Gen. reserve fund, £140,000 ; life ass. fund, £225,966 ; cap., £250,000 ; paid up, £50,000.

AZIENDA INSURANCE COMPA-NIES OF VIENNA, 31, Lombard-st. Estab. 1882. Capital 12,000,000 of florins.

CALEDONIAN FIRE AND LIFE INSURANCE CO., 82, King William-st, E.C., and 14, Waterloo-pl, S.W Estab. 1805. Annual income, £260,000 ; accumulated funds, £1,160,000.

CHURCH OF ENG. LIFE AND FIRE ASS., TRUST, AND ANNUITY INST., 9, King-st, Cheapside. Est. 1840. Accumulated funds on 31st Dec., 1886, £783,286.

CITY OF GLASGOW LIFE ASSURANCE CO., 12, King William-st, E.C. Established 1838. Funds exceed £1,483,000. Premium income, £150,000.

CLERICAL, MEDICAL, AND GENERAL LIFE ASSURANCE SOC., 15, St. James's-sq, S.W. City Branch, Mansion House-bdgs. Established 1824. Financial position on the 30th June, 1887, was : subsisting assurances and bonuses, £6,849,646.

COMMERCIAL UNION FIRE, LIFE, AND MARINE ASSURANCE CO. LIM., 19 & 20, Cornhill. Established 1861. Capital paid-up, £250,000. Reserves in hand, £1,070,064, in addition to which there is a special reserve for the exclusive security of the life policy holders of £1,105,035.

COUNTY FIRE OFFICE, 50, Regent-st, W., and 14, Cornhill. Established 1806.

CROWN LIFE OFF., 188, Fleet-st. Estab. 1825. Funds, £1,885,129.

EAGLE INSURANCE CO. (for Lives only), 79, Pall Mall, S.W. Established 1807. Funds in hand 31st Dec., 1887, £2,871,674.

ECONOMIC LIFE, 6, New Bridge-st, Blackfriars. Established 1823. Mutual. Accumulated funds, £3,562,753.

EDINBURGH LIFE ASSURANCE CO., 11, King William-st, E.C. Established 1825.

EMPIRE FIRE ASSOCIATION, LIMITED, 66, Finsbury-pavement, E.C.

EQUITABLE FIRE INS. CO. LIM., 11 & 13, St. Ann-st, Manchester; London Office, 69, Lombard-st, E.C. Financial position on the 31st December, 1887 : Capital subscribed, £263,335 ; capital paid up, £52,667 ; gross income, £83,674 ; reserve funds, £32,798. Total assets, including uncalled capital, £300,517 8s. 7d.

EQUITABLE LIFE ASSURANCE SOC., Mansion House-st. Established 1762. Mutual invested capital (exclusively from premiums received), £4,250,000. The recent division showed a clear surplus of £1,893,700.

EQUITABLE LIFE ASSURANCE SOCIETY OF THE UNITED STATES,

Established 1859. London Office, 81, Cheapside, E.C. Accumulated funds, £12,117,067.

EQUITY AND LAW LIFE ASSURANCE SOC., 18, Lincoln's-inn-fields. Established 1844. Accumulated funds, £2,111,862.

FIRE INSURANCE ASSO., 66, Cornhill, E.C.

GENERAL LIFE AND FIRE CO., 103, Cannon-st, E.C. Established 1837. Capital and accumulated funds exceed £2,100,000.

GUARDIAN FIRE & LIFE ASSURANCE CO., 11, Lombard-st, and 21, Fleet-st. Established 1821. Paid up capital, £1,000,000 ; funds in hand, £3,999,000.

HAND-IN-HAND FIRE AND LIFE INSURANCE SOCIETY, 26, New Bridge-st, Blackfriars. Est. 1696. Accumulated funds, £2,280,731. Rate of bonus return varies from 20 to 50 per cent. in the Fire, and from 45 to 75 per cent. in the Life Department.

IMPERIAL FIRE INSURANCE COMPANY, 1, Old Broad-st, E.C., and 22, Pall Mall, S.W.

IMPERIAL LIFE INSURANCE COMPANY, 1, Old Broad-st, E.C., and 22, Pall Mall, S.W.

KENT INSURANCE CO. Established 1802. FIRE, LIFE, AND ANNUITIES. Head office, Maidstone. Branches : London, 124, Cannon-st, E.C. ; Manchester, 1, Cooper-st. Funds, nearly £800,000.

LANCASHIRE FIRE AND LIFE INSURANCE CO., 14, King William-st, E.C. Established 1852. Reserve in hand : Fire and General, £356,990 ; Life, £759,271.

LAW FIRE INSURANCE SOC., 114, Chancery-la. Established 1845. Capital, £5,000,000. Paid up, and in reserve, £304,083.

LAW LIFE ASS. SOC., 187, Fleet st. Est. 1823. Assets on 31st Dec., 1887, £5,218,687.

LAW UNION FIRE AND LIFE INSURANCE CO., 126, Chancery-la. Estab. 1854. Reserve in hand on 30th Nov., 1887, £996,908.

LEGAL AND GENERAL LIFE ASSURANCE SOC., 10, Fleet-st. Established 1836. Empowered by Act of Parliament. Net assurance fund, £1,957,170. Share capital, fully subscribed, £1,000,000 ; paid up, £160,000.

LIFE ASSO. OF SCOTLAND, 5, Lombard st, E.C., and 123, Pall

Mall, S.W. Established 1838 Accumulated fund, £2,507,433.

LION FIRE INSURANCE COMPANY LIMITED, 83, Queen-st, E.C. Subscribed capital, £825,000 ; Paid up, £112,013 15s.

LIVERPOOL AND LONDON AND GLOBE INSURANCE CO., 7 and 8, Cornhill, and Charing ✠. Established 1836. Fire and Life. Total invested funds, £7,324,034, of which general reserve and fire re-insurance fund, £1,870,000.

LONDON AND LANCASHIRE FIRE INSURANCE CO., 74, King William-st, E.C. Estab. 1862. Funds in hand, over £550,000. The comp. transacts fire business only.

LONDON ASSURANCE CORPORATION, for Marine, Fire, and Life Assurances, 7, Royal Exchange. Incorporated 1720. Funds in hand, £3,432,140 12s. 9d.

LONDON LIFE ASSO., 81, King William-st, E.C. The accumulated fund exceeds £3,925,000. Its gross income from premiums and interest is more than £490,000, of which income the amount returned to members in reduction of their premiums is upwards of £217,000. The new assurances effected in the last year amounted to £201,600, and the corresponding annual premiums were £7,470.

MANCHESTER FIRE ASSURANCE CO., 98, King-st, Manchester, and 96, Cheapside, E.C. Established 1824. Capital paid up, £100,000 ; reserve fund, £140,000.

METROPOLITAN LIFE ASSURANCE SOC., 3, Princes-st, Bank. Established 1835. Sum now assured, £5,200,000 ; annual income, £236,502 ; assurance and reserve funds, £1,853,000.

MIDLAND COUNTIES INSURANCE CO., Gresham-bdgs, Basinghall-st. Est.1851. Reserve in hand £65,502. Capital paid up, £32,500

MUTUAL ACCIDENT ASSOCIATION LIMITED. Head Office, 32, Brown-st, Manchester ; London Office, 10, King William-st, E.C. Established1881. Guarantee fund, £100,000.

MUTUAL FIRE INSURANCE CORPORATION LIMITED. Head Office, Brown-st, Manchester ; London Office, 10, King William-st. Est, 1870. Reserve fund, £136,951. Guarantee fund, £100,000.

MUTUAL LIFE ASSURANCE SOC., 39, King-st, Cheapside. Estab.

1834. The assets on 31st Dec., 1887, were £1,179,503, being over fourteen years' premium income, and equal to £42 5s. 3d. for every £100 assured.

NATIONAL ASSURANCE CO. OF IRELAND, 33, Nicholas-lane, E.C. Established 1822. Authorised capital, £2,000,000.

NATIONAL FIRE INSURANCE CORPORATION LIMITED, 72, King William-st., E.C. Established 1876. Capital and reserve funds, £187,000.

NEW YORK LIFE INSURANCE Co. Chief Office for Gt. Britain and Ireland, 76 and 77, Cheapside. Accumulated fund on the 31st Dec., 1887, £16,976,616.

NORTH BRITISH AND MERCANTILE INSURANCE CO., 61, Threadneedle-st., E.C., and 8, Waterloo-pl, Pall Mall, S.W. Established 1809. Paid up capital and reserve in hand, £1,664,128.

NORTHERN ACCIDENT INSURANCE CO., LIM., 224, Piccadilly, W., and 37, Queen Victoria-st, E.C.

NORTHERN ASSURANCE CO., 1, Moorgate-st, E.C. Estab. 1836. Accumulated funds, £3,297,000.

NORWICH UNION FIRE INS. SOC., 50, Fleet-st, 19, Serjeants-Inn, and 18, Royal Exchange. Estab. 1797. Capital, £1,100,000.

NORWICH UNION LIFE INSURANCE SOC. (on the principles of Mutual Assurance), 50, Fleet-st, and 19, Serjeants Inn. Estab. 1808. Accumulated Funds, nearly £2,000,000.

PELICAN LIFE INSURANCE CO., 70, Lombard-st, E.C., & 57, Charing ✝, S.W. Established 1797. Accumulated funds, £1,333,290.

PHŒNIX FIRE OFFICE, 19, Lombard-st, E.C., and 57, Charing ✝, S.W. Established 1782. Losses already paid, over £16,000,000.

POSITIVE GOVERNMENT SECURITY LIFE ASS. CO. LIM, 34, Cannon-st, E.C. Est. 1870. Policy-holders' premium funds reserved on 31st Dec., 1887, £318,958 14s. od.; policy-holders' guarantee fund on 31st Dec., 1887, £43,476 1s. 7d. Special feature of the Company: Investment in names of trustees for policy-holders of the entire net premiums paid.

PROVIDENT CLERKS' AND GENERAL GUARANTEE ASSO, LIMITED,

61, Coleman-st. E.C. Capital subscribed, £100,000. Amount called up and paid, £60,000.

PROVIDENT CLERKS' AND GENERAL ACCIDENT INSURANCE CO. LIMITED, 61, Coleman-st, E.C. Capital subscribed, £50,000.

PROVIDENT CLERKS' MUTUAL LIFE ASSURANCE ASSOCIATION, 27, Moorgate-st, E.C. Established 1840. Invested fund, £1,234,231. Annual premium income, £111,440.

PROVIDENT LIFE OFFICE, 50, Regent-st, W., and 14, Cornhill. Assets, £2,501,300.

PROVINCIAL LIFE INS. CO., 7, Queen Victoria-st, E.C. Estab. 33 years. Funds, £332,118.

PRUDENTIAL ASSURANCE CO. (LIM.), Holborn Bars. Assurance funds, £8,000,000.

QUEEN INSURANCE COMPANY, 60, Gracechurch-st, E.C., and Dale-st, Liverpool. Established 1857. Annual income, £736,392; funds in hand, £1,296,062; claims paid, £6,131,959.

RELIANCE MUTUAL LIFE ASSURANCE SOC., 71, K. William-st, E.C. Established 1840. The surplus funds are divided amongst the members, who incur no liability beyond their premium payments.

ROCK LIFE ASSURANCE CO., 15, New Bridge-st, Blackfriars. Established 1806. Accumulated fund, £3,079,937.

ROYAL EXCHANGE ASSURANCE, for Fire, Life, and Marine Insurances. Chief Office, Rl. Exchange; Branch Office, 29, Pall Mall. Incorporated 1720. Total funds in hand exceed £4,000,000. For further particulars, see Advertisement, page 309.

ROYAL FARMERS' AND GENERAL INS. CO., FIRE, LIFE, & HAIL, 3, Norfolk-st, Strand. Est. 1840. Reserve in hand, £328,540.

ROYAL INSURANCE CO., 28, Lombard-st, 33, Chaucery-la, W.C., and 35, St. James's-st, S.W. Established 1845. Funds in hand December, 1883, £5,672,040.

SCEPTRE LIFE ASSO. LIMITED, 40, Finsbury-pavement, E.C. Established 1864. Reserve in hand, £320,000.

SCOTTISH AMICABLE LIFE ASSURANCE SOC., 1, Threadneedle-st. Established 1826. Accumulated funds, £2,800,000,

SCOTTISH EQUITABLE LIFE ASSURANCE SOC., 69, K. William-st, E.C. Established 1831. Funds in hand on 1st March, 1887, £2,889,114.

SCOTTISH IMPERIAL LIFE INSURANCE CO., 4, K. William-st, E.C. Established 1865. Total assets, £242,634.

SCOTTISH METROPOLITAN LIFE ASSURANCE CO., 79, Cornhill, E.C. Established 1876. Assets, £102,590.

SCOTTISH PROVIDENT INST., 17, K. William-st, E.C. Instituted 1837, incorporated 1848. The realised fund, which at the close of the previous year was £4,736,292, was largely increased during the year; the amount at 31st Dec., 1884, being upwards of £5,000,000.

SCOTTISH PROVINCIAL ASSURANCE CO., 64, Cannon-st, E.C. Established 1825. Total assets on 31st Jan., 1887, £1,693,455.

SCOTTISH UNION AND NATIONAL INSURANCE OFFICE (Fire, Life, and Annuities), 3, K. William-st, E.C. Established 1824. Total invested funds, £8,500,000.

SCOTTISH WIDOWS FUND. Established in 1815 for mutual life insurance. London office, 28, Cornhill, E.C. On the 31st Dec., 1887, the funds of the society amounted to upwards of £9,653,000, and the annual income to upwards of £1,150,000.

STANDARD LIFE ASSURANCE CO., 83, K. William-st, E.C., and 3, Pall Mall-east, S.W. Established 1825. Invested funds, £6,000,000; annual revenue, £900,000.

STAR LIFE ASSURANCE SOC. (Life and Annuities), 32, Moorgate-st, E.C. Established 1843. Assurance and annuity fund, £2,606,573 17s. 5d.

SUN FIRE OFFICE, 63, Threadneedle-st; 60, Charing ✝; and Oxford--st, corner of Vere-st. Established 1710.

SUN LIFE ASSURANCE SOC., 63, Threadneedle-st, E.C.; 60, Charing ✝; and at Oxford-st, corner of Vere-st. Established 1810. Total funds, £2,212,283.

UNIVERSAL LIFE ASSURANCE SOC., 1, K. William-st, E.C. Established 1834. Funds invested, £1,102,100.

VICTORIA MUTUAL LIFE AS

SURANCE SOC., LIMITED, Finsbury-sq-bdgs, E.C. Established 1860. Funds in hand, 31st Dec., 1887, £43,158. Premium income, £8,900.

WESTMINSTER AND GENERAL LIFE ASS. ASSO., 28, King-st, Covent-gdn, W.C. Established 1836. Amount of funds, £506,018; subscribed capital not called up, £95,000. Premium income, £48,435.

WESTMINSTER FIRE OFFICE, 27, King-st, Covent-gdn, W.C. Established 1717.

WEST OF ENGLAND INSURANCE CO., 20, New Bridge-st, E.C. Established 1807. Reserve in hand, £1,042,375; capital, £600,000.

International Club, corner of Northumberland-avenue and Trafalgar-sq.—Founded in 1888, for the association of gentlemen, without regard to nationality, politics, or religion. Annual subscription : Town members, £5 5s ; country, foreign, and colonial members, £3 3s. No other liability and no entrance fee at present. Full particulars from secretary on application.

Invalid Carriages and Chairs are supplied in endless variety ; and for the convenience of those who fortunately have only temporary need of such assistance, arrangements are also made for their hire. A self-propelling chair can be obtained at from 32s. to 42s., a mechanical invalid's bed at from 42s. to 63s., and a bath-chair at 42s. per lunar month. There are but few houses in the trade, whose names will be readily found in the Post Office Directory.

Irish Exhibition in London.—(See under OLYMPIA in APPENDIX.)

Irish Office.—The office of the Chief Secretary to the Lord-Lieutenant is at 17 and 18, Great Queen-st, S.W., and the hours are from 11 to 5. NEAREST Ry. Stn., St. James's-pk (Dis.) ; Omnibus Rtes., Victoria-st and Westminster-br ; Cab Rank, Tothill-st.

Ironmongers' Company (The) possess a broad frontage in Fenchurch-st, and a large though somewhat gloomy hall. In the court-room a number of the original charters of the company are to be seen hanging on the walls, together with an autograph letter from the notorious Judge Jeffrey.

In the hall is a portrait of Isaac Walton, and among other interesting paintings are a likeness of Mr. John Nicholl who wrote a history of the company, and Gainsborough's portrait of Lord Hood. Mrs. Margaret Dane is also represented. This worthy person bequeathed to the company a sum of money, the interest of which was to be spent in the purchase of faggots for the burning of witches. Nowadays the Ironmongers do not advocate extreme measures, and the money is devoted to the warming, not the burning, of the poor. The most admirable thing in the Ironmongers' Hall is the wood-carving round and about the fire-place—date about 1747.

Isle of Dogs.—An uninviting title euphemistically derived from " Isle of Ducks," and applied to what was at one time about the best imitation on a small scale of the Great Dismal Swamp to be found in England. The place was not until late years an island at all, but simply a peninsula jutting out into the river between Limehouse and Blackwall. Just at the beginning of the present century, however, the Corporation cut a canal through the neck of the "unlucky Isle of Doggs," as Master Pepys hath it, and so opened a short cut for ships bound up or down the river. Apparently, however, the new road was not found satisfactory, for it has been long since closed and sold to the East and West India Dock Company, who in 1870 converted it into the magnificent South-West India Dock, one of the finest of their splendid system. The isle itself is pretty well covered with ship-building and engineering yards, and was a few years since one of the busiest spots on the river bank. Strikes and trade quarrels have for the last few years considerably mitigated its prosperity, and the Isle of Dogs has at present a decided air of having been gathered to its godfathers, which, let us hope, it will soon again lay aside. Among things not generally known in this connection may be mentioned the very useful little railway forming part of the Great Eastern system, which runs right down the middle of the island, through the East and West India Docks, where there is a station, and past the Millwall Docks, where there is another, to a point on the river-

bank just opposite Greenwich, with which there is communication by steam ferry on the arrival and departure of each train.

Isthmian Club, Piccadilly, W. Established 1882. — Proprietary. For "Gentlemen who have been educated at one of the universities or public schools, and for officers of the army and navy." The election of members is by ballot, and vested in the committee. Subscription : Town members, £10 10s., country members (who must reside not less than 50 miles from London), £7 7s. The club is non-political, and formed for the association of gentlemen interested in rowing, cricket, and other sports.

Italian Exhibition (The), Earl's-ct, West Brompton.—(See APPENDIX.)

Italy. — EMBASSY, 24, Kensington - gate, S.W. NEAREST Ry. Stn., High-st Kensington ; Omnibus Rte., Kensington-rd ; Cab Rank, Queen's-gate, S.W. CONSULATE, 31, Old Jewry. NEAREST Ry. Stns., Mansion House (Dis.) and Moorgate-st (Met.); Omnibus Rtes., Cheapside and Moorgate-st ; Cab Rank, King-st.

ITALIAN BENEVOLENT SOCIETY, initiated by the Government of H.M. the King of Italy, and under the presidency of His Majesty's ambassador in London. Secretary, Signor P. F. Righetti, 10, Greville-st, Hatton-gdn, E.C. Relieving office of the Society, 10, Greville-st, Hatton-gdn. Hours of attendance, on Wed. and Sat. from 11 till 1 p.m. No Italian is excluded on account of his religious or political opinions. His moral character, however, will be considered in giving relief. The objects of the Society are :— To provide needy Italians with bread and lodging. To assist poor Italians who wish to return to their country, principally those in ill-health and women or children in distress. To help poor Italians to assistance from other charitable institutions. To procure medical and surgical attendance and medicine for the sick ; in case of death to provide decent burial. To give weekly assistance in cases of chronic disease, old age, &c. To procure places of nightly refuge, especially for Italian boys ; to use means to prevent ill-treatment of these boys by their masters, and to take legal measures to have justice done them. To direct those who give a satisfactory account of their conduct how to find employment. To do other beneficent works according to circumstances and means.

ITALIAN COURIERS' SOCIETY, 38, Golden-sq, W.C.

ITALIAN RESTAURANTS (CHEAP). The Café de la Paix (G. Pirovano's), 203, Oxford-st, and the Hotel d'Italie and Restaurant, 52, Old Compton-st, Soho, have been recommended to the EDITOR as good and cheap.

PREVITALI'S HOTEL, 14 to 18, Arundell-st, Coventry-st.

PROVISION DEALER: B. Perelli Rocco, 8, Greek-st, Soho.

SCUOLA SERALE E DOMENICALE GRATUITA PER GL' ITALIANI IN LONDRA, Little Saffron Hill, Hatton-gdn.

SOLFERINO HOTEL, 7 and 8, Rupert-st, Haymarket.

Japan.—MINISTRY, 9, Cavendish-sq, W. NEAREST *Ry. Stn.*, Portland-road (Met.); *Omnibus Rtes.*, Oxford-st and Regent-st; *Cab Rank*, Regent-st. CONSULATE, 84, Bishopsgate-st-within, E.C. NEAREST *Ry. Stn.*, *Omnibus Rte.*, and *Cab Rank*, Bishopsgate-st.

Jews.—The tangible benefits which flow from civil and religious liberty may be seen in the improved social and political status of the Jews of London, since the abolition of the Test Acts and the passing of the Jewish Emancipation Bill. Until within a comparatively recent period the Jews were deprived of the privileges of the universities; and as that of the capital was the first to break down the barrier of caste, the Jews affect the University of London more than any other seat of learning in the United Kingdom. A large number of Jewish youths pass through the City of London School, whence they have carried off many of the most important prizes, scholarships, &c. The community have their own colleges for the study of the Hebrew language and Rabbinical law in St. James's-place, Aldgate, and at Tavistock House, Tavistock-sq. Within the memory of living man the Jews of the metropolis were scarcely ever to be found resident outside their own quarter, at the east end of the City, embracing Bevis Marks, Aldgate, Houndsditch, the Minories, Haydon-sq (thirty years ago a garden surrounded with

substantial houses, now a busy railway centre), Goodman's-fields, Whitechapel, Petticoat-lane (since called Middlesex-st, but dear to the heart of Israel as "the lane"), part of Spitalfields, &c. A large number of rich Jewish families have migrated from the "four streets" (rows of handsomely appointed residences, which encompassed Goodman's-fields, formerly a green space used as a military exercising ground, but since built over), and taken up their quarters in Bayswater, Bloomsbury, and Maida-vale. So plentiful are Jewish households in the west district, that certain streets and terraces where they have formed colonies are playfully called the "New Jerusalem." Social persecution kept the chosen people together as in a sort of Ghetto; but the large spirit of toleration has scattered them broadcast over the City. Rag Fair, as it is called, the greatest old clothes market of the metropolis, is held in an open space close to Houndsditch. Sunday morning is its busiest time. There are also Sunday morning bazaars, for the sale of second-hand jewellery and plate, held in public rooms of certain well-known Jewish coffee-houses of the district, where valuable and portable property readily changes hands. Houndsditch is the head-quarters of the fancy warehousemen, mostly Jews, who supply the hawkers and small shopkeepers of London with combs, razors, sponges, and mock jewellery for the ornamentation of the ambitious poor and others. An immense trade in new and second-hand clothing, and in new boots, shoes, furs, caps, &c., for exportation to the colonies, is carried on in this quarter. The London artisan often purchases the tools of his trade in Petticoat-lane on Sunday mornings; where also may be bought the highly spiced confectionery in which the children of Israel delight—the brown and sweet "butter cake," the flaccid "bola," the "stuffed monkey," and a special pudding made of eggs and ground almonds. The poorer Jews of London eat Spanish olives and Dutch cucumbers pickled in salt and water, as food rather than as a relish. They love herrings steeped in brine, German sausage, the dried flesh of beef and mutton, smoked salmon, and, indeed, fish of all sorts, stewed with lemons and

eggs, or fried in oil. Every Jewish luxury may be obtained in perfection in Petticoat-lane, besides "cosher" meat, and matsoth or unleavened cakes, used at the Feast of the Passover, which falls about Eastertide. The Jews slaughter their beasts by cutting the animal's throat; the slaughterers being officials of the community, who affix seals to every portion of the carcase. The rabbis are also most particular in supervising the manufacture of the unleavened bread for the Passover. Raw and fried fish are staple commodities of "the lane," and several fried-fishmongers have been known to amass large fortunes. "Cosher" rum and shrub, and liqueurs, such as cloves, aniseed, noyeau, &c., of which the Jews are exceedingly fond, may be obtained in this quarter. Drunkenness, however, is an offence all but unknown. The Jews of London are among the best fathers, sons, and husbands in the metropolis. They are a most affectionate, home-staying, sober people; but their wealth has been much overrated. Since the persecution of the Jews of Russia in 1881, large numbers of their co-religionists, not over-burdened with worldly possessions, have settled in this country. Their poverty, however, is seldom obtrusive because of their many noble charities, the personal generosity of the great families among them, and their own natural thrift. There are shops for the sale of Hebrew books, and articles used in the rites of the synagogue, in Bevis Marks and in the streets abutting on Whitechapel and Commercial-road. The Jews of London support two newspapers, *The Jewish Chronicle* and *The Jewish World*, and they have several burial grounds devoted exclusively to their own use. They have no need of funeral reform, their religion enjoining the greatest simplicity in burying the dead; the use of feathers and bands is never permitted, and the coffin is always of plain unpainted and undraped wood. Thus, the Jews of London, even when ostentatious in life, practise humility in death.

HISTORY AND STATISTICS.— The question when the Jews first settled in England has not yet been satisfactorily answered. But it is beyond question that, soon after the Conquest, William I. invited large numbers of them to come over from Normandy. It is said that he appointed for their residence that part of the City termed the Old Jewry, and that their first synagogue was erected in the N.W. corner of the street. Their burial-ground, called "the Jews' Garden," was in St. Giles's, Cripplegate, on the spot now occupied by Jewin - st. After suffering great persecution, the Jews, numbering about 16,000, were banished from England by Edward I. in the year 1290, and for a period of 365 years but few Jews resided in this country. When Oliver Cromwell became Lord Protector, he was induced by Manasseh ben Israel, a rabbi of Amsterdam, to permit the Jews to return. In February, 1657, a piece of land was granted them for a burial-ground, and in the same year a synagogue was erected in King-st, Duke's-pl, by Jews who had originally come from Spain and Portugal. They were, at that time, treated by the law as aliens ; but every restriction has gradually been removed, and they are now placed on a footing of perfect equality with their fellow-citizens. The number of Jews resident in the metropolis is probably not less than 50,000.

RELIGIOUS ORGANISATION.— 1. The great majority of English Jews are Ashkenazim, whose ancestors came over from Germany (Ashkenaz), Holland, and Poland. They are under the spiritual supervision of the Chief Rabbi, Rev. Dr. Nathan Marcus Adler (formerly Chief Rabbi of Hanover), who was installed in his office in 1845. His health having begun to fail, he asked, in 1879, for a suffragan to aid him in the discharge of his duties. His son, the Rev. Dr. Hermann Adler, Chief Minister of the Bayswater Synagogue, was accordingly appointed his delegate.

The principal synagogues belonging to the Ashkenazim were incorporated into the United Synagogue by Act of Parliament, dated 14th July, 1870, 33 and 34 Vict. c. 116. The president of the United Synagogue is Lord Rothschild, and the secretary Dr. A. Asher. The synagogues at present comprised in the Union are : The Great Synagogue, St. James's-pl, Aldgate, E.; Hambro', Church-row, Fen-

church - st, E.C.; New, Great St. Helen's, E.C.; Bayswater, Chichester - pl, Harrow - rd, W.; Central, Great Portland-st, W.; Borough, Vowler-st, Walworth-rd, S.E.; North London, John-st-west, Thornhill-road, Barnsbury, N.; East London, Rectory-sq, Stepney-gn, E.; St. John's Wood, Abbey-rd, St. John's Wood, N.W.; New West End, St. Peters-burg-pl, Bayswater, W., and the Dalston Synagogue, Poet's-road, Canonbury, N. The following synagogues, though under the spiritual supervision of the Chief Rabbi, are not consti-tuents of the United Syna-gogue : Western Synagogue, St. Alban's-pl, S.W.; Maiden Lane, Maiden-lane, Covent-gdn, W.C.; Besides the above, there are over fifty minor synagogues, which have recently been united. The president and vice-president of this federation of Chevras (as they are termed), are Lord Roths-child and S. Montagu, Esq., M.P., respectively.

2. The Sephardim Community includes those Jews whose an-cestors originally came from Spain and Portugal. The Sephardim differ from the Ashkenazim in the pronunciation of Hebrew and in some points of liturgy. Their lead-ing member was Sir Moses Monte-fiore, Bart., who died 28th July, 1885, in his 101st year. Their ecclesiastical chief is the Rev. Dr. Moses Gaster, who was appointed in 1887. Their place of worship is in Bevis Marks, with a branch syna-gogue in Upper Bryanston-st, W. In addition to these places of wor-ship, there is the West London Synagogue of British Jews, in Upper Berkeley-st, W., the members of which differ from the before - mentioned congregations in some matters of ritual. Their Chief Minister is the Rev. Prof. Marks.

These synagogues furnish sitting accommodation for about 15,000 adults.

The Jewish Cemeteries in London are : Willesden-lane, Wil-lesden; Forest-gate, West Ham; Mile End-rd, E.; Kingsbury-rd, Ball's-pond; Bancroft-rd, Mile End ; and Jeremy's-green-lane, Edmonton.

EDUCATIONAL INSTITUTIONS. —The following is a list of the more important Jewish educa-

tional institutions in the metro-polis :—The Beth Hamidrash College, St. James's-pl, Aldgate, at which classes are held three times a week for the exposition of biblical and post-biblical works in Hebrew ; lecturer and librarian, the Rev. Dayan Spiers. Jews' College, Tavistock-ho, Tavistock-sq, for the training of Jewish ministers ; prin-cipal, Dr. Friedländer. Jews' Free School, Bell-lane, Spitalfields ; the largest elementary school in Eng-land, the average daily attend-ance being 3,150 children. The Government grant received by the school in 1885 was £2,988. Head master, Mr. M. Angel. Jews' Infant Schools, Commercial-st, E., and Tenter-st, Goodman's-fields, E. Jews' Hospital and Orphan Asylum, Lower Norwood, "for the support of the aged, and the maintenance, education, and em-ployment of youth ;" 250 inmates. Jews' Deaf and Dumb Home, Walmer-rd, Notting-hill. Stepney Jewish Schools, Stepney-gn, E. Westminster Jews' Free School, Hanway-pl, Oxford-st. Borough Jewish Schools, Heygate-st, Wal-worth. Bayswater Jewish Schools, St. James's-ter, Harrow-rd, W. High Class School for Girls, Chenies-st, Tottenham-ct-rd. The following schools are attached to the Spanish and Portuguese Jews' Synagogue : College, Heneage-la ; "Gates of Hope" Incorporated School, Heneage-la ; National In-fant and Villareal Girls' School ; Spanish and Portuguese Jews' Orphan Inst. In addition to these schools there are the following in-stitutions : Jews' College Literary Society. This society has been organised with the object of delivering lectures and reading papers on subjects connected with Hebrew literature and Jewish history. The Association for the Diffusion of Religious Know-ledge. Under the auspices of this association, Sabbath schools are held every Saturday. The association has also formed classes for instruction in Hebrew and the Jewish religion in connection with several Board schools. Jewish Working Men's Club, 45, Great Alie-st, E.; Working Lads' Institute, Hutchison-st, Aldgate ; Girls' Club. There are libraries containing the standard works of Hebrew literature at the Beth Hamidrash, Jews' College, Jews' Free School, and the New West End Synagogue.

CHARITIES AND OTHER ASSO-
CIATIONS.—The more important
of these associations are as follows :
*The London Committee of Depu-
ties of the British Jews*, consisting
of representatives of the metropolitan and provincial congregations
of Jews. It is the purpose of this
board to "watch over the interests
of the Jews in this empire, and
deliberate on what may conduce
to their welfare and improve their
general condition. The board also
use their influence and exertions
in favour of Jewish communities
or individuals in foreign countries
in cases of oppression, wrong, or
misfortune which may come under
their notice." President, Arthur
Cohen, Esq., Q.C., *The Anglo-
Jewish Association*, "for the promotion of the moral and social
advancement of the Jews throughout the world, and for the removal
of the disabilities under which
they are still labouring in many
countries." President, Sir Julian
Goldsmid, M.P. *The Board of
Guardians*, for relief of the Jewish
poor, Devonshire-sq, Bishopsgate,
E. President, Benjamin L. Cohen,
Esq. *Bread, Meat, and Coal
Charity*; the expenditure £1,700
per annum. President, J. De
Castro, Esq., *Institute for the
Relief of the Indigent Blind*.
President, Alderman Sir B. S.
Phillips. *Jewish Ladies' Benevo-
lent Loan Society*. President,
Lady de Rothschild. *Jewish
Convalescent Home*, Portland-rd,
S. Norwood ; founded in memory
of Judith, Lady Montefiore ; Presi-
dent, Mrs. Adler. *Convalescent
Home for Infants*, Lower Tooting.
*Jewish Home for the Aged and
Disabled*, Stepney-gn, E. *Hand-
in-Hand Asylum*, for reduced
Jewish tradesmen. *Poor Jews'
Temporary Shelter*, Leman-st, E.,
and *Jewish Ladies' Association
for Preventive and Rescue Work*.
President, Lady Rothschild.
Various almshouses to accommodate about 150 inmates. The
Spanish and Portuguese "*Beth
Holim*" *Hospital*, Mile-end-rd, E.
Three of the great London hospitals have specially-endowed
wards set apart for Jewish
patients, viz., the London, Metropolitan Free, and Evelina
Hospitals. The latter was
founded by Baron Ferdinand
de Rothschild in memory of his
wife, whose name it bears. Besides
the above, there are upwards of
a hundred minor charitable and

friendly societies, chiefly in the
east of London, in connection with
the Jewish community.

**Judge Advocate-Gene-
ral's Office.**—This department
is charged with the administration
of military law. The office is at
35, Great George-st, S.W., and
the hours are from 10 to 4.
NEAREST *Ry. Stn.*, Westminster-
br ; *Omnibus Rtes.*, Whitehall and
Victoria-st ; *Cab Rank*, Palace-yd.

**Junior Army and Navy
Club,** 10, St. James's-st, S.W.—
Members must be commissioned
officers in the Regular Army, Royal
Navy, Royal Marines, and Royal
Indian Forces, and those who may
have retired from the same. The
admission of candidates is now
vested in the committee. Number
of members, 1,500. Entrance fee,
£21 ; subscription, £8 8s.

Junior Athenæum Club,
116, Piccadilly, W.—Members of
both Houses of Parliament,
members of the universities,
fellows of the learned and
scientific societies, and gentlemen,
are eligible for election. The
committee elect. Number of
ordinary members, 1,000. Subscription, £10 10s.

Junior Carlton, 30, Pall
Mall, is a political club in strict
connection with the Conservative
party, and designed to promote its
objects. Gentlemen of position who
acknowledge the recognised leaders
of the Conservative party are alone
eligible as candidates. Entrance
fee (including subscription to
library), £38 17s. ; subscription,
£10 10s.

**Junior Constitutional
Club,** 14, Regent-st, W.—Established in 1887 as a political club
for gentlemen professing Conservative principles. No entrance fee
at present. Annual subscription :
town members, £3 3s. ; country
members, £1 1s.

Junior Garrick Club,
1A, Adelphi-terrace.—Proprietary.
"All members of the dramatic
profession, or any branch of the
dramatic art, as actors, vocalists,
dramatic authors, managers of
theatres, acting managers, com-
posers, instrumental performers,
and scenic artists, practically pursuing or having practically followed as their vocation any of the
above branches of dramatic profession shall always be eligible for
admission as members of the club."
The committee elect. No en-

trance fee at present ; subscription,
£3 3s. ; country members, £2 2s.
It is also open to *non*-members of
the above professions.

Junior Travellers' Club,
96 & 97, Piccadilly, W.—Established in 1886 on a similar basis to
that of the Travellers' Club. Proprietary, and distinctly non-political. Entrance fee, £10 10s ; annual
subscription, £8 8s. for members
living in London, £5 5s. for
country members. Full information from secretary.

**Junior United Service
Club,** 11 & 12, Charles-st, St.
James's, consists of the princes of
the blood royal, commissioned
officers of the Navy, Army, Marines, Royal Indian Forces, and
Regular Militia, Lord-Lieutenants
of Counties, second-lieutenants in
the Army, and midshipmen in the
Navy. No officer is eligible for
admission to the club who is not
on full, half, or retired full pay
of the Navy, Army, Marines, or
Royal Indian Forces ; or who, if
an officer of Militia, has not one
year's embodied service or attended
six regular trainings, certified by
the commanding officer, adjutant,
or paymaster of the regiment.
Militia candidates may be proposed after serving one training, or
one month's service. No retired
officer can be entered as a
candidate unless his name
appears in the official Army List,
and he has served for five years
previous to retirement ; and no
officer of Militia who has not previously belonged to the regular
forces unless he is actually serving.
Entrance fee, £40 ; subscription,
£7 7s. Every member has the
privilege of introducing three
friends to breakfast, lunch, or dine
with him. Election by ballot of the
members during February, March,
April, May, June, and July. One
black ball in ten excludes.

Kennel Club, 6, Cleveland-
row, St. James's, S.W., endea-
vours in every way to promote
the general improvement of dogs,
dog-shows, and dog trials. The
election of members is vested
solely in the committee, and is
made by ballot, three members of
the committee being a quorum at
such ballot, and two black balls
excluding. Entrance fee, £5 5s. ;
subscription, £5 5s. Any member
violating the rules and regulations
of the club for the time being in
force, is liable to be expelled by

he committee; and any member of the club who shall be proved to the satisfaction of the committee to have in any way misconducted himself in connection with dogs or dog-shows, or to have in any way acted in opposition to the fundamental rules and principles upon which the club has been established, or in any other manner which would make it undesirable that he should continue to be a member, is to be requested to retire from the club; and if a resolution to that effect shall be carried by three-fourths of the committee present at the meeting duly summoned to consider the case, the member so requested to retire thenceforth ceases to be a member of the club, and his subscription for the current year shall not be returned to him. No member of the club shall, under any circumstances, knowingly, either enter or exhibit a dog, or dogs, at any competition under a false name, age, pedigree, breeder, or description. The rules of the club as to dog-shows, field-trials, &c., which have been very carefully framed, may be obtained on application to the secretary.

Kennington Park (Map 13) is little more than a large square, and contains only about a dozen acres. It is, however, prettily planted, and occupies the site of the old Kennington Common, the scene of the memorable Chartist *fiasco* of 1848. NEAREST *Ry. Stn.,* Walworth-rd ; *Omnibus Rtes.,* Harleyford-rd, Kennington-rd, and Kennington-pk-rd.

Kensington Gardens (Map 5) adjoin Hyde-pk. from which they are divided by a haha and sunk well. They are thickly wooded, almost the only open space being that occupied by that favourite resort of skaters, the Round Pond, with the vista leading from it in the direction of the park. It has to some extent a mildly scientific character, a large proportion of its trees and shrubs having labels attached showing their Linnæan classification, country of origin, &c., and the collection of flowering trees along the north walk is in springtime almost worth a run up from the country to see.

Kensington Palace (Map 5) —A heavy brick building in the comfortable commonplace style of Queen Anne, chiefly noteworthy as having been the birthplace of her present most gracious Majesty. The north row of big houses known as Palace-gdns occupies the site of the old garden of the palace, the former proportions of which—never very magnificent — have been of late years much contracted in many ways. NEAREST *Ry. Stn.,* High-st, Kensington, and Notting Hill - gate; *Omnibus Rtes.,* Kensington · rd and Uxbridge-rd ; *Cab Rank,* Kensington-rd.

Kew Gardens are not only among the most favourite resorts of the London holiday maker, but have special value to the botanist and horticulturist. The judicious expenditure of public money has made the gardens and houses at Kew almost unique among public institutions of the kind. Here are to be seen flourishing in an atmosphere of their own, though in an uncongenial climate, the most beautiful tropical palms, plants, ferns, fern-trees, and cacti ; and the pleasure grounds and arboretum contain in endless and exhaustive profusion specimens of the flowers, shrubs, and trees indigenous to Great Britain. Attached to the gardens is a valuable museum of useful vegetable products. The gardens are at present open free to the public every day in the week at noon, as well as on Sunday afternoons ; the morning hours being reserved for the necessary work of the gardeners, curators, and students. From Waterloo (40 min.), 1st, 1/2, 1/9 ; 2nd, 1/-, 1/4 ; 3rd, -/9, 1/2.

King's College, Strand (Map 7).—The work of the coll. is carried on in eight departments, viz. : (1) The theological department, morning and evening classes ; (2) The department of general literature and science ; (3) The department of engineering and applied sciences ; (4) The medical department ; (5) The work of the evening classes embraces classes of all kinds, corresponding to those in the regular departments ; (6) The Civil Service Department, in preparation for the upper and lower branches of the Home Civil Service ; (7) The department for ladies, carried on at 13, Kensington-sq ; (8) The School. Although by the creation of the above departments the studies are classified as a direction to the students, yet occasional students are admitted to any one or more classes without any restriction or qualification. Rooms are provided within the walls of the coll. for the residence of a limited number of matriculated students. The censor of the coll. lives within its walls, and has the superintendence of all resident students. Students also may be received by leave of the council as boarders in certain private families. Full information about the coll. can be obtained from the separate prospectus of each department, and from the Calendar (3s. by post), for which application should be made to the Sec. NEAREST *Ry. Stn.,* Temple (Dis.) ; *Omnibus Rte.,* Strand ; *Cab Rank,* Catherine-st.

King's College School, Strand. In connection with King's Coll.—The school is divided into (1) The Clinical Division ; (2) Mathematical Division ; (3) Mercantile Division ; (4) Lower or Preparatory Division. The general age of admission is from 8 to 16 years. The fees for the whole regular course of instruction in either division, including stationery and use of books, amount to £8 per term for those entering under 16 years of age ; £10 per term for those entering over 16 years of age. The entrance fees amount to £2 13s. 6d. Boys may be received as boarders. All further information may be obtained of the Sec., at the school. NEAREST *Ry. Stn.,* Temple (Dis.) ; *Omnibus Rte.,* Strand ; *Cab Rank,* Catherine-st.

King's Cross (Map 3) ; once called Battlebridge, and decorated with a statue of George IV., which has been relegated to limbo ; is situate at the east end of the Euston-road, at its junction with the York and Gray's-inn roads. Here is the externally hideous but inwardly commodious terminus of the Great Northern Railway, and nearly opposite is a station of the Metropolitan Railway, so that King's Cross is an even more convenient neighbourhood from which to escape to any other part of the world, than most places in London. Just outside the station is the Great Northern Hotel. NEAREST *Ry. Stn.,* King's ✠ (Met.) ; *Omnibus Rtes.,* Euston-rd and Gray s-inn-rd ; *Cab Fare* to Bank or Charing ✠, 1/6.

Ladies Shopping without male escort, and requiring luncheon, can safely visit any of the great restaurants — care being always taken to avoid passing through a drinking-bar. In some cases a separate room is set apart for ladies, but there is practically no reason why the public room should be avoided. At some of the great "omnium gatherum" shops, and at institutions such as South Kensington and the Rl. Academy, luncheon can be obtained, while several confectioners at the West End particularly study the comfort of ladies, who are also specially catered for at Verrey's Restaurant in Regent-st.

Ladies' Victoria Club, 3, Old Cavendish-st, W. A residential club exclusively for ladies, who are admitted members on the recommendation of a patroness, member, or other suitable reference. Subscription, £2 2s. Entrance fee, £2 2s. Family tickets, £5 5s. Bedrooms can be had for long or short periods.

Lady Artists, Society of. Pictures received early in March. Fee paid by all exhibitors, members or otherwise, 2s., to be returned if the work be not placed. Number of members, 31; associates, 25. Non-professional exhibitors pay a fee of half-a-guinea for the placing of one or two pictures; for more than two, one guinea. Exhibitors are charged 10 per cent. on the price of works sold. The exhibitions of the society are held in the Drawing-room Gallery, Egyptian Hall, Piccadilly. All particulars can be obtained by sending a stamped and directed envelope addressed to the secretary, Miss Fanny E. Partridge, 2, York-pl, Portman-sq, or to the agents, Messrs. Jennings, 16, Duke-st, Manchester-sq. Admission to the exhibition, 1s.; catalogues, 6d. each.

Lambeth Bridge (Map 13) is perhaps the ugliest ever built. It was also—when it was built, at all events — supposed to be the cheapest. It is a suspension-bridge of three spans, and one great economy in its construction consists in the use of wire cables in place of the usual chains. It connects Westminster with Lambeth, where it lands close by the Archbishop's Palace. NEAREST Ry. Stn., South side as for Lambeth

Palace. North side, Ry. Stn., St. James's-pk (Dis.); Omnibus Rte., Victoria-st.

Lambeth Palace (Map 13). — This building, for centuries the official residence of the Archbishops of Canterbury, is situate nearly opposite to the Houses of Parliament. The Lollards' Tower, the chapel, the great hall, the great dining-room, and the magnificent library, which contains a remarkable collection of MSS., black-letter tracts, &c., are the principal attractions. The picture-gallery and the guard chamber contain many curious portraits. Few of the London sights are better worth a visit than Lambeth Palace. NEAREST Ry. Stns., Westminster-br (Dis.) and Vauxhall; Omnibus Rtes., Westminster-br-rd, Kennington-rd, Palace-rd, and Harleyford-rd.

Lancaster Club, Lancaster House, Savoy, established in 1882 "upon a non-political and social basis, and intended to meet the requirements of those who wish for the comforts and conveniences of a first-class West End club." Election by ballot, at present vested in the committee. Annual subscription, town members £3 3s., country members £2 2s., the first 250 being admitted without entrance fee, members incurring no responsibility beyond payment of their subscriptions.

La Plata.—(See ARGENTINE REPUBLIC.)

Law Courts.—Prior to the Conquest there was only one superior court of justice in the kingdom. This court, called the curia regis, originally sat at Westminster, where the king had a palace, and his treasury and exchequer. It seems to have been originally held at Westminster in a chamber called the Exchequer Chamber (or chamber ornamented with stars), which was probably the chamber in which in Edward III.'s time the king sat with his council to levy fines and amercements for the exchequer. Here, too, subsequently sat the celebrated Star Chamber. The hall of Westminster, or, as it is now called, Westminster Hall, was built in the time of William Rufus; and it was in this hall up to the year 1820 that the courts were held. The curia regis being bound to follow the king in his progresses, the trial of common causes was found

much delayed; and it was therefore enacted in Magna Charta that the Common Pleas should sit certo loco. This place was Westminster, and from that time the Common Pleas sat in Westminster Hall. The King's Bench and the Exchequer still continued to follow the king to any place where he might be; but, as time went on, the courts became separated, and the King's Bench appears to have sat in Westminster Hall from the time of Henry III. The Chancery was separated from the curia regis as early as the reign of Richard I., but it was not until about the reign of Henry VIII. that the Chancery sat regularly in the Hall, and then only in term time. Out of term the Chancellors sat at various places, sometimes at their own houses.

The appearance of the courts as they were held in the Hall up to the year 1820 is well represented in the familiar drawing of Gravelot. Each court consisted of a simple bench raised within a canopy and side curtain, a bench beneath for the officers of the court, a bar within which were assembled the Queen's Counsel, and outside stood the barristers and the public. The Chancery and King's Bench were stationed at the extreme end of the Hall, opposite the great door, near which, in the north-western corner, was the Common Pleas. The rest of the Hall was taken up by the stalls of booksellers, fruiterers, and others, who plied their trade with as much zeal and noise as did the advocates higher up the Hall. It is not quite known where the Exchequer was; it was probably held, at least ordinarily, in the Exchequer Chamber, which was also used for the arguments of great questions of law.

So matters stood up to 1820 when the courts lately in use were built. The pressure of business, however, soon drove the Chancery Court to Lincoln's-inn, where new courts were erected for the administration of that branch of the law. The new courts at Westminster were also soon found inadequate for the business of the common law, and they had not been built ten years when a violent dispute arose as to their capacity for the constantly increasing business. This agitation gradually increased until it culminated in the scheme of the new Palace of Justice, Fleet-st (Map 7), completed in 1882,

---

The present courts in the metropolis are the following:

HOUSE OF LORDS (THE).—The court of ultimate appeal in the kingdom sits in the House of Lords itself to hear appeals from the courts of appeal in England, Scotland and Ireland. The House sits not only during the sittings of Parliament, but also during the prorogation at times appointed by the House during the previous session, while the Queen has power, by writing under her sign manual, to authorise them to hear appeals during a dissolution. The appeals are by case, and are regulated by the standing orders of the House, which must be strictly followed. The House of Lords at present in use was opened for judicial business in the year 1847, the old house having been destroyed by fire in the year 1834.

JUDICIAL COMMITTEE OF THE PRIVY COUNCIL (THE) hears appeals from the colonies as well as ecclesiastical cases. It sits in Downing-st, and presents this extraordinary feature, that the judgment of the majority is given as the judgment of the whole court, dissenting judges having no power to express their dissent in any shape or way. Besides the judges who are appointed to sit in the Privy Council, the bishops and archbishops sit as assessors in ecclesiastical cases.

SUPREME COURT OF JUDICATURE (THE), as at present constituted, consists of the *Court of Appeal* and the *High Court of Justice*. The former takes appeals from the Common Law Division, the latter from the Chancery Divisions, including Bankruptcy Appeals. The *High Court of Justice* consists of five Divisions, viz.: the Chancery, Queen's Bench, Common Pleas, Exchequer, and Probate, Divorce, and Admiralty Divisions.

The Queen's Bench Division still retains exclusive jurisdiction over the civil and criminal proceedings previously exercised by the Crown side of the Court of Queen's Bench; the Common Pleas Division retains jurisdiction over appeals from Revising Barristers; while the Exchequer retains its powers as a Court of Revenue.

The sittings of the High Court of Appeal, and the sittings in London and Middlesex of the High Court of Justice, are four in number, viz.: The Michaelmas Sittings, commencing on the 2nd of November, and terminating on the 21st of December; the Hilary Sittings, commencing on the 11th of January, and terminating on the Wednesday before Easter; the Easter Sittings, commencing on the Tuesday after Easter week, and terminating on the Friday before Whit Sunday; and the Trinity Sittings, commencing on the Tuesday after Whitsun week, and terminating on the 8th of August. The Common Law Divisions sit at 10.30 daily, and rise at 4, except on Saturdays, when they rise at 2. The different Courts of the Chancery Division generally sit at 10. The Vacations of the Supreme Court are four in number, the Long Vacation, commencing on the 10th of August, and terminating on the 24th of October; the Christmas Vacation, commencing on the 24th of December, and terminating on the 6th of January; the Easter Vacation, commencing on Good Friday and terminating on Easter Tuesday; and the Whitsun Vacation, commencing on the Saturday before Whit Sunday, and terminating on the Tuesday after Whit Sunday. During the Long Vacation two judges sit occasionally, generally once a week, to dispose of pressing business, and these Vacation judges (chosen at the beginning of the year) have likewise the power to dispose of such business during other parts of the year when the Courts are not sitting, at times which may not strictly be in vacation. The sittings of the Courts are interrupted at intervals by reason of the Judges having to go on the various circuits, which are now held four times a year. Certain of the Judges are also selected to hear election petitions.

COURT FOR THE CONSIDERATION OF CROWN CASES RESERVED (THE) sits from time to time in each sitting, to hear appeals on questions of law in criminal cases, there being no appeal in such cases on questions of fact.

LONDON BANKRUPTCY COURT (THE) is held in Lincoln's-inn-fields, the public entrances being 5, Portugal-st, and 34, Lincoln's-inn-fields. The court is open during vacation, when the office hours are 11 till 2; in term they are 10 till 4, except on Sat., when they are 10 till 2.

SHERIFFS' COURT (THE), Red Lion-sq, is held merely for the assessment of damages, in cases in which the liability is admitted, and the sole question is the amount of damages to be awarded, as well as in cases for the assessment of compensation under the Lands Clauses Act. It has no fixed sessions, but when any assessment of any nature has to be made, an appointment for the hearing is fixed at the office.

RAILWAY COMMISSIONERS (THE) were appointed in 1873 for the purpose of carrying into effect the provisions of the Railway and Canal Traffic Act, 1854, whereby railway and canal companies are required, amongst other things, to afford all reasonable facilities for the forwarding of traffic, and to give no undue preference in favour of any particular person. The commissioners are three in number, and sit from time to time at Westminster.

WRECK COMMISSIONERS' COURT (THE) is held at Westminster and other places, when requested by the Board of Trade, to hold investigations into shipping casualties and the same are generally held by one of the Wreck Commissioners (of whom there cannot be more than three in existence at one time) sitting with assessors. The court derives its powers from the Merchant Shipping Act, 1876.

ECCLESIASTICAL COURTS (THE) are two in number:

Arches Court (The) is a Court of appeal belonging to the Archbishop of Canterbury. It is held in Westminster, and it has jurisdiction to try appeals from each of the diocesan courts within the province, the diocesan courts taking cognizance of all ecclesiastical matters arising within their respective limits.

Consistory Court of London (The) is the ordinary court of the bishop, in which all the ecclesiastical causes within his jurisdiction are tried. It is generally held at the Chapter House, St. Paul's, but not always.

CENTRAL CRIMINAL COURT (THE) is held at the Old Bailey. It has jurisdiction to try all treasons, murders, felonies, and misdemeanours committed within the city of London and county of Middlesex, and certain parts of Essex, Kent, and Surrey. The commissions of Oyer and Terminer are issued annually, and on the first day of the Michaelmas sittings the commissioners assemble to fix the sittings, which must be at least twelve in every year, and to appoint the judges who are to attend them according to a certain rota. The list of sittings can always be obtained on application to the clerk of the court.

Two judges attend every session to try the more serious offences, while the Recorder, Common Serjeant, and Judge of the Sheriffs' Court preside over the other. In each court one alderman at the least must be present.

Besides this jurisdiction, it may be mentioned that the court has an additional jurisdiction, to try offences committed on the high seas, within the jurisdiction of the Admiralty of England.

POLICE COURTS (THE).—(See POLICE.) — The magistrates of these courts are all stipendiaries, and may do any act directed to be done by more than one justice, except at petty sessions. Within the City of London there are two police-courts, viz., the Mansion House and Guildhall. In these courts the Lord Mayor and Aldermen of the City are empowered to act alone, and to do all things which are otherwise required to be done by more than one justice. Within the City, too, any two justices having jurisdiction therein have all the powers which any one magistrate of the before-mentioned police-courts has; while outside the districts assigned to the police-courts, but within the Metropolitan District, two magistrates, besides having the ordinary county jurisdiction, have also, when sitting together, the powers of a single magistrate in the same way as two justices within the City of London. The limits of the Metropolitan Police District exclude the City of London, but include the whole of Middlesex and parts of Surrey, Hertford, Essex, and Kent, within a radius of about 15 miles from Charing-✝. The police-courts are regulated by 2 & 3 Vict. c. 71, and 3 & 4 Vict. c. 84, while the City Police is regulated by 2 & 3 Vict. c. 44. The magistrates sitting in the police-courts have a summary and regular jurisdiction. This jurisdiction is regulated by various Acts of Parliament, and enables them to dispose of cases coming within it in a summary manner. Such proceedings in respect of a variety of minor offences, which are prohibited only

under pecuniary penalties. This power they can also exercise in cases of larceny, when the value of the property stolen does not exceed 5s., provided that the person charged consent to that course being adopted, and provided also that the offence is not one which, owing to a previous conviction, is punishable with penal servitude, in which case the magistrate can sentence the prisoner to three months' imprisonment. In cases of simple larceny exceeding 5s., if the case be one which may be properly disposed of in a summary manner, and if the prisoner plead guilty, the magistrates have power then to sentence him to six months' imprisonment. In cases beyond the summary jurisdiction, they are bound, if a sufficient case be made out, to commit the prisoner for trial.

MIDDLESEX SESSIONS (THE) are held at the Sessions House, Clerkenwell-gn, and at the Sessions House, Westminster; at the former the court sits to try criminal cases and to transact county business, at the latter to hear appeals. The list of sittings for the year is made up in December, and can be obtained at the office of the clerk of the peace, Clerkenwell-gn. A general and adjourned general sessions are held in each month, except in those months appointed for the ordinary quarter sessions, when the quarter sessions and an adjourned quarter sessions are held. There are thus twenty-four sessions in the year. The grand jury are summoned on the Mon., when they take the men's cases, the bills for the women's cases are taken on the Tu., and a special day is fixed for the bail cases. The court consists of a bench of magistrates, presided over by the Assistant-Judge. The appeal days will also be found on the printed list, and are fixed generally in the months of January, April, July, and October; while the applications for licences for music and dancing are generally fixed for a day in October.—(See SESSIONS.)

GENERAL ASSESSMENT SESSIONS (THE) for the metropolis, are held in February in each year in the Westminster Sessions House, before three justices of Middlesex (of whom the Assistant-Judge must be one), two of London, two of Kent, and two of Surrey, who are appointed yearly in October, for determining appeals against the Valuation List made

under the Valuation Act, 1869. These lists are made up every five years during which time they form the basis on which the hereditaments therein valued are to be rated. The first list under the Act came into operation on the 6th April, 1871, so it is from this date the quinquennial period is to be calculated. During this quinquennial period, however, supplemental lists are made each year to meet the cases where alterations in the lists have taken place in the preceding twelve months, or of houses which have been built or altered between the times at which the valuation list is made out. It is for the purpose of hearing appeals from these various lists that the assessment sessions are held.

GENERAL ANNUAL LICENSING MEETING (THE) for Middlesex and Surrey, is required, by 9th Geo. IV. c. 61, to be held within the first ten days of March in each year. The day, hour, and place of such meeting must be fixed by the justices, 21 days before the meeting. At this meeting the justices assembled are likewise to appoint not less than four or more than eight special sessions for transferring licences from one person to another and for other contingencies. By long usage the general annual licensing meeting for the City of London is held on the second Monday of the month of March, the Act of 9th Geo. IV. c. 61, not applying to the City of London. If the justices refuse to grant a new licence there is no appeal, and even if they grant one it will not be valid until it be confirmed by the Confirming Committee. The only appeal is against the refusal to renew or transfer a licence, in which case an appeal lies to the quarter sessions.

CONFIRMATION COMMITTEE (THE) is held to confirm the grant of new licences to sell liquor to be consumed on the premises without which such grant would not be valid.

SURREY SESSIONS (THE) are held at Newington. There are at least twelve sessions a year, and generally thirteen, and sometimes fourteen— the two latter being for gaol deliveries prior to the assizes. The list of sittings can be obtained at the court. Its proceedings are substantially the same as the Middlesex Sessions, the annual licensing meeting being regulated by the same Acts as regulate the holding of the same in Middlesex.

SPECIAL SESSIONS are also held at the different special sessional divisions in the metropolis for various purposes, such as the poor rates, highways, and others. These are always fixed by the justices of special sessions, and particulars of them can be obtained upon application to the clerks of the several sessional divisions.

COURTS WITHIN THE CITY.—
The Lord Mayor's Court.—This is an inferior court, but has jurisdiction over all actions without any limitation as to the amount of the debt or damages claimed, provided that in cases where the claim is over £50 the whole cause of action arose within the City. In cases under £50 no objection to the jurisdiction can be taken, provided that the defendant dwells or carries on his business within the City at the time of action brought, or provided he shall have done so within six months before that time, or if the cause of action either wholly or in part arose therein. This court also awards compensation under the Lands Clauses Act. The court sits every month at the Guildhall, the judge being the Recorder, the Common Serjeant, or a deputy appointed by them. In certain cases there is an appeal to the superior courts. The procedure of this court is regulated by the Mayor's Court Procedure Act. 1857 (20 & 21 Vict. . 157).

City of London Court (The), formerly called the Sheriffs' Court of the City of London, is now practically a county court, and is held at the Guildhall-bdgs in the City of London ; the offices being open from 10 till 4, except on Sat., when they are open from 10 till 1. It has jurisdiction up to £50, and is regulated by 15 & 16 Vict. c. 77.

Secondaries' Court (The) is a Sheriffs' Court, and is held in the City of London, at the Guildhall. It occupies the same position in the City as the Sheriffs' Court, and Lion-sq, does in the county of Middlesex, with the exception that it does not assess damages under the Lands Clauses Act, which cases are heard in the Mayor's Court.

City Sessions (The) are held for the purpose of granting and transferring licences within the City of London. They are held at the Guildhall from time to time, and information as to them can always be obtained upon application at the Guildhall.

Hustings Court, an ancient court in the City, now obsolete.

The NEW LAW COURTS (for description, see DICKENS'S DICTIONARY OF LONDON for 1880) were opened by the Queen on December 4th, 1882, and are now the head-quarters of the legal business of London. NEAREST (to the Palace of Justice) *Ry. Stn.,* Temple (Dis.) ; *Omnibus Rtes.,* Strand, Fleet-st, and Chancery-la ; *Cab Rank,* St. Clement's Church.

Lawn Tennis. —(*See* ALL ENGLAND.)

Law Society (Incorporated) of the United Kingdom, 103 to 113, Chancery-la.—This society of attorneys, solicitors, and proctors was established in 1827, and was incorporated by charter in 1831. In 1833 it instituted courses of lectures for articled clerks and students ; in 1836 the judges issued regulations, under which the council, jointly with the masters of the courts, act as examiners of candidates for admission on the roll ; in 1843, it was appointed Registrar of Attorneys, under the 6 & 7 Vict. c. 73 ; in 1845, it obtained a second charter containing extended powers ; and in 1872 a supplemental charter enlarging its constitution. Additional powers and duties were conferred on the society by the 23 & 24 Vict. c. 127. All persons are examined before entering into and also during their articles of clerkship. In 1877, the power of making regulations for the conduct of the preliminary, intermediate, and final examinations, and of appointing examiners, was practically vested in the Incorporated Law Society, under 40 & 41 Vict. c. 25 (The Solicitors Act, 1877). *Admission fee :* If the solicitor is proposed as a member within five years from his first certificate, £2 town, £1 country. After that time, £5 town, £2 country. *Annual subscription :* town members, £2 ; country, £1. The institution comprises the following departments : The Hall, open daily from 9 a.m. till 9 p.m., is furnished with the votes and proceedings of Parliament, the *London Gazette,* morning and evening newspapers, reviews, and other publications. The library is open daily from 9 a.m. to 9 p.m., except from August 10th to October 24th, when it is closed at 6 p.m., and on Saturdays, when it is closed at 4 p.m. It comprises upwards of 24,000 volumes, and is divided into two parts : the north and south wings are for the exclusive use of members. The articled clerks of members are admitted to the law library on payment of an annual subscription of £2. Lectures on the different branches of the law are delivered in the hall on each Thursday from November to June inclusive. The members are entitled to attend gratis, and their clerks (whether articled or not) are admitted on payment of £1 11s. 6d. for each set of lectures, or £3 3s. for the whole. The clerks of gentlemen not members pay £2 2s. for each set, or £4 4s. for the whole ; and other students, not falling within either of those classes, are admitted on paying £2 12s. 6d. for each set, or £5 5s. for the whole. Law classes have also been instituted for the purpose of facilitating the acquisition of legal knowledge by the articled and other clerks of solicitors. The classes are held from November to June inclusive, and the fee payable by each subscriber is £2 12s. 6d. for each branch, or £5 5s. for the whole course. The registry office, for the use of members and their clerks, is open daily from 9 a.m till 6 p.m., except on Saturdays, when it is closed at 2 p.m.

THE CLUB consists of members of the society ; entrance £10 10s., subs., £6 6s. for town members, and £4 4s. for country members. NEAREST *Ry. Stn.,* Temple (Dis.); *Omnibus Rtes.,* Chancery - la, Fleet-st, and Strand ; *Cab Rank,* Serle-st.

Leicester Square (Map 7) dates from 1635, when the first house was built by Robert Sydney, Earl of Leicester. In 1671, the south side was completed. Even at this early date the square had particular attraction for foreigners. Colbert, the French ambassador, resided here ; and Leicester House sheltered Prince Eugene, and saw the end of the troublous life of the Queen of Bohemia. Later Leicester House became the court of George II., when Prince of Wales, who in turn was succeeded in opposition by his own son Prince Frederick. Perhaps the first theatrical performance known in the square was when a company of amateurs, including the future George III., played Addison's tragedy of Cato. But Leicester-sq has more interesting memories than these. At No. 47, on the west side, lived and worked Sir Joshua Reynolds, and on the opposite side, close to the present Alhambra, Hogarth spent some of the best years of his life. Next door to Hogarth lived John Hunter, and, hard by, Sir Isaac Newton had his observatory. Later on Newton's house was occupied by Dr. Burney, better known as the father of Madame d'Arblay, the authoress of the now almost forgotten "Evelina." Many celebrated shows have had their habitation in the square. Miss Linwood's gruesome exhibition of worsted work; the earliest idea of hatching chickens by steam; assaults at arms; and even prize-fights; at various times appealed for public support in Savile House, on the north side. The Gordon Rioters sacked Savile House, and the complete destruction which even they were unable to effect was some years ago consummated by the fire which entirely destroyed it. In the north-east corner of the square flourished for many years one of the best exhibitions in London, Burford's Panorama; and in the middle of the square the Great Globe itself was set up, until the too sensitive feelings of the inhabitants could bear it no longer. On its removal literally a wreck was left behind. The most hideous statue in London, which Mr. Wyld's enterprise had relegated to a temporary retirement, made its unwelcome reappearance. At last a band of practical jokers, under cover of a fog, worked such pranks on the mutilated statue, that even he sense of humour of the authorities was excited, and a preliminary clearance was made. Nowadays the square is neat and orderly. Leicester-sq is still the capital of the great foreign settlements about Soho.

Liberia, Republic of.—MINISTRY. Letters should be addressed to the care of the Consul-General, Office, 15, Abchurch-lane, E.C. NEAREST *Ry. Stn.*, Cannon-st (S.E.); *Omnibus Rte.* and *Cab Rank*, Cannon-st.

Libraries (Circulating). —The principal circulating libraries for general literature, especially the more recently published works, are:—W. H. SMITH and SON'S, 186, Strand ; MUDIE'S, 30 to 34, New Oxford-st ; and the GROSVENOR GALLERY LIBRARY, 137, New Bond-st. Terms for W. H. Smith and Son's:—1. Subscribers can only change their books at the depôt where their names are registered. A Subscriber may exchange once a day ; the clerk in charge will obtain from London any work in the Library which a subscriber may desire to have. Novels exchanged only in unbroken and complete sets. London subscribers transferring their subscriptions to a country depôt, of which there are more than 500, will be entitled only to the number of volumes which the country terms assign to the amount they subscribe ; similarly, country subscriptions transferred to town become subject to the London regulations. Terms:—1. For subscribers obtaining their books from a London terminus, or 186, Strand :

		Six Months.	Twelve Months
1 Vol. at a time	..	£0 12 0	£1 1 6
2 Vols.	,,	0 17 6	1 11 6
4 ,,	,,	1 3 0	2 2 0
8 ,,	,,	1 15 0	3 3 0
15 ,,	,,	3 0 0	5 5 0

2. From a Country Bookstall :

		Six Months.	Twelve Months
1 Vol. at a time	..	£0 12 0	£1 1 0
2 Vols.	,,	0 17 6	1 11 0
4 ,,	,,	1 3 0	2 2 0
6 ,,	,,	1 8 0	2 10 0
8 ,,	,,	1 15 0	3 3 0
12 ,,	,,	3 0 0	5 5 0

MUDIE'S SELECT LIBRARY, 30 to 34, New Oxford-street. Terms of subscription for subscribers obtaining their books from the central office :—

		Three Months.	Six Months.	Twelve Months.
1 Vol.	..	£0 7 0	£0 12 0	£1 1 0
2 Vols.	..	0 10 6	0 18 0	1 11 6
4 ,,	..	0 14 0	1 4 0	2 2 0
6 ,,	..	1 1 0	1 16 0	3 3 0
8 ,,	..	1 8 0	2 8 0	4 4 0
10 ,,	..	1 15 0	3 0 0	5 5 0

2 Vols. for each additional Guinea per Annum.

Branch Offices, 281, Regent-st, 2, King-st, Cheapside, and 241, Brompton-rd, South Kensington. A supply of books, consisting chiefly of popular works available for the immediate use of subscribers, is always kept in reserve and replenished from day to day. When the books desired are not in stock,

they are obtained from the head office with as little delay as possible

		Three Months.	Six Months.	Twelve Months
1 Vol.	..	£0 7 6	£0 12 6	£1 1
2 Vols.	..	0 11 0	0 19 0	1 11
3 ,,	..	0 15 0	1 5 0	2 2
6 ,,	..	1 1 0	1 18 0	3 3

2 Vols. for each additional Guinea per Annum.

The London Book Society for the weekly delivery of books in London and the Suburbs :

		Three Months.	Six Months.	Twelve Months
3 Vols.	..	£0 15 0	£1 5 0	£2 2
6 ,,	..	1 1 0	1 18 0	3 3

2 Vols. for each additional Guinea.

GROSVENOR GALLERY LIBRARY —The Library Department contains an ample supply of the best and newest literature, both English and Foreign, and a library of vocal and instrumental music Subscription to the Circulating Library from 16s. per annum All the books in the library both English and Foreign, are available for subscribers, without distinction as to amounts of subscription, and subscribers, at their option, may have volumes of music instead of books.

TERMS OF SUBSCRIPTION.

TOWN.

	Half Year.	One Year
1 Vol.	£0 10 0	£0 16 0
2 Vols.	0 16 0	1 7 6
3 Vols.	1 2 0	1 18 6
4 Vols.	1 6 6	2 6 0
6 Vols.	1 16 0	3 3 0
8 Vols.	2 8 0	4 4 0
10 Vols.	3 0 0	5 5 0
Each addl. 2 Vols.	0 12 0	1 1 0

Subscribers for 3 or more vols are entitled to free delivery once in every week in London and suburbs.

CLUBS AND LITERARY INSTITUTIONS

			One Year
12 Vols.	..	..	£4 4 0
20 Vols.	..	..	6 6 0

10 Vols. for each additional 3 Guineas The books to be exchanged in complete sets, as issued.

COUNTRY.

	Half Year.	One Year
5 Vols.	£1 4 0	£2 2 0
9 Vols.	1 16 0	3 3 0
12 Vols.	2 8 0	4 4 0
15 Vols.	3 0 0	5 5 0
18 Vols.	3 12 0	6 6 0
Each addtl 3 Vols.	0 12 0	1 1 0

Books to be exchanged in complete sets not oftener than once a week.

Boxes for the conveyance of books to country subscribers are provided by the library free of charge, but the charge for carriage to and fro is payable by the subscriber Of the current periodicals one only at a time will be allowed to each Town subscription. Each number of a review or magazine counts as a volume.

For more substantial works, the LONDON LIBRARY, 14, St. James's-sq. Subscription, payable annually in advance, £2. Entrance £6, or £3 annually without entrance fee. Members may commute their annual subscriptions by payment of £20, or £26. Persons who wish to become subscribers must send their names, accompanied by an introduction from an existing member of the society, to the librarian, to be submitted to the committee. Members residing within 10 miles of the General Post Office, London, are entitled to take out ten volumes; and members residing at a greater distance, fifteen at a time; to be exchanged as often as required. Members desirous of taking out more may, upon payment of an increased subscription, claim an additional number of volumes of old works, or one extra copy of any new work in the library for every additional pound per annum. The time allowed for the perusal of new books (i.e. books published within the last two years) is fourteen days, to be reckoned from the day of issue, without reference to any summons for the return of the book. Older books are allowed to be kept two months.

LONDON INSTITUTION, Finsbury-cir, E.C. — The London Institution " for the advancement of literature and the diffusion of useful knowledge " is an association of 450 proprietors, incorporated by Royal Charter, and extending their advantages to subscribers. No pecuniary profit accrues to the proprietors or any other persons concerned in its management. Subscribers pay £2 12s. 6d. or £2 2s. a year, according as they do or do not wish to attend the lectures. The circulating library consists of nearly 70,000 volumes, and is supplemented by large subscriptions to trade circulating libraries, general, foreign, scientific, and musical. The best new books are added daily, and each subscriber may borrow 10 vols. There are excellent reading-rooms for books, periodicals, and newspapers, with a writing-room. The lectures are given twice a week on Mon. at 5 p.m. and Thur. at 4 p.m.) during four winter months by men of distinction in science,

art, and literature. All letters should be addressed " Superintendent," London Institution, Finsbury-cir, E.C. Personal application may be made in the library between 9.30 a.m. and 9 p.m. (Sat. 3 p.m.)

CHARLES WOOLHOUSE'S UNIVERSAL CIRCULATING MUSIC LIBRARY, 81, Regent-st, W., embraces all the works of every eminent composer, both English and foreign. New compositions of merit and general interest, published in England or abroad, are added to the library immediately on their appearance. Subscribers, at the expiration of their subscription, are entitled to select music to the extent of one-half of the amount of their subscriptions, at full price. The prices of works marked " Net " are to be doubled.

TERMS OF SUBSCRIPTION.

Per Annum	..	..£2 2 0
„ Half-Year	..	.. 1 8 0
„ Quarter ..	..	.. 0 16 0
„ Month	..	.. 0 8 0

Including the above-mentioned Presentation.

Town subscribers are supplied with £2 2s. worth of music at a time, which may be exchanged once a week; country subscribers with £4 4s. worth of music at a time, which may be exchanged every month; or £6 6s. worth of music, which may be exchanged every two or three months. Subscribers buying music are charged half-price. The presentation music must be taken out at the end of every subscription.

LEWIS'S MEDICAL AND SCIENTIFIC LIBRARY, 136, Gower-st, W.C., established 1852, contains all the standard works in medical literature, general science, &c., and new books and new editions are added as soon as published. Books may be kept as long or changed as often as desired. Special terms to book clubs and institutions throughout the country.

TERMS.

For subscribers in town and country (the year commencing at any date):

		Per Ann.
1 Vol. at a time	..	..£1 1 0
2 Vols. „	..	.. 1 10 0
4 „ „	..	.. 2 2 0
7 „ „	..	.. 3 3 0
14 „ „	..	.. 5 5 0
20 „ „	..	.. 7 7 0
30 „ „	..	.. 10 10 0

5 Vols. for every additional Guinea.
Prospectus of the library post free.

Catalogue of the library, 5s.; 2s. to subscribers.

ROLANDI'S FOREIGN SUBSCRIPTION LIBRARY, 20, Berners-st.— Exclusively for the circulation of foreign works.

TERMS OF SUBSCRIPTION.

Commencing at any date, and including books in the French, German, Italian, and Spanish languages :

One Year	..	..£2 2 0
Six Months	..	.. 1 2 6
Three Months	..	.. 0 12 0
One Month ..	..	.. 0 4 6

A Yearly Subscription (entitling to 1 work at a time) 1 1 0

Library hours 9 a.m. to 7 p.m. 1. Yearly and half-yearly subscribers are entitled to 6 vols. at a time in town, and to 12 in the country. 2. A guinea yearly subscription entitles to one work at a time. 3. Quarterly subscribers are entitled to two works at a time in town, and to four in the country. 4. Monthly subscribers are entitled to one work at a time in town, and to two in the country. 5. Double subscriptions may be entered, allowing an increased number of books. 6. Expenses incurred for carriage, porterage, booking, &c., are charged to the account of the subscriber.

There are also several smaller libraries, which themselves subscribe to one or other of the large establishments, re-lending the books to their own subscribers.

Libraries (Public):—

BETHNAL GREEN LIBRARY, The Hall, London-st.

BIRKBECK LITERARY AND SCIENTIFIC INSTITUTION, 29, Southampton-bdgs, Chancery-la.

BRITISH MUSEUM (which see).

DR. WILLIAMS'S LIBRARY, formerly in Redcross-st, now removed to a noble building erected for its reception, 14 & 18, Grafton-st, near University College, especially intended for the Nonconforming clergy, on whose recommendation strangers are admitted to its use.

GUILDHALL LIBRARY AND READING ROOM, recently built, also the museum, chiefly of British antiquities. Open free.—(And see CITY OF LONDON.)

LONDON INSTITUTION LIBRARY, 11, Finsbury-cir.

PATENT OFFICE LIBRARY AND READING ROOM, 25, Southampton-bdgs, Chancery-lane, where the specifications of patents may be perused. There is also an extensive general and technical library, and the scientific and technical periodicals of all the world are laid on the table and filed for reference. Free. Closes 4 p.m.

SION COLLEGE LIBRARY, Victoria Embankment, E.C. All the London clergy are *ex officio* members and can borrow the books. Others admitted to read on the recommendation or introduction of a clergyman. This was one of the eleven libraries which formerly were entitled to claim a copy of every book published, a privilege which was commuted for an annual grant of money from the Treasury, based on the average value of the books actually claimed and received. In this case the sum is £365 odd shillings.

ST. PANCRAS LIBRARY, 29, Camden-st.

WORKING MEN'S COLLEGE LIBRARY, 46, Great Ormond-st, W.C.

Lincoln's Inn.—(*See* INNS OF COURT.)

Liverpool Street Station (Map 8).—Built as a terminus by the Great Eastern Railway when the station at Shoreditch proved inadequate for the purpose. The main line offices and platforms are on the right, and those for the suburban traffic on the left of the entrance. NEAREST *Ry. Stns.*, Broadst (N.L.), and Moorgate-st (Met.); *Omnibus Rte.*, Bishopsgate-st; *Cab Fare*, to Bank 1/-; to Charing + 1/6.

Lloyd's.—This establishment, which has risen to the dignity of a corporation, with rights assigned to it by special Act of Parliament, occupies a great portion of the first floor of the Royal Exchange, Cornhill. It is still frequently spoken of by old-fashioned people and foreigners, as Lloyd's Coffeehouse ; Edward Lloyd having been the name of the enterprising proprietor of a coffee-house in Tower-st, once much patronised by shipowners and merchants. The first mention of it is to be found in the *London Gazette* of 21st February, 1688. During the reign of Charles II., and towards the close of the seventeenth century, merchants, like their more fashionable contemporaries farther west, greatly affected coffee-houses, though it was not until 1691 or 1692, when Mr. Lloyd removed to the corner of Abchurch-la and Lombard-st, that his house became the headquarters of ship sales, and of

marine insurance with which the name of "Lloyd's" is now associated. Previous to his settling in Lombard-st, the chief resort of ship-brokers and owners was "John's" (surname unknown), in Birchin-la, but Mr. Lloyd succeeded in attracting to his house the best of the shipping fraternity, and before long it became their chief place of meeting. For many years, and even after the middle of the eighteenth century, the transactions carried on seem to have been of a nondescript character, and, according to existing records, many of the everyday occurrences were of an order calculated to wound deeply the susceptibilities of the respectable body of gentlemen who at present preside over the destinies of Lloyd's. In addition to the sale of ships, all sorts of articles were put up to auction, varied by an occasional raffle of a horse, 60 members at £1 1s., which it was prudently stipulated must be paid in advance. Another form of speculation in which our ancestors indulged was effecting insurances on the lives of public men ; the chances of persons in bad health, or who had infringed the laws of the country, being alike made the medium of gambling. Steele, in "The Tatler," and Addison in "The Spectator," notice Lloyd's coffee-house as the resort of merchants and shipowners, and the latter's paper, No. 46, April 23, 1711, gives a very good insight into the manners and customs of its frequenters. The miscellaneous forms of betting and gambling in vogue seem to have made the respectable *habitués* ashamed of their surroundings, and about 1770 the notion, which had been taken up and abandoned more than once, of making Lloyd's, hitherto open to all comers, a society confined to qualified members of repute and means, was again brought on the *tapis*, chiefly through the energy of John Julius Angerstein, a German by descent, whose talent and integrity had raised him to a foremost position amongst underwriters. Martin Kuyck von Mierop, considerably Angerstein's senior, and a man of weight, presided at the first meeting, held towards the close of 1771, when 79 gentlemen put down £100 apiece towards uniting themselves into a society, then mentioned as "New Lloyd's," though before long the adjective was dropped. After

temporary occupation of a place i[n?] Pope's Head-alley, Cornhill, which proved inadequate to their pu[r]poses, "New Lloyd's," on the 7[th?] March, 1774, entered into posse[s]sion of premises on the first flo[or] of the old Royal Exchange (sin[ce] burnt down), previously occupie[d] by the British Herring Fisher[y] Society. Established in suitabl[e] quarters, Lloyd's rapidly increase[d] in importance and reputation, an[d] membership became, and has bee[n] ever since, a guarantee of hig[h] commercial standing. In 1811 i[ts] arrangements were reorganise[d] and the first regular secretary a[p]pointed. Sixty years later Lloyd['s] succeeded in getting an Act passe[d] constituting it a corporation, an[d] giving it many important facilitie[s].

At the present day those wh[o] have the *entrée* of Lloyd's room are : members entitled to unde[r]write ; members not so entitle[d] subscribers ; and substitutes. Th[e] expenses of the corporation in tel[e]graphy, &c., are very considerabl[e] and the records, kept in alpha[?] betical order, of the voyages of a[ll] vessels, with the other miscell[a]neous requirements of a larg[e] establishment, involve the emplo[y]ment of an extensive staff, rangin[g] from expert linguists to tiny me[s]sengers. The underwriting bus[i]ness, *i.e.* the insurance against lo[ss] or damage of ships and cargoes [?] and from all parts of the world, carried on in two rooms of nobl[e] proportions, while another is d[e]voted to files of commercial paper[s] lists of shipping intelligence, wri[t]ten and printed, and seats an[d] tables for reading and writin[g]. This is called the merchants' roo[m] distinguishing it from the unde[r]writing rooms where the chi[ef] business of the place goes o[n.] Beyond the merchants' room is [a] large apartment, used as a resta[u]rant and luncheon-bar, and know[n] as the captains' room, from th[e] fact that masters of ships frequen[t] it when vessels are put up to au[c]tion. These sales take place [in?] the luncheon-room usually at 2.3[0?] p.m. There is also a library, we[ll] stocked with books of referenc[e] on many subjects, and containin[g] amongst other curiosities, quai[nt?] old policies of assurance, one [of?] which bears date 16th Augu[st] 1708, while the other insure[s] Napoleon I.'s life and freedom u[p] to the 21st June, 1813, and som[e] pieces of splendid black oak furn[i]ture, made from the wreck [of?]

H.M.S. *Lutine*, a frigate bound fo Texel, which was lost off the Dutch coast on the 9th October, 1799, with a large quantity of specie and bar gold and silver on board. From time to time efforts were made, with varying success, to recover portions of the treasure, until, Lloyd's underwriters having longsince paid the amounts assured, the *Lutine* affair became forgotten; but about five-and-twenty years ago energetic measures were again taken to make further search, and with so much effect that over £20,000 was eventually secured. NEAREST *Ry. Stns.*, Mansion House (Dis.) and Moorgate - st (Met.) ; *Omnibus Rtes.*, Cheapside, Moorgate-st, and Queen Victoria-st; *Cab Rank*, Bartholomew-la.

Local Government Board, Whitehall, S.W. Hours 10 to 4. NEAREST *Ry. Stn.*, Westminster-br (Dis.) ; *Omnibus Rtes.*, Whitehall and Strand ; *Cab Ranks*, Horse Guards and Palace-yard.

Local Marine Board.—Office for examination of masters and mates, St. Katharine Dock House, Tower-hill. Hours 10 to 4, Saturdays 10 to 2. NEAREST *Ry. Stn.*, Tower-hill (Met.) ; *Omnibus Rte.*, Fenchurch-st ; *Cab Rank*, Royal Mint-st.

Lodging Houses (Common). — Every establishment of this kind throughout the metropolis is now under direct and continual police supervision ; every room being inspected and measured before occupation, a placard being hung up in each stating the number of beds for which it is licensed, calculated upon the basis of a minimum allowance of space for each person. Every bed, moreover, has to be furnished weekly with a complete supply of fresh linen, whilst careful provision is made for the ventilation of the rooms, the windows of which are also thrown open throughout the house at 10 a.m. In its way there are few things more striking, than the comparative sweetness of these dormitories, even when crowded with tramps and thieves of the lowest class. The common sitting - rooms on the ground floor are not, it must be confessed, always equally above reproach. In all cases the men's and women's dormitories are separate ; rooms devoted to married couples being partitioned off in the fashion of the old, square-pewed churches, and into separate pens upon about the same scale. The mixed lodging - houses — or those at which both sexes are received—are comparatively few, the general practice being for each house to confine itself to one class. All have a common sitting-room on the ground floor, with a fire at which the lodgers can cook their own victuals. In a few instances these supplies can be obtained in the house itself. About the best sample of this kind of establishment extant will be found at St. George's Chambers, St. George's-st, London Docks (*vulgo*, Ratcliff-highway), a thorough poor man's hotel, where a comfortable bed, with use of sitting - room, cooking apparatus and fire, and laundry accommodation (soap included), can be had for 4d. a night ; all kinds of provisions being obtainable in the bar at proportionate rates. To any one interested in the condition of the London poor, this establishment is well worth a journey to the East End to visit. On the other hand, the following is a list of streets or places in the metropolis in which common lodging houses of the lower class are situate :

POLICE DIV.	STREET OR PLACE.	PARISH.
A	Old Pye-st, St. Ann-st, Gt. Smith-st, Dacre-st, Gt. Peter-st, Artillery-row, and Strutton-ground	Westminster.
B	Turk's-row, Kepple-st, Pimlico-rd, Church-st, Lawrence-st, and Cheyne-row ..	Chelsea.
C	Castle-st, Whitcomb-st, and St. Martin's-st ..	St. Martin's.
	Litchfield-st and George-yd	St. Anne's, Soho.
D	Bell-st, Little Grove-st, Molyneux-st, Circus-st, Gee's-ct, Barrett's-ct, Whitfield-pl	St. Marylebone.
E	Macklin-st, Short's-gdns, Parker-st, Queen-st, Dyott-st, Kennedy-ct, Kemble-st, Maras-bdgs, Betterton-st, and Newton-st, Black Horse-yd ..	St. Giles's.
	Fulwood's-rents and Took's-ct	Holborn.
	Market-st, Charlotte-pl, Euston-rd, and Tonbridge-st	St. Pancras.
	New Church-st	St.My. le Strnd.
	Holles-st, Vere-st, Sardinia-st, Wych-st, Gilbert-passage, Drury-la ..	St. Clemt. Danes
F	Hanover-ct, Langley-ct, Harvey's-bdgs, and Lumley-ct	St. Martin's.
F	Edgware-rd and Queen's-rd	Paddington.
	Peel-st, Blenheim-cres, Clarendon-rd, and High-st	Kensington.
G	Golden-la, New-ct, Twister's-alley, Middle-row, Greenarbour-ct, Banner-st, Gt. Arthur-st, and Dufferin-st	St. Luke's.
	Portpool-la, Holborn-bdgs, Brooke-st, Greville-st, Gt. Saffron-hill, and Vine-st	Holborn.
	Clerkenwell-close, Pentonville-rd, Clerkenwell-gn, Hermes-hill, and Cyrus-st ..	Clerkenwell.
	Alexandra-bdgs, Market-st, Scrutton-st, Craven-st, Dunloe-st, Kingsland-rd, and Hoxton-st	Shoreditch.
	Cow Cross-st and St. John-st	St. Sepulchre.
	Gray's Inn-rd	St. Pancras.
	York-rd	Islington.
H	Flower and Dean-st, Dorset-st, Paternoster-row, Thrawl-st, Keate-st, Brick-la, Princes-st, White's-row, Hanbury-st, George-st, Pearl-st, Wentworth-st, Heneage-st, Brushfield-st, Wheeler-st, and Mount-st	Christchurch.
	Nicoll's-row, White-st, and Church-st	Bethnal Gn.

POLICE DIV.	STREET OR PLACE.	PARISH.
H	Wellclose-sq, Leman-st, Osborne-pl, Well-st, Dock-st, Grace's-alley, and Bull-st	Whitechapel.
		Shoreditch.
	Hare-alley, Boundary-st	Old Artill'ry-gd.
	Gun-st	St. George's E.
	St. George's-st, Ship-alley, Princess-sq, Cable-st, North East-passage, Ratcliff-st, and Pell-st	Ratcliff.
	London st, Stepney-causeway, Broad-st, and Narrow-st	Shadwell.
	High-st, Cable-st, King David's-la, and Baroda-pl	Mile End Old-tn
	Turner-st, Lucas-st, Commercial-rd, Greenfield-st, and Lady Lake's-grove ..	Wapping.
	East Smithfield, Upper Well-alley, and St. George's-st	Bethnal Gn.
J	Globe-rd, Bethnal Green-rd, and Pritchard's-rd	Hackney.
	High-st and Sylvester-rd	Shoreditch.
	Dunston-st	Limehouse.
K	St. Ann-st and West India-rd	Ratcliff.
	Stepney-causeway and Medland-st	Poplar.
	High-st, Manchester-rd, Pennifields, Finch-st, East India-dk-rd, and Emmet-st	Bow.
	Bow-rd and Burdett-rd	N. Woolwich.
	Albert-rd	Christchurch.
L	Broadwall, Gt. Charlotte-st, Stamford-st, and Collingwood-st ..	
	Hooper-st, Tower-st, Cox's-bdgs, Granby-pl, Broadwall, Lambeth-walk, Kennington-rd, Paradise-st, and Belvedere-rd	Lambeth.
		St. George's.
	Gray-st and Webber-row	Camberwell.
	Camberwell-rd	Newington.
M	Walworth-rd and Princes-st	
	Mint-st, Tabard-st, Orange-st, Union-st, Red Cross-sq, Collier's-rents, Queenst, Harrow-st, Red Cross-st, and George-st	Southwark.
	Gravel-la and Princes-st	Rotherhithe.
	Bermondsey-rd and Long-wk	Bermondsey.
N	New North-rd and Islington-gn	Islington.
P	Meeting House-la, Church-st, Old Kent-rd, High-st, Peckham, and Lordship-la	Camberwell.
		Newington.
	East-st	Lewisham.
	High-st	Battersea.
R	Arpley-rd	Deptford.
	Mill-la, New King-st, Watergate-st, Church-st, Baildon-st, and Gove-st	Woolwich.
	Canon-row, Rope Yard-rails, Nile-st, lower end of High-st, and Market-hill ..	EastGreenwich.
	Lower East-st, Thomas-st, and Beresford-st	Hampstead.
S	Bank-bdgs, Brewhouse-la, Holly-mount, and Hampstead-rd	Hammersmith.
T	Brook Green-pl, Queen-st, and King-st	Fulham.
	Stamford-rd, King's-rd, and Greyhounds-rd	Starch Green.
	Gayford-rd	Wandsworth.
V	Princes-pl, Iron Mill-rd, Grottan-rd, and Church-row	Battersea.
	High-st, Clarence-ter, and Usk-rd	Lambeth.
W	Wandsworth-rd, Vauxhall, Railton-rd, and New Park-rd	Kensington.
X	Bangor-st, Crescent-st, St. Clement's-rd, and Walmer-rd	Paddington.
	Clarendon-st	Chelsea.
	Kensal-rd, Falcon-ter, and Church-pl	
	Wormington-rd, Portobello-rd, Bramley-rd, Hesketh-pl, St. Clement-rd, and Mary-pl	Kensington.
	St. Ann's-rd, Latimer-rd, and Norland-rd	Hammersmith.
Y	Queensland-rd, Holloway, and Gordon-pl, Highgate	Islington.
	Pancras-rd and Eve-pl	St. Giles's
	Harmood-st, Prince of Wales'-rd, Circus-rd, Pratt-st, Litcham-rd, & Rochford-st	St. Pancras.

Lodgings.—The immense extension of late years of the metropolitan railway system has thrown open to those in search of lodgings a much wider field than heretofore, even when sight-seeing is the object, and time pressing. To those who are very hard pushed in the latter respect, or who contemplate being out late at night after the trains have ceased running, a central situation is, of course, still of importance; and those would do well to confine themselves — if economically disposed — to the streets between the river and the Strand, where they will get tolerable accommodation at about 30s. to 50s. a week, or to those on either side of New Oxford-st, where the charges will run a few shillings lower. In Bloomsbury, again, a little farther north, but still within easy reach of the amusement centre, will be found a whole region, the chief occupation of which is the letting of lodgings, and where the traditional bed and sitting room can be obtained at almost any price from one guinea to two and a half. Those who wish to be central, and are not particular as to the price they pay, should prosecute thei search in the streets between Pall Mall and Piccadilly, including the former, where they will find as a rule small rooms, often shabbily furnished, but good cooking, first-class attendance, and a general flavour of "society." Prices here are a good deal influenced by the "season," this being the special resort of fashionable bachelors who live at their clubs ; but the weekly rent of a bed and sitting room may be taken at from three to six or eight guineas; "extras" also, of course, being in proportion. On the other side of Piccadilly, prices are much the same, or, if anything, rather higher ; but you get larger rooms for your money, the increased distance from the more fashionable clubs rendering them relatively somewhat cheaper. Beyond Oxford-st, again, there is a considerable drop, becoming still more decided on the farther side of Wigmore-st, where very good lodgings can be had for 30s. to 40s. a week. We have here, however, got beyond the region of male attendance, and must be content with the ministrations of the ordinary lodging-house "slavey." The streets running immediately out of Portland-pl may be taken as belonging to the category of those between Wigmore-st and Oxford-st, averaging, say, from about 30s. to 60s. per week. Turning southwards again we have the large districts of Brompton and Pimlico ; a good deal farther off in point of absolute distance, but with the advantage of direct communication with the centre both by rail and omnibus, and the houses are newer and of better appearance. Visitors, however, having their families with them will do well to make enquiry either of some well-informed friend or some respectable house-agent in the neighbourhood before settling down in any particular street. The prices here will be found much the same as in the two districts last mentioned, varying of course with the accommodation, which has here a greater range than in most districts. Those who desire still cheaper accommodation must go farther afield, the lowest-priced of all being in the north-east and south-east districts, in either of which a bed and sitting room may be had at rents varying from 10s., or even less, to 30s. In the extreme west, south-west, and north-west, rents are a little higher, 15s. a week being about the minimum. In all cases, except perhaps that of the Pall Mall district, these prices should include kitchen fire, boot-cleaning, hall and staircase gas, attendance, and all extras whatsoever. It will, however, be necessary to stipulate for all these things individually. The mere word "inclusive" means nothing, or less, being very commonly taken as an indication that the enquirer either does not know what extras mean, or is too shy to formulate his requirements categorically. Set everything out in plain terms and in black and white. Stipulate also at the same time and in the same way as to the prices to be charged for gas and coal for private consumption ; the former being usually charged at the rate of 6d. per week per burner, and the latter at the rate of 6d. per scuttle. It may be as well to remember, too, if bent on rigid economy, that scuttles vary in size. Finally, you will find it necessary, if in the habit of dining late—*i.e.* after 1 or 2 p.m.—to make distinct stipulations to that effect, not only generally, but, if you so desire, with special regard to Sunday. In first-class districts this does not so much apply, though even in them there is no harm in mentioning it. But in houses of the lower classes, this will almost invariably be found a difficulty, a very large proportion flatly declining to furnish late Sunday dinners on any terms. The usual mode of hiring lodgings is by the week, in which case a clear week's notice, terminating on the same day of the week as that on which possession was taken, is necessary before leaving. If you wish to be at liberty to leave at shorter notice, or to give the week's notice from any other day, it will be necessary to have an express stipulation to that effect in writing.

Lodging Houses, Model.
—(*See* MODEL LODGING HOUSES.)

London Bridge (Map 8)—
built in 1824-27 from the designs of John Rennie, architect of Southwark and Waterloo Bridges, partly by himself, partly by his son, Mr. J. Rennie. The cost, from various causes, was enormous, and a good deal of misapprehension seems to exist upon this point ; some authorities placing it at a little under a million and a half, while others give it at over two and a half millions. It is built of granite in five arches ; the centre arch being 152 ft., the two next 140 ft., and the two shore arches 130 ft. each, in span. In order to facilitate traffic, police-constables are stationed along the middle of the roadway, and all vehicles travelling at a walking pace only are compelled to keep close to the kerb. There are still, however, frequent blocks, and the bridge should be avoided as much as possible, especially between 9 and 10 a.m. and 4 and 6 p.m. This periodical congestion of London-bridge, and, still more, of its approaches, is a very serious matter, and various schemes have been proposed for widening the bridge so that all the existing space could be devoted to vehicular traffic, while the pedestrians could be relegated to what may be called *annexes*, but for some reason or other they have all fallen through. The accepted scheme is that for building a bridge lower down, which is now in progress. NEAREST *Ry. Stns.*, Cannon-st (S.E.) and Monument (Met. and Dis.) (north side), and London-br (S.E. and L.B. & S.C.) (south side) ; *Omnibus Rtes.*, Cannon-st, King William-st, London-br, and Southwark-st.

London Bridge Station
(Map 14).—The South Eastern Railway Company formerly had their London terminus here, but since the establishment of Cannon-st and Charing Cross, the very inconvenient arrangement of platforms, which still officially ranks as a terminus, is practically only a local station. Side by side with the South Eastern Station is one of the London termini of the London, Brighton, and South Coast Railway, both for the main and Crystal Palace Victoria lines. Adjoining the Brighton Station again is the Terminus Hotel, which, as well as the Bridge House Hotel, just across the road, is convenient for travellers whose business lies in the Borough and its neighbourhood.

London Crystal Palace,
Oxford-cir, and 9, Great Portland-st, Oxford-st.—A bazaar for the sale of toys and the cheaper kind of fancy goods. Open from 10 to 6 daily, except on Sat. when it is closed at 5. NEAREST *Ry. Stn.*, Portland-rd ; *Omnibus Rtes.*, Oxford-

st, Regent-st, and Gt. Portland-st; *Cab Rank*, Oxford Market.

London Stone, in the wall in the front of St. Swithin's Church, Cannon-st. Supposed to be the centre mile-stone from which the Romans measured distance. NEAREST Ry. Stn., Cannon-st (S.E.); *Omnibus Rtes.*, Cannon-st, Qn. Victoria-st, and K. William-st; *Cab Rank*, Opposite.

Lord Advocate's Office, Home Office, Whitehall, S.W.— "No regular office hours. Attendance usually given from 11 to 5 when Parliament is sitting. When Parliament is not sitting the whole work of the office is done in Edinburgh." NEAREST Ry. Stn., Westminster-br (Dis.) *Omnibus Rtes.*, Whitehall and Strand; *Cab Rank*, Horse Guards.

Lord Chamberlain's Department, Stable-yd, St. James's Palace (hours 11 till 4), is a branch of Her Majesty's Household, and includes among other officers the Lord Chamberlain, Vice-Chamberlain, Comptroller of Accounts, Master of the Ceremonies, Lords and Grooms in Waiting, Poet Laureate, Examiner of Plays,&c.—NEAREST Ry.Stn., St. James's-pk (Dis.); *Omnibus Rtes.*, Piccadilly, Grosvenor-pl, and Victoria-st; *Cab Rank*, St. James's-st.

Lord Great Chamberlain's Office, Royal Court, Palace of Westminster, S.W. Hours 10 to 4, Sat. only.—Tickets are issued here gratis every Sat. to view the new Palace of Westminster. — NEAREST Ry. Stn., Westminster-br (Dis.); *Omnibus Rtes.*, Whitehall, Victoria-st, and Strand; *Cab Rank*, Palace-yard.

Lord Mayor's Show.—The dull monotony, which is one of the saddest features of the life of the hard-working lower orders of London, is relieved by so little in the way of pageant or show, that it is no wonder that the most insignificant mercies are received with disproportionate gratitude. It is necessary to bear this well in mind in endeavouring to account for the continued popularity of the procession which blocks some of the principal City streets annually on the 9th of November. One redeeming point may be noticed. There are always plenty of bands and some military display; and there is so little to enliven the usual dinginess of a London November day, that the streaming flags and ban-

ners give unwonted life and colour to the dingy scene. It may, after all, be doubted whether he is not the wisest Lord Mayor who relies on the personal attractions of the *person-nel* of the City for his show. Quite enough wonderful things have been exhibited by ambitious and æsthetic Lord Mayors in the way of beery knights in armour, circus elephants, and shivering ladies from the back rows of the ballet, to prove that whatever qualities may be requisite to secure civic honours, the organisation of shows finds no place amongst them. The course of the procession in the City proper, and the inconvenience to which men of business are put during its progress, depend upon the ward of which the Lord Mayor is alderman. In any case Fleet-street and the Strand are sure to have all the benefits and all the disagreeables of the show. It is, perhaps, a thing to see once. A single experience will show that it is undesirable to take any trouble to see it twice. The best point of view is from the window of a friend who occupies rooms along the line of route, more especially if he have liberal ideas on the subject of lunch. The kerb-stone can in no way be recommended. The 9th of November is pickpockets' carnival, and one of the very worst mobs in London is that which closes up behind the final escort, and follows the procession with howls and horseplay.

Lost Property. — Persons losing property in cabs, omnibuses, and trams would do well to apply at 21, Whitehall-place, where, if drivers or conductors have been honest, and have complied with the police regulations, lost articles can be recovered on payment of a very moderate reward.

Lowther Arcade (Map 7), Strand, opposite Charing ✠ Stn. —A bazaar principally for cheap toys and mosaic jewellery. Open from 8.30 a.m. until 9 p.m. NEAREST Ry. Stns., Charing ✠ (S.E. & Dis.); *Omnibus Rtes.*, Parliament-st, St. Martin's-la, and Strand; *Cab Rank*, Charing ✠.

Ludgate Hill (Map 8).—The appearance of this, the western approach to St. Paul's, has been marred by the railway-bridge of the L. C. & D. Ry., which crosses it at its lower end and destroys the view from Farringdon-cir at

its foot. Ludgate-hill is stee and in slippery weather hors with heavy waggons have serio difficulty in getting up it, thoug the difficulty and danger ha been much lessened by the layir down of the new wood pavemer Some houses recently built ne the foot of the hill, on the sou side, have been thrown back som feet, and it is hoped that eventual the improvement will be carrie out throughout the whole leng of the street. From Ludgate-hi only can a good view be obtaine of the grand western façade of S Paul's Cathedral, a view that h been greatly improved by the clea ing away of the iron railings, s leaving the west front open t Ludgate-hill. Few improvemen in a small way have been as val able and effective as this.

Lunacy Commissioners 19, Whitehall-pl, S.W. Hou 10 to 4; Saturdays, 10 to NEAREST Ry. Stns., Charing ✠ (S.E. & Dis.); *Omnibus Rtes.*, Whitehall and Strand; *Cab Rank* Horse Guards. The offices of th Masters in Lunacy, the Lunatic Visitors, and the Registrar i Lunacy, are at the Royal Cour of Justice, W.C. Hours of bus ness generally from 10 till 4, bu fewer in the vacation. NEAREST Ry. Stn., Temple (Dis.); *Omni bus Rtes.*, Strand, Fleet-st, an Chancery - la; *Cab Rank*, S Clement's Church.

Lyceum Theatre, We lington-st, Strand (Map 8).—This i one of the prettiest houses in Lon don, and while large enough t enable the poetical drama, even i the case of the heaviest Shake spearean play, to be effectivel mounted, is not too large for the re quirements of a modern audience It is worth notice that the Lyceum occupying a perfectly isolated po sition with a street on each of it four sides, offers special facilitie for egress in case of alarm, while the saloon and lobby accom modation is on an unusuall handsome scale. The convenienc and safety of the public, as wel as the beauty of the house, wer greatly enhanced by the extensiv alterations, which have been mad by Mr. Irving at various times NEAREST Ry. Stns., Templ (Dis.) and Charing ✠ (S.E. & Dis.); *Omnibus Rte.*, Strand *Cab Ranks*, Burleigh-st and We lington-st.

Lyric Club, Piccadilly East, and St. Anne's, Barnes, S.W., "was established in March, 1880, for the social assembly of musical artists and amateurs, and to meet the long felt want of a West End musical club." It was opened in January, 1885. Proprietary. Soirées are given to which ladies may be invited, and smoking concerts weekly during the season. Annual subscription : town members, £10 10s. ; country members, £5 5s. No entrance-fee at present.

Madagascar.—Consulate, 5, East India-avenue, Leadenhall-st. Nearest Ry. Stn., Fen-church-st ; Omnibus Rte., Grace-church-st and Cornhill ; Cab Rank, Leadenhall-st.

Magistrates.—(See Middle-sex and Surrey.)

Mansion House (Map 8).—This official palace of the City is about 120 years old, and was built by Dance on the site of the old stocks market. Its principal feature is a Corinthian portico with six fluted columns, but the broad staircase which should lead up to them is missing ; and the portico, approached by two little side flights, has a drolly inconsequent air perched up some dozen feet or so over the heads of passers-by. The building itself has something of the general air of a Roman palazzo, and had originally a central courtyard ; this, however, has now been roofed in, and so converted into what is known as the Egyptian Hall. It contains some statues by British artists – Foley, Bailey, Marshall, and others—and affords a fine dining-hall for the great City banquets. It is also frequently used for large charitable and other meetings. Nearest Ry. Stns., Mansion Ho. (Dis.) and Cannon-st (S.E.) ; Omnibus Rtes., Cheapside, Qn. Victoria-st, King William-st, Cornhill, Threadneedle-st, and Moorgate-st ; Cab Rank, King William-st.

Mansion House Street (Map 8).—Many Londoners would deny that such a street exists, but the few houses at the end of the Poultry, facing the Mansion House, and the Mansion House itself, officially stand in Mansion House-st. We apply the term for convenience to the open space in front of the Mansion House, where Cheapside, Princes-st, Threadneedle-st, Cornhill, Lom-bard-st, King William-st, and Queen Victoria-st unite. As Charing ✠ is the heart of all London, this great junction is the heart of the City, and the traffic that meets and crosses here is bewildering. With the exception, to some extent, of Lombard-st, all these streets are main arteries of traffic, and their united flow is so confusingly great that a timid person would find it absolutely impossible to effect a crossing from the Bank to the Mansion House without assistance. Here are the three great centres of City life : The Bank of England, the Royal Exchange—which contains Lloyd's—and the Mansion House. In the streets around are all the great banking establishments of London, and the wealth within a quarter of a mile radius of this spot is incalculable. Of all the sights of London there is nothing that fills a foreigner with such a sense of amazement and admiration as the mighty ceaseless flow of traffic in front of the Mansion House.

Maps.—The ordinary Ordnance maps of London and its environs are, according to information furnished from the office : 1. One on a scale of one inch to a mile, which shows the environs stretching some eighteen miles to east and west, and twelve or thirteen north and south, of the City, sold at 2s. 6d. per copy, and dating about fifty years back. 2. The same map on four quarter sheets at 1s. per quarter, showing improvements up to 1872. 3. A map contained on four sheets, scale six inches to a mile, price 1s. per sheet, which sheets are also published in four quarters at the same price, on a scale of twelve inches. Both the latter are what are known as skeletons—that is to say, only showing streets, roads, and rivers, without houses or other characteristics. The next size is a map on a scale of twenty-five inches to a mile, published in eighty-nine sheets, at 2s. 6d. each, which gives full details of houses, &c.; and the last and largest on a scale of five feet to a mile, in 327 sheets, at 2s. each. These form the basis of most, if not of all, the private maps published, the skeletons being filled up in each case in accordance with the special object in view. Dealing first with what may be termed the normal map, which gives streets, squares, buildings, &c., without any very specially distinguishing method of treatment, Reynolds's Coloured Map of London is one of the most comprehensive of those that have as yet come into our hands, being, indeed, with the exception of Messrs. Bacon's and of the splendid District Railway Map, the only one which takes any account of that not very fashionable, but very populous district fast springing up west of Shepherd's Bush-gn, and fast joining London to Acton as it has already joined it to Richmond. It is divided into quarter-miles, and has an illustrated index of streets, &c. Messrs. W. H. Smith & Son's New Plan of London is a remarkably clear and well-printed skeleton map, extending from Hammersmith to Blackwall, and from Upper Holloway to Brixton. It is very lightly and judiciously coloured, all water being tinted blue, and all grass green ; whilst omnibus and tramway routes are traced out in yellow. The number of these routes, and the way in which they permeate every section of the town, is one of the most striking features of London, and comes out in this map with especial clearness. Another good point is the distinguishing between underground and surface railways, not in the ordinary fashion by eliminating the former altogether, but by differently coloured lines. Altogether this map, which is divided into half-mile squares, calculated from St. Paul's, is one of the most generally useful we have received. Collins's Standard Map of London, with illustrated guide, is a large, useful map, boldly printed, and with the stations, railways, docks, canals, &c., brought prominently forward by means of colour. It is divided into mile squares, indicated at the top and bottom by letters, and at the sides by figures, and has attached to the wrapper a small pamphlet, with woodcuts of some of the principal places of interest, and brief notes upon them. Philip's Map of London for Visitors is of a similar kind, but on a somewhat smaller scale, more lightly printed, and with a less free use of colour. It is divided on the same principle, but into half-mile squares, and is printed on rather thicker paper. Bacon's Extended Map of

LONDON is on the 4-in. scale extending west as far as Holland-pk, the only difference between it and the same firm's SHILLING MAP OF LONDON being that the latter does not reach quite so far south. Their NEW MAP OF LONDON AND SUBURBS is a fine bold map on the 4-in. scale, extending from Shepherd's Bush to the Docks, and corrected up to within the last three or four years. Their large map of LONDON AND SUBURBS on the 4-in. scale, extending from Kingsbury to Leytonstone, and mounted in four folding sheets for convenience of reference, is corrected up to date, giving the Harrow extension of the Metropolitan Railway. WALTHAM BROTHERS' POCKET MAP OF LONDON (C. Smith and Co.) is a rough-and-ready little article about the size of a small cotton pocket-handkerchief, mounted on strong calico, and folding into almost the compass of a rather small purse. It is a skeleton map, but is very clear and good, the railways and stations being printed in red. HOUL-STON'S HANDY MAP OF LONDON is very similar, but on paper only, and folding into a paper wrapper. THOMAS LETTS'S SOUTH LONDON, and OXFORD AND CAMBRIDGE BOAT-RACE MAPS are, as their names imply, partial in their bearing. The former, indeed, which is on the 1-in. scale, has a rather more ambitious scope than its title would necessarily imply, being, in fact, a map not so much of South London as of the Southern environs extending a mile or two beyond Croydon and Cheam. It is a very handy little map, about three inches square when folded in its cloth case, and very clearly drawn. The boat-race map is about the same size or a trifle bigger, and deals exclusively with that section of the river between Putney and Mortlake, over which the famous race is rowed. It is on the 6-in. scale, giving roads, paths, &c., in considerable detail, and is a very useful companion for any stranger bent on assisting at the great aquatic event of the London year.

We come next to three railway maps, all of considerable interest in relation to the subject with which they more especially deal. MESSRS. W. H. SMITH & SON'S RAILWAY STATION MAP OF LON-DON AND ITS ENVIRONS, on the scale of one inch to one mile, extends from Windsor to Chisle-hurst, and from a little north of Edgware to about a mile south of Epsom Downs. The tinting here is in counties, but is put in very lightly, thus throwing up the heavily-marked railway lines, which are the especial feature of the map. Following out the same idea, the names of railway stations are printed in a blacker type than that used for other places, the various indications of parks, gentlemen's seats, roads, &c., being also kept under as much as possible. One peculiar feature of this map is the unusually elaborate manner in which it is marked off for the calculation of distances. It is divided not only into three-mile squares, but into mile circles, the starting-point in each case being St. Paul's. Altogether, for railway use, one of the best maps of the series. AIREY'S RAILWAY MAP is almost unique in its way, devoting itself to its subject with a singleness of purpose which is really almost sublime, and absolutely ignoring all such minor features of the country it portrays as hills, roads, streets, churches, public buildings, and so forth. It is rather startling at first to find the Metropolitan Railway pursuing its course through a country as absolutely devoid of feature as was the "Great Sahara" in the good old African maps of the Pre-Spekian period. But, as a matter of fact, it is only by such means that Mr. Airey attains, or can attain, his object, which is just to convey in simple but unmistakable form a considerable amount of curious information as to the ownership of the various lines which honey-comb the metropolis in every direction. LONDON RAILWAYS SIMPLIFIED AND EXPLAINED is a trifle less rigid in the simplicity of its adherence to one idea, inasmuch as it devotes a plain thin line—a mere scratch such as in ordinary maps of Europe serves to denote a fourth-rate river—to the tracing out of the more important streets and roads. But with it, as with Mr. Airey's, the railway system is the be-all and the end-all of its existence, and from it may in like manner be extracted a large store of useful and interesting information. The map distinguishes each separate railway according to its proprietary by a double system of colours and con-tinuous or broken lines. Where the trains of one company have running powers over the metals of another, the same coloured or marked line is continued alongside of that proper to the railway itself, but of a lighter type. In some instances five or six different lines may be seen wending their way side by side, while the uninitiated student is astonished to find the Midland, the North-Western, and so forth, stretching out their feelers half way between London and Brighton, whilst on the other hand the London and Brighton line burrows under the river on its way to Liverpool-st, and the ubiquitous London, Chatham, and Dover thinks nothing of thrusting out its tentacles to Palmer's Green or Colney Hatch. A map of the same character, but better for ordinary purposes than any of these, is BACON'S LONDON RAILWAYS AND STATIONS AT A GLANCE, which gives the railways in strong black lines, dotted or broken or otherwise characterised to distinguish each, with a very good skeleton map of the principal streets in pale blue. If that portion were brought up a little more to date, this map would be, for its purpose, as nearly perfect as a map often is. THE ILLUSTRATED MAP OF LONDON (C. Smith and Son) is another specialty map, and of a very curious appearance, being printed on a solid orange ground, as of a glorified London fog. It is, however, one of the most useful maps that the tourist visitor could well carry about with him, every building of any importance, from his point of view, being given *in propriâ personâ* on Brobdingnagian scale, whilst the omission of all ordinary houses, &c., and of all but the really important streets, reduces the problem of finding the way to a really charming simplicity; and the whole map, which is by no means unwieldy in size, and which is strongly mounted on stiff cotton, is a capital companion. So, too, is the INDICATOR MAP OF LONDON and VISITORS' GUIDE of the same firm, which has for specialty a good tape arrangement, by grace of which and of the alphabetical list of some 7,000 streets pasted into the cover, any required place can be found in a moment. The Indicator map, indeed, requires to be laid upon a table when consulted, and so far, for use at street corners, its orange-coloured competitor would probably have the advantage of it. But, on the other hand, the Indicator will conduct the enquirer at once to thousands of places with which the other does not profess or care to deal. BACON'S PICTORIAL MAP OF THE ENVIRONS OF LONDON seems intended rather to assist the enquiring mind of the potential tourist. Its special feature is the insertion every here and there in its appropriate place of a tiny picture of church, or house, or tree, or other noteworthy feature of local scenery.

Arriving now at the maps of the country immediately around London, one of the handiest little sheets of really pocket size is LETTS'S ENVIRONS OF LONDON, on the inch scale, which folds up into a little cloth case of between three and four inches square, and is exceedingly clear and legible. It extends from Hanwell to Erith Marshes, and from about a mile north of Friern Barnet to about half a mile south of Norwood Junction, the railways being coloured red except when underground. It may, perhaps, be questioned whether this exception is not a mistake, the almost entire disappearance of the Metropolitan Railway thus produced having a rather curious effect. HOULSTON'S HANDY MAP OF SURREY is another of the same kind, quite small enough for the waistcoat pocket, yet containing all necessary detail. LETTS'S SURVEY OF THE COUNTRY ROUND LONDON, to the distance of thirty-two miles from St. Paul's, is, of course, a much larger sheet, though on a slightly smaller scale. It contains also rather more detail, but dispenses altogether with the use of colour. STANFORD'S MAP OF TWELVE MILES ROUND LONDON, on the other hand, which is on a considerably larger scale, uses colour freely, to distinguish between the various counties; the railways also being laid down in red, while the parks, river, &c., are shown similarly distinguished. BACON'S ENVIRONS OF LONDON is a good pocket map on the inch scale, brought up to within the last two or three years. MESSRS. W. H. SMITH & SON'S MAP OF THE ENVIRONS OF LONDON, on the scale of one inch, extends from Windsor to East Wickham, and from South Mimms to Epsom Downs. It is coloured in counties, of which it contains por-

tions of no fewer than eight, the railways being strongly marked in red. The roads, parks, gentlemen's seats, &c., with all the natural features of the country, are clearly distinguished, the names of all places of any importance being printed in type of a size very acceptable to eyes that have lost something of their first vigour. THE EXCURSIONIST'S MAP OF THE ENVIRONS OF LONDON is on the half-inch scale, and uses colour for the boundaries of counties only. It is a useful map for its purpose, and giving fewer details than that last mentioned, is to some extent easier of reference. On the other hand REYNOLDS'S OARSMAN'S AND ANGLER'S MAP OF THE RIVER THAMES, from its source to London-br, and the same firm's COLOURED CHART OF THE THAMES ESTUARY, with map of the river from London to Gravesend, abound in detail; the former especially having its wide margin studded thick with useful hints as to islands, weirs, ferries, currents, favourable fishing-grounds, preserves, &c.

Among the finest maps that have come into our hands are STANFORD'S ENVIRONS OF LONDON, extending twenty-five miles from the metropolis, and the same firm's six-inch scale map of London in twenty-four sheets. It is hardly necessary to say that neither of them is strictly adapted — or intended—for casual study at street corners, but for home use they are excellent, while their scale admits of an amount of detail which in smaller sheets would be hopelessly confusing. And finally the best and most practically useful of all is beyond question the improved map of the DISTRICT RAILWAY CO. This is a map which may be fairly said to be absolutely indispensable to anyone who wants to understand the extraordinary ramifications of the interior railway system of London. Looked at from the point of view of the time-tables, such a journey as that from the Old Kent-rd to Willesden, or from Kew Bridge to Dalston, is not to be contemplated without dismay; but when the thing is studied with the assistance of this map, even experienced Londoners will be surprised to see how simple a business it really is. A clearer and better map of London does not exist.

Marble Arch (Map 6) at the

west end of Oxford-st, nearly opposite Edgware-rd. Formerly stood outside Buckingham Palace. —NEAREST Ry. Stn., Edgware-rd (Met.); Omnibus Rtes., Edgware-rd, Oxford-st, and Baker-st.

Markets.—The following are the metropolitan markets, particulars of the chief of which will be found under their respective headings.

BERMONDSEY (Skin), S.E.

BILLINGSGATE (Fish), E.C.

BOROUGH (Fruit and Vegetable), S.E.

CLARE (General), W.C.

COLUMBIA (Fish and General), Baroness-rd, E.

COVENT GARDEN (Fruit, Vegetable, and Flower), W.C.

CUMBERLAND (Hay), Regent's-pk, N.W.

FARRINGDON (Fruit, &c.), E.C.

FOREIGN CATTLE, Dock-st, Deptford, S.E.

GREAT NORTHERN RAILWAY (Potato), York-rd, N.

LEADENHALL (Meat, Poultry, and Live Stock), E.C.

LONDON CENTRAL (Meat, Fish, &c.), Smithfield, E.C.

METROPOLITAN (Cattle), Holloway, N.

NEWPORT (Meat), W.C

PORTMAN (Hay and Vegetable), N.W. Office, 64, Carlisle - st N.W.

SMITHFIELD (Hay), E.C.

SOUTH LONDON (General), New Kent-rd.

SPITALFIELDS (Vegetable), E.

STRATFORD, Stratford-br (Vegetable, and Agricultural Produce), E.

WHITECHAPEL (Hay and Straw), 114, Whitechapel High-st, E.

Marlborough Club, 52, Pall Mall.—No particular qualification. Entrance fee, £31 10s.; subscription, £10 10s.

Marlborough House, the residence of H.R.H. the Prince of Wales, is at the extreme west end of Pall Mall on the south side of the street.

Marylebone Theatre, Church-st, Edgware-rd (Map 1).— NEAREST Ry. Stn., Edgware-rd (Met.); Omnibus Rtes., Church-st and Edgware-rd.

Medical Education and Registration (General

Council of), 299, Oxford-st, W. Hours 10 to 4. NEAREST *Ry. Stn.*, Portland-rd (Met.); *Omnibus Rtes.*, Baker-st, Oxford-st, and Regent-st ; *Cab Rank*, Gt. Portland-st.

Mendicity Society.—(*See* BEGGARS.)

Mercers' Company (The) has its home in Ironmonger-la, overlooking Cheapside. The Mercers have a chapel of their own, in which divine service is held every Sunday evening, and attended by a congregation of 100 persons and upwards — a respectable gathering for the City of London, where there are comparatively but few residents. Until recently the company had the entire management of St. Paul's School, which was founded by Dean Colet, whose father was a mercer. At the present time they are patrons of three livings, managers of several schools and hospitals, and possess a large number of exhibitions to the two Universities. There are three old pictures of special interest in the court-room : Holbein's portrait of Sir Thomas Gresham, Dean Colet, and Whittington, who is represented as a sedate and prosperous-looking person caressing a cat. A portrait of Lord Selborne has lately been added to the collection. Perhaps the most noteworthy objects in the place are the wood carving, and an ancient gateway which contains a shutter in the form of a portcullis. This machine is elaborately carved, and was one of the few things that escaped destruction in the Great Fire. Near the present hall stood the house of Gilbert a' Beckett, mercer, in which his son Thomas was born.

Merchant Taylors (The) are the old rivals of the Fishmongers, and profess Conservative politics. Their hall, Threadneedle-st, which is on the ground-floor, is stated by its admirers to be the largest of all the City halls ; by ordinary persons it might perhaps be considered the ugliest. It was built after the Great Fire by Jarman. The latest addition to the portrait gallery is a likeness of Lord Justice Baggallay by J. Sant, R.A. Busts of Sir J. Pollock and the late Lord Derby stand in the vestibule before the drawing-room ; and portraits of Wellington by Wilkie, and Pitt by Hoppner, are hanging in the gallery over-

looking the hall. Many royal personages, eleven in all, have belonged to the company, and a large number of peers and peeresses. Sir John Hawkwood, the famous freelance, was a Merchant Taylor, as also was Stow, the historian. The master of the company used to be called the pilgrim, having to travel for his associates.

Merchant Taylors' Sch. (Map 8) occupies the buildings formerly devoted to Charterhouse School, Charterhouse-sq, is one of the best of the public schs. of London, and has little to fear in any competition. The ancient motto of the sch., *Homo plantat Homo irrigat, sed Deus dat Incrementum*, well expresses the aspiration of the "pious founders ;" and the following extract from the old statute of 1561 sets forth the origin of the sch. : "The Grammar-Schoole, founded in the Parish of St. Laurence Pountney, in London, in the Yere of our Lord God one thousand, fyve hundred, sixty-one, by the Worshipfull Company of the Marchaunt Taylors, of the Citty of London, in the honour of Christ Jesu." Presentations to the sch. are in the gift of the members of the court of assistants of the Merchant Taylors' Co. The sch. is divided primarily into upper and lower ; and the upper sch. into two divisions, called the classical side and the modern side. The lower sch. is preparatory to the upper, promotions being made from the lower to the upper twice a year according to individual proficiency. The half of Monday is, throughout the sch., devoted to religious instruction. The dues are a fee of £4, and £12 12s. per annum, paid quarterly in advance, by boys in the lower, or £15 15s. per annum by boys in either department of the upper sch. This includes every charge for education, except books. There is no boarding system, but boarders are received by the assistant-masters, and by other persons, with whom special arrangements must be made. No boy can be admitted unless he be over nine and under fourteen years of age, and pass the entrance examination to the satisfaction of the head-master. The list of the scholarships and exhibitions to the Universities is amazing, and the sch. scholarships themselves are of great importance. Such a list as that which is here appended is probably unparalleled :

Fifteen junior scholarships of £100 per annum, tenable for five years under certain conditions at St. John's Coll., Oxford ; four senior scholarships of £150 per annum to be held at St. John's Coll , Oxford, for four years by scholars educated at Merchant Taylors', who have pa-sed all examinations required for the degree of B.A.; four Parkyn exhibitions of £90 for four years to Cambridge, for mathematics ; five Andrew exhibitions of £86 per annum for five years tenable at St. John's Coll., Oxford, for history and modern languages ; two Fish exhibitions of £80 per annum for four years, tenable at St. John's Coll., Oxford, for Hebrew and Divinity ; two Stuart exhibitions, one to Cambridge, of about £60, for four years, and one to Oxford, of £50, for eight years ; four Co.'s exhibitions of £40, for four years, to either Oxford or Cambridge ; one sch. exhibition, of about £26, for four years, tenable at Oxford ; two Pitt Club exhibitions, of about £30, for four years, tenable at Oxford or Cambridge ; and one free medical and surgical scholarship of £125 annually at St. Thomas's Hospital. All boys who have been in the sch. two years are eligible to the twenty-one scholarships at St. John's Coll., Oxford, until the 11th of June preceding their nineteenth birthday. Candidates for other sch. exhibitions may in some cases have passed their nineteenth birthday, but must have been a certain time in the sch. and attained a certain rank in it, and passed certain examinations. At least ten scholarships are awarded annually by competition to boys who have been at least one year in the sch. Four of these, called senior scholarships, are open to boys under sixteen, and are of the value of £30 per annum, and tenable as long as the holder remains in the sch. One at least of these senior scholarships is awarded every year for modern subjects. The remaining scholarships, called junior scholarships, are open to boys under fourteen, and are of the value of £15 15s. (the equivalent of a free education in the upper sch.), tenable for two years, or until the holder is elected to a senior scholarship. Besides these there are two entrance scholarships of £12 12s., tenable for two years for boys under 12 years of age. It is not surprising that ith advantages such as these ae list of distinguished Taylorians aould comprise the names of a many remarkable men. All formation can be obtained from e secretary at the sch. NEAREST y. Stn., Omnibus Rte., and Cab ank, Aldersgate-st.

Meteorological Office,
6, Victoria - st, Westminster.— Not open to the public. Persns having business with the ffice are requested to call between e and 2." NEAREST Ry Stn., ictoria ; Omnibus Rte., Victoria-st ; Cab Rank, Army and avy Stores, Victoria-st, Westminster, S.W.

Metropolitan Board of Works, Spring-gdns, S.W.—
ours 9 till 4 ; Sat., 9 till 2. The earest approach to a municipal ody in London outside the City. reat public works, such as the ain drainage scheme, the emankments, the making of important new thoroughfares, &c., are ntrusted to the Board ; and a st of minor duties, involving uch work for the members and eavy charges on the ratepayers, e devolve upon them. NEAREST y. Stns., Charing ✚ (S.E. and is.); Omnibus Rtes., Cockspurst, Strand, and Whitehall ; Cab ank, Trafalgar-sq.

Mexico.—MINISTRY, 175,
romwell-rd, S.W. NEAREST Ry. in., South Kensington (Dis.) ; nnibus Rte., Brompton-rd ; Cab ank, Cromwell-rd. CONSULATE, Great Winchester-st, E.C. EAREST Ry Stn., Bishopsgate ; nnibus Rtes., Old Broad-st and ishopsgate - st ; Cab Rank, ishopsgate-st.

Middle Class Hospital.—
ee HOSPITALS, Home Hospital ssociation.)

Middlesex County fficers.
ustos Rotulorum and Lord Lieutenant—The Earl of Strafford.
hairman of the Court—Colonel Sir F. B. Morley, K.C.B.. 14, Norland-pl, Notting-hill, W.
ssistant Judge—P. H. Edlin, Esq., Q.C., 64, Queensboro'-ter, Hyde-pk, W.
hairman of the Committee for Accounts and for General Purposes—Sir W. H. Wyatt, 88, Regent's-pk-rd.

Chairman of the Second Court— J. D. Fletcher, Esq., 12, Westbourne-ter, W.
Clerk of the Peace—Sir Richard Nicholson, Sessions House, Clerkenwell.
Assistant ditto—C. Threlfall, Esq.
Clerks in the Office of ditto—Mr. Hodgkinson, Clerk of Second Court ; Mr. Wm. Champion, W. C. Sage, W. Tyler, and H. J. Baker.
County Treasurer—George Allen, Esq., Guildhall, Westminster.
Clerk to ditto—Mr. Farmer.
Surveyor of County Bridges— Fred. H. Pownall, Esq., 33A, Montagu-sq, W.
Analyst for the extra Metropolitan part of Middlesex— Dr. T. Redwood, 17, Bloomsbury-sq.
Clerk to Committees of the Court —Mr. Charles Wright, Sessions House, Clerkenwell.
Acting Clerk to ditto—Mr. E. W. Beal.
Crier of the Court—Mr. Arthur Rumbelow.
Crier of the Second Court.—Mr. Geo. Smith.

Middlesex County Magistrates.

A LIST OF THE ACTING MAGISTRATES OF THE COUNTY OF MIDDLESEX, 1888.
Strafford, The Earl of, Lord Lieutenant and Custos Rotulorum, 34, Wilton-pl, S.W.
Acworth, NathanielBrindley,Esq., The Hook, Northaw, near Barnet, N.
Adair, Captain Allan Shafto, Barnet.
Adams, William, Esq., Tower Lodge, Regent's-pk-rd, N.W.
Adeane, Captain Edward Stowley, R.N., 28, Eaton-pl, S.W.
Agnew, William, Major-General, 6, Belsize-pk-gdns, N.W.
Allen, James Henry, Esq., 2, Chester-ter, Regent's-pk.
Alston, Sir Francis Beilby, K.C.M.G., 69, Eccleston-sq, Pimlico, S.W.
Amherst, William Amherst Tyssen, Esq., Didlington-pk, Norfolk.
Annesley, Colonel The Hon. Algernon Sydney Arthur, 57, Belgrave-rd, S.W.
Antrobus, Robert Crawford, Esq., 27, Eccleston-sq, S.W.

Armstrong, Sir Alex., K.C.B., D2, Albany, Piccadilly.
Arnold, Augustus Walter, Esq., 9, Sussex-pl, Hyde-pk, W.
Arundell of Wardour, Lord, Wardour Castle, Salisbury.
Ashby, John, Esq., M.P., The Close, Staines.
Atkinson, H. J., Esq., M.P., Gunnersbury House, Acton.
Baggallay, Ernest, Esq., West Ham Police-court.
Baptie, Thomas Procter, Esq., Highgate Keep, N.
Baring, Thomas Charles, Esq., 1, Grafton-st, W.
Barnard, Herbert, Esq., 23, Portland-pl.
Barreto, The Baron Henry, Berkeley House, Cambridge-st, Hyde-pk, W.
Barter, Henry, Esq., 16, Airliegardens, Campden-hill, W.
Bartley,George ChristopherTrout, Esq., M P., St. Margaret's House, Victoria-st, S.W.
Bashford, Charles Brome, Esq., Copthorne House, Worth, Sussex.
Bashford, Wm. Charles Lake, Esq., Copthorne House, Worth, Sussex, and Brunswick-square, Brighton.
Bayley, Edmund Kelly, Esq., Arnolds, Holmwood, Surrey.
Beaumont, Captain Wm. Spencer, Arthur's Club, S.W.
Beetham, Albert Wm., Esq., 11, South-sq, Gray's-inn, W.C.
Bennett, Henry Curtis, Police Court Hammersmith.
Berners, Capt. Hume, R.N., 12, Eaton-sq, S.W.
Bethel, The Hon. Slingsby, Chelsea Lodge, Chelsea Embank.
Bevan, Robert Cooper Lee, Esq., 31, Prince's-ga, W.
Bickerstaff, Wm. Martin, Esq., 1, Avenue-rd, Regent's-pk.
Bingham, Lord,32, Portland-pl,W.
Bird, William, Esq., Bute House, Hammersmith, W.
Bodkin, Wm. Peter, Esq., Westhill, Highgate, N.
Borthwick, Sir Algernon, Bart., M.P., 139, Piccadilly, W.
Bosanquet, Percival, Esq., Ponfield, Hertford.
Boscawen, The Hon. Hugh Le Despencier, 20, South-st, Parklane, W.
Boulnois, E., Esq., 15, Cavendishrd, Regent's-pk.
Bousfield, William, Esq., 33, Stanhope-gdns, S.W.
Bowles,Henry Carrington Bowles, Esq., Myddleton House, Waltham ✚.

Brandreth, Joseph Edward Lyall, Esq., 32, Elvaston-pl, Queen's-ga, S.W.

Bridge, J., Esq., Bow-st Police Court, W.C.

Bridgwater, Dr.Thomas, Harrow, and Beaufort Club, Dover-st,W.

Britten, Daniel, Esq., 7, Hanover-ter, Regent's-pk, N.W.

Bromley, Edward, Esq., 12, Eccleston-sq, S.W.

Brooke, Edward, Esq., 51, Nevern-sq, South Kensington.

Bros, James R.W., Police Courts, Clerkenwell and Dalston.

Browell, Edward M., Esq., Board of Green Cloth, Buckingham Palace, S.W., and Feltham, Middlesex.

Brownrigg, General John Studholme, C.B., 28, Lowndes-st, S.W.

Bruce, Lord Charles, 77, Pall Mall, S.W.

Bruce, Col. Robert, C.B., 6, Warwick-sq, S.W., and Army and Navy Club, Pall Mall.

Burgess, Philip Blunt, Esq., 22, Carlyle-sq, Chelsea.

Burke, Charles G., Esq., 68, Holland-rd, W.

Burt, George, Esq., 19, Grosvenor-rd, S.W.

Bushby, H. J., Esq., Police Court, Worship-st, E.C.

Busk, Thomas Teshmaker, Esq., Ford's Grove, Winchmore Hill, N.

Byles, Walter Barnard, Esq., 3, Prince's-gdns, Hyde-pk.

Byng, Colonel the Hon. Henry William John, 20, Carlton House-ter, S.W.

Cadogan, The Hon. Fred. Wm., M.P., 72, South Audley-st, W.

Cadogan, The Earl, Chelsea House, Cadogan-pl, S.W.

Campbell, Charles Hallyburton, Esq., 64, Cromwell-rd, S.W.

Campbell, James, Esq., Arkley, Barnet, N.

Campbell, Sir George, K.C.S.I., M.P., 13, Cornwall-gdns, S.W.

Carr, John, Esq., 40, Bloomsbury-sq, W.C.

Carnarvon, The Right Hon., the Earl of, 43, Portman-sq, W.

Carr, John, Esq., 40, Bloomsbury-sq, W.C.

Cater, John White, Esq., West Lodge, Barnet, N.

Cave, Thomas, Esq.

Cecil, Lieut.-Col. Lord Eustace, 32, Eccleston-sq, S.W.

Chambers, Henry, Esq., 671, Commercial-rd, E., and Manor House, Sydenham.

Chapman, Francis Stewart, Esq., 36, Stanhope-gdns, W.

Charles, James, Esq., Kennet House, Harrow.

Charrington, John, Esq., Upper Clapton, E., and Ratcliff, E.

Churchill, Lord Alfred Spencer, 16, Rutland-ga, Hyde-pk, W.

Clarke, Thomas Truesdale, Esq., Swakeleys, near Uxbridge.

Clarke - Thornhill, Wm. Capel, Esq., Rushton Hall, Kettering, Northamptonshire.

Clitherow, Col. Edward John Stracey, Boston House, Brentford.

Clode, Charles Matthew, Esq., C.B., 14, Ashley-pl, Victoria-st, S.W.

Cocks, Thomas Somers, Esq., 42, Great Cumberland-pl, W.

Colebrooke, Sir Thomas Edward, Bart., 14, South-st, Park-la, W.

Colville of Culross, Lord, 42, Eaton-pl, S.W.

Cook, Major Arthur Bott, 37, Great Cumberland-pl, W.

Cook, Edward Rider, Esq., Woodford, Essex.

Cooke, William Major, Esq., Marylebone Police Court, W.

Copeland, Wm. Fowler Mountford, Esq., Russell Farm, Watford, Herts.

Cotton, William James Richmond, Esq. (Alderman of London), 27, St. Mary Axe, E.C.

Cox, Frederick, Esq., 9, Ennismore-gdns, Princes-ga, W.

Cox, Irwin Edward Bainbridge, Esq., Ivor House, Barnet-ga, Barnet, Herts.

Cox, Richard Henry, Esq., Craig's-ct, S.W.

Craven, Wm. George, Esq., 38, Hertford-st, Mayfair, W.

Creyke, Ralph, Esq., 28, Ennismore-gdns, S.W.

Crowder, Augustus George, Esq., 65, Portland-pl, W.

Cundy, Charles F., Esq., 26, Wilton-pl, S.W.

Curtis, Spencer Hy., Esq., Totteridge House, Herts.

Cust, Robert Needham, Esq., 63, Elm-pk-gdns, Fulham-rd, S.W.

Dakin, Alderman Sir Thomas, Tooting, Surrey.

Dalbiac, Henry Eardley Aylmer, Esq., Durrington, near Worthing, Sussex.

Daley, F. H., Esq., M.D., 185, Amhurst-rd, Hackney Downs.

Damer, Captain L. S. Dawson.

Daniell, Alfred B., Esq., 93, Finchley-rd, N.W.

Daubeney, General Sir H. B., K.C.B., Osterley Lodge, Isleworth.

Davis, Maurice, Esq., M.D., 11, Brunswick-sq, W.C.

Deane, Francis Henry, Esq., East View, Uxbridge.

Deedes, Henry Charles, Esq., 7, Queen-st, Mayfair, W.

De Salis, W. F., Esq., Dawley Court, Uxbridge.

D'Eyncourt, L. C. T., Esq., Westminster Police Court, W.

De Rutzen, A., Esq., Marylebone Police Court, W.

Dickson, Lieut.-Colonel Lothian, Sheffield.

Dilke, The Right Hon. Sir Charles W., Bart, 76, Sloane-st, S.W.

Dimsdale, The Hon. Robt. Baron, Carlton Club, Pall Mall.

Dixon-Hartland, Fred Dixon, Esq., M.P., 14, Chesham-pl, S.W.

Dodd, George Ashley, Esq., Surrenden Dering, Ashford, Kent.

Doe, Joseph B., Esq., Causey Ware Hall, Lower Edmonton.

Donnithorne, Lieut. Col. Edward, Twickenham.

Down, John Langdon, Esq., 81, Harley-st, W.

Downes, Commissary General Arthur Wm., C.B., 28, Charleville-rd, West Kensington.

Dufferin, The Earl of, The Travellers' Club, Pall Mall.

Duncombe, Vice-Admiral the Hon. Arthur, 37, Hill-st, Berkeley-sq, W.

Ebury, The Rt. Hon. Lord, 35, Park-st, Grosvenor-sq, W.

Edlin, Peter Henry, Esq., Q.C. (Assistant Judge), 64, Queenborough-ter. Hyde-pk, W.

Edwards, Sir Henry, 53, Berkeley-sq, W.

Evans, Edward Prichard, Esq., Tintern House, Primrose Hill-rd, N.W.

Fane, Charles Thorold, Esq., 1, Fleet-st, and 7, Norfolk-cres, Hyde-pk.

Farquhar, Horace B. T., Esq., 4, Berkeley-st, W.

Farquhar, Sir Walter Rockliffe, Bart., 18, King-st, St. James's.

Faulconer, Thos., Esq., 8, St. John's Wood-pk, N.W.

Fenwick-Fenwick, E., Esq., Hammersmith Police Court.

Finnis, George Carruthers, Esq., 13, York-ter, Regent's-pk.

Fitz-Gerald, Sir Gerald, K.C.M.G., 30, Pont-st, Belgrave-sq.

Fleming, John, Esq., 82, Lancaster-ga, Hyde-pk, W.

Fletcher, Alexander Pearson, Esq., 7, Abercorn-pl, N.W.

Fletcher, John Dunnington, Esq., 13, Glendower-pl, South Kensington.

Fletcher, John S., Esq., Treherne House, West End, Hampstead.

Fletcher, John Thompson, Esq., The Birches, Upper Norwood, S.E.

Ford, Edward, Esq., Old Park, Winchmore Hill, N.

Ford, John Walker, Esq., Chase Park, Enfield.

Forster, Sir Charles, Bart., M.P., 35, Queen's-ga, S.W.

Forsyth, William, Esq., Q.C., 61, Rutland-ga, S.W.

Fortnum, Charles Drury Edward, Esq., Stanmore-hill.

Fowler, Sir Robert Nicholas, Bart., (Alderman of London), 50, Cornhill.

France, John Frederick, Esq., 2, Norfolk-ter, Bayswater, W.

France, G. F., Esq., 40, South-st, W.

Fraser, Sir Wm. Aug., Bart., Carlton Club, Pall Mall.

Fremantle, Major-Gen. Arthur L., C.B., 5, Tilney-st, Park-la.

Fremantle, The Hon. Charles Wm., Royal Mint, E.

Gabriel, Sir Thomas, Bart., Commercial-rd, Lambeth, S. (Alderman of London).

Gadesden, Augustus William, Esq., Ewell Castle, Surrey.

Galsworthy, Edwin Henry, Esq., 18, Park-cres, Portland-pl.

Gardiner, General Henry Lynedoch, 109, Cromwell-rd, S.W.

Garford, Francis, Esq.,2, Courtland-ter, The Mall, Bayswater.

Gibbons, Sir John, Bart., Stanwell-pl, Staines.

Gibbs, Henry Hucks, Esq., St. Dunstan's, Regent's-pk.

Gillespie, Robert, Esq., 33, Palmeira Mansions, Brighton.

Glover, John, Esq.,Merton Lodge, West Hill, Highgate, N.

Glyn, The Hon. Pascoe Charles, 54, Lowndes-sq, S.W.

Goode, Joseph John, Esq., Caxton House, Queen's-rd, Brownswood-pk, N.

Goodson, James, Esq., 32, Kensington-gdns-sq, W.

Gordon, General, the Hon. Alex. Hamilton, K.C.B., 34, Lennox-gdns, Sloane-st, S.W.

Gostling-Murray, Colonel Charles Edward, Whitton-pk, Hounslow

Gotto, Edward, Esq., The Logs, East Heath-rd, Hampstead.

Grant, Colonel William Lewis, 44, Gloucester-sq, Hyde-pk, W.

Gray, John, Esq., 4, Westbourne-ter-rd, W.

Green, Henry, Esq., Blackwall-yard.

Green, Joseph Edwin, Esq., 12A, Myddelton-sq, E.C.

Greville, Lt.-Col. Arthur Charles, Hillingdon, Uxbridge.

Greville, The Hon. George, 4, Chester-sq, S.W.

Griffith, Henry, Esq., 30, Prince's-gdns, Hyde-pk, W.

Grosvenor, The Hon. Algernon Henry, 25, Park-st, Grosvenor-sq, W.

Guest, Montague John, Esq., 3, Saville-row, W.

Gwynne, James Eglinton Anderson, Esq., F.S.A., 97, Harley-st, Cavendish-sq, W.

Hall, Major-Genl. H., 90, Eaton-pl, S.W.

Hallett, James Alfred, Esq., 7, St. Martin's-pl, Trafalgar-sq.

Halswell, Hugh Beauchamp,Esq., 26,Kensington-ga, Hyde-pk,W.

Hamilton, The Rt. Hon. Lord George Francis, M.P., 17, Montagu-st, Portman-sq, W.

Hanbury, Charles Addington, Esq., Belmont House, East Barnet, Herts, N.

Hankey, Thomson, Esq., 59, Portland-pl, W.

Hannay, James L., Esq., Police Court, Worship-st, E.C.

Hanson, Alderman Sir Reginald, Bart., 4, Bryanston-sq, W.

Hardcastle, Henry, Esq., 38, Eaton-sq, S.W.

Hardman, Sir William, 81, St. George's-rd, S.W.

Hardwick, Philip Charles, Esq., 2, Hereford-gdns, Park-la, W.

Harrison, William, Esq., 23, Highbury Quadrant, N.

Harvey, Richard Musgrave, Esq., 13, Devonshire-st, Portland-pl.

Hazard, Richard, Esq., 126, Albion-rd, Stoke Newington, N.

Headley, Lord, 7, Astwood-rd, Cromwell-rd, S.W.

Heberden, Colonel Henry, R.A., 3C, Oxford and Cambridge Mansions, Marylebone, W.

Henry,Mitchell, Esq., Stratheden House, Knightsbridge.

Hill, Charles, Esq., Rockhurst, West Hoathly.

Hillingdon, Lord, Camelford Hse, Park-la, W.

Hoare, Gerard Noel, Esq., 47, Cleveland-sq, Hyde-pk, W.

Hoare, Samuel, Esq., M.P., 7, Hereford-gdns. Park-la, W.

Hobart, Robert Henry, Esq., C.B., 54, Chester-sq, S.W.

Hogarth, Major John H.H.S.D., Junior United Service Club, S.W., and Heston Hall, W.

Hogarth, John Rayer, Esq., Heston Hall, W.

Holland, Sydney George, Esq., Llangallock Park, Crickhowell.

Holland, John Robt., Esq., 1, Upper Berkeley-st, W.

Holms, John, Esq., 16, Cornwall-gdns, Queen's-ga, W.

Homan, Ebenezer, Esq., Friern Watch, Finchley, N.

Hornby, Vice-Admiral William Windham, 6, Roland Houses, Kensington, W.

Horsley, Charles, Esq., 174,Highbury New-pk, N.

Hosack, John, Esq., Clerkenwell Police Court, E.C.

Howard, John Morgan, Esq., Q.C., M.P., 22, Gloucester-st, S.W.

Howard, Joseph, Esq., M.P., The Green, Tottenham.

Hubbard, Alex., Esq., Derwentwater House, Acton, W.

Hughes-Hughes, William Esq., 5, Highbury Quadrant, N.

Hunt, Sir Henry Arthur, C.B., 54, Eccleston-sq, and 45, Parliament-st.

Hunter, Walter, Esq., 48, Bowrd, E.

Ingham, Sir James Taylor, Bow-st Police Court, W.C.

Jennings, Richard, Esq., 60, Portland-pl, W.

Jersey, Right Hon. The Earl of, 3, Great Stanhope-st, W.

Johnson, Edmund Charles, Esq., 4, Eaton-pl, Belgrave-sq, S.W.

Johnston, Alexander Rose, Esq., Fairfield, Harrow Weald.

Johnston, Capt. James Gilbert, 39, Hyde-pk-sq, W.

Johnstone, Major-General John Julius, 1, York-ter, Regent's-pk.

Jones, John, Esq., 12, Northumberland Houses, King Edward-rd, South Hackney, E.

Jones, William Samuel, Esq., 17, Bolton-gdns, South Kensington. S.W.

Kemble, Horatio, Esq., 103,Cromwell-rd, S.W.

Kendall, Captain Clarence Peter Trevelyan, 6, Wilton-pl, S.W.

Kerr, Robert Malcolm, Esq., 7, Chester-ter, Regent's-park, N.W.

Kitching, Albert George, Esq., Chace Court, Enfield.

Knight, Alderman Sir Henry Edmund, 6, Stratford-pl,W.

Lafone, Alfred, Esq., M.P., Hanworth Park, Feltham.

Lamplough,Charles Edward,Esq. 72, Cornhill, E.C.

Latham, Morton, Esq., 23, Norfolk-st, Park-la, W.

F

Laurie, Reginald P. Northall, Esq., Palace Chambers, Westminster, S.W.

Lawrence, Sir James Clarke, Bart., Alderman of London), 75, Lancaster-ga, Hyde-pk.

Lawrence, Sir William, (Alderman of London), 75, Lancaster-ga, W.

Lawrence, The Lord, 66, Pont-st, S.W.

Lee, Henry, Esq., 25, Highbury-quadrant, N.

Lermitte, James Hy., Knightons, East Finchley, N.

Lescher, Joseph Francis, Esq., South Weald, Brentwood.

Levick, James, Esq., 9, King's Arms-yd, Moorgate-st, E.C.

Lewis, Alfred David, Esq., 34, Leinster-gdns, W.

Lilly, William Samuel, Esq., 27, Michael's-gr, Brompton.

Littler, R. D. M., Esq., Q.C., 4, Temple-gdns, E.C.

Lucan, General George Charles, Earl of, 12, South-st, W.

Lucas, Arthur Charles, Esq., 30, Wilton-cres, S.W.

Lucas, Sir Thomas, Bart., 12, Kensington Palace-gdns, W.

Lushington, Franklin, Esq., Thames Police Ct., Stepney, E.

Lusk, Sir Andrew, Bart. (Alderman of London), 15, Sussex-sq, W.

Lyall, Charles, Esq., 55, Sussex-gdns, Hyde-pk, W.

Lyon, Major William, 2, South-st, Park-la, W.

McCall, John, Esq., Stadacona House, Amhurst-pk, Hackney.

MacGregor, Evan, Esq., C.B. Red Lodge, Priory-gr, South Kensington.

MacInnes, Miles, Esq., M.P., Rickerby, Carlisle.

Mackinnon, Lauchlan, Esq. Reform Club, Pall Mall.

Mackinnon, William Alexander, Esq., 4, Hyde-pk-pl, W.

Mackintosh, George G., Esq., Richmond House, Twickenham.

McMurdo, Gen. Sir Montague Scott, K.C.B., Rose Bank, Fulham.

Magheramorne, The Lord, 17, Grosvenor-gdns, S.W.

Mansfield, John Smith, Esq., Marlborough Police Court, W.

March, Thomas C., Esq., Board of Green Cloth, Buckingham Palace.

Marshall, James, Esq., 37, Grosvenor-rd, S.W.

Martineau, Philip Meadows, Esq., 6, Christian-st, St. George's East.

Master, Robert Edward, Esq., Hillingdon, Parke, Hillingdon.

Mayne, Rear-Adml. Richard C., C.B., 101, Queen's-ga, Hyde-pk.

Meyer, James, Esq., Forty Hall, Enfield, N.

Miller, Alexander Edward, Esq., Q.C., Clonara, Stanmore, N.W.

Miller, Geo. Taverner, Esq., 7, Millbank-st, S.W.

Miller, Colonel James, 84, Portland-pl, W.

Milman, Major-General George Brian, C.B., Queen's House, Tower of London.

Milltown, The Right Hon. the Earl of, Palace-gdns, Kensington.

Mitchison, William Anthony, Esq., Manor House, Sunbury, S.W.

Monkswell, Lord, Chelsea Embankment, S.W.

Montagu Stuart-Wortley, the Hon. Francis Dudley, 68, Longbridge-rd, South Kensington.

Montefiore, Joseph Sebag, 40, Westbourne-ter, W.

Moon, John Francis, Esq., 33, Park-st.

Morley, Col. Sir Francis Brockman, 14, Norland-pl, Notting-hill, W., Chairman of the Court.

Morley, John, Esq., Upper Clapton, E.

Morris, Edward Robert, Esq., Manor Place, Highbury, N.

Mosley, Ernald, Esq., Woodlands, Ivy Heath, Uxbridge.

Mundella, The Right Hon. Anthony John, M.P., 16, Elvaston-pl, S.W.

Munro, George Lawson, Esq., 96, Highbury New-pk, N.

Nash, Henry, Esq., 15, Sussex-gdns, Hyde-pk, W.

Nelson, Lieut.-General Alexander Abercromby, C.B., The Cedars, Southall.

Nelson, Edward Montague, Esq., Hanger Hill House, Ealing, W.

Newdigate, Lieut.-Colonel Francis Wm., 26, Seymour-st, W.

Newton, Robert Milnes, Esq., Great Marlborough - st Police Court, W.

Nicholl, Hume, Esq., 23, Connaught-sq, Hyde-pk.

Nicholson, Cornelius, Esq., Ashleigh, Ventnor.

Nicoll, Donald, Esq., Oaklands, West End, Kilburn, N.W.

Noble, John, Esq., Park Place, Henley-on-Thames.

Noel, E. F., Esq., Manor House, Stanmore.

Noel, The Hon. Henry Lewis, 17, Westbourne-ter, W.

Norris, Edwd. Samuel, M.P., 24, Chester-ter, Regent's-pk.

North, Lieut.-Col. John Sidney, 16, Arlington-st, S.W.

North, Lord, 51, Cromwell Houses South Kensington, W.

Orton, Frederick, M.D., Esq. Crouch End, Hornsey.

Otway, Sir Arthur Bart., 13 Eaton-pl, S.W.

Paget, John, Esq., Hammersmith Police Court, W.

Palliser, Capt. Arthur, 1, Bryanston-pl, W.

Parker, Henry, Esq., Parkfield Potter's Bar, N.

Partridge, William, Esq., Westminster Police Court, S.W.

Peck, Cuthbert Edgar, Esq. Wimbledon House, Surrey.

Pellew, Henry Edward, Esq.

Pender, John, Esq., 18, Arlington st, W.

Penton, Capt. Frederick T., M.P. Sutton Park, Sandy, Beds.

Peto, Sir Samuel Morton, Bart. Blackhurst, Tunbridge Wells.

Phillips, Sir Benjamin Samuel (Alderman of London), 17, Grosvenor-st, W.

Phillips, Henry Dominic, Esq. The Maples, Hampton Wick.

Pinhey, Robert Hill, Esq., 18 Bassett-rd, Notting-hill, W.

Pixley, Stewart, Esq., 21, Leinster gdns, W.

Plowden, Trevor Chichele, Esq. 14, Redcliffe-sq, S. Kensington

Plowden, Sir Wm. Chichele, M.P. 12, Queen's-ga-pl, S.W.

Plucknett, Geo., Esq., Manor House, Finchley, N.

Pollington, John Horace Savile Viscount, 8, John-st, Berkeley sq.

Pollock, Major - Gen. Sir F Richard, K.C.S.I., 12, Cambridge-sq, W.

Ponsonby, The Hon. Ashley John Geo., 9, Prince's-gdns, Kensington, S.W.

Ponsonby, Edward, Esq., 15, Queen Anne-st, W.

Portman, Viscount, 5, Prince's-gate Hyde-pk, S.W.

Powell, Geo. Holt, Esq., Cedar Lawn, Hampstead.

Power, Major - General Edward Henry, 3, Gledhow-gdns, South Kensington.

Pownall, Henry Harrison, Esq. 19, Old-sq, Lincoln's Inn, W.C.

Pownall, John Fish, Esq., 19 Old-sq, Lincoln's Inn, W.C. and 63, Russell-sq, W.C.

Prendergast, Colonel Lennox, 22 Grosvenor-gdns, S.W.

Price, John Blount, Esq., 8 Highbury-hill, N.

Rashleigh, Jonathan, Esq., 3 Cumberland - ter, Regent's-pk. N.W.

Reade, Charles Darby, The Rev., 83, Holland-rd, Kensington.

Reckitt, Francis, Esq., Caen Wood Towers, Highgate, N.

Rintoul, Lieut.-Col. Robert, 28, Carlyle-sq, Chelsea, S.W.

Ritchie, The Right Hon. Chas. Thompson, M.P., Wetherby-gdns, S.W.

Ritchie, James Thompson, Esq., 72, Queensborough-ter, Hyde-pk.

Ross, Major Alex. Henry, M.P., 9, Upper Berkeley-st, W.

Ryder, The Hon. Henry Dudley, 27, Queen's-ga-gdns, W.

Salisbury, The Marquis of, K.G., 20, Arlington-st, W.

Salomons, Sir David Lionel, Bart., Broom-hill, Tunbridge Wells.

Sandhurst, Lord, 4, Manchester-sq, W.

Sandford, John Douglas, Esq., 16, Onslow-gdns, S.W.

Sanford, Colonel Henry Ayshford, 55, Ennismore-gdns, S.W.

Saunders, Thomas Wm., Esq., Thames Police Court, E.

Sayer and Sele, The Lord, Casket Hill, Reading.

Scott, Montague David, Esq., M P., Hove, Brighton.

Scott, Thomas, Esq., Nevill-pk, Tunbridge Wells.

Sedgwick, John Bell, Esq., 1, St. Andrew's-pl, Regent's-pk.

Seymour, Hugh Horatio, Esq., 30, Upper Brook-st, W.

Sharpe, Montague, Esq., Han-well-pk, Hanwell.

Sheil, James, Esq., Hammersmith Police Court, W.

Shepheard, Charles, Esq., Beau-mont House, Grange-rd, Ealing.

Sheridan, H. Brinsley, Esq., 6, Colville-gds, Kensington-pk, W.

Shore, Richard Nowell, Esq., 16, Nevern-sq, Earl's Court, S.W.

Sidney, Thomas, Esq., Bowes Manor, Southgate (Alderman of London).

Slade, Sir Alfred, Bart., Re-ceiver-General's Office, Somerset House, W.C.

Smith, Basil Woodd, Esq., Branch-hill Lodge, Hampstead-heath.

Smith, Horace, Esq., Police Court, Dalston.

Smith, Rt. Hon. William Henry, 3, Grosvenor-pl, S.W.

Smyth, Gen. Sir Edward Selby, K.C.M.G., Darby House, Sun-bury-on-Thames.

Somerset, Lieut. - Col. Alfred Plantagenet, Enfield Court, N.

Somerset, Admiral L. E. H., 44, Curzon-st, Mayfair.

Somes, Samuel Francis, Esq., Fortismere, Muswell-hill, N.

Sotheby, Major C. W. H., E4, Albany, W.

Spearman, Edmund Robert, Esq., 3, Grenville-pl, Cromwell-rd, S.W

Spicer Edward, Esq., 188, Crom-well-rd, S.W.

Spicer, Richard Wm., Esq., 3, Chesham-pl, S.W.

Stapylton, Henry E. Chetwynd, Esq., 72, Warwick-sq, S.W.

Stedall, Col., The Priory, High-gate, N.

Stewart, Alexander John Robert, Esq., 12, Palmeira-sq, Brighton.

Stewart, John Archibald Shaw, Esq., 71, Eaton-pl, S.W.

Stirling, Sir Walter George, Bart., 36, Portman-sq, W.

Strafford, The Right Hon. the Earl of (Lord Lieutenant), 34, Wilton-pl, S.W.

Stuart-Wortley, Hon. F. D.M., 68, Longridge-rd, Sth. Kensington, S.W.

Talbot, John G., Esq., M.P., 10, Great George-st, Westminster.

Tanqueray, John Samuel, Esq., Llangollen.

Taylor, Hugh, Esq., Church End, Finchley, N.

Taylor, Major R. K., Grovelands, Southgate, N.

Tewart, Edward, Esq., 16, York-pl, Portman-sq, W.

Thompson, Archibald, Esq., Myn-wood, Bell Bar, Hatfield.

Thompson, Col. Robert, Kneller Hall, Whitton, Hounslow.

Tilley, Sir J., K.C.B., 73, St. George's-sq.

Todhunter, R. F., Esq., Cham-pions, Shenley, Barnet.

Townsend, The Marquis, Balls Park, Hertford.

Tremenheere, General George Borlase Spring-gr., Isleworth, W.

Trench, Colonel the Hon. William Le Poer, 3, Hyde-pk-gdns, W.

Trotter, Major Frederick, Dyr-ham Park, Barnet.

Truscott, Sir F. W., 103, Victoria-st, S.W.

Tufnell, Thomas Robert, Esq., 18, Moorgate-st, E.C.

Tweedmouth, Lord, Brook House, Park-la, W.

Twining, Richard, Esq., 215, Strand, W.C.

Tyler, Sir James, Pine House, Holloway, N.

Vaughan, James, Esq., Bow-st Police Court, W.C.

Verney, Lt. Col. Geo. Hope, The Cedars, Esher.

Vincent, Lieut.-Col. Charles E. H., M.P., 1, Grosvenor-sq, W.

Wakefield, Charles Marcus, Esq., Belmont, Uxbridge.

Waldegrave, Wm. Fredk., Earl, 13, Montagu-pl, W.

Waller, Fred., Esq , Q.C., 6, Chester-sq, S.W.

Walshe, E. F. Devenish, Esq., St. George's Club, 2, Savile-row.

Walter, John, Esq., 40, Upper Grosvenor-st, W.

Waterlow, Sir Sydney Hedley, Bart., Fairseat, Highgate, N. (Alderman of London).

Waterlow, Walter Blandford, Esq., 5, Storey's-gate, St. James's-pk.

Webb, Capt. J., Riversdale, Twickenham.

Webb, Col. Richard F., 6, West Cromwell-rd, South Kensington.

Webster, Robert Grant, Esq., M.P., 83, Belgrave-rd, S.W.

West, Sir Algernon, K.C.B., Am-bassador's Court, St. James's Palace.

Whatman, George Dunbar, Esq., 8, Queensberry-pl, Kensington.

White, Henry, Esq., 30, Queen's-ga, South Kensington.

Wigram, Charles Hampden, Esq., 8, Manchester-sq, W.

Willans, William Henry, Esq., 23, Holland-pk, Kensington.

Willcocks, Fred. Wm., Esq., 132, Queen's-rd, Finsbury-pk, N.

Willes, Admiral Sir Geo., K.C.B., 68, Cadogan-pl, Chelsea, S.W.

Willett, E. S., Esq., M.D., Wyke House, Isleworth.

Williams, William Walter, Esq., 29, Highbury-quadrant, N.

Wilson, Cornelius Lea, Esq., The Cedars, Beckenham, Kent, S.E.

Wilson, Fleetwood Pellew, Esq., 30, Portman-sq, W.

Wolff, Sir Henry Drummond, 4, Chesham-pl, S.W.

Wood, Sir Charles Alexander, 11, Elvaston-pl, Queen's-ga, S.W.

Wood, Edward, Esq., Hanger Hall, Ealing.

Wood, Thomas, Esq., Gwernyfed Park, Breconshire.

Worms, Baron George de, 17, Park-cres, Portland-pl.

Worms, Baron Henry de, M.P., 42, Grosvenor-pl, S.W.

Wyatt, Sir William Hy., 88, Re gent's-pk-rd, N.W.

Young, Frederick, Esq., 5 Queensberry-pl, S.W.

Young, John, Esq., Bush Hill, Winchmore-hill, N.

Young, Major-Gen. Ralph, 70, Finchley New-rd, N.W.

Middlesex Sessions House, Clerkenwell - gn, near Farringdon-rd (Map 7), stands nearly on the site of Hicks's Hall, the famous old mansion built in 1612 by Sir Baptist Hicks, silk mercer

F 2

to accommodate the magistrates of Middlesex at the times of sessions. The new hall, which cannot be numbered among the most successful of the architectural features of London, was built in 1782. For many years the name of "Hicks's Hall" stuck to it, and it is said that, even now, the criminal classes who are most familiar with the Sessions House on Clerkenwell-gn continue to call it by the old name, although it may reasonably be supposed that their ideas as to who Hicks was, and what he did, are but hazy. NEAREST *Ry. Stn.*, Farringdon-st (Met.); *Omnibus Rtes.*, Exmouth-st and Goswell-rd; *Cab Rank*, Opposite.

Military and Royal Naval Club, 16, Albemarle-st, W.—Proprietary. For officers of the Army, Navy, Royal Marines, and Auxiliary Forces, and those retired from the same. Annual subscription, £6 6s; members on service abroad, £1 1s. No liability beyond subscription, and no entrance fee before 1st October.

Military Home District (*Head Quarters, Horse Guards, London*), comprising Berkshire, Buckinghamshire, City of London, Middlesex, Oxfordshire, Surrey, Tower Hamlets, and Woolwich, including Victoria and Royal Albert Docks, and North Woolwich.

TROOPS QUARTERED IN THE COMMAND.—CAVALRY: 1st and 2nd Life Guards, Royal Horse Guards, and 10th Hussars. ARTILLERY: B Brigade, B Battery, Horse Artillery, and Coast Brigade, No. 6 Division. ENGINEERS: 3 companies. COMMISSARIAT AND TRANSPORT: 3 companies. INFANTRY: 1st, 2nd, and 3rd Battalions Grenadier Guards, 1st Battalion Coldstream Guards, and 1st and 2nd Battalions Scots Guards.

REGIMENTAL DISTRICTS. No. 2 (GUILDFORD). — *Territorial Regiment*, the Royal West Surrey. *Volunteers*, 1st, 2nd, 3rd, and 4th West Surrey. Nos. 7 and 57 (HOUNSLOW).—No. 7. *Territorial Regiment*, the Royal Fusiliers. *Volunteers*, 1st and 2nd Fusiliers. No. 57.—*Territorial Regiment*, the Middlesex. *Volunteers*, 3rd, 8th, 11th, and 17th Middlesex. No. 31 (KINGSTON). — *Territorial Regiment*, the East Surrey. *Volunteers*, 1st,

2nd, 3rd, and 4th Surrey. No. 43 (OXFORD). — *Territorial Regiment*, the Oxfordshire Light Infantry. *Volunteers*, 1st 2nd, and 4th Oxford, and 1st Bucks. No. 49 (READING).—*Territorial Regiment*, the Berkshire Regiment. *Volunteers*, 1st Berks.

The following regiments of Auxiliary Forces are attached to the Brigade of Foot Guards :—To GRENADIER GUARDS — *Militia Battalion*, 4th Battalion Royal Fusiliers. *Volunteers*, 1st, 2nd, and 3rd London, 12th and 25th Middlesex (attached), and 15th and 24th Middlesex. To COLDSTREAM GUARDS — *Militia Battalion*, 7th Battalion King's Own Rifle Corps. *Volunteers*, 4th Middlesex, 6th and 1st Middlesex (attached), and 16th, 18th, 19th, 21st, and 22nd Middlesex. To SCOTS GUARDS — *Militia Battalions*, 5th and 7th Battalions Rifle Brigade. *Volunteers*, 2nd Middlesex, 5th and 9th Middlesex (attached), 7th, 13th, 14th, and 20th Middlesex, and 1st and 2nd Tower Hamlets.

WOOLWICH—TROOPS QUARTERED IN THE COMMAND.— CAVALRY: 20th Hussars. ARTILLERY: Riding Establishment. Horse Artillery, A Brigade, A Battery; B Brigade, F Battery; A and B Batteries Depot; 1st Brigade, J and K Batteries; 2nd Brigade, C, I, and L Batteries; 3rd Brigade, E Battery; 4th Brigade, A and D Batteries, No. 10 Battery, 1st Brigade, Cinque Ports Division, No. 10 Battery, London Division, No. 10 Battery, Western Division. Depot London Division. District Staff, A and B Divisions. ENGINEERS: Detachment. COMMISSARIAT AND TRANSPORT: 2nd Company (Depot), and 6th, 13th, 14th, 26th, 33rd, and 34th Companies. ORDNANCE STORE CORPS: A, B, and D Companies. INFANTRY: 2nd Battalion, the Rifle Brigade.

Milk.—London milk-sellers are supplied partly from cow-sheds in London itself, partly from numerous farms in all parts of the country, brought within easy reach by the railway system. Milk is, unfortunately, as recent experience has proved, often the means of spreading serious epidemics of typhoid, diphtheria, and scarlatina. The Adulteration Act made it a penal offence to sell milk and

water as "milk," and an Order in Council now enforces the registration, regulation, and cleansing of dairies, milk-shops, &c. It is almost impossible for small proprietors of milk businesses to properly carry out the sanitary arrangements necessary to secure freedom from contamination. A medical inspector to frequently inspect and report upon the farms from whence the supplies are obtained; an engineer to supervise the water supply and drainage; care taken of the employés in London, by giving them suitable dwellings for themselves and families, so as to avoid the probability of their living in wretched and crowded tenements; and a staff of inspectors to guard against malpractices on the part of the milk-carriers, are precautions that can rarely be adopted by private milk-sellers. It is only in companies with large capital at command that the necessary precautions and supervision can be thoroughly carried out. A system comprising such arrangements as given above may be seen in operation in the establishments of the London and Provincial Dairy Company, and the Aylesbury Dairy Company, though the arrangements for checking the sophistication of the article on its road to the consumer still seem to leave something to be desired. Much confusion was caused by an ingenious person who discovered an ambiguity in the Adulteration Act, and who unfortunately succeeded in inducing several magistrates to adopt his views. According to the judgments delivered in accordance with this reading of the Act, no public inspector, buying goods for the purpose of analysis, could be prejudiced if they were adulterated, and consequently no penalties could be enforced. This for a time frustrated the undoubted object of the legislature. Fortunately in March, 1879, the superior court, on appeal, adopted the common-sense view, and the provisions of the Act are now in useful operation.

Millbank Prison (Map 13), on the river bank, near Vauxhall-bridge, was built, a good many years ago, on Bentham's "Panopticon" plan, six different buildings radiating from a common centre. The building, which it has been announced is to be shortly pulled down, and its site converted into an open space, or used for the erecion of artisans' dwellings, was capable of holding 1,000 prisoners, and cost the enormous sum of half-a-million of money.

Mines, Royal School of, Jermyn-st.—The School of Mines which was established in 1851, was really a product of the geological survey of the United Kingdom, begun by Sir Henry de la Beche in 1834. The principal object of the institution has always been, and is, to discipline the students thoroughly in the principles of those sciences upon which the operations of the miner and metallurgist depend. The professors attached to the school lecture on the following subjects : Mining, mineralogy, chemistry, general natural history, physics, applied mechanics, metallurgy, geology, and mechanical drawing. The fee for a course of 40 or more lectures is £4 ; for 30, and under 40, £3. Students passing the examination of the third year in the first class receive an official certificate as Associates of the Royal School of Mines. There are various exhibitions, scholarships, and free admissions attached to the school, as to which information can be obtained of the registrar. At suitable periods during the year lectures are given in the evening to working men. These courses are systematic, and are so arranged as to illustrate, within two years, the principal subjects taught at the institution. — (*See* GEOLOGICAL MUSEUM.)

Mint, Royal, Little Tower-hill (Map 8). Hours 10 till 4.—Contains some of the most beautiful automatic machinery in the world. The process of converting bar gold into coins of exactly the same size, and the same weight to half a grain, can be seen here in perfection. Formerly the Royal Mint was the only place whence gold coinage was issued having currency in the United Kingdom and its colonies, but for many years mints have been established in Sydney and in Melbourne, whence by every mail arrives a large influx of colonial gold coin. Applications to view the Mint should be made in writing to the Chancellor of the Exchequer. The orders are, however, rather charily given. — NEAREST *Ry. Stns.,* Mark - la (Met. and Dis.) and Fenchurch-st ; *Omnibus Rtes.,* Fenchurch-st and Aldgate; *Cab Rank,* Royal Mint-st.

Missionary Museum, Blomfield-st, Finsbury.—An exhibition of interesting objects collected by missionaries of the London Society. Open free, from 10 to 4 daily ; Sat. 10 to 2. NEAREST *Ry. Stn.,* Bishopsgate ; *Omnibus Rtes.,* Old Broad-st and Bishopsgate-st ; *Cab Rank,* New Broad-st.

Model Lodging-Houses. —So many of the poorer among the working classes of London are absolutely compelled to live within easy distance of their work, that a serious problem is added to the many difficulties which arise when great metropolitan improvements are in contemplation. The destruction of whole quarters of the town, which house, however inadequately, many families, is not an enterprise to be undertaken without due regard being had to the requirements of those whose little homes are taken from them, and who, if matters are left to take their own course, have no choice but to seek refuge in the already overcrowded streets and alleys which remain untouched. Fortunately this is a question which early attracted the attention of practical philanthropists, and several associations now exist which have its solution for their object. Of these it will be sufficient to mention three of the best known, and some extracts from their respective reports will be read with interest. THE METROPOLITAN ASSOCIATION FOR IMPROVING THE DWELLINGS OF THE INDUSTRIOUS CLASSES, Offices, 8, Finsbury-circus, E.C., established in 1841, and incorporated by Royal Charter in 1845, had, at the date of its last report, 14 blocks of buildings and groups of cottages, accommodating 1,432 families, in such diverse regions of the town as Mile End, Penge, Mayfair, Pimlico, Bermondsey, Old Pancras-rd, &c., and it is stated that in every instance the operations of the association have produced general improvement in the neighbourhood. Wisely recognising the undesirability of any stigma of charitable relief applying to their houses, the association goes on the principle of dividing among its shareholders a fair interest on the capital invested. This may be roughly stated at about 5 per cent., the charter limiting the dividend to that rate. The balance of profit over 5 per cent. is carried to a

guarantee fund. The tenants of the association are of a most miscellaneous kind, and there is no doubt that, to a very large extent, its benefits are really available for the classes whom it is intended to serve. The average rate of mortality in the buildings of the association has been 6 per 1,000 less than that of the whole of the metropolis—a sufficient testimony of itself to the character of the buildings. THE TRUSTEES OF THE PEABODY DONATION FUND, whose offices are at 64, Queen-st, Cheapside, started with sums given and bequeathed by Mr. Peabody, amounting in all to half-a-million of money. The added money received for rent and interest has brought this capital to the magnificent sum of (in round numbers) £935,500, the total capital including money borrowed being £1,239,000. The principle of this fund is to devote the profits gradually to the purchase of land and the erection of buildings. Up to the present time the trustees have provided for the artisan and labouring poor of London 11,150 rooms, exclusive of bath-rooms, laundries, and wash-houses. These rooms comprise 5,614 separate dwellings, occupied by upwards of 20,200 persons. It was for some time feared that the class of accommodation provided was somewhat too good, and consequently too expensive for the actual artisan and labouring classes. But the table showing the employ of the tenants, which is appended to the report for 1887, is reassuring on this head. Bricklayers, cabmen, charwomen, letter-carriers, messengers, needle-women, police-constables, porters, &c., comprise large numbers of persons who can afford to pay but very moderate rentals. The average weekly earnings of the head of each family were £1 3s. 9¾d. The average rent of each dwelling was 4s. 9¼d. per week, and if it be considered that these rents are somewhat too high, it must be remembered that many of the dwellings comprise as many as three rooms, and that the free use of water, laundries, sculleries, and bath-rooms is included. The cheapest lodgings are naturally in Shadwell, where the rents are, for one room, 2s. to 2s. 3d. ; two rooms, 3s. 3d. to 3s. 6d.; and three rooms, 4s. to 4s. 6d. In Southwark-st the charges for the same accommodation are respectively 3s., 4s. 3d. to 4s. 9d., and 5s. 3d. to 5s. 9d. The same average prevails in Pimlico, where there are also sets of four rooms at 7s. 6d. The death-rate of the Peabody-bdgs in 1887 was about 0·85 per 1,000 below London. THE ARTIZANS, LABOURERS, AND GENERAL DWELLINGS CO.— In the words of its prospectus, " this company was established for the erection of improved dwellings near to the great centres of industry, but free from the annoyances arising from the proximity of manufactures." Large estates have been secured near Clapham Junc., the Harrow-rd, and the Green Lanes Stn. on the Great Eastern Ry. The first, called Shaftesbury-pk, is now covered with 1,200 houses ; whilst the second, called Queen's-pk, Harrow-rd, now completed, contains 2,220 houses ; and on the third estate, called Noel - pk, 1,238 houses have been already built, and when completed this estate will comprise about 2,600 dwellings. The estates have been laid out with every regard to the latest sanitary improvements. The Shaftesbury-pk Estate is readily accessible from Kensington, Victoria, Waterloo, Ludgate-hill, and London-br, at low fares ; while the Westbourne-pk Stn. on the Metro. Dis. and Gt. Western Rys., and the Kensal Gn. Stn. on the Hampstead Junc. and N. London Rys., and the new station on the London and N. Western main line, with a good service of omnibuses, make the Queen's-pk Estate at Harrow-rd almost equally accessible. At Noel-pk there is a stn. of the G.E.R., while Woodgn and Hornsey on G.N.R., and Haringay- pk on Midland, are quite near. The sale of intoxicating liquor is altogether excluded. The company reserves the right to prohibit sub-letting, or to limit the number of lodgers. On the two completed estates the School Board for London has provided ample school accommodation. At Noel-pk, the local School Board has purchased an acre of land for the erection of schools. At Queen's-pk a large hall for religious services, public meetings, entertainments, etc., has been erected. The houses are divided into five classes, according to accommodation and position. The smallest —fifth-class—contains four rooms on two floors ; the fourth, five rooms on two floors. A third-class house has an additional bedroom. In the second-class house there is an extra parlour, making in all seven rooms ; while a house of the first-class has eight rooms— a bath-room being the additional accommodation. The present weekly rentals, which include rates and taxes, are as follows: An ordinary fifth-class house, 6s. ; fourth-class, 7s. 6d.; third-class, 9s.; second-class, 10s.; first-class, 11s. There are also some double tenement houses with complete separate accommodation for two families at 4s. 6d. and 5s. The shops, corner houses, those with larger gardens than ordinary, and some other exceptional houses, are subject to special rental. The company has extended its operations to block-buildings in London, having erected at Lisson-gr buildings to accommodate about 300 families. Buildings are also nearly completed at Gray's-inn-rd, and Coldbath-sq, having frontages to a new street from Holborn Town Hall to Islington. These will accommodate 250 families. Buildings upon other sites are in progress. It is claimed for these Dwellings that for domestic convenience, sanitary arrangements, for architectural appearance, and for lowness of rent, they compare favourably with any previously erected. The company pays a dividend of 5 per cent. on its ordinary and 4½ on its preference capital. Authority has recently been taken to increase the ordinary capital from £1,000,000 to £2,000,000. All applications to rent houses must be made to the offices on the estates, and must contain a stamped envelope for reply. Full information may be obtained at the chief office, 16, Great George-st, S.W.

Monte Video.—(See URUGUAY.)

Monument, Fish-st-hill (Map 8), was erected by Wren to commemorate the Great Fire. It is of Portland stone, and 202 feet high. On the pedestal there was at one time an inscription attributing the fire of 1666 to "the treachery and malice of the Popish faction, in order to carry out their horrid plot for extirpating the Protestant religion and old English liberty, and the introducing Popery and sla- very," but this absurdity has been very properly cancelled, and London's column, though still "pointing to the skies," no longer "like a tall bully lifts its head and lies." The charge of admission is 3d., and the hours from 8 to 6 from March 25 to September 29, and from 9 to 4 from September 29 to March 25, daily, Sun. excepted. It will be remembered that, according to "Martin Chuzzlewit," the man in charge considered it quite worth twice the money not to make the ascent. NEAREST *Ry. Stns.*, Cannon-st (S.E.) and Monument (Met. & Dis.); *Omnibus Rtes.*, Cannon-st, K. William-st, Gracechurch-st, and Fenchurch-st ; *Cab Rank,* Opposite.

Moving.—The inconveniences which are, under the best of circumstances, inseparable from the process of moving are now reduced to a minimum. There are several respectable firms who take all trouble and responsibility at inclusive rates. No attempt can be made here to give a list of charges, as these necessarily vary according to the circumstances of each particular case. But the inexperienced householder may be cautioned not to be satisfied with a simple estimate at so much per van load, but to insist upon a contract limiting distinctly the number of loads that will be necessary.

Museums.—(See ARMOURERS' CO., BETHNAL GREEN, BRITISH, CHRISTY, COLLEGE OF SURGEONS, GEOLOGICAL, GREENWICH HOSPITAL, HERALDS' COLLEGE, INDIA, KEW, MISSIONARY, PATENT, SOANE, S. KENSINGTON, TOWER, UNITED SERVICE, WOOLWICH.)

Music.—(See CONCERTS ; GUILDHALL SCHOOL OF MUSIC ; MUSIC, ROYAL ACADEMY OF ; and TRINITY COLLEGE.)

Music Halls.—The music hall, as it is at present understood, was started many years ago at the Canterbury Hall over the water. The entertainments proving popular the example was speedily followed in every quarter of the town. It is to be regretted that the absurd and anomalous Acts of Parliament, by which public entertainments are regulated, practically prohibit music-hall managers from giving anything which may, by any exercise of ingenuity, be called "an entertainment of the stage." It is time that a change took place in this matter. Among he principal halls may be mentioned the Alhambra and the Empire, in Leicester-sq; the Bedford, in Camden Tn.; the Canterbury, Westminster-br-rd; the Foresters, Cambridge-rd, E.; Gatti's, Westminster-br-rd; the London Pavilion, at the top of the Haymarket; the Metropolitan, Edgware-rd; the Oxford, Oxford-st; the Cambridge, 136, Commercial-st; the Paragon, Mile End-rd; the Royal Albert, Victoria-dock-rd; the Royal, High Holborn; the South London, London-rd, S.E.; and in the New Cut, Lambeth, formerly the well-known Victoria Theatre, and still earlier the still better known Coburg, now converted into a music hall on "temperance" principles. Of these the Alhambra, the Canterbury, the Metropolitan, and the South London have a specialty for ballet on a large scale. The Canterbury has an arrangement for ventilation peculiar to itself. A large portion of the roof is so arranged as to admit of its easy and rapid removal and replacement. The entertainments at the other halls vary only in degree. The operatic selections which were at one time the distinguishing feature of the Oxford have of late years been discontinued. A curiosity in the way of music halls may be found by the explorer at the "Bell," in St.George's-st, Ratcliff Highway, where, contrary to precedent, the negro element preponderates among the audience instead of on the stage. The hours of performance at most music-halls are from about 8 till 11.30, and the prices of admission vary from 6d. to 3s. Private boxes, at varying prices, may be had at nearly all the music-halls.

Music, Royal Academy of, Tenterden-st, Hanover-sq.—All branches of music are taught at the academy, and students may choose any one for their principal study. In addition to this there are other obligatory classes. Candidates for admission must be recommended, and, on presenting themselves for admission, must take music they can perform. The principal scholarships are the Westmorland for vocalists, open to ladies between the ages of 17 and 20; the Potter, open to ladies and gentlemen; the Sterndale Bennett; the Parepa Rosa; the John Thomas (Welsh); the Henry Smart; the

Sainton Dolby; the Sir John Goss; the Thalberg; the Lady Goldsmid; the Balfe; the Hine Gift; and the Liszt. There is in addition a long list of prizes and medals for proficiency in every branch of the musical art, and under the most varied conditions. Application for admission should be made to the sec., Mr. John Gill, at the academy, who will also furnish all particulars that may be desired. NEAREST *Ry. Stn.*, Portland-rd; *Omnibus Rtes.*, Oxford-st and Regent-st; *Cab Ranks*, Oxford-market and Conduit-st.

National Church Club.—
(*See* CLERGY CLUB.)

National Club, 1, Whitehall · gdns. — Every member is understood to concur in the following fundamental principles:— 1 That it is essential to the due administration of public affairs throughout the empire, that the Protestant principles of the Constitution, the Protestant reformed faith, as established by law, shall be maintained. 2. That the authority of Holy Scripture ought to be recognised in any system of national education, as the only infallible standard of faith and morals. 3. That it is the duty of all persons to endeavour to improve the moral and social condition of the people. Entrance fee for laymen, £5 5s.; subscriptions, Town members, £6 6s.; country members, £4 4s.; clerical members, £1 1s. less that above rates.

National Conservative Club, 9, Pall Mall, S.W.—A political club, established in 1886 for gentlemen professing Conservative opinions. Entrance fee, £10 10s; subscription, £6 6s.

National Gallery, Trafalgar-sq (Map 7).—It was not until the year 1824 that a national gallery of pictures was founded in England. The purchase of the collection of Mr. J. Angerstein formed the nucleus of the present collection. A grant of £60,000 was originally voted by Parliament to provide for the acquisition of the pictures and the incidental expenses. The collection was first exhibited in Mr. Angerstein's house in Pall Mall, and many presents and bequests of more or less value were made during the next few years. The present building was opened to the public in 1838, altered and

enlarged by Sir James Pennethorne in 1860 and 1869. Five rooms were added on the departure of the Royal Academy of Arts. In 1876 a new wing, designed by E. M. Barry, R.A., was built. Sight-seers should not judge of the building by its exterior, from which point of view it is one of the most unfortunate specimens of English architecture. The interior, however, is well adapted for its purpose, the rooms being well-proportioned, carefully ventilated, and admirably lit. It is impossible to attempt anything like a description of the many important works contained in the gallery. The authorised catalogues, which may be obtained on the spot, are both historically and descriptively exhaustive, but are not absolutely necessary, as the frames of all the pictures are inscribed with subject and painters' names. The gallery is open to the public on Mon., Tu., Wed., and Sat. throughout the year during the following hours: Jan. from 10 till 4; Feb., Mar., and Apr., from 10 till 5; May, June, July, and Aug., from 10 till 6; Sept., Oct., Nov., and Dec., from 10 till dusk. The gallery is open to students on Th. and Fri. during the above-mentioned months during the hours named, the public being admitted on these days from 12 o'clock, on payment of 6d. NEAREST *Ry. Stns.*, Charing ✠ (S.E. & Dis.); *Omnibus Rtes.*, Charing ✠, Haymarket, St. Martin's-la; *Cab Rank*, Trafalgar-sq.

National Liberal Club, Victoria Embankment, W.C.—Established to further the interests of the Liberal cause, and intended to be a centre in the metropolis for Liberals throughout the kingdom. In January, 1886, there were nearly 6,000 members. Entrance fee for town members, £10 10s; annual subscription, £6 6s. For country members the subscription is £3 3s. Election is by committee; the control of elections rests with the general committee, a body of one hundred and twenty gentlemen from all parts of the United Kingdom; affiliated clubs and associations are represented on the general committee.

National Portrait Gallery, Exhibition-rd, South Kensington (Map 5).—The collection of National Portraits has been temporarily transferred by consent

of the trustees, to the Bethnal Green Branch of the South Kensington Museum (*which see*), and now occupies the entire range of the picture gallery there. NEAREST *Ry. Stn.*, South Kensington; *Omnibus Rtes.*, Kensington Gore and Brompton; *Cab Rank*, Cromwell-rd.

National Union Club, (The), 23, Albemarle-st, W.—Established in 1887. "Has for its primary object the association of gentlemen of all shades of political feeling, who desire to preserve intact the unity and integrity of the British Empire." No entrance fee at present. Annual subscription: town members, £5 5s; country members, £3 3s; colonial and foreign members, £2 2s.

Natural History Museum, SOUTH KENSINGTON (Map 5), comprises specimens brought together by Sir Hans Sloane, mammals, &c.; Colonel Montagu, ornithology; Hardwicke, Indian animals; Hodgson, mammals and birds; Yarrell, fishes; Ross and Belcher, antarctic specimens; Stephens, entomology, 88,000 specimens; Bowring, entomology; Reeves, vertebrate animals from China; Clark, coleoptera; Hugh Cuming, shells, the largest collection ever formed, acquired in 1866; A. R. Wallace, birds; Dr. Bowerbank, sponges; the specimens collected during the Transit of Venus Expedition (1875), and the recent Arctic exploration; and the zoological collections transferred in 1880 from the India Museum. NEAREST *Ry. Stn.*, South Kensington (Dis.); *Omnibus Rtes.*, Brompton-rd and Kensington-rd; *Cab Rank*, opposite.

Naval and Military Club, 94, Piccadilly.—For officers and ex-officers of the Army and Navy. Entrance fee, £36 15s.; annual subscription, £8 8s. Qualification: The club shall consist of Commissioned officers in the Army, Royal Navy, and Royal Marines on full pay, retired pay, or half pay at the date of their names being entered in the candidates' book, and of Midshipmen who have attained the age of seventeen years, and are in the service at the date of their ballot. The election is by ballot of members. Thirty at least must vote, and one black ball in seven excludes.

Naval School, Royal.—(*See* ROYAL NAVAL SCHOOL.)

Needlework (Art), Royal School of, Exhibition - road, South Kensington.—Show rooms open 10 a.m to 6 p.m. in summer, and 5 p.m. in winter. Close on Sat. at 2 p.m. Letters to be addressed to "The Secretary."

Netherlands. — MINISTRY, 40, Grosvenor-gdns, S.W. NEAREST *Ry. Stns.*, Victoria (Dis., L.B. & S.C., L.C. & D.); *Omnibus Rtes.*, Grosvenor-pl, Victoria-st, and Vauxhall-br-rd; *Cab Rank*, at Station. CONSULATE, 40, Finsbury-cir, E.C. NEAREST *Ry. Stns.* Moorgate-st (Met.) and Mansion House (Dis.); *Omnibus Rtes.*, Moorgate-st and Old Broad-st; *Cab Rank*, Finsbury-pavement.

New Club, Covent-gdn.— Proprietary. Election by ballot in committee, two black balls to exclude. Annual subscription, £10; for members abroad, £1. "After the election of the first hundred members, an entrance fee of £10, in addition to the subscription, shall be paid by the next three hundred, after which the subscription and entrance fee will be raised if considered desirable." The club possesses a handsome theatre and ball-room, in which entertainments are given from time to time.

Newgate (Map 8).—A gloomy building of granite, constructed, after the old style, with a single eye to the security of its prisoners. Improvements have been made of late in its sanitary arrangements, but modern requirements can never be satisfied in the present building. The existing structure dates from 1782, Newgate having been attacked and partly burned by the Gordon rioters in 1780, whilst still incomplete. Shortly after, the execution of capital sentences, which till then had taken place at or in the immediate neighbourhood of Tyburngate, about fifty yards west of the present Marble Arch, was transferred to the open space in front of Newgate, the scaffold being erected before the low door, called the Debtors'-door, which may still be seen. Since 1868 executions have taken place within the prison. Only the officials and the representatives of the press are admitted, unless by special order. The prison is now only used for the reception of prisoners for trial

at the Central Criminal Court. A very interesting and exhaustive history of Newgate, by Major Arthur Griffiths, was published in 1884 by Messrs. Chapman and Hall. Application to view the prison should be addressed to the Home Secretary, who alone can give the necessary permission. NEAREST *Ry. Stns.*, Holborn-viaduct (L. C. & D. and Met.); *Omnibus Rtes.*, Newgate-st and Ludgate-hill; *Cab Rank*, Old Bailey.

Newgate-street (Map 8).— Few streets have been more improved of late years than this, which fifteen years ago was little better than a lane running by the side of the dreary wall of Newgate Prison, and the greasy neighbourhood of Newgate Market. The impediment to traffic was, however, so great that it was determined to widen the street, and the whole of the N. side has now been thrown back some 20 feet. At the point where Holborn-viaduct ends and Newgate-st begins the street called Old Bailey runs in front of Newgate Prison. Giltspur-st, which is a continuation of the Old Bailey, leads to Smithfield Market. On the N. of Newgate-st is the Blue-coat School, or Christ's Hospital (*which see*); the play-ground of the school facing the street. Many propositions have been made for the removal of the school into the country, as the land upon which it stands is of great value, and no doubt ere long the change will be brought about. On the N. corner, where Newgate-st runs into the end of St. Martin's-le-Grand, is the new Post Office, an imposing pile of buildings dedicated to the especial service of the Telegraph and Money-order Departments. To the S. of Newgate-st, behind Newgate Prison, was Newgate Market, which has for some years been abolished, although many butchers still retain shops in their old premises.

New Granada. — (*See* Colombia.)

New Jerusalem Church (commonly called **Swedenborgians**).

1. HISTORY.—Swedenborg died in London in 1772; and the history of his followers, who were not at first connected in Church membership in any way, dates from 1783, when 16 persons, drawn by public advertisement, assembled together, and thereafter met at intervals. In

the following year they assumed the name of "The Theosophic Society," to which belonged John Flaxman the sculptor, William Sharpe the engraver, and Lieut.-Gen. Rainsford, afterwards Governor of Gibraltar. In 1788 the first church was opened for regular public worship in Great East Cheap. The Rev. M. Sibly was appointed pastor; and after several changes a church was erected for his congregation in Friar-st in 1803. From this the society moved in 1844 to the handsome church, now standing, in Argyle-sq. The church in Cross-st, Hatton-gdn, was the first specially erected for this body in the metropolis, in 1797. Owing to pecuniary difficulties it was sold to the Caledonian Asylum, and occupied by the celebrated Edward Irving. When he and his congregation moved to the larger church in Regent's-sq in 1827, it was by a great effort repurchased for the New Church, and remained in its hands until it was found necessary to follow its members, when in 1874 it removed to a handsome Gothic building adjoining the Athenæum in Camden-rd. With this church some of the most noted preachers and theologians of the body have been connected. It possesses a baptismal font presented to it by Flaxman, and an extensive library bequeathed by the Rev. S. Noble. In 1872 the church in Palace-gdns-ter, Kensington, was purchased and handsomely endowed by J. Finnie, Esq., of Bowden, at a cost of £12,050. Two bas-reliefs by Flaxman, illustrating two of the petitions in the Lord's Prayer, are its features of interest to the general public.

2. ITS BELIEF IS—That Jesus Christ is the only God, and that in Him is a Trinity not of persons but of essentials. That the Scriptures contain an internal or spiritual meaning, which is their soul, and is what exists among the angels. The key to this inner sense is called the correspondence of natural with spiritual things. That salvation is attained by shunning evils as sins, and not simply by faith. That a man has a spiritual body, and, after he has cast off his natural body at death like a worn-out garment, he continues to live on without interruption in the spiritual world in which he then finds himself. That in the world of spirits which he first enters everything in a man is brought

into harmony with his ruling love, and according as that is good or evil, he is thereby prepared either for heaven or hell. The Second Coming of the Lord and the Last Judgment are believed to be spiritual events which are now accomplished.

3. CHURCHES in London and its suburbs:

Anerley, Waldegrave-rd.
Brixton, Brixton Hall, Acre-la.
Bromley, West-st.
Camberwell, Flodden-rd.
Dalston, Albion Hall, Albion-sq.
Deptford, Warwick-st.
Holloway, Camden-rd.
Islington, Devonshire-st.
Kensington, Palace-gdns-ter.
King's-cross, Argyle-sq.
Willesden, Parker's Hall.

4. MISSIONARY and OTHER INSTITUTIONS. A New Church College, though initiated in 1845, was really established as to collegiate buildings and teaching appliances only in 1867. It has small but handsome buildings. The Swedenborg Society, British and Foreign, instituted in 1810, publishes and circulates the works of Swedenborg only. Every free library in the country as it is formed is offered a set of its publications, and its operations are world-wide. The languages in which it keeps the works of Swedenborg are Latin, English, French, German, Italian, Swedish, Polish, Danish, Icelandic, Russian, Marathi, and Welsh. At present translations are being made into Hindi and modern Greek. It is well endowed, and has contributors among all the receivers of Swedenborg's teachings, whether separatists from the Established Church, or non-separatists, the latter having been from the earliest times a very numerous and influential class. The Missionary and Tract Society was formed in 1821. It was at first a branch of an older institution in Manchester, but soon became quite independent. It circulates about 5,000 volumes annually, and 50,000 tracts and pamphlets. It has a staff of paid and volunteer missionaries, whose objects are not only to break new ground when needed, but also to assist small societies in the country which are unable to afford the services of a paid pastor. The other metropolitan institutions are the Students' and Ministers' Aid Fund Committee; the Na-

tional Missionary Institution, founded in 1857 to commemorate the centenary of the New Church; the New Church Orphanage, established in 1881; the New Church Evidence Society (formerly called the Auxiliary Missionary and Tract Society), composed principally of young men, who make it their business to look after published statements respecting the views of their Church and its founder, and who have done much by their emendations of notices in encyclopædias, biographical works, &c., to correct the wildly inaccurate statements which not long ago almost universally prevailed. They also keep a sharp eye on the religious press, and are active in introducing by letter, tract, or book their own views to the authors of most new books, whether these contain approximations to their views or the reverse.

5. HEADQUARTERS.—These are for nearly every institution of the church at 36, Bloomsbury-st, Oxford-st, W.C. The building is pre-eminently the headquarters for the publications of the body. From it the "Morning Light," a weekly journal, is issued; a monthly called the "New Church Magazine," a modification to modern necessities of one started in 1812; and a juvenile magazine started in 1840. Most of the committees of the institutions named above meet in the Swedenborg Society's rooms, where also a valuable collection of portraits, books, and other curiosities has been collected. Its committee-room is adorned with a very fine bust of Swedenborg, executed by Mr. Preston Powers, the son of the better-known Hiram Powers, who was himself a most zealous member of this Church.

New Law Courts. — (See LAW COURTS.)

New Oxford and Cambridge Club, 20, Albemarle-st, W. Established in 1885. For members of either university. No entrance fee. Annual subscription: Town members, £8 8s; country members, £5 5s. Full information from secretary.

New River.—Was started in 1608 by Sir Hugh Myddelton. He was not Sir Hugh then, however, but a simple "citizen and goldsmith," the baronetcy being a subsequent reward for the success of his great undertaking. The New River is carried from the springs and chalk wells some twenty miles from London to the great reservoirs, 40 acres in extent, at Stoke Newington; thence, after time to clear itself, to the New River Head by Sadler's Wells Theatre—which in the old times had a special connection therewith, and could turn its stage into a huge tank for nautical exhibitions—and thence direct to the lower portions of the city or to the high-level reservoirs in Claremont-sq and at Highgate.—(*See also* WATER.)

New Road, or, as it is now called, the Marylebone and Euston roads, forms, with its continuation, the City-rd, the northern alternative route from the City to the West End. It starts from Moorgate-st by way of Finsbury-sq, and debouches into the Edgware-rd about half a mile from the Marble Arch. It has no very special character beyond the semi-suburban character of most of its houses, each with its little patch of garden in front, and its little cluster of tombstone-makers about Tottenham-court-rd. The Metropolitan Ry. runs under it for nearly its whole length.

New Sadler's Wells Theatre, St. John-st-rd, E.C. (Map 3).—The famous old house of Grimaldi and of Phelps, at one time known as the "Water Theatre," its position right on the New River affording an opportunity for nautical displays not to be had elsewhere. Its chief modern interest, however, is to be found in the Shakespearian revivals which so honourably distinguished the management of the late Mr. Phelps and raised this little outlying place of entertainment into the front rank of the London theatrical world. Subsequently Sadler's Wells fell on evil days, till in 1879 it was taken by Mrs. Bateman, and entirely rebuilt on a larger and most liberal scale. After Mrs. Bateman's death it was carried on under the management of her daughters. They, however, retired, after but a brief experience of the cares of management, and the theatre has not offered anything remarkably attractive since. NEAREST *Ry. Stns.*, King's ✠ (G.N. & Met.) and St. Pancras (Mid.); *Omnibus Rtes.*, City-rd, High-st, Islington, Pentonville-rd, and Goswell-rd.

New Salisbury Club.—(*See* SALISBURY CLUB.)

New South Wales.—AGENCY-GENERAL, 5, Westminster-cham, S.W. NEAREST *Ry. Stn.*, St. James's-pk (Dis.); *Omnibus Rtes.*, Victoria-st and Parliament-st; *Cab Rank*, Palace-yard.

Newspapers.—The following are the principal newspapers published in London, with their offices, price, and specialties :

Morning.

DAILY CHRONICLE, 1d., 80, Fleet-st .. .. Radical
   ,,   NEWS, 1d., 67, Fleet-st, and 19 to 22, Bouverie-st .. .. Liberal
   ,,   TELEGRAPH, 1d., 135, Fleet-st.. .. .. .. Independent Liberal
CONTINENTAL TIMES, 1d., 137, Strand .. .. General.
FINANCIAL NEWS, 1d., 11, Abchurch-la, E.C. .. .. .. Financial
FINANCIER, 2d., 2, Royal Exchange-bdgs .. .. .. Financial
MORNING ADVERTISER, 3d., 127, Fleet-st .. .. .. Organ of licensed victuallers
   ,,   POST, 1d., 12, Wellington-st, Strand .. .. Fashion and foreign affairs
   ,,   SHIPPING LIST, 2d., 28, Bishopsgate-st-within.. .. .. Shipping
POST OFFICE DAILY LIST, £1 per annum, 14, Bartholomew-close, E.C. .. .. Official List of Mails, &c.
PUBLIC LEDGER, 2½d., 6, St. Dunstan's-alley, E.C. .. .. .. Commercial
SPORTING LIFE, 1d., 148, Fleet-st .. .. Sport
SPORTSMAN, 1d., 139, Fleet-st .. .. Sport
STANDARD, 1d., 104, Shoe-la .. .. Conservative
TIMES, 3d., Printing House-sq, E.C. .. .. General

Evening.

ECHO, ½d., 22, Catherine-st, Strand .. .. Radical
EVENING CORN TRADE LIST, £5 15s. per annum, 28, Bishopsgate-st-within .. .. Commercial
EVENING NEWS, ½d., 12, Whitefriars-st, E.C. .. .. .. Conservative
   ,,   POST AND DAILY RECORDER, 1d., Fleet-st, E.C. .. Financial
   ,,   STANDARD, 1d., 104, Shoe-la .. .. Conservative
GLOBE, 1d., 367, Strand .. .. Conservative
PALL MALL GAZETTE, 1d., 2, Northumberland-st, Strand .. Radical
ST. JAMES'S GAZETTE, 1d., Dorset-st, E.C. .. .. .. High-class Liberal
SHIPPING AND MERCANTILE GAZETTE, 5d., 54, Gracechurch-st, E.C. .. .. Shipping
STAR, ½d., established in 1888, Stonecutter-st, E.C. .. .. .. Radical

Weekly, etc.

ACADEMY, 3d., 27, Chancery-lane, W.C. .. .. Literary and critical
ACCOUNTANT, 6d., 34, Moorgate-st, E.C. .. .. Professional
ADMIRALTY AND HORSE GUARDS GAZETTE, 6d., 9, Catherine-st, W.C. .. .. Professional
AFRICAN TIMES, 4d., 121, Fleet-st, E.C. .. .. Neutral

AGRICULTURE, *1d.*, Wych-st, W.C.	Agricultural
AGRICULTURAL GAZETTE, *4d.*, 9, New Bridge-st	Illustrated—trade
ALLEN'S INDIAN MAIL, *6d.*, 13, Waterloo-pl, S.W.	Indian news
AMERICAN TRAVELLER, *3d.*, 4, Langham-pl, S.W.	American news and List of American Travellers
ANGLO-AMERICAN TIMES, *4d.*, 26, Basinghall-st, E.C.	American news and Articles
ARCHITECT, *4d.*, 175, Strand	Professional
ARMY AND NAVY GAZETTE, *6d.*, 16, Wellington-st, Strand	Professional
ATHENÆUM, *3d.*, 22, Took's-ct, Chancery-lane	Critical, literary, and scientific
AUSTRALIAN AND NEW ZEALAND TRADES' JOURNAL, monthly, *1s.*, 72, Leadenhall-st, E.C.	Colonial
BANNER, *1d.*, 10, Southampton-st, W.C.	Church and Constitution
BAPTIST, *1d.*, 61, Paternoster-row	Denominational
BAYSWATER CHRONICLE, *1d.*, 97, Westbourne-grove	Local—Bayswater, Paddington, Hyde-pk, &c.
BAZAAR AND EXCHANGE AND MART, *2d.*, 170, Strand	Advertisements of articles for sale or exchange
BELL'S WEEKLY MESSENGER, *5d.*, 145, Queen Victoria-st, E.C.	Agricultural
BICYCLING NEWS AND TRICYCLING GAZETTE, *1d.*, 98, Fleet-st	Bicycling
BIRD OF FREEDOM, *1d.* 52, Fleet-st	Sporting
BOARD OF TRADE JOURNAL, *6d.*, Great New-st, E.C.	Commercial
BONDHOLDERS' REGISTER, *3d.*, 2, Royal Exchange-bdgs	Foreign investments
BOOKSELLER, *6d.*, 12, Warwick-la, E.C.	Trade
BOOT AND SHOE TRADE JOURNAL, *2d.*, 9, St. Bride's Avenue, E.C.	Trade
BREWERS' GUARDIAN, *1s.*, 5, Bond-ct, Walbrook	Trade
,, JOURNAL, *2s.*, Eastcheap-bdgs, E.C.	Trade [chester, &c.)
BRITISH ARCHITECT, *4d.*, 15, King William-st, W.C.	Professional (Liverpool, Man-
BRITISH AUSTRALIAN, *4d.*, 157, Strand	Colonial matters
BRITISH AND COLONIAL PRINTER AND STATIONER, BOOKSELLERS' CIRCULAR AND PAPER TRADE REVIEW, *4d.*, 24, Bouverie-st, E.C.	
BRITISH AND FOREIGN CONFECTIONER, *6d.*, 188, Strand, W.C.	Trade
BRITISH JOURNAL OF PHOTOGRAPHY, *2d.*, 2, York-st, Covent-gdn	Organ of Photos.—Edinburgh
,, MAIL, monthly, *1s.*, 12 & 14, Catherine-st, W.C.	Chambers of Commerce
,, MEDICAL JOURNAL, *6d.*, 429, Strand	Organ of British Medical Association
,, MERCANTILE GAZETTE, *1s.*, 19, Ludgate-hill, E.C.	Commercial
,, TRADE JOURNAL, monthly, *6d.*, 113, Cannon-st	Price current of British goods
,, WEEKLY, *1d.*, 27, Paternoster-row	Liberal
BRIXTON NEWS, *1d.*, 34, Brixton-rd, S.W.	Local
BROAD ARROW, *6d.*, 6, Lancaster-pl, W.C.	For military, naval, & civil ser
BUILDER, *4d.*, 46, Catherine-st, Strand	Technical
BUILDERS' WEEKLY REPORTER, *2d.*, 30, Poppin's-ct, Fleet-st	Trade
BUILDING AND ENGINEERING TIMES, *2d.*, 149, Aldersgate-st	Trade
,, NEWS, *4d.*, 332, Strand, W.C.	Technical
,, WORLD, *6d.*, 31, Southampton-st	Technical
BULLIONIST, *6d.*, 27, Throgmorton-st, E.C.	Financial
CABINET MAKER, *6d.*, 42, City-rd, E.C.	Trade
CAMBERWELL NEWS, *1d.*, Portslade-rd, Wandsworth-rd	Local—for South London
CANONBURY AND HIGHBURY ADVERTISER, *½d.*, 313, Essex-rd, N.	Local
CATHOLIC PRESS, *2d.*, 130, Strand	Independent
,, TIMES, *1d.*, 92, Fleet-st	Denominational
CHARITY RECORD, *2d.*, 160, Fleet-st, E.C.	Charity Work
CHEMICAL NEWS, *4d.*, 3, Boy-ct, Ludate-hill	Scientific
CHRISTIAN, *1d.*, 12, Paternoster-bdgs	Undenominational
CHRISTIAN AGE, *1d.*, 1, St. Bride-st, E.C	Family and Religious
,, COMMONWEALTH, *1d.*, 73, Ludgate-hill	
,, GLOBE, *1d.*, 168, Fleet-st	Undenominational
,, LIFE, *2d.*, 123, Fleet-st	
,, MILLION, *1d.*, 20, St. Bride's-avenue, E.C.	
,, UNION, *1d.*, 8, Salisbury-sq, Fleet-st	Undenominational
,, WORLD, *1d.*, 13, Fleet-st	Protestant
CHURCH BELLS, *1d.*, 12, Southampton-st, W.C.	Church of England
,, OF ENGLAND TEMPERANCE CHRONICLE, *1d.*, Paternoster-sq, E.C.	Temperance, not teetotal

CHURCH REVIEW, *1d.*, 11, Burleigh-st, Strand	.. .. ..	Anglo-Catholic
,, TIMES, *1d.*, 32, Little Queen-st, W.C.	.. .. ..	Anglo-Catholic
CITIZEN, *1d.*, 68, Leadenhall-st..	.. .. ..	Local
CITY PRESS, *1d.*, 148 and 149, Aldersgate-st		Local—City of London
CIVILIAN, *3d.*, 6, St. Bride-st, E.C.	.. .. ..	Professional
CIVIL SERVICE GAZETTE, *3d.*, 12, Fetter-la, E.C.	.. ..	Professional
,, ,, TIMES, *1d.*, Wine Office-ct, E.C.	.. ..	Professional
CLAPHAM CHRONICLE, *1d.*, Portslade-rd, S.W.	..	Local—Clapham, Lambeth, &c.
COLLIERY GUARDIAN, *5d.*, 49, Essex-st, Strand	..	Technical
COLLIERY MANAGER, *6d.*, 32, Bouverie-st, E.C.	..	Technical
COMMERCIAL GAZETTE, *42s.* per annum, 58, New Broad-st		Business matter
COMMERCIAL WORLD, *3d.*, 10, Adam-street, Adelphi	..	Mercantile
CONTRACT JOURNAL, *6d.*, 139, Salisbury-ct, E.C.	..	
COUNTY COURTS CHRONICLE, *1s. 6d.*, 10, Wellington-st, Strand		County court reports
,, GENTLEMAN, *2d.*, 136, Strand	.. ..	Sport, etc.
COURIER AND EAST LONDON ADVERTISER, *½d.*, Canning-town, E.		Independent
COURIER DE LONDRES, *2d.*, 76, Finsbury-pav, E.C.	..	Financial and General
COURSE OF EXCHANGE, *6d.*, 4, Copthall-bdgs, E.C.	..	Financial
COURT AND SOCIETY REVIEW, *6d.*, 142, Strand, W.C.	..	Society
,, CIRCULAR, *5d.*, 2, Southampton-st, Strand	..	Fashionable
,, JOURNAL, *5d.*, 13, Burleigh-st, W.C...	..	Fashionable
CRYSTAL PALACE DISTRICT TIMES, *1d.*, Westow-st, Upper Norwood		Local
CYCLING TIMES, *1d.*, East Temple Chambers, Whitefriars-st	..	Cyclists
DECORATION *6d.*, York st, W.C.	.. .. ..	Art Manufactures
DETROIT FREE PRESS, *1d.*, 325, Strand, W.C.	.. ..	
DRAMATIC REVIEW, *1d.*, 12, Catherine-st, W.C.	.. ..	Theatrical
EAST END NEWS, *6d.*, 46, High-st, Poplar	.. .. ..	Shipping
EAST LONDON ADVERTISER, *1d.*, 96, Mile End-rd..	.. ..	Local
EAST LONDON OBSERVER, *1d.*, 260A, Whitechapel-rd	..	Local—East London
ECCLESIASTICAL GAZETTE, *6d.*, 291, Strand, W.C.	..	
ECONOMIST, *8d.*, 340, Strand	.. ..	Commercial and Financial
EDUCATIONAL TIMES, *6d.*, 89, Farringdon-st, E.C. ..		Technical
ELECTRICAL REVIEW, *4d.*, 22, Paternoster-row	.. ..	Scientific
ELECTRICIAN, *4d.*, 1, Salisbury-ct, E.C.	.. ..	Scientific
EMPIRE, *3d.*, 4, Brown's-bdgs, St. Mary Axe, E.C.	..	Home news for South Africa and Australia
ENGINEER, *6d.*, 163, Strand	.. ..	Professional
ENGINEERING, *6d.*, 35 & 36, Bedford-st, Covent-gdn	..	Professional
ENGLAND, *1d.*, 291, Strand	.. ..	National and Conservative
ENGLISH CHURCHMAN, *1d.*, 2, Tavistock-st, Covent-gdn	..	Establishment
,, MECHANIC AND WORLD OF SCIENCE, *2d.*, 332, Strand, W.C.		Applied Science
ENTR'ACTE, *1d.*, 3, Catherine-st, Strand	.. ..	Theatrical
ERA, *6d.*, 49, Wellington-st	.. ..	Theatrical
ESTATES GAZETTE, *3d.*, 22, St. Bride-st, E.C.	..	Sales and letting
EUROPEAN MAIL, *12s.* per annum, 161, Queen Victoria-st ..		Home news for colonies each mail
FARMER, *3d.*, 291, Strand, W.C.	.. .. ..	Illustrated—country pursuits
FIELD, *6d.*, 346, Strand	.. .. ..	Country pursuits
FINANCE CHRONICLE, *4d.*, 8, John-st, Adelphi	..	Finance and banking
FINANCIAL WORLD, *1d.*, 3, Broad-st-buildings, E.C.	..	Finance
FISHING GAZETTE, *2d.*, 12 & 13, Fetter-la	.. ..	Fishing
FREEMAN, *1d.*, 21, Furnival-st, Holborn	.. ..	Baptist
FREEMASON, *3d.*, 16, Great Queen-st, W.C.	.. ..	Masonic
FRIEND, *6d.*, 5, Bishopsgate-st-without	.. ..	Quaker
FUN, *1d.*, 153, Fleet-st	.. ..	Comic
FUNNY FOLKS, *1d.*, Red Lion-ct, Fleet-st	.. ..	Comic
FURNITURE GAZETTE, *4d.*, 74 & 75, Great Queen-st, W.C.	..	Sheets of practical designs
GARDEN, *4d.*, 37, Southampton-st, Strand	.. ..	Illustrated—horticultural
GARDENERS' CHRONICLE, *5d.*, 41, Wellington-st, Strand	.. ..	Illustrated—horticultural

GARDENER'S MAGAZINE, 2d., 4, Ave Maria-la	Illustrated—horticultural
GARDENING, 1d., 37, Southampton-st, Strand	
GENERAL WEEKLY SHIPPING LIST, 4d., 13, St. Mary Axe	Commercial
GOOD TEMPLAR'S WATCHWORD, 3d., 3, Bolt-ct, E.C.	Teetotal
GRAPHIC, 6d., 190, Strand	Illustrated
GROCER, 4d., Eastcheap-bdgs, E.C.	Trade
GROCERS' GAZETTE, 1d., 35, Eastcheap, E.C.	Trade
GROCERS' JOURNAL, 1d., 40, Whitefriars-st, E.C.	Trade
GUARDIAN, 6d., 5, Burleigh-st, Strand	High Church
HACKNEY AND KINGSLAND GAZETTE, ½d., 440-2, Kingsland-rd	Local—for N.E. London
HACKNEY EXAMINER AND NORTH-EAST LONDON CHRONICLE, ½d., 107, New North-rd, N.	Local
HAIRDRESSERS' WEEKLY JOURNAL, 1d., 51, Frith-st, Soho	Trade
HAMPSTEAD AND HIGHGATE EXPRESS, 1d., High-st, Hampstead	Local—for North-west London
HEALTH, 2d., 34, Paternoster-row,	Sanitary
HOLLOWAY AND HORNSEY PRESS, ½d., 382, Hornsey-rd, N.	Local
HOME NEWS, 6d., 55, Parliament-st	India, Australia, & N. Zealand
HOME AND COLONIAL MAIL, 6d., 188, Strand	Home News
HOMEWARD MAIL, 6d., 65, Cornhill	Indian News
HORNSEY AND FINSBURY PARK JOURNAL, 1d., 1, Stapleton-ter, Crouch End, N.	Local
ILLUSTRATED LONDON NEWS, 6d., 198, Strand	
" POLICE NEWS, 1d., 286, Strand	Sensational
" SPORTING AND DRAMATIC NEWS, 6d., 148, Strand	
INDICATOR, ½d., 250, Harrow-rd	Local
INQUIRER, 2d., Essex-st, Strand	Unitarian
INSURANCE GAZETTE, 2d., 34, Cursitor-st, E.C.	Insurance
" GUARDIAN, 1d., Ave Maria-la, E.C.	Agents' organ
" JOURNAL, 4d., 80, Fleet-st, E.C.	Commercial
" RECORD, 2d., 13, York-st, Covent-gdn	Advocacy of insurance
INVENTION, 3d., 54, Fleet-st	Criticism of companies
INVESTORS' GUARDIAN, 6d., 6, St. Swithin's-la, King William-st	Technical
IRON, 6d., 161, Fleet-st	Trade
" AND COAL TRADES' REVIEW, 26s. per annum, 342, Strand	Trade
IRONMONGERS' JOURNAL, 6d., 2, Fenchurch-bdgs, E.C.	Trade
IRON AND STEEL TRADES' JOURNAL, 6d., 82, Cannon-st, E.C.	Trade
ISLINGTON GAZETTE, ½d., 10, High-st, Islington	Local—for N. London (Liberal)
" NEWS, 1d., 10, High-st, Islington-gn	Local—for N. London (Indepen.
JEWISH CHRONICLE, 2d., 2, Finsbury-sq	Denominational
" WORLD, 1d., 8, South-st, Finsbury	Denominational
JOHN BULL, 5d., 6, Whitefriars-st, E.C.	Constitutional Toryism
JOURNAL OF GAS LIGHTING, 6d., 11, Bolt-ct, Fleet-st	Gas
" HORTICULTURE, 3d., 171, Fleet-st	Horticulture, bees, and poultry
" THE SOCIETY OF ARTS, 6d., 4 & 5, York-st, Covent-gdn	Scientific
JOURNALIST, 1d., Savoy House, Strand	Professional
JUDY, 2d., 99, Shoe-la, Fleet-st	Comic
JUSTICE OF THE PEACE, 5d., 7, Fetter-la	Legal
KENSINGTON NEWS, 1d., 4, Bedford-ter, Church-st, Kensington	Local—for West London
KENSINGTON AND HAMMERSMITH REPORTER, 1d., 96, The Grove, Hammersmith	Conservative
KILBURN TIMES, 1d., 4, Cambridge-rd, Kilburn	Local—for North-west London
LABOUR NEWS, 1d., 7, Gough-sq, E.C.	Industrial
LABOUR TRIBUNE, 1d., 63, Fleet-st	The Rights of Labour
LADIES' PICTORIAL, 6d., 172, Strand, W.C.	
LANCET, 7d., 423, Strand	Medical
LAND AGENTS' RECORD, 6d., 75, Fleet-st	Trade
" AND WATER, 6d., 182, Strand	Field sports and natural history
LAW JOURNAL, 6d., 5, Quality-ct, Chancery-la, W.C.	Notes of important decisions
" TIMES, 1s., 10, Wellington-st	Law reports
LEATHER TRADE CIRCULAR, 5s. per annum, 24, Birchin-la, E.C.	Trade

LICENSED VICTUALLERS' GAZETTE, 2d., 26, Southampton-st, Strand..			Sporting
,, ,, MIRROR, 1d., 9, Catherine-st, Strand ..		..	Sporting
LIFE, 6d., 434, Strand, W.C.			Society
LIVE STOCK JOURNAL, 4d., 9, New Bridge-st			Technical
LLOYD'S WEEKLY LONDON NEWSPAPER, 1d., 12, Salisbury-sq, Fleet-st..			Radical
LOCAL GOVERNMENT CHRONICLE, 3d., 90, Fleet-st			Local Government topics
LONDON AND CHINA EXPRESS, £3 3s. per annum, 79, Gracechurch-st..			Home news for China
,, ,, TELEGRAPH, 9d., £2 2s. per annum, 79, Grace-church-st		..	China news
,, COMMERCIAL RECORD, 5s. per quarter, 11, Jewry-street, Aldgate		..	Merchant law and economy
,, FIGARO, 1d., 2, Tavistock-st, W.C.		..	Society
,, GAZETTE, 1s., 45, St. Martin's-la		..	Official Government organ
LONDONER ZEITUNG, 2d., 40, Finsbury-cir		..	German organ in London
MAGNET, 3½d., 19, Exeter-st, Strand		..	Agriculture
MAIL, 2d., Printing House-sq, Blackfriars		..	Partial reprint from *Times*
MARK-LANE EXPRESS, 3d., Clement's House, Clement's Inn-passage, W.C.		..	Corn trade
MARYLEBONE MERCURY, 1d., 102, High-st, Marylebone		..	Marylebone and neighbourhood
MEDICAL PRESS AND CIRCULAR, 5d., 20, King William-st		..	Professional
METHODIST RECORDER, 1d., 161, Fleet-st		..	Denominational
,, TIMES, 1d., 125, Fleet-st ..		..	Denominational
METROPOLITAN, 2d., Dorset House, Salisbury-sq		..	Corporation, Board of Works, Vestries, &c.
MID-SURREY GAZETTE, 1d., 12, Falcon-rd, Battersea		..	Local
MILLER, 5d., 24, Mark-la		..	Trade
MINING JOURNAL, 6d., 18, Finch-la		..	Mines and railways
,, WORLD, 6d., Gresham House, Old Broad-st		..	Technical
MODERN SOCIETY, 1d., 9, Crane-ct, Fleet st		..	
MONEY, 4d., 27, Change-alley, E.C.		..	Financial
,, MARKET REVIEW, 6d., 2, Royal Exchange-bdgs ..		..	Financial
MONTHLY STATEMENT, COLONIAL AND FOREIGN PRODUCE, 10s. 6d. per annum, 11, Jewry-st ..			Commercial
,, STATEMENT, DRUGS, 10s. 6d. per annum, 11, Jewry-st			Commercial
MOONSHINE, 1d., 130, Fleet-st		..	Comic
MUNICIPAL REVIEW, 4d., 12, Catherine-st, W.C.		..	Local Government
MUSICAL STANDARD, 3d., 23, Red Lion-st		..	Critical
,, TIMES, 4d., 1, Berners-st, Oxford-st		..	Contains anthems, glees, &c.
,, WORLD, 3d., 12, Catherine-st, W.C.		..	Critical
NATIONAL CHURCH, 1d., 9, Bridge-st, Westminster		..	Church of England
,, REFORMER, 2d., 63, Fleet-st		..	Secularist and republican
NATURE, 6d., 29, Bedford-st, Strand		..	Scientific
NEWS OF THE WORLD, 1d., 19, Exeter-st, Strand		..	Radical
NONCONFORMIST, 6d., 13, Fleet-st		..	
NORTH LONDON NEWS, ½d., 433, Caledonian-rd		..	Local
,, MIDDLESEX CHRONICLE, 1d., 353, Upper-st, Islington		..	Local—for Northern suburbs
,, WESTERN GAZETTE, 1d., 134, High-st, Camden Town		..	Local
NORWOOD NEWS, 1d., South Norwood		..	Local
NOTES AND QUERIES, 4d., 22, Took's-ct, Chancery-la		..	Literary
OBSERVER, 4d., 396, Strand		..	Sunday—general
OFFICIAL PRICE CURRENT AND COMMERCIAL REGISTER, 1s., 65A, Leadenhall-st, E.C. ..			
ORCHESTRA, 3d., 185, Fleet-st ..		..	Music and drama
OVERLAND MAIL, £1 12s. 6d. per annum, 65, Cornhill		..	Home news for India
PADDINGTON MERCURY, 1d., 62, Porchester-rd, W.		..	Local
,, TIMES, 1d., 30, Praed-st, Paddington		..	Local
PALL MALL BUDGET, 3d., 2, Northumberland-st, Strand ..			Weekly edition of P.M.G.
PAPER-MAKERS' CIRCULAR, 6d., 160A, Fleet-st		..	Trade
PAPER AND PRINTING TRADES' JOURNAL, 2s. per annum, 50, Leadenhall-st ..			Trade
PAWNBROKERS' GAZETTE, 2d., Eagle-ct, Dean-st, High Holborn		..	Trade
PENNY ILLUSTRATED PAPER, 1d., 10, Milford-la, Strand ..	,,	,,	

PENNY PICTORIAL NEWS, *1d.*, Red Lion House, Fleet-st, E.C...	Illustrated
PEOPLE, *1d.*, 110, Strand, W.C.	Conservative
PHARMACEUTICAL JOURNAL, *4d.*, 11, New Burlington-st	Pharmaceutical Society
PHOTOGRAPHIC JOURNAL, *3d.*, 59, Pall Mall..	Organ of Photographic Society
„ NEWS, *3d.*, 5, Furnival-st, E.C.	Artistic and scientific
PICTORIAL WORLD, *6d.*, 149, Strand, W.C.	Illustrated
PLUMBER AND DECORATOR, *6d.*, 24, Wellington-st, W.C.	Trade
POLICE GAZETTE, Scotland-yard, S.W.	Private circulation only
POOR LAW UNIONS GAZETTE, *2d.*, 68, Wardour-st	Runaways
POST MAGAZINE, *1d.*, 4, Wine Office-ct, Fleet-st	Insurance
POTTERY GAZETTE, *8d.*, 19, Ludgate-hill	Trade
PRESS NEWS, *2d.*, 8, Windsor-ct, Strand	Professional
PRIMITIVE METHODIST, *1d.*, 4, Wine Office-ct, Fleet-st	Denominational
PRINTERS' REGISTER, *3d.*, 33A, Ludgate-hill	Trade
PRINTING TIMES & LITHOGRAPHER, *6d.*, 73, Ludgate-hill, E.C.	Trade
PRODUCE MARKET REVIEW, *2d.*, 121, Cannon-st	Commercial
PROTESTANT TIMES, *1d.*, 37, Aldermanbury, E.C.	Independent
PUBLIC OPINION, *2d.*, 11, Southampton-st, Strand	Extracts and digests
PUBLISHERS' CIRCULAR, *8s.* per annum, St. Dunstan's House, Fetter-la, E.C.	List of all new books
"PUMP COURT," The Temple Newspaper and Review, *6d.*, 33, Exeter-st, W.C..	The organ of the Bar
PUNCH, *3d.*, 85, Fleet-st	Comic
QUEEN, *6d.*, 346, Strand	Fashions, &c.
RACING CALENDAR, *£1 5s.* per annum, 6, Old Burlington-st	Sporting
RAILWAY HERALD, *2d.*, 61, Fleet-st	Technical
„ NEWS, *6d.*, 3, Whitefriars-st, Fleet-st	Technical
„ RECORD, *2d.*, 2, Whitefriars-st	Technical
„ TIMES, *5d.*, 2, Exeter-st	Technical
RECORD, *4d.*, 1, Red Lion-ct, Fleet-st	"No Government interference
REFEREE, *1d.*, 20, Wine Office-ct, Fleet-st	Protestant
REVIEW, *6d.*, 74 & 75, Great Queen-st	Sport and gossip
REYNOLDS'S WEEKLY NEWSPAPER, *1d.*, 313, Strand	Insurance
RICHMOND TIMES, *1d.*	Democratic
ROCK, *1d.*, 7, Southampton-st, Strand	Local
	Protestant
SADDLERS' GAZETTE, ETC., *4d.*, 46, Cannon-st	Trade
ST. JAMES'S BUDGET, *6d.*, Dorset-st, Whitefriars	Cuttings from St. James's Gazette
ST. PANCRAS GAZETTE, *1d.*, 80, High-st, Camden Tn.	Local
„ GUARDIAN, *1d.*, 35, High-st, Camden Tn	Local
SANITARY RECORD, *1s.*, 15, Waterloo-pl	Hygiene
SATURDAY REVIEW, *6d.*, 38, Southampton-st, Strand	General Criticism
SCHOOL BOARD CHRONICLE, *3d.*, 72, Turnmill-street	Official Organ of School Boards
„ GUARDIAN, *1d.*, Depository, Sanctuary, Westminster	Organ of National Society
SCHOOLMASTER, *1d.*, 14, Red Lion-ct, Fleet-st	Professional
SCHOOLMISTRESS, *1d.*, 15, Wine Office-ct	Professional
SCIENTIFIC NEWS, *1d.*, 138, Fleet-st	Science
SEWING MACHINE AND CYCLE NEWS, *1d.*, 2, Whitefriars-st, E.C.	Trade
SHOE AND LEATHER RECORD, *1d.*, 30, Finsbury-pav, E.C.	Trade
SOCIETY, *1d.*, 172, Strand	Social
SOLICITORS' JOURNAL, *6d.*, 27, Chancery-la	Professional
SOUTH AMERICAN JOURNAL AND BRAZIL, ETC., 37, Walbrook, E.C.	South American
SOUTH LONDON CHRONICLE, *1d.*, 44, Camberwell-rd, S.E.	Local
„ „ GAZETTE, *1d.*, Portslade-rd, Wandsworth	Local
„ „ OBSERVER, *1d.*, 84, Church-st, Camberwell	Local
„ „ PRESS, *2d.*, Red Lion-ct, E.C.	Local—with magazine articles
„ WESTERN STAR, *1d.*, Portslade-rd, Wandsworth-rd	Local
SPECTATOR, *6d.*, 1, Wellington-st, Strand	Literary and General Review
SPORTING CLIPPER, *2d.*, 145, Fleet-st	Sport
„ TIMES, *2d.*, 52, Fleet-st	Sport
STAGE, *2d.*, Clement's-inn-passage, Strand	
STATIONER AND FANCY TRADES REGISTER, *6d.*, 160A, Fleet-st..	Trade
STATIST, *6d.*, 1, Salisbury-ct, Fleet-st	Commercial
STOCKKEEPERS' AND FANCIERS' CHRONICLE *3d.*, 139, Fleet-st	Horses, Cattle, &c.

Sunday School Chronicle, 1d., 56, Old Bailey..		For teachers, &c.
Sunday Times, 1d., 2, Salisbury-ct, E.C...		General
Sunday Words, 1d., 26, Wellington-st, W.C.		For Sunday reading
Surrey County Observer, 1d., 152, Manor-st, Clapham		Local
Tablet, 5d., 27, Wellington-st, Strand		Roman Catholic
Tailor and Cutter, 2d., 93, Drury-la		Trade
Telegraphic Journal, see Electrical Review.		
Temperance Record, 1d., 337, Strand		Organ of Temperance League
Timber Trades' Journal, 4d., 14, Bartholomew-close..		Trade
Tobacco, 3d., 90, Gracechurch-st, E.C.		Trade
Tobacco Trade Review, 6d., 28, Eastcheap-bdgs, E.C...		Trade
Topical Times, 1d., Catherine-st, W.C.		Gossip
Tottenham and Edmonton Herald, 1d., Lower Tottenham		Local
Tower Hamlets Independent, 1d., 306, Mile End-rd		Local
Truth, 6d., 10, Bolt-ct, Fleet-st		Society
United Service Gazette, 6d., 6, Catherine-st, W.C.		Naval and Military
Universe, 1d., 310, Strand		Ultramontane
Vanity Fair, 1s., 12, Tavistock-st, Covent-gdn		Society
Volunteer Service Gazette, 4d., 121, Fleet-st		Professional
Wandsworth & Battersea Times, 1d., 138, High-st, S.W.		Local
War Cry, 1d., 101, Queen Victoria-st, E.C.		Salvation Army
Warehousemen and Drapers' Trade Journal, 3d., 148 & 149, Aldersgate-st		Trade
Weekly Budget, 1d., Red Lion-ct, Fleet-st		Working class
" Dispatch, 1d., 20, Wine Office-ct		Working class
" Notes, 1s., 27, Fleet-st		Law Decisions, &c.
" Register, 3d., 43, Essex-st, W.C.		Ultramontane
" Reporter, 1s., 27, Chancery-la ..		Law Reports up to previous Wed-
" Times, 1d., 332, Strand		Radical [nesday
West London Advertiser, 1d., The Grove, Hammersmith ..		Local
" Observer, 1d., Broadway, Hammersmith		Local
" Middlesex Advertiser, 1d., 30, Sloane-sq, Chelsea ..		Local
Westminster and Lambeth Gazette, 1d., 154, Westminster-br-rd		Local
Whitehall Review, 6d., Savoy House, W.C.		Society
Willesden and Kilburn Chronicle, 1d., 4, Cambridge-rd, Kilburn		Local
Wine and Spirit Trade Monthly Circular, 5s. per annum, 27, Crutched Friars, E.C.		Trade
Wine Trade Review, 2s., 28, Eastcheap-bdgs, E.C. ..		Trade
Wit and Wisdom, 1d., 3, St. Bride-st, E.C.		
Wool and Textile Fabrics, 6d., 6, Helmet-ct, Strand		Trade
World, 6d., 1, York-st, Covent-gdn..		Society

New Thames Yacht Club, Club Houses, Gravesend. — The object of the club is the encouragement of yacht building and sailing on the river Thames ; and the funds of the club are appropriated, after payment of the necessary expenses, to the providing of prizes in money or otherwise to be sailed for by yachts on the river Thames. The members elect, and one black ball in five excludes. The club is managed by commodore, vice-commodore, rear-commodore, and treasurer, who are *ex officio* members of every committee, with a sailing committee of fourteen, and a house committee of six. Subscription, £3 3s. The club burgee is blue with gold

phœnix ; ensign, blue with gold phœnix in fly.

New University Club, 57, St. James's-st.—The constitution of this club provides that it shall be composed of 550 members of the University of Oxford, and 550 of the University of Cambridge. All persons are qualified to become members of the club who shall have resided for one year at least as a member of some college or hall in either university, or shall have received the honorary degree of M.A., or of Doctor, in either university. Election by ballot. Twenty members must vote, and one black ball in ten excludes. Entrance, £31 10s. : subs. £8 8s.

New Zealand. — Agency-General, 7, Westminster-chambers, Victoria-st, S.W. Nearest Ry. Stn., St. James's-pk (Dis.); Omnibus Rtes., Victoria-st and Parliament-st; Cab Rank, Palace-yard.

Nicaragua, Republic of. —Consulate, 22, Great Winchester-st, E.C. Nearest Ry. Stn., Bishopsgate; Omnibus Rtes., Bishopsgate-st and Old Broad-st ; Cab Rank, Bishopsgate-st.

Northbrook Indian Club, 3, Whitehall-gdns, S.W. — Established "for the use of Indian gentlemen residing in England, and of others who have resided in India, or who take an active interest in Indian affairs, and with the object of promoting social intercourse between persons of these classes." Proprietary. Annual subscription, £3 3s.; country members, £2 2s.

North London Collegiate School for Girls, Sandall-rd, Camden-rd, N.W.—Estab. 1850. Endowed 1875. Head Mistress, Miss Buss, F.C.P. Fees £17 11s. to £20 14s. per annum according to age. Entrance fee £1. Boarders are received by the head mistress at her private residence, and by other ladies. Further information may be obtained from the Secretary, Miss Mary E. Warne. NEAREST *Ry. Stns.*, Camden-rd (Midland) and Camden Town (North Lond.); *Omnibuses* from Charing ✠ to the Brecknock; *Tramcars* from Euston-rd to Holloway.

CAMDEN SCHOOL FOR GIRLS, Prince of Wales-rd, N.W.— Established 1871. Superintendent, Miss Buss, F.C.P. Head Mistress, Miss Lawford. Fees from £5 2s. to £7 4s. per annum, according to age. Entrance fee, 5s. The names of ladies who receive boarders will be given on application. Further information may be obtained from the Secretary, Miss A. Elford. NEAREST *Ry. Stn.*, Kentish Town (North Lond.); *Omnibuses*, Elephant and Castle to Shipton; *Tramcars*, King's Cross to Gospel Oak.

North London Collegiate School, High-st, Camden Tn. (Founded in 1850). — Principal : Rev. C. W. Williams, D.D., F.R.A.S. Is divided into commercial and classical departments. There is also a junior school for little boys. The fees are £2 10s., £3, and £3 10s. per term, payable in advance; boys entering when fifteen, £4 4s. per term. Fees in the junior school, £2 2s. per term, inclusive. Boys may be boarded, and dinner is provided at 1s. for day boys. All further particulars may be obtained of the Principal at the school. NEAREST *Ry. Stns.*, Gower-st (Met.), Camden, Euston, and St. Pancras ; *Omnibus and Tram Rtes.*, Camden Tn. High-st ; *Cab Rank*, Mornington-cres, High-st.

Novelty Theatre, Great Queen-st, Lincoln's - inn - fields (Map 7).—A handsome theatre,

capable of holding about 1,000 persons, from the designs of Mr. Thomas Verity. First opened 9th Dec., 1882, but after a couple of weeks the new theatre closed its doors, to re-open for an almost equally brief term as the Folies Dramatiques. About the end of 1883 it was again opened for a short time under its original designation, and in the spring of 1888 it was once more opened under the management of Messrs. George Giddens and T. G. Warren, but after an unsuccessful season of only a few weeks' duration it had again to be closed. NEAREST *Ry. Stns.*, Temple (Dis.) and Charing ✠ (S.E.); *Omnibus Rtes.*, High Holborn and Strand ; *Cab Rank*, Lincoln's-inn-fields.

Nuisances. — A few of the *désagrémens* to which metropolitan flesh is heir have been legally settled to be "nuisances."

(*a*) THE FOLLOWING WILL be summarily suppressed on appeal to the nearest police-constable :

Abusive language ; Advertisements, carriage of (except in form approved) ; Areas left open without sufficient fence.

Baiting animals ; Betting in streets ; Bonfires in streets ; Books, obscene, selling in streets.

Carpet-beating ; Carriage, obstruction by ; Cattle, careless driving of ; Coals, unloading, between prohibited hours ; Cock-fighting ; Crossings in streets, obstructing.

Defacing buildings ; Deposit of goods in streets ; Dogs loose or mad ; Doors, knocking at ; Drunk and disorderly persons ; Dust, removal of, between 10 a.m. and 7 p.m.

Exercising horses to annoyance of persons ; Exposing goods for sale in parks.

Firearms, discharging ; Fireworks, throwing in streets ; Footways, obstructions on ; Footways unswept ; Furious driving ; Furniture, fraudulent removal of, between 8 p.m. and 6 a.m.

Games, playing in streets.

Indecent exposure.

Lamps, extinguishing.

Mat-shaking after 8 a.m. ; Musicians in streets.

Obscene singing ; Offensive mat-

ters, removal of, between 6 a.m. and 12 night.

Posting bills without consent ; projections from houses to cause annoyance.

Reins, persons driving without ; Ringing door bells without excuse ; Rubbish lying in thoroughfare.

Slides, making, in streets ; Stone-throwing.

Unlicensed public carriage.

(*b*) THE FOLLOWING WILL require an application to the police-courts :

Cesspools, foul ; Cock-crowing.

Dead body, infectious, retained in room where persons live ; Disease, persons suffering from infectious, riding in public carriage, or exposing themselves, or being without proper accommodation ; Disorderly houses ; Drains foul.

Factory, unclean or overcrowded Furnace in manufactory not consuming its own smoke ; Food unfit for consumption, exposing.

Gaming houses.

Houses filthy or injurious to health.

Infected bedding or clothes, sale of.

Letting infected house or room ; Lotteries.

Manufactures (making sulphuric acid, steeping skins, &c.) ; Manure, non-removal of ; Milk, exposing, unfit for consumption.

Obstructions in highways, bridges, or rivers ; Overcrowding of house.

Powder magazine, or keeping too large a quantity of powder.

Theatres, unlicensed ; Trades, offensive (keeping pigs, soaphouse, slaughter-house, or manufactures in trade causing effluvia, &c.).

Want of reparation of highway Warehousing inflammable materials ; Water, fouling or polluting.

(*c*) THE FOLLOWING WILL require a summons in the County Court: Any of those nuisances next mentioned where the value or the rent of the premises in dispute, or in respect of which and over which the easement is claimed, shall not exceed £20 per annum ; or where damages in a personal action not exceeding £50 are sought to be recovered, unless by consent of both parties.

(d) THE FOLLOWING WILL require a regular action at law :

Buildings from which water falls on to another house.

Commons, injury to soil, digging turf, injuring pasture.

Drainage, interruption of.

Encroachments on highways, rivers, streets, or squares.

Gas company fouling any stream.

Lights, obstruction of.

Party wall, paring off part of ; Publication of injurious advertisements.

Rivers, pulling down banks of ; Right of way, interruption of.

Sewage, conducting, into river ; Stream, pollution or diversion of.

(e) THE FOLLOWING HAVE NOT been definitely settled either way, but may be worth the cost and trouble of a trial :

Church bell-ringing.

Hospital, infectious.

Manufactory, near house, introducing more noisy machinery, or new way of working it ; Music, powerful band near house.

Rifle practice ; Rockets or fireworks, letting off, frequently.

Sewage contributed by several persons, amount contributed by each not being sufficient to cause a nuisance.

Nurses.—HAMILTON ASSOCIATION FOR PROVIDING TRAINED MALE NURSES, 69, South Audley-st, W. Established in 1885 for the purpose of training and providing male nurses as attendants on male patients in hospitals, infirmaries, or chambers, and on male members of private families, also to nurse gratuitously the sick poor. For full information apply to Secretary.

INSTITUTION FOR NURSES FOR NERVOUS AND MENTAL DISORDERS, PARALYSIS, AND EPILEPSY, 1, Northop-st, Park-st, Grosvenor-sq, W.—Number of nurses unlimited. Terms : £1 2s., £1 6s., £1 11s. per week. The nurses are only engaged to attend on ladies.

LONDON ASSOCIATION OF NURSES, 62, New Bond-street ; branch office, 86, Kennington-park-road.—Number of nurses over 100. Terms, from £1 1s. to £4 4s. per week. Medical nurses, from £1 1s. to £2 2s. per week; mental nurses, from £1 1s. to £3 3s. per week ;

monthly nurses, from £4 4s. to £21 per month ; surgical nurses and male attendants, from £2 2s. to £3 3s. per week ; fever and small-pox nurses, £1 1s. to £3 3s. per week. In connection with the Association of Nurses there are "Home Hospitals," where patients can be received under the care of their own physicians, each patient being provided with a separate room. Terms, from £4 4s. to £12 12s. per week.

METROPOLITAN AND NATIONAL NURSING ASSOCIATION FOR PROVIDING TRAINED NURSES FOR THE SICK POOR, the Superior, 23, Bloomsbury-sq.— Terms, gratis. Where artisans or others are able, they contribute small sums weekly. No cases are nursed where the patient is able to board and pay a resident nurse. Ladies when trained live in a district home under a lady superintendent trained like themselves.

MR. WILSON'S INSTITUTION FOR HOSPITAL TRAINED NURSES, 96, Wimpole-st, Cavendish-sq, W. Established 1867. — The nurses reside when disengaged at the Institution, 96, Wimpole-st. Medical, surgical, monthly, mental, dipsomania, and fever nurses. Also male attendants for mental, dipsomania, medical, and surgical cases. Nurses are sent to all parts of England, America, and the Continent. The nature of the case, age, and sex should be described to Mr. Wilson, or to the lady superintendent, so that a suitable nurse may be selected.

NORTH LONDON NURSING ASSOCIATION FOR PROVIDING TRAINED NURSES FOR THE SICK POOR IN THEIR OWN HOMES, 413, Holloway-rd, London, N.—Nine nurses. Terms : Free to the sick poor in their own homes. Paying cases are not taken. The institution is entirely dependent on voluntary contributions.

NURSING INSTITUTE, Great Ormond-st, W.C.—(See HOMŒOPATHIC HOSPITAL.)

ST. JOHN'S NURSING COMMUNITY, 68, Drayton-gdns, S.W.; Branch, 210, East India Dock-rd, E.—Over 100 nurses. From 30s. to £2 2s. per week. Nurses (sick or monthly) sent to cases, at home or abroad, on application to the lady superior. The sisterhood has a maternity home at 42, Gunter-gr, Chelsea, for the recep-

tion of poor respectable married women, and for the training re-monthly nurses. Ladies and of spectable women received for training in all branches of nursing.

ST. MARY MAGDALENE'S HOME FOR TRAINED NURSES, 3, Delamere-crescent, Paddington, W. —Forty nurses. Terms on application to lady superior.

WESTMINSTER TRAINING SCHOOL AND HOME FOR NURSES, 27, Queen Anne's-gate, S.W. Founded (1874) by Lady Augusta Stanley. — Number of nurses varies. The whole nursing staff of the Westminster Hospital is provided by this institution. The committee beg to call the attention of medical men to the fact that thoroughly trained private nurses are supplied at the shortest notice for medical, surgical, and fever cases. Apply to Miss Pyne, Matron and Superintendent of Nurses, Westminster Hospital, S.W.— Charge per week, £1 11s. 6d. ; for surgical, mental or infectious cases, £2 2s. ; to cover expenses of disinfection, £1 1s.

Oil Colours, Institute of Painters in.—The exhibitions are held in the Galleries of the Royal Institute of Painters in Water Colours in Piccadilly. They are open to the works of all artists, subject to selection, and members are elected from the works exhibited. The exhibitions are annual, and commence in November or December, the admission being 1s. Illustrated Catalogues, 1s. President, James D. Linton ; Vice-President, Frank Walton ; Treasurer, Wm. L. Thomas ; Secretary, H. F. Phillips ; Curator, Alfred Everill.

Old Bailey (Map 8), the street which gives the familiar name to the great criminal court of the country, properly and officially styled the Central Criminal Court, which stands on its east side under the same roof with Newgate Prison. It derives its name from the ballium or open space in front of the old City Wall, along which it ran from Lud Gate to New Gate. In the old days of public executions, Monday morning was often high festival in the Old Bailey, and Tom Noddy and McFuze, and Lieutenant Tregooze, and their friend Sir Carnaby Jenks of the Blues, would

y fabulous sums for a window in
ne of the public-houses opposite,
om which to witness the edifying
pectacle. There is nothing now
o be seen on "hanging mornings"
ut a black flag, and the occupa-
on of the tumbledown old taverns
to that extent gone. They are
ar from desolate, however, find-
g ample scope for their energies
 providing for the smaller carry-
g trade of London, of which
he Old Bailey may be roughly
eckoned as the head-quarters.
lmost every house in the street is
 booking-office and place of call
or at least a score or two of
teady-going Barkises, who make
eir daily journeys to districts
gnored by railways, and the
tudent of eccentricities might
aste his time to less purpose
 many a more pretentious
treet.

Old Paulines' Club.—This
lub consists exclusively of gentle-
en who have been educated at St.
aul's School, London. The annual
ubscription is 5s., entrance fee 10s.
ife subscription £5 5s. Gentle-

men desirous of becoming members should communicate with
the hon. secretary, G. B. Long,
Esq., Marlborough House, Pall
Mall, S.W.

Olympia.—(*See Appendix.*)

Olympic Theatre, Wych-st,
Drury-lane (Map 7).—A pretty
little theatre, memorable for the
triumphs of Vestris and Robson.
In the palmy days of extravaganza
disputed the lead in that class of
entertainment with the Lyceum.
But it never took kindly to the
modern vulgarities of burlesque,
and of late years has eschewed that
line altogether, and addicted itself
chiefly to strong drama of a more
or less romantic type. For some
time the theatre has not been particularly flourishing. NEAREST
Ry. Stn., Temple ; *Omnibus
Rte.*, Strand; *Cab Rank*, St.
Clement's Church.

Omnibuses. — The omnibus
service of London is chiefly in the
hands of the London General Omnibus Company (Limited), whose
carriages traverse the leading
thoroughfares in every direction at

regular intervals from early morn
to midnight. Besides the company there are also on the principal routes one or two large
private proprietors, and a considerable number of smaller owners,
who run their vehicles more or
less at discretion, as well as lines
between the great railway-stations.

The London General Omnibus
Company has lately met with fresh
competition in the London Road
Car Company (Limited), which has
offices at 9, Grosvenor-rd, Westminster, and at the present time
has convenient vehicles running on
the following five lines : Victoria
Stn., *via* Charing ✠, Fleet-st, and
Bank, to Broad-st Stn., every
8 min. Hammersmith-broadway,
via Piccadilly-circus, Tottenham-
court-rd to Offord Arms. West
Kensington,*via* Piccadilly,Strand,
etc., to Liverpool-st & London-br.
Walham-gn, *via* Fulham-rd and
Piccadilly to London-br. Walham-
gn, *via* King's-rd, Sloane-sq, Victoria, and Strand to Liverpool-st.

The following are the principal
lines :

LINE.	COLOUR, &c.	START.	ROUTE.	FARES.
ABNEY-PK (Weavers' Arms) to ICTORIA STN.	*Green.* "Favorite."	8 a.m. & every 15 min. to 10.40 p.m.	Church-st,Albion-rd,Essex-rd,Angel, St.John's-st-rd, Gray's inn-rd,Hol-born, Chancery-la, Strand, Char-ing ✠, Victoria-st.	To Angel 3d. Balls-pond-gate to West-minster 4d. All way 6d.
ANGEL (Islington) to LONDON-BR.	*Green.* "Favorite."	8.20 a.m. and every 5 min. to 11.10 p.m.	City-rd, Finsbury-sq, Moorgate-st, Bank, K. William-st, London-br Stn.	All way 3d.
BANK to SOUTH HACKNEY.	*Red.* "South Hackney."	8.15 a.m. and every 10 min. to 11.35 p.m.	Royal Exchange, Threadneedle-st, Bishopsgate, Norton Folgate, Shoreditch, Hackney-rd, Victoria-pk-rd, Laureston-rd.	Durham-st, Hackney-rd, to The Albion 2d. All way 3d.
BARNSBURY (Pocock Arms) KENNINGTON.	*Brown.* "Islington."	7.45 a.m. and every 10 min. to 10.55 p.m.	Offord-rd, Liverpool-rd, Angel, Gos-well-rd, Ludgate-hill, London-rd, and Kennington-pk-rd.	To Angel 2d, to Lud-gate - hill 4d. All way 5d.
BERMONDSEY to GRACE-CHURCH-ST.	*Green.* "Bermondsey"	8 a.m. and every 15 min. to 11.15 p.m.	Grange-rd, Bermondsey-st, Tooley-st, London-br Stn., K. William-st.	All way 4d.
OLD FORD to SAND'S END.	*Chocolate.* "Chelsea."	8 a.m. and every 17 min. to 10.58 p.m.	Bethnal Gn.-rd, Church-st, Bishops-gate, Cornhill, Cheapside, Fleet-st, Strand, Piccadilly, Sloane-st.	Bank 2d, Bank to Charing ✠ 1d, to Sloane-st 3d, Char-ing ✠ to Sand's End 4d. All way 6d.
BLACKWALL to PICCADILLY CIRCUS.	*Blue.* "Blackwall."	7.50 a.m. and at frequent intervals to 10 p.m.	East India-rd,Commercial-rd,White-chapel, Aldgate, Cornhill, Queen Victoria-st, Fleet-st, Strand.	To Bank 3d, Com-mercial-rd to Char-ing ✠ 4d. All way 6d.

LINE.	COLOUR, &c.	START.	ROUTE.	FARES.
Bow to Charing ✠.	*Green.* "Bow."	7.50 a.m. and every 7 min. to 10.25 p.m.	Mile End-rd, Whitechapel, Cornhill, Cheapside, Fleet-st, Strand, Charing ✠.	Post Office 4d, Whitechapel Ch. 4d. All way 6d.
Brixton Ch. to Charing ✠.	*Green.* "Brixton."	8.10 a.m. and every 10 min. to 10.30 p.m.	Brixton-rd, Kennington-rd, Westminster-br, Parliament-st.	Brixton to Kennington - pk 2d. All way 3d.
Brixton Ch. to Grace-church-st.	*Green.* "Paragon."	8 a.m. and every 10 min. to 10.20 p.m.	Kennington-rd, Elephant and Castle, Borough High-st, London-br.	To Eleph. and Castle 3d. All way 4d.
Brixton Ch. to Norwood.	*Green.* "Brixton Ch."	10 a.m. and every 30 min. to 10 p.m.	Brixton Church, Effra-rd, Tulse-hill.	Upper Tulse-hill to Norwood 3d. All way 6d.
Brixton Ch. to Oxf.-cir.	*Green.* "Brixton."	8.10 a.m. and 11 p.m.	Kennington-rd, Westminster-br, Charing ✠, Haymarket.	To Charing ✠ 3d. All way 4d.
Broad-st Stn. to Brompton.	*White.* "Brompton."	8.45 a.m. and about every 6 m. to 12.10 night	Broad-st, Cheapside, Fleet-st, Strand, Charing ✠, Piccadilly, Brompton-rd.	Broad-st to Char. ✠ 1d. Char. ✠ to Bromp. 4d. Reg.-cir. to Bromp. 4d. All way 6d.
Broad-st Stn. to Cannon-st Stn.	*Brown and White.*	8.30 a.m. and every 5 min. to 7.30 p.m. Wkdays only.	Old Broad-st, Royal Exchange, K. William-st, Cannon-st (except Sunday).	All way 1d.
Broad-st Stn. to Hammersmith.	*Red.* "Hammersmith."	8.48 a.m. and every 10 or 12 min. to 11.50 p.m.	Broad-st, Cheapside, Ludgate-hill Stn., Fleet-st, Strand, Charing ✠, Piccadilly, Kensington.	Broad-st to Char.✠ 1d, Char. ✠ to Kensgt. Ch. 4d, Kensgtn-Ch to Hammersmith 3d All way 6d.
Broad-st Stn. to Walham-gn.	*White.* "Brompton," &c.	8.45 a.m. and every 6 min. to 12.5 night	Cheapside, Fleet-st, Strand, Charing ✠, Piccadilly, Brompton-rd.	Charing ✠ 1d. All way 6d.
Brompton to Broad-st Stn.	*White.* "Brompton," &c.	7.45 a.m. and every 6 min. to 11 p.m.	Brompton-rd, Piccadilly, Charing ✠, Strand, Fleet-st, Cheapside, Broad-st.	To Reg.-cir 3d, Char.✠ 4d, Char ✠ to Broad st 3d. All way 6d.
Brompton to Holloway.	*Blue.* "Favorite."	7.55 a.m. and every 7 or 8 m. to 10.46 p.m.	Brompton-rd, Piccadilly, Regent-st, Portland-rd, King's ✠, Caledonian-rd.	To Oxford-cir 3d. All way 6d.
Brompton (Queen's Elm) to Islington.	*Blue.* "Islington & Brompton."	8.29 a.m. and every few min. to 12.9 night	Brompton-rd, Piccadilly, Regent-st, Portland-rd Stn., Euston-rd.	To Oxford-cir 3d. All way 6d.
Camberwell-gate (Red Lion) to Camden Tn.	*Blue.* "Waterloo."	8.8 a.m. and every few min. to 11.35 p.m.	Walworth-rd, London-rd, Waterloo-br, Strand, Regent-st, Portland-pl, Albany-st.	Cambrwll.-gn to Char. ✠ 2d, Waterloo-br to Camden Tn. 4d Char. ✠ to Camden Tn. 3d. All way 6d
Camberwell (The Green) to Grace-church-st.	*Yellow.* "Camberwell."	7.45 a.m. and every 6 min. to 10.10 p.m.	Walworth-rd, Elephant and Castle Newington-causeway, Boro', London-br.	All way 3d.
Camberwell-gate (Red Lion) to Hackney-rd.	*Yellow.* "Hackney-road."	7.30 a.m. and every 8 or 9 min. to 11.7 p.m.	Elephant and Castle, Boro', London-br, Gracechurch-st, Bishopsgate, Shoreditch.	Camberwell - gate to Cornhill 2d, Cornhill to Hackney-rd 2d.

LINE.	COLOUR, &c.	START.	ROUTE.	FARES.
AMBERWELL-GATE to ST. JOHN'S WOOD.	*Green.* "Atlas."	8.20 a.m. and every 8 min. to 11.30 p.m.	Walworth-rd, London-rd, Westminster-rd and br, Whitehall, Charing ✠, Regent-st, Oxford-st, Orchard-st, Baker-st, Park-rd.	Oxford-cir to Eyre Arms 3d. All way 6d.
CAMDEN TN. (Britannia) to CAMBERWELL-GATE.	*Blue.* "Waterloo."	8.18 a.m. and every 6 or 8 min. to 11.35 p.m.	Park-st, Albany-st, Portland-pl, Regent-st, Charing ✠, Strand, Waterloo-br.	To Charing ✠ 3d, to Waterloo-br 4d. Charing ✠ to Camberwell-gate 2d. All way 6d.
CAMDEN TN. (The Castle, Kentish Tn-rd) to KENNINGTON-PK.	*Green.* "King's ✠."	8.24 a.m. and every few min. to 11.10 p.m.	Gt. College-st, Euston-rd, Gray's-inn-rd, Holborn, New Bridge-st, Blackfriars-br.	To King's ✠ 2d, to Bridge-st 3d. King's ✠ to Eleph. & Castle 3d. All way 5d.
CAMDEN TN. (Britannia) to RICHMOND-RD	*Claret.* "Camden Tn."	9.30 a.m. and every 15 min. to 11.25 p.m.	Park-st, St. John's Wood-rd, Grove-rd, Church-st, Paddington-gn, Bishop's-rd.	Lord's Cricket-ground to Royal Oak 2d. All way 4d.
CAMDEN TN. (Britannia) to OLD KENT-RD.	*Blue.* "Waterloo."	8.24 a.m. and every 7 min. to 11.10 p.m.	Albany-st, Portland-pl, Regent-st, Charing ✠, Strand, Waterloo-br.	To Charing ✠ 3d, to Waterloo-br 4d. All way 6d.
CAMDEN TN. to VICTORIA STN.	*Yellow.* "Camden."	7.40 a.m. and every 7 min. to 11.30 p.m.	Hampstead-rd, Tottenham-court-rd, St. Martin's-la, Whitehall, Victoria-st.	To Oxford-st 2d, to Trafalgar-sq 3d. All way 4d.
CANNON-ST to BROAD-ST	*Br. & White*	8.40 a.m. every 5 m. to 7.45 p.m.	Cannon-st, K. William-st, Royal Exchange, Old Broad-st, except Sun.	All way 1d.
CHARING ✠ to Bow.	*Green.* "Bow and Charing ✠."	8.50 a.m. and every 7 min. to 11.35 p.m.	Regent-st, Charing ✠, Strand, Fleet-st, Cheapside, Whitechapel, Mile End-rd, Bow-rd.	To Whitechapel Chur. 4d. Post Office to Bow 3d. All way 5d.
CHARING ✠ (Trafalgar-sq) to BRIXTON.	*Green.* "Brixton."	8.45 a.m. and every 10 min. to 12 night.	Whitehall, Westminster-br.	To Kennington-pk 2d, to Brixton 3d.
CHARING ✠ (Trafalgar-sq) to KENNINGTON-PK.	*Red.* "Kennington-pk and Charing ✠."	8.20 a.m. and every 5 min. to 11.40 p.m.	Whitehall, Westminster-br and rd, Kennington-rd	All way 2d.
CHARING ✠ to KENSAL GN. (William IV.)	*Red.* "Kensal-gn and Charing ✠."	8.51 a.m. and every 12 min. to 11.35 p.m.	Regent-st, Oxford-st, Edgware-rd, Bishop's-rd, Harrow-rd.	To Oxford-cir 1d, Edgware-rd 2d, Royal Oak 3d, Prince of Wales 4d.
CHARING ✠ STN. to KILBURN.	*Red.* "Charing ✠ & Kilburn."	8.47 a.m. and every 15 min. to 11.15 p.m.	Trafalgar-sq, Waterloo-pl, Regent-st, Oxford-st, Edgware-rd.	To Regent-cir 2d, to Chapel-st 3d. All way 5d.
CHARING ✠ STN. to NOTTING HILL	*Red.* "Charing ✠ & Rl. Oak."	8.37 a.m. and ev. 6 or 7 min. to 11.40 p.m.	Regent-st, Oxford-st, Edgware-rd, Praed-st, Eastbourne-ter, Bishop's-rd, Westbourne-gr, Archer-st.	To Oxford-cir 2d, to Chapel-st, Edgware-rd 3d. All way 4d.
CHELSEA (Sand's End) to OLD FORD.	*Chocolate.* "Chelsea."	8 a.m. and every 18 min. to 10.58 p.m.	King's-rd, Sloane-st, Piccadilly, Strand, Fleet-st, Cheapside, Cornhill, Bishopsgate.	To Charing ✠ 3d, Charing ✠ to Bank 1d. All way 6d.
CLAPHAM-COM. to GRACE-CHURCH-ST	*Chocolate.* "Clapham."	8 a.m. and every 8 to 10 min. to 10.15 p.m.	Stockwell, Kennington-pk-rd, Elephant and Castle, Borough, London-br.	To Elephant & Castle 2d. All way 4d.

LINE.	COLOUR, &c.	START.	ROUTE.	FARES.
CLAPTON to OXFORD-CIR.	*Green.* "Clapton and Oxford-cir."	7.58 a.m. and ev. 15 or 20 m. to 10.12 p.m.	Hackney-rd, Shoreditch, Bank, Cheapside, Holborn.	To Hackney 3d, Bank 4d. All w 6d.
CLAPTON to OXFORD-CIR.	*Dark Green.* "Clapton and Oxford-cir."	8.40 a.m. and every 20 min. to 10.20 p.m.	Dalston-la, Essex-rd, Angel, Euston-rd, Gt. Portland-st.	Hackney to Oxf.-c 6d, Angel to Oxf.-c 3d.
DEPTFORD to GRACE-CHURCH-ST.	*Green.* "Deptford."	8.30 a.m. and every 30 min. to 9.30 p.m.	Rotherhithe, Lower-rd, Tooley-st, London-br, Gracechurch-st.	To Dockhead 2d. A way 4d.
ESSEX-RD to OLD KENT-RD.	*Green.* "Islington and Old Kent-rd."	7.45 a.m. and ev. 6 or 7 min. to 10.40 p.m.	New North-rd, East-rd, City-rd, Moorgate-st, K. William-st, London-br, Boro'.	To London-br Ry. 3 Bank to Lord Nelso 3d. All way 5d.
ELEPHANT & CAS. to FARRINGDON-RD.	*Red.* "Metropolitan Ry."	7.50 a.m. and ev. 5 or 6 min. to 11.4 p.m.	London-rd, Blackfriars-br, Farringdon-rd.	Start from Elephan and Castle Stn. A way 1d.
ELEPHANT & CAS. to KINGSLAND-GA.	*Green.* "Kingsland."	8.6 a.m. and every 6 min. to 11.50 p.m.	Boro', London-br, Gracechurch-st, Bishopsgate, Kingsland-rd.	Cornhill to Kingslan 2d. All way 3d.
ELEPHANT & CASTLE to BROAD-ST.	*Red.* Plain.	7.50 a.m. and every 5 min. to 10.36 p.m.	Boro', London-br, King William-st, Old Broad-st.	
FARRINGDON-RD to EL. & CAS.	*Red.* "Metropolitan Ry."	8.48 a.m. and every 5 or 6 min. to 11.24 p.m.	Farringdon-rd, Blackfriars-br, London-rd.	All way 1d.
FENCHURCH-ST STN. to KILBURN.	*Dark Green.* "Kilburn."	8.50 a.m. and every 6 or 7 min. to 11.25 p.m.	Cornhill, Cheapside, Holborn, Oxford-st, Edgware-rd.	To Oxford-cir 4d, t Chapel-st, 5d. A way 6d.
FULHAM (Putney-br) to LONDON-BR.	*White.* "Putney-br."	7.35 a.m. and every 16 to 18 m. to 10.35 p.m.	Fulham-rd, Brompton-rd, Piccadilly, Strand, Fleet-st, Cheapside.	To South Kensingto 3d, to Charing ✠ 4 All way 6d.
GENERAL POST OFFICE to HOLLOWAY.	*Red.* "Favorite."	At short intervals morning and evening.	Aldersgate-rd, Goswell-rd, Angel, Holloway-rd.	Angel to Nag's Hea 2d. All way 3d.
GRACE-CHURCH-ST to BERMONDSEY.	*Green.* "Bermondsey," &c.	8.14 a.m. and every 15 min. to 11.14 p.m.	K. William-st, London-br, Tooley-st, Bermondsey-st, Grange-rd.	All way 4d.
GRACE CHURCH-ST to BRIXTON.	*Green.* "Paragon."	8.40 a.m. and every 10 min. to 11 p.m.	London-br, Boro', Elephant and Castle, Kennington-rd, Brixton-rd.	Elephant and Castl to Brixton Churc 3d. All way 4d.
GRACE-CHURCH-ST to CAMBERWELL.	*Yellow.* "Camberwell."	8.30 a.m. and every 6 min. to 11.15 p.m.	London-br, Boro' High-st, Elephant and Castle, Walworth-rd.	All way 3d.
GRACE-CHURCH-ST to CLAPHM.-COM.	*Chocolate.* "Clapham."	8.40 a.m. and every 10 min. to 11 p.m.	London-br, Boro', Elephant and Castle, Kennington-pk-rd.	Elephant and Castl and Clapham 3 All way 4d.
GRACE-CHURCH-ST to PECKHAM.	*Dark Green.* Plain.	9.15 a.m. and every 30 min. to 10.15 p.m.	London-br, Boro', Elephant and Castle, Walworth-rd	To Camberwell-gn 3 Camb.-ga to Peck ham 2d. All way 5
GRACE-CHURCH-ST to ROTHER-HITHE.	*Green.* "Rother-hithe."	8.15 a.m. and every 15 min. to 11.15 p.m.	London-br, Tooley-st, Southwark-pk, Lower-rd	Southwark-pk to Ro therhithe 2d. Al way 4d.
GRACE-CHURCH-ST to STREATHAM.	*Green.* "Paragon."	8.40 a.m. and every 10 min. to 9.15 p.m.	London-br, Boro', Elephant and Castle, Kennington-pk-rd, Brixton-hill.	Brixton Church t Streatham 3d. Al way 6d.
GRACE-CHURCH-ST to TULSE-HILL.	*Green.* "Norwood."	Sun. 1hr. later. 10.15 a.m. abt, ev. 15 m. to 8.45 p.m.	London-br, Boro', Elephant and Castle, Kennington-rd, Brixton-rd,	Brixton Church t Tulse-hill 3d. Al way 6d.

LINE.	COLOUR, &c.	START.	ROUTE.	FARES.
GRACECH.-ST to WANDSWORTH-RD.	Chocolate. "Wandsworth."	8.45 a.m. and every 15 min. to 11.30 p.m.	London-br, Southwark-st, Stamford-st, York-rd, Albert-embankment.	York-rd to Wandsworth 2d. All way 4d.
HACKNEY to OXFORD-ST.	Green. "Hackney & Oxford-st."	8.40 a.m. and every 30 min. to 10.20 p.m.	Dalston-la, Ball's-pond-rd, Essex-rd, Angel, King's ✠, Euston-rd, Portland-pl.	To Angel, Islington, 4d, Angel to Oxford-cir 3d. All way 6d.
HACKNEY-RD to CAMBERWELL-GATE.	Yellow. "Hackney-rd."	7.30 a.m. and every few min. to 11.8 p.m.	Bishopsgate, Cornhill, Gracechurch-st, London-br, Boro'.	To Cornhill 2d, Cornhill to Camberwell-gate 2d.
HACKNEY, SOUTH, to BANK.	Red. "South Hackney."	7.45 a.m. and every 10 min. to 10.55 p.m.	Laureston-rd, Victoria-pk-rd, Hackney-rd, Shoreditch.	To Durham-st, Hackney-rd 2d. All way 3d.
HAMMERSMITH to BROAD-ST STN.	Red. "Hammersmith."	8 a.m. and every 10 min. to 10.29 p.m.	Kensington, Piccadilly, Charing ✠, Strand, Fleet-st, Cheapside.	To Knsngtn.Ch.3d,K. Ch.to Charing ✠ 4d, Char. ✠ to Broad-st 1d. All way 6d.
HAMPSTEAD (High-st) to PICCADILLY CIRCUS.	Yellow. "Hampstead."	8.15 a.m. and every 15 min. to 10.40 p.m.	Haverstock-hill, Camden Tn., Hampstead-rd, Tottenham-court-road, Charing-✠-rd.	All way 4d.
HARROW-RD (Pr. of Wales, St. Peter's-pk) to LONDON-BR.	Yellow. "Paddington."	7.15 a.m. and every 5 min. to 10.13 p.m.	Porchester-rd, Bishop's-rd, Edgware-rd, Oxford-st, Cheapside, K. William-st.	To Edgware-rd 2d, to Oxford-cir 3d, Oxford-cir to Chancery-la 2d. All way 6d.
HAVERSTOCK-HILL (High-st) to VICTORIA STN.	Yellow. "Haverstock-hill."	8.25 a.m. and every 5 min. to 11 p.m.	Hampstead-rd, Tottenham-court-rd, Oxford-st, St. Martin's-la, Whitehall, Victoria-st.	To Tottenham-ct-rd 2d, to Victoria Stn. 4d.
HIGHGATE (Duke of St. Albans) to OXFORD-ST.	Yellow. "Highgate."	8.5 a.m. and every 10 min. to 11.40 p.m.	Kentish Tn.-rd, Camden Tn., Hampstead-rd, Tottenham-court-rd.	Hampstead-rd to Tottenham-ct-rd 2d, to Oxford-st 3d.
HOLLOWAY (Nag's Head) to BROMPTON.	Blue. "Favorite."	8 a.m. and every few min. to 10.58 p.m.	Caledonian-rd, Portland-rd, Regent-st, Piccadilly, Brompton-rd.	Oxford-cir to Brompton 3d. All way 6d.
HOLLOWAY (Nag's Head) to LONDON-BR.	Green. "Favorite."	8 a.m. and every 5 min. to 10.50 p.m.	Grove-rd, Holloway-rd, City-rd, Moorgate-st, K. William-st.	To Angel, Islington 2d. All way 5d.
HOLLOWAY to VICTORIA STN.	Green. "Favorite."	8.5 a.m. and every 7 min. to 10.54 p.m.	Angel, St. John-st-rd, Gray's-inn-la, Chancery-la, Fleet-st, Parliament-st, Victoria-st.	To Angel 2d, Chancery la to Victoria Stn. 3d. All way 6d.
HORNSEY (Seven Sisters'-rd) to LONDON-BR.	Green. "Favorite."	8.2 a.m. and at frequent intervals to 11.3 p.m.	Holloway-rd, Angel, City-rd, Moorgate-st, K. William-st.	Highbury to Angel 2d. Angel to London-br 3d, Bank to London-br 1d. All way 6d.
HORNSEY-RISE to VICTORIA STN.	Green. "Favorite."	8 a.m. and at frequent intervals to 10.35 p.m.	Hornsey-rd, Seven Sisters'-rd, Holloway-rd, Angel, St. John's-st-rd, Gray's-inn-la, Chancery-la, Fleet-st, Parliament-st, Victoria-st.	To Angel 2d, Angel to Fleet-st 3d, Chancery-la to Victoria Stn. 3d. All way 6d.
HOXTON to PARSON'S GREEN.	Chocolate. "Chelsea."	8 a.m. and every 18 min. to 10.52 p.m.	Pitfield-st, Moorgate-st, Cheapside, Fleet-st, Strand, Waterloo-pl, Piccadilly-cir, Sloane-st.	To St. Paul's 3d, Bank to Charing ✠ 1d. All way 6d.
ISLINGTON (Duke of York) to BROMPTON.	Blue. "Islington and Brompton."	8.17 a.m. and ev. 6 or 7 min. to 11.52 p.m.	Euston-rd, Portland-rd, Regent-st, Piccadilly, Brompton-rd.	Oxford-cir to Brompton 3d. All way 6d.

LINE.	COLOUR, &c.	START.	ROUTE.	FARES.
ISLINGTON to KENNINGTON-PK.	*Brown.* "Islington."	7.45 a.m. and every 10 min. to 11.10 p.m.	Offord-rd, Thornhill-rd, Liverpool-rd, Angel, Goswell-rd, Aldersgate-st, Ludgate-hill, Blackfriars-br.	To Angel 2d, to Ludgate-hill 3d. All way 6d.
ISLINGTON to OLD KENT-RD.	*Green.* "Islington and Kent-rd."	7.45 a.m. and ev. 6 or 7 min. to 10.40 p.m.	New North-rd, East-rd, City-rd, Finsbury-sq, K. William-st, London-br.	To London-br Stn. 3d, Bank to Old Kent-rd 3d. All way 5d.
KENNINGTON to BARNSBURY.	*Brown.* "Islington."	8.46 a.m. and every 10 min. to 11.14 p.m.	London-rd, Blackfriars-br, Ludgate-hill, Post Office, Goswell-rd, Angel, Liverpool-rd.	Kennington to Ludgate 2d, to Angel 3d, Angel to Barnsbury 2d. All way 5d.
KENNINGTON (The Park) to CHARING ✠.	*Red.* "Kennington-pk and Charing ✠."	a.m. and every 5 min. to 11.15 p.m.	Westminster-rd and br, Parliament-st, Whitehall.	All way 2d.
KENNINGTON to KENTISH TN.	*Green.* "King's ✠."	8.8 a.m. and every 8 or 9 min. to 10.45 p.m.	Elephant and Castle, London-rd, Blackfriars-br, New Bridge-st, Ludgate-cir, Holborn, Gray's-inn-rd.	Ludgate-hill Stn. to King's ✠ 2d, King's ✠ to College-st 2d. All way 5d.
KENNINGTON-PK to CAMDEN TN.	*Green.* "King's ✠."	8 a.m. and every 8 or 9 min. to 11.15 p.m.	Elephant and Castle, London-rd, Blackfriars-br, New Bridge-st, Holborn, Gray's-inn-rd.	Elephant and Castle to King's ✠ 3d, Bridge-st to Camden Tn. 3d, King's ✠ to Camden Tn. 2d. All way 6d.
KENNINGTON-PK to ISLINGTON.	*Brown.* "Islington."	8.46 a.m. and every 10 min. to 11.14 p.m.	Blackfriars-br, Ludgate-hill, Aldersgate-st, Liverpool-rd.	To Ludgate-hill 3d, Angel to Barnsbury 2d. All way 6d.
KENSAL GN. (William IV.) to CHARING ✠.	*Red.* "Kensal-gn. and Charing ✠."	8 a.m. and every 12 min. to 10.40 p.m.	Harrow-rd, Bishop's-rd, Edgware-rd, Oxford-st, Regent-st.	To Prince of Wales 1d, Royal Oak 2d, Praed-st 3d, Oxf-cir 4d, Charing ✠ 5d.
KENSAL GN. (William IV.) to LONDON-BR.	*Yellow.* "Paddington."	8.41 a.m. and every 12 min. to 9.58 p.m.	Harrow-rd, Porchester-rd, Bishop's-rd, Edgware-rd, Oxford-st, Holborn, Cheapside, K. William-st.	To Rl. Oak 2d, Rl. Oak to Oxford-cir 2d. All way 6d.
KENTISH TN. (Castle Tav.) to KENNINGTON.	*Green.* "King's ✠."	8.24 a.m. and every 8 or 9 min. to 11.10 p.m.	Gt. College-st, King's ✠, Gray's-inn-rd, Holborn, Ludgate-cir, Blackfriars-br.	College-st, to King's ✠ 2d, King's ✠ to Ludgate-hill Stn. 2d. All way 5d.
KENTISH TN. to TRAFALGAR-SQ.	*Yellow.* "Carlton."	7.40 a.m. and abt. ev. 15 m. to 11.30 p.m.	Haverstock-hill, High-st, Camden Tn., Hampstead-rd, Tottenham-ct-rd, St. Martin's-la.	To Oxford-st 2d. All way 3d.
KILBURN to CHARING ✠.	*Red.* "Kilburn and Charing ✠."	8 a.m. and every 15 min. to 10.20 p.m.	Edgware-rd, Oxford-st, Regent-st, Waterloo-pl.	To Oxford-cir 4d, Oxford-cir and Charing-✠ 2d. All way 5d.
KILBURN to FENCHURCH-ST.	*Dark Green.* "Kilburn."	7.44 a.m. and ev. few min. to 10.5 p.m.	Edgware-rd, Oxford-st, Holborn, Cheapside, Cornhill.	To Chapel-st 3d, to Oxford-cir 4d. All way 6d.
KILBURN to VICTORIA STN.	*Red.* "Kilburn and Victoria Stn."	8.10 a.m. and every 6 min. to 11.35 p.m.	Edgware-rd, Park-la, Grosvenor-pl.	To Marble Arch 3d. All way 5d.
KILBURN AND FULHAM.	*Light Blue.* "Kilburn and Kensington."	8 a.m. and every 15 min. to 11 p.m. From Fulham 8.20 to 11.30.	Cambridge-rd, Walterton-rd, Gt. Western-rd, Richmond-rd, Notting-hill Gate, Silver-st, High-st, Kensington.	
KINGSLAND-GATE to EL. & CAS.	*Green.* "Kingsland."	7.37 a.m. and every 6 min. to 11.32 p.m.	Kingsland-rd, Shoreditch, Gracechurch-st, K. William-st, Borough.	To Cornhill 2d. All way 3d.
LIVERPOOL-ST to NOTTING HILL.	*Dark Green.* "Bayswater."	8.13 a.m. and every few min. to 11.28 p.m.	K. William-st, Cheapside, Holborn, Oxford-st, Edgware-rd, Bishop's-rd, Westbourne-gr.	To Oxford-cir 3d, Clarendon-rd to Edgreroad 2d, to Oxford-cir 3d. All way 6d.

LINE.	COLOUR, &c.	START.	ROUTE.	FARES.
LIVERPOOL-ST to PIMLICO.	*Chocolate.* "Westminster."	8 a.m. and every 6 min. to 12 night.	Queen Victoria-st, St. Paul's, Fleet-st, Strand, Charing ✠, Whitehall, Vauxhall-br-rd, Warwick-st.	Somerset House to Warwick-st 3d. All way 4d.
LIVERPOOL-ST to SHEPHERD'S BUSH.	*Green.* "Bayswater."	8.35 a.m. and every 10 min. to 11.20 p.m.	Cheapside, Newgate-st, Viaduct, Holborn, Oxford-st, Bayswater-rd, Notting-hill, Uxbridge-rd.	To Oxford-cir 4d. All way 6d.
LIVERPOOL-ST Stations to STARCH-GN.	*Green.* "Bayswater."	9.2 a.m. and every 12 min. to 11.28 p.m.	Cheapside, Holborn, Oxford-st, Uxbridge-rd, Goldhawk-rd.	To Oxford-cir 4d. All way 6d.
LIVERPOOL-ST to WESTMINSTER.	*Chocolate.* "Westminster."	8 a.m. and every 6 min. to 12 night.	Queen Victoria-st, Ludgate-hill, Fleet-st, Strand, Charing ✠, Whitehall, Parliament-st, Vauxhall-br-rd.	Charing ✠ to Westminster 2d. All way 4d.
LONDON-BR to ACTON.	*Green.* "Bayswater."	11.50 a.m. and 5.20 p.m.	K. William-st, Cheapside, Holborn, Oxford-st, Bayswater, Shep. Bush.	Oxford-cir to Acton 6d. All way 9d.
LONDON-BR to ANGEL.	*Green.* "Islington."	8.48 a.m., ev. 3m.to11.52p.m.	K. William-st, Bank, Moorgate-st, Finsbury-sq, City-rd.	All way 3d.
LONDON-BR to HARROW-RD.	*Yellow.* "Paddington."	8.16 a.m. and every 6 min. to 11.26 p.m.	K. William-st, Cheapside, Holborn, Oxford-st, Edgware-rd, Bishop's-rd.	To Oxford-cir 3d. Chancery-la to Oxford-cir 2d, Edgware-rd to Prince of Wales 2d. All way 6d.
LONDON-BR to HOLLOWAY.	*Green.* "Favorite."	8.48 a.m., at freq. inter. to 11.40 p.m.	K. William-st, Moorgate-st, City-rd, Holloway-rd.	Angel, Islington, to Nag's Head 2d. All way 5d.
LONDON-BR to HORNSEY.	*Green.* "Favorite."	8.40 a.m., at freq. inter. to 11.40 p.m.	K. William-st, Moorgate-st, City-rd, Angel, Holloway-rd.	London-br and Bank 1d, London-br and Angel 3d, Angel and Highbury 2d. All way 6d.
LONDON-BR to KENSAL GREEN.	*Yellow.* "Paddington."	8.16 a.m. and every 12 min. to 11.26 p.m.	K. William-st, Cheapside, Holborn, Oxford-st, Edgware-rd, Bishop's-rd, Harrow-rd.	Oxford-cir to Rl. Oak 2d, Rl.Oak to Kensal Gn. 2d. All way 6d.
LONDON-BR to RICHMOND-RD	*Green.* "Paddington," *via* New-rd.	9.5 a.m. and every 10 min. to 11.50 p.m.	K. William-st, Moorgate-st, City-rd, Euston-rd, Chapel-st, Bishop's-br.	To Bank 1d, to Angel, Islington 3d, to Rl. Oak 6d.
LONDON-BR (*via* Oxford-st) to ROYAL OAK.	*Yellow.* "Rl. Oak and London-br."	8.15 a.m. and every 5 min. to 11.25 p.m.	K. William-st, Cheapside, Holborn, Oxford-st, Edgware-rd, Bishop's-rd.	To Bank 1d, to Oxford-cir 3d. All way 6d.
LONDON-BR to ST. JOHN'S WOOD.	*Green.* "City Atlas."	9 a.m. and every 8 to 12 min. to 10.45 p.m.	K. William-st, Cheapside, Holborn, Oxford-st, Baker-st, Park-rd.	Chancery-la to Swiss Cottage 5d, Oxford-cir to Swiss Cottage 3d. All way 6d.
MILE END-RD (Burdett-rd) to SHEPHERD'S BUSH (Wellington Tav.)	*Green.* "Bayswater."	6.52 a.m. and every 5 or 6 min. to 9.18 p.m.	Mile End-rd, Aldgate, Bank, Cheapside, Holborn, Oxford-st, Bayswater-rd.	To Bank 1d, Bank to Oxford-cir 3d, Oxford-cir to Notting Hill-gate 3d. All way 6d.
NORWOOD (Cemetery) to BRIXTON CHURCH.	*Green.* "Brixton Ch. and Norwood Cemetery."	10 a.m. and every 30 min. to 10 p.m.	Tulse-hill, Effra-rd.	Upper Tulse-hill 3d. All way 6d.
NOTTING HILL (Earl of Lonsdale, Archer-st) to CHARING ✠.	*Red.* "Charing ✠."	7.54 a.m. and every few min. to 10.50 p.m.	Westbourne-gr, Bishop's-rd, Eastbourne-ter, Praed-st, Edgware-rd, Oxford-st, Regent-st, Waterloo-pl.	To Edgware-rd 2d, to Oxford-cir 3d. All way 4d.

LINE.	COLOUR, &C.	START.	ROUTE.	FARES.
NottingHill (LancasterHtl) to Liverpool-st.	*Dark Green.* "Bayswater."	8 a.m. and every few min. to 10.20 p.m.	Westbourne-gr, Bishop's-rd, Eastbourne or Westbourne-ter, Edgware-rd, Oxford-st, Holborn, Cheapside, K. William-st.	To Rl. Oak 2d, to Oxford-cir 3d, to Chancery-la 5d. All way 6d.
Notting Hill to Mile End-rd.	*Green.* "Bayswater."	8 a.m. and every 15 min. to 11.10 p.m.	Bayswater-rd, Oxford-st, Holborn, Cheapside, Cornhill, Mile End-rd.	To Oxford-cir 3d. All way 6d.
Old Ford to Rl. Exchange	*Yellow.* "Old Ford and Bank."	7 a.m. and every 5 min. to 11.6 p.m.	Victoria-pk, Bethnal Gn.-rd, Church-st, Shoreditch.	All way 2d.
Old Kent-rd (The Swan) to Camden Tn.	*Blue.* "Waterloo."	8.28 a.m. and every 7 min. to 11.27 p.m.	New Kent-rd, London-rd, Waterloo-br, Strand, Charing ✠, Regent-st, Portland-pl, Albany-st.	Waterloo to Camden Tn. 4d, Charing ✠ to Camden Tn. 3d. All way 6d.
Old Kent-rd (Lord Nelson) to Essex-rd.	*Green.* "Islington and Old Kent-rd."	7.54 a.m. and every few min. to 10.8 p.m.	Dover-rd, Borough-rd, London-br, K. William-st, Moorgate-st, City-rd, East-rd, New North-rd.	Lord Nelson to Bank 3d. London-br Stn. to Essex-rd, Islington 3d. All way 5d.
Oxford-cir to Acton (Sun.).	*Light Green.* "Bayswater."	10, 10.30, 10.50, 11.30 a.m., 2, 2.30, 3, 6, 8.50 p.m.	Oxford-st, Bayswater, Shepherd's-bush.	All way 6d.
Oxford-cir to Brixton.	*Green.* "Brixton."	9 a.m. and 12 night.	Regent-st, Haymarket, Whitehall, Westminster-br, Kennington-rd.	To Charing ✠ 2d. Charing ✠ to Brixton 3d. All way 4d.
Oxford-cir to Clapham-common.	*Chocolate.* "Clapham."	12 a.m. and 7 p.m.	Regent-st, Whitehall, Parliament-st, Westminster-br, Kennington, Stockwell.	Charing ✠ to Kennington-ga 2d, Kennington-ga to Clapham 2d. All way 4d.
Oxford-cir to Clapton.	*Green.* "Clapton and Regent-cir."	9.15 a.m. and ev. 15 or 20 m. to 11.35 p.m.	Oxford-st, Holborn, Newgate-st, Cheapside, Threadneedle-street, Bishopsgate, Shoreditch, Hackney-rd.	To Bank 3d, Bank to Hackney 2d, Hackney to Clapton 3d. All way 6d.
Oxford-cir (Green Man) to Clapton.	*Dark Green.* "Clapton and Regent-cir."	9.45 a.m. and ev. 20 min to 11.25 p.m.	Regent-st, Gt. Portland-st, Euston-rd, Angel, Essex-rd, Ball's-pond-rd, Dalston-la, Hackney.	To Angel 3d, to Hackney 6d.
	Last three	Omnibuses	from Piccadilly-circus, 10.55, 11.15,	11.35.
Oxford-cir to Hackney.	*Green.* "Hackney & Oxford-st."	9.45 a.m. and every 30 min. to 11.25 p.m.	Portland-rd, Euston-rd, Angel, Essex-rd, Ball's-pond-rd, Kingsland-gate, Dalston-la.	Oxford-cir to Angel 3d. Angel to Hackney 4d. All way 6d.
	Last three	Omnibuses	from Piccadilly-circus, 10.55, 11.15,	11.35.
Oxford-cir to Peckham (Rye-la).	*Green.* "Times."	10 a.m. and every 60 min. to 11 p.m.	Regent-st, Whitehall, Westminster-br, Elephant and Castle, Camberwell-gn, Peckham-rd.	Elephant and Castle to Peckham 3d. All way 5d.
Oxford-cir to Victoria.	*Blue.* "Rl. Blue."	8.25 a.m. and every 10 min. to 11.50 p.m.	Regent-st, Bond-st, Piccadilly, Grosvenor-pl.	All the way 2d.
Oxford-st (Tott-ct-rd) to Highgate.	*Yellow.* "Highgate."	9 a.m. and every 12 min. to 11.40 p.m.	Hampstead-rd, Camden Tn., Kentish Tn.-rd.	Tottenham-ct-rd to Hampstead-rd 2d. All way 3d.
Parson's Gn (King's-rd) to Hoxton.	*Chocolate.* "Chelsea."	8.3 a.m. and every 17 min. to 11 p.m.	King's-rd, Sloane-st, Piccadilly, Strand, Fleet-st, Cheapside, Moorgate-st.	To Charing ✠ 3d, St. Paul's to Hoxton 3d. All way 6d.

LINE.	COLOUR, &c.	START.	ROUTE.	FARES.
PECKHAM (King's Arms) to GRACE-CHURCH-ST.	*Dark Green.* "Plain."	8 a.m. and every 30 min. to 9.30 p.m.	Peckham-rd, Walworth-rd, Elephant & Castle, Borough, London-br.	Camberwell-gate 2d. Camberwell-gn to City 3d. All way 5d.
PECKHAM (Rye-la) to OXF.-CIR.	*Green.* "Times."	9 a.m. and every 60 min. to 10 p.m.	Peckham-rd, Camberwell-gn, Elephant and Castle, Westminster-br-rd, Charing ✠, Regent-st.	Elephant and Castle 3d. All way 5d.
PICCADILLY CIRCUS to BLACKWALL.	*Blue.* "Blackwall."	8.57 a.m. and every 6 or 7 min. to 11.16 p.m.	Whitehall, Charing ✠, Strand, Fleet-st, St. Paul's, Cheapside, Cornhill, Aldgate, Whitechapel, Commercial-rd, East India-rd.	Charing ✠ to Commercial-rd 4d, Bank to Blackwall 3d. All way 6d.
PICCADILLY CIRCUS to HAMPSTEAD.	*Yellow.* "Hampstead"	9.5 a.m. and every 15 min. to 11.30 p.m.	Charing ✠-rd, Tottenham-ct-rd, Hampstead-rd, Camden Tn., High-st, Haverstock-hill.	Tottenham-ct-rd to Hampstead 3d. All way 4d.
PICC.-CIR to PORTLAND-RD STN.	*Yellow.*	8.45 a.m. and every 5 min. to 7.45 p.m.	Regent-st, Oxford-cir, Regent-st, Portland-rd. Week days only.	2d and 3d.
PIMLICO (Monster) LIVERPOOL-ST.	*Chocolate.* "Westminster."	8.10 a.m. and every 6 min. to 11.10 p.m.	Vauxhall - br - rd, Parliament - st, Whitehall, Strand, Fleet-st, Ludgate-hill, Queen Victoria-st.	To Charing ✠ 2d, Cha. ✠ to Ludgate-hill 1d. All way 4d.
PORTLAND-RD STN to PICC.-CIR.	*Yellow.*	8.30 a.m. and every 5 min. to 7.20 p.m.	Portland-rd, Regent-st, Oxford-cir. Week days only.	All the way 2d and 3d.
PUTNEY-BR to LONDON-BR.	*White.* "Putney-br."	7.40 a.m. and about every qr. of an hour to 10.40 p.m.	Fulham-rd, Brompton-rd, Piccadilly, Charing ✠, Strand, Fleet-st, St. Paul's.	To South Kensington Mus. 3d, Charing ✠ to London-br 2d. All way 6d.
RICHMOND-RD to CAMDEN TN.	*Claret.* "Camden Tn."	9.24 a.m. and every 15 min. to 11.20 p.m.	Westbourne-gr, Bishop's-rd, Church-st, Grove-rd, St. John's Wood-rd.	Rl. Oak to Lord's Cricket Ground 2d. All way 4d.
RL. EXCH. to OLD FORD.	*Yellow.* "Old Ford and Bank."	7.25 a.m. and every 5 min. to 12 night.	Threadneedle - st, Bishopsgate - st, Shoreditch, Bethnal Gn.-rd, Victoria-pk.	All way 3d.
RL. EXCH. to SOUTH HACK-NEY.	*Red.* "South Hackney."	8.15 a.m. and every 10 min. to 11.35 p.m.	Threadneedle-st, Bishopsgate, Hackney-rd, Cambridge Heath, Victoria-pk-rd.	All way 3d.
ROTHERHITHE to GRACE-CHURCH-ST.	*Green.* "Rotherhithe."	8 a.m. and every 15 min. to 11.10 p.m.	Lower-rd, Southwark-pk, Bermondsey, Tooley-st, London-br.	To Southwark-pk 2d. All way 4d.
ROYAL OAK (Bayswater) to LONDON-BR.	*Yellow.* "Rl. Oak and London-br."	7.25 a.m. and every 5 min. to 10.20 p.m.	Bishop's-rd, Edgware-rd, Oxford-st, Holborn, Cheapside, K. William-st.	To Oxford-cir 2d, Holborn-cir 4d. All way 6d.
ST. JOHN'S WD. to CAM-BERWELL-GA.	*Green.* "Atlas."	8.20 a.m. and every 8 min. to 11.30 p.m.	Finchley-rd, Park-rd, Baker-st, Oxford-st, Regent-st, Charing ✠, Whitehall, Westminster-br.	Eyre Arms to Oxford-cir 3d. All way 6d.
ST. JOHN'S WOOD to LON-DON-BR.	*Green.* "City Atlas."	8 a.m. and ev. 8 to 12 m. to 9.30 p.m.	Marlborough-rd, Park-rd, Baker-st, Oxford-st and circus, Holborn, Cheapside, K. William-st.	Swiss Cottage to Oxford-cir 3d, to Chancery-la 5d. All way 6d.
ST. JOHN'S WOOD to WAL-WORTH-RD.	*Green.* "Atlas."	8.25 a.m. and every 8 min. to 11.30 p.m.	Finchley-rd, Park-rd, Baker-st, Oxford-st, Regent-st and circus, Charing ✠, Whitehall, Westminster-br.	To St. John's Wood Ch. 2d, to Oxford-cir 3d, to Charing ✠ 4d. All way 6d.

LINE.	COLOUR, &c.	START.	ROUTE.	FARES.
SHEPHERD'S BUSH to LIVERPOOL-ST.	*Green.* "Bayswater."	7.35 a.m. and every 10 min. to 10.5 p.m.	Uxbridge-rd, Bayswater-rd, Oxford-st, Holborn, Cheapside.	To Notting-hill 2d, to Oxford cir 4d. All way 6d.
S. HACKNEY to RL. EXCHANGE.	*Red.* "South Hackney."	7.45 a.m. and every 10 min. to 10.55 p.m.	Victoria-pk-rd, Hackney-rd, Shoreditch, Threadneedle-st.	All the way 3d.
STARCH-GN to LIVERPOOL-ST STNS.	*Green.* "Bayswater."	7.55 a.m. and every 12 min. to 9.58 p.m.	Goldhawk-rd, Uxbridge-rd, Bayswater-rd, Oxford-st, Holborn, Cheapside.	To Notting-hill 3d, to Oxford-cir 5d, to Bank 6d.
STOKE NEWINGTON to VICTORIA STN.	*Green.* "Favorite."	8 a.m. and every 15 min. to 10.40 p.m.	Essex-rd, Angel, St. John-st-rd, Gray's-inn-rd, Chancery-la, Strand, Whitehall, Victoria-st.	Abney-pk to Angel, 3d, Charing ✠ 5d Victoria Stn. 6d.
STONEBRIDGE-PK to OXFORD-CIR.	*Red.* "Harlesden-gn."	8.4 a.m. and every hour to p.m.	Kensal-gn, Harrow-rd, Bishop's-rd, Edgware-rd, Oxford-st.	To Kensal-gn 1d, P. of Wales 2d, Rl. Oak 3d, Chapel - st 4d, Oxford-cir 5d.
TOLLINGTON-PK. TO VICTORIA STN.	*Green.* "Favorite."	8.5 a.m., freq. inter. to 10.40 p.m.	Seven Sisters'-rd, Holloway-rd, Angel, Gray's-inn-rd, Chancery-la. Strand, Whitehall, Victoria-st.	Holborn 4d, Charing ✠ 5d, Angel to Holborn 2d. All way 6d.
TRAFALGAR-SQ.to KENTISH TN.	*Yellow.* "Carlton."	8 a.m., ev. 12 or 15 m. to 12 night.	St. Martin's-la, Tottenham-ct-rd, Hampstead-rd, Haverstock-hill.	To Euston-rd 2d. All way 3d.
TULSE-HILL to GRACE-CHURCH-ST.	*Green.* "Norwood."	8.10 a.m. and every 40 min. to 9.15 p.m.	Brixton-rd, Kennington-rd, Elephant and Castle, Boro', London-br.	Tulse-hill to Brixton Ch. 3d. All way 6d.
UXBRIDGE-RD to CHARING ✠.	*Green.* "Bayswater."	7.50 a.m. and every 20 min. to 10.31 p.m.	Shepherd's Bush-gn, Notting-hill, Bayswater-rd, Oxford-st, Regent-st, Charing ✠,	To Shepherd's Bush 1d, Notting-hill 2d, Marble Arch 3d, Oxford-cir 4d, Charing ✠ 5d, Ludgate-cir 6d.
VICTORIA STN. to ABNEY PK.	*Green.* "Favorite."	9.16 a.m. and every 15 min. to 11.56 p.m.	Victoria-st, Charing ✠, Chancery-la, Gray's-inn-rd, St. John-st-rd, Angel, Essex-rd,	Victoria to Balls-pd 4d, Angel to Abney-pk 3d. All way 6d.
VICTORIA STN. to CAMDEN TN.	*Yellow.* "Camden Tn."	8 a.m. and every 7 min. to 12 night.	Victoria-st, Parliament-st, Charing-✠, St. Martin's-la, Tottenham-ct-rd, Hampstead-rd.	Trafalgar-sq to Camden Tn. 3d, Oxford-st to Camden Tn. 2d. All way 4d.
VICTORIA STN. to HAVERSTOCK-HILL.	*Yellow.* "Haverstock-hill."	9 a.m. and every 5 min. to 11.40 p.m.	Victoria-st, Parliament-st, Charing-✠, St. Martin's-la, Tottenham-ct-rd, Hampstead-rd.	Tottenham - ct - rd to Haverstock-hill 2d. All way 4d.
VICTORIA STN. to HOLLOWAY.	*Green.* "Favorite."	9.10 a.m. and at freq. int. to 12 night.	Victoria-st, Whitehall, Strand, Fleet-st, Chancery-la, Gray's-inn-la, St. John-st-rd, Angel, Holloway-rd.	To Chancery-la 3d, Angel to Holloway-rd 2d. All way 6d.
VICTORIA STN. to HOLLOWAY.	*Green.* "Favorite."	9.10 a.m. and at frequent intervals to 12 night.	Victoria-st, Parliament-st, Charing-✠, Strand, Chancery-la, Gray's-inn-rd, St. John-st-rd, Angel, High-st.	To Angel 4d, Westminster Abbey to Highbury 4d, Angel to Highbury 2d. All way 6d.
VICTORIA STN. to HORNSEY-RISE.	*Green.* "Favorite."	9.12 a.m. and at frequent intervals to 11.54 p.m.	Victoria-st, Parliament-st, Charing-✠, Strand, Fleet-st, Chancery-la, Gray's-inn-la, St. John-st-rd, Angel, Holloway-rd.	To Chancery-la 3d, Fleet-st to Angel 3d, Angel to Hornsey 3d. All way 6d.

LINE.	COLOUR, &c.	START.	ROUTE.	FARES.
VICTORIA STN. to KILBURN.	*Red.* "Kilburn and Victoria Stn."	8 a.m. and every 6 min. to 11.30 p.m.	Grosvenor-pl, Park-la, Edgware-rd, Maida-vale.	Marble Arch to Kilburn 3d. All way 5d.
VICTORIA STN. to KING'S ✠	*Green.* "Victoria Stn. and King's ✠."	7.55 a.m. and every 10 min. to 10.45 p.m.	Hyde-pk-cor, Piccadilly, Leicester-sq, Long-acre, Great Queen-st, Southampton-row, Russell-sq, Judd-st	
VICTORIA STN. to OXF.-CIR.	*Blue.* "Rl. Blue."	8 a.m. and every 10 min. to 11.20 p.m.	Grosvenor-pl, Piccadilly, Bond-st, Oxford-st.	All the way 2d.
VICTORIA STN. to STOKE NEWINGTON.	*Green.* "Favorite."	9.16 a.m. and every 15 min. to 11.56 p.m.	Victoria-st, Whitehall, Strand, Fleet-st, Chancery-la, Gray's-inn-rd, St. John-st-rd, Angel, Essex-rd, Newington-gn-rd, Albion-rd, Church-st.	Charing ✠ to Angel 3d, to Abney-pk 5d, Angel to Abney-pk 3d. All way 6d.
VICTORIA STN. to TOLLINGTON-PK.	*Green.* "Favorite."	8.30 a.m. and at frequent intervals to 11 p.m.	Victoria Stn., Whitehall, Strand, Chancery-la, Gray's-inn-rd, St. John-st-rd, Angel, Holloway-rd.	Charing ✠ to Tollingpk 5d, Holb. to Tolling.-pk 4d, Holb. to Angel 2d. All way 6d.
VICTORIA to WESTBOURNE-PK. (Ledbury-rd.)	*Red.* "Victoria Stn."	8 a.m. and every 6 min. to 11.25 p.m.	Grosvenor-pl, Park-la, Edgware-rd, Praed-st, Eastbourne-ter, Bishop's-rd.	Victoria Stn. to Edgware-rd 2d. All the way 4d.
WALHAM-GN. to BROAD-ST STN.	*White.* "Brompton."	7.45 a.m. and every 16 or 18 m. to 11 p.m.	Brompton-rd, Piccadilly, Charing ✠, Strand, Fleet-st, Cheapside.	Walham-gn to St. George's-pl 3d, to Charing ✠ 4d, to Broad-st Stn. 6d.
WALWORTH-RD to ST. JOHN'S WD.	*Green.* "Atlas."	8.25 a.m. and every 8 min. to 11.30 p.m.	London-rd, Westminster-br, Whitehall, Charing ✠, Regent-st, Oxford-st, Baker-st, Park-rd.	Swiss Cot. to St. John's Wd. Ch. 2d, to Oxford-cir 3d, to Char. ✠ 4d. All way 6d.
WANDSWORTH RD to GRACECHURCH-ST.	*Chocolate.* "Wandsworth."	8 a.m. and every 15 min. to 10.30 p.m.	Albert Embankment, York-rd, Stamford-st, Southwark-s London-br.	To York-rd 2d. All the way 4d.
WATERLOO STN. to KING'S CROSS.	*Red.* Waterloo Stn. and King's ✠.	8 a.m. and every 15 min. to 10.30 p.m.	Fleet-st, Chancery-la, Holborn, Gray's Inn-rd.	To Fleet-st, 2d. All the way 3d.
WATERLOO (Loop Line Stn) to LIVERPOOL-ST STN.	*Chocolate.*	Every few min.	Over Blackfriars-br, and Queen Victoria-st.	All the way 3d.
WESTBRNE-PK (Ledbury-rd) to VICTORIA.	*Red.* "Victoria Stn."	8.30 a.m. and every 6 min. to 11.50 p.m.	Bishop's-rd, Eastbourne-ter, Praed-st, Edgware-rd, Park-la, Grosvenor-pl.	To Edgware-rd 2d. All the way 4d.
WEST KILBURN to CHARING ✠.	*Red.* "West Kilburn."	7.45 a.m. and every 20 min. to 10.53 p.m.	Shirland-rd, Harrow-rd, Edgware-rd, Oxford-st, Regent-st.	
WEST KILBURN to LONDON BRIDGE.	*Yellow.* "Paddington."	8.3 a.m. and every 10 min. to 10.20 p.m.	Shirland-rd, Harrow-rd, Edgware-rd, Oxford-st, Holborn, Cheapside, K. William-st.	
WESTMINSTER (Warwick-st) to LIVERPOOL-ST.	*Chocolate.* "Westminster"	8.10 a.m. and every 6 min. to 11.10 p.m.	Vauxhall-br-rd, Whitehall, Strand, Fleet-st, Queen Victoria-st.	To Charing ✠ 2d. All the way 4d.

Opera Comique, 299, Strand (Map 7).—A roomy and handsome theatre, built end to end with the Globe, their stages being separated by a party-wall only. This theatre had no pit until it was reconstructed by Mr. David James in 1885. NEAREST *Ry.* Stn., Temple (Dis.); *Omnibus Rte.,* Strand ; *Cab Rank,* St. Clement's.

Orange Free State.— CONSULATE, 2, Sinclair-gdns, Kensington, W.

Oriental Club, 18, Hanover-sq, is "composed of noblemen, M.Ps., and gentlemen of the first distinction and character." The members elect by ballot ; one black ball in ten excludes. Entrance fee, £31 ; subscription, £9 9s.

Orleans Club, 29, King-st, S.W.—Proprietary, the number of members being limited to 550, who pay an entrance fee of £21, and an annual subscription of £8 8s. Election by committee. Each member, in addition to all the privileges of the club, is entitled to admit two ladies to the ladies' coffee-room and private dining-rooms.

Oxford and Cambridge Club, 71 to 76, Pall Mall, S.W.— For the association of gentlemen educated at these Universities. Qualification for membership : A degree ; passage of examinations required for a degree ; or two years' residence. Entrance fee, £42 ; subscription, £8 8s.

Oxford Street (Map 6)— De Quincey's stony-hearted stepmother—ought to be, if it be not, the finest as well as the longest and straightest of the main arteries of London. With one end reaching through its extensions—Holborn, Newgate-st, and Cheapside—to the City, with the other continued by the Bayswater-rd by the side of Hyde-pk, through Notting-hill, and out, with scarce a curve, to the far west, it ought to be the finest thoroughfare in the world. As a matter of fact it is not so by any means, and though it is, like all the other thoroughfares, improving, it still contains many houses which even in a third-rate street would be considered mean.

Oysters.—The best places for oysters are Wilton's, 1, Bury-st, St. James's ; Rule's, in Maiden-la, at the back of the Adelphi and Vaudeville ; Lynn's, about the middle of the south side of Fleet-st ; Smith's, in the Strand, near the Lyceum ; Pimm's, in the Poultry ; Scott's at the top of the Haymarket ; H. Prosser's, 84, Chancery-la ; J. S. Prosser's, 6, High Holborn ; and Sweeting's, 158, Cheapside.

Packing.—Any of the colonial outfitters have a staff of packers.

Paddington Station (Map 5). — When railways were first made, it was the fashion to put the stations on the outskirts of towns, and it was in obedience to this rule that the Great Western Railway Co. established their fine London terminus in the then remote district of Paddington. The establishment of the Metropolitan and District Railways has, to some extent, neutralised the inconvenience of the situation, which, however, still remains considerable. The Great Western Hotel immediately adjoins the station. NEAREST *Ry. Stn.,* Paddington (Met.) ; *Omnibus Rte.,* Edgware-rd ; *Cab Fare* to Bank, 2/6 ; to Charing ✠, 1/6.

Paintings and Sculpture. —The works of the following artists may be found as under.
   * Sculptors.   † Frescoes.
Abbott, National Portrait Gallery
Allan, Sir W., Apsley House
Angelico, Fra, National Gallery
Antonello da Messina, Nat. Gal.
Backhuizen, Bath House ; Bridgewater House ; Mrs. H. T. Hope ; Munro Collection ; Nat. Gal.
Bacon (the elder), Guy's Hospital ; Hampton Court Palace
Banks, T., National Gallery*
Basaiti, Marco, National Gallery
Beale, Mrs.,College of Physicians ; Lambeth Palace
Beechey, Sir W., Drapers' Hall ; Fishmongers' Hall ; National Port. Gallery ; Hampton Court
Behnes, College of Physicians*
Bell, St. Stephen's Hall*
Bellini, Giov., Mid. Temple Hall ; Nat. Gal. ; Hampton Court
Berchem, M., Bath Ho. ; Bridgewater Ho. ; Mar. of Bute ; Nat. Gal. ; Dulwich.
Bird, E., Nat. Gal. ; Stafford Ho.
Bleeck, P. van, Garrick Club
Bockman, Greenwich Hospital ; Hampton Court
Bonheur, Rosa, National Gallery
Bordone, Paris, Merchant Taylors' Hall ; Hampton Ct. ; Nat. Gal.
Borgognone, Amb., Nat. Gal.

Both, Dorchester House ; Dulwich
Bouts, Dierick, National Gallery
Briggs, Merchant Taylors' Hall
Bubb, Guy's Hospital*
Buonarotti, M.,Apsley Ho. (doubtful); Nat. Gal.; R. Academy*
Burnet, Apsley House
Callcott, Sir A. W., Nat. Gal.
Canaletto, Nat. Gal. ; Hampton Court; Soane Museum
Canova, Apsley House*; Holderness House*
Capelle, Van de, National Gallery
Caracci, An., Bath Ho. ; Bridgewater Ho. ; Nat. Gal.
Caracci, L., Bridgewater House
Chantrey, Apsley Ho.* ; College of Physicians* ; Goldsmiths' Hall * ; Guildhall * ; Holderness House * ; Soane Museum*
Charpentier, Salters' Hall
Cimabue, National Gallery
Claude, Apsley Ho. ; Bridgewater Ho.; Mar. of Bute ; Dorchester Ho. ; Grosvenor Ho. ; Mrs. H. T. Hope; Nat. Gal.; Baring Gal.
Clint, Garrick Club
Clostermann, Guildhall
Cocques, Gonzales, Nat. Gal.
Collins, Baring Gal. ; Ld. Northbrook ; Nat. Gal.
Constable, Nat. Gal. ; S. Ken. Mu.
Cooke, E. W., N. Gal. ; S. Ken. Mu.
Cooper, Sidney, National Gallery
Cope, Ho. of Lords† ; Poet's Hall†
Copley, Guildhall ; Nat. Gal.
Cornelis, Hampton Court
Correggio, Apsley House ; Bath House ; Nat. Gal.
Credi, Lorenzo di, Nat. Gal.
Creswick,T.,Nt. Gal.; S. Ken. Mu.
Crivelli, Carlo, National Gallery
Cross, Westminster Palace
Cuyp, Baring Gal. ; Ld. Northbrook ; Bath Ho. ; Bridgewater Ho. ; Mar. of Bute ; Dorchester Ho.; Grosvenor Ho.; Mrs. Hope; Nat. Gal. ; Rothschild, Baron ; Dulwich
Dahl, Greenwich Hospital
Damer, Mrs., Guildhall*
Danby, F., Nat. Gal. ; S. Ken. Mu.
Dance, Sir N., Greenwich Hospital ; Lincoln's Inn Hall
David, J. L., Apsley House
Delaroche, Paul, Bridgewater Ho.; Hertford Ho.; Stafford Ho.
De Wint, Garrick Club
Dobson, Devonshire House
Dolci, Carlo, Nat. Gal. ; Dulwich
Domenichino, Baring Gal. ; Lord Northbrook ; Bath Ho.; Bridgewater Ho.; Mrs. Hope ; Dulwich
Dow, G., Baring Gal. ; Lord Northbrook ; Bath Ho. ; Bridgewater Ho. ; Mar. of Bute ; Grosvenor Ho.; Mrs. H. T. Hope ; Nat. Gal. ; Dulwich

Dürer, Albrecht, Stafford House
Dyce, House of Lords †; Westminster Palace †
Dyckmans, National Gallery
Eastlake, M. Temp. Hall; Na. Gal.
Egg, Augustus, National Gallery
Etty, National Gallery
Evans, Greenwich Hospital
Eyck, Jan van, National Gallery
Flaxman, University College*
Foley, St. Stephen's Hall*
Francia, F., Na. Gal.; Hampton Ct.
Frith, Nat. Gal.; Sth. Ken. Mus.
Gainsborough, Col of Phy.; Foundling; Garrick; Grosvenor Ho.; Ironmongers' Hall; Nat. Gal.; Sth. Ken. Mus.; Hampton Ct.; Dulwich
Gerard, Mark, Hampton Court
Gibson, Westminster Hall
Giorgione, Bath Ho.; Ho.of Lords; Nat. Gal.; R.Acad.; Hampt. Ct.
Goodall, F., National Gallery
Gozzoli, Benozzo, National Gallery
Graham, Stationers' Hall
Grant, F., Apsley House
Greuze, Baring Gal.; Lord Northbrook; Dorchester Ho.; Dudley Ho.; Nat. Gal.; Rothschild, Baron; Hampton Ct.; Hertford Ho.
Grisoni, Garrick Club
Guercino, Bath Ho.; Bridgewater Ho.; Mar.of Bute; Stafford Ho.; Dulwich
Guido, Bridgewater Ho.; Grosvenor Ho.; Nat.Gal.; Stafford Ho.; Dulwich
Guzzardi, Leonardo, Admiralty
Gysels, P., Mrs. H. T. Hope
Hals, Franz, Hampton Court
Harlowe, Garrick; Lin. Inn Hall
Haydon, National Gallery
Hayman,
Hayter, Goldsmiths' Hall
Haytley, Foundling
Helst, Van der, Mrs. H. T. Hope; Hampton Court
Herbert, Poets' Hall†; West. Hall
Heyden, Van der, Apsley House; Bath House; Nat. Gal.
Hickey, Garrick   [Hall
Highmore, Foundling; Stationers'
Hobbema, Bath Ho.; Bridgewater Ho.; Mar. of Bute; Dorchester Ho.; Grosvenor Ho.; Hertford Ho.; Mrs. Hope; Nat. Gal.; Dulwich.
Hogarth, Foundling; Grosvenor Ho.; Lansdowne Ho.(?); Nat. Gal.; Nat. Por. Gal.; Norfolk Ho.; St. Bartholomew's; Soane Mus.; Sth. Ken. Mus.
Holbein, Barber Surgeons' Hall; Bath Ho.; Lambeth Pal.; Norfolk Ho.; Hampton Ct.
Honthorst,   Stafford   House; Hampton Court
Hooghe, P. de, Bath Ho.; Mar.

of Bute; Mrs. Hope; Nat. Gal.; Rothschild, Baron
Hoppner, Merchant Taylors' Hall; Hampton Court
Horsley, H.of Lords†; Poets' Hall†
Howard, Norfolk House
Hudson, B. Mus.; Goldsmiths' Hall
Huysmans, National Gallery
Huysum, Jan van, Bath Ho.; Grosvenor House; Dulwich; Na.Gal
Isabey, Soane Museum   [Ho.
Jackson, Ho. of Lds.; Lansdowne
Janssen, C., Goldsmiths' Hall
Jardin, Karel du, Baring Gal.; Ld. Northbrook; Bath Ho.; Nat. Gal.; Dulwich
Jervas, Lansdowne House
Jordaen, Devonshire House
Joseph, S., National Gallery*
Kauffmann, Ang., Hampton Ct.
Kirke, Greenwich Hospital
Kneller, Sir G., Charterhouse; Coll. of Phy.; Devonshire Ho.; Garrick; Greenwich Hos.; Nat. Por. Gal.; St. Bartholomew's; Hampton Court; R. Society
Landseer, Sir E., Apsley House; House of Lords; Nat. Gal.; South Kensington Museum
Lawrence, Sir T., Chesterfield Ho.; Garrick; Merch. Taylors' Hall; Nat. Gal.; Nat. Por. Gal.; Norfolk House; St. Bartholomew's; Soane Mus.; Sth. Kens. Mus.; Stafford Ho.; Royal Society
Le Brun, Grosvenor Ho.; Dulwich
Lee, F. R., National Gallery
Leiden, L. van, Norfolk House
Lely, Sir P., Bridgewater Ho.; Devonshire Ho.; Greenwich Hos.; Nat. Por. Gal.; Hampton Ct.; Rl. Society; Barbers' Hall
Leslie, G. R., Lansdowne Ho.; Nat. Gal.; Sth. Kens. Mus.
Lingelbach, Jan, National Gallery
Linnell, J., National Gallery
Lippi, Filippo, National Gallery
Loutherbourg, Greenwich Hospital; National Gallery
Luini, Bath House, 82, Piccadilly
Maas, N., Bridgewater House; National Gallery
Maclise, House of Lords†; Nat. Gal.; Westminster Pal.†
Mantegna, And., Baring Gallery; Lord Northbrook; Hampton Ct.; Nat. Gal.
Marshall, St. Stephen's Hall*
Martin, National Gallery; Stafford House
McDowell, Greenwich Hospital*; St. Stephen's Hall*
Meissonier, Hertford House
Memling, National Gallery
Mercier, Garrick
Metzu, Bridgewater Ho.; Baring Gal.; Ld. Northbrook; Hertford Ho.; Mrs. Hope; Nat. Gal.

Mieris, F., Mar. of Bute; Mrs. Hope; Nat. Gal.
Mieris, W., National Gallery
More, Sir Antonio, British Museum; Society of Antiquaries
Moroni, G. B., Nat. Gal.
Mortimer,—, Garrick; Stafford H.
Moucheron, National Gallery
Murillo, Baring Gal.; Ld. Northbrook; Bath Ho; Grosvenor Ho.; Hertford Ho.; Holland Ho.; Lansdowne Ho.; Nat. Gal.; Stafford Ho.; Dulwich
Mulready, Baring Gal.; Ld.Northbrook; Nat. Gal.; S. Kens. M.
Murray, British Museum; Fishmongers' Hall
Mytens, Norfolk Ho.; Hampton Ct.
Nasmyth, P., National Gallery; National Portrait Gallery
Netscher, Bath Ho.; Mrs. H. T. Hope; Nat. Gal.
Newton, G. S., Bridgewater Ho.; Ho. of Lords; Nat. Gal.
Nollekens, Apsley Ho*; Rl. Soc.*
Northcote,   Goldsmiths'   Hall; Guildhall
Opie, Garrick; Overstone, Lord, 2, Carlton-gdns; National Gallery
Orcagna, National Gallery
Os, Jan van, National Gallery
Ostade, A., Apsley Ho.; Baring Gal.; Bath House; Bridgewater Ho.; M.of Bute; Hertford Ho.; Mrs. H. T. Hope; Nat. Gal.; Dulwich
Ostade, J., Baring Gal.; Bath Ho.; Dorchester Ho.; Nat. Gal.
Palma Vecchio, Hampton Court
Parmegiano, Stafford House
Pellegrino, National Gallery
Perugino, Pietro, National Gallery
Pickersgill, F. R., Westmins Pal.
Pierce, E., Fishmongers' Hall
Piombo, Seb. del, Baring Gal.; Bridgewater Ho.; Lansdowne Ho.; Nat. Gal.
Pollajuolo, Ant., National Gallery
Potter, Paul, Baring Gallery; Bath Ho.; Grosvenor Ho.; Mrs. H.T. Hope; Nat. Gal.
Poussin, G., Bridgewater House; Grosvenor House; Nat. Gal.; Stafford House; Dulwich
Poussin, N., Bridgewater House; Grosvenor House; Nat. Gal.; Stafford Ho.; Hampton Court; Dulwich
Ramsay, Allan, Foundling; Goldsmiths' Hl.; Merch. Taylors' Hl.
Raffaelle, Baring Gallery; Bridgewater Ho.; Grosvenor House; Lansdowne Ho.; Munro Collection; Nat. Gal.; S. Kens.; Stafford Ho.; Hamp. Ct.; Dulwich
Rauch, Apsley House; Lansdowne House*
Rembrandt,   Bath   Ho.;   Bridge-

Pall Mall (Map 6) is the nearest approach in London to a street of palaces. Every political celebrity belongs to one or other of the clubs which occupy the principal portion of its space. The Army and Navy, and the United Service embrace all the men illustrious in arms; while the Church and learning are represented by the Athenæum, and the Oxford and Cambridge. Fond as are the people of this country of Gothic architecture, that style has no representative in Pall Mall. Here everything is classical, although the degree to which the classical architecture is adhered to differs widely between the chaste Italian of the Reform and the florid display of its next-door neighbour, the Carlton. One blot in the street is the property of the nation. The War Office is altogether out of keeping with the clubs upon the same side of the way. The building is already doomed, and some day, when times are better, a building more worthy of its purpose and surroundings will no doubt rise in its place. Marlborough House, the residence of the Prince of Wales, is not visible from the street. It stands within the walls at the corner of the road into the park, facing St. James's Palace. The following is the order in which the clubs on the south side are situated, beginning from Marlborough House: The Unionist, the Guards, the Oxford and Cambridge; then, next to the War Office, the Carlton, then the Reform, the Travellers', and the Athenæum, opposite to which, across Waterloo-pl, stands the United Service. On the north side, the new National Conservative Club is at the corner of Waterloo-pl. The Junior Carlton is next to George-st, and the Army and Navy stands at the opposite corner, its entrance being in George-st, and the Marlborough next door to the Institute of Painters in Water Colours.

Pall Mall Club, 7, Waterloo-pl, S.W., is established "to facilitate the association of gentlemen who wish to enjoy the social advantages of a club having no political bias." The election of members is vested solely in the committee, and is decided by ballot. Five members of the committee form a quorum, and two black balls exclude. The entrance is at the discretion of the committee from time to time, and is at present £10 10s. Subscription: Town members, £8 8s.; country members, £6 6s.; foreign members, £1 1s.

Paraguay.—CONSULATE, 7 and 8, Great Winchester-st, E.C. NEAREST *Ry. Stns.*, Broad-st (N.L.) and Moorgate-st (Met.); *Omnibus Rtes.*, Bishopsgate-st and Moorgate-st; *Cab Rank*, Broad-st Station.

Parcels.—The principal London Parcels Agencies are:

Carter, Paterson & Co., 126, Goswell-rd, E.C.; George Yard, Aldermanbury; Peel-st, Notting Hill-gate, W.; 32, Chalk Farm-rd, N.W.; 182, High-st, Deptford, S.E.; 151, Bermondsey-st, S.E.; 8, Milner-st, Chelsea, S.W.; High-st, Brentford; and 46, Millbank-st, Westminster.

Crouch's Universal Parcels Conveyance, 13, Gutter-la, E.C.

Foster's Parcels Express Co., 80, Fore-st, E.C.; and 18, Carlisle-st, Soho.

Globe Parcels Express Co., 44, St. Paul's Churchyard; 5, Finsbury-st, E.C.; and 13, Woodstock-st, Oxford-st, W.

London Parcels Delivery Co., 12, Rolls-bdgs, Fetter-la; 45, Leadenhall-st, E.C.; Church-st, Deptford; 88, Marlborough-rd, Chelsea; 81, High-st, Hampstead; Cranmer-rd, N. Brixton; Mildmay-avenue, Balls

Pond, N.; 11, Lawton-rd, Mile End-rd, E.; 149, Lancaster-rd, W.; Asgill-la, Richmond, W.

Pickford & Co., 57, Gresham-st, E.C.; 24, Rood-la, E.C.; Castle Inn, Wood-st, E.C.; Dumpton-pl, Regent's-pk; 56, Warwick-st, W.; 62, Berwick-st, Soho; 29, Blackman-st, S.E.; 29, Union-st, S.E.; Long-la, Bermondsey; Walham-gn, S.W.; York-rd, City-rd, E.C.; Praed-st, Paddington; 6, Wood-st, Westminster; Haydon-sq, E.; Oval-rd, N.W.; Whitechapel, E.; Nine Elms, S.W.; Preston's-rd, Poplar; Lett's-rd, Stratford; King-st, Poplar; 83, Willow-walk, Bermondsey; 156, Brompton-rd; 34, Queen-st, E.C.; 107, Poplar High-st, E.; and Broad-st Ry. Office, Eldon-st, E.C.

All of these have almost innumerable local collecting offices, full information as to which can be obtained on application.

Parcels Post.—The delivery of parcels by post in the metropolis is subject to the general regulations which obtain throughout the country, and full information on this subject will be found in the Post Office Guide. For the rules to be observed in regard to parcels addressed "Poste Restante," see *under head* POSTE RESTANTE.

Parkes Museum of Hygiene, 74, Margaret-st, S.W. —Open daily from 10 till 7. A valuable institution, of which full particulars can be had from secretary on application.

Parliamentary Constituencies (*See* CONSTITUENCIES).

Parliamentary Papers. —Old blue books and parliamentary papers, otherwise difficult to obtain, can generally be bought of Mr. King, Canada-bdgs, King-st, Westminster.

Parochial District Establishments.

BETHNAL GREEN. — *Workhouse*, Bonner's Hall Field, Bethnal-gn, E. *School*, Leytonstone.

CAMBERWELL. — *Workhouses*, Havil-st, Camberwell, S.E., and Gordon-rd, Peckham, S.E. *Infirmary*, separate infirmary at Havil-st. *School*, South Metropolitan District School at Sutton.

CHELSEA.—*Workhouse*, Chelsea, Arthur-st. *Infirmary*, Cale-st, Chelsea. *School*, Kensington and Chelsea District School.

FULHAM.—*Workhouse*, Hammersmith. *Infirmary*, adjoins Work-

house. *School*, West London District School at Ashford.

GREENWICH.—*Workhouse*, Greenwich. *Infirmary*, separate infirmary at Greenwich. *School*, South Metrop. Dis. School at Sutton.

HACKNEY.—*Workhouse*, Sydney-road, Homerton. *Infirmary*, High-st, Homerton, E. *School*, Forest Gate District School.

HAMPSTEAD.--*Workhouse*, Hampstead, N.W. *School*, Hendon Workhouse.

HOLBORN.—*Workhouses*, Gray's Inn-rd and Shepherdess-walk, N. *Infirmary*, Highgate. *School*, Mitcham.

ISLINGTON. — *Workhouses*, St. John's-rd and Cornwallis-rd, N. *Infirmary*, separate infirmary, St. John's-rd. *School*, Hornsey.

KENSINGTON.—*Workhouses*, Marloes-rd, Kensington, and Mary-pl, Notting-hill, W. *Infirmary*, Marloes-rd. *School*, Kensington and Chelsea District School.

LAMBETH.—*Workhouses*, Renfrew-rd, Lower Kennington-la, and Prince's-rd, S.E. *Infirmary*, Brook-st, Kennington-rd. *School*, Norwood.

LEWISHAM.—*Workhouse*, Lewisham. *School*, North Surrey District School at Anerley.

LONDON, CITY OF.—*Workhouse*, Homerton. *Infirmary*, separate infirmary at Bow. *School*, Central London District School at Hanwell.

MILE END.—*Workhouse*, *Infirmary*, *and School*, Bancroft-rd, Mile End.

PADDINGTON.—*Workhouses*, Harrow-rd, W., and King's-rd, N.W. *School*, West London District School at Ashford.

POPLAR. — *Workhouse*, Poplar. *Infirmary*, 45, Upper North-st, Poplar, E. *School*, Forest Gate District School.

ST. GEORGE'S. — *Workhouses*, Wallis-yd, Buckingham Palace-rd, and Fulham-rd, S.W. *Infirmary*, Fulham-rd. *School*, West Lond. Dist. School at Ashford.

ST. GEORGE'S-IN-THE-EAST.— *Workhouse*, Princes-st, Old Gravel-la. *Infirmary*, separate infirmary at Princes-st. *School*, Plashet.

ST. GILES-IN-THE-FIELDS AND ST. GEORGE, BLOOMSBURY.— *Workhouse*, Endell-st, W.C. *Infirmary*, Central London Dis. Sick Asylum. *School*, Strand Union School at Edmonton.

ST. MARYLEBONE.—*Workhouse*, Northumberland-st, W. *In-*

firmary, Ladbroke-grove-rd, W. *School*, Southall.

ST OLAVE'S. — *Workhouses*, Parish-st, Tooley-st, S.E., Tanner-st, Bermondsey, and Lower-rd, Rotherhithe. *Infirmary*, Lower-rd, S.E. *School*, South Metrop. Dist. School at Sutton.

ST. PANCRAS.—*Workhouse*, St. Pancras-rd, St. Pancras. *Infirmary*, Dartmouth-pk-hl, Highgate. *School*, Leavesden.

ST. SAVIOUR'S. — *Workhouses*, Marlboro'-st, Blackfriars-rd, S.E., Mint-st, Southwark, S.E., and Westmoreland-st, Walworth, S.E. *Infirmary*, Champion-hill, East Dulwich, S.E. *School*, Central London District School at Hanwell.

SHOREDITCH.—*Workhouse*, Hoxton, N. *Infirmary*, Hoxton-st, N. *School*, Brentwood District School.

STEPNEY.—*Workhouse*, St. Leonard-st, Bromley. *Infirmary*, Stepney District Sick Asylum. *School*, South Metropolitan District School at Sutton.

STRAND. — *Workhouse*, Edmonton. *Infirmary*, Central London District Sick Asylum. *School*, Edmonton.

WANDSWORTH AND CLAPHAM.— *Workhouse*, St. John's-hill, S.W. *Infirmary*, separate infirmary at St. John's-hill. *School*, North Surrey Dist. School at Anerley.

WESTMINSTER.—*Workhouse*, 48, Poland-st, W. *Infirmary*, Central London District Sick Asylum. *School*, St. James's-rd, Upper Tooting.

WHITECHAPEL. — *Workhouse*, South-grove, Mile-end-rd, E. *Infirmary*, Baker's-row, Whitechapel. *School*, Forest Gate District School.

WOOLWICH. — *Workhouse*, Plumstead. *Infirmary*, separate infirmary at Plumstead. *School*, South Metropolitan District School at Sutton.

And see ASYLUMS (MET. DISTRICT).

Parochial School Districts.

CENTRAL LONDON.—City of London, St. Saviour's. *School*, Hanwell.

FOREST GATE.—Poplar, Whitechapel. *School*, West Ham.

KENSINGTON AND CHELSEA.— Kensington, Chelsea. *School*, Banstead.

NORTH SURREY—Croydon, Lewisham, Richmond, Wandsworth, Clapham. *School*, Anerley, S.E.

SOUTH METROPOLITAN.—Camberwell, Greenwich, St. Olave's, Woolwich, Stepney. *Schools*, Sutton ; Banstead-rd, S.E. ; Herne Bay ; Witham, Essex.

WEST LONDON.—Fulham, Paddington, St. George's. *School*, Ashford.

Parochial Sick Asylum Districts.

CENTRAL LONDON. — Strand, Westminster, St. Giles and St. George, St. Pancras. *Asylum*, Cleveland-st, Fitzroy-sq, W.

POPLAR AND STEPNEY.—Poplar, Stepney. *Asylum*, Bromley, E.

Patent Museum, South

Kensington (Map 5), was, by the Act of 1883, transferred to the South Kensington Museum, and now forms part of the science collections. It occupies a portion of the south galleries, and is under the same regulations as those which govern the Museum generally. There are few institutions more worthy of a visit. There are mechanical inventions of all kinds, some exhibited in model, some of full size. There are locomotive and marine engines, pumps, bridges, docks, and machinery of all sorts. Of special interest are the primitive steam-engines from which have sprung the enormous development with which we are familiar. There is Stephenson's "Rocket," which won the prize at the competition in 1829, and whose velocity was at that time looked upon as alarming. Close by it is the "Sans Pareil," of Hawksworth, of Darlington, a competitor with the "Rocket." Even of higher interest is "Puffing Billy," the first locomotive ever built, having been at work on a colliery line in 1813. There is Watt's first "Sun and Planet" engine for winding and pumping. The patent was taken out in 1760, and the engine was erected in 1795. Near it is Newcomen's Cornish pumping-engine, patented in 1769. Of equal interest, as the progenitors of our cotton industry, are Arkwright's carding and spinning machines, patented in 1769, and close by is Buchanan's original carding-engine, patented in 1824. This may be considered the first carding machine of the type now in use. Newsham's fire-pump, patented in 1721, affords a striking contrast to the steam fire-engines of the present day, but the advance

that has been made is still more strongly shown in Robertson's original engine, built for Bell's *Comet*, the first steamboat that ever ran in British waters. Close by the *Comet* engine is the first hydraulic pump ever made, by Bramah, in 1795. A conspicuous object is the great clock of Glastonbury Abbey, constructed by Lightfoot, one of the monks of the convent in 1325, and still working and keeping time. The sight of these remarkable objects only makes one regret more strongly that so little has been done to preserve the early patents. A museum containing examples of the gradual progress which has been made in all our various manufactures would have been of immense value and interest. The museum is open to the public every day, admission free. NEAREST *Ry. Stn.*, South Kensington (Dis.) ; *Omnibus Rtes.*, Brompton-rd and Fulham-rd ; *Cab Rank*, Opposite.

Patent Office, 25, Southampton-buildings, Chancery-la. Hours 10 to 4.—The Free Library in the Patent Office was opened to the public in March, 1855, and consisted at that time of the printed records of the office, the patent publications of a few foreign states, and a small collection of works of reference. At the present day the library contains upwards of 80,000 volumes of printed records, and scientific and technical literature in all languages. The Patent Office Library has become celebrated for its collection of transactions of learned societies and scientific and technical journals, all in an unusually complete state. The facilities afforded for the consultation of these works, as well as the records of the office (with their indices), dating from the reign of James I., and, above all, their prompt supply, have made the library a place of resort for all interested in the progress of patented and scientific invention. The great drawback is the want of space for the accommodation of upwards of 700 readers weekly. NEAREST *Ry. Stn.*, Temple (Dis.) and Farringdon-st (Met.); *Omnibus Rte.*, Holborn ; *Cab Rank*, Holborn (Fetter-la).

Paternoster Row (Map 8), the headquarters of the book trade once, is no longer so in the sense in which the phrase is commonly understood. In the latter part of the last and the first part of the present century, "the Row" was the literary heart of London, and its history is bound up with that of the great publishing firms and the great literary enterprises of that period. But nowadays the publishing stream has worn for itself fresh channels, and the bulk of the great publishers are to be found in or about Piccadilly, Regent-st, or the Strand. As a rule, however, these only deal directly with their authors, the greater portion of their sales being carried on through the medium of two or three great book merchants who supply the retail trade, and whose location in "the Row" makes it in truth the great book-market of London.

Paulatim Club, 39, Fitzroy-sq, W.—This Club was established to promote social intercourse among former pupils of University College School and their friends, and now numbers between 300 and 400 members. Entrance fee, £1 1s.; subscription, £2 2s.

Pavilion Theatre, Whitechapel-rd (Map 4).—A large East End theatre, capable of holding considerably over 3,000 persons. Melodrama of a rough type, farce, pantomime, &c. NEAREST *Ry. Stns.*, Aldgate (Met.) and Whitechapel (E. Lon.); *Omnibus Rtes.*, Whitechapel - road; *Cab Rank*, Aldgate.

Pentonville Prison(Map 3) —known as the Model Prison— in Caledonian-rd, about 200 yards S.E. of the Cattle Market. It consists of a central hall, with five radiating wings, contains a thousand cells, and is conducted on a modification of the silent and solitary systems. Orders to view from the Home Office. NEAREST *Ry. Stn.*, Barnsbury (N. Lon.); *Omnibus Rte.*, Caledonian - rd ; *Cab Rank*, Offord-rd.

People's Palace (The) (BEAUMONT TRUST), Mile End-rd,;E.—The germ of this institution was the bequest of £12,250 by Mr. Barber Beaumont, towards the founding of a Philosophical Institution for the benefit of the inhabitants of Beaumont-sq, Mile End. Since then the trust has been much extended and has erected palatial buildings for the advantage of the East End poor, out of funds subscribed by the public ; the Drapers' Company having alone contributed the

munificent sum of £60,000. The scheme of the trust includes the provision of a great central hall, large library, swimming baths, technical trade and science schools, gymnasia, billiard and refreshment rooms, great exhibitions, winter gardens, &c. ; the aim, in short, being to provide a place of recreation and university for the poor of East London. Since Oct., 1887, when active operations began, three quarters of a million people have attended the palace, and there are now nearly 3,000 students in the evening classes. The palace is, indeed, well worthy a visit from all. NEAREST *Ry. Stn. and Omnibus Rte.*, Mile End-rd.

Persia.—MINISTRY, 80, Holland-park. NEAREST *Ry. Stns.*, Notting Hill - gate (Dis.) and Uxbridge - rd (Met.); *Omnibus Rte.*, Uxbridge-rd ; *Cab Rank*, Uxbridge - rd. There is no Persian Consulate in London.

Peru.—MINISTRY, 13, Comeragh - road, West Kensington. NEAREST *Ry. Stn.*, West Kensington (Dis.); *Omnibus Rtes.*, Kensington-gore and Hammersmith-rd. CONSULATE, 9, New Broad-st. NEAREST *Ry. Station and Omnibus Rte.*, Bishopsgate-st ; *Cab Rank*, New Broad-st.

Petty Sessional Divisions in the Metropolitan Police District.—In those portions of the Sessional Divisions which are within the limits of any metropolitan police-court, the criminal business is taken to the police-court ; but Petty Sessions are held for all parochial or other civil business.

BEACONTREE HALF HUNDRED, Essex (J, K, and N divs.), Petty Sessions Room, Magistrates Court, Eastern-rd, Stratford, daily at 9.30, Saturdays 11.

BLACKHEATH DIVISION, Kent (K, P,and Rdivs.),GreenManHotel, Blackheath, second Tu. in each month. For civil business only.

BRENTFORD DIVISION, Middlesex (T and X divs.), Town Hall, New Brentford, Mon. and Sat. at 11 a.m.

BROMLEY DIVISION, Kent (P and R divs.), every Monday at the Court House, Bromley. The whole of the petty sessional div.is within the metro. police district, excepting the parishes of Chelsfield, Cudham, and Knockholt.

CHESHUNT DIVISION, Herts (Y

div.), Sessions Room, St. Mary's Hall, Cheshunt, alternate Wednesdays at 11 a.m.

CHIPPING BARNET DIVISION, Herts(S and Y divs.),Town Hall, Chipping Barnet, Mon. at 11 a.m. Police cases are occasionally taken from parts of Finchley and Friern Barnet, in the Highgate div. (County of Middlesex), and Shenley and Totteridge (County of Herts), to the Chipping Barnet Petty Sessions.

CROYDON DIVISION, Wallington Hundred, Surrey (P, V, and W divs.),Town Hall,Croydon,Wed. at 10, and Sat at 11 a.m.

DARTFORD DIVISION, Kent (R div.), Court House, Dartford, every Sat. at 1 p.m. ; Local Board Office, Erith, last Tues. in the month, at 3.30 p.m. Charges taken in the parishes of East Wickham, Bexley, Crayford, and Erith, are heard at Woolwich Police Court. Summonses are decided at Dartford Petty Sessions on alternate Saturdays at 1 p.m. Offences under Metropolitan Police Act, Local Board Office, Erith, at 3 p.m., last Wednesday in month.

EDGWARE DIVISION (Gore Hundred), Middlesex (S and X divs.), Court House, Edgware, every Wed. at 11 a.m. The greater portion of the criminal business from Willesden in the Kensington div. (all the other parishes of which are in a police-court district) is taken to the Edgware Petty Sessions, but all the parish business, &c., which must be done in the div., is transacted at the Vestry Hall, Kensington, at appointed times throughout the year. The whole of Harrow is in this div. for civil business.

EDMONTON HUNDRED, Middlesex (N and Y divs.), County Court, Edmonton, Thurs. at 10 a.m. The whole of Enfield is in this div. for civil business.

ENFIELD, Middlesex (Y div.), Clerk's Office, Enfield Town, Mon. at 10 a.m.

EPSOM DIVISION, Copthorne Hundred, Surrey (V and W divs.), Petty Sessions Court, Epsom, every Mon. at 10.30 a.m., except Bank Holidays, when the Sessions are held on Wed.

FINSBURY.—*See* HIGHGATE GORE HUNDRED.—*See* EDGWARE.

G 2

HAMPSTEAD, Middlesex (S div.), Police-stn., Hampstead, every Wed. at 10 a.m.

HANOVER-SQUARE DIVISION, Middlesex (B and C divs.), Board Room, Mount-st. For civil business only.

HAVERING-ATTE-BOWER, Essex, at County Court, Romford, every Thurs. This div. includes Romford, Hornechurch, & Havering.

HIGHGATE OR FINSBURY DIVISION, Middlesex (S and Y divs.), Police Stn., Highgate, Mon. at 10 a.m. For police cases only. Police cases which arise in parts of Finchley and Friern Barnet are occasionally taken before the justices sitting at the Barnet Petty Sessions.

DITTO (G, N, S, and Y divs.), Sessions House, Clerkenwell, occasionally on Thurs. at 10.30 a.m. For civil business only.

HOLBORN DIVISION, Middlesex (C, D, E, G, and S divs.), Holborn Town Hall, Gray's-inn-rd. For civil business only.

KENSINGTON DIVISION, Middlesex (B, T, and X divs.), Vestry Hall, Kensington. First Tu. in month. For civil business only.

KINGSTON, BOROUGH OF (V div.), the Petty Sessions are held in the Town Hall every Wed. at 10 a.m.

KINGSTON AND ELMBRIDGE HUNDREDS, Surrey (V div.), the Petty Sessions for the Hundred are held in the Assize Court, Kingston-upon-Thames, every Thurs. at 11 a.m

MARYLEBONE DIVISION, Middlesex (D and S divs.), Court House, Marylebone-la. For civil business only.

NEWINGTON DIVISION, Surrey (L, M, P, R, V, and W divs.), Sessions House, Newington, specially at appointed times throughout the year. For civil business only.

PADDINGTON DIVISION, Middlesex (D and X divs.), Vestry Hall, Paddington-gn. For civil business only.

RICHMOND DIVISION, Surrey (V div.), Petty Sessions Court, Richmond, Wed. at 11 a.m.

ST. JAMES'S DIVISION, Middlesex (C div.), St. James's Vestry Hall, Piccadilly. Civil business only.

ST. MARGARET'S DIVISION, Middlesex (A and B divs.), Sessions House, Westminster. For civil business only.

ST. PANCRAS DIVISION, Middlesex (D, E, G, S, and Y divs.), 23, Gordon-st, W.C. For civil business only. Part of this parish is in the Finsbury Div. for police cases. Those parts of the parishes of Hampstead and St. Pancras which are not included in a police-court district come within this division occasionally.

SOUTH MIMS DIVISION, Middlesex (S div.). The ordinary magisterial business of this division is transacted at the Town Hall, Barnet, every Mon. at 11 a.m. Special Sessions for parochial business are held at appointed times throughout the year at the Hart's Horns Inn, High-st, Barnet.

SPELTHORNE DIVISION OR HUNDRED, Middlesex (T div.), Town Hall, Staines ; Red Lion Inn, Hampton ; Running Horse Inn, Sunbury Common, alternate Mon. at 12 a.m.

STRAND DIVISION, Middlesex (E div.), Vestry Rooms, St. Martin's - in - the - Fields. For civil business only.

TOWER DIVISION, Middlesex (G, H, J, K, and N divs.), County Court, Great Prescot-st, Whitechapel, E. For civil business only

TOWER OF LONDON, LIBERTY OF (H div.), Court House, Wellclose-sq, E.

UXBRIDGE DIVISION (Elthorne Hundred), Middlesex (T and X divs.), Public Rooms, Uxbridge, Mon. at 11 a.m.

WALTHAM ABBEY DIVISION (Epping Hundred), Essex (N and K divs.), County Court, Waltham Abbey, Tu. at 10.30 a.m.

WANDSWORTH DIVISION, Surrey (V div.), County Court House, Wandsworth, specially, at appointed times throughout the year. For civil business only.

Piccadilly (Map 6). — The great street leading from the Haymarket and Regent - st westward to Hyde-pk-corner. From Hyde-pk-corner to Devonshire House the houses are confined to the north side, the Green-pk forming, to that point, the southern side, which, for a considerable distance, is lined by foliage trees of some antiquity, and of great beauty. Being the high road to the most fashionable quarters in the west and south-west of London, Piccadilly, during a great portion of the year, presents a bright and lively, not to say kaleidoscopic, appearance ; and even when the great stream of " West End " London life seems to have nearly run dry elsewhere it is still to be found, though perhaps but a rivulet, in Piccadilly. Few streets in town have so many associations. Here, or hard by, at one time or another, have lived such people as Byron, Scott, Sir Wm. Petty, Lord Eldon, Nelson's Lady Hamilton, Verrio, Sir Francis Burdett, Lord Palmerston, and "Old Q." Piccadilly is one of the few streets left in London which are remarkable both from a commercial and from a "society point of view. Eastward the double row of houses is almost entirely devoted to trade, and westward a few shops are still dotted amongst the stately abodes which overlook the Greenpk. From the " White Horse Cellar " to the mansion of the Rothschilds, and Apsley House ; from the butcher's shop to Devonshire House ; from the tavern to the club-house, every kind of edifice is represented. On a fine summer's morning the departure of the coaches from the " White Horse Cellar " is an amusing and interesting sight, unique of its kind in these railway times—(See COACHES). Among the principal public buildings are Sir Christopher Wren's brick church, dedicated to St. James, certainly not one of the master's happiest efforts so far as its exterior is concerned ; the Geological Museum, which abuts on the southern side ; the new buildings of the Institute of Painters in Water Colours ; and Burlington House, the home of the Royal Academy and of many learned societies.

Picture Galleries. — The following is a list of the Picture Galleries in London which belong to the nation, and of those which may be fairly described as public. They will be found fully described under their respective headings:—

British Artists, Society of.
City of London Society of Artists.
Dudley Gallery.
Dulwich Gallery.
Grosvenor Gallery.
Lady Artists, Society of
National Gallery.
National Portrait Gallery.
Royal Academy.
Royal Institute of Painters in Oil Colours.
South Kensington
Water Colours, Institute of Painters in.
Water Colours, Society of Painters in.

In addition to these there is a vast number of picture shows always on view, in the neighbourhood principally of Bond-st and Pall Mall, which are run for the most part by picture-dealers. The most important of these is undoubtedly the French Gallery of Messrs. Wallis, in Pall Mall East, where periodical exhibitions of pictures of the highest class have been held for some years. The Doré Gallery, 35, New Bond-st, is devoted, as its name imports, to the works of Gustave Doré. At Messrs. Agnews', 39B, Old Bond-st, Messrs. Boussod & Co.'s, 116, New Bond-st, Mr. McLean's, 7, Haymarket, the Galleries, 168, New Bond-st, and Messrs. Tooths', Haymarket, among others, there are frequently special exhibitions of pictures. All the picture shows will be found advertised in the front pages of the daily papers. To see everything of interest in the way of works of art during the season in London is an expensive matter; for, in addition to all the above-mentioned galleries, the price of admission to each of which may be taken at a shilling, not to mention the charge for occasional catalogues, there is a sort of guerilla contingent of single pictures which fight for their own hand, and the toll for seeing which is a further succession of shillings. In these cases, it is generally desirable to turn a deaf ear to the blandishments of the polite gentlemen who tout for the engraving which is to be published at some future and uncertain date. Of course, cases occur when visitors really wish to subscribe, but in most cases the unsuspecting victim is overpersuaded into the purchase of something he does not want, and which he probably forgets all about until the bill comes in for payment

(*And see* PAINTINGS AND SCULPTURE.)

Pigeon Clubs.—There are many societies in London for promoting the pigeon fancy. The first of these is the Peristeronic, meeting fortnightly during the winter months at Freemasons' Tavern, and having an annual exhibition at the Crystal Palace in January. There is also the City Columbarian, meeting in London Wall, and several in the suburbs.

Pigeons.—(*See* POULTRY.)

Police.—The police force of London comprises the Metropolitan Police and the City Police. The latter have jurisdiction in the City of London proper, covering about 1 square mile, and consisting of about 900 men. The Metropolitan Police District extends to a radius of about 15 miles from Charing ✠, and covers more than 700 square miles. The force in the beginning of 1888 consisted of 13,346 men, distributed into 23 divisions, not including 760 men doing duty in the five Dockyards. Each sergeant and constable bears the letter of his division and number on his collar, which should be taken down if any complaint has to be preferred. Within a reasonable distance of nearly every house in any populous district there is, besides the local police-station, a fixed police point (*see* FIXED POINTS), at which a constable may always be found from 9 a.m. to 1 a.m. If the constable at the fixed point be called away on special duty, his place is taken by the first patrol who arrives at the vacant post. Every householder should learn where is the nearest police-station and fixed point. If police assistance be required on some special occasion, such as a party, personal or written application should be made to the superintendent of the division on which the ground is situated. Such duty is done by men in their own time, and from 5s. to 10s. is generally given by the person interested.

SPECIAL DUTIES.—The following questions have also been submitted to the Metropolitan Police Department, and have received the annexed replies:

Whether, when application is made at a station for a married constable to take charge of an empty—furnished—house, any and what responsibility is undertaken by the department, and what are the general terms and conditions on which such applications are entertained?

Police sergeants or constables are permitted by the commissioner to take charge of unoccupied furnished houses on the recommendation of the superintendent of the division, provided they have undivided charge; that no servants remain; and that there are no valuables or plate therein. No responsibility whatever is undertaken by the police department. There are no other set terms or conditions. If the man's wife is employed to keep the house clean, it becomes a matter of arrangement between the parties. Sergeants and constables are allowed by the divisional superintendents to occupy unfurnished houses, or houses that have not been inhabited, provided they are reported, on inspection, as not likely to be prejudicial to the health of the officer.

Whether the police on ordinary night duty are allowed to be made available for calling private individuals in time for early trains, &c.?

The police are not only allowed, but are taught that they are bound to render this or any other service in their power to the inhabitants.

Whether any arrangement is practicable—short of hiring a special constable—by which a house can safely be left empty for a few hours?

Certainly not. The custom, unfortunately, is a very prevalent one notwithstanding numerous official cautions, and a large number of offences are traceable to it, as it affords every facility for thieves and housebreakers.

Police Courts.—Bow STREET: Bow-st, Covent-gdn. Chief Police Magistrate, Sir J. T. Ingham; Magistrates, J. Vaughan, Esq., and J. Bridge, Esq. Chief Clerk, J. Alexander, Esq. Hours 10 to 5. Application for summonses to be made at 10 a.m.; summonses heard at 2 p.m.; remands and charges from 10 a.m. till 5 p.m. NEAREST *Ry. Stn.*, Temple ; *Omnibus Rtes.*, Strand and Oxford-st ; *Cab Rank*, Catherine-st, Strand.

CLERKENWELL: King's ✠-rd. Magistrates, T. I. Barstow, Esq., and James R.W. Bros, Esq. Chief Clerk, H. Cavendish, Esq. Hours 10 to 5. Application for summonses to be made at 10 a.m. NEAREST *Ry. Stns.*, King's ✠ and Farringdon-st ; *Omnibus Rtes.*, Gray's-inn-rd, Exmouth-st, Euston-rd, and Pentonville-rd ; *Cab Rank*, Gray's-inn-rd, Met. Ry. Stn.

DALSTON: Close to Dalston Junction (N.L) Magistrates, T. I. Barstow, Esq., Horace Smith, Esq., and James R. W. Bros, Esq. Chief Clerk, — Titterton, Esq. Hours 10 to 5.

GREENWICH: Magistrates, R. H. B. Marsham, Esq., and E. Fenwick - Fenwick, Esq. Chief Clerk, H. P. Newton, Esq. Hours 10 to 1.30. Applications for summonses to be made at 12 noon. NEAREST *Ry. Stn.*, Greenwich.

GUILDHALL JUSTICE-ROOM; Magistrates, Aldermen. Chief Clerk, Herbert George Saville, Esq. Hours 10 to 4. Applications for summonses to be made at 1 p.m.; summonses, remands, and charges are heard from 12 noon. NEAREST *Ry. Stns.*, Mansion House and Moorgate-st; *Omnibus Rtes.*, Cheapside and Moorgate-st; *Cab Rank*, Lothbury.

HAMMERSMITH: Vernon-st, Hammersmith-rd. Magistrates, J. Paget, Esq., Montagu Williams, Esq., Q.C., and H. Curtis-Bennett, Esq. Chief Clerk, G. A. Bird, Esq. Hours 10 to 2. Applications for summonses to be made at 10 a.m.; remands and summonses heard at 11 a.m.; charges from 10 a.m. to 1.30 p.m. NEAREST *Ry. Stn.*, West Kensington; *Omnibus Rte.*, Hammersmith-rd; *Cab Rank*, Red Cow-la.

LAMBETH: Renfrew-rd, Lower Kennington-la. Magistrates, Geo. Chance, Esq., and R. J. Biron, Esq.,Q.C. Chief Clerk,T. C. Martin, Esq. Hours 10 to 5. Applications for summonses at 10 a.m. NEAREST *Ry. Stn.*, Elephant and Castle; *Omnibus Rtes.*, Newington-bts and Kennington-pk-rd; *Cab Rank*, High-st, Newington-butts.

MANSION HOUSE JUSTICE-ROOM. Magistrates, Lord Mayor and Aldermen. Chief Clerk, Cecil Douglas, Esq. Hours 10 to 4; Saturdays, 10 to 2; affidavits taken between 12 and 2. Summonses, remands, and charges are heard from 12 noon. NEAREST *Ry. Stns.*, Mansion House and Moorgate-st; *Omnibus Rtes.*, Cheapside, Moorgate-st, Qn. Victoria-st, and King William-st; *Cab Rank*, Lothbury.

MARLBOROUGH-ST: Gt. Marlborough-st. Magistrates, R. M. Newton, Esq., and J. S. Mansfield, Esq. Chief Clerk, J. R. Lyell, Esq. Hours 10 to 5. Applications for summonses to be made at 10 a.m. and 12 noon; summonses heard at 2 p.m.; remands at 12 noon; and charges from 10 a.m. to 5 p.m. NEAREST *Ry. Stns.*, Portland-rd and Charing ✠ (Dis. & S.E.); *Omnibus Rtes.*, Regent-st and Oxford-st; *Cab Ranks*, Conduit-st and Oxford-market.

MARYLEBONE: Seymour-pl, Bryanston-sq. Magistrates, A. de Rutzen, Esq., and W. M. Cooke, Esq. Chief Clerk, W. Tate, Esq. Hours 10 to 5. Application for

summonses to be made at 10 a.m.; summonses heard at 2 p.m.; remands at 11 a.m.; and charges from 10 a.m. to 5 p.m. NEAREST *Ry. Stn.*, Edgware-rd; *Omnibus Rtes.*, Edgware-rd and Marylebone-rd; *Cab Rank*, Gt. Quebec-st, Marylebone-rd.

SOUTHWARK: Blackman-st, Borough. Magistrates, W. Slade, Esq., and J. Sheil, Esq. Chief Clerk, H. Nairn, Esq. Hours 10 to 5. Applications for summonses to be made at 10 a.m.; summonses heard at 2 p.m.; remands at 12 noon; and charges from 10 a.m. to 5 p.m. NEAREST *Ry. Stn.*, Borough-rd; *Omnibus Rtes.*, Blackman-st and Boro'; *Cab Rank*, Boro'-rd, Newington-causeway.

THAMES: Arbour-st-east, Stepney. Magistrates, T. W. Saunders, Esq., and F. Lushington, Esq. Chief Clerk, J. R. Sayer, Esq. Hours 10 to 5. Applications for summonses to be made at 10 a.m. and 12 noon; summonses heard at 2 p.m.; remands at 11 a.m.; and charges from 10 a.m. to 5 p.m. NEAREST *Ry. Stns.*, Stepney and Shadwell; *Omnibus Rtes.*, Commercial-rd-east, Burdett-rd, and Mile End-rd; *Cab Rank*, Mile End-rd.

WANDSWORTH: Love-la,Wandsworth. Magistrates, Montagu Williams, Esq., Q.C., J. Paget, Esq., and H. Curtis-Bennett, Esq. Chief Clerk, G. A. Bird, Esq. Hours 10 to 5. Applications for summonses to be made at 2.30 p.m.; summonses heard at 4 p.m. remands at 3 p.m. NEAREST *Ry. Stn.*, Wandsworth; *Omnibus Rte.*, Wandsworth-rd.

WEST HAM: Stratford. Magistrate, Ernest Baggallay, Esq. Chief Clerk, W. H. Fowler, Esq. Hours 10 to 5. NEAREST *Ry. Stn.*, Stratford.

WESTMINSTER: Vincent-sq. Magistrates, L. C. T. D'Eyncourt, Esq., and W. Partridge, Esq. Chief Clerk, A. H. Safford, Esq. Hours 10 to 5. Summonses heard at 2 p.m.; remands at 12 noon; NEAREST *Ry. Stn.*, Victoria; *Omnibus Rtes.*, Rochester-row and Vauxhall-br-rd; *Cab Rank*, Victoria-st.

WOOLWICH: Woolwich. Magistrates, R. H. B. Marsham, Esq., and E. Fenwick - Fenwick, Esq. Chief Clerk, H. P. Newton, Esq. Hours 2.30 to 5.

WORSHIP-ST: Finsbury. Magistrates, H. J. Bushby, Esq., and J. L. Hannay, Esq. Chief Clerk,

E. Leigh, Esq. Hours to to 5. NEAREST *Ry. Stns.*, Broad-st (N.L.) and Liverpool-st (G.E.); *Omnibus Rtes.*, City-rd and Norton Folgate.

Police Force (City), 1888.—

The City Police Force comprises 1 commissioner, 1 chief superintendent, 1 superintendent, 14 inspectors, 92 sergeants, and 781 constables. The following is a list of the divisions, with addresses of stations:—

1. CRIPPLEGATE, Moor-la.
2. SNOW HILL, Snow-hill.
3. BRIDEWELL PLACE, Bridewell-pl.
4. CLOAK LANE, Queen-st.
5. TOWER STREET, Seething-la.
6. BISHOPSGATE, Bishopsgate-st.

Police Force (Metropolitan).—

The following is the Divisional distribution of the Metropolitan Police Force, with names of Superintendents and strength of Divisions:—

C. O. OR COMMISSIONERS' OFFICE.—Charles H. Cutbush, Supt. Executive Branch; Edward Ware, Supt. Public Carriage Branch; John Shore, Supt. Criminal Investigation Dept.; Inspectors 43, sergeants 63, constables 120. Total 229.

A OR WHITEHALL DIVISION. Joseph Henry Dunlap, Supt., also Charles Fraser, King-st, Westminster.—Inspectors, 38; sergeants, 60; constables, 835. Total, 935.

B OR CHELSEA DIVISION. Chas. W. Sheppard, Supt.,Walton-st, Brompton.—Inspectors, 22; sergeants, 52; constables, 560. Total, 635.

C OR ST. JAMES'S DIVISION. William G. Hume, Supt., Little Vine-st,Piccadilly.—Inspectors, 17; sergeants, 37; constables, 386. Total, 441.

D OR MARYLEBONE DIVISION. George Draper, Supt., Marylebone-la.—Inspectors, 23; sergeants, 40; constables, 467. Total, 531.

E OR HOLBORN DIVISION. Rich. W. Steggles, Supt., Bow-st.—Inspectors, 17; sergeants, 50; constables, 447. Total, 515.

F OR PADDINGTON. Philip Giles, Supt., Paddington-gn.—Inspectors, 21; sergeants, 41; constables, 377. Total, 440.

G OR FINSBURY DIVISION. Charles Hunt, Supt., King's ✠-rd, Clerkenwell. — Inspectors,

23; sergeants, 46; constables, 480. Total, 550.

H OR WHITECHAPEL DIVISION.
Thos. Arnold, Supt., Leman-st, Whitechapel. — Inspectors, 30; sergeants, 44; constables, 473. Total, 548.

J OR BETHNAL GREEN DIVISION.
James Keating, Supt., Bethnal Gn-rd. — Inspectors, 38; sergeants, 56; constables, 522. Total, 617.

K OR BOW DIVISION.
George Steed, Supt., Bow-rd.— Inspectors, 48; sergeants, 71; constables, 619. Total, 739.

L OR LAMBETH DIVISION.
James Brannan, Supt., Lower Kennington-la. — Inspectors, 22; sergeants, 35; constables, 346. Total, 404.

M OR SOUTHWARK DIVISION.
Denis Neylan, Supt., Blackman-st, Southwark. — Inspectors, 28; sergeants, 43; constables, 429. Total, 501.

N OR ISLINGTON DIVISION.
William J. Sherlock, Supt., Stoke Newington High-st. — Inspectors, 37; sergeants, 66; constables, 536. Total, 640.

P OR CAMBERWELL DIVISION.
Thomas Butt, Supt., High-st, Peckham—Inspectors, 44; sergeants, 68; constables, 599. Total, 712.

R OR GREENWICH DIVISION.
Christopher McHugo, Supt., Blackheath - rd, Greenwich.— Inspectors, 38; sergeants, 71; constables, 476. Total, 586.

S OR HAMPSTEAD DIVISION.
William Harris, Supt., Albany-st, Regent's-pk. — Inspectors, 42; sergeants, 80; constables, 613. Total, 736.

T OR HAMMERSMITH DIVISION.
Wm. Fisher, Supt., Broadway, Hammersmith.—Inspectors, 52; sergeants, 75; constables, 623. Total, 751.

V OR WANDSWORTH DIVISION.
David Saines, Supt., West-hill, Wandsworth. — Inspectors, 36; sergeants, 59; constables, 561. Total, 657.

W OR CLAPHAM DIVISION.
Stephen Lucas, Supt., Brixton-rd. —Inspectors, 39; sergeants, 72; constables, 571. Total, 683.

X OR KILBURN DIVISION.
Frederick Beard, Supt., Carltonter, Harrow-rd.—Inspectors, 40; sergeants, 53; constables, 469. Total, 563.

Y OR HIGHGATE D.VISION.
William J. Huntley, Supt., Kentish Town - road. — Inspectors, 46;

sergeants, 73; constables, 607. Total, 727.

THAMES DIVISION.
George Skeats, Supt., Wapping, near the river.—Inspectors, 49; sergeants, 4; constables, 147. Total, 201.

WOOLWICH DOCKYARD DIVISION.
Thomas E. Hindes, Supt., Woolwich Arsenal.—Inspectors, 8; sergeants, 25; constables, 140. Total, 174.

PORTSMOUTH DOCKYARD DIV.
Wm. Ventham, Supt., Portsmouth. —Inspectors, 8; sergeants, 29; constables, 171. Total, 209.

DEVONPORTDOCKYARD DIVISION.
William Wakeford, Supt., Devonport.—Inspectors, 7; sergeants, 19; constables, 128. Total, 155.

CHATHAM DOCKYARD DIVISION.
Geo. Godfrey, Supt., Chatham.— Inspectors, 6; sergeants, 24; constables, 157. Total, 188.

PEMBROKE DOCKYARD DIVISION.
No Superintendent.—Inspectors, 2; sergeants, 4; constables, 28. Total, 34.

Total strength of all ranks, including superintendents, 14,106.

Police Office (City), 26, Old Jewry, E.C.—Commissioner, Col. Sir James Fraser, K.C.B.; Chief Supt., Major Henry Smith; Receiver, J. W. Carlyon-Hughes, Esq. Chief Clerk, John Whatley, Esq. NEAREST *Ry.Stns.*, Broad-st, Cannon-st, Mansion House, and Moorgate; *Omnibus Rtes.*, Cheapside, King William-st, and Moorgate-st; *Cab Rank*, Lothbury.

Police Office (Metropolitan), 4, Whitehall-place, S.W.— Commissioner, Colonel Sir Charles Warren, G.C.M.G.; Assist. Commissioners, Lieut.-Col. R. L. O. Pearson, A. C. Bruce, Esq., and J. Monro, Esq.; Legal Adviser, J. E. Davis, Esq.; Chief Constables, A. C. Howard, Esq., Lt.-Col. Roberts, Lt.-Col. B. Monsell, Major W. E. Gilbert, and A. F. Williamson, Esq. (Criminal Investigation Department); Chief Clerk, W. F. M. Staples, Esq.; Receiver for the Metropolitan Police District and Courts of Metropolis, Alfred Richard Pennefather, Esq.; Chief Clerk, E. Mills, Esq.; Surgeon-in-Chief, A. O. Mackallar, Esq.; Acting Surveyor, J. Butler, Esq.; Engineer under Smoke Nuisance Abatement Acts, W. R. E. Coles, Esq.; Storekeeper, Mr. J. Mole; Criminal Investigation Department, Superintendent, John Shore; Executive Branch and Common Lodging Houses Branch

Chief Inspector Cutbush; Public Carriage Branch, Chief Inspector Ware; Lost Property Office, Chief Inspector Beavis.

Police Orphanage (Metropolitan and City), Twickenham.—President, Col. Sir Charles Warren, G.C.M.G.; Vice-Presidents, Lieut.-Col. Pearson, A. C. Bruce, Esq., J. Monro, Esq., and Col. Sir James Fraser, K.C.B. (City Police); Chairman of Board of Managers & Treasurer, Lt.-Col. Monsell; Sec., Arthur J. Kestin.

Portland Club, 1, Stratford-pl, W., is at present limited to 250 members, paying an entrance fee of £10 10s., and an annual subscription of £7 7s. Election by ballot. Twenty members, at least, must vote. If to every ten votes "For" the admission of the candidate, there be one "Against" it, he is not elected. No game of hazard shall be played, nor shall dice be used in the club.

Portugal. — MINISTRY, 12, Gloucester-pl, Portman-sq. NEAREST *Ry. Stn.*, Baker-st (Met.); *Omnibus Rtes.*, Baker-st, Marylebone-rd, and Oxford-st ; *Cab Rank*, Baker-st, Portman-sq. CONSULATE, 3, Throgmorton-av, E.C. NEAREST *Ry. Stns.*, Broad-st and Moorgate-st ; *Omnibus Rtes.*, Moorgate-st and Cornhill ; *Cab Rank*, Bartholomew-la.

Postage and Inland Revenue Stamps.—Stamped envelopes, stamped newspaper wrappers, and inland and foreign post cards, are sold at the chief office between the hours of 6.45 a.m. and 10 p.m. ; at Lombard-st between 7 a.m. and 7.45 p.m. ; at the W. district office between 7 a.m. and 11 p.m. ; at the other district offices and Charing ✠, Gracechurch-st, Eastcheap, Mark-la, Throgmorton-av, Leadenhall-st, Queen Victoria-st, and Ludgate-circus, the branch offices, and receiving houses, between 8 a.m. and 8 p.m., and at Fleet-st, between 8 a.m. and 3 a.m. except Saturday, when the office closes at midnight. Postage stamps can, however, be purchased at any office during the hours in which attendance is given for telegraph business, and inland revenue stamps at all London post offices between the hours of 8 a.m. and 8 p.m. At every money order office the postmaster is required to keep a sufficient stock of these stamps

Postal Regulations—

Relating specially to the London District. Any postal information which it has not been possible to include in this book will readily be found in the Post Office Guide, published by Messrs. Eyre & Spottiswoode, Great New-st, Fetter-la, price 6d., by post 8½d.

Postal Districts. — London and its environs are divided into eight postal districts. The following are the names of the districts, with their abbreviations, viz :

Eastern Central	E.C.
Eastern	E.
Northern	N.
North-Western	N.W.
South-Eastern	S.E
South-Western	S.W.
Western	W.
Western Central	W.C.

By the addition of the initials of the postal district to the address of a letter for London or its neighbourhood, increased security is afforded against misdelivery or delay, and the work of the Post Office is facilitated.

Town Deliveries.—The portion of each district within about 3 miles of the General Post Office is designated the town delivery, and the remainder the suburban delivery. Within the limits of the E.C. District there are daily twelve deliveries, and within the town limits of the other districts eleven deliveries; the first, or general post delivery, including all inland, colonial, and foreign letters arriving in sufficient time, commences about 7.20 a.m., and, except on Mon., or on other days when there are large arrivals of letters from abroad, is generally completed, throughout London, by 9 o'clock. In the E.C. district the second delivery begins at about 8.30 a.m., and includes the correspondence received by night mail from Ireland and by the north mails arriving at 8 a.m.; and the third delivery in this district, corresponding with the second delivery in other districts, is made at about 10 a.m., and includes the letters collected in London generally at 8.45 a.m., and the correspondence by the Scotch mail arriving about 9 a.m. The next nine deliveries are made in every district hourly, and include all letters reaching the General Post Office, or the district offices, in time for each despatch. The last delivery, extending to all the districts, begins at about 7.45

p.m. Each delivery within the town limits occupies about an hour. The provincial day mails are due at various times, and letters are included in the next delivery after their arrival in London. The day mails from Ireland, France, and the Continent generally, and the letters received from Brighton and other towns which have a late afternoon communication with London, are delivered the same evening in London and in the suburbs within the six-mile circle.

Suburban Deliveries.—There are six despatches daily to most suburban districts. The first (at 6.30 a.m.) is to all places within the London district; and includes the correspondence by the night mails from the provinces, and by any colonial or foreign mails arriving in sufficient time. The delivery is generally completed in the nearer suburbs by 9 a.m., and at the more distant between 9 and 10 a.m. The second despatch (at 9.30 a.m.) is to the nearer suburban districts only. The third despatch (at 11.30 a.m.) comprises, with a few exceptions, every part of the London district. Except to isolated places, the fourth despatch (at 2.30 p.m.) is to most of the suburban districts. The fifth despatch (at 4.30 p.m.) extends to the whole of the suburban districts; and, except in the remoter rural places, the letters are delivered the same evening. The sixth despatch is at 7 p.m. Letters for this despatch posted at the town receiving houses and pillar boxes by 6 p.m., or at the chief office of the district to which they are addressed by 7.30 p.m., are delivered the same evening, except at a few distant places, where the delivery is made early the following morning. The deliveries in the suburban districts begin from one to two hours after the stated time of despatch, according to the distance from London; the deliveries in rural parts of the remoter suburban districts being necessarily fewer than in the towns and villages.

Collections from the Town and Suburban Branch Offices and Receiving Houses, &c.— The latest times for posting letters at the chief and district offices and at the branch offices and receiving houses and pillar letter boxes for the London and suburban despatches and for the inland, colonial, and foreign mails,

are fully stated in the table of Late Letter Posting (*which see*). Letters brought to the branch offices and receiving houses and pillar boxes after the fixed time of posting has expired cannot be forwarded till the next despatch. Letter-carriers are not permitted to take charge of letters to be posted on their route. As a general rule the number of despatches from any place is the same as the number of deliveries there. At the district offices, and at the town receiving houses, separate boxes are provided for "London District" and "General Post" letters. The inscription on the "London District" box is in red letters, and that on the "General Post" box in black letters. In the town districts generally, and in certain suburbs where there is a collection from the pillar boxes at 3 a.m., the receiving office letter boxes are closed during the night and on Sundays, in order that letters may not be posted there, but in the pillar boxes, and so have the advantage of such early collection.

Night Mails from London. —These mails leave the General Post Office at 8 p.m., and arrive at almost all important towns in England and Wales in time for a morning delivery, beginning before 9 o'clock. The arrival at Edinburgh, Glasgow, and Dublin is also in time for a similar delivery.

Delivery.—All Letter Carriers are prohibited from distributing any letters, newspapers, &c., except such as have passed through a Post Office. Nor are they allowed to receive any payment beyond the postage for the delivery or collection of any letter, &c.; nor to deviate from the route laid down for them. The prohibition from receiving payment in addition to the postage does not, however, extend to Christmas-boxes. No person living within a Town free delivery, or within the limits of a Rural Post free delivery, unless he rent a private box, can claim to have his letters delivered at the office window if a delivery by letter carrier or a despatch by messenger is about to take place; but letters which arrive by a mail, and after which there is no immediate delivery by letter carrier, may be obtained by any person on application at the office window, so long as the office is open for delivery.

LATE LETTER POSTING.—The following table shows the latest times for posting Ordinary Letters, &c., without or with Late Fees, for the Night Mails (Inland and Foreign) at the principal Post Offices, &c. in London. Letters for the Provinces posted in the Metropolitan District up to midnight, and in the Suburbs at or before midnight, are now included in the despatches by early (newspaper) trains in advance of the ordinary morning mails.

OFFICES.	LETTERS AND POST CARDS.						NEWSPAPERS AND BOOK PACKETS.			
	Inland and Foreign Mails.	Inland Mails only.	Mails for Foreign Countries generally.			Mails for Continent of Europe only.	Inland Mails.	Foreign Mails.	Inland and Foreign Mails	
	Without Fee	With ½d Fee	With 1d. Fee	With 2d. Fee	With 3d. Fee	With 6d. Fee	Without Fee	Without Fee	With ½d. Fee	With ½d. Fee
	h. m.	h. m.	h. m.	h. m.	h. m.	h. m.　h. m.	h. m.	h. m.	h. m.	h. m.
GENERAL POST OFFICE (St. Martin's-le-Grand).	6 0	7 45	7 0	7 15	7 30	—	5 30	6 0	6 45	7 15
EASTCHEAP (Branch).										
FLEET-ST (Branch).										
GRACECHURCH-ST (Branch)										
LOMBARD-ST (Branch).										
LEADENHALL-ST (Branch).										
LUDGATE-CIR (Branch).	6 0	7 0	7 0	—	—	—	5 30	5 30	—	—
MARK-LANE (Branch).										
QUEEN VICTORIA-ST (Branch).										
THROGMORTON-AVENUE.										
CHARING CROSS (Branch).										
*W.C. DISTRICT OFFICE (Holborn).										
N. DISTRICT OFFICE (Islington).										
E. DISTRICT OFFICE (Commercial-rd-east).										
S.E. DISTRICT OFFICE (Blackman-st, Borough).	6 0	7 30	7 0	—	—	—	5 30	5 30	—	—
*S.W. DISTRICT OFFICE (Buckingham-gate).										
*W DISTRICT OFFICE (Vere-st).										
*N.W. DISTRICT OFFICE (Eversholt-st).										
CANNON-ST RAILWAY STATION.	Special Letter Boxes for Continental Mails only.					7 30 to 8 0				
CHARING CROSS RAILWAY STATION.						7 0 to 8 0				

* NOTE.—Letters for places served by the undermentioned Railways (by direct despatch from the District Offices) can be posted as under :—

At S.W. District Office for South Western Railway .... } if bearing ½d. extra Stamp, till { 8 0 p.m.

W. do. { Great Western Railway .... }   { 8 0 p.m.

    { Midland and North Western Railways...........   7 45 p.m.

N.W. do. Midland and London and North Western Railways   8 0 p.m.

    { Great Eastern Railway...........................   7.45 p.m.

W.C. do. { Great Western, North Western, Great Eastern, and Midland Railways .... } Letters, Book Packets, &c., if handed in at the counter prepaid and bearing ½d. extra in Stamps, till 7.45 p.m.

LATEST TIME FOR REGISTER-
ING LETTERS. — For the night
mails the latest time for registering both inland and foreign and
colonial letters at St. Martin's-le-
Grand, and at the head district
offices and at Lombard-st, Gracechurch-st, Mark-la, Eastcheap,
Fleet-st, Ludgate-cir, Leadenhall-
st, Queen Victoria-st, Throgmor-
ton-avenue, Charing ✠, and Paddington, on payment of the fee of
2d., is 5.30 p.m. ; or, on payment
of a late fee of 2d. in addition to
the registration fee, the latest time
is 6 p.m., and at the chief office
only, between 6 and 6.30 p.m. on
payment of a late fee of 4d., between 6.30 and 7 p.m. on payment
of a late fee of 6d., and between
7 and 7.30 p.m. on payment of a
late fee of 1s. in addition to the
ordinary fee and postage. At the
town branch offices and town receiving houses the latest time for
registering letters for the night
mails is 5 p.m. For the day
mails to the provinces, Ireland,
Scotland, France, and the Continent generally, and for the
colonial and foreign mails, *via*
Southampton, letters can be registered, on payment of the ordinary fee, at the chief office till
10 p.m., and at all head district
post-offices up to 8 p.m. At all
other branch and receiving offices,
letters can be registered so long as
the offices are open to the public
for postal business. But to ensure
a due despatch by the above-named
mails, such letters should be tendered not later than 7.45 p.m.
For the first London District Delivery letters can be registered, on
payment of the ordinary fee, at
the chief office till 10 p.m., and at
the head district offices till 8 p.m. ;
at the branch offices in Lombard-
st, Gracechurch-st, Mark-la, Eastcheap, Fleet-st, Ludgate - cir,
etc. (as above), and at all other
branch offices and receiving
offices, till 7.45 p.m. ; and for
the other London district deliveries half an hour before the
latest time for posting ordinary
letters. An exception to this is
that letters for delivery the same
night in the London District can
be registered at all head district
offices up to 6.30 p.m. No letter
can be registered at the chief office
or the Lombard-st post-office before
7 a.m., or the western district office
before 7.30 a.m., or at any of the
other offices in London before 8
a.m. At the suburban offices the

latest time for registering is half
an hour before the fixed time for
clearing the box for each despatch, except that no letter can
be registered before 8 a.m. or
after 8 p.m.

BUSINESS RELATING TO MONEY
ORDERS, SAVINGS BANKS, &c., is
transacted at the chief district
offices and at the post-offices in
Lombard-st and Charing ✠ between 10 a.m. and 4 p.m. except
on Sat.,when such business ceases
at 1 p.m., except at Lombard-st,
where the time is 2 p.m. At Gracechurch-st, Mark - la, Eastcheap,
Fleet-st, Ludgate-cir, Leadenhall-
st, Queen Victoria-st, and Throgmorton-av post-offices, the branch
offices, and receiving houses in the
town districts, the time is between
10 a.m. and 4 p.m. ; at branch
offices in the W. and S.W. suburban districts between 10 a.m. and
5 p.m., and in other suburban
districts, between 9.30 a.m. and 5
p.m. ; and at receiving houses in
the suburban districts between 9
a.m. and 6 p.m. Although, however, general savings-bank business
ceases at the hours named, yet
savings-bank *Deposits* are received at district and branch
offices until 8 p.m. on Sat., and
at receiving houses, as a rule,
both on Fri. and Sat. until 7 p.m.
—(*For further information see*
POSTAGE STAMPS, PRIVATE LET-
TER BOXES, TELEGRAPH OFFICES,
PRIVATE WIRES.

SATURDAYS.—Letters for the
country posted in London or the
London districts on Sat. too late
for the ordinary evening mails, but
in time for the last evening collections, are delivered next morning,
if for places within the range of
the midnight despatches ; if for
places beyond that range, they are
delivered on Mon.

ON SUNDAYS all post-offices in
the London district are closed, with
the exception of those which are
open for the receipt and despatch
of telegrams during the hours
stated in Table of Telegraph
Offices (*which see*). Letters posted
in the pillar boxes within the
town limits, and in some of the
nearer suburbs, on Sun., are collected early on Mon. morning in
time for the general day mails
and for the first London district
delivery.

ON BANK HOLIDAYS the postal
and telegraph arrangements in
London are of an exceptional character, and due notice is given of

them by means of notices to the
public exhibited at metropolitan
post-offices.

ENQUIRIES for MISSING LET-
TERS, &c., should be made at the
Secretary's Office, New Building,
between 10 a.m. and 4 p.m. (Sat.
between 10 and 1).

THE RETURNEDLETTEROFFICE
is in Telegraph-st, Moorgate-st.

THE MONEY ORDER OFFICE is
at St. Martin's-le-Grand.

THE POST OFFICE SAVINGS
BANK is 144A, Queen Victoria-st.

Poste Restante.—LETTERS
"TO BE CALLED FOR."—There is
a Poste Restante both at the
General Post Office, St. Martin's-
le-Grand, and at the Charing ✠
post-office, where letters or parcels
"to be called for" can be obtained
between the hours of 8 a.m. and
8 p.m. at the G.P.O., and between
8 a.m. and 5 p.m. at Charing ✠.
No letters, &c. (except communications from the Savings
Bank Department), are taken in
"to be called for" at the other
district or branch offices, and
any so directed are sent to the
Returned Letter Office to be returned to the writers. The Poste
Restante being intended solely
for the accommodation of strangers
and travellers who have no permanent abode in London, letters
for residents must not be addressed to the post-office "to be
called for ;" and any letters for a
resident so addressed, although
delivered at the post-office for
one week, are, after that time,
sent out by the letter-carriers.
Even strangers are not, as a rule,
allowed to use the Poste Restante
for more than two months at the
end of which time they are expected to have their letters sent
to a private address. Letters, &c.,
addressed to initials or to fictitious names at the Poste Restante are not taken in, but are at
once sent back to the writers.
Letters,&c., may not be re-directed
from a private address to the Poste
Restante. Letters, &c., intended
to be called for at the General
Post Office should have the words
"to be called for" added to the
address, otherwise such letters
are sent round, in the first instance, to the several departments
of the General Post Office, to
ascertain whether they are intended for any of the officers, and
therefore may not be at hand
when applied for. All persons ap-

plying for letters, &c., at the Poste Restante must be prepared to give the necessary particulars to the clerk on duty, to prevent mistakes and to ensure the delivery of the letters to the persons to whom they properly belong. If the letters be for a subject of the United Kingdom he must be able to state from what place or district he expects them, and must produce some proof of identification; and if he sends for his letters, the messenger, besides being furnished with this information, must have a written authority to receive them. If the applicant be a foreigner he must produce his passport; or if he send for his letters the messenger must produce it. Subjects, however, of States not issuing passports, are treated as subjects of the United Kingdom. Letters from abroad addressed to the Poste Restante, London, are retained for two months. Letters from provincial towns similarly addressed are retained one month, and letters posted in London one fortnight; all such letters, at the end of these periods, being sent to the Returned Letter Office for disposal in the usual manner. None of the letter receivers in the London district are required to take charge of letters to be called for; and all newly-appointed letter receivers are forbidden to do so. Those who have been for some time in the service are for the present permitted to take in such letters (charging a fee for the accommodation), provided that the letters are addressed " Post Office," and that the persons seeking such accommodation are known to them or have previously made a like application, and that the receiver is satisfied that proper use will be made of the privilege. When, however, letters for strangers are presented without the receiver's consent having been first obtained, or, when there is reason to suspect that the receiving house is being made to serve improper ends, the receiver is instructed to refuse to take them in. Letters may not be re-directed from the Poste Restante to a receiving house, or from one receiving house to another in the London district. This regulation does not apply to communications from the Savings Bank Department addressed to receiving houses to

be called for, letter receivers being required to take in such communications, but without requiring any payment from the depositors.

Post Office, St. Martin's-le-Grand, E.C.—(*See* GENERAL POST OFFICE.)

Post Office Savings Bank Department, 144, Queen Victoria-st, E.C. — (*See* GENERAL POST OFFICE.)

Poultry and Fancy Fowls.—At Stevens's Auction Rooms, King-st, Covent-gdn, there is on nearly every Tu. a sale of poultry and pigeons, where good specimens may often be obtained cheaply. Amongst the London dealers, Baily, of Mount-st, is most reliable. Birds may be obtained of many dealers in Leadenhall Market. At the Poultry Show, held annually in November at the Crystal Palace, there are always large sale classes containing good birds, both fowls and pigeons, at moderate prices. The live pigeons sold in London may be arranged under two or three distinct heads. A very large trade is done in blue rocks and other dovecote birds for the supply of the pigeon shooting matches at the Gun Club, Hurlingham, &c. Fancy pigeons may be obtained, though rarely of high quality, of the dealers in Seven Dials and Club-row, Spitalfields. Homing birds can hardly be obtained of good quality except by application to a known amateur—the birds advertised being generally common farmyard pigeons imported from Belgium for the gun clubs.

Pratt's Club, 14, Park-pl, St. James's.—Election by ballot in committee, which consists of 20 members, five forming a quorum. One black ball in the quorum of five excludes, two in the whole committee. One of the rules provides " That no member bring a stranger into the Club under any pretence whatever." Entrance, £2 2s.; subscription, £5 5s.

Presbyterian Church of England (The) is diffused over all the country, but has its main strength in London, Lancashire, and the northern counties of Northumberland, Cumberland, and Durham. Of the 10 Presbyteries into which it is divided, the largest is the Presbytery of London, which has on its roll 88 congre-

gations and preaching stations' with about 18,279 communicants. During the year 1887, these congregations raised the sum of £91,659 3s. 6d. for religious and charitable uses. There are throughout England 288 congregations, with a membership of 61,781, which contributed in 1887, for all purposes, £219,585 3s.7d. The English Presbyterians, like the Scotch, always call their places of worship churches, not chapels. The Theological College for the training of ministers is at Queen Square House, Guilford-st, W.C. The Secretary is the Rev. John Black, 7, East India-avenue, E.C. "The Presbyterian Church acknowledges the Word of God contained in the Scriptures as the only rule of faith and duty. The interpretation which it attaches to the Word of God, or the theology it draws from Holy Writ, is just that Trinitarian and Evangelical theology which was common to all the Reformed Churches of the 16th century, and was expressed with remarkable unanimity in their Confessions, including among them the Doctrinal Articles of the Church of England. These Confessions, it need hardly be added, pre-suppose and affirm the doctrine of the earlier creeds known as the Apostles' and the Nicene. The document by which the teaching from Presbyterian pulpits in this country is liable to be tested is the Confession of Faith framed by the Assembly of Divines, at Westminster, in the 17th century. This Confession forms at the present day the doctrinal standard (in subordination to Holy Scripture) of all Presbyterian Churches that use the English language in the British Islands, in the Colonies and Dependencies of the Empire, and in the United States of America. The tenor of doctrine in the Confession is popularly known through the ' Shorter Catechism ' composed by the same Assembly of Divines." A board of elders, presided over by the minister, takes charge of each congregation, and this is called the session or congregational presbytery. A group of congregations is placed under a district presbytery, in which sit the ministers with an equal number of elders who are chosen at stated times by the sessions as their representatives. The district presbytery hears and settles complaints and appeals, examines and approves new preachers, ordains ministers and missionaries, &c. ; and to one of these presbyteries every preacher or minister is answerable for his doctrine and life. "Above the presbyteries is the synod, which has the supreme power of direction and legislation in the Church, and to which all the missionary work and the arrangements for the education and support of the ministry are reported and submitted. In the synod, as in the presbyteries, ministers and elders sit in equal numbers, with equal rights of speech and vote, and no clerical or lay parties exist."

The following is a list of the principal English Presbyterian churches in London :—

Belgrave: Halkin-st - west, Belgrave-sq, S.W.
Bermondsey: Southwark-pk-rd, Bermondsey, S.E.
Blackheath: Charlton-rd, S.E.
Bow: Bow-rd, corner of Mornington-rd, Bow, E.
Brockley: Brockley, S.E.
Camberwell: Brunswick-sq, S.E.
Camden-rd: Camden - pk - rd, Camden-rd, N.W.
Canonbury: Trinity,Church-rd,N.
Clapham-rd: Trinity, S.W.
Clapton: Downs-pk-rd, Hackney Downs, E.
Crouch Hill: Holly-pk, N.
Croydon: St. George's, Oakfield-rd, Croydon.
Ealing: St. Andrew's, Broadway, Ealing, W.
East India-rd: Plimsoll-st, E.
Forest Hill: St. John's, Devonshire-rd, Forest-hill, S.E.
Greenwich: St. Mark's, South-st, Greenwich, S.E.
Hammersmith: St. Andrew's, Goldhawk-rd, Hammersmith, W.
Hampstead: Trinity, Hampstead.
Highbury: Park Church, Grosvenor-rd, Highbury New-pk, N.
Islington: Colebrooke-row, N.
Kensington: Allen-st, Kensington, W.
Kentish Tn.: Trinity, Kentish Tn.-rd, N.W.
Kingston-on-Thames: Fife - rd, Kingston-on-Thames
Marylebone: Upper George-st, Bryanston-sq, W.
Millwall: St. Paul's, West Ferry-rd, Millwall, E.
New Barnet: Augustine, Somerset-rd
Notting-hill: Trinity, Kensington-pk-rd, Notting-hill, W.
Oxendon: Haverstock-hill, N,W,

Putney, Granard: Putney-pk-la, S.W.
Regent-sq: Regent-sq, W.C.
Richmond: Hill-st, S.W.
St. John's Wood: Marlborough-pl, St. John's Wood, N.W.
Silvertown: Newlands - st, Tate-rd, Silvertown, E.
Somers Tn.: Ossulton-st, Somers Town, N.W.
South Kensington: Cornwall-gdns, Emperor's-gate, S.W.
Southwark: St.George's,Borough-rd, Southwark, S.E.
Stepney: John Knox, Oxford-st, Stepney, E.
Stoke Newington: Assembly Rooms, Defoe-rd, Church-st, N.
Stratford: Trinity, Maryland-point, Stratford, E.
Streatham: Trinity, Angles-rd, Streatham, S.W.
Tooting: Defoe Church, High-st, Tooting, S.W.
Tottenham: St. John's, High-rd, Tottenham, N.
Upper Norwood: Upper Norwood, S.E.
Victoria Docks: Hack-rd, Victoria Docks, E.
Wandsworth: Merton-rd, Wandsworth, S.W.
Westbourne-gr: St. Paul's, Westbourne-gr-ter,Westbourne-gr,W.
Whitfield: Whitfield, Wilson-st, Drury-la, W.C.
Willesden: Harrow - rd, near Junction, N.W.
Wimbledon: Drill-hall,Wimbledon
Wood Gn.: St. James's, Southgate-rd, Wood Gn., N.
Woolwich: New-rd, Woolwich, S.E., and St. Andrew's, Angle-sea-hill, Woolwich, S.E.

Press Club, 107, Fleet-st, E.C.—For London and country journalists. Entrance, £1; subscription, £3 3s. for town, and £1 1s. for country members.

Primitive Methodist Connexion.

1. HISTORY. — In December, 1822, Leeds Circuit sent two missionaries (Messrs. P. Sugden and W. Watson)to London. "So small was the amount of money with which they were furnished, that on arriving in the metropolis they had only one shilling in their pockets. The coachman bowed, and solicited a gratuity. They gave him their only shilling. Next came the guard and begged for a similar favour. They frankly told him who they were, and what were the circumstances in which they were placed. He happened to be a professor of

religion, a member of the Baptist denomination. He sympathised with them in their difficulties, and with true Christian catholicity took them to his house, gave them breakfast, and purchased some books of them in order to relieve them."

For many years the poverty of the missionaries and the churches organised by them prevented their erecting, purchasing, or renting suitable places of worship, and the growth of the denomination was slow. In 1844 the membership was only 434. In 1864 the membership had risen to 2,914, and in 1879 to 4,621. In 1864 there were but 4 circuits, 1 branch and 2 missions in London : in 1879 11 circuits and 4 missions. The London Second Circuit then numbered 700 on its roll of membership ; now the Second and the Ninth Circuits, which have been divided since 1864, number 1,256. London Third Circuit then numbered 817 members ; but now there are in London Third, Fifth, and Eighth, which then formed part of the circuit, 1,327. Croydon Mission then numbered 80 members : it is now London Sixth, with 183 members. Hammersmith Mission had then 149 members ; it now numbers 372 : and London Twelfth Circuit, with 133 members, has been made from it. Tottenham, which then was a branch of London First Circuit, has become London Tenth Circuit, and reports 201 members. Trinity Street, Southwark, Walthamstow, North Bow, and Surrey Chapel are Missions of recent date ; they have an aggregate membership of 303 members.

2. CHAPELS.—The following is a list of the principal chapels in the London Circuits and Missions :—
        London First Circuit.
Memorial Church, the Oval, Hackney-rd, E.
Hackney: London Fields, E.
Kingsland : Castle-st, E.
        London Second Circuit.
Islington: South-st, New North-rd, E.
King's-✝ : Winchester-st, Pentonville, N.
Caledonian-rd : op. St. James's-rd.
Holloway: Durham-rd, Seven Sisters'-rd, N.
Dartmouth Park, N.W.
        London Third Circuit.
Stepney Green Tabernacle, Stepney-gn, Mile End-rd, E.
        Bromley and Stratford Br.
Bromley: Powis-rd, Bruce-rd.
Stratford : New-tn, Henniker-rd,

London Fourth Circuit.
Walworth: 113, East-st, S.E.
Lennington: Thomas-st, Kennington-pk, S.E.
Peckham: Sumner-rd, S.E.
Rotherhithe: Union-rd, S.E.
Forest-hill: Stanstead-rd, S.E.

London Fifth Circuit.
Plumstead: Robert-st, Glyndon-st.
Woolwich: Union Chapel, Sun-st.
Erith: High-st.
Belvedere: Picardy-hill.

London Sixth Circuit.
Croydon: Laud-st.
Sutton: Lind-rd.

London Seventh Circuit.
Hammersmith: Dalling-rd, W.
Battersea: Knox-rd, Plough-la.
,, New-rd, Wandsworth-rd.
Wandsworth: High-st.

London Eighth Circuit.
Poplar: Chrisp-st, East India-rd.
Canning Tn.: Mary-st, Barking-rd.
Cubitt Tn.: Manchester-rd, E.
Millwall: Maria-st, West Ferry-rd.
Forth Woolwich: Story-st and Elizabeth-st, E.
Plaistow: West Ham-pk, Stratford-rd, E.
Sutton-st: Commercial-rd, E.

London Ninth Circuit.
Camden Tn.: Little King-st, N.W.
Kentish Tn.: Grafton-rd, N.W.
Marylebone: Seymour-pl, Bryanstone-sq, W.
Harrow-rd: near Royal Oak Stn.
Hampstead: Little Church-row.
Notting Hill: Fowell-st, Lancaster rd, W.

London Tenth Circuit.
Tottenham: Northumberland-pk.

London Twelfth Circuit.
Crayshott - rd, Shaftesbury - pk, Lavender-hill, S.W.

Missions.
Surrey Chapel: Blackfriars-rd, S.E.
St. James's Hall, Southwark-pk-rd
Trinity-st Church, Southwark, S.E.
Walthamstow: Higham-hill, Gloucester-rd.
North Bow: Driffield-rd, Roman-rd, E.

In addition to these there are about 50 smaller chapels or rooms. The increased value of Connexional property during the last fifteen years is above £65,000, and sitting accommodation has been provided during that time for 44,123 adults. The present value of property held by the Connexion is about £85,000, and there is sitting accommodation for about 80,000 adults.

3. HEAD QUARTERS.—The headquarters were at Sutton-st, Commercial-rd, E., for many years, but

when the Rev. Newman Hall and his congregation removed to Christ Church, he and his deacons arranged that the connexion should have Surrey Chapel upon advantageous terms during the remainder of the lease, and the General Committee, the Missionary Committee, and several other committees, now meet weekly in the library of Surrey Chapel for the transaction of business. The book-room is still at Sutton-st, where a large business is carried on ; the gross receipts last year were above £25,000, and the net profits over £3,500. 108,000 periodicals of five different kinds were issued monthly. There is also a Quarterly Review issued, which commands a large sale. 46,026 congregational hymn-books, 33,536 Sunday-school hymn-books, and 2,300 revival hymn-books were sold during the year.

Primrose Club, 4, Park-pl, St. James's-st, S.W.—Established in 1887, as a social club, in connection with the Conservative party. Annual subscription: Town members, £5 5s.; country members, residing not less than 20 miles from London, £3 3s. Members incur no other liability.

Primrose Hill (Map 2) is a high mound at the north side of Regent's-pk, whence a good view may be obtained. It is the centre of a great population, and is very popular with holiday makers who are unable to get out of town, although, with the exception of a rather small open-air gymnasium, there is nothing to contribute to the public amusement. NEAREST *Ry. Stns.*, Chalk Farm (N.L.) and St. John's Woodrd (Met.) ; *Omnibus Rte.*, Albert-rd ; *Cab Rank,* Zoological-gdns (near new north entrance).

Prince of Wales's Theatre, Coventry-st (Map 7), opened, for the first time, 18th January, 1884, with " The Palace of Truth." This handsome and commodious structure was built for Mr. Edgar Bruce, from the designs and under the direction of Mr. C. J. Phipps, F.S.A. The building is lighted throughout by electricity, gas being retained in case of need. There is a spacious pit, eight rows of stalls, balcony, first circle, and gallery, with eight private boxes on each side the proscenium. The theatre succeeded, almost from the first, in becoming popular.

NEAREST *Ry. Stns.*, Charing ✠ (S.E. and Dis.); *Omnibus Rtes.*, Haymarket and Piccadilly ; *Cab Rank,* Coventry-st.

Princess's Theatre, Oxford-st (Map 6).— The large theatre, memorable for the Shakespearean revivals of the late Mr Charles Kean, was demolished in 1880, and rebuilt from the designs of Mr. C. J. Phipps. The new theatre was opened on the 6th November, 1880, on which occasion Mr. Edwin Booth appeared as Hamlet, the American actor subsequently playing a round of legitimate parts during the following four or five months. After Mr. Booth's departure the theatre was taken by Mr. Wilson Barrett, under whose management it was for several years most successful. The specialty of the theatre lies in melodrama of strong incidents and effects. The new Princess's, although a handsome theatre, did not meet with unqualified public approval, the extreme height of the auditorium, and the consequent steepness of the various circles, being considerably objected to. NEAREST *Ry. Stns.*, Portland-rd (Met.) and Charing ✠ (S.E.); *Omnibus Rte.*, Oxford-st ; *Cab Rank,* Oxford-market.

Prisons.—*(For particulars of the several prisons, see under their respective heads.)* — The prisons and sessions houses of London are known by the following cant names : Central Criminal Court as " The Start "; the Old Bailey as " The Gate "; Sessions House, Clerkenwell, as " X's Hall " ; Surrey Sessions House as " The Slaughter House." The convict and other prisons are commonly called " Jugs."

Private Letter Boxes.— Private letter boxes may be rented at the General Post Office, at the Lombard-st, Gracechurch-st, and Mark-lane branch offices, and at any district office. The charge for a private box is £3 a year, payable in advance ; and no box can be rented for less than a year. Private box holders can obtain their letters between 7.30 a.m. and 7.45 p.m. At sub-district offices, private bags are made up for a payment in advance of £2 per annum.

Private Theatricals.— There is no difficulty in making comfortable and convenient arrangements for private theatricals in London. Messrs. Harrison Bros. of Bow-st ; Mr. May, of Bow-st ; and Messrs. Nathan, of Tichborne-st, may safely be consulted as to matters connected with "fit up" theatres and costumes, and a perfect theatre may be arranged, with little trouble and no damage, in any good-sized room, by either of these firms. For wigs and "make up" the amateur may depend upon Mr. Clarkson, of Wellington-st; Mr. Fox, Russell-st, Covent-gdn ; and Mr. Rickards, Bow-st, Covent-gdn. Mr. French, of the Strand, sells all sorts of plays and books connected with theatricals. Should the contemplated performance be intended to be on an ambitious scale, professional supervision is desirable and the stage managers of many of the theatres are specialists in this department. If the assistance of professional ladies be desired, the advertising columns of the *Era* (published weekly at Wellington-st, Strand) should be consulted, and the answers to correspondents in the same excellent journal will always furnish the enquirer with every kind of information in regard to theatrical matters.

Private Wires.—The Post Office Telegraph Department undertakes to construct and afterwards maintain, upon the payment of an annual rental, a line of private wire between the place of business or residence of a firm or private individual and a Postal Telegraph Office, or between two or more places of business or residence. In any town where a sufficient number of wires are led into the Head Postal Telegraph Office, the Department is prepared to provide a means whereby any two wires may be joined together at will, in order that messages may be transmitted by one renter to another direct without the necessity for repetition at the Postal Telegraph Office. The Department also undertakes to supply Greenwich mean time by electric current every hour in the day in London. All applications or communications in regard to private wires or time signals should be addressed to "The Secretary, General Post Office, London, E.C."

REGULATIONS AND CONDITIONS.—(*a*) An Instrument in a Postal Telegraph Office elsewhere than in London, where special rates are charged.—For desk accommodation and clerk's services, the charge is £5 5s. per annum. (*b*) Delivery of Local Messages.—A charge of 3d. each is made upon messages sent over a private wire and intended to be delivered within the local free delivery for telegrams ; beyond that boundary the ordinary rates for delivery are charged. Local messages to the renter are sent over the private wire free, and messages called for at the post office are also delivered free. (*c*) Messages to be forwarded as Letters.—These messages, if sent over a private wire to a post office before the hour for closing the ordinary letter box to the public, are subject to a fee of 1d. in addition to the charge for postage ; and if sent after the closing of the ordinary box, but before the late box is closed, they are subject to a fee of 3d. in addition to the charge for postage. (*d*) Extension of an Existing Line.—If the extension increases the rental, the cost is borne by the Department ; if not, it is borne by the renter. (*e*) Maintenance of Lines and Apparatus not the property of the Department will be undertaken for any period of not less than one year ; the annual charge is calculated at £1 less, per mile, than the rates set forth under "wire rental scale," and at reduced charges for apparatus, but the line and apparatus must be put into thorough order by the proprietor at his own expense before the Department will undertake to maintain them. The Department cannot allow the erection on its poles of a wire not belonging to it. (*f*) Agreement.—A simple form of agreement has been prepared, which every renter will be required

TIME SIGNALS. FROM LONDON TO THE COUNTRY.

		10 a.m. Signal £ s. d.	1 p.m. Signal £ s. d.	
Including the rental and maintenance of a private wire, from the Local Head Postal Telegraph Office to the renter's house, of ¼ mile in length		12 0 0	27 0 0	If the private wire exceed one mile in length, the ordinary tariff rate will be charged in addition to £10 for the 10 a.m. signal, or £25 for the 1 p.m. signal.
Do. do. do. ½		14 0 0	29 0 0	
Do. do. do. ¾		16 0 0	31 0 0	
Do. do. do. 1		17 0 0	32 0 0	

TABLE OF CHARGES FOR RENTAL OF PRIVATE WIRES (A), INSTRUMENTS, ETC. (B), AND INTERCOMMUNICATION (C).

A.—WIRE RENTAL.

—	In London.	Other Parts of the Kingdom.	—
	Per mile, per annum.		
	£ s. d.	£ s. d.	*** The minimum charge generally is for one mile, advancing beyond that distance by quarter-miles ; any less distance than a quarter-mile being counted as a quarter-mile.
1. Over house, or underground	8 0 0	7 0 0	
2. On the roads - -	6 0 0	5 0 0	NOTE.—The Department, however, reserves
3. Under water - -	Special rates, according to circumstances.		to itself the right to vary these rates under special circumstances.

B.—Instrument Rental, &c.

	A B C. Per Set of 1 Communicator, 1 Indicator, and 1 Bell.	1 Single Needle, and 1 Battery.	1 Printer and 1 Battery.	Telephone. Per Set of 1 Transmitter 1 Receiver, 1 Bell, 1 Battery.
	Rental per annum.			
	£ s. d.	£ s. d.	£ s. d.	£ s. d.
I. If rented from the Department, per annum - — *(This includes maintenance, repairs, and renewals, in each case.)*	6 0 0 — Extra Bell 1 0 0	3 0 0 *	10 0 0 *†	4 0 0 — Extra Bell 1 0 0 *
II. If the property of the renter, per annum -	3 10 0 — Extra Bell 0 15 0	2 10 0 *	7 10 0 *†	2 10 0 — Extra Bell 0 15 0

Ordinary switches, when required, will be supplied and afterwards maintained by the Department at an annual rental of 10s. each. Switches, if specially made to suit the requirements of the renter, will be charged for specially.

* Including renewal of battery.
† Including supply of paper ribbon.

C.—For Wire and Instruments on a System of Intercommunication Elsewhere than in London.

	Rental per annum. With A B C.	With Telephones.
	£ s. d.	£ s. d.
Single wire not exceeding half a mile	19 5 0	14 10 0
Do. do. do. a mile	22 15 0	18 0 0
Double do. do. a quarter mile	—	14 10 0
Do. do. do. half a mile	—	16 5 0
Do. do. do. a mile	—	21 10 0

to sign. This agreement, as a rule, will be for not less than three years, and will be determinable at three months' notice, given previous to the end of the fixed term; or failing such notice, on payment of such sum as the Department may agree to accept in lieu thereof; but where the expense of construction is considerable, the term must not be less than from five to seven years; the latter period being stipulated for when the proposed line will be in an outlying district, and will be specially provided for a single renter, and when it is not probable that there will be other renters. (*g*) Payment of Rental.—The rental is, in all cases, payable yearly, in advance. (*h*) Deposit Account.—A deposit, to cover charges for messages forwarded over the public wires, &c., is required in cases where a wire is led into a post-office.

Privy Council Office, Whitehall, S.W. Hours 10 to 5. Agricultural Department, 44, Parliament-st, S.W. Hours 11 to 5. Nearest *Ry. Stn.,* Westminster-br; *Omnibus Rtes.,* Whitehall and Strand; *Cab Rank,* Horse Guards.

Prussia.—(*See* German Empire.)

Public Halls.—The principal halls available for amateur and other performances are :

Exeter Hall, Strand, formerly the great place for the "May Meetings" of religious societies. Recently presented by six gentlemen, at a cost of £25,000, to the Young Men's Christian Asso.

Ladbroke Hall, 14, Ladbroke-grove-rd, seats about 400 persons ; the charges being, concert or reading, £3 ; dramatic performance, £3 10s.; ball, £4 4s.

Langham Hall, 43, Gt. Portland-st, will accommodate about 600 persons ; the charge being £5 5s. an evening, and £3 3s. for an afternoon concert.

Prince's Hall, Piccadilly.—No information.

St. George's Hall, Langham-pl, will accommodate from 800 to 900 persons ; the charges being, dramatic performances, £15 15s.; evening concerts, &c., £10 10s.; morning concerts, &c., £7 7s. Vacancies in each week: Mon., Tu., Wed., and Fri. afternoons, Th. and Sat. evenings. The minor hall can be had occasionally ; terms, £3 3s.

St. James's Hall, Piccadilly and Regent-st, will seat from 1,800 to 2,000 people. Rent for afternoons, £21 ; for evenings £26 5s.; for meetings £31 10s., with a hall-keeper's fee of £1 1s. The smaller hall is permanently occupied by the Moore and Burgess Minstrels.

Steinway Hall.—The handsome and commodious room in Lower Seymour-st seats about 600 persons, is in connection with the London Branch Establishment of Messrs. Steinway & Sons, of Steinway Hall, New York, and can be engaged for high-class concerts, recitals, lectures, &c.

Store-street Hall, Bedford-sq, also seats from 600 to 700 persons ; the fee being, with use of piano, £5 5s.; without it, £4 4s.

Westbourne Hall, Westbourne-gr, seats 500 people, at a charge per night of £3 3s.

Public Offices.—(*See under their respective Heads.*)

Public Schools' Club.—(*See* UNIVERSITY AND PUBLIC SCHOOLS' CLUB.)

Public Works Loan Board, 3, Bank-buildings, E.C. Hours 10 to 4.—NEAREST *Ry. Stns.*, Mansion House (Dis.) and Moorgate - st (Met.); *Omnibus Rtes.*, Moorgate-st, Cheapside, Cornhill, and Old Broad-st; *Cab Rank*, Bartholomew-la.

Putney Embankment, opened in 1888, extends for about half a mile towards Barnes, and has a carriage way of thirty-five, and a footway of ten feet wide, and is an immense advantage to this large and growing locality. Reached by steamer, or by rail from Waterloo.

Queen Anne's Bounty, and First Fruits and Tenths Office, next to 3, Great Dean's-yd, Westminster.—Hours 10 to 4; Sat. 10 to 2.—NEAREST *Ry. Stn.*, Westminster-br; *Omnibus Rtes.*, Victoria-st and Parliament-st; *Cab Rank*, Palace-yard.

Queensland. — AGENCY-GENERAL, 1, Westminster-chambers, Victoria-st, S.W. NEAREST *Ry. Stn.*, St. James's-park (Dis.); *Omnibus Rtes.*, Victoria and Parliament streets; *Cab Rank*, Tothill-st

Racing.—There is no lack of racecourses in the neighbourhood of London, and scarcely a week elapses in the racing or steeple-chasing seasons without some opportunity being given the turfite for the pursuit of his favourite amusement in almost every form. Between the Ascot week and a day's plating at one of the smaller meetings there is a very considerable range, and the Londoner has only to take his choice. The most famous of the metropolitan race-courses is Epsom, with its time-honoured traditions of Derby and Oaks; and one of *the* London weeks is the "Derby week," which is at the end of May or beginning of June. There is also a very pleasant two days' meeting at Epsom in the early spring, on the second of which the popular City and Suburban Handicap is decided. The pretty little town of Epsom is easily and conveniently reached from Waterloo by the L. & S. W. and from Victoria and London-br by the L. B. and S. C. Ry. The latter has also a station on Banstead Downs, within a quarter of a mile of the course. The stations in the town itself are rather more than a mile from the Grand Stand, the road being, for the most part, very steep. Plenty of vehicles are always in waiting at the railway stations to convey the traveller to the scene of action, and prices range from 1s. to 5s. each passenger, according to circumstances. On an off day in fair weather "a bob a nob" is generally the correct thing. Half-a-crown to five shillings may be taken as the normal tariff on "big days," but, of course, the weather and the great "law of supply and demand" have to be taken into consideration. The Epsom Grand Stand is fairly convenient, but the managers charge high prices both for admission and for any extra accommodation that may be required. A new subscription lawn and new stands next the winning-post are the latest Epsom improvements.

Far superior to Epsom for the general quality of its sport and of its visitors, is Ascot, where the races take place a fortnight after the Derby. The Cup Day (Thurs.) is considered the great day; but to the lover of racing for itself, as distinguished from the ordinary pleasure-seeker, the Tues. is far preferable. The important and valuable stakes contended for on that day almost invariably attract the cream of the best horses in training. Indeed, even as regards the attendance of visitors, the Tues. has of late years been running the Cup Day very close. The show of ladies' dresses in the royal enclosure, and on the carriages and drags opposite the stand, on either the Tues. or Thurs., is one of the most extraordinary sights of the season. Ascot can be reached by the G.W.R. to Windsor, where omnibuses, &c., meet every train. The drive from Windsor to Ascot-heath (about five or six miles) is charming, but this is not a very convenient route, especially on the return journey The other route to Ascot is by the L. & S. W. R., from Waterloo, and the journey in the race week probably costs more money and occupies more time than any journey of a similar length in England. The very unsatisfactory nature of the railway service is, indeed, the great drawback to Ascot. The L. & S.W. station is a quarter of a mile from the Grand Stand, which is an exceedingly well-arranged and convenient building, or rather series of buildings, and the charges for admission, &c., are not so exorbitant as at some other places. At the Grand Stands at Epsom and Ascot private boxes and stalls may be engaged, but very early application to the managers is necessary, and even then they are difficult to obtain. The price of admission to the stands varies in proportion to the interest of the day's sport, but may be roughly said to vary from ten shillings to a guinea.

A pretty and very fashionably attended racecourse is that at Sandown-pk, within a very short distance of the Esher Stn. of the L. & S. W. R., where races—both on the flat, over hurdles, and over the steeplechase courses—take place at frequent intervals. A similar institution has also been inaugurated at Kempton-pk, near the Sunbury Stn. on the Thames Valley Line. At both places the public are admitted to the ground on payment, but the best of the stands are reserved for the members of the two clubs who have a proprietary interest in the grounds. Among other gate-money meetings are those of Croydon and the Alexandra-pk. Racing also takes place after Ascot at Windsor and Egham; and before Epsom Summer Meeting, at Harpenden, on the G.N.R.; and the excellent service of the L.B. & S.C.R. makes it possible to include the pretty course at Brighton in the metropolitan list. Goodwood-pk (the private racecourse of the Duke of Richmond) is not so easy of access, but deserves a visit if only from the fact that it is *the* fashionable meeting of the racing season. Newmarket itself is within two hours of London by the G.E.R., and thus the best racing in the world is brought within easy reach of the Londoner. The exact dates of all these meetings are published in the sporting papers, and will also be found in the Calendar at the beginning of this book; and for the special train arrangements, which may vary occasionally, the advertisements in the daily, as well as in the sporting papers should be referred to. It is useful to remember that racecourse refreshments are almost always abominable, and that it is as well to have as little to do with them as possible. At Ascot perhaps they are better than at most places; and at Newmarket and Sandown-pk, Messrs. Bertram and Roberts are in power, and a very much better state of things exists. But, as a rule, the Grand Stand bar reminds one of the average theatre saloon, nothing worse than which has ever been invented by the ingenuity of man.

There are, probably, even more welshers and thieves at the London race meetings than elsewhere, because the meetings, being more numerous and close at home, afford more constant employment to these industrious classes. The visitor who wants a wager should be very shy of depositing his money with anybody he does not know, and unless he be acquainted with a respectable bookmaker, ought to keep his money in his pocket. If not he will most assuredly never see it again. The three-card men, and the gentlemen who invite the stranger to ring the bull and to prick the garter, are more strictly looked after by the police than was formerly the case, and are not quite so obstructive as of yore. But let the uninitiated beware when a gentleman in the railway carriage lays a great-coat, or a rug, over his knees, and producing some cards, begins, the moment the train has started, with "Well, gentlemen, and what do you say to a little game of cards to while away the tedium of the journey?" or words to that effect. Still more let him take heed to his actions if a gentleman opposite starts an animated conversation with him, and if another gentleman in a distant part of the carriage begins to contradict, and even to make a show of a quarrel with the card-player. A stony silence, and the manifestation of an absorbing interest in the landscape, may be prescribed in most cases of this kind. The innocent who begins to talk is lost, and is not unlikely to be robbed, even if he does not bet. In any such case it is wise to leave the carriage at the next station if possible.

The Victoria Club, in Wellington-st, Strand, is the principal resort of professional racing-men in London, and a great part of the commission betting of Europe is done there. It is, however, a strictly private club, and in no sense what the law understands by a betting-house. The Subscription Room, at Tattersall's, is also a private club (subscription £3 3s.,

election by committee) for the purposes of betting, but differs from the Victoria in that it is not a social club as well. Strict observance of Sir Alexander Cockburn's Act has almost entirely stopped ready-money betting in London as elsewhere, and, as has been said above, the intending backer, who is unacquainted with a respectable bookmaker, had better avoid the dangers of the "lists."

Railway Commissioners, W. Front Committee Room, House of Lords, S.W.—Hours 10 to 5 ; Saturdays 10 to 2. NEAREST *Ry. Stn.,* Westminster-br (Dis.); *Omnibus Rtes.,* Parliament-st and Victoria-st ; *Cab Rank,* Palace-yd.

Railways.—It would be difficult to attempt by any mere verbal explanation to describe the "iron roads" of the metropolis, and all efforts in that direction would be futile but for the one or two maps (*see* MAPS) specially devoted to the elucidation of the labyrinth of stations, junctions, tunnels, viaducts, embankments, and cuttings, running in such quick succession as to make one marvel at the amount of ingenuity, skill, labour, and capital which must have been expended to obtain such results.

Recent years have seen considerable development, and especially in what is commonly called the "Underground" Railway, a term which originated with the construction (entirely in tunnels beneath the Marylebone and Euston rds) of the line between Farringdon-st and Bishop's-rd, the first of its kind in the world ; but a term, however, now falling rapidly into disuse owing to the numerous suburban branches which have since been constructed.

The lines are owned by two companies—viz., the District Ry. and the Metropolitan Ry. ; and the most recent development of these systems has been the completion of what is known as the "Inner Circle"—*i.e.,* the coupling-up of the line in the east end of London between Mansion House and Aldgate, by which means a circular system of trains is now running continuously throughout the day in both directions, connecting all the termini of the great railways, and enabling anyone to pass direct to or from the "Underground" systems entirely under cover with one exception—viz., between Fenchurch-st Stn.

and Mark-lane, about a three minutes' walking distance.

These particular systems are, however, of such vast importance to Londoners—as is evidenced by the number of passengers carried by them annually, which reached in 1884 to the enormous figure of over 110,000,000—that a short description of them will be useful. Starting, therefore, say, from the Mansion House Stn. (District Ry.), we pass westward to Blackfriars, thence under the Thames-embankment to Temple (for the theatres and Law Courts), Charing ✠ (for Sth.-Eastern Ry. and the theatres), Westminster (for the Houses of Parliament and Government offices), thence under Parliament-sq, skirting Westminster Abbey, to St. James's-pk, Victoria (for the London, Chatham, and Dover, London, Brighton, and South Coast, and Crystal Palace Rys.), Sloane-sq, South Kensington (a subway connects this station with the Natural History and South Kensington Museums, the Exhibition Buildings, and the Albert Hall), Glo'ster-rd (several important branches diverge at this station—*see below*),thence to High-st (Kensington), Notting Hill Gate, Bayswater, Praed-st, Paddington (for Great Western Ry.), Edgware-rd (a junction for other branches), Baker-st (another junction), Portland-rd, Gower-st (for London and North-Western Ry.), King's ✠ (for Great Northern and Midland Rys.), Farringdon-st, Aldersgate-st, Moorgate-st, Bishopsgate (for Great Eastern Ry.), Aldgate, Mark-la (for the Tower and Fenchurch-st Ry. terminus), Monument (for London-br Rys.), to Cannon-st (for South-Eastern Ry.), and thence back to the Mansion House. This is called the "Inner Circle."

What is known as the "Middle Circle" commences at Mansion House, and embraces the same stations as given above for the "Inner Circle" up to Glo'ster-rd, where the line diverges southward and passes through Earl's Ct. (an important junction), to Addison-rd (another important junction), Uxbridge-rd (for Shepherd's Bush), thence to Latimer-rd, Notting Hill and Ladbroke-grove, Westbourne Pk. (for Great Western line), Royal Oak, and Bishop's-rd (for Great Western terminus), to Edgware-rd, and thence over the "Inner Circle," through Aldgate, back to Mansion House.

The "Outer Circle" takes the same route as the "Middle Circle" from the City as far as Uxbridge-rd, whence its direction is through Wormwood Scrubs to Willesden Junction (for London and North Western Ry.), Kensal Gn., Brondesbury, Finchley-rd, Hampstead Heath, Kentish Tn., Camden Tn., Islington and Highbury, Dalston Junction, and thence to Broad-st.

At Earl's Ct. the line diverges in two other directions, one through West Brompton and Walham Gn. to Putney-br (shortly to be extended to Wimbledon and Surbiton), the other through West Kensington and Hammersmith, and thence through Shaftesbury-rd and Turnham Gn., where it again diverges in two directions, one going south-westerly through Gunnersbury and Kew Gardens to Richmond, the other north-westerly through Acton Gn. to Mill Hill-pk, where it again diverges into two lines, one going through Ealing, and forming a junction there with the Great Western line to Southall, West Drayton, Slough, and Windsor, and the other to South Ealing, Boston-rd, Osterley and Spring Grove, to Hounslow (Town and Barracks Stns.).

Latimer-rd on the "Middle Circle" is the junction for a line which after passing through Shepherd's Bush to Hammersmith, connects near the latter place with the line to Richmond above described.

Baker-st on the "Inner Circle" is the junction for St. John's Wood, Swiss Cottage, Finchley-rd, West Hampstead, Kilburn-Brondesbury, Kingsbury-Neasden, and Harrow.

The foregoing exhausts the whole of the line of the "Underground" system with one important exception, only recently opened, viz., on the "Inner Circle" line between Bishopsgate and Mark-la. Here two lines leave the "Inner Circle" and connect with one another at Aldgate East, from which point they pass through St. Mary's to Whitechapel—Mile-End.

At St. Mary's the line diverges to Shadwell and Wapping, and passes thence through the Thames Tunnel to Rotherhithe, Deptford-rd, and New ✠, where it connects with the South Eastern and London, Brighton, and South Coast Railway systems.

Railway Stations with the companies to which they belong:

ABBEY WOOD	S. Eastern
ACTON	Gt. Western
,,	N.L.&S.W. junc.
,, -GREEN	District
,, MILL-HILL-PK	,,
ADDISON-RD	,,
ALDERSGATE-ST	Metropolit.
ALDGATE	Dist. & Met.
,, EAST	,,
ALEXANDRA PALCE.	Gt. Northn.
ANGEL-RD	Gt. Eastern
BAKER-ST	Metropolit.
BALHAM & UPPER TOOTING	L. B. & S.C.
BARKING	L. T. & S.
,, -RD (Canning Tn)	Gt. Eastern
BARNES	S. Western
BARNET, NEW	Gt. Northn.
,, HIGH	,,
BARNSBURY	N. London.
BATTERSEA	W. L. Ext.
,, PK	L. B. & S.C.
,, ,,	L. C. & D.
BAYSWATER	Metropolit.
BECKENHAM	S. Eastern
,,	L. C. & D.
BELVEDERE	S. Eastern
BENFLEET	L. T. & S.
BERMONDSEY, S.	L. B. & S.C.
,, SPA-RD	S. Eastern
BETHNAL GN. JUNC.	Gt. Eastern
BISHOPSGATE	,,
,,	Metropolit.
BISHOP'S-RD	Gt. Western.
BLACKFRIARS-BR	District
BLACKHEATH	S. Eastern
,, HILL	L. C. & D.
BLACKWALL	Gt. Eastern
,,	N. London
BOROUGH-RD	L. C. & D.
BOSTON-RD (for Brentford and Hanwell)	District
BOW	N. London
BOWES-PK	Gt. Northn.
BRENTFORD	Gt. Western
BRENTFORD, BOSTON-RD	District.
BRENTWOOD and WARLEY	Gt. Eastern
BRIMSDOWN	,,
BRIXTON	L. C. & D.
BROAD-ST	N. London
,,	L. & N. W.
BROMLEY	S. Eastern
,,	L. C. & D.
,, -BY-BOW	L. T. & S.
,, SOUTH	N. London
BROMPTON, WEST	District
,,	W. L. Ex.
,, GLO'STER-RD	Dis. & Met.
BRONDESBURY	L. & N. W.
BUCKHURST-HILL	Gt. Eastern
BUSHEY	L. & N. W.
BUSH HILL-PARK	Gt. Eastern

CAMBERWELL NEW-ROAD	L. C. & D.
CAMBRIDGE-HEATH	Gt. Eastern
CAMDEN-RD	Midland
,, TN.	N. London
,,	L. & N. W.
CANNING TN.	Gt. Eastern
CANNON-ST	Dist. & Met.
,,	S. Eastern
CANONBURY	N. London
CARSHALTON	L. B. & S.C.
CASTLE-HILL	Gt. Western
CHALK FARM	N. London
,,	L. & N. W.
CATERHAM	S. Eastern
,,	L. B. & S.C
CATERHAM JUNC.	S. Eastern
CATFORD-BR	,,
CENTRAL-ST (Royal Albert Dock)	Gt. Eastern
CHAMPION-HILL	L. B. & S.C.
CHARING ✠	District
,,	S. Eastern
CHARLTON	,,
CHEAM	L. B. & S.C
CHELSEA	W. L. Ext.
,, (Sloane-sq)	District
,, (Walham-gn)	,,
CHIGWELL-LANE	Gt. Eastern
CHILD'S-HILL	Midland
CHINGFORD	Gt. Eastern
CHISLEHURST	S. Eastern
CHISWICK	S. Western
,, (Turnham-gn)	,,
CLAPHAM	L. C. & D.
,, JUNCTION	L. B. & S.C
,, ,,	S. Western
,, ,,	L. C. & D.
CLAPTON	Gt. Eastern
COBORN-RD (for Old Ford)	,,
CONNAUGHT - ROAD (Rl. Albert Dock)	,,
CRICKLEWOOD	Midland
CROUCH END	Gt. Northn.
CROUCH-HILL	Midland
CROYDON (Addis-combe-rd)..	S. Eastern
CROYDON (EAST)	,,
,, ,,	L. B. & S. C.
,, (NEW)	,,
,, (SOUTH)	,,
,, (WEST)	,,
CRYSTAL PALACE	,,
,,	L. C. & D.
CUSTOM HOUSE	Gt. Eastern
DALSTON JUNCTION	N. London
DENMARK-HILL	L. C. & D.
,,	L. B. & S.C.
DEPTFORD	S. Eastern
DEPTFORD-RD	District
,,	L. B. & S.C.
,,	Metropolit.
DUDDING-HILL	Midland
DULWICH	L. C. & D.
,, NORTH	L. B. & S.C.
EALING	District
,,	Gt. Western

Ealing-common	District
Earl's Court	,,
Earlsfield and	
Summers Tn.	S. Western
East End, Finchley	Gt. Northn.
East Ham	L. T. & S.
Edgware	G. Northn.
,, -rd	Metropolit.
Elephant&Castle	L. C. & D.
Enfield	Gt. Eastern.
,,	Gt. Northn.
,, Lock	Gt. Eastern.
Epsom Town	L.B. & S.C.
,, ,,	S. Western.
,, Downs	L.B. & S.C
Euston-sq	L. & N. W.
Ewell	L.B. & S.C.
,,	S. Western.
Farringdon-st	Metropolit
Fenchurch-st	Gt. Eastern.
,,	L. T. & S.
Finchley	Gt. Northn.
,, -rd	Metropolit.
,, ,, and	
Frognal	L. & N. W.
Finchley-rd	Midland
Finsbury-pk	Gt. Northn.
Forest-gate	Gt. Eastern
,, hill	L.B. & S.C.
Fulham	District
Gallions(Rl.Albert	
Dock)	Gt. Eastern
Gipsy-hill	L.B. & S.C.
Globe-rd and De-	
vonshire-st	Gt. Eastern
Gloucester-rd	Dist. & Met.
Gospel Oak	L. & N. W.
Gower-st	Metropolit.
Gravesend	S. Eastern
Greenhithe	,,
Green-lanes and	
Noel Park	Gt. Eastern
Greenwich	S. Eastern
Grosvenor-rd	L.B. & S.C.
,,	L. C. & D.
Gunnersbury	L. & S. W.
Hackney	N. London
Hackney-downs	Gt. Eastern
Hadley Wood	Gt. Northn.
Haggerston	N. London
Hammersmith	District
,,	Gt. Western
,,	Metropolit.
Hampstead-heath	L. & N. W.
Hampton	S. Western
,, Court	,,
,, Wick	,,
Hanwell	Gt. Western
,, (Boston-rd)	District
Haringay Park	Midland.
Harrow	L. & N. W.
,,	Metropolit.
Hatfield	Gt. Northn.
Hayes	Gt. Western
Hendon	Midland
Herne-hill	L. C. & D.
Highbury and Is-	
lington	N. London

Highgate	Gt. Northn.
,, -rd	Midland
Holborn-viaduct	L. C. & D.
Holloway	Gt. Northn.
Holloway, Upper	Midland
Homerton	N. London
Honor Oak	L. C. & D.
Hornsey	Gt. Northn.
,, -rd	Midland
Hounslow & Whit-	
ton	S. Western
,, Town..	District
,, Barracks	,,
Ilford	Gt. Eastern
Isleworth	S. Western
Islington(Highby.)	N. London
Junction-rd	Midland
Kenley	S. Eastern
Kensal-gn	L. & N. W.
Kensington,(Addi-	
son-rd)	District
,,	Gt. Eastern
,,	S. Western
,,	L. & N. W.
,,	L.B. & S.C.
,, High-st	Dist. & Met.
,, South	,,
,, West	District
Kent House (Penge)	L. C. & D.
Kentish Tn.	L. & N. W.
,,	Midland
Kew-br	N. L.& S.W.
	junc.
,,	S. Western
,, Gardens	L. & S. W.
Kilburn	L. & N. W.
,, -Brondesbury	Metropolit.
King's	,,
,,	Gt. Northn.
Kingsb'y-Neasden	Metropolit.
Kingston	S. Western
Ladywell	S. Eastern
Langley	Gt. Western
Latimer-rd	G.W.& Met.
Lea-bridge	Gt. Eastern
Leatherhead	S. Western
,,	L.B. & S.C.
Lee	S. Eastern
Leigh	L. T. & S.
Leman-st	Gt. Eastern
LewishamJunction	S. Eastern
,, -rd	L. C. & D.
Leyton	Gt. Eastern
Leytonstone	,,
Limehouse	,,
Liverpool-st	,,
London-br	L.B. & S.C.
,,	S. Eastern
London-fields	Gt. Eastern
Lordship-lane	L. C. & D.
Loudoun-rd	L. & N. W.
Loughton	Gt. Eastern
Lower Edmonton.	
Lower Norwood	L.B. & S.C.
Lower Sydenham	S. Eastern
Low-st	L. T. & S.
Ludgate-hill	L. C. & D.
Malden, New	S. Western

Malden, New	L. B. & S. C.
Manor-pk	Gt. Eastern
Mansion House	District
Mark-la	Dist. & Met.
Marlborough-rd	Metropolit.
Maryland-point	Gt. Eastern
Maze-hill	S. Eastern
Merton, Lower	L. B. & S. C-
,,	S. Western
Mildmay-pk	N. London
Mile End (White-	
chapel)	District
Mill-hill	Midland
,,	Gt. Northn.
,, Park	District
Millwall Junction	Gt. Eastern
Mitcham	L. B. & S. C
Monument	Dist. & Met.
Moorgate-st	Metropolit.
Muswell-hill	Gt. Northn.
New	District
,,	L. B. & S. C.
,,	Metropolitn.
,,	S. Eastern
New Croydon	L. B. & S. C.
New Southgate	Gt. Northn.
Norbiton	S. Western
Norbury	L. B. & S. C.
North Weald	Gt. Eastern
North Woolwich	,,
NorwoodJunction	L. B. & S. C.
,, ,,	L. C. & D.
Notting Hill	G.W. & Met.
,, ,, gate	Metropolit.
Nunhead	L. C. & D.
Oakleigh-pk	Gt. Northn.
Old Ford	N. London
Old Kent-rd	L. B. & S. C.
Osterley & Spring	
Grove	District
Paddington	Gt. Western
Palmer's-gn	Gt. Northn.
Park	Gt. Eastern.
Parson's-gn	District
Peckham (Qn's.-rd)	L. B. & S. C.
,, rye	L. C. & D.
,, ,,	L. B. & S. C.
Penge	,,
,,	L. C.'& D.
Pinner	L. & N. W.
Plaistow (Essex)	L. T. & S.
,, (Kent)	S. Eastern
Plumstead	,,
Ponder's End	Gt. Eastern
Pope-st	S. Eastern
Poplar	N. London
,,	Gt. Eastern
Portland-rd	Metropolit
Potter's Bar	Gt. Northn.
Praed-st	Metropolit.
Putney	S. Western
,, -br	District
Queen's-pk(W. Kil-	
burn)	L. & N. W.
,, rd(Peckham)	L. B. & S. C.
,, ,, (Battersea)	S. Western
,, ,,(Bayswater)	Metropolit.
Rayne's-pk	S. Western

RICHMOND	District
" ..	Metropolit.
"	S. Western
ROMFORD	Gt. Eastern
ROTHERHITHE ..	Dist. & Met.
"	L. B. & S.C.
ROYAL OAK ..	Gt. Western
ST. ANN'S-RD ..	Midland
ST. JAMES'S-PK ..	District
ST. JOHN'S	S. Eastern
ST. JOHN'S WOOD-RD	Metropolit.
ST. MARY'S, White-chapel	Dist. & Met.
ST. PAUL'S.. ..	L. C. & D.
SEVEN SISTERS(Tottenham	Gt. Eastern
SHADWELL	District
"	E. London
SHAFTESBURY-RD..	District
"	S. Western
SHEPHERD'S BUSH	G.W. & Met.
"	S. Western
SHEPPERTON ..	"
SHOREDITCH ..	N. London
" ..	Dist. & Met.
" ..	L. B. & S.C.
SILVER-ST (for Upper Edmonton) ..	Gt. Eastern
SILVERTOWN ..	"
SLOANE-SQ ..	District
SLOUGH	Gt. Western
SNARESBROOK ..	Gt. Eastern
SNOW-HILL.. ..	L. C. & D.
SOUTH ACTON ..	N.L. & S.W. Junc.
SOUTH BROMLEY ..	N. London
SOUTHALL	Gt. Western
STH. BERMONDSEY	L.B. & S.C.
STH. EALING ..	District
STH. KENSINGTON	Dist. & Met.
SPA-RD	S. Eastern
STAMFORD-HILL ..	Gt. Eastern
STEPNEY	
"	L. T. & S.
STOCKWELL, NTH. }	L. C. & D.
" STH J	L. C. & D.
STONEBRIDGE-PK ..	Midland
STRATFORD ..	Gt. Eastern
STRAWBERRY-HILL..	S. Western
STREATHAM ..	L. B. & S.C.
" -HILL ..	"
" -COMMON ..	"
STROUD GREEN ..	Gt. Northn.
SUDBURY	L. & N. W.
SUNBURY	S. Western
SURBITON	
SUTTON	L. B. & S.C.
SWISS COTTAGE ..	Metropolit.
SYDENHAM	L. B. & S.C.
" -HILL ..	L. C. & D.
" LOWER	S. Eastern
" UPPER..	L. C. & D.
TEDDINGTON ..	S. Western
TEMPLE	District
THAMES DITTON ..	S. Western
THORNTON-HEATH	L. B. & S.C.
TIDAL BASIN, VICTORIA DOCKS ..	Gt. Eastern
TOTTENHAM HALE	Gt. Eastern
TOTTENHAM,SOUTH	Midland
TOTTERIDGE ..	Metropolit.
TULSE HILL ..	L. B. & S.C.
TURNHAM-GN ..	District
"	S. Western
TWICKENHAM ..	"
UPPER HOLLOWAY	Midland
UPPER NORWOOD..	L. B. & S.C.
UPPER SYDENHAM	L. C. & D.
UPTON-PK	L. T. & S.
UXBRIDGE	Gt. Western
" -RD ..	"
" " ..	W. L." Ext.
" " ..	L. & N. W.
VAUXHALL.. ..	S. Western
VICTORIA	District
"	Gt. Western
"	L. B. & S.C.
"	L. C. & D.
"	L. & N. W.
VICTORIA-PK ..	N. London
"	Gt. Eastern
WALHAM-GN ..	District
WALTHAM ✠ ..	Gt. Eastern
WALWORTH-RD ..	L. C. & D.
WANDSWORTH ..	S. Western
" -COM.	L. B. & S.C.
" -RD	
" "	L. C. & D.
WAPPING	District
"	L. B. & S.C.
"	Metropolit.
WATERLOO ..	S. Western
WATERLOO JUNCTION	S. Eastern
WATFORD	L. & N. W.
WELSH HARP ..	Midland
WESTBOURNE-PK ..	Gt. Western
" ..	G.W. & Met.
WEST BROMPTON ..	District
" and LILLIE BRIDGE ..	W. Lon.Ext.
WEST DRAYTON ..	Gt. Western
WEST END	Midland
WEST HAMPSTEAD	Metropolit.
WEST INDIA DOCKS	Gt. Eastern
WEST KENSINGTON	District
WESTMINSTER-BR..	"
WHITECHAPEL ..	"
" ..	L. B. & S.C.
" ..	Metropolit.
" (Mile End)	District
" (St. Mary's)	Dist. & Met.
WHITE HART-LANE (Tottenham) ..	Gt. Eastern
WHITTON (Hounslow)	S. Western
WILLESDEN JUNC.	L. & N. W.
" -GN ..	Metropolit.
WIMBLEDON ..	S. Western
" ..	L. B. & S.C.
WINCHMORE-HILL ..	Gt. Northn.
WINDSOR	Gt. Western
"	S. Western
WOODFORD	Gt. Eastern
WOOD-GN	Gt. Northn.
WOODSIDE	S. Eastern
WOODSIDE-PARK ..	Gt. Northn.
WOOD-ST(Walthamstow)	Gt. Eastern
WOOLWICH TOWN..	"
" NORTH	"
" ARSENAL	S. Eastern
" DOCKYD.	"
WORCESTER-PK ...	S. Western
WORMWOOD SCRUBS	L. & N. W.
YORK-RD(Battersea)	L. B. & S.C.
" "	L. C. & D.

Railway Ticket Offices.

—Branch offices for the sale of tickets, and for receiving parcels, have been opened by several of the principal railway companies as under:

GREAT EASTERN.—West End Office, 61, Regent-st, opposite the Café Royal; Blossoms-inn, Lawrence-la, Cheapside; Billiter Ho., Billiter-st; Spread Eagle, 3, Whittington-avenue, Leadenhall-st; "Swan with Two Necks," Gresham-st; Messrs. Cook & Son, Ludgate-cir, Fleet-st; First Avenue Hotel, Holborn; 82, Oxford-st; Messrs. Gaze & Son, 142, Strand; 16, Holborn; Messrs. Cook & Son, Hotel Metropole, Charing✠; 9, Grand Hotel-bdgs, Charing✠; "Golden ✠," Charing ✠; 70, St. Martin's-la; 28, Regent-st; Messrs. Gaze & Sons, Piccadilly-cir (next door to the "Criterion"); 34, Albert-ga, Knightsbridge; 33, High-st, Kensington; Mr. Whiteley, Westbourne-gr; 241, Oxford-st; Hotel "Windsor," Victoria-st, Westminster.

GREAT NORTHERN.—43 and 44, Crutched Friars, E.C.; 16, Fish-st-hill, E.C.; "Bee Hive," White Cross-st, E.C.; 80, Bishopsgate-st-without, E.C.; 3, King Edward-st, E.C.; Moorgate-st Stn. (G.N. Office); Farringdon-st (next to Met. Ry.), E.C.; 230, Essex-rd, Islington, N.; 95, High-st, Borough, S.E.; 44, Bread-st, E.C.; George Inn, Borough, S.E.; *Blackfriars (L. C. & D.) Goods Stn., S.E.; 190, Westminster-br-rd, S.E.; 90, Tottenham-ct-rd; 264, High Holborn, W.C.; 111, Strand, W.C.; 32, Piccadilly-cir, W.; 285, Oxford-st, W.; Royal Oak Office, 6, Porchester-rd, Westbourne-gr, W.; 3, Charing ✠; Albert Gate Office, 1, William-st, Lowndes-sq, S.W.; Royal Mint-st Stn., Minories, E.; *East India Docks Stn., Poplar, E.; *West India Docks Stn., Poplar, E.;

* For goods only,

*Poplar Docks Stn., E. ; *Hackney Wick, E. ; * Victoria Dock Stn., E.

GREAT WESTERN.—5, Arthur-st-east, London-br ; 29,Charing-✠; Cheapside;43&44,Crutched Friars; 67, Gresham-st ; 193, Oxford-st ; Bartlett's-bdgs, Holborn-cir; Kingston's Booking-office, Fitzroy-sq ; 82, Queen Victoria-st ; 23, New Oxford-st ; 407, Oxford-st ; 6, Camden-rd, N.W.; Messrs. Cook's, Ludgate-cir; and 26, Regent-st.

LONDON and NORTH WESTERN.— Chief Office, Broad - st Stn., Eldon-st, E.C.; "Spread Eagle," 3, Whittington-avenue, Leadenhall-market, E.C. ; Hambro'-wharf, Upper Thames-st, E.C. ; "Cross Keys," Wood-st, E.C. ; "Swan with Two Necks," Gresham-st, E.C. ; "Bolt-in-Tun," Fleet-st, E.C. ; 22, Aldersgate-st, E.C. ; 30, Smithfield West, E.C. ; 8 and 9, Clerkenwell-gn, E.C. ; 65, Aldgate, E. ; 43, New Oxford-st (late 474½, Oxford-st), near the British Museum, W.C. ; "Golden -✠," Charing -✠, W.C. ; Victoria-st, Westminster (under Army and Navy Hotel), S.W. ; 70, St. Martin's-la, W.C. ; "George and Blue Boar," High Holborn, W.C.; 16, Holborn, E.C. ; "White Horse," Fetter-la, E.C. ; Universal Office, "Spread Eagle," Piccadilly-cir, W. ; 496, Oxford-st (near the Marble Arch), W. ; 231, Edgware-rd, W.; "Griffin's Green Man and Still,"241,Oxford-st, W. ; "The Lion," 108, New Bond-st, W. ; Atlas Office, 167, Tottenham-ct-rd, W.C. ; Universal Office, 117, Borough, S.E.; Surrey Ry. Office, 138, Newington-causeway, S.E. ; 233 and 234, Blackfriars-rd, S.E. ; 34, Albertga, Knightsbridge, S.W. ; 33, Hereford - rd, Bayswater, W.; 33, High-st, Kensington, W.; "Angel," 5, Pentonville-rd, Islington, N. ; 194, Westminster-br - rd, S.E. ; Railway Arch, Great Eastern-st, Shoreditch, E. ; The Universal Office,Kilburn Stn., N.W.; Broad-st Stn., N. L. Ry., E.C.; Willesden Junc. Stn., L. & N. W. Ry., N.W.; Bow Stn., N. L. Ry., E.; Highbury Stn., N. L. Ry., Islington, N.; Dalston Stn., N. L. Ry., E.; Shoreditch Stn., N. L. Ry., E.; Poplar Stn., N. L. Ry., E.; Camden Town, N. L. Ry., Universal Goods and Parcels Office, N.W.; Hammersmith and Chiswick Stn., N. & S.W. J. R.; Acton Stn., N. & S.W. J. R.

* For goods only.

LONDON AND SOUTH WESTERN. — 30, Regent-st, Piccadilly-cir ; Exeter-bdgs, Arthur-st-west ; 9, Grand Hotel-bdgs, Trafalgar-sq.

LONDON, BRIGHTON, AND SOUTH COAST, AND ISLE OF WIGHT.—28, Regent-circus, Piccadilly ; 8, Grand Hotel-bdgs, Trafalgar-sq ; Messrs. Cook & Son, Tourist Office, Ludgate-cir ; Messrs. Gaze & Son, Tourist Office, 142, Strand ; "Red Cap," Camden-rd, N.W.; Hay's Booking Office, 4, Royal Exchange-bdgs, Cornhill ; City General Enquiry Office, 18, Fish-st-hill.

LONDON,CHATHAM AND DOVER. —105, Ludgate-cir.

LONDON, TILBURY, AND SOUTH-END.—28, Regent-cir, W. ; 8, Grand Hotel-bdgs, Trafalgar-sq ; 4, Royal Exchange-bdgs, E.C.

METROPOLITAN. — Piccadilly - cir and Regent-cir.

MIDLAND.—445, West Strand ; 5, Charing -✠; 272, Regent-cir ; 35, Piccadilly ; 33, Cannon-st ; 99, Gracechurch-st ; 28, Regent's-cir, W.; 8, Grand Hotel-bdgs, Trafalgar-sq ; 10A, New Bond-st ; and 495, Oxford-st.

SOUTH EASTERN.—371, Strand. DISTRICT.—51, Queen Victoria-st, E.C.

Raleigh Club, 16, Regent-st, S.W. — No candidate is eligible for ballot unless he shall have reached the age of 21 years, or shall have served .not less than one year in the army, the militia, or civil service, or five years in the navy, or be already a member of one of certain first-class London clubs. The kitchen is closed at 2 a.m. ; the bar, card, and billiard rooms at 4 a.m. ; and no fresh rubber of whist, game of cards, or billiards, shall be commenced after 3.30 a.m. Entrance fee, £15 15s. ; subscription, £10 10s.

Ranelagh Club, Barn Elms.—This club is instituted for the purpose of affording an agreeable riverside resort to gentlemen desirous of dining out of London, and participating in the games of cricket, polo, lawn-tennis, &c. The entrance fee is £15 15s., and the annual subscription £7 7s. Members are entitled to admit two ladies with free passes, and may give vouchers of admission on payment to as many friends as they please. The price of admission to members' friends is ten shillings, except on such days as the committee may

appoint, when it is raised to twenty. No person is eligible for membership who is not received in general society. The election is in the hands of the committee. At least five members must vote, and one black ball in five excludes.

Ratcliff Highway (Map 9). —This, which until within the last few years was one of the sights of the metropolis, and almost unique in Europe as a scene of coarse debauchery, is now chiefly noteworthy as an example of what may be done by effective police supervision thoroughly carried out, though the dancing-rooms, music-halls, and foreign cafés of the Highway—now re-christened St. George's-st—are still well worthy of a visit from the student of human nature. The performances in the various places of entertainment are, perhaps, not of a refined description, nor is the audience ; but it is just possible that, from an exclusively moral point of view, the advantage may even be proved to be not altogether on the side of the higher refinement. The casual ward of St. George's Workhouse, at the bottom of Old Gravel-la, is well worth a visit, and so, if it be not too late in the evening, is the mission church of St. Peter's, London Docks, hard by, where you will find in full work an agency which, if the people of the neighbourhood are to be believed, has had in the marvellous transformation which has taken place a more potent influence even than police and parliament combined. Returning thence to Shadwell High - st, you may visit the "White Swan," popularly known as "Paddy's Goose," once the uproarious rendezvous of half the tramps and thieves of London, now quite sedate, and, to confess the truth, dull—very dull. Down to the right here, again, is the little waterside police-station where the grim harvest of the "drag," the weird flotsam and jetsam of the cruel river, lies awaiting the verdict that will— let us hope—"find it Christian burial." And so back into the High-way again, and up Cannon-st-rd, where stands St. George's Church, the scene of the famous riots of 1858-59, which gave the first popular impulse to the "ritualistic" movement, and out into wide Commercial-rd, the boundary of "Jack's" dominion, beyond which again lie the bustling

"Yiddisher' quarter of White-chapel and the swarming squalor of Spitalfields.

Reading Rooms.—AMERICAN EXCHANGE AND READING ROOMS, 449, Strand.—Terms : 5s. per month (or less term); £2 a year. The largest collection of American newspapers on this side the Atlantic (*and see* UNITED STATES).

DEACON'S INDIAN & COLONIAL ROOMS, 154, Leadenhall-st. — Terms : Open free for the use of the customers of the firm. Strangers pay 30s. per annum. The proprietors, Messrs. Samuel Deacon and Co., act as agents for numerous English, Colonial, and Foreign papers, copies of which are filed by them, and they receive advertisements for the same. Established in 1822, and carried on uninterruptedly to the present time.

SEAMEN'S CHRISTIAN FRIEND SOCIETY'S SAILORS' READING ROOMS, 215, St. George's-st, London Docks, E.—Free.

Record Office, Fetter - la, Fleet-st (Map 7).—Open daily. Hours 10 to 4, Sat. 10 to 2, except Sun., Christmas Day to New Year's Day inclusive, Good Friday and the Sat. following, Easter Mon. and Tu., Whit Mon. and Tu., Her Majesty's Birthday and Coronation Day, and days appointed for public fasts, &c.—Collection of Manuscripts, &c., including Domesday Book. With the exception of the search-rooms the building is not generally open to inspection. The search-rooms are approached from the entrance in Fetter-la. The visitor, on entering the building, faces a bust of Lord Langdale, "first statutory keeper of the Rolls," and, taking the passage to the right, will find a book in which it is necessary to inscribe name and address. Just beyond this, to the left, is the entrance to the search-rooms. Each searcher is to write his name and address daily in the attendance-book. Searchers are not allowed to inspect any documents upon which restrictions are placed, without obtaining permission of the department to which they appertain. The designation of each record required is to be written by the searcher on a separate ticket, unless it extends to more than one part of a roll or volume, in which case the several parts or volumes may be asked for

on a single ticket. Each searcher is allowed to have three documents, books, rolls, or parts of rolls at a time. The officer has power to increase, at his discretion, the number. Documents are not to be taken into the search-rooms unless stamped. A searcher may take notes or a full copy of any record, and examine the same with the record ; but no officer may examine, correct, or certify such copy or extracts. No officer is allowed to act as a record agent, or to make a search or copy for his own profit. Tracings are not allowed without permission. Office copies are to be made and delivered according to priority of application, except in special cases. Fees are to be paid in advance, together with the expenses of the officer on attendances. No mark in pencil or ink, or otherwise, is permitted to be made on any record, document, or book ; and any searcher damaging a record with ink will be deprived of the privilege of using ink in future, unless by permission of the Master of the Rolls, in writing. The paper on which a searcher is writing must not be placed on any record or book, nor pens containing ink on the desks or tables. Records, documents, books, or other articles belonging to the Public Record Office, are not to be taken out of the search-rooms. Searchers are to replace the calendars or indexes which they have been using, and to return the records, documents, and books they have received to the officers.

TABLE OF FEES.—For authenticated copies per folio of seventy-two words : Documents to the end of the reign of George II., 1s. Documents after the reign of George II., 6d. Authenticated copies of plans, drawings, &c., per hour, 2s. 6d. Attendance at either House of Parliament to be sworn, £1 1s. Attendance at either House of Parliament, or elsewhere, to give evidence, or with ten records or less number, per diem, £2 2s. For each additional record each day, 2s. Attendance on the Master of the Rolls as a Vacatur, £1 1s. Attendance to receive mortgage-money, 5s. Attendance on payment of mortgage-money, 10s. 6d. There is a " Handbook of the Public Records" by F. S. Thomas, Secretary of the Public Records, published by Eyre and Spottiswoode. NEAREST *Ry. Stns.*, Blackfriars

(Dis.), Farringdon-st (Met.), Ludgate-hill (L. C. & D.); *Omnibus Rtes.*, Fleet-st, Holborn, Chancery-la, and Farringdon-st ; *Cab Ranks*, Farringdon-st and Holborn.

Reform Club, 104, Pall Mall.—Is instituted for the purpose of promoting the social intercourse of the Reformers of the United Kingdom. Candidates must be Reformers and socially eligible. Entrance fee, £40 ; subscription, £10 10s.

Regent Circus (Map 6).—A name given at the first formation of Regent-st to two different sites at the opposite ends of that thoroughfare : the one where it crosses Oxford-st, the other its point of intersection with Piccadilly. The eternal fitness of things has by this time vindicated itself, and the two circuses are known respectively as Regent and Piccadilly Circus. NEAREST *Ry. Stns.*, Charing ✠ (S.E. & Dis.); *Omnibus Rtes.*, Piccadilly, Haymarket, and Regent-st ; *Cab Rank*, Haymarket.

Regent's Park (Map 2) is nearly three miles round, but its space is a good deal taken up by the grounds of the Zoological and Botanical Societies, the Baptist College, and sundry private villas. It affords a pretty drive, and is surrounded by terraces of good but rather expensive houses, but is quite outside the fashionable world. It is a great place for skating. A band plays near the broad walk on Sunday in the summer, and a vast amount of cricket of a homely class enlivens the northern portion of the park on Saturday afternoons. NEAREST *Ry. Stns.*, Portland-road and St. John's Wood-rd (Met.) ; *Omnibus Rtes.*, Marylebone-rd, Albany-st, and Park-rd; *Cab Ranks*, Zoological Gns, York and Albany, St. John's Wood Chapel, and Portland-rd.

Regent Street (Map 6) was planned and built by Nash in 1813, and has something of that uniformity of design which is by some considered the highest beauty of street architecture. Viewed from this standpoint it is the handsomest street in London, as it is certainly, with the one exception of Portland-pl, the broadest. Foreign visitors, however, will probably not consider that this is very much to say on either head. Starting from the south end of Portland-pl it crosses Oxford-st, and runs for some distance in an almost straight line until it reaches Vigo-st. Here begins the bold curve known as the Quadrant, each side of which in its early days formed an arcade. The interception of light caused by this arrangement, and the too convenient shelter it afforded for undesirable company, caused the removal of these structures many years ago, and the Quadrant no longer bears any distinctive title, the houses being simply numbered into Regent-st, which at its south-eastern end takes a short turn to the right, opening out a view of the towers of the new Palace at Westminster, broken by the Guards' Memorial and the Duke of York's Column. From this point Regent-st, crossing Piccadilly and the Circus, is continued down a sharpish incline by Waterloo-pl past Pall Mall to the steps leading to St. James's-pk. No thoroughfare in London is more thronged during the season, or presents a gayer aspect. In the busiest time of the afternoon, from four to six, two great tides of carriages ebb and flow, north and south, east and west, along and across the broad track of Regent-street. Pedestrians of every class, from the fashionable lounger to the street Arab; from the duchess to the work-girl; from the bewigged and padded *roué* to the bright and rosy boy fresh from school; from the quietly-dressed English gentleman to the flashily-arrayed foreign count of doubtful antecedents; from the *prima donna assoluta* to the "lion comique"; from the county magnate to the shoddy millionaire, surge and jostle along the crowded footway. As is the case with the other great thoroughfares in London Regent-st has its favourite side, and although some of the handsomest and most attractive shops, even in this street of tradesmen's palaces, are on the western side, it is comparatively deserted by passengers, as are the southern sides of Oxford-st and Piccadilly, the western side of St. James's-st, and the sunny north side of Pall Mall. Regent-st is not distinguished for public buildings: Langham Church, with its singularly sharp pointed extinguisher spire, at the extreme north end; Hanover Chapel, close to Hanover-st; and Archbishop Tenison's Chapel, opposite New Burlington-st, are all that it is necessary to mention. The principal places of

public amusement are St. George's Hall and St. James's Hall.

Registers of Births, Marriages, and Deaths are

now kept at Somerset House (*which see*).

Restaurants.—A very few years ago the expectant diner, who required, in the public rooms of London, something better than a cut off the joint, or a chop or steak, would have had but a limited number of tables at his command. A really good dinner was almost entirely confined to the regions of club-land, with one or two exceptions, respectable restaurants, to which a lady could be taken, may be said hardly to have existed at all. Artful seekers after surreptitious good dinners, who knew their London well, certainly had some foreign houses in the back settlements of Soho or of Leicester-square, to which they pinned their faith, but the restaurant, as it has been for many years understood in Paris, practically had no place in London. Time, which has changed the London which some of us knew, as it has changed most of the habits of society, has altered all this. It is probably true that, even now, it is impossible to dine in public in London as well as that important ceremony can be performed in Paris. We have still no Café Riche or Café Anglais. The Maison Dorée of London that shall compare with that gilded and delightful, but all too expensive show in Paris, has still to be organised. But so much has been done in twenty years, that those among us who are still respectably young, may look forward to the day when the glories—and the prices—of the Boulevard des Italiens may be ours. However that may be, one thing is certain; that if you know where to go, and how to arrange your campaign, you can dine as well in London, in all styles and at all prices, as any reasonable *gourmet* can wish. Whether the hungry man or woman choose to dine *à la carte* or on the *table d'hôte* system, he or she must be difficult to please if London cannot produce something satisfactory. All that we propose to attempt in this article is to give some guide to the gastronomic chart of London. To box the entire compass would be impossible in the space at our

command, and we must still leave whole continents to the curious explorer. If any *table d'hôte* Stanley, or *à la carte* Cameron, will communicate their future discoveries to us, the compilers of the DICTIONARY will do their best in future editions to keep the public properly posted on this most important subject.

Perhaps the oldest of the real restaurants in London is Verrey's, in Regent-st, which still holds a first-class position among the *à la carte* houses. Somewhat in the line of Verrey's, though on a larger scale, is Nicols's, Café Royal, 68, Regent-st. At both these houses, people who know how to order their dinners will be thoroughly well served. It should be noted that the visitor who wishes to dine well at the Café Royal, or to dine in a private room, should go upstairs. Then there are to be noted the recently re-constructed and palatial Holborn Restaurant, 218, High Holborn; Spiers and Pond's, Criterion, Piccadilly; and the St. James's Hall, Regent-st and Piccadilly. At the Holborn, the *table d'hôte* dinner (3s. 6d.), which consists of a judicious mixture of the French and English styles of cookery, is served daily from 5.30 to 8.30, and the diner has, besides an excellent meal, the opportunity of listening to a selection of first-class instrumental music, which is performed during the *table d'hôte* hours by an efficient band. Private parties can also dine comfortably and conveniently in the other departments of the Holborn. At the Criterion the *table d'hôte* is served daily in the Grand Hall from 5.30 to 8 (on Sun. at 6), at 3s. 6d.; the French dinner at the same hours, in the West Room, is 5s. per head. There is also a "joint" dinner at 2s. 6d. in the room on the right of the Piccadilly entrance hall. The *'able d'hôte* at the St. James's Hall is served from 5.30 to 9, and the price is 3s. 6d., and for the French dinner 5s. The Burlington, at the corner of New Burlington-st and Regent-st, is also well known for its excellent set dinners at 5s., 7s. 6d., and 10s. 6d. The *table d'hôte* dinner at the Hotel Continental (1, Regent-st) is good though undeniably expensive, and the same remark applies to that at the Bristol in Burlington-gdns. There is also a varied choice at the Café Monico, Tichborne-st, Haymarket; and at

Gatti's, 436, Strand. Bertram and Roberts, at the Royal Aquarium, provide two excellent dinners, one at 3s. 6d. and the other at 5s. The restaurant can now be entered without going through the Aquarium, to which diners at the *table d'hôte* have the right of free entrance afterwards. The "Piccadilly," at the corner of Shaftesbury Avenue, has been opened recently. At the following, among other hotels, strangers (even if not staying in the house) can also dine in the coffee-rooms, or at the *table d'hôte* dinners: the Langham, 6s., at 6 o'clock; the First Avenue Hotel, and the Hotels Métropole and Victoria, Northumberland-avenue, 5s., from 6 to 8 o'clock; Grand Hotel, 5s., at 6 o'clock; Inns of Court Hotel, 5s., at 6 o'clock; the Midland (6 and 7.30; on Sat. and Sun. at 6 only), at 5s.; and for a quieter dinner, Dieudonné's, in Ryder-st, at 6.30, for 4s., is well spoken of. It is worth a pilgrimage to the City to taste turtle soup and "fixings" at the "Ship and Turtle," Leadenhall-st. Among other dinners may be mentioned the *table d'hôte* at the Gaiety Restaurant of Messrs. Spiers and Pond, adjoining the Gaiety Theatre (3s. 6d.); of the "Cavour," in Leicester-sq (3s.); of the "Horse-shoe," Tottenham-ct-rd (2s. 6d.). The Caledonian Hotel, Robert-st, Adelphi, also offers a 2s. 6d. *table d'hôte* at 6 o'clock. Houses of a foreign type are very numerous, and of every order of merit; Kettner's, Church-st, Soho (*table d'hôte*, also *à la carte*), and Previtali's, 14, Arundel-st, Coventry-st (excellent *table d'hôte*, from 6 o'clock, at 3s. 6d.), enjoy as good a reputation as any. The "Globe," 4, Coventry-st; the "Solferino," 7, Rupert-st; and the Sablonière Hotel, Leicester-sq, are alternative foreign houses, where a dinner may be had at moderate prices. At Romano's Vaudeville Restaurant, 399, Strand, a well-cooked dinner and good wine may be relied on. Here also are private rooms. At the Adelphi Restaurant, 68, Strand, will also be found good foreign cooking and excellent wines at very reasonable prices, as well as a grill. Pagani's Restaurant, 48 and 54, Great Portland-st, W., is very well spoken of. Among the latest

additions to the restaurants of London is that on the Duval system, opposite the Royal Courts of Justice in the Strand, which was opened in the spring of 1886, by Messrs. Spiers and Pond. The old-fashioned fish and joint dinner still holds its own here and there. The best houses of this class are the "Albion," Russell-street (opposite Drury Lane Theatre), which passed into the hands of Messrs. Spiers and Pond at the end of 1885; Simpson's, Strand; and the "Rainbow," Fleet-street. The average charge for joint, cheese, &c., may be taken at 2s. 6d., with fish usually 1s. extra. "The King's Head," 265, Strand, for many years well known as "Carr's," has the credit of having been the first house in London to recognise the public want of a cheap bottle of claret. It must be specially remembered, in ordering dinner *à la carte* at the foreign houses, that, as a general rule, "what is enough for one is enough for two." If the waiter, on taking an order for two persons, enquires whether you wish one portion or two, it is certain that one is enough. If the point be not raised by the waiter, the enquiry should be made by the diner.

It will be gathered from the foregoing summary that there are plenty of good dinners to be got in London, but unfortunately there is one point on which the conservatism of London caterers has not yet given way. The prices charged for wines—except so far as regards the light kinds of claret, &c.—are uniformly absurd. It seems preposterous that a man should be charged twice as much for a bottle of champagne at a restaurant as it will cost him if supplied by his own wine merchant. Such matters as interest of money, &c., are always brought forward in justification of exorbitant prices for wines. When you come to vintage clarets and old bottled ports, this is no doubt all very well; but when you are called upon to pay 10s. or 12s. a bottle for wine bottled a year or two ago, it would certainly seem as if there must be something wrong somewhere. — (*Also see* CHOPS AND STEAKS, DINNERS, FISH DINNERS *and* VEGETARIAN RESTAURANTS.)

Riding Horses and Schools.—One of the best

establishments in town is that of Mr. Haines (late Allen), at 70, Seymour-pl, Bryanston-sq, which has as good a covered school as can be found. In this case, as in all matters of education, much must depend upon circumstances; but it may be roughly said that two dozen lessons from a competent instructor will cost 7 guineas in the school, and 11 guineas on the road. The hire of a riding-horse, like everything else in London, varies almost absurdly according to the time of year; a useful horse, which out of the season can be hired at from 5 to 7 guineas per month, will cost between the middle of April and the middle of July from 10 to 12 guineas. These prices at a first-class house include every charge from corn to shoes.

Roumania.—LEGATION, 50, Grosvenor-gdns, S.W. NEAREST *Ry.Stn.*, Victoria; *Omnibus Rtes.*, Buckingham Palace-rd, Grosvenor-pl, and Victoria-st; *Cab Rank*, Victoria Stn. CONSULATE, 37, Old Jewry, E.C. NEAREST *Ry. Stns.*, Cannon-st (S.E.R.) and Moorgate-st (Met.); *Omnibus Rte.*, Cheapside; *Cab Rank*, Lothbury.

Rowing. — Full particulars about rowing and rowing clubs, canoeing, &c., on the Thames will be found in DICKENS'S DICTIONARY OF THE THAMES. There are also good clubs on the Lea, head-quarters as a rule at Lea-br, either at the "Jolly Anglers," Wicks's, or Green's, and at Verdon's, Upper Clapton. The principal Lea clubs are the Albion, Alexandra, Elvington, Phœnix, and Vesper. Information as to rowing matters may be readily found in all the sporting papers, the reports of races in the *Field* being exceptionally well done. The "Rowing Almanack," an annual published at the *Field* office, is edited by one of the best practical judges of rowing and matters aquatic in England.

Royal Academy of Arts, Burlington House, Piccadilly (Map 6).—The annual exhibition, which is open from the beginning of May to the end of July, and the winter exhibitions of loan pictures, are too well known to require any description here. But it is perhaps not generally known that the interesting collection of pictures presented by Academicians on receiving that distinction, known as the diploma pictures, may be seen daily from 11 till 4 (free). In addition to providing one of the largest picture shows in the world —from the proceeds of which its income is derived—the Royal Academy fulfils important functions as an educational establishment. Teachers and professors of painting, sculpture, architecture, and anatomy are appointed by the academy, and medals and prizes are annually awarded to successful students. NEAREST *Ry. Stns.*, Charing ✠ (S.E.) & St. James's-pk (Dis.); *Omnibus Rte.*, Piccadilly; *Cab Rank*, Piccadilly (Albany).

Honorary Members. — The Archbishop of York, Chaplain ; Rt. Hon. W. E. Gladstone, M.P., Professor of Ancient History ; the Dean of Christchurch, Professor of Ancient Literature; Robt. Browning, Secretary for Foreign Correspondence ; Sir C. T. Newton, K.C.B., Antiquary.

Honorary Retired Academicians.—Cope, C. W. ; Herbert, John Rogers; Pickersgill, F. R. ; Redgrave, Richard, C.B. ; Richmond, George.

Honorary Foreign Academicians. — Gérôme, Jean Léon ; Guillaume, Claude Jean Baptiste Eugène; Henriquel-Dupont, Louis Pierre ; Knaus, L. ; Meissonier, Jean Louis.

Academicians.—Alma-Tadema, Lawrence ; Armitage, Edward ; Armstead, Henry Hugh ; Barlow, Thomas Oldham ; Boehm, Joseph Edgar ; Calderon, Philip H., Keeper and Trustee ; Cole, Vicat ; Cooper, Thomas Sidney ; Davis, Henry W. B. ; Dobson, William Charles Thomas ; Faed, Thomas ; Fildes, S. Luke; Frith, William Powell ; Gilbert, Sir John ; Goodall, Frederick ; Graham, Peter ; Hodgson, John Evan, Librarian ; Holl, Frank; Hook, James Clarke; Horsley, John Callcott, Treasurer and Trustee ; Leslie, George Dunlop; Leighton, Sir Fredk., Bart., President and Trustee ; Long, Edwin ; Marks, Henry Stacy; Marshall, William Calder; Millais, Sir John Everett, Bart., Trustee ; Orchardson, William Quiller ; Ouless, Walter William, Auditor ; Pearson, John Loughborough ; Pettie, John; Poynter, Edward J. ; Riviere, Briton ; Sant, James ; Shaw, Richard Norman ; Stocks, Lumb ; Stone, Marcus ; Thornycroft, W. Hamo ; Waterhouse, Alfred, Auditor ; Watts, George

Frederick ; Wells, Henry Tanworth, Auditor; Woolner, Thomas; Yeames, William Fredk.

Associates.—Aitchison, George ; Birch, Charles Bell ; Blomfield, Arthur William ; Boughton, George H.; Brett, John ; Brock, Thomas ; Burgess, John Bagnold ; Burne-Jones, E.; Crofts, Ernest ; Crowe, Eyre ; Dicksee, Frank; Ford, E. Onslow ; Gilbert, Alfred ; Gow, Andrew C.; Gregory, E. J. ; Herkomer, Hubert ; Hunter, Colin ; Leader, Benj. W. ; Lucas, J. Seymour ; Macbeth, R. W. ; McWhirter, John; Moore, Henry; Morris, Philip Richard; Prinsep, Valentine Cameron ; Richmond, Wm. B. ; Stacpoole, Frederick ; Storey, George Adolphus ; Waterhouse, John Wm. ; Woods, Henry.

Honorary Retired Associates. —Le Jeune, H. ; Nicol, E. ; Woodington, W. F.

Professors. — Of Painting, J. E. Hodgson, R.A. Of Sculpture, vacant. Of Architecture, G. Aitchison, A. R. A. Of Anatomy, John Marshall, F.R.S. Of Chemistry, A. H. Church, M.A.

Secretary.—Frederick A. Eaton, M.A.

Royal Academy of Music.
—(*See* MUSIC, ROYAL ACADEMY OF.)

Royal Botanic Society.—
(*See* BOTANIC SOCIETY.)

Royal College of Surgeons.—(*See* COLLEGE OF SURGEONS.)

Royal Colonial Institute.
—(*See* COLONIAL INSTITUTE.)

Royal Courts of Justice
(Map 7).—(*See* LAW COURTS.)

Royal Exchange, The
(Map 8), was opened on January 1st, 1845. The old Exchange, which occupied the same site, was built after the Great Fire, and again suffered from the same element in 1838. The first Exchange was opened in 1579 by Queen Elizabeth, who, by her herald, declared the house to be "The Royal Exchange." Sir Thomas Gresham introduced exchanges into England, but they had been popular in most of the commercial cities of Italy, Germany, and the Netherlands, many years previous to their adoption here. The present edifice is almost an oblong, and encloses a roofed-in courtyard, round which

is an ambulatory 170 ft. long by 113 ft. In the centre of the open space is a marble statue of Her Majesty, and about this image of the Queen merchants and traders meet at certain hours to transact business and discuss matters affecting finance and commerce. The ceiling of the ambulatory is worth looking at. It is divided by beams and panelling, and lavishly decorated. In the four angles are the arms of Edward the Confessor, Edward III., Queen Elizabeth, and Charles II. Busts and armorial bearings of eminent persons abound, including those of Whittington and Gresham. The west front, which is the principal entrance, is by far the most impressive. It consists of a Corinthian portico, with columns upwards of 40 feet high. On the frieze is an inscription in Latin, explaining that the Exchange was founded in the thirteenth year of Queen Elizabeth, and restored in the seventh of Queen Victoria. The apartments above the ambulatory are occupied, for the most part, by large insurance companies, and by "Lloyd's" rooms.—(*See* LLOYD'S.) NEAREST *Ry Stns.*, Mansion House (Dis.), Moorgate-st (Met.), and Cannon-st (S.E.) ; *Omnibus Rte.*, Bank ; *Cab Rank*, Bartholomew-la.

Royal Horticultural Society.—(*See* HORTICULTURAL SOCIETY.)

Royal Institution, 21, Albemarle-st, Piccadilly.—*Subscription.* Members, entrance fee, £5 5s. ; first annual subscription, £5 5s. ; or £63 in lieu of all payments. Annual subscribers pay £5 5s., and £1 1s. as entrance fee ; they are admitted to lectures, libraries, and newspaper rooms, but not to evening meetings. Members have the right of introducing two friends by ticket to evening meetings ; tickets for lectures are issued to their wives, sons, and daughters on payment of £1 1s. for all courses of lectures, and 10s. for a single course, and to subscribers, on payment of £2 2s. for all courses of lectures, and £1 1s. or 10s. 6d. for single courses. *Objects:* To promote scientific and literary research; to teach the principles of induction and experimental science ; to exhibit the application of these principles to the various arts of life ; and to afford opportunities for study. The Institution comprises

two laboratories for the promotion of chemical and physical science, a model room, a library of about 50,000 volumes, a reading room for study, newspaper room, &c. The weekly meetings are held every Friday during the session. NEAREST *Ry. Stns.*, Charing ✠ (S.E. & Dis.) and St. James's-pk (Dis.); *Omnibus Rtes.*, Piccadilly and Bond-st; *Cab Ranks*, St. James's-st and Piccadilly.

Royal London Yacht Club, 2, Saville-row, W.—The object of this club is the improvement of yacht building and the encouragement of yacht sailing. The election is by ballot, one black ball in four excludes. The officers are commodore, vice-commodore, rear-commodore, and cup-bearer. The general affairs of the club are managed by a committee consisting of the flag officers, cup-bearer, and not exceeding twenty-four members, of whom three shall form a quorum. No entrance fee; subscription, £6 6s. Burgee, blue with crown over City arms; ensign, blue with crown over City arms in the fly.

Royal Naval School, New ✠.—This school was established for the sons of officers in the Royal Navy and Marines of ward-room rank, and it is the only one in the United Kingdom where the sons of naval men can obtain a good education at *cost price*. Even this charge is reduced (when the funds of the school permit) in the case of officers who are very badly off. Sons of military men and of civilians are admitted on remunerative terms, in limited numbers. The following is the scale of charges for boarders: for sons of naval and Marine officers of ward-room rank, £52 10s.; for all others, £73 10s. per annum. For day scholars under 12 years of age, £15 15s.; over 12 years of age, £18 18s. per annum. It is important to note that 4 nominations for Naval Cadetships, and 1 nomination for an Assistant Clerkship, R.N., are given yearly, by the Lords of the Admiralty, and awarded at the discretion of the Council. The education given is of the usual public school character, boys being prepared for the Universities, for the Naval, Military, E. I. Civil Services, &c. NEAREST *Ry. Stns.*, New ✠ (L. B. & S. C. and S.E.). Trains from Charing ✠ every 20 minutes.

Head Master and Chaplain, Rev. James White, M.A.; Secretary, Lieut. Henry Chamberlain, R.N.; Office, 32, Sackville-st, Piccadilly.

Royal Palace of Justice (Map 7).—(*See* LAW COURTS.)

Royal Society of British Artists.—(*See* SOCIETY OF BRITISH ARTISTS.)

Royal Society (The), Burlington House, Piccadilly.—This, the leading scientific society of Europe, was incorporated by Charles II. in 1662. The Society originally occupied a house in Crane-ct, Fleet-st. In 1780, by grant from George III., it was lodged in Somerset House; a move was made to Burlington House in 1857, and in 1873 the Fellows took possession of their present convenient quarters in the east wing. Meetings for reading and discussion of scientific papers take place weekly, from the third Thurs. in November to the third Thurs. in June, at 4.30 p.m., the hour of meeting having been changed from the time-honoured 8.30 p.m., in April, 1882. The President is at present Professor George Gabriel Stokes, M.A., D.C.L., LL.D. (M.P. for Cambridge University), and the number of Fellows, including 50 foreign, is 527. Candidates for the fellowship have to be proposed and recommended by a certificate in writing, the blank forms for which are granted only on the personal or written request of a Fellow of the society. After this is filled up it must be signed by six or more Fellows, of whom three at least must have personal knowledge of the candidate. Certificates for any session are not received after the first Thurs. in March. The annual subscription is £3. The rooms of the society contain numerous busts of past presidents, and a number of portraits, some of great interest, of eminent scientific men. Among these may be mentioned a curious head of Copernicus on panel, by Lorman of Berlin, in the library; a very quaint Tycho Brahe by Mierevelt; and Galileo after Sustermans, in the anteroom. Over the President's chair in the meeting-room is a fine portrait of Newton by Vanderbank. The collection further includes good specimens of Kneller, Lawrence, Lely, and Reynolds. On the stairs is a bust of Charles II. by Nollekens. The library contains about

40,000 vols. of scientific books, including, of course, a complete set of the Philosophical Transactions, the first volume of which was published in 1666. In the library is preserved an interesting collection of relics of Sir Isaac Newton, such as the original MS. of the "Principia;" a lock of the philosopher's hair; his watch; a plaster cast of his face, which belonged to Roubilliac; the first reflecting telescope made by Newton's own hands in 1671; and a dial cut by him, when a boy, in the wall of the house in which he was born, at Woolsthorpe. The popular idea that men of science are not as a rule men of business is oddly confirmed by an order, preserved here, addressed by Newton to Dr. John Francis Ffouquier to invest money in the South Sea Bubble; and to make the matter worse, the day selected for the speculation was the 27th July, 1720, when South Sea Stock was almost, if not quite, at its very highest price. Sundry pieces of the Woolsthorpe apple-tree are also shown. The visitor may please himself on the question of believing them to be pieces of the tree from which the celebrated apple did, or did not, fall. Permission to view the Society's rooms is granted to visitors provided with a Fellow's order. Bishop Sprat's history, published 1667; Doctor Birch's history, published in 1756–7; and that of Mr. Weld, published by Parker in 1848, contain full information as to the history, &c., of the Royal Society NEAREST *Ry. Stns.*, Charing ✠ (S.E. & Dis.); *Omnibus Rtes.*, Piccadilly and Bond-st; *Cab Rank*, Piccadilly (The Albany).

Royal Thames Yacht Club, 7, Albemarle-st, W. Commodore, H.R.H the Prince of Wales.—The object of this club is the encouragement of yacht building and sailing on the river Thames, and the funds are appropriated, after payment of necessary current expenses, to the purchase of prizes to be sailed for. The officers are a commodore, vice-commodore, rear-commodore, three trustees, secretary, cup-bearer, and two auditors. The secretary is a paid officer. The subscriptions are, for members who have joined the club since the 1st May, 1874, £7 7s., except in the case of a candidate owning, on being elected a member, a yacht of or exceeding the lowest tonnage classed in the club matches, whose subscription shall be £5 5s. The entrance fee is £21, except in the case of yacht owners, who only pay £15 15s. The election is by ballot in committee; eight members form a quorum, and one black ball in four excludes. The general committee of management consists of twenty-one members exclusive of the *ex officio* members, five to form a quorum. The ensign and burgee of the club are thus defined by Rule 21: The club flag shall be the blue ensign of Her Majesty's fleet, agreeably to a warrant dated 24th July, 1848, granted to the club by the Lords Commissioners of the Admiralty; the burgee shall be blue with a white cross, and a red crown in the centre; the hoist of the ensign to be two-thirds of the length, the burgee to be always hoisted with the club ensign.

Royalty Theatre, Dean-st, Soho —(Map 7). — Formerly known as the "Soho," and earlier still as "Miss Kelly's." Rebuilt in 1882-83. NEAREST *Ry. Stns.*, Charing ✠ (S.E. & Dis.) and Portland - rd ; *Omnibus Rtes.*, Oxford - st, Regent - st, and St. Martin's-la ; *Cab Rank,* Dean-st.

Russia.—EMBASSY, Chesham House, Belgrave-sq. NEAREST *Ry. Stns.*, Victoria (Dis. & L.C. & D.); *Omnibus Rtes.*, Knightsbridge, Sloane-st, and Grosvenor-pl ; *Cab Rank,* Pont-st. CONSULATE, 17, Winchester-st, E.C. NEAREST *Ry. Stns.*, Broad-st (N.L.) and Moorgate - st (Met.); *Omnibus Rtes.*, Bishopsgate-st and Moorgate-st ; *Cab Rank,* Broad-st Stn.

Sadler's Wells Theatre. —(*See* NEW SADLER'S WELLS.)

St. George's Club, 4, Hanover-sq, W. The club is proprietary and non-political. It was founded with a view of providing a centre where residents in England, Americans, Colonials, and Anglo-Indians, might meet in social intercourse. There are 40 bedrooms for the use of members. Entrance fee, £10 10s ; colonial and foreign members, £5 5s. Subscription, for town members, £8 8s., country members £5 5s., foreign members £2 2s. Application for membership, etc., should be addressed to the secretary.

St. George's Hall, Langham-pl, W. (Map 6).—In this commodious hall are given the entertainments long known as Mr. and Mrs. German Reed's, and now

under the management of Messrs. Alfred Reed and Corney Grain. The performances, as a rule, take place on Mon., Wed., and Fri. evenings at 8, and on Tues., Thurs., and Sat. afternoons at 3. The prices of admission are 1s. and 2s.; Stalls, 3s. and 5s. (*and see* PUBLIC HALLS). NEAREST *Ry. Stn.*, Portland-rd; *Omnibus Rtes.*, Mortimer-st and Oxford-st ; *Cab Rank,* opposite.

St. James's Club, 106, Piccadilly, W.—Ordinary members of this club are elected by ballot, but members of the *corps diplomatique*, of the English diplomatic service, and of the diplomatic establishment of the Foreign Office, may be admitted without ballot, under certain restrictions. The entrance fee is £26 5s. ; the subscription, £11 11s.; and carefully considered reductions are made in the case of members of the English diplomatic service who are employed abroad. The election is by ballot in committee ; "six shall be a quorum, one black ball in nine, if repeated, and two above nine, shall exclude." The club occupies the premises once tenanted by the defunct Coventry Club.

St. James's Hall, entrances in Regent-st and Piccadilly (Map 6). — One of the finest public halls in London. Some of the best concerts in London are given here (*see* CONCERTS) at varying seasons, and in the smaller hall are permanently located the minstrels of Messrs. Moore and Burgess, whose entertainment has for many years been deservedly most popular (*and see* APPENDIX). A good restaurant is attached to the Hall (*see* RESTAURANTS *and* PUBLIC HALLS). NEAREST *Ry. Stns.*, Charing ✠ (S.E. & Dis.) ; *Omnibus Rtes.*, Piccadilly and Regent-st ; *Cab Rank,* Piccadilly.

St. James's Palace (Map 6) is the oldest of the royal palaces in London, but has long since ceased to be used by royalty for any but ceremonial purposes, though custom still recognises it as the nominal head-quarters of English Royalty, and the English court is always diplomatically referred to as the Court of St. James's. NEAREST *Ry. Stn.*, St. James's-pk (Dis.); *Omnibus Rtes.*, Piccadilly, Regent-st, and Strand ; *Cab Rank,* St. James's-st.

St. James's Park (Map 6) joins the south-east corner of the Green-pk, and is little more than an

enclosed garden, nearly half o which is occupied by a shallow piece of water, probably the safest for skating in London. The Mall, a broad walk planted with elms, limes, and planes, runs along the north side, and gets its name from the game formerly played there. On the east side is the parade-ground of the Horse Guards, where the guard is trooped daily at 11 a.m. NEAREST *Ry. Stn.*, St. James's-pk (Dis.); *Omnibus Rtes.*, Regent-st, Parliament-st, and Victoria - st ; *Cab Ranks,* Horse Guards and Trafalgar-sq.

St. James's Street (Map 6).—Although the splendour of the clubs of Pall Mall has eclipsed those of St. James's-st, yet the latter can boast an historical interest all their own. White's was founded in 1730, the Cocoa Tree in 1746, Brooks's in 1764, Arthur's a year later, while of the Pall Mall clubs the oldest, the Guards, did not come into existence until fifty years afterwards, namely, in 1813. The bow window of White's is historical. From it generations of statesmen have calmly surveyed the passing world ; and though coat - collars are not worn high, frilled shirts have been abandoned, and the general style of dress is easier and more comfortable nowadays, yet in other respects the quiet elderly gentlemen who still gaze from the windows of the St. James's club-houses can differ but little from those who looked out a hundred years ago. The house at the corner of Piccadilly, now the Devonshire, was once Crockford's. There are comparatively new clubs in St. James's, but these belong to the new *régime*, and have nothing in common with the quiet and the fogeydom of the old clubs.

St. James's Theatre, King-st, St. James's (Map 6).—At the back of Pall Mall ; built by Braham, the singer. After undergoing many vicissitudes, and remaining almost continuously closed for a very long period, it has been for some years successfully managed by Messrs. Hare and Kendal, by whom it was structurally altered very much for the better. NEAREST *Ry. Stn.*, Westminster-br (Dis.); *Omnibus Rtes.*, Piccadilly, Regent-st, and Strand ; *Cab Rank,* St. James's-st.

St. John of Jerusalem in England (Order of).—

This order was founded about the year 1092, for the maintenance of an hospital at Jerusalem; and, subsequently, for the defence of Christian pilgrims on their journeys to and from the Holy Land. It afterwards became a knightly institution, but ever preserved its hospitals, and cherished the duty of alleviating sickness and suffering. The order was first planted in England in the year 1100, and raised the noble structure which once formed the Priory of Clerkenwell, of which the gateway now alone remains to attest the importance of the chief house of the order in England. The order of St. John held high place in this country until the year 1540, when it was despoiled, suppressed, and its property confiscated by Act of Parliament. In 1557 it was restored by Royal Charter, and much of its possessions re-granted; but only to be again confiscated within the subsequent two years by a second statute, which did not, however, enact the re-suppression of the fraternity. Still, with the loss of possessions, and the withdrawal of most of its members to Malta—then the sovereign seat of the order—it became practically dormant in England. Many fluctuations have marked the fortunes of an institution which played a prominent part in most of the great events of Europe, until its supreme disaster in the loss of Malta, in 1798, after which the surviving divisions of the order had each to perpetuate an independent existence, and to mark out the course of its own future. It is more than half a century ago that a majority of five of the seven then existing remnants of the institution decreed the revival of the time-honoured branch of the order in England, since which event it has, so far as means permitted, pursued, in spirit, the original purposes of its foundation—the alleviation of the sickness and suffering of the human race. The following are some of the objects which have engaged the attention of the order in England: 1. Providing convalescent patients of hospitals (without distinction of creed) with such nourishing diets as are ordered by the medical officers, so as to aid their return, at the earliest possible time, to the business of life and the support of their families. 2. The institution in England of what is now known as the "National Society for Aid to Sick and Wounded in War." 3. The foundation and maintenance of cottage hospitals and convalescent homes. 4. Providing the means and opportunities for local training of nurses for the sick poor, and founding what is now known as the Metropolitan and National Society for training and supplying such nurses. 5. The promotion of a more intimate acquaintance with the wants of the poor in time of sickness. 6. The establishment of ambulance litters, for the conveyance of sick and injured persons in the colliery and mining districts, and in all large railway and other public departments and in towns, as a means of preventing much aggravation of human suffering. 7. The award of silver and bronze medals, and certificates of honour, for special services on land in the cause of humanity. 8. The initiation and organisation, during the Turco-Servian war, of the "Eastern War Sick and Wounded Relief Fund." 9. The "British Ophthalmic Hospital at Jerusalem," established in the Holy City under the management of the Chapter, for the alleviation of the terrible sufferings caused by diseases of the eye and ignorance of its treatment. 10. The institution of the "St. John Ambulance Association" for instruction in the preliminary treatment of the injured in peace and the wounded in war. Although initiated less than eight years ago the movement has already attained very great success. Upwards of 200 local centres have already been formed in important towns and districts in all parts of the kingdom, and many others are in course of formation. Among the more notable classes are those for the instruction of the Royal Navy; Royal Military College, Sandhurst; Guards; Royal Artillery, and other regiments; Metropolitan and City Police; County Constabulary; Metropolitan and Provincial Fire Brigades; Royal Naval Artillery Volunteers; the War Office; Admiralty; Somerset House, and other Government departments; the Customs House; East and West India Docks; Surrey Commercial Docks; Victoria Docks; Mercantile Marine; Great Northern, London and North Western, Great Eastern, South Eastern, and other railway companies' *employés*, and numerous public and private institutions. Her Majesty the Queen has been graciously pleased to make donations each of £25, to the Shetland Islands Centre and to No. III. District of the Metropolitan Centre, of both of which H.R.H. Princess Beatrice is the President. T.R.H. the Duke of Edinburgh, the Duke of Connaught, H.S.H. the Duke of Teck, H.S.H. Prince Edward of Saxe-Weimar, also hold the office of President at various country centres. Certificates have more than once been presented to the Windsor classes by H.R.H. Princess Christian, and at Kensington and Richmond by H.R.H. the Duchess of Teck. Princess Christian had not only been awarded both the preliminary and nursing certificates after passing the prescribed examinations, but has translated from the German a course of lectures by Professor Esmarch on "First Aid to the Injured," copies of which can be obtained at St. John's Gate. The Order of St. John has no connection whatever with any of the associations or fraternities similar or not in name to its own, which have been formed for the promotion of charitable or otherwise benevolent purposes, nor is it confined to any sect or party, or to any religious denomination; but it is thoroughly universal, embracing among its members and associates those who, in the spirit of our Divine Master, are willing to devote a portion of their time or their means to the help of the suffering and the sick, and to labour earnestly *Pro Utilitate Hominum*. Communications may be addressed to the Secretary of the Order of St. John, St. John's Gate, Clerkenwell.

St. Pancras (Map 3), the

terminus of the Midland Railway, is, with the exception of the new Gt. Eastern terminus at Liverpool-st, the largest and handsomest railway-station in England. It is built of iron and glass, in a single span. The girders of the roof do not, as in most cases, extend from side to side, supported by abutments at either end, like the girders of an ordinary house, but spring straight from the ground in pairs from either side of the building, the upper ends curving over and meeting in the middle. Each girder is broad at the base, tapering gradually as it bends over to meet its fellow, and the whole station is thus simply a vast roof springing directly from the ground, the brick walls at the side being in fact mere screens of no structural value in the way of support. This peculiar form of girder, giving the arch of the roof a somewhat pointed instead of the usual rounded contour, has a quaintly Gothic effect, which harmonises well with the gorgeous architecture of the huge hotel (*see* HOTELS) which forms the Euston-rd façade of the structure. The station entrance for cabs and carriages is on the west side of the station from Euston-rd, whence also on the east side a subway for foot passengers only leads at a sharp incline up to the end platform, connecting the departure with the arrival side. The booking offices are all on the west side, opening direct from the carriage way. NEAREST *Ry. Stns.*, King's ✠ (Met. & G.N.); *Omnibus Rte.*, Euston-rd; *Cab Fares*, to Bank, 1/6 ; to Charing ✠, 1/-.

St. Paul's Cathedral (Map 8), the most conspicuous building in London, takes rank amongst the world's largest churches. Tradition has it that the original building was erected in the second century, that it was destroyed during the reign of the Roman Emperor Diocletian, rebuilt subsequently, and again desecrated by the Saxons, who held impious revelry within its walls. William the Conqueror gave a charter which conferred the property in perpetuity upon the cathedral, and solemnly cursed all who should attempt to diminish the property. In 1083, and again in 1137, St. Paul's suffered from fire, and in the Great Fire was once more totally destroyed. In 1673 Sir Christopher Wren was employed to build a new edifice, and years later the present St. Paul's was completed. The upper portion is of a composite order of architecture ; the lower, Corinthian. Built in the form of a cross, an immense dome rises on 8 arches over the centre. Over the dome is a gallery, and above the gallery is the ball and the gilded cross, the top of which is 404 feet from the pavement beneath. The most attractive views of the cathedral are obtained from the river and from the west front, in Ludgate-hill, whence

admission is to be gained after ascending a flight of stone steps. The west front opens at once into the nave. Immediately on the right is a recess, not unlike the private chapels in Westminster Abbey, containing a monument to the great Duke of Wellington. A figure representing Arthur Wellesley lies under a canopy of bronze, and the names of his many victories are sculptured below. On the other side of the nave, to the left, is a military memorial ; the colours of the 58th Regiment hang over it, and a marble bas relief in commemoration of the members of the Cavalry Brigade who fell in the Crimea. A little farther on are two brass tablets, one on each side of the black doors which are sacred to the memory of the two Viscounts Melbourne. These tablets bear the details of the loss of H.M.S. *Captain*, September 7, 1870. An illustration of the ship is engraved on the brass, and the names of the officers and men who perished with her. Although there is no dearth of "storied urn and animated bust" in St. Paul's, it must be confessed that the general impression produced by the inside of the cathedral is a gloomy one. The interior is chiefly remarkable for its dearth of stained glass, and the few frescoes which decorate the supporting arches of the dome only serve to illustrate the poverty of the cathedral in artistic effort. It is impossible, too, to forget that St. Paul's is a show, despite the notices displayed everywhere which beseech the visitor to remember the sacred character of the edifice. Nothing of any passing interest is to be seen in the nave, but the active visitor may, after paying a fee of 6d., ascend a winding staircase to the whispering-gallery, which runs round the base of the dome. As this is perfectly circular, a whisper may be heard round the wall from one side to the other, and an intelligent attendant will explain certain experiences of his own anent this curiosity in architecture. On a level with the whispering gallery will be found the clock and the canon's library. The latter is not particularly interesting, but the clock is worth a visit, though we do not advise persons with delicate ears to approach it about the time of its striking the hour. Above is a stone gallery, whence, if the day

be clear, a fair view of London and the Thames may be obtained ; and if the visitor be still more ambitious, he may ascend more winding stairs, and reach the golden gallery far above the dome. Thence he may climb yet more steps until he reach the ball, an expedition which may be undertaken once in youth, but hardly again. The ball is hollow. It is large enough to hold several people, and a visit to it entails the payment of another fee. As fine a view, however, as is necessary for ordinary people may be obtained as already suggested from the golden gallery, which is, by the way, no inconsiderable journey from the nave. A still further fee of sixpence will admit the visitor to the crypt, which lies underneath the nave and chapel. Behind an iron railing, which however, may be entered, stands a porphyry sarcophagus, in which are the mortal remains of the Duke of Wellington. Farther on is the sarcophagus containing the body of Nelson, and this lies exactly under the dome. To the left of Nelson is Collingwood, and to the right is Cornwallis. At the end of the crypt is the funeral car on which Wellington's coffin was carried to its last resting-place. The car was made from the cannon taken by the Duke from the French, and cost some £13,000 to construct. Just outside the railing is a granite tomb, under which is buried Picton, who fell at Waterloo, and on the south side of the altar is the painters' corner. Here are buried Dance, West, Wren, Sir T. Lawrence, Turner, James Barry, Sir Joshua Reynolds, Opie, J. Dawe, Fuseli, Rennie, Cockerell, Cruikshank, and Sir Edwin Landseer. Services are held daily in the cathedral, to which the public are admitted. During these hours no one is allowed to visit the sights. NEAREST *Ry. Stns.*, Mansion House or Blackfriars (Dis.), and Ludgate-hill (L. C. & D.); *Omnibus Rtes.*, Newgate-st, Ludgate-hill, and Aldersgate-st ; *Cab Rank*, St. Paul's Churchyard.

St. Paul's Churchyard.— In olden time St. Paul's Churchyard was one of the great business centres of London. About the church men met to discuss the doings of the day, the last piece of news from Flanders, France, or Spain, or the rumours from the country. Here the citizens gathered angrily when there was any talk of an invasion of their cherished liberties, grumbled over a benevolence demanded by his majesty for the pay of the troops engaged in the French war, or jeered at some poor wretch nailed by his ears in the pillory. Here the heralds would proclaim the news of our victories by sea and land; here the public newsmen would read out their budgets; vendors of infallible nostrums would wax eloquent as to the virtues of their wares; and the wives and daughters of the citizens gather to gossip and flirt. It was at once the exchange, the club, and the meeting-place of London. Paul's Cross was the heart of the City; here men threw up their bonnets when they heard of Crecy and of Agincourt; here they listened to the preachings of the first followers of Wycliffe; here they erected their choicest pageants when a new sovereign visited the City for the first time, or brought his new-made spouse to show her to his lieges; and gathered with frowning brows beneath iron caps when London threw in its lot with the Parliament, and the train-bands marched off to fight the King's forces. The business mart of the City lies now in front of the Mansion House, but a great deal of business is still done under the shadow of the Cathedral. On the south side are several very large and important warehouses, while on the north are some of the largest drapers and silk-mercers in the metropolis. St. Paul's Churchyard is the only spot inside the City in which establishments of this kind are gathered, and it is almost singular, turning out of Cheapside and other thoroughfares in which very few women are to be met with, to find so large a number before the shops in the narrow footway north of St. Paul's. As is the case with so many other London churchyards, that of St. Paul's Cathedral is now laid out with shrubs and flower-beds, and provided with a sufficiency of comfortable seats. — *For* NEAREST Stns., &c., *see* ST. PAUL'S CATHEDRAL.

St. Paul's School (Founded 1512 by John Colet, D.D., Dean of St. Paul's), Hammersmith-rd, West Kensington, W. — There are 153 scholars on the foundation, who are entitled to en-tire exemption from school fees. Vacancies are filled up at the commencement of each term according to the results of a competitive examination. Candidates must be between 12 and 16 years of age, but some scholarships are reserved for boys under 12, if of promising ability. Capitation scholars pay £24 a year. The governors of this school are appointed by the Mercers' Co. and the Universities of Oxford, Cambridge, and London. The sum of £1,500 is annually devoted by the governors to the establishment of seven exhibitions, varying in value from £80 to £40 a year, and tenable at either university. To the University of Cambridge there are the following exhibitions: Two exhibitions at Trinity, founded by Mr. Perry in 1696, of the value of £40, tenable for two years. An exhibition, founded by Mr. Stock in 1780 at Corpus Christi, of the yearly value of £30, given to a scholar recommended by the high master. An exhibition in the same college, founded by Mr. George Sykes in 1766, value £36 a year. An exhibition founded by Mr. Barnes in 1844, value £60 a year for four years. The Keen Scholarship of £30 for one year, is given to a scholar proceeding to Oxford or Cambridge for proficiency in mathematics. NEAREST *Ry. Stns.*, West Kensington (Dis.), Addison-rd (Dis.), and Hammersmith (Dis., Met., and S. W.); *Omnibus Rte.*, Hammersmith-rd.

St. Stephen's Club, 1, Bridge-st, Westminster, limited to 1,500 members. — The only persons eligible for membership are those who profess and maintain Constitutional and Conservative principles. The committee have power to select for ballot twenty candidates annually from those duly proposed and seconded, who shall be called selected members. The election of members is by ballot in committee. Entrance, £21; subscription, £10 10s.

Salisbury Club (New), 12, St. James's-sq. — This club was established in 1880, converted into a members' club in 1886, and reorganised in 1888 as the New Salisbury Club; is described as being instituted upon a social and non-political basis. It extends to members the privilege of introducing as visitors, ladies as well as gentlemen. The election is in the hands of the committee. Subscription: Town members, £10 10s.; country members, £5 5s.; foreign members, £2 2s.

Salters' Company (The) do not possess a strictly beautiful building, however commodious and comfortable it may be. It was built in 1827, and is notable for its acoustic properties. A portrait of Sir Sills Gibbons, ex-lord mayor, painted by Wells, R.A., hangs in an ante-room, and a portrait of the Duke of Wellington on horseback is on the staircase. A fine old carved chair, once the master's, now the hall porter's, stands in the vestibule; and the details of a bill of fare for fifty salters in the year 1560 are interesting, as illustrating the rise in price of provisions during the last three centuries. The trade of a salter nowadays includes cochineal, logwood, and chemical preparations.

Salvation Army. — Headquarters, 101, Queen Victoria-st.

San Domingo. —CONSULATE, 18, Coleman-st, City. NEAREST *Ry. Stns.*, Broad-st and Moorgate-st; *Omnibus Rte.*, Moorgate-st; *Cab Rank*, Lothbury.

San Salvador, Republic of. —CONSULATE, 7, Jeffreys-sq, E.C. NEAREST *Ry. Stn., Omnibus Rte.*, and *Cab Rank*, Fenchurch-st.

Sanger's Amphitheatre (late Astley's) (Map 13). —A theatre and hippodrome on the Surrey side, about a couple of hundred yards from Westminster-br; formerly known as Astley's, now in the hands of Messrs. Sanger, who have introduced a large menagerie element into the performances. NEAREST *Ry. Stn.*, Westminster-br; *Omnibus Rte.*, Westminster-br-rd.

Sanitary Assurance Association.—(*See* HOUSES.)

Savage Club, Lancaster House, Savoy, Strand. — Qualification: To be a working member in the fields of literature, science, music, or art. Candidates, after notice of vacancy, are invited to use the club as much as possible, for a certain time, previous to going up for election, in order that they may become known to the club. The committee elect; one black ball in five excludes. Entrance fee, £5 5s.; subscription, £5 5s.

Savile Club, 107, Piccadilly, W.—The object of the club is good fellowship, as is set forth in its motto, *sodalitas convivium*. Election by committee. Entrance fee, £10 10s.; subscription, £5 5s.

Savoy Theatre (Map 7).— Entrance for foot passengers, Beaufort-bgs,Strand; carriage entrance, Thames Embankment. This theatre was built by Mr. D'Oyly Carte from designs by Mr. C. J. Phipps, mainly for the performance of the Gilbert and Sullivan form of comic opera, which has been so popular during the last few years. The theatre, which is of fair size, is one of the most convenient and most elegantly decorated houses in London. The Savoy Theatre enjoys the distinction of having been the first theatre in London—if not in the world—to be lighted throughout by the electric light, and the experiment has proved a most signal success. It was first opened on Monday the 10th of October, 1881, with Messrs. Gilbert and Sullivan's "Patience," which had already enjoyed a long and successful career at the Opera Comique. NEAREST *Ry. Stns.*, Charing ✠ (Dis. & S.E.); *Omnibus Rte.,* Strand; *Cab Rank*, Burleigh-st.

Scandinavian Club, 80 & 81,Strand.—The object of this club is to promote social intercourse among Scandinavians. There is no entrance fee, and the yearly subscription is £4 4s.

School Board.—Has in operation 401 schools, accommodating 407,104 children. The average gross annual cost per child on the average attendance at the London Board Schools was at March, 1887, £3 3s. 0d. The average salary of a head master is £275 4s. 3d. ; of a head mistress £194 15s. 2d.; of an assistant master £112 15s. 1d.; and of an assistant mistress £85 13s. 11d. The average percentage of passes in the three primary subjects is higher in the London Board Schools than the average in all schools in England and Wales, the figures being according to the last return: reading, 95'7 ; writing, 90'6 ; arithmetic, 87'3.

The members of the Board are divided into nine standing committees, namely, statistics, works, school management, compulsory bye-laws,industrial schools, educational endowments, finance, store,

and evening classes. The reports of these committees, which are issued for the most part yearly, contain exhaustive information and very copious statistics upon all matters connected with the work of the Board, and are sold by Messrs. Hazel, Watson, and Viney (Ltd.), 52, Long Acre, W.C. The offices of the Board are on the Victoria Embankment,near the Temple Stn. of the District Ry. (Map 13), and the hours of attendance are from 10 to 5 ; on Saturdays from 10 0 2. The clerk is G.H.Croad,Esq.,B.A.

School Board Committees.—(*See* CONSTITUENCIES.)

School Board Constituencies.—(*See* CONSTITUENCIES.)

School Board, Members of.—(*See* CONSTITUENCIES.)

Scotland Yard (Great), connecting Northumberland-avenue and Whitehall, is very different from the queer little settlement much frequented by coalheavers, which was described in the "Sketches by Boz." Its principal importance consists in the fact of its containing several of the offices of the head-quarters' staff of the Metropolitan Police. These are the Criminal Investigation Department and the Executive Branch, which are always open, and the Public Carriage (Licensing) Branch, which is open to the public from 10 to 3.30. The offices for the property left in public carriages are (*a*) for the public, 21, Whitehall-pl, S.W., and (*b*) for drivers and conductors, Middle Scotland-yd. Office hours, 10 to 5.

Scottish Club, 39, Dover-st, Piccadilly. Proprietary.—The club is non-political, and those who are eligible for membership are landowners of Scotland or gentlemen otherwise connected with the country, as by property or marriage. At present the entrance fee is £10 10s. Subs., for town members, £7 7s. ; country members, £6 6s. ; if members of certain clubs in Scotland, £5 5s.

Sea-water Baths.—The question of the possibility of providing the regular supply of sea-water to the metropolis for bathing purposes has long exercised the ingenuity of projectors. Indeed, things at one time went so far, that it was in contemplation to

form a company to lay a gigantic pipe to Brighton for the purpose of turning the Channel waters on to London in much the same way as the waters of Loch Katrine are laid on to Glasgow. For the present, however, this and other schemes of almost equal grandeur remain in abeyance—possibly in consequence of that uncomfortable want of confidence with which the investing public has of late years been so much afflicted. It has occurred to the manager of the Great Eastern Railway Company that, if the sea cannot be brought to London wholesale, something might be done to organise its transmission by instalments. Accordingly, sea-water from Lowestoft will be delivered daily, except Sundays, at any station on the railway, or at any address within the ordinary cartage delivery of the Company in London or the country at one uniform price of sixpence for every three gallons, payable on delivery. The vessels containing the water are perfectly tight, well corked, and fitted with a handle to admit of their being easily carried upstairs ; they are left by the Company's carman, if required, for the convenience of the consignee, and called for afterwards without extra charge. Orders can be sent by post to the Sea-Water Office, Liverpool Street Station, E.C.; to the stationmaster at Lowestoft, or given verbally to any station-master on the railway, or to the carmen when delivering or fetching the vessels. The water is got from the sea at Lowestoft by means of pipes extending into deep water, and is brought into London by the night mail passenger train. Hotels, schools, hospitals, and other places in London requiring large quantities of sea-water can be supplied by water-carts filled from tank trucks specially constructed for plying between Lowestoft and London.

Servants vary even more than most commodities. The best way to get one is to select from the advertisements in the daily papers. The next best, to advertise your wants (*see* ADVERTISING), though this will expose you to the attacks of a considerable class who will call simply for the purpose of extorting their "expenses." In either case insist upon a personal character. Written characters are not worth reading. A false character—written or personal—is an indictable offence, and the London courts will convict both the servant who uses and the person who gives it. It is not a safe plan to go to a Registry unless you know all about it first, though there are some which are really trustworthy. But a servant who once finds his or her way to a Registry Office is almost always unsettled, and no sooner in a place than looking out for another. The average London wages may be set down as: Butlers, £40 to £100; Footmen, £20 to £40; Pages, £8 to £15; Cooks, £18 to £50; Housemaids, £10 to £25; Parlourmaids, £12 to £30; "General Servants," *Anglicé* Maids of all Work, £6 to £15. A month's notice is required before leaving or dismissing; but in the latter case a month's wages will suffice. For serious misconduct a servant can be discharged without notice or its equivalent. If economy is necessary, bear in mind that the payment of commissions from tradesmen to servants is an almost universal London custom, and a fruitful source of deliberate waste. "Kitchen stuff" is another expensive institution, specially designed to facilitate the consumption of articles on the replacing of which cook may make her little profit. Dripping, which is a perquisite for which almost all cooks will make at least a fight, not only means a good deal more than its name would imply, but leads to the spoiling of your meat by surreptitious stabbings that the juice may run away more freely. This ingenious arrangement is also much favoured of late years by the butcher, who nowadays in "jointing" always cuts well into the meat. The avoidance of these and other similar forms of robbery requires a little intelligence and a good deal of firmness. Give good wages, and let it be clearly understood before hiring that no perquisites are permitted. A serious mistake, and one too often made, is to lay down the hard-and-fast rule, "no followers allowed." Servants always have had and always will have followers whether their masters and mistresses like it or not. It is much wiser to recognise this fact, and to authorise the visits of the "follower" at proper times and seasons, first ascertaining that his antecedents and character are good.—(*See also* HOUSEHOLDERS, HINTS TO.)

Servia.—MINISTRY, 7, Gloucester-pl, Hyde-pk. NEAREST *Ry. Stns.*, Edgware-rd (Met.) and Paddington (G. West.); *Omnibus Rte.* and *Cab Rank*, Uxbridge-rd. CONSULATE, 76, Cannon-st, E.C. NEAREST *Ry. Stn.*, *Omnibus Rte.*, and *Cab Rank*, Cannon-street.

Sessions of the Peace, 1888.—

CENTRAL CRIMINAL COURT, 1888.

Monday ..	..	..	..	9th January.
Monday ..	..	..	..	30th January.
Monday ..	..	..	..	27th February.
Monday ..	..	..	..	19th March.
Monday ..	..	..	..	23rd April.
Monday ..	..	..	..	28th May.
Monday ..	..	..	..	2nd July.
Monday ..	..	..	..	30th July.
Monday ..	..	..	..	17th September.
Monday ..	..	..	..	22nd October.

MIDDLESEX.

	At the Sessions House Clerkenwell.	At the Sessions House Westminster.
January quarter session (criminal business) ..	Monday, 2nd January.	
Appeal day		Saturday, 7th January.
January adjourned quarter session (criminal business)..	Monday, 16th } January.	
County day	Thursday, 19th }	
February general session (criminal business) ..	Monday, 6th }	
February adjourned general session (criminal business)..	Monday, 20th } February.	
County day	Thursday, 23rd }	
March general session (criminal business) ..	Monday, 5th } March.	
March adjourned general session (criminal business) ..	Monday, 19th }	
April quarter session (criminal business)	Tuesday, 3rd April.	
Appeal day		Saturday, 7th April.
April adjourned quarter session (criminal business) ..	Monday, 16th } April.	
County day	Thursday, 19th }	
May general session (criminal business) ..	Monday, 7th }	
May adjourned general session (criminal business) ..	Tuesday, 22nd } May.	
County day	Thursday, 24th }	
June general session (criminal business)	Monday, 4th } June.	
June adjourned general session (criminal business) ..	Monday, 18th }	
July quarter session (criminal business)	Monday, 2nd July.	
Appeal day		Saturday, 7th July.
July adjourned quarter session (criminal business) ..	Monday, 16th } July.	
County day	Thursday, 19th }	
August general session (criminal business).. ..	Tuesday, 7th }	
August adjourned general session (criminal business) ..	Monday, 20th } August.	
County day	Thursday, 23rd }	
September general session (criminal business) ..	Monday, 3rd } September	
September adjourned general session (criminal business)	Monday, 24th }	
October quarter session (Applications for licences for music, dancing, and racecourses)	Thursday, 4th } October.	
Criminal business	Monday, 8th }	

MIDDLESEX.	At the Sessions House Clerkenwell.	At the Sessions House Westminster.
Appeal day	.. ..	Saturday, 13th October.
County day	Thursday, 18th October.	
October adjourned quarter session (criminal business) ..	Monday, 22nd October.	
November general session (criminal business)	Monday, 5th	
November adjourned general session (criminal business)	Monday, 19th ⎱ November.	
County day	Thursday, 22nd ⎰	
December general session (criminal business)	Monday, 3rd ⎱ December.	
December adjourned general session (criminal business)	Monday, 17th ⎰	

SURREY.—To be holden at the Sessions House, Newington.

EPIPHANY	General quarter session ..	Tuesday, January 3, 1888.
	Special adjourned session..	On the fourth day (excl. Sun.) before the Assize.
	Adjourned session	Monday, February 6, 1888.
	The like	Monday, March 5, ,,
EASTER ..	General quarter session ..	Tuesday, April 3, ,,
	Adjourned session	Monday, May 7, ,,
	The like	Monday, June 4, ,,
MIDSUMMER ..	General quarter session ..	Tuesday, July 3, ,,
	Special adjourned session..	On the fourth day (excl. Sun.) before the Summer Assize.
	Adjourned session	Monday, September 3, 1888.
MICHAELMAS ..	General quarter session ..	Tuesday, October 16, ,,
	Adjourned session	Monday, November 5, ,,
	The like	Monday, December 3, ,,

Business will be disposed of as follows : County business on the first day of each quarter session ; and the trials of prisoners on the second and subsequent days thereof. At the adjourned sessions, business referred by the original quarter session and the trials of prisoners. Prosecutors and witnesses should have notice to attend on the second day of each general quarter session, and on the first day of each adjourned session, at 10 o'clock. Appeals, road proceedings, &c., on the first Monday after the commencement of each general quarter session, at 10 o'clock. Music, dancing, and racecourse licenses on Thursday, October 18, at 10 o'clock.

NOTE.—The Epiphany general quarter session for 1889, will commence on Tuesday, January 1, 1889.

Seven Dials.

Seven Dials.—This locality is celebrated as the heart of one of the poorest districts in London. Of late years various improvements have been made in the neighbourhood, and the Dials are now traversed by omnibuses, and have made considerable progress towards civilisation. But the locality is still a singular one, and as it lies in close proximity to the West End, can be easily visited by those curious to see one of the seamier sides of the inner life of London. The readiest approach to it is from St. Martin's-la, crossing between Cranborne-st and Long Acre. Turning up northwards here, the stranger finds himself in a street altogether unique in its way. It is the abode of bird-fanciers. Every variety of pigeon, fowl, and rabbit can be found here, together with hawks and owls, parrots, love-birds, and other species native and foreign. There is a shop for specimens for the aquarium, with tanks of water - beetles, newts, water-spiders, and other aquatic creatures. Others are devoted to British song birds, larks, thrushes, bull-finches, starlings, blackbirds, &c. Here and there are shops filled with cages of every kind, and one or two dog-fanciers have also settled here. Passing through this lane we are in the Dials, a point where seven streets meet. If it be desired to see poor London, it is better not to go straight on, but to turn up any of the side streets. Here poverty is to be seen in some of its most painful aspects. The shops sell nothing but second or third hand articles—old dresses, old clothes, old hats, and at the top of the stairs of little underground cellars, old shoes, so patched and mended that it is questionable whether one particle of the original material remains in them. These streets swarm with children of all ages, engaged in every kind of game which childhood is capable of enjoying without the addition of expensive apparatus. Tip-cat and battledore and shuttlecock are great favourites about the Dials, and the passer-by must guard his face or take the consequences. Children sit on door-steps and on the pavement, they play in the gutter, they chase each other in the road, and dodge in and out of houses. It is evident that the School Board has not much power in the neighbourhood of the Dials. Public-houses abound, and it is clear that whatever there may be a lack of in this territory of St. Giles, there is no lack of money to pay for drink. At night the public-houses are ablaze with light, and on Saturday evenings there is a great sound of shouting and singing through the windows, while the women stand outside and wait, hoping against hope that their husbands will come out before the week's money is all spent. Nowhere within reach of the West End of London can such a glimpse of the life of the poorer classes be obtained as on a Saturday evening at the Dials.

Sharpers.—The tricks of these gentry are too numerous to particularise, for they comprise all the snares that human ingenuity can set for credulity. To avoid them there is but one maxim—be on your guard. There is the confidence trick, wherein two confederates obtain possession of the greenhorn's purse, ostensibly for a few minutes, "just to show his confidence" in one of them, who has previously entrusted him with

H

his purse, filled probably with fictitious notes on "The Bank of Elegance," or some other imaginary name, the alleged proceeds of a legacy which he is anxious to divide with his new-found friend, from charitable motives. These confidence-trick people lurk about Westminster Abbey, the British Museum, the Zoological Gardens, and other places visited by strangers. They sometimes spend days in the company of a dupe before they put his credulity to a test. Then there is the ring-dropping trick, by which a dupe is induced to buy a worthless ring, purporting to be a diamond, by a man who pretends to find it just in front of his victim, but alleges he has neither time nor inclination to seek a better market. The three-card trick, and other tricks with cards, practised often in railway trains, may cost an innocent man, who is so foolish as to play with strangers, all he possesses. The painted-bird trick, whereby a worthless sparrow is passed off as a valuable piping-bullfinch or canary, ensnares many ladies. People who consider themselves knowing in horseflesh are often entrapped by horse-copers, who, by a variety of artful means, make worthless horses appear valuable. In these cases the story generally is that the sale only takes place on account of the death of a relation. Every trial is promised; the horses will be taken back, and the money returned within a month, if the purchaser wishes; a veterinary warrant is to be given. Such are the falsehoods which ensure a constant supply of victims, who are afterwards ashamed to expose their folly in a court of law. The trial is put off on various excuses, the veterinary certificate is written by a confederate, and the guarantee is worthless.

Shoeblacks.—The red uniform of the Shoeblack Brigade is now so familiar to Londoners that they are apt to forget how recently it has appeared in the streets, and to whom is due the initiation of the system which has worked so well. The first society to start the system of shoeblack brigades was that of the Ragged Schools, Saffron-hill. The wants of London pedestrians are now supplied by nine such societies, whose object it is, not only to find employment for poor and honest boys as shoeblacks, but also to

educate them, and to give them a start in the world. The average earnings of the 400 boys on the lists of these societies are nearly £12,000 a year; a fourth of which amount is earned by the red-uniformed boys of the Saffron-hill brigade, which is between 60 and 70 strong. Of this number more than 40 boys sleep on the premises. All the lads belonging to the societies are licensed by the chief commissioners of the City and Metropolitan Police, under the provisions of 30 & 31 Vict. c. 134. Licenses are also granted to boys not belonging to any society, and a guerilla horde of unlicensed shoe-blacks, who are subject to no discipline or supervision, infest the streets and annoy the passenger.

Siam.—MINISTRY, 23, Ashburnham-pl, South Kensington. NEAREST *Ry. Stn.*, South Kensington; *Omnibus Rte.*, Brompton-rd; *Cab Rank*, Cromwell-rd. CONSULATE, 6, Great Winchester-st. NEAREST *Ry Stns.*, Broad-st (N.L.) and Moorgate-st (Met.); *Omnibus Rtes.*, Old Broad-st and Moorgate-st; *Cab Rank*, Liverpool-st.

Sight-Seeing.—Sight-seeing, in the opinion of many experienced travellers, is best avoided altogether. It may well be, however, that this will be held to be a matter of opinion, and that sight-seeing will continue to flourish until the arrival of that traveller of Lord Macaulay's, who has found his way into so many books and newspapers, but whose nationality shall not be hinted at here. One piece of advice to the intending sight-seer is at all events sound. Never go to see anything by yourself. If the show be a good one, you will enjoy yourself all the more in company; and the solitary contemplation of anything that is dull and tedious is one of the most depressing experiences of human life. Furthermore, an excellent principle—said to be of American origin—is never to enquire how far you may go, but to go straight on until you are told to stop. The enterprising sight-seer who proceeds on this plan, and who understands the virtue of "palm oil," and a calm demeanour, is sure to see everything he cares to see.
—(*See also* AMUSEMENTS.)

Sion College, Victoria Emb., E.C.—(*See* LIBRARIES, PUBLIC.)

Skating Club Archers' Hall,

Regent's-pk, and 1, Devonport-st, Hyde-pk.—Estab. 1830. Limited to 150 gentlemen and 25 ladies. Entrance, £3 3s.; sub., £2 2s.; for ladies, £1 1s. Object: For practice of "figure" skating.

Skinners' Hall (The) is by no means as pleasant an apartment as the drawing-room of the company, which is lavishly decorated, and built entirely of cedar-wood. The hall, which dates from the Fire, is situated at No. 8, Dowgate Hill, and was redecorated some ten years ago. A portrait of Mr. T. G. Kensett, formerly clerk to the company, painted by Richmond, R.A., is the latest addition to the art collection. The company possesses fifteen university exhibitions and four free schools. Skinners' Hall was frequently used by the Lord Mayor as a residence before the present Mansion House was built. When a master of the company is to be elected, the ex-holder of the office tries on a cap, which he declares to be a misfit. The cap is then passed from one to another till it reaches the person for whom it has been made, who declares it to be a fit, and so becomes master. The trade of skinner has decreased in importance latterly. The first exhibition of the City of London Society of Artists was inaugurated here in March, 1880. NEAREST *Ry. Stns.*, Cannon-st (S.E.) and Mansion House (Dis.); *Omnibus Rtes.*, Cannon-st, Queen Victoria-st, and Cheapside; *Cab Rank*, Cannon-st Stn.

Smithfield Club, Office, 12, Hanover-sq, W.—Strictly speaking, not so much a club as an agricultural society for offering prizes for improvements in feeding and fattening of cattle, &c. Its annual show takes place at the Royal Agricultural Hall, Islington, and is known as the Christmas Fat Cattle Show, held in December. The subscription is £1 1s. per annum, or life, £10 10s. No entrance fee. Qualification: Being proposed by any member of the club, or on payment of £2 2s by non-members for privilege of exhibiting live stock.

Soane Museum, 13, Lincoln's-inn-fields (Map 7).—Antique sculptures, models of temples, &c., pictures, illuminated MSS., antique gems and cameos, and a library containing many rare architectural works, including many folio volumes of drawings by the Brothers Adam, the celebrated architects and decorative artists of the last century. The museum is open free to the public on Tu., Wed., Th., and Sat., in April, May, June, July, and Aug., and on Tu. and Th. in February and March, from 11 to 5. Cards for private days and for students to be obtained of the curator at the museum. Perhaps the most remarkable object in this museum is the magnificent sarcophagus, nine feet in length, carved out of one block of translucent oriental alabaster. It contained the body of Sethos, or Osirei Meneptha, the father of the great conqueror Ramses II., and is covered both inside and out with hieroglyphic writing and figures from the mythology of Egypt, representing the judgment of the dead, and other subjects. This sarcophagus was discovered by Belzoni in the year 1817, and purchased by Sir John Soane from Mr. Salt in 1824 for the sum of £2,000. Among the pictures may be particularly noticed those by Hogarth, who is here seen at his strongest in the series known as "The Rake's Progress," the truest and most tremendous work of any satirist since the days of Juvenal himself; and the great master is seen in his broader and more distinctly humorous view in his "Election" pictures. In addition to the Hogarths, is a fine example of Sir Joshua Reynolds, "The Snake in the Grass;" a fine picture by Watteau; a view on the Grand Canal, Venice, by Canaletti, formerly in the possession of William Beckford, of Fonthill, and considered the finest example known by this master. There are also two good pictures by Calcott, and a very remarkable Turner, "Van Tromp's Barge Entering the Texel in 1645." NEAREST *Ry. Stn.,* Temple (Dis.); *Omnibus Rtes.,* Holborn and Strand; *Cab Rank,* High Holborn.

Society of Arts, John-st, Adelphi (Map 7). President: H.R.H. the Prince of Wales; Sec., Mr. H. Trueman Wood.—Subscription: £2 2s. Life Sub., £21. No entrance fee. Founded in 1754, and incorporated by Royal Charter in 1847, for "The encouragement of the arts, manufactures, and commerce of the country, by bestowing rewards for such productions, inventions, or improvements as tend to the employment of the poor, to the increase of trade, and to the riches and honour of the kingdom; and for meritorious works in the various departments of the fine arts; for discoveries, inventions, and improvements in agriculture, chemistry, mechanics, manufactures, and other useful arts; for the application of such natural and artificial products, whether of home, colonial, or foreign growth and manufacture, as may appear likely to afford fresh objects of industry, and to increase the trade of the realm by extending the sphere of British commerce; and generally to assist in the advancement, development, and practical application of every department of science in connection with the arts, manufactures, and commerce of the country." The session commences in November, and ends in June. The number of meetings held during the session amounts to between 70 and 80. The "ordinary" meetings are held on Wed. evenings at 8 p.m. Meetings of the Indian, the Foreign and Colonial sections, and of the section of Applied Art are also held. At these meetings papers are read and discussed on subjects of applied science, art, &c. The public are admitted to the meetings by a member's order. There are three or more courses of "Cantor Lectures," given under a bequest from the late Dr. Cantor, during the session, and a short course of Juvenile Lectures during the Christmas holidays. Other meetings are also held for the discussion of special subjects, and additional courses of lectures are occasionally given. The journal of the society is published weekly, and contains full reports of the society's proceedings, as well as a variety of information connected with arts, manufactures, and commerce. After having occupied several houses, the society moved, in 1774, into their present building, which was erected for them by the Brothers Adam. A few years afterwards, James Barry, R.A., undertook to decorate the meeting-room with paintings "analogous to the views of the institution," and these pictures still continue to be a distinguishing feature of the room. The public are admitted to see the pictures on presentation of a visiting card. The earliest exhibitions of pictures, out of which grew the annual exhibitions of the Royal Academy and other artistic associations, were held in the rooms of the Society of Arts. NEAREST *Ry. Stns.,* Charing ✠ (S.E. & Dis.); *Omnibus Rte.,* Strand; *Cab Rank,* Burleigh-st.

Society of British Artists (Royal), Suffolk-st, Pall Mall-east, was first started in the year 1822, by several artists of eminence, amongst whom were the late Clarkson Stanfield and David Roberts, afterwards Royal Academicians, and Mr. Linton the landscape painter, in consequence of the small amount of space available for artists not members of the Royal Academy. In the year 1847, Her Majesty the Queen was pleased to grant the Society a Charter of Incorporation. It is governed by a Council, presided over by John Burr, Esq., with a Vice-President, W. Holyoake, Esq., and other members (12 in number) who are elected annually, and it is supported by annual subscriptions of the whole body of members, who at present are 85 in number. A meeting for the election of members is held yearly, in the latter end of March, when the names of all candidates are submitted to the ballot. Two exhibitions are held in the year, the principal one in the spring; the days for sending in works of art for which are the fourth Mon. and Tu. in March. The days for receiving works for the Winter Exhibition, are the first Mon. and Tu. in November. Admission 1s., catalogue 1s. A member on his election pays no entrance fee, and is at liberty to terminate his membership at any time, by giving six months' notice to that effect. About 1,700 works are annually exhibited in the Society's galleries; many eminent artists, now members of the Royal Academy and of the two Water-Colour Societies, have exhibited their works in these exhibitions previous to their election to these last-named societies. NEAREST *Ry. Stns.,* Charing ✠ (S.E. & Dis.); *Omnibus Rtes.,* Pall Mall, Haymarket, and Waterloo-pl; *Cab Rank,* Haymarket.

Soho Bazaar, 77, Oxford-st (Map 7).—The best and oldest bazaar in London, chiefly devoted to the supply of the requirements of ladies and children Open at 10; closes at 5 in winter, at 6 in summer. NEAREST *Ry. Stn.,* Gower-st (Met.); *Omnibus Rtes.,*

Gt. Portland-st, Oxford-st, Tottenham-ct-rd ; *Cab Rank*, Dean-st.

Somerset House, Strand (Map 7), is the one memento left of the succession of palaces which once lined the Middlesex bank of the Thames between London and Westminster. It is only a memento, not a relic ; the old Somerset House, built in the middle of the sixteenth century for the Protector Somerset, by John of Padua, having been pulled down in 1775, when Buckingham House was settled upon Queen Charlotte in its stead. The present building is the work of Sir W. Chambers, and was erected with an express view to the purpose to which it has ever since been devoted, viz. the accommodation of various Government and semi-public offices. It is a fine work of its kind, though the effect of the river front, which is its finest visible façade, is naturally not improved by the removal of the river. It is in the Italian style, with capitals of various Grecian orders copied from original antiques. Bacon, Banks, Carlini, Flaxman, Geraeci, Nollekens, and Wilton all had a hand in the ornamental portion of the work. Its chief point of practical interest to the general public is the collection of Wills and Registers of Births, Marriages, and Deaths, which may be searched over any period not exceeding 5 years on payment of the fee of 1s. If a certified copy of any entry be required, the charge, in addition to the 1s. for the search is 2s. 7d., which includes stamp duty of 1d. The registers contain entries of all births, deaths, and marriages registered since 1st July, 1837. It is not generally known that on going to the General Register Office to search for a death, it may at the same time be ascertained whether a Will has been proved, or letters of administration granted for the disposal of the deceased's effects. There are also local registry offices in every district, where the ordinary business of registration can be effected. NEAREST *Ry. Stn.,* Temple (Dis.) ; *Omnibus Rtes.,* Strand and Wellington-st ; *Cab Rank,* Catherine-st.

South African Republic. —CONSULATE, 118, Stoke Newington-rd, N.

South Australia.—AGENCY-GENERAL, 8, Victoria-chambers, Victoria-st.—NEAREST *Ry. Stn.,*

St. James's-pk (Dis.) ; *Omnibus Rtes.,* Victoria-st and Parliament-st ; *Cab Rank,* Victoria-st.

South Kensington Museum (Map 5) stands on twelve acres of land, acquired by the Government at a cost of £60,000 ; these are a portion of the estate purchased by the Commissioners for the Exhibition of 1851 out of the surplus proceeds of that undertaking. Here, in 1855, a spacious building was constructed, chiefly of iron and wood, under the superintendence of the late Sir W. Cubitt, C.E., at a cost of £15,000 ; which was intended to receive several miscellaneous collections of a scientific character, mainly acquired from the Exhibition of 1851, and which had been temporarily housed in various places. In addition to the collections already alluded to, the whole of the Fine Art collections which had been exhibited at Marlborough House since 1852 were also removed to South Kensington ; and these were supplemented by numerous and valuable loans from Her Majesty the Queen and others. This iron building was opened on June 22, 1857, as the South Kensington Museum. It occupied the site of the new South Court, in which the cast of the Trajan Column and other architectural works are now exhibited. Immediately after the opening of the museum, the erection of permanent buildings was commenced ; and the Picture Galleries, the Schools of Art, the North and Central Courts, the Keramic Gallery, Lecture Theatre, and Refreshment Rooms were completed and opened in successive years. The iron building was removed in 1865, and has been re-erected as a branch museum at Bethnal-green. The MUSEUM is open daily ; free on Mon., Tu., and Sat. On students' days, Wed., Th., and Fri., the public are admitted on payment of sixpence each person. The hours on Mon., Tu., and Sat. are from 10 a.m. till 10 p.m. ; on Wed., Th., and Fri. from 10 a.m. till 4, 5, or 6 p.m., according to the daylight. Tickets of admission to the museum, including the library and reading-rooms, and the Bethnal Green Museum, are issued at the following rates: Weekly, 6d. ; monthly, 1s. 6d. ; quarterly, 3s. ; half-yearly, 6s. ; yearly, 10s. Yearly tickets are also issued to any school at £1,

which will admit all the pupils of such school on all students' days. Tickets to be obtained at the catalogue sale stall of the museum.

THE COLLECTION OF BRITISH PICTURES at South Kensington was commenced by the gift of Mr. Sheepshanks, who, in presenting his pictures to the nation, stipulated that they should be kept in a suitable building in the immediate neighbourhood of Kensington. This gift was followed by other donations of pictures, and the galleries now contain 617 oil paintings and 1,291 water-colour drawings, specimens of the works of the best British Masters, nearly all contributed by private individuals for the advancement of the public art-education in this country.

THE COLLECTIONS OF SCULPTURE consist chiefly of decorative sculpture of the Renaissance period in marble, stone, and terra-cotta, including numerous specimens of the glazed terra-cotta of the 15th century, known as Della Robbia ware.

THE EDUCATIONAL COLLECTION was begun by the Society of Arts, and first exhibited in St. Martin's Hall, in 1854, after which exhibition numerous objects were presented to the Government to form the nucleus of an educational museum. The library contains upwards of 36,000 volumes of educational books, and the collections of scientific apparatus, models, and appliances for educational purposes, number some thousands of specimens.

MATERIALS FOR BUILDING AND CONSTRUCTION.—The nucleus of this collection was formed partly by gifts and purchases from the Exhibition of 1851 and from the Paris Exhibition of 1855. It comprises samples of building stones, cements, terra-cottas, bricks, fire-proof floors, ornamental tiles, enamelled slate, specimens of woods for construction, &c.

REPRODUCTIONS by electrotype, by casting, and by photography of historical art-monuments and of art-objects existing in the collections of other countries, have been obtained and used, not only for exhibition in the South Kensington Museum, but to furnish models for the use of the students in the schools of art in the provinces.

NAVAL MODELS.—In the year 1864 the collection of the naval models belonging to the Admiralty was removed from Somerset House to South Kensington. This collection has, for educational purposes, since been transferred to the Royal Naval School at Greenwich. During the time of its remaining in the galleries at South Kensington, however, many acquisitions were made ; these are still exhibited at South Kensington, and comprise several important models, and various appliances for modern warfare.

LOANS FROM PRIVATE COLLECTORS.—In addition to those important collections of art-objects acquired by the State, the South Kensington Museum contains in one of its courts, especially devoted for this service, a large collection of art-objects on loan from various private owners, who desire to co-operate with the Government in carrying on the art-education of the public.

RULES RESPECTING THE RECEPTION BY THE SOUTH KENSINGTON MUSEUM, AND ITS BRANCH MUSEUM AT BETHNAL GREEN, OF OBJECTS GIVEN, LENT, OR SENT ON APPROVAL FOR PURCHASE.—Whilst every care is taken of objects lent for exhibition, or deposited on approval for purchase, the Museum (following the rule of the Royal Academy and other bodies) cannot be responsible for loss or damage. No object can be received on approval for purchase unless the price be named before or on delivery ; and it is to be understood that the Museum has the first right of making a purchase at any time within the period for which the objects are lent. Photographs, copies, or casts are made of such loans as may be useful for instruction in schools of art, unless the lender objects in writing. Two copies of each photograph are sent to the lender. Permission to copy or photograph objects on loan is not granted to private persons without the sanction in writing of the lender. For convenience of reference and comparison, objects submitted for purchase are liable to be photographed solely for official purposes, and not for sale, unless an objection in writing be made by the proprietor at the time of the delivery of the objects. When photographs are taken, two copies will be given to the proprietor of the object photographed.

REGULATIONS FOR COPYING IN THE SOUTH KENSINGTON MUSEUM.—Any person may, at any time when the Museum is open to the public, sketch or make notes of any objects in the Museum (see exceptions below), provided such copying do not necessitate his or her using an easel or extra seat, or otherwise obstructing the circulation of visitors. Any person wishing to copy by using an easel, &c., can do so on any students' day, under proper arrangements to prevent inconvenience to the public. The following are the exceptions referred to : *a.* The paintings in water colours, to copy which no permission is granted. *b.* Objects on loan can only be copied on the production of the written permission of the owners, which will be retained by the department. *c.* Pictures in the Sheepshanks' Gallery, to copy which special permission must be obtained, in accordance with the following conditions : Forms of application for permission to copy are supplied by the attendant in the gallery, or will be sent in reply to a letter addressed to the Director, S. Kensington Museum, London, S.W. No application to copy the works of any living artist can be entertained unless it be accompanied by the written permission of such artist. Such permission will only allow of works being copied by means of water colours, or on porcelain, or by drawing or engraving, copying in oil not being permitted. Applicants must, if required, send specimens of their competency. No copying can be permitted except on the days devoted to study ; and not more than four persons can be admitted at the same time to work in any apartment. No work can be removed from the walls for the purpose of copying.

THE LIBRARY is contained in rooms on the west side of the north court, and is entered through a door in the west arcades.—(*See* ART TRAINING SCHOOL.)

THE EDUCATIONAL READING ROOM is at present situated in a temporary building at the extreme western side of the museum, and is entered from the west corridor. On students' days the reading-room is open to all visitors ; on free days admission is restricted to clergymen, teachers of schools for the poor, or holders of tickets.

Among the most noteworthy and interesting objects are : In the ARCHITECTURAL COURT, a rood loft of alabaster and coloured marbles, with sculptured decoration ; a fine specimen of Flemish architecture, brought from the cathedral at Bois-le-Duc, North Brabant, and dated 1625. In the SOUTH COURT Dr. Schliemann's (loan) collection of antiquities from Hissarlik. Against the west wall is a fine marble sculpture of the 4th century B.C., representing Phœbus Apollo driving the horses of the sun, originally forming a metope of the Doric temple of Phœbus Apollo at Ilium ; beside it it is a stele or memorial pillar with Greek inscription, found on the site of the temple of the Ilium Minerva. In front of the colossal figure of a Bodhisatura, or sacred person destined to become a Buddha, is a case containing a sea-eagle, or osprey, with outspread wings, and standing on a rock, the work of the famous Japanese sculptor Miyochin Muneharu, a specimen of Japanese ironwork of the 16th century. In the ORIENTAL COURTS the cases contain weapons of war, swords, &c., showing the peculiarities of ancient construction or artistic decoration. One case is filled with steel coffers, some of them remarkable for their large and intricate locks ; other cases with examples of metal work, chiefly art bronzes, statuettes and groups, inkstands, candlesticks, snuffers, ewers, mortars, door-knockers, handles, lock plates, a pair of gilt bronze (16th century) fire dogs, or andirons, lent by the Queen, a statuette of Ceres (17th century), a cupid holding a dolphin ascribed to Donatello. Especially to be noticed are the candlesticks and other objects in bronze from the Soulages collection. Here also are salvers of pewter by, or in the manner of, François Briot, a French goldsmith of the 17th century ; also damascened salvers and ewers, Saracenic and Venetian. In cases in this row are a collection of English and foreign gold and silver coins, given by the Rev. R. Brooke, and others bequeathed by the late Mr. T. Millard ; a collection of snuff-boxes, bequeathed by Mr. G. Mitchell ; also snuff-boxes and etuis in gold, enamelled, jewelled, &c., and miniatures in oil and water-colour, lent by Mr. C. Goding. Fine Italian bronze busts of the 16th century, ascribed to Bernini, are placed on pedestals near here. In the NORTH COURT two fine examples of the peculiar flat relief introduced by Donatello should be studied. On brackets and screens on the left or west side of this court are placed several terra-cotta busts, chiefly contemporary portraits of Florentine citizens of the 15th century. Near these are bas-reliefs, figures and groups, chiefly in unglazed terra cotta, some of singular beauty. Here also is a large collection of sculpture in terra cotta, both plain and enamelled. Of the enamelled terra cotta known as Della Robbia ware, the museum possesses more than fifty examples. A very important example is an altar-piece representing the Adoration of the Magi, and containing upwards of twenty figures. Another very beautiful example of Della Robbia ware is a full-length figure of the Virgin, with the Infant Saviour in her lap, under an arched border of fruit and flowers, and supported on a triangular bracket. The EAST ARCADE is divided into several bays by transverse - walls, into which are built several fine carved stone chimney-pieces. In the READING-ROOM of the ART LIBRARY is a harpsichord, formerly the property of Handel, presented to the Museum by Messrs. Broadwood and Sons. Near it is a spinet made by Annibale de Rossi, of Milan, and dated 1577. A spinet in leather case, decorated in coloured glass, made at Murano towards the end of the 16th century, and said to have belonged to Elizabeth, Queen of Bohemia, daughter of James I.; and two other Italian spinets, dated 1555 and 1568, stand close by; and a small German finger-organ of the 16th century; this organ was said by its late owner to have once belonged to Martin Luther. A virginal, signed "John Loosemore, fecit 1655," stands near. Close by is a cabinet of marqueterie, the fronts of the drawers carved with emblematic groups of figures in high relief. This is said to have been made from the designs of Hans Holbein for Henry VIII. In the PERSIAN COURT is arranged the fine collection of Persian textiles, given by H.I.M. the Shah; the earthenware tiles, metal work, carpets, &c., purchased in Persia by Major R. Murdoch Smith, R.E., and M. Richard. In the PRINCE CONSORT GALLERY are placed many of the most interesting and costly possessions of the museum,

including a valuable collection of ancient enamelled objects, chiefly of ecclesiastical use. The eight cases immediately following contain numerous examples of the various classes of enamel, ancient and modern. Pre-eminent among those are the painted enamels of Limoges of the 16th and 17th centuries. These consist of plaques, salvers, ewers, salt-cellars, caskets, &c.; and furnish to the art student a very complete illustration of this manufacture. The most important example in these cases is the large casket, enamelled on plates of silver, on which is painted a band of dancing figures. It is attributed to Jean Limoson, about the close of the 16th century. Another remarkable enamel is the large medallion portrait of Charles de Guise, Cardinal de Lorraine. In a case, among several examples of engraved crystal, the most remarkable is a ewer of Byzantine workmanship of the 9th or 10th century. It is difficult to conjecture how such a vessel could be carved and hollowed out in so hard a substance. A cup of oriental sardonyx is distinguished for the beauty of its mounting, which bears the English hall-mark for the year 1567. Objects in the precious metals, generally combined with other materials, as wood, ivory, nautilus shells, cocoa-nut shells, fill another case. The celebrated Martelli Bronze or mirror cover, which has been reproduced in electrotype by Messrs. Franchi, is placed in the case in the centre. This work of the Italian sculptor Donatello was made about the year 1440 for the Martelli family of Florence. A case beside it contains examples of damascened work. A metallic mirror, in a lofty and elaborate stand of steel damascened with gold and silver, is one of the finest existing specimens of the damascened work of Milan. Two large plaques damascened in gold and silver, with views of the cities of Urbino and Pesaro, are from a piece of furniture made for one of the Dukes of Urbino in the 16th century. In the GALLERY OF WATER-COLOUR DRAWINGS is a collection of precious stones, jewellery, &c., amongst which will be found the gold missal case said to have belonged to Henrietta Maria, the queen of Charles I. It is covered with delicately-chased figures encrusted with brilliant translucent

enamels of various colours. It is Italian work, about the year 1580. Of the same date is a beautiful example of English work, a miniature case of gold, enamelled, the front set with diamonds and rubies; it contains a miniature, by Hilliard, of Queen Elizabeth, wearing a jewelled crown and necklace. NEAREST *Ry. Stn.*, S. Kensington; *Omnibus Rtes.*, Brompton-rd and Kensington-rd; *Cab Rank*, Opposite. *And see* INDIAN SECTION.

Southwark Bridge (Map 8) has of late years been much improved by the introduction of a little colour into the painting of its arches, which were formerly all in solemn black, and had a very heavy appearance. The credit of being the handsomest iron bridge across the river rests between it and Blackfriars-br; and, on the whole, though the latter is the more gorgeous, the former is perhaps, from the simplicity of its contour, the more striking. The length is 708 ft., or little more than half that of Waterloo. The arches, three in number, rest on stone piers; the centre arch having a span of 402 feet—the longest ever attempted until the adoption of the tubular principle — and the two shore arches 210 ft. each. From the inconvenience of its approaches this handsome bridge has been from the first comparatively valueless as a practical connection between the two shores. NEAREST *Ry. Stns.* (N. side), Mansion House (Dis.); *Omnibus Rte.*, Cannon-st; *Cab Rank*, Cannon-st. (S. side) London-br (S.E. & L.B.&S.C.); *Omnibus Rte.* and *Cab Rank*, Southwark-st.

Southwark Park has been formed within the last dozen years or so, in the once dreary district beyond the Bermondsey tan-yards. NEAREST *Ry. Stns.*, Spa-rd and South Bermondsey; *Omnibus Rtes.*, Deptford - rd and Blue Anchor-rd.

Spain.—EMBASSY, 50, Onslow-gdns, S.W. NEAREST *Ry. Stn.*, Sth. Kensington (Dis.); *Omnibus Rtes.*, Brompton-rd and Kensington-rd; *Cab Rank*, Sth. Kensington Stn. CONSULATE, 21, Billiter-st. NEAREST *Ry. Stns.*, Fenchurch - st and Cannon - st (S.E.); *Omnibus Rtes.*, Leadenhall-st and Fenchurch-st; *Cab Rank*, Fenchurch-st

Standard Theatre, Shoreditch (Map 8), one of the principal East End theatres, as well as one of the largest in London, just opposite the old terminus of the G.E.R., the site of which is now occupied by the magnificent new goods station of that company. Provides at times a rather higher class of performance than is customary in these districts, with leading actors, or at times whole companies, from the best West End houses. NEAREST *Ry. Stns.*, Bishopsgate (G.E.) and Shoreditch (N.L. & E.L.); *Omnibus Rte.*, Shoreditch.

Stationery Office, Prince's-st, Storey's-gate, Westminster, S.W. Hours 10 till 4.30. NEAREST *Ry. Stn.*, Westminster-br (Dis.); *Omnibus Rtes.*, Parliament-st and Victoria-st; *Cab Rank*, Palace-yd.

Statues. — Unfortunately London is not celebrated, although it may be notorious, for its public statues. They are to be encountered in all quarters of the town, from the melancholy effigy of Cobden in Camden Tn., to the uncomfortable seated figure of Peabody at the back of the Royal Exchange, or the still more forlorn Dr. Jenner in Kensington-gdns. It is difficult to go very wrong with a simple column, and as the statues which crown the York and Nelson columns are out of the reach of inspection, these monuments are not without merit. At the foot of the Nelson column are Sir Edwin Landseer's four colossal lions, perhaps the most artistic effigies in the streets of London. The equestrian statue of Richard Cœur de Lion, by Baron Marochetti, in Palace-row, Westminster, and Sir Gilbert Scott's Crimean memorial to officers educated at Westminster School, which is to be found in Broad Sanctuary, Westminster, are well worthy of a special visit. The curious history of the equestrian statue of Charles I., at Charing ✠, gives it a peculiar interest quite apart from considerations of art. The same cannot be said of the statue of the Duke of Wellington removed in 1883 from Hyde-pk-corner. The Guards' Memorial at the foot of Waterloo-pl is not without a certain massive effect. The National Memorial to the Prince Consort in Hyde-pk, should by all means be seen, if only as a warning that the expenditure of vast sums of money does not necessarily lead to satisfactory results. At the junction of Hamilton-pl and Park-

la is an important work by Thos. Thorneycroft in the form of a fountain, dedicated to "the fathers of English poetry," the gift of Mrs. Brown, 1875. This displays three seated figures, representing Tragedy, Comedy, and Poetry. Above are Shakespeare, Chaucer, and Milton, and the whole is surmounted by a somewhat conventional figure of Fame. The work is more ambitious in design than most of the London open-air sculpture, and, so far as its statues of Shakespeare, Chaucer, and Milton are concerned, is a very creditable performance. There is an almost grotesque statue of Queen Anne (restored by Mr. Belt), absurdly dwarfed by the great west front of St. Paul's Cathedral. Wayfarers in the squares should by no means be tempted to inspect the statues by which many are adorned, although the accumulated smoke of years has happily, to a large extent, concealed the sculptors' intentions

The following are the principal open-air statues, monuments, and memorials of the metropolis:

ACHILLES, Hyde-pk.

ALBERT MEMORIAL, Kensington-gore.

ANNE (QUEEN), Queen - square Bloomsbury; Queen-sq, Westminster; and St. Paul's-church-yard.

BARRY, Westminster.

BEACONSFIELD (EARL OF), Palace-yard.

BEDFORD (DUKE OF), Russell-square.

BENTINCK (LORD GEORGE), Cavendish-sq.

BRUNEL, Victoria Embankment.

BURNS (ROBERT), Victoria Embankment.

BYRON, (LORD), Hamilton - gdns, Hyde-pk-corner.

CANNING (GEO.), New Palace-yd.

CARLYLE (THOMAS), Chelsea Embankment.

CHARLES I., Charing ✠.

CHARLES II., Chelsea Hospital.

CLEOPATRA'S NEEDLE, Victoria Embankment.

CLYDE (LORD), Waterloo-pl.

COBDEN, Camden Tn.

CORAM (CAPT.), Foundling Hospital.

CUMBERLAND (DUKE OF). Cavendish-sq.

DERBY (EARL OF), Parliament-sq.

EDWARD VI., Christ's, St. Bartholomew's, and St. Thomas's.

ELEANOR CROSS, Charing ✠ Station.

FOX, Bloomsbury-sq.

FRANKLIN (SIR JOHN), Waterloo-place.

GEORGE I., Grosvenor-sq.

GEORGE II., Golden-sq.

GEORGE III., Somerset House and Cockspur-st.

GEORGE IV., Trafalgar-sq.

GUARDS' MEMORIAL, Waterloo-place.

GUY (THOMAS), Guy's Hospital.

HAVELOCK (GENERAL), Trafalgar-square.

HENRY VIII., St. Bartholomew's.

HERBERT (LORD), War Office, Pall Mall.

HILL, ROWLAND, Ryl. Exchange-buildings.

JAMES II., Whitehall.

JENNER (DR.), Kensington-gdns.

KENT (DUKE OF), Portland-pl.

MARBLE ARCH, Oxford-st.

MILL (JOHN STUART), Victoria Embankment.

MONUMENT, Fish-st-hill.

MYDDLETON (SIR HUGH), Islington-gn.

NAPIER (GENERAL SIR CHARLES) Trafalgar-sq.

NELSON, Trafalgar-sq.

OUTRAM (SIR J.), Victoria Embankment.

PALMERSTON (LORD), Palace-yd.

PAXTON (SIR J.), Crystal Palace.

PEEL (SIR ROBERT), Cheapside and Palace-yard.

PEABODY (GEORGE), Royal Exchange.

PITT (WILLIAM), Hanover-sq.

POET'S FOUNTAIN, Hamilton-pl.

PRINCE CONSORT, Holborn-viaduct, Horticultural Gardens, and Albert Memorial.

RAIKES (ROBERT), Victoria Embankment.

RICHARD I., Old Palace-yard.

SHAKESPEARE, Leicester-sq.

SLOANE (SIR HANS), Botanic Gardens, Chelsea.

STEPHENSON (ROBERT), Euston-square.

TEMPLE BAR MEMORIAL, Fleet-street.

TYNDALE (WILLIAM), Victoria Embankment.

VICTORIA (QUEEN), Royal Exchange.

WELLINGTON (DUKE OF), St. James's Pk, Tower-gn, and Rl. Exchange.

WESTMINSTER SCHOOL CRIMEAN MEMORIAL, Broad Sanctuary.

WILLIAM III., St. James's-sq.

WILLIAM IV., King William-st.

YORK (D. OF), Carlton House-ter.

Steamboats.-(*See* DICKENS'S DICTIONARY OF THE THAMES.)

Stock Exchange (Map 8). —The London market for the purchase and sale of public stocks, shares, and similar securities, is situated in Capel-court, and Shorter's-court, close to the Bank of England. The earliest minutes bearing upon the origin of the Stock Exchange are those of 1798 (although in them mention is made of a similar association as having existed in 1773), and from them it appears that the business of stockbrokers and jobbers was conducted towards the end of the eighteenth century partly in the Rotunda of the Bank of England, but chiefly in the rooms at the Stock Exchange Coffee House in Threadneedle-st, to which admission could be obtained on payment of sixpence. At the beginning of this century the greatly increasing business became too much for the rooms, and the indiscriminate admission of the public was calculated to expose the dealers to the loss of valuable property. Accordingly, a body of gentlemen acquired a site near Capel-ct, raised a capital of £20,000, and erected a new and spacious building for the accommodation of the new undertaking. A Committee for General Purposes was formed, and new members elected by ballot at a subscription of £10 10s. The objects of the undertaking are described by Mr. Levien, the secretary to the General Purposes Committee, to be (1) to provide a ready market, and (2) to make such regulations as would ensure the prompt and regular adjustment of all contracts. The administration of the Stock Exchange is in the hands of two bodies with distinct functions. The Managers represent the shareholders (the 400 shares have now been subdivided into 20,000), and are the executive of the proprietors of the building, but have no control over the business transacted by the members. All matters belonging to this department are in the hands of the Committee for General Purposes, who represent the subscribers or members of the Stock Exchange, and are elected by them annually. The subscriptions of members (who also have to be elected annually) are taken by the Managers, and constitute, in fact, the rent paid for the building. Candidates for election as members must be recommended by three members of not less than four years' standing, who must have personal knowledge of the applicant and his circumstances, and who engage to pay £500 each to the creditors in case the member so recommended be declared a defaulter within four years from the date of his admission. The entrance fee in this case is £315, and the subscription £31 10s. If the candidate has been a clerk in the Stock Exchange for four years previous to his application, he requires two sureties only for £300 each for four years, his entrance fee is £131 5s., and subscription £31 10s. The members are divided into brokers and jobbers or dealers ; the former buying and selling for clients, the latter being always ready to "make a price," and to buy and sell almost any quantity of current securities, looking for their profit to the difference between the price they can obtain, and that at which they can buy. There is no official tariff for commissions, this being a matter which is left for arrangement between brokers and their principals. It should be noted that, although all brokers necessarily take out a licence from the Corporation (under a penalty of £105), the possession of such a licence, which costs £5, carries with it no right of admission to the Stock Exchange, which is entirely in the hands of the Committee. This licence had long been a source of annoyance and irritation in the Mincing Lane and Stock Exchange markets, and recent consultations between their representatives and those of the Corporation led to a settlement of the question, the Corporation agreeing not to oppose the Bill which passed through both Houses of Parliament, abolishing the broker's rents, or tax of £5, in the year 1886. It should be borne in mind that the Committee of the Stock Exchange strictly forbid any members to advertise. Members unable to fulfil their engagements are publicly declared defaulters by direction of the chairman, deputy-chairman, or any two members of the committee. Defaulters are only eligible for re-admission when they have paid at least one-third of the balance of the loss caused by their failure, independently of the security money, or when they have re-couped the sureties one-third of the amount paid by them when the debts have been less than the amount secured. Further, they must have failed in one of two classes : the first for failures arising from the default of principals, where no bad faith or breach of rules has been practised, and where the operations have been in fair proportion to the defaulter's means ; the second for cases which have been marked by indiscretion and the absence of reasonable caution. Re-admission is entirely in the hands of the Committee for General Purposes, by whom also are settled all disputes between members, and between members and non-members, if the latter be willing. The names of defaulters are now officially communicated to the daily papers. The members of the Stock Exchange number about 2,600 (of whom 1,100 are brokers and the remainder jobbers). Some of the members act as clerks to others, in which case they are not allowed to transact business for themselves. The total number of clerks, including members who act in that capacity, is about 1,800. The total revenue accruing to the managers is some £126,000, which leaves a net balance of some £95,000. The shares are valuable, and the building account having been cleared off will probably be still more so. Strict privacy is maintained on the Stock Exchange, and visitors are not admitted.

Strand (Map 7).—The Strand, one of the historical streets of London, was formerly the waterside road between London and Westminster. Hence its name. Between it and the river lay the palaces of the great nobles, and on the other side the green fields stretched away without a break to the north. The road was bad then, and people who could afford it took boat for the City at Westminster-stairs, in preference to picking their way along the ill-paved streets, with the chance of being pushed aside by the numerous lackeys and retainers into the deep holes that abounded in every direction. As the steamers have driven the watermen from the river, so the growth of London has swept away the palaces, and the names of the streets alone mark where they stood. The Strand is a great thoroughfare still, and the connecting link between the City and the West. Fashion seldom goes east of Charing +, and the great drapery shops of the West End have no counterpart in the Strand ; nor upon the other hand does business, in the City man's sense of the word, come west of Temple-bar. Hence the Strand is a compromise. There is somehow an air of greater lightness and gaiety than is apparent in the City. There are more women among the foot passengers, more looking into shop windows, and an absence of that hurried walk and preoccupied look which prevail in the City proper. The difference will at once strike the observer, and is the main characteristic of the street. The stranger will probably be disappointed at his first visit to the Strand, and in truth the houses which line it are still for the most part unworthy of its position as a portion of the greatest thoroughfare in London. Nor, with the exception of the New Law Courts at its eastern end, the Charing + Hotel, the newly erected Grand Hotel, and a few private shops, has much been done in the way of improvement in the Strand. When the two churches of St. Clement Danes and St. Mary-le-Strand are swept away, and Booksellers'-row disappears, the Strand may become a noble thoroughfare; but at present there is no street of equal importance in any capital of Europe so unworthy of its position. The Strand is essentially the home of theatres. The Adelphi, Lyceum, Gaiety, Vaudeville, Strand, Terry's, and Opera Comique are in the street itself, while hard by are the Globe, the Olympic, the Savoy, the Avenue, and Toole's Theatre. Exeter Hall is also in the Strand.

Strand Theatre, on the south side of the Strand, just east of Somerset House (Map 7). Rebuilt in 1882. Specialty, comedy, burlesque, and opera bouffe, particularly the two latter. NEAREST *Ry. Stn.,* Temple (Dis.) ; *Omni-*

bus Etc., Strand ; *Cab Rank,* St. Clement's Church (N. side).

Stratford Market, FOR VEGETABLES AND AGRICULTURAL PRODUCE. — This market, established by the G.E.R. Co. on their own premises, is likely to effect an important revolution in the vegetable trade of the East End. The stalls are most conveniently arranged with a platform running along the back, to the side of which the laden trucks from the country are brought immediately on arrival, whilst in front every convenience is afforded for loading direct into the purchasers' carts. The saving of time and expense in thus avoiding the middle journey between railway and market is very great, and the new Market can hardly fail to exercise an important influence in prices throughout its neighbourhood, if not, indeed, farther west.

Streets.—It may by some be considered superfluous to give any directions for the guidance of footpassengers in the streets, but in a city where the traffic is so large, and the press and hurry so great, as is the case in London, a few words of caution will be found not to be without their use. The first thing to recollect is, that people who are only bent on pleasure should give way to those who clearly have some business object in view. What is called in America mere " loafing " should always be avoided. Not only is the " loafer " always in everybody's way, but he is invariably the favourite mark for the pickpocket. Perhaps no custom contributes more to the support of London thieves than the practice in which many ladies indulge of carrying their purses in their hands. Be very chary of strangers who accost you in the streets. It is possible that they only wish to know the time or to ask the way. It is, however, quite as likely that they belong to the great fraternity of sharpers and swell mobsmen, and are only paving the way to the ultimate transaction of business. A street row or crowd should always be avoided. If there be really some difficulty on hand, private interference can do no good, and police intervention is sure not to be long delayed. But it very frequently happens that a disturbance is created by street thieves solely with a view to their own profit. It

is well to give houses building o under repair a wide berth. Bricks, lumps of plaster, paint, workmen's tools, &c., are easily dropped from the ladder or scaffolding and may cause a lifelong injury. Visitors to London in the spring, when cleaning and repainting are the fashion, should be on their guard against wet paint. Coal-flaps and gratings of all kinds should be distrusted. A butcher with his tray, a sweep with his brush, a carpenter with his saw protruding from his basket, and a scavenger ladling mud into his cart, must be treated with the greatest respect— they will treat you with none. Scarcely less dangerous are the ladies and gentlemen who persist in swinging umbrellas, parasols, and sticks about to the common danger, without the slightest idea of the damage they may do. It is desirable, where possible, for foot passengers to keep to the right It is hardly necessary to add that any form of street altercation or quarrel should be most carefully avoided, and that in this, as most other matters, the man who knows how to give and take fairly will get through London with the least trouble and inconvenience to himself and others. Crossing, although a matter that has been lately much facilitated by the judicious erection of what may be called "refuges," and by the stationing of policeconstables at many of the more dangerous points, still requires care and circumspection. Many a general action is fought with a smaller list of killed than this class of accident annually supplies in London. One of the most fatal errors is to attempt the crossing in an undecided frame of mind, while hesitation or a change of plan midway, is ruinous. To the wary wayfarer London is the safest promenade in the world. To drive along its streets at all, a man must have his eyes about him, and his horses in hand. He will make believe to be going to run over you, no doubt, and, if you derange his calculations by suddenly pulling up or turning back, may very probably do so. But the fault will have been your own. Make up your mind before you leave the kerb what line you mean to take, and when you leave it pursue that line calmly and inexorably, and you may zigzag through any street in London every day of your life, withou the smallest fear for your bones, hatever may be the trials of nerve or ear.—(*For a description of some of the principal streets of London see under the respective names.*)

Sunday is not a pleasant day for a stranger in London. Shops and places of amusement are shut. A very large proportion of eating-houses of every kind also close entirely during Sunday, whilst many of those which open at all only do so in the evening. In the summer afternoons, however, there is generally music in the parks, especially Regent's, Victoria, and Battersea, and a Fellow's order will admit to the Zoological Gardens. It has for some inscrutable reason become fashionable to be seen on foot in Hyde-pk on Sun. Anyone studying London life should, especially in summer, visit Victoria-pk in the evening; and there are also at times preachings in some of the East End theatres. Most of the railways—especially the southern—run fast excursion trains to various points, leaving at from 7 to 9 a.m., and returning about 10 p.m., at exceedingly low fares. Sunday is also a great day for the river, now more than ever accessible from all parts of London by the new lines of the District Ry. to Richmond and Putney.

Suppers. — "Legislature's harsh decree," as Mr. Henry S. Leigh has it, and the late hours at which theatrical managers close their houses, have almost had the effect of ousting supper from its old position as a cheery public meal. Suppers, of course, can still be had in public, but there is generally, and certainly after twelve o'clock, an uncomfortable feeling that the proceedings are in some way obnoxious to the law, and as the minutes go by, the uneasiness of the head waiter is apt to damp the spirits of the *convives*. The Albion, Russell-st, opposite Drury Lane Theatre ; the Gaiety, the Criterion, and the St. James's Hall Restaurants; the Café de l'Europe, adjoining the Haymarket Theatre ; Romano's in the Strand ; Rule's in Maiden-lane ; and the Cavour in Leicester-sq, are all good houses for suppers. Most of the oyster houses can also be relied upon for a good midnight meal. The effect of the early closing Act, and one

perhaps not contemplated by its promoters, has been the establishment of an enormous number of minor clubs, whose principal business is transacted at night. It by no means follows that the Londoner who is turned out of his tavern or restaurant goes home to bed. On the contrary, he is much more likely to adjourn to his club, where he can—and does—enjoy himself until the small hours grow large again. It may be added that the rules of many of these clubs are easy, and their committees kind. Little difficulty need therefore be apprehended in obtaining admission to one or other of these *quasi* taverns.

Surgical Aid Society, The (Established 1862), Salisbury-sq, Fleet-st.—Supplies every kind of mechanical support to the afflicted poor, without limit as to locality or disease. Water-beds and invalid couches, &c., are lent upon the recommendation of subscribers. By special grants to urgent and deserving cases, the committee ensure that every patient receives prompt assistance.

Surrey County Officers. —The following is a list of the officers for the county of Surrey, 1888 :

Lord Lieutenant and Custos Rotulorum.—The Earl of Lovelace, East Horsley Towers, Leatherhead Station.

High Sheriff.—Walter Blandford Waterlow, High Trees, Redhill.

Chairman of Quarter Sessions.—E. H. L. Penrhyn, East Sheen.

Chairmen of the Courts at Newington. — 1st Court, Sir W. Hardman, 81, St. George's-rd, South Belgravia; 2nd ditto, G. Somes, Spencer Lodge, Roehampton, S.W.

Deputy Chairmen of Courts at Newington.—J. Mews, 103, Westbourne-ter; H. Yool, Oakfield, Weybridge.

Clerk of the Peace.—Sir R. H. Wyatt, Sessions House, Newington.

County Treasurer. — F. H. Beaumont, Sessions House, Newington.

Under Sheriff.—C. J. Abbott, 8, New-inn, Strand, W.C.

Clerk to Lieutenancy.—Sir R. H. Wyatt, Sessions House, Newington.

Chief Constable.—H. C. Hastings, Guildford.

County Surveyor. — C. H. Howell, 3, Lancaster-pl, Strand.

Coroners.—Camberwell, G. P. Wyatt, Esq., 33, Wiltshire-rd, S.W.; Croydon District, W. P. Morrison, Reigate ; Newington District, W. Carter, Althorp House, New Wandsworth ; Kingston District, A. B. Hicks, Kingston on-Thames; Southwark and Duchy of Lancaster, Sam. F. Langham, Esq., 10, Bartlett's-bdgs, Holborn.

County Asylum, Cane Hill.—Medical Superintendent, J. M. Moody, L.R.C.P.; Chaplain, Rev. J. C. Crawford, M.A.; Clerk to Visitors, F. Hooper.

County Asylum, Wandsworth. — Medical Superintendent, J. Strange Biggs, M.D. ; Senior Assistant Medical Officer, F. H. Ward, M.R.C.S.; Chaplain, Rev. C. E. Casher; Clerk to Visitors, J. Cartledge.

County Asylum, Brookwood.—Medical Superintendent, J. E. Barton, L.R.C.P. ; Senior Assistant Medical Officer, F. G. Gayton, M.B.; Chaplain, Rev. W. S. Sutthery, M.A. ; Clerk to Visitors, J. Cartledge.

Clerks to Justices of Divisions. —Chertsey, T. M. Jenkins ; Croydon, H. Seale ; Dorking, J. Hart ; Epsom, T. Bell ; Farnham, R. Mason ; Godstone, Alex. F. Rooke, Westerham, Edenbridge ; Guildford, F. F. Smallpeice; Kingston, J. Bell; Newington, G. C. Whiteley, Town Hall Chambers, Borough; Reigate, J. M. Head ; Richmond, J. Cartledge ; Wandsworth, A. A. Corsellis.

Surrey Magistrates.—The following are the acting magistrates of the county of Surrey, 1888: The Earl of Lovelace, Lord Lieut. and Custos Rotulorum, East Horsley Towers, Leatherhead Station.

Abinger, Ld., 46, Cromwell-gdns, S.W.

Adams, John Wood Richards, Springhill, Winkfield.

Antrobus, Sir Edmund, Bart., 11, Grosvenor-cres, S.W.

Appleyard, Major-Gen. Fredk. E., Yardkai, Surbiton.

Arbuthnot, G., Elderslie, Dorking.

Baggallay, Rt. Hon. Sir R., Kt., 55, Queen's-ga, S. Kensington.

Balfour, Jabez Spencer, 4, Marl-borough-gate, W.

Barclay, Henry Albert, Under-hill, Bletchingley, Redhill.

Barnard, H., 23, Portland-place, W.

Barrow, R. V., Engadine, Croy-don.

Baynes, Sir W. J. W., Bart., Forest Lodge,West-hill, Putney-heath.

Beaufoy, M. H., South Lambeth.

Beddington, Maurice, The Limes, Carshalton.

Bennett, Henry Curtis, Wands-worth Police-courtt.

Beresford, Marcus (Col.), Up-lands, Guildford.

Besley, Frederick John, Viewfield, Kenley, Surrey.

Bevington, James Buckingham, Merle Wood, Sevenoaks.

Bevington, Samuel Bourne (Col.), St.Thomas's-st,Southwark,S.E.

Bidder, George Parker, Q.C., Ravensbury Park, Mitcham.

Biron, Robert John, Q.C., Lam-beth Police-court.

Blackburn, Joshua, Brockwell Hall, near Dulwich, S.E.

Blenkinsop, W. E. B., 15, Earls-field-rd, Wandsworth-com,S.W.

Bonham, Sir G. F., Bt.,Cranleigh, Knowle-pk, Guildford.

Bourke, the Hon. Henry Lorton, Milburn, Esher.

Boutcher, E., Bermondsey, S.E.

Braby, James, Maybanks, Rudg-wick, Sussex.

Brand, J., Bedford-hill, Clapham.

Bridge, John, Headley, Epsom.

Brocklehurst, Edward, Kinners-ley Manor, near Reigate.

Brodrick, the Hon. W. St. J. F., M.P.,Peper Harow, Godalming, and 29, Lower Seymour-st, W.

Brooksbank, T.,Bermondsey, S.E.

Broomhall, John, Fairholme, Sur-biton.

Brown, W. S., 6, Sussex-sq, Hyde-park.

Bruce, L. B. K., Roehampton, S.W.

Buller, James Hornby (Col.), Down Hall, Epsom.

Bulpett, George.

Burdett, Sir Francis, Bart.(Lieut.-Col.), Ancaster House, Rich-mond-hill, Surrey.

Burnett, J. R. F., 2, College-villas-rd, S. Hampstead, N.W.

Byrne, Major-Gen. Thomas Ed-mund, Yekels Castle,Camberley, Surrey.

Byron, E.,Coulsdon Court, Surrey.

Calvert, Archibald Motteux (Lieut.-Colonel), Ockley Court, Dorking.

Carpenter, A., M.D., Croydon.

Cattley, John Garratt, Shabden, Merstham, Surrey.

Cave,Thomas,Queensbury House, Richmond, Surrey.

Cazalet, William Clement, Grene-hurst, Ockley Station, Surrey.

Chambers, J. H. (Lieut.-Col.), Putney House, Putney, S.W.

Chambers, William Edward, Sut-ton, Surrey.

Chance, George, Lambeth Police-court.

Churchill, Charles, Weybridge-pk, Surrey.

Churchill, H., Clapham-com,S.W.

Clark, Gordon Wyatt, Mickleham Hall, Dorking.

Clay, Sir A. T. F., Bart., Shere, Guildford.

Cockburn, William Yates, Lincoln House, Surbiton.

Colebrooke, Sir Thomas Edward, Bart., 37, South-street, W.

Collambell, Charles, 148, Lam-beth-rd, Lambeth, S.E.

Collyer, William James, Hale-bourne, Chobham.

Combe, C., Cobham-pk, Surrey.

Combe, R. H., Pierrepont House, Frensham, Farnham.

Cooper, John, jun., Hooley House, Purley, Surrey.

Corry, John, Rosenheim, Park-hill-rd, Croydon.

Coutts, Francis Burdett Money, Ancoate, Weybridge.

Cubitt, The Right Hon. George, M.P., 17, Prince's-gate, S.W.

Cunliffe, Roger, 10, Queen's-gate, S.W.

Currie, B. W., Coombe Warren, Kingston-upon-Thames.

Davis, Robert,Wandsworth-com.

De Cetto(Col.), L.C.A.A., Brook Lodge, Holmwood, Surrey.

De Salis, Rev. Henry, Portnall Park, Virginia Water, Staines.

Dingwall, Charles, Portley, Cater-ham, Surrey.

Durnford, F. A. (Lt.-Col.), Rose-dale, Walton-upon-Thames.

Eastwood, Francis Edmund, Gos-den House, Guildford.

Eastwood, J. F., Esher Lodge, Esher.

Eccles, Charles.

Edridge, Sir T. R., Elms, Croydon.

Edwards, Sir Henry, 53, Berkeley-sq, W.

Edwards, Samuel, Wood Lodge, Streatham, S.W.

Egerton, The Hon. Francis (Rear-Admiral), M.P., Devon-shire House, Piccadilly, W.

Egmont, Earl of, Nork House, Epsom.

Evelyn, W. J., Wotton, Dorking.

Evill, William, 51, St. John's-hill, New Wandsworth, S.W.

Farmer, William Robert Gamul, Nonsuch Park, Cheam, Sutton.

Farquhar, Sir Walter Rockliffe, Bart., 18, King-st, St. James's, S.W.

Farrer, Sir Thomas Henry, Bart., Abinger Hall, Dorking.

Fenton, Myles, Ridge Green House, Nutfield, Surrey.

Field, J., 108, Westminster-br-rd.

Fielden, Joshua, Nutfield Priory, Redhill.

Fletcher, Sir Henry, Bart., Ham Manor, Arundel, Sussex.

Foley, Lord, 7, Audley-sq, W.

Foley, The Hon. Fitzalan, 7, Audley-sq, W.

Francis, Frederick, East Molesey Court, Surrey.

Frankland, Edward, D.C.L., The Yews, Reigate-hill.

Freshfield, Charles Kaye, Upper Gatton-pk, Reigate.

Gabriel, Sir Thomas, Bart. Edge-combe Hall, Wimbledon, S.W.

Gabriel, Thomas, Elmstead, Leigham-ct-rd, Streatham, S.W.

Gadesden, Augustus William, Ewell Castle, Ewell.

Gassiot, John Peter, The Culvers, Carshalton.

Gatty, Charles Henry, Felbridge Park, East Grinstead.

Giffard, Admiral Sir George, K.C.B., Brightleigh, Outwood, Redhill.

Gleig, Colonel A. C., Ashtead, Epsom.

Godman, J., Park Hatch, Godalming.

Godwin-Austen, H. H. (Lt.-Col.), Shalford House, Guildford.

Goodall, George, Frensham, Farnham.

Goodson, Thomas, Hill Farm, Carshalton.

Gower, G. W. G. Leveson, Titsey Park, Godstone, Redhill.

Gower, Hon. Edward F. Leveson, 14, South Audley-st, W.

Grissell, Thomas De la Garde, Norbury Park, Dorking.

Halsey, E. J., Pirbright, and 9, Drayton-gardens, S.W.

Hambro, E. A., Roehampton, S.W.

Hampton, John Vivian, Oakdale, The Holmwood, Dorking.

Hankey, Fred. Alers, M.P., 44, Lowndes-sq, S.W.

Hankey, John Barnard, Fetcham Park Leatherhead.

Hardman, Sir William, 81, St. George's-rd, South Belgravia, S.W.

Harrison, James Fortescue, 41, Ovington-sq, S.W.

Hartopp, Sir J. W. C., Bt., King's Wood Warren, Epsom.

Healey, Edward Charles, Wyphurst, Cranley, Guildford.

Heaming, Wm. Walter, Woodhill, Wonersh, Surrey.

Heath, D. D., Kitlands, Dorking.

Heath, Henry H., The Rylands, Upper Norwood, S.E.

Heath, Sir L. (Rear - Admiral, K.C.B.), Holmwood, Dorking.

Henderson, John Effingham, Crawley Down, Crawley.

Hetley, F., M.D., Norbury Lodge, Upper Norwood, S.E.

Hoare, H. G., 37, Fleet-st, E.C.

Hoare, Thomas Rolls, Marlow House, Kingston-upon-Thames.

Hodgson, James Stewart, Denbigh, Haslemere.

Holland, The Right Hon. Sir H. T., Bart, M.P., 65, Rutland-gate, S.W.

Hollings, Herbert J. B., The Watchetts, Frimley.

Hopgood, J., Clapham-com, S.W.

Hornidge, Marmaduke, Milbourne House, Barnes, S.W.

Howard, Robert Mowbray, Hampton Lodge, Farnham.

Hutton, Charles William Cookworthy, Belair, Dulwich, S.E.

Hyslop, Akroyd, Hilton Grange, Sutton.

Hylton, Lord, 16, Stratton - st, Piccadilly, W.

Ingram, William James, *Illustrated London News* Office, 198, Strand, W.C.

Judd, James, South Knoll, Upper Norwood, S.E.

Keene, Samuel Wolfe, Mill Lodge, Barnes, S.W.

Kemmis, Arthur Henry Nicholas, Croham Hurst, Croydon.

King, Hugh Fortescue Lock, Brooklands, Weybridge.

Knight, Charles Raleigh, Tekells Frimley, Farnboro' Station.

Lainson, Henry, Colley Manor, Reigate.

Landell, William Wright, Thomas-st, Horselydown, S.E.

Latrobe-Bateman, John Frederick, F.R.S., Moor Park, Farnham, and 18, Abingdon-st, S.W.

Lawrence, Henry W., Alenko, Ridgeway, Wimbledon.

Lawrence, Sir J. C., Bt., Pitfield-wharf, Waterloo-br, S.E.

Lawrence, Sir Trevor, Bart., M.P., 57, Prince's-gate, S.W.

Leckie, Patrick Comrie, 15, Ashburn-pl, Cromwell-rd, S.W.

Le Marchant, Sir H. D., Bart., Chobham-pl, Wokingham.

Lindsay, Charles Robert, Glen Lea, Dulwich-com, S.E.

Lodwick, Robert William.

Lovelace, The Earl of (Lord-Lieutenant), East Horsley Towers, Leatherhead Station.

Lloyd, Lewis, Monk's Orchard, Beckenham.

Lucas, Charles Thomas, Warnham Court, Horsham.

Lucas, Thomas, 37, Great George-st, S.W.

Lushington, Edward Harbord, Brackenhurst, Cobham, Surrey.

McArthur, Alexander, M.P., Raleigh Hall, Brixton, S.W.

Macdonald, Sir A. K., Bart., Woolmer Lodge, Liphook, Hants.

Macdonald, Duncan, Weybank Lodge, Guildford.

Margary, Alfred Robert (Major), Chartham Park, East Grinstead.

Marsack, Major-Genl. Augustus

Becker, Elstead Lodge, Godalming.

Marshall, Frederick (General), Broadwater, Godalming.

Maxwell, Sir John Robert Heron, Bart., Hamilton House, Lower Tooting, S.W.

Mews, J., 107, Westbourne-ter, W.

Midleton, The Viscount, 89, Eaton-sq, S.W.

Morgan, Octavius Vaughan, 13, The Boltons, S.W.

Mortimer, C., Streatham, S.W.

Murray, George James, Mytchett Place, Frimley, Surrey.

Murray, John, 50, Albemarle-street, W.

Murray, Robert Hay, Godington Park, Ashford, Kent.

Nicholson, Samuel, Union Club, Trafalgar-sq, W.C.

Northey, Rev. Edward Wm., Woodcote House, Epsom.

Northumberland, The Duke of, Albury Park, Guildford.

Ogg, Sir W. A., Oakfield, College-rd, Dulwich, S.W.

Ogilvie, Glencairn Stewart, Athol House, Surbiton-rd, Kingston.

Ommanney, Octavius (Lieut.-Col.), Bloxham, Banbury, Oxon.

Onslow, Earl of, 7, Richmond-ter, Whitehall, S.W.

Onslow, Pitcairn (Major), Dunsboro' House, Woking Station.

Oxenbridge, Viscount, 29, Belgrave-sq, S.W.

Palmer, William, Market-st, Bermondsey, S.E.

Pares, John, The Cedars, Farnham.

Pattison, H. J., Kingston-upon-Thames.

Pawle, F. C., Northcote, Reigate.

Peek, Sir Henry William, Bart., Wimbledon House, S.W.

Pennington, Frederick, Broom Hall, Dorking.

Penrhyn, Edward Hugh, Leycester, East Sheen, S.W.

Percy, Lord Algernon, Merrow Grange, Guildford.

Percy, The Earl, Albury Park, Guildford.

Pilcher, John G., Englefield-gn, Surrey.

Pinckard, George Henry, Combe Court, Godalming.

Pocock, Thomas Willmer, Glenridge, Virginia Water, Staines,

Pollock, Sir C. E. (one of the Barons of the Court of Exchequer), The Croft, Putney, S.W.

Powell, A., Milton Heath, Dorking.

Porcelli, Captain Allan Roger Charles, Hill House, Lyndhurst, Hants.

Ralli, Pandeli, 17, Belgrave-sq, S.W.

Ramsden, John C. F. (Capt.), Busbridge Hall, Godalming.

Rate, Lachlan Mackintosh, Milton Court House, Dorking.

Rennie, John Keith, 6, Holland-st, Blackfriars, S.E.

Renton, John Thomson, Bradstone Brook, Shalford, Guildford.

Revelstoke, Lord, Coombe Cottage, Kingston-upon-Thames.

Ricardo, Percy, Bramley Park, Guildford.

Ross, John Stephen (Colonel H. M. Indian Army), Rydal, Wimbledon, S.W.

Rothery, Henry C., 94, Gloucester-ter, Hyde-pk-gardens, W.

Rowcliffe, Edward Lee, 1, Bedford-row, W.C.

Rowe, Captain Edward Fisher, Thornecombe, Bromley, Surrey.

Rugge-Price, Charles, Spring-gr, Richmond, Surrey.

Russell, Sir Charles, Q.C., M.P., 86, Harley-st, W.

Sassoon, Joseph Sassoon, Ashley Park, Walton-on-Thames.

Saunders, Charles Burslem, C.B., Westbourne Lodge, College-rd, Dulwich, S.E.

Saunders, Thomas, 120, Holland-rd, Kensington, W.

Scott, Harry Warren, Forbes House, Ham, Richmond.

Scott, W. C., 14, Brechin-pl, South Kensington.

Scovell, George, 25, Grosvenor-pl, Hyde-pk-cor, S.W.

Scovell, George Thomas (Capt.), Woodcote, Dorking.

Seymour, Leopold R. (Lieut.-Col.), Brockham Park, Betchworth.

Sharpe, Captain Marcus, White's Grounds, Bermondsey, S.E.

Sheil, James, Southwark Police Court.

Sherbrooke, Viscnt., 34, Lowndes-sq, S.W.

Sherrard, James Corry, 7, Oxford-sq, Hyde-pk, W.

Sibley, Thomas Harmer (Major-Gen.), Shirley Goss, Caterham.

Simmonds, John Whately, 132, York-rd, Lambeth, S.E.

Simmons, James, Cherrimans, Haslemere, Surrey.

Smith, Charles Edward, Silvermere, Cobham, Surrey.

Smith, Samuel.

Smyth, J. H. (Major-Gen., C.B.), Frimhurst, Farnboro' Station.

Somes, George, Spencer Lodge, Roehampton, and 62, Great Cumberland-pl, W.

Soper, William Garland, Harestone, Caterham Valley.

Spence, Frederick (Major-Gen., C.B.), Lime Lodge, Englefield-gn, Staines.

Spring, Robert (Major).

Steere, L., Jayes, Ockley, Dorking.

Stern, Sydney, 10, Great Stanhope-street, W.

Stone, David Henry, St. Thomas's Hospital, S.E.

Stone, W. H., Lea Park, Godalming.

Stonor, His Honour, Judge, 1, Stafford-ter, Kensington, W.

Stopford, Robert Fanshawe (Admiral), Mount Ararat, Richmond, Surrey.

Strafford, The Earl of, 34, Wilton-pl, S.W.

Stringer, Miles (Colonel).

Strong, Richard, 3, Champion-pk, Denmark-hill, S.E.

Sumner, Arthur Holme, Hatchlands, Guildford.

Tate, Henry, Park-hill, Streatham, S.W.

Terry, T. H. C. (Lieut.-Colonel), Burvale Hersham, Walton-on-Thames.

Thornton, Thomas Henry, C.S.I., D.C.L., 23, Bramham-gardens, South Kensington.

Thring, Lord, 5, Queen's-gate-gdns, S.W.

Topham, Sir William (Lieut.-Colonel), Noirmont, Weybridge.

Tredcroft, Charles Lennox (Major), Glen Ancrum, Guildford.

Tritton, Henry John, Ewell House, Ewell.

Truscott, Sir Francis Wyatt, 103, Victoria-st, S.W.

Turney, George Leonard, The Grove, Camberwell, S.E.

Vade-Walpole, Charles C, B., Broadford, Chobham,

Vincent, Sir Wm., Bart., Comportsfield, Ashstead, Surrey.

Waterfield, Ottiwell Charles, Nackington, nr. Canterbury.

Webb, Robert William, Milford House, Godalming.

Webster, James Hume, Mardea Deer Park, Caterham.

Weeding, Thomas Weeding, Les Rochers, Addlestone, Surrey.

Welch, Stanley Kemp, 55, Cornwall-gdns, South Kensington.

Weston, Lieut.-Col. William, Bramley, Guildford.

White, George Frederick, 1, Porchester-gate, Hyde-pk, W.

White, Sir William, C.B., Stonehill, Upper Sheen, S.W.

Williams, Montagu, Q.C., Police Court, Wandsworth.

Wilson, John, The Laurels, Upper Tooting, S.W.

Wilson, John Walter, The Beeches, Oatlands-park, Weybridge.

Worms, Baron G. de, 17, Parkcres, Portland-pl, N.W.

Wrottesley, The Hon. E. B., Middleton Lodge, Bournemouth.

Yool, Henry, Oakfield, Weybridge.

Young, John, Kenley, Surrey.

Young, W., Stanhill Court, Charlwood, Surrey.

Surrey Theatre, Blackfriars-rd (Map 13).—The principal Surrey-side theatre, standing just at the junction of the great roads from Westminster, Waterloo, and Blackfriars bridges. Specialty, melodrama, farce, and pantomime. NEAREST Ry. Stn., Borough-rd (L.C.&D.); Omnibus Rtes, Blackfriars-rd, Waterloo-rd, and West minster-br-rd.

Surveyors.—(See VESTRIES.)

Sweden and Norway.—MINISTRY, 47, Charles-st, Berkeley-sq. NEAREST Ry. Stn., St. James's-pk (Dis.); Omnibus Rtes., Piccadilly, Park-la, Oxford-st, and Regent-st; Cab Rank, Piccadilly. CONSULATE, 24, Great Winchester-st. NEAREST Ry. Stns., Bishopsgate (G.E.) and Mansion House (Met.); Omnibus Rtes., Moorgate-st, Old Broad-st, and Cheapside; Cab Rank, New Broad-st.

Swedenborgians. — (See NEW JERUSALEM CHURCH.)

Switzerland.— CONSULATE, 25, Old Broad-st. NEAREST Ry.

Stns., Broad-st (N.L.) and Bishopsgate-st (G.E.);
Omnibus Rtes., Old Broad-st, Moorgate-st, and
Cheapside ; *Cab Rank*, Liverpool-st.

Telegraph Department (Government
Indo-European), 49 and 50, Parliament - st, S.W.
Nearest *Ry. Stn.*, Westminster-br ; *Omnibus
Rtes.*, Parliament-st, Strand, Victoria-st, West-
minster-br ; *Cab Rank*, Palace-yd.

Telegraph Offices are, as a rule, open from
8 a.m. to 8 p.m. on week days, and from 8 a.m.
to 10 a.m. on Sundays. The following offices are
open later :—

Name of Office.	Week-day Attendance.	Sunday Attendance.
	a.m. p.m.	a.m. p.m.
Blackheath Village	8 to 10	8 to 8
Blackwall	8 ,, 10	8 ,, 8
Bow	7 ,, 11	8 ,, 10
Brixton Rise	8 ,, 9	..
Camberwell	8 ,, 11	8 ,, 10
Camden-rd	7 ,, 11	8 ,, 8
Cen. Telegraph Stn.	Open always.	
Chalk Farm	8 ,, 11	8 ,, 8
Clapham Common.	8 ,, 10	8 ,, 10
Ealing	8 ,, 10	8 to 10, 5 to 6
Eastern Dis. Office	7 ,, 11	8 to 8
Euston-sq	6 ,, 11	8 ,, 10
Fleet-st	8 a.m. to 3 a.m.	..
Forest Hill	8 to 10	..
Fulham-rd, 262	8 ,, 11	8 ,, 8
Greenwich (Nel-son-st)	8 ,, 10	8 ,, 10
Hammersmith	8 ,, 11	8 ,, 8
Hampstead-gn	8 ,, 11	8 ,, 8
*Holborn Viaduct (L.C.&D.R.Stn.)	8 ,, 9	..
Holloway-rd, 422	8 ,, 11	8 ,, 10
Kensington (Young-st)	8 ,, 11	8 ,, 8
King's ✠ (G.N.R.)	Open always.	
Kingsland High-st	8 ,, 11	8 ,, 10
Lambeth, 42, Ken-nington-rd	8 ,, 9	..
*London Bridge (L.B. & S.C.R.)	Open always.	
Lower Thames-st.	6 ,, 8	..
*Ludgate Hill Stn. (L.C. & D.R.)	8 ,, 10	9 to 10 { 1 to 3 { 6 to 8
Moorgate-st-bdgs	Open always.	
N. Dis. Office	7 ,, 11	8 to 10
Norwood Dis. Office	8 ,, 10	8 ,,
Notting-hill (near Archer-st)	8 ,, 11	8 ,, 8
Paddington (Lon-don-st)	7 ,, 11	8 ,, 8
*Paddingtn.(G.W.)	Open always.	
Peckham	8 ,, 9	..
Putney	8 ,, 10	8 to 10, 5 to 6
St. John's Wood (Circus-rd)	8 ,, 11	8 ,, 10
*St Pancras Stn. (Midland Ry.)	Open always.	
S.E. Dis. Office	7 ,, 11	8 ,, 8

Name of Office.	Week-day Attendance	Sunday Attendance.
	a.m. p.m.	a.m. p.m.
South Kensington (Exhibition-rd)	8 to 11	8 to 8
S.W. Dis. Office	7 ,, 11	8 ,, 8
Stratford	8 ,, 10	8 ,, 8
Swiss Cottage	8 ,, 11	
Victoria Docks	8 ,, 10	
*Victoria Station (L.B. & S.C.R.)	4 a.m. to 1 a.m.	
*Victoria Station (L.C. & D.R.)	Open always.	
*Waterloo Station (L. & S.W.R.)	6 a.m to mid.	8 ,, 11
W. Dis. Office	7 to 11	8 ,, 8
W.C. Dis. Office	7 ,, 11	8 ,, 8
West Strand	Open always.	
White Hart - lane, Tottenham	8 ,, 10	8 to 10, 5 to 6
Wimbledon	8 ,, 10	8 ,, 10, 5 ,, 6

* These offices only collect telegrams.

Telephones.—(*See* United Telephone Co.)

Temperance Restaurants.—(*See* Coffee
Public Houses.)

Temple.—(*See* Inns of Court.)

Terry's Theatre, 105, Strand (Map 7).—A
handsome and commodious building, fitted with all
modern improvements and appliances ; built and
designed by Mr. Walter Emden, and opened for the
first time on 17th October, 1887, under the management of Mr. Edward Terry, Sole Lessee. Nearest *Ry.
Stns.*, Charing ✠ (Dist. and S.E.); *Omnibus Rtes.*,
Strand and St. Martin's-la ; *Cab Rank*, Bedford-st.

Thames, The.—Every detail of interest connected with the river, from its source to the Nore,
including reports of regattas, articles on rowing,
bathing, camping-out, the favourite trips from Lech-
lade to Richmond, and similar matters, will be found
fully set forth in Dickens's Dictionary of the
Thames, price 1s.; sold everywhere. There are also
full descriptions of Oxford city, and of all the Colleges of the University, as well as of Abingdon,
Wallingford, Reading, Henley, Windsor and
Windsor Castle, Richmond, Gravesend, Southend,
etc., etc., with exhaustive articles by well-known
specialists on the ornithology, geology, etc., of the
Thames Valley.

Thatched House Club, 86, St. James's-st.—
A social club with no political bias. The election of
members is vested in an election committee. One
black ball in five excludes. Entrance fee, £26 5s.;
subscription, £10 10s.

Theatres.—(*See* Appendix.)

Toole's Theatre, King William-st, Strand
(Map 7).—This pretty theatre—formerly the " Folly,"
and at one time the " Charing Cross "—was enlarged
and improved by Mr. Toole in the winter of 1881-2,
and reopened on Thursday, the 16th of February,
1882. The name of the theatre sufficiently indicates
the class of entertainment which it offers to the
public. Nearest *Ry. Stns.*, Charing ✠ (Dis. &
S.E.); *Omnibus Rtes.*, Strand and St. Martin's-la ;
Cab Rank, Duncannon-st.

Tourist Agencies have of late years assumed a rather important place in the economy of London. The system was originally started by Messrs. Cook & Son, formerly of Leicester, now of Ludgate-cir. For some time they had a practical monopoly of the business, and the "Cook's Tourist" has for years been a recognised feature of Continental travel. Messrs. Gaze & Son, 142, Strand, who now divide the business with them, have not achieved quite so wide a notoriety, but provide the intending tourist with the same facilities, both for ordinary expeditions and for those joint-stock journeyings known as "personally conducted parties." A comparison of the books of fares issued by the two firms shows, that while a variation now and then occurs of a penny, or even a shilling, upon their respective charges, the prices are practically, and in most cases identically, the same. The charge is about 8s. a day for bedroom, lights, service, plain breakfast or tea, and dinner at the *table d'hôte*. A second meat meal involves the additional daily expenditure of from 6d. to 9d. It should be noted that Messrs. Gaze dispose of their coupons to all comers, Messrs. Cook only to those travelling with the tickets of the firm. Messrs. Swan & Leach (Lim.), of Charing ✠ and Piccadilly-cir, also transact a large business as tourist-agents, and have several country branches.

Tower of London (Map 8), once a fortress, a royal residence, a court of justice, and a prison, is now a government storehouse and armoury, and a show place for visitors. The most conspicuous part of the series of buildings enclosed by the moat is the White Tower, whose founder, tradition has it, was Julius Cæsar. William the Conqueror was the authentic builder of the structure, which was subsequently improved upon by Henry III. Inside is the chapel of St. John, the most perfect specimen of Norman architecture in the kingdom. Surrounding the White Tower is a series of battlements now used for government purposes, flanked by a number of smaller towers, many of which are celebrated for the captives who have been imprisoned in them. For instance, in the Well Tower Queen Elizabeth was immured; in the

Devereux Tower the Earl of Essex; and in the White Tower Sir Walter Raleigh. In the Bloody Tower the two sons of Edward IV. were murdered; and in Bowyer's Tower Clarence is supposed to have been drowned in a butt of malmsey wine. The Beauchamp Tower was built probably by Henry III. The last executions took place after the rebellion of 1745, when Lords Lovat, Balmerino, and Kilmarnock were beheaded for high treason. The latest occupants of the Tower as state prisoners were Sir Francis Burdett, and the gang of ruffians known as the Cato Street Conspirators. The regalia or jewel-house is a show place, and contains the royal crowns and sceptres and other jewels, whilst in the armoury is as magnificent a collection of armour and weapons as there is extant. The Tower is open to the public from 10 till 4. Admission to the Armouries, 6d., and to the Jewel House, 6d.; free on Mon. and Sat.; and open from 10 till 6 on these days from May to September inclusive. NEAREST *Ry. Stns.*, Mark-la (Dis. & Met.) and Cannon-st (S.E.); *Omnibus Rtes.*, Fenchurch-st and Aldgate High - st; *Cab Rank*, Great Tower-st.

Tower Subway.—A curious feat of engineering skill, in the shape of an iron tube seven feet in diameter driven through the bed of the Thames between Great Tower - hill and Vine-st. The original intention was to have passengers drawn backwards and forwards in a small tram omnibus. The tunnel is now used as a footway. NEAREST *Ry. Stns.*, Mark-la (Dis. & Met.) and Fenchurch-st (G.E.); *Omnibus Rtes.*, Aldgate High-st and Fenchurch-st; *Cab Rank*, Tower Hill.

Trafalgar Square (Map 7) has been called the finest site in Europe, but it is, even now, far from having been utilised to the extent of its possibilities. The National Gallery and St. George's Barracks occupy the whole of the upper or N. side of the square: the church of St. Martin-in-the-Fields stands in the N.E. corner; on the E. side are the premises occupied by the Royal Humane Society, and Morley's Hotel; on the W. side are the Royal College of Physicians and the Union Club; on the

S. side of the square are the Grand Hotel on the site of Northumberland House, and the plot between Northumberland-avenue and Parliament-st, on which the National Liberal Club now stands; while W. of Parliament-street are some shops and insurance offices as far as the entrance to Spring-gdns. Nelson's monument with its four lions, is the most conspicuous feature of the square, which contains, moreover, statues of Napier, Havelock, and other worthies. The fountains, which ought to add to the appearance of the place, in reality detract from it, by the ridiculous insufficiency of their jets of water; and it is to be hoped that the flight of time will materially improve the appearance of the trees. NEAREST *Ry. Stns.*, Charing ✠ (Dis. & S.E.); *Omnibus Rtes.*, St. Martin's-la and Charing ✠; *Cab Rank*, Trafalgar-sq.

Tramways.—The following information respecting the principal tramways has been furnished, on request, by the respective companies:—

On Sundays and Bank Holidays the cars start one hour later in the morning, and cease running the same time at night.

‡ The penny fares and the transfer tickets are suspended on Sundays and Holidays, including the Bank Holidays.

The North Metropolitan Tramways Company.

BALLS POND LINE.—*Colour*, Green. *Route*, Graham - rd, Ball's Pond-rd, Essex-rd, and Goswell-rd. (3½ miles, 35 minutes.) *Fares*, Mare-st, Hackney, and Aldersgate, 3d.; Mare-st, Hackney, and Angel, 2d.; Dalston Junction and Aldersgate, 2d.; ‡Dalston Junction and Mare-st, 1d. First car from Mare-st, 7.20; last, 11.10. First car from Aldersgate-st, 7.58; last, 11.51.

BARKING-ROAD LINE.—*Colour*, Red. *Route*, Canning Town Station to Greengate. (1⅓ miles, 12 minutes.) *Fare*, any distance, 1d. First car from Canning Town, 5.25; last, 11.13. First car from Greengate, 5.5; last, 10.53.

BARKING BUSSES.—From Poplar Stn. to Canning Town Stn. (¾ mile, 10 min.) *Fare*, ½d. First bus from Poplar Station, 7.50; last, 11.5. First bus from Canning Town Station, 8.6; last, 11.21.

BISHOPSGATE LINE. — *Colour*, White. *Route*, Stoke Newingtn-rd, High-st, Kingsland-rd, Shoreditch. (3miles, 30minutes.) *Fare*, Weaver's Arms and Norton Folgate, 2d. First car from Weaver's Arms, 7.38; last, 10.42. First car from Norton Folgate, 8.12; last, 11.16.

CANONBURY LINE. — *Colour* Chocolate. *Route*, Seven Sisters-rd, Holloway-rd, Canonbury-rd, New North-rd, East-rd, and City-rd. (4 miles, 40 minutes.) *Fares*, Finsbury-pk and Moorgate-st, 3d.; Finsbury-pk and Essex-rd, 2d.; Highbury-stn and Moorgate-st, 2d. ‡Finsbury-pk and Nag's Head, 1d.; ‡Nag's Head and Highbury-stn, 1d. First car from Finsbury-pk, 7.50; last, 11.4. First car from Moorgate, 8.25; last, 11.51

DALSTON-LANE AND HOLBORN. —*Colour*, Yellow. *Route*, Mare-st, Hackney-road, Old-st, and Clerkenwell-rd. (3¾ miles, 37 minutes.) *Fares*, Dalston-la and Holborn, 3d.; Dalston-la and Goswell-rd, 2d.; Well-st and Holborn, 2d.; ‡Hackney Station and Cambridge Heath, 1d.; City-rd and Holborn, 1d. First car from Dalston-la, 7.7; last, 11.3. First car from Holborn, 7.50; last, 11.49.

FINSBURY PARK AND MOORGATE-ST.—*Colour*, Yellow. *Route*, Seven Sisters-rd, Holloway-rd, Upper-st, and City-rd. (4¼ miles, 42 minutes.) *Fares*, Finsbury-pk and Moorgate, 3d.; Finsbury-pk and Angel, 2d.; ‡Finsbury-pk and Nag's Head, 1d.; ‡Nag's Head and Highbury-stn, 1d.; ‡Highbury-stn and Angel, 1d. First car from Finsbury-pk, 7.5; last, 11.4. First car from Moorgate, 7.50; last, 11.53.

HIGHGATE AND ALDERSGATE-ST.—*Colour*, Red.—*Route*, Upper Holloway, Holloway-rd, Upper-st, and Goswell-rd. (3¾ miles, 38 minutes.) *Fares*, Highgate and Aldersgate, 3d.; Highgate and Angel, 2d.; Highbury-stn and Aldersgate, 2d.; ‡Highgate and Nag's Head, 1d.; ‡Nag's Head and Highbury-stn, 1d; ‡Highbury-stn and Angel, 1d. First car from Highgate, 7.45; last, 10.46. First car from Aldersgate, 8.26; last, 11.30

HIGHGATE AND MOORGATE-ST.—*Colour* Blue. *Route*, Upper Holloway, Holloway-rd, Liverpool-rd, and City-rd. (4¼ miles, 42 minutes.) *Fares*, Highgate and Moorgate, 3d.; Highgate and

Angel, 2d.; Station-rd, Highbury, and Moorgate, 2d.; ‡Highgate and Nag's Head, 1d.; ‡Nag's Head and Station-rd, 1d.; ‡Station-rd and Angel, 1d. First car from Highgate, 7; last, 11.8 First car from Moorgate, 7.45; last, 11.57.

KING'S ✛ LINE.—*Colour*, Red, light-band. *Route*, Seven Sisters-rd, Holloway-rd, Camden-rd, Caledonian-rd. (2¾ miles, 27 min.) *Fares*, Finsbury-pk and King's ✛, 3d.; Finsbury-pk and Offord-rd, 2d.; Nag's Head and King's ✛ 2d.; ‡Finsbury-pk and Nag's Head, 1d.; ‡Nag's Head and Offord-rd, 1d.; ‡Offord-rd and King's ✛, 1d. First car from Finsbury-pk, 7.43; last 11.43. First car from King's ✛, 8.13; last 12.13.

KINGSLAND LINE. — *Colour*, Red. *Route*, Stamford-hill, Stoke Newington-rd, High-st, Kingsland-rd, Old-st, and City-rd. (4 miles, 41 minutes.) *Fares*, Stamford-hill and Moorgate, 3d.; Stamford-hill and Shoreditch, 2d.; Weaver's Arms and Moorgate, 2d.; ‡Brooke-rd and Stamford-hill, 1d.; First car from Stamford-hill, 7.20; last, 11.1. First car from Moorgate, 8.4; last, 11.49.

LEYTONSTONE LINE.—*Colour*, Blue. From Stratford, *via* Leytonstone-rd to Green Man. (2¼ miles, 22 minutes.) *Fares*, Stratford to Leytonstone, 2d.; ‡Stratford and Plough and Harrow, 1d.; ‡Plough and Harrow and Green Man, 1d. First car from Stratford, 7; last, 11.5. First car from Green Man, 7.30; last, 11.35.

LOWER CLAPTON AND BLOOMSBURY. — *Colour*, Blue. *Route*, Lower Clapton-rd, Mare-st, Hackney-rd, Old-st, Clerkenwell-rd, Theobald's-road. (5¼ miles, 52 min.) *Fares*, Lea-bridge-rd and Bloomsbury, 3d.; Lea-bridge-rd and Shoreditch, 2d.; Median-rd and Goswell-rd, 2d.; Well-st and Bloomsbury, 2d.; City-rd and Bloomsbury, 1d.; ‡Lea-br-rd and Hackney-stn, 1d.; ‡Hackney-stn and Cambridge Heath, 1d. First car from Lea-br-rd, 6.52; last, 10.58. First car from Bloomsbury, 7.43; last, 11.58.

MANOR HOUSE LINE.—*Colour*, Green. *Route*, Green-lanes, Southgate-rd, Bridport-pl, Mintern-st, East-rd, and City-rd. (3¾ miles, 38 minutes.) *Fares*, Manor House and Moorgate, 3d.; Manor House and Balls Pond-rd, 2d.; Riversdale-rd and Sturt Arms, 2d.; Newington-gn and Moorgate-

st, 2d.; ‡Riversdale-rd and Manor House, 1d. First car from Manor House, 7.58; last, 10.55. First car from Moorgate, 8.39; last, 11.59.

MUSEUM LINE.—*Colour*, Red. *Route*, Mare-st, Cambridge-rd, Mile End-rd, Whitechapel. (2¼ miles, 23 minutes.) *Fares*, Well-st, Hackney, and Aldgate, 2d.; ‡Well-st and Bethnal Green-rd, 1d. First car from Well-st, 7.30; last, 11.4. First car from Aldgate, 7.56; last, 11.32.

POPLAR LINE.—*Colour*, Yellow. *Route*, East India-rd and Commercial-rd (2¾ miles, 29minutes.) *Fares*, Poplar and Aldgate, 2d.; ‡Poplar and Burdett-rd, 1d.; ‡North-st and Stepney-stn, 1d; ‡Burdett-rd and George, 1d.; ‡Stepney-stn and New-rd 1d.; ‡George and Aldgate, 1d. First car from Poplar, 7; last, 11.29. First car from Aldgate, 7.32; last, 12.3.

ROMFORD-ROAD LINE.—*Colour*, Red. From Stratford, *via* Romford-rd to White Post-la, Manor-pk. (2 miles, 21 minutes.) *Fares*, Stratford and Manor-pk, 2d.; Princess Alice and Manor-pk, 1d.; Princess Alice and Stratford, 1d. First car from Stratford, 7.30; last, 11. First car from Manor-pk, 7.55; last, 11.25.

STAMFORD HILL AND HOLBORN.—*Colour*, Green. *Route*, Stamford-hill, Stoke Newington-rd, High-st, Kingsland-rd, Old-st, and Clerkenwell-rd. (4¾ miles, 47 minutes.) *Fares*, Stamford-hill and Holborn, 3d.; Stamford-hill and Shoreditch, 2d.; Weavers' Arms and Goswell-rd, 2d.; Dalston Junction and Holborn, 2d.; City-rd and Holborn, 1d.; ‡Brooke-rd and Stamford-hill, 1d. First car from Stamford-hill, 7.26; last, 10.57. First car from Holborn, 8.19; last, 11.54.

STRATFORD LINE. — *Colour*, Blue. *Route*, High-st, Bow-rd, Mile End-rd, and Whitechapel. (3¾ miles, 38 minutes.) *Fares*, Stratford and Aldgate, 3d.; Stratford and Burdett-rd, 2d.; Bowbridge and Aldgate, 1d. First car from Stratford, 5.55; last, 11.25. First car from Aldgate, 6.40; last, 12.10.

UPPER CLAPTON AND MOORGATE. — *Colour*, White. *Route*, Upper Clapton-rd, Lower Clapton-rd, Mare-st, Hackney-rd, Old-st, and City-rd. (4½ miles, 48 minutes.) *Fares*, Upper Clapton and Moorgate, 3d.; Clapton and Cambridge

Heath, 2d. ; Lea-bridge-rd and Shoreditch, 2d.; Median-rd and Moorgate, 2d.; ‡ Upper Clapton and Lea-bridge-rd 1d. ; ‡Lea-bridge-rd and Hackney-stn, 1d.; ‡Hackney - stn and Cambridge Heath, 1d. First car from Upper Clapton 7.45; last, 10.56. First car from Moorgate, 8.36 ; last, 11.52.

VICTORIA-PARK LINE.—*Colour*, Yellow. *Route*, Cassland-rd, Victoria-pk, Grove-rd, and Burdett-rd. (2¾ miles, 28 minutes.) *Fare*, Cassland-rd and West India Dk, 2d. ; Cassland-rd and Mile End-rd, 1d. ; Roman-rd and Burdett-rd Station, 1d ; Mile End-rd and West India Dock, 1d. First car from Cassland-rd, 7 ; last, 10.54. First car from West India Dock 7.36 ; last, 11.30.

London Street Tramways Co.

CLERKENWELL-RD AND HOLLOWAY-RD.—*Route*—King's ✠-rd and Caledonian-rd. *Fares*—Holloway-rd and Clerkenwell-rd, 2d. ; Copenhagen-st and Clerkenwell-rd, 1d. *Week Days*—8.25 a.m. to 11.5 p.m. *Sundays*—9.53 a.m. to 11.5 p.m.

HAMPSTEAD HEATH AND ANGEL. — *Route* — Southampton-rd, Shipton, Prince of Wales's -rd, Kentish Town-rd, and Gt. College-st, Pancras-rd, King's ✠, and Pentonville. Cars run every 5 minutes in each direction from 7.45 a.m. until 3 p.m., and then every 3 mins. until 10.56 p.m., after which cars at intervals of 7 mins. run from Shipton to Angel until 11.20 p.m.

HIGHGATE AND EUSTON-RD.—*Route*—Highgate Archway, Junction-rd, Kentish Town-rd, High-st (Camden Tn.), and Hampstead-rd to Euston-rd. Cars run every 5 minutes in each direction till 4.30 p.m., then every 4 mins. to 9 p.m. *Week days*—Archway to Euston-rd, 7.45 a.m. to 11.32 p.m.; Euston-rd to Archway, 8.21 a.m. to 12.9 p.m. *Sundays*—Archway to Euston-rd, 9.20 a.m. to 11 p.m.; Euston-rd to Archway,10.13 a.m. to 11.37 p.m. *Fare*—Between Highgate Archway and Euston-rd, 2d.

HOLLOWAY AND EUSTON-RD. – *Route* – Parkhurst-rd, Camden-rd, High-st (Camden Tn.), Hampstead-rd to Euston-rd. Cars run every five minutes. *Week days* —Nag's Head to Euston-rd, 7.35 a.m. to 11.40 p.m. ; Euston-rd to Nag's Head, 8.7 a.m. to 12.20 p.m. *Sundays*—Nag's Head to Euston-rd, 9.22 a.m. to 11.10 p.m.; Euston-

rd to Nag's Head, 9.54 a.m. to 11.40 p.m. *Fare*—Nag's Head to Euston-rd, inside or outside, week days 2d., Sundays 3d.

KING'S ✠ & FINSBURY PARK. *Route*—Caledonian-rd, Camden-rd, Holloway - rd, and Seven Sisters-rd. *Fares*—King's ✠ and Offord-rd, 1d. ; Offord-rd and Nag's Head, 1d. ; Nag's Head to Finsbury-park, 1d. ; Finsbury-park to Offord-rd, 2d. ; Nag's Head and King's ✠, 2d ; Finsbury-park and King's ✠, 3d. *Week days*, 8.17 a.m. to 12.9 a.m. *Sundays*, 9.53 a.m. to 12.9 a.m.

London Tramways Co.

BRIXTON AND BLACKFRIARS-BRIDGE. — *Route* — Brixton - rd, Kennington-pk, Kennington-pk-rd,Newington-butts, Elephant and Castle, London-rd, Blackfriars-rd, to Blackfriars - br (Surrey side). From Brixton every 7½ minutes from 7.15 a.m. to 10.57 p.m. From Blackfriars every 7½ minutes from 7.58 a.m. to 11.33 p.m. *Fare*, 2d.

BRIXTON AND ST. GEORGE'S CHURCH, BOROUGH. — *Route* — Brixton-rd, Kennington-pk, Kennington-pk-rd, Newington-butts, Elephant and Castle, Newington-causeway, Blackman-st, St. George's Church. From St. George's Church every 7½ minutes from 6.37 a.m. to 9.33 p.m. From Brixton every 7½ minutes from 7.15 a.m. to 10.32 p.m. *Fare*, 2d.

BRIXTON AND WESTMINSTER-BRIDGE. — *Route* — Brixton - rd, Kennington-pk, Kennington-rd, and Westminster-rd, to Westminster-br (Surrey side). From Brixton every 7½ minutes from 7.51 a.m. to 11.20 p.m. From Westminster every 7½ minutes from 8.5 a.m. to 11.57 p.m. *Fare*, 2d.

CAMBERWELL-GREEN AND VICTORIA STATION, *via* cars and omnibuses.—*Route*.—Camberwell New-rd, Kennington Oval, Harley-ford-rd, over Vauxhall-br, through Vauxhall - br - rd. From Camberwell every 3 minutes from 7.25 a.m. to 11.13 p.m. From Victoria every 5 minutes from 7.25 a.m. to 11.20 p.m. *Fare*, 2d.

CLAPHAM AND BLACKFRIARS. –*Route*—Clapham-rd, Kennington-pk, Kennington-pk-rd, Newington-butts, Elephant and Castle, London - rd, Blackfriars - rd, to Blackfriars-br(Surrey side). From Clapham every 7½ minutes from 7.15 a.m. to 11.2 p.m. From Blackfriars every 7½ minutes from 7.54 a.m. to 11.34 p.m. *Fare*, 2d.

CLAPHAM AND ST. GEORGE'S CHURCH, BOROUGH. — *Route*— Clapham-rd, Kennington-pk, Kennington-pk-rd, Newington-butts, Elephant and Castle, Newington-causeway, Blackman-st, St. George's Church. From Clapham every 7½ minutes from 6.45 a.m. to 10.52 p.m. From St. George's Church every 7½ minutes from 7.54 a.m. to 11.23 p.m. *Fare*, 2d.

CLAPHAM AND WESTMINSTER-BRIDGE. — *Route* — Clapham - rd, Kennington- pk, Kennington - rd, Westminster-rd, to Westminster-br (Surrey side). From Clapham every 7½ minutes from 7.35 a.m. to 11.59 p.m. From Westminster every 7½ minutes from 8.5 a.m. to 12.2 p.m. *Fare*, 2d.

GREENWICH AND BLACKFRIARS-BRIDGE.—*Route*—Trafalgar - rd, Nelson-st, London-st, Greenwich-rd, Broadway, New ✠-rd, Hatcham, Old Kent-rd, New Kent-rd, London-rd, Blackfriars-rd, to Blackfriars-br(Surrey side). From Greenwich every 10½ minutes from 7.12 a.m. to 10.33 p.m. From Blackfriars every 10½ minutes from 8.10 a.m. to 11.44 p.m. *Fare*, 3d. all the way.

GREENWICH AND WESTMINSTER-BRIDGE. — *Route* — Trafalgar - rd Nelson-st, London-st, Greenwich-rd, Broadway, New ✠-rd, Hatcham, Old Kent-rd, New Kent-rd, London-rd, Westminster-rd, to Westminster - br (Surrey side). From Greenwich every 6 minutes from 7.4 a.m. to 10.46 p.m. From Westminster every 6 minutes from 8.13 a.m. to 11.57 p.m. *Fare*—3d. all the way.

NEW ✠ AND BLACKFRIARS *via* PECKHAM. — *Route* — Queen's-rd, High-st, Peckham-rd, Church-st, Camberwell-rd, Walworth-rd, London-rd, Blackfriars-rd,to Blackfriars-br (Surrey side). From New ✠ every 5 minutes from 7.48 a.m. to 11.3 p.m. From Blackfriars every 5 minutes from 7.54 a.m. to 11.53 p.m. *Fare*, 2d. First car leaves Queen's-rd Stn. at 7.12 a.m.

NEW ✠ AND WESTMINSTER *via* PECKHAM. — *Route* — Queen's-rd, High-st, Peckham-rd, Church-st, Camberwell-rd, Walworth-rd, London - rd, Westminster - rd, to Westminster - br (Surrey side). From New ✠ every 5 minutes from 7.55 a.m. to 11.6 p.m. From Westminster every 5 minutes from 7.59 a.m. to 11.58 p.m. *Fare*, 2d. First car leaves Queen's-rd Stn. at 7.17 a.m.

New ✠ Gate and St. George's Church. — *Route* — High-st, Peckham-rd, Church-st, Camberwell-rd, Walworth-rd, Newington Causeway, Blackman-st, to St. George's Church. From St. George's Church every 5 minutes from 7 a.m. to 11.52 p.m. From Rye-la, Peckham, every 5 minutes from 7 a.m. to 11.35 p.m. *Fare*, 2d.

Busses in connection with the cars run over Blackfriars, Vauxhall, and Westminster Bridges Fare, ½d.

Travellers' Club, 106, Pall Mall.—The following is the form of recommendation of candidates for this club : " A. B. being desirous of becoming a member of the Travellers' Club, we, the undersigned, do, from our personal knowledge, recommend him to that honour, subject to the qualification of Rule 15." The provision of Rule 15 is "that no person be considered eligible who shall not have travelled out of the British Islands to a distance of at least 500 miles from London in a direct line." The members elect by ballot. When 12 and under 18 members ballot, one black ball, if repeated, shall exclude ; if 18 and upwards ballot, two black balls exclude, and the ballot cannot be repeated. The presence of 12 members is necessary for a ballot. Each member on admission is required to pay £42, which sum includes his subscription for the current year. Each subsequent annual subscription is £10 10s.

Treasury, Whitehall, S.W., and Treasury Chambers, Whitehall (Map 13).—Hours 11 to 5. Nearest *Ry.Stn.,* Westminster-br(Dis.); *Omnibus Rtes.,* Whitehall and Strand; *Cab Rank,* Horse Guards. The office of Parliamentary Counsel at 18, Qn. Anne's-ga, Westminster; of the Receiver of Fines and Penalties at 2, St. Martin's-pl ; and of the Examiner of Criminal Law Accounts and Sheriffs' Accounts, at 109, Victoria-st, Westminster.

Tricycling.—(*See* Bicycling.)

Trinity College, Mandeville-pl, Manchester-sq, W., has "for its objects the advancement of musical and general education, by (1 organising classes and lectures ; (2) holding examinations, at which diplomas, certificates, and prizes are given to the successful candidates ; and (3) doing all other such lawful things as are calculated to promote the objects in view. Full particulars, respecting fees for students, resident or otherwise, will be found in the " College Calendar," which is published by Mr. Reeves, 185, Fleet-st. to which book, also, reference should be made for all details as to classes, scholarships, diplomas, &c. Honorary membership of the college is obtainable by election, and on payment of an annual subscription of £1 1s. Honorary members have free access to the college library ; the privilege of competing for scholarships and prizes ; the " Calendar and College Journal " (monthly), gratis ; free enrolment of an institution in union ; the electoral privilege of the college senate ; right of attendance at the usual public meetings of the college. " House members " have in addition (on payment of a further annual subscription of £1 1s.) the free use of the reading-rooms of the college, &c. There are now about six hundred honorary members.

Trinity House, Tower-hill (Map 8), is a building of the Ionic order, erected at the close of the last century by Samuel Wyatt. It has some interesting busts of naval celebrities, with, amongst other pictures, a huge Gainsborough, upwards of twenty feet in length, and representing the Trinity Board of the day. The Board has control of the pilotage, beaconage, &c., of the United Kingdom. (*See* Dickens's Dictionary of the Thames). Nearest *Ry. Stns.,* Cannon-st (S.E.) and Mark-la (Dis. & Met.) ; *Omnibus Rtes.,* Fenchurch-st and Aldgate High-st ; *Cab Rank,* Tower Hill.

Trotting is not very much patronised in London, but good sport is afforded at the meetings which occasionally take place on the track in the grounds of the Alexandra Palace.

Turf Club, 47, Piccadilly, W.—Formerly the Arlington Club. No special qualification. Each member playing at whist, humbug, piquet, écarté, &c., shall, prior to leaving the club, pay to the porter 1s. 6d. If only two play, the charge to be 5s. Each member playing at dummy to pay 2s. Gentlemen calling for fresh cards must have two packs, which will be charged 5s. "The Laws of Whist," edited by John Loraine Baldwin, were adopted in 1866. "The Laws of Piquet," and "The Laws of Écarté," edited by Cavendish, were adopted in 1873 and 1877. For the convenience of members. the committee engage a cashier, whose duty it is to settle the whist accounts between the members, but the club is not responsible for the acts of such whist cashier. The members leave their money in his hands on their own responsibility. The election is by ballot in committee, two black balls exclude. The entrance fee is £31 10s., and the subscription for the first eight years, £15 15s., after which it will be reduced to £12 12s.

Turkey.—Embassy, 1, Bryanston-sq. Nearest *Ry. Stn.,* Edgware-rd (Met.) ; *Omnibus Rtes.,* Edgware-rd, Oxford-st, and Marylebone-rd ; *Cab Rank,* Seymour-pl. Consulate, 5, Union-court, Old Broad-st, E.C. Nearest *Ry. Stns.,* Broad-st (N.L.) and Liverpool-st (G.E.) ; *Omnibus Routes,* Old Broad-st and Moorgate-st ; *Cab Rank,* Liverpool-st.

Tussaud's Exhibition of Waxworks and Napoleonic Relics, one of the oldest exhibitions in London, and for many years situated in Baker-st, is now in magnificent new quarters in the Marylebone-rd. The nearest station is Baker-st (Met.), close to the building. Omnibuses run along the Marylebone-rd, and the "Atlas" and "City Atlas" lines along Baker-st are also handy. The prices are 1s. a head, with 6d. extra for Napoleon Room and Chamber of Horrors.—(*And see* Appendix).

Tyburn Gate (Map 6).—The real site of this spot is matter of dispute. An iron slab opposite the end of Edgware-rd, and about 50 yards W. of the Marble Arch, professes to designate the precise situation ; but No. 49, Connaught-sq, some two or three hundred yards N.W. of that spot, disputes with it the doubtful honour, as does also the portion of the Edgware-rd at the corner of Bryanston-st. Nearest *Ry. Stn.,* Edgware-rd ; *Omnibus Rtes.,* Edgware-rd and Uxbridge-rd ; *Cab Rank,* opposite.

Union Club, Trafalgar-sq.—No special qualification. Election is by ballot of members. Forty members must ballot, and one black ball in ten excludes, but "should there be any box in which forty balls at the least are not found, the candidate shall be put up again at the next ballot." Entrance fee, £31 10s.; subscription, £7 7s.

Unionist Club, 68, Pall Mall (adjoining Marlborough House), established in 18·7 "to assist in preserving the union of the British Empire." Annual subscription, £4 4s. A limited number of bed-rooms provided for members. Full information from hon. sec.

United Club, Charles-st, St. James's, S.W. — Proprietary. Social. No special qualification. This club was founded in 1865, and is established on the premises of, and in connection with, the United Hotel, in Charles-st, St. James's-sq, having exclusive use of spacious club-rooms for dining, reading, writing, &c. No entrance fee. Subscription, £5 5s. for the first year, and £3 3s. for each subsequent year.

United Service Club, 116, Pall Mall.—For officers not under the rank of commander in the navy, or major in the army, or retired officers who have held those ranks. In addition to these, "all such officers as have been or may be in charge of any of the following civil departments at home: — Chaplain, commissary, paymasters, directors-general of the medical department of the army and navy, as well as the retired inspectors - general (who have served in that rank), and surgeons-general of the army, and inspectors-general of hospitals and fleets of the navy, the treasurers of the club, the three surgeons-major of the Guards, and the principal veterinary surgeon shall be eligible to become members." There is also a considerable list of officers and others who may be invited by the committee as visitors for any period not exceeding three months at a time. Election by ballot, fifty members at least to vote. Each candidate must have at least fifty votes to constitute his election, and one black ball in ten excludes. "Admission money," £40; subscription, £7 7s., beginning with the second year.

United Service Institution (Royal), Whitehall - yd (Map 13). Founded 1831. Granted a Royal Charter 1860. Design:

To promote naval and military art, science, and literature by means of a library containing works on naval, military, and standard subjects in all languages; the delivery of lectures; the exhibition of inventions; the publication of a journal; and a museum containing naval and military models, arms, relics, and trophies All officers of the navy, the army, colonial and reserved forces, are eligible to become members. Entrance fee, £1. Annual subscription, £1. Life membership, including entrance fee. £10. The United Service Museum is situated in Whitehall-yard.— Upon entering, the visitor finds himself in a room devoted to arms from New Zealand, the Sandwich and other islands in the Pacific Ocean, and Africa. There are spears and assegais of all shapes and sizes, belonging to the tribes of Abyssinia, Ashanti, Central and Southern Africa. Upon the floor stands a great variety of war-drums of various forms; these are looked upon by African tribes in much the same light in which European troops regard their standards. There are many shields of different kinds, among them one with silver ornaments, formerly the property of a great chief in Abyssinia. There are also some suits of curious armour made of plaited cane. In the African department are some Moorish guns and matchlocks, inlaid with silver. The next room is devoted to modern arms. There is a collection of the rifles employed by the different governments of Europe, and a great many other forms of breechloader and magazine rifles. In the same room are obsolete fire-arms, flint-locks, and other weapons. The next room is devoted to Asiatic arms. There are some curious Chinese and Indian cannon and gingals, some suits of Indian chain-armour, together with primitive weapons from Borneo and the Polynesian islands. Beyond the Asiatic room is that devoted to the marine branch of the United Service. There are a great variety of fine models of ships of all shapes. Among them a melancholy interest attaches to one or two fine models of ironclads upon his own design, presented by Captain Cowper Coles, who went down in the *Captain*. In this room are some Gatling guns and mitrailleuses of various patterns. At

one end are models of small craft of all kinds, from the Cingalese outrigger and the Venetian gondola to the Chinese junk. In the next room is a model upon a large scale of the Battle of Trafalgar, showing the exact position of the various vessels of the united French and Spanish fleets, and of those composing the two British columns of attack. Returning back to the first room, the visitor will find to his left two rooms filled with models of all the different descriptions of ordnance in use in the British army and navy, together with the shot and shell fitted for them. Upstairs there are several rooms with noteworthy military trophies, the most interesting object in the whole museum being a model of the field and battle of Waterloo, executed with a marvellous accuracy and fidelity. The United Service Museum is open daily, except Fri., the admission being by ticket obtainable from members, or by written or personal application to the secretary enclosing stamped envelope. From January to July papers are read on naval and military subjects, and inventions of interest to the two services are exhibited in the theatre. Special lectures to volunteer officers and to military students attending the classes of the garrison instructor are also occasionally given; particulars may be had of the secretary. NEAREST *Ry. Stns.,* Westminster-br and Charing ✠ (Dis. & S.E.); *Omnibus Rtes.,* Whitehall and Strand; *Cab Rank,* Horse Guards.

United States.—LEGATION, Victoria-st, S.W. NEAREST *Ry. Stn.,* St. James's-pk; *Omnibus Rtes.,* Victoria-st and Parliament-st; *Cab Ranks,* Tothill-st and Palace-yd. CONSULATE GENERAL, 12, St. Helen's-pl, E.C. NEAREST *Ry. Stn., Omnibus Rte.,* and *Cab Rank,* Bishopsgate-st.

AMERICAN CLUB.—(*See* ST. GEORGE'S CLUB, Hanover-sq.)

AMERICAN EXCHANGE & READING ROOMS (H. F. Gillig, manager), 449, Strand, W.C., with leading American and Colonial papers, Exchange and News Rooms, reading and writing rooms for ladies and gentlemen, ladies' toilet rooms, gentlemen's smoking room, lavatory, &c. Financial, commission, and despatch departments. 5s. per month, or £2 per year. Special cable code, 5s.

AMERICAN FORWARDING AGENCY, G. W. Wheatley & Co., 10, Queen-st, Cheapside, E.C., and 23, Regent-st, S.W.

AMERICAN PRESS ASSOCIATION OF NEW YORK, 34, Throgmorton-st, and 153, Fleet-st, E.C.

AMERICAN TRAVELLER, READING, AND RECEPTION ROOMS, 4, Langham-pl.

ANGLO-AMERICAN TELEGRAPH Co. General office, 26, Old Broad-st, E.C.; office for messages, 23, Throgmorton-st, E.C.

BARING BROTHERS & Co., 8, Bishopsgate-st-within.

BENNETT - MACKAY CABLES, 23, Royal Exchange, E.C.

DIRECT UNITED STATES CABLE Co. Head office, 34, Throgmorton-st, E.C. (always open).

LANGHAM HOTEL, Langham-pl.

MORGAN, J. S. & Co., 22, Old Broad-st.

NEW YORK HERALD, 33, Cornhill, E.C.

NEW YORK TRIBUNE, 26, Bedford-st, W.C.

STEAMERS.—Allan Line, Chief office, 103, Leadenhall-st, E.C.—Anchor Line, 48, Fenchurch - st, E.C.—Cunard Line, 6, St. Helen's-pl, E.C., and 28, Pall Mall, S.W.—Guion Line, 5, Waterloo-pl, S.W.—North German Lloyd, 5 & 7, Fenchurch-st, E.C., and 32, Cockspur-st.—White Star Line, 34, Leadenhall-st, E.C.

United Telephone Co. (Lim.), Oxford-ct, Cannon-st, E.C.

—It is a remarkable instance of the speed with which discoveries in connection with electricity are being developed, that the telephone, which, when the first edition of the DICTIONARY OF LONDON was published in 1879, was little more than a scientific toy, is now the means of instantaneous communication from one end of London to another. The United Telephone Co., which was established in 1880, offers to its subscribers either private wires for exclusive communication between two or more fixed points, or wires connected with the nearest exchange — the latter method affording direct communication with every other subscriber to the exchange system. The renter of a private wire has the communicating apparatus entirely under his own control, and can use it, day or night, without the intervention of any of the company's servants. The charge for private lines is at a fixed annual

rental, payable in advance, varying with the situation and the distance apart of the points connected.

The exchange system enables any subscriber to be put into immediate and direct communication with any other subscriber to the system. The charge for such communication, within a radius of five miles from the General Post Office, is £20 per annum, payable in advance, and includes erection and maintenance of line and instruments. The mode of working is as follows: Each subscriber is furnished with a set of instruments —consisting of transmitter, receiver, and signal-bell—which is connected into a wire communicating with the exchange or switch-room nearest his address. To each subscriber a number is assigned, by which his name and line are known. These exchanges or switch-rooms—of which there are now sixteen in full working order throughout the metropolis—are connected together by cables or trunk lines, and each switch-room is provided with a switching apparatus, by means of which the attendants can connect any two wires with each other, answer calls, and ring up subscribers. A subscriber, on wishing to talk with another, rings up the exchange to which he himself belongs, and, on being answered by one of the attendants, he names the number he wants, and is at once connected with the wire of the other subscriber with whom he desires to communicate. Conversation is then carried on in the ordinary tone, and when the conversation is finished, each of the two subscribers who have been talking presses his bell—the signal that he has finished talking and that he may be disconnected. This disconnection is accomplished in an instant, and each of the two subscribers can then, on ringing up again, be connected afresh with another line. The calls—that is, each time one subscriber rings up another and enters into conversation with him—now average upwards of 10,000 a day, or allowing for one answer to each enquiry, equal to 20,000 messages a day.

The London exchange stations, which are open from 9 a.m. to 7 p.m. (Saturdays until 5 p.m.), are as follows: 36, Coleman-st, Leadenhall - st, Cornhill, Queen Victoria-st, Eastcheap, Chancery-

la, Westminster, South Kensington, Regent-st, East India-avenue, Hop Exchange, Eastern, Millwall, London Docks and Shadwell, Stratford, Victoria Docks. Further particulars can be obtained on application to the head office in London.

United University Club,

1 and 2, Suffolk-st.—Established 1822.—For 500 members of the University of Oxford and 500 of the University of Cambridge. The members elect by ballot, one black ball in ten excludes. Entrance fee, £31 10s.; subscription, £8 8s.

University College, Gower-st (Map 2).

—Divided into faculties of arts, laws, science (including the Indian School, the department of applied science and technology, and the Slade School of Fine Arts), and medicine. Students are admitted without examination to any class or classes. Before finally selecting their classes students are recommended to consult the professors of the subjects they propose to study. Classes in all subjects of instruction within the faculties of arts, and laws, and of science, are open to both men and women, who are taught in some classes together and in others separately. The deans and vice-deans attend in the council-room from 10 a.m. till 2 p.m. on the first two days of the session for the purpose of giving advice and information to students attending the college. No female student is admitted to the college, except upon the recommendation of the Lady Superintendent, and upon producing a satisfactory reference or introduction. Class examinations take place at the end of each session, when prizes and certificates of honour are awarded. For examinations for degrees, see UNIVERSITY OF LONDON. A library is open to students on week days throughout the session. University Hall, adjoining the college, is designed for the residence of men studying in the University, and a register of persons who receive boarders is kept in the office of the college, and College Hall, Byng-place, W.C., offers the advantages of collegiate residence to the women students; full information as to terms, etc., may be obtained in the college office. The following is a list of prizes and scholarships in the faculties of arts, &c:

ANDREWS PRIZES.—(a) *Prizes for New Students.*—Three prizes

of £30 each awarded annually upon examination, as follows : One for classics, one for any two of the three subjects, mathematics, physics, chemistry ; one for three languages : (1) English, (2) either Latin or Greek, (3) French, German, or Italian. The competition is limited to those who have not previously been students of the college ; and no competitor can obtain more than one prize.

(b) *Prizes for Students of One Year's standing.*—At the end of each session two prizes of £30 will be awarded to those first-year students who shall be recommended to the council by the Faculties of Arts, and Laws, and of Science, as having distinguished themselves most by their answers at the sessional examinations of the classes, and by their good conduct during the session.

(c) *Prizes for Students of Two Years' standing.*—At the end of each session, one prize of £50, and one of £40, will be awarded to those second-year students who shall in the same way have been recommended to the council by the aforesaid Faculties.

CLOTHWORKERS' CO.'s EXHIBITIONS.—The Company has founded in University Coll. two exhibitions of £50 a year, one for proficiency in Chemistry, and one for proficiency in Physics.

FIELDEN SCHOLARSHIPS IN GERMAN AND FRENCH.—At the close of every session two scholarships, one of £15 and one of £10, will be given in the junior classes of German and French respectively, and one scholarship of £25 in the senior class of each of these subjects.

GILCHRIST ENGINEERING SCHOLARSHIPS. — An entrance scholarship of the value of £35 a year, tenable for two years, and a senior scholarship of the value of £80, will, during the pleasure of the Gilchrist trustees, be annually offered for competition.

HEIMANN MEDAL.—A silver medal in memory of the late Professor Heimann, founded by his children, will be awarded annually as the first prize in the senior class of German.

HOLLIER SCHOLARSHIPS, ONE FOR GREEK AND ONE FOR HEBREW.—Tenable for one year only; their value is at present about £60 each.

JEWS' COMMEMORATION SCHO-LARSHIP.—£15 a year, tenable for two years.

JOHN STUART MILL SCHOLARSHIP IN PHILOSOPHY OF MIND AND LOGIC.—A scholarship of £20 tenable for one year.

JOSEPH HUME SCHOLARSHIPS.—A scholarship in jurisprudence, of £20 a year, tenable for three years ; a scholarship in political economy, of £20 a year, tenable for three years.

MALDEN MEDAL AND SCHOLARSHIP.—For the most distinguished third-year's student of the Faculty of Arts.

MAYER DE ROTHSCHILD EXHIBITION.—Of the annual value of about £60 ; is awarded as the highest prize in the classes of pure mathematics.

RICARDO SCHOLARSHIP IN POLITICAL ECONOMY.—Of £20 a year, tenable for three years.

SLADE SCHOLARSHIPS.—Under the will of the late Mr. Felix Slade, six scholarships of £50 per annum each, tenable for three years, have been founded in the college to be awarded to students in Fine Arts not more than 19 years of age at the time of the award, for proficiency in drawing, painting, and sculpture. Two of these scholarships may be awarded every year. Ladies as well as gentlemen, not being more than 19 years of age at the date of election, are eligible. Should competitors be unable to produce evidence of having passed such an examination in general knowledge as may be deemed satisfactory by the council, they will be required to pass an examination of an elementary kind, which will be held in January each year. Prizes and medals are given to students who have attended one at least of the Slade classes during the whole session.

SLADE TRAVELLING SCHOLARSHIP.—Of £150 per annum, tenable for two years, to be open to past and present students of the Slade School, not over 30 years of age.

MORRIS BURSARY.—Of £25 a year, tenable for two years.

TREVELYAN GOODALL SCHOLARSHIP IN FINE ART.—Of £20 a year, tenable for three years.

CASE EXHIBITION.—£20 for one year.

THE WEST SCHOLARSHIP IN ENGLISH.—£30 for one year.

ELLEN WATSON MEMORIAL SCHOLARSHIP.—£12 for one year.

TUFFNELL SCHOLARSHIP. — A Tuffnell Scholarship of £100, tenable for two years, may be awarded annually, alternately for distinction in analytical and practical and in general chemistry.

UNIVERSITY COLLEGE SCHOOL SCIENCE FUND. — £10 for one year, a bronze medal, and a book prize of the value of £2.

THE FACULTY OF MEDICINE.—The dean, vice-dean, and sub-dean attend specially to give information and advice to intending students or their friends in the last days of September. The following scholarships, exhibitions, &c., are annually awarded :

Three entrance exhibitions, of the respective value of £100, £60 and £40, are annually awarded for proficiency in science, upon examination by written papers, to gentlemen who are about to commence their first winter's attendance in a medical school.— Atkinson-Morley Surgical Scholarships, for the promotion of the study of surgery amongst the students of University Coll., London. They are of the present value of £45 per annum, and are tenable for three years ; and one (or more) of them may be awarded every year. Sharpey Physiological Scholarship, established by the subscribers to the Sharpey Memorial Fund, for the promotion of biological sciences especially by the encouragement of the practical study of physiology in the college. The annual income of the scholarship is about £70.—Filliter Exhibition. A prize of £30 awarded annually in July, founded for the encouragement of proficiency in pathological anatomy, by George Filliter, Esq., in memory of his deceased son, Dr. William Filliter.—Clinical Medals founded by Dr. Fellowes. Dr. Fellowes's clinical medals, one gold and two silver, with certificates of honour, are awarded at end of each winter and summer session.—Medal founded in honour of the late Professor Liston. The Liston gold medal and certificates of honour will be awarded at the end of the session to the pupils who shall have most distinguished themselves by reports and observations on the surgical cases in the hospital.—Alexander Bruce Gold Medal for proficiency in pathology and surgery, is awarded at the close of the winter session.—Cluff Memorial Prize will be awarded every other year to the student deemed by the faculty of medicine the most proficient in anatomy, physiology, and chemistry. The next award will take place in 1889.—An Atchison Scholarship, value about £59 per annum tenable for two years, may be awarded annually after the close of the winter session. — The Erichsen Prize, value £10 10s., awarded yearly in May for proficiency in practical surgery, and the Tuke Silver Medal for proficiency in practical pathology. Gold and silver medals, or other prizes, as well as certificates of honour, are awarded, after competitive examinations, to those students who most distinguish themselves in particular branches of study in the college or hospital. Prizes to the value of £10 will be given in the class of hygiene. Libraries and museums are open to students in the medical faculty.

The value of Scholarships, &c., annually offered is about £2,000. Nearly all those in the Faculties of Arts, Laws, and Science, are open to women.

There are many other prizes and certificates. All information may be obtained from the Sec. at the college. NEAREST *Ry. Stn.*, Gower-st (Met.); *Omnibus Rtes.*, Euston-rd, Tottenham-ct-rd ; *Cab Ranks*, Tottenham-ct-rd and Euston-rd.

University College School, Gower-st. In connection with University Coll.—The usual branches of a liberal education are taught in this school ; religious instruction is left entirely to parents. The age of admission is between 9 and 15. The work of some of the higher classes is arranged with a special view to matriculation at the London University. The fee for each term is £8 8s. Four Entrance Scholarships of £4 4s. per term, tenable at the school for three years, will be awarded annually in July to boys of good character, between the ages of 12 and 14 on July 1st, whether already in the school or not. Dinners are provided for day boarders at 1s. 2d. each ; also light refreshments. Boarders are received in some of the masters' houses; terms, as well as all further particulars, may be obtained of the Sec. to the council at the school. NEAREST *Ry. Stns.*, Gower - st, Euston, King's +, and St. Pancras ; *Omnibus Rtes.*, Euston-rd, Tottenham-court-rd ; *Cab Rank*, Tottenham-court-rd.

University of London, Burlington - gardens, Piccadilly (Map 6).—Incorporated by Royal Charter in the first year of the present reign. The charter gave the governing body the power after examination to confer the degrees of Bachelor of Arts, Master of Arts, Bachelor of Laws, Doctor of Laws, Bachelor of Medicine, and Doctor of Medicine. In the 13th Victoria their powers were enlarged. Further letters patent were issued in the 21st Victoria giving the governing body power to confer the degrees of Bachelor, Master, and Doctor in Arts, Laws, Science, Medicine, Music, and also in such other departments of knowledge, except theology, as the governing body should from time to time determine. In 1863 the present charter was granted with a view to " ascertaining by means of examination the persons who have acquired proficiency in literature, science, arts, and other departments of knowledge by the pursuit of such course of education, and of rewarding them by academical degrees and certificates of proficiency as evidence of their respective attainments and marks of honour proportioned thereunto." Provision is also made by the present charter for granting the additional degrees of " Master in Surgery, and for the improvement of medical education in all its branches, as well in medicine as in surgery, midwifery, and pharmacy." There is no special provision for Music. Power to grant degrees in Music was contained in the charter of 21st Victoria. A supplemental charter of 27th August, 1868, gave the governing body the power to hold special examinations for women being candidates for certain certificates of proficiency, and to grant such certificates. These powers were further extended by another supplemental charter, dated March 4, 1878, under which the governing body has power after examination to grant to women any degrees or certificates of proficiency which they have the power to grant to men. Women, however, are not in all respects on an equality with men, inasmuch as it is provided that " no female graduate of the said University shall be a member of the Convocation of the said University, unless and until such Convocation shall have passed a resolution that female graduates be admitted to Convocation." The governing body consists of the Chancellor, Vice-Chancellor, and 36 Fellows.

There are two examinations for matriculation in each year, one commencing on the second Monday in January, and the other on the third Monday in June. Candidates must have completed their sixteenth year, and the necessary certificate must be transmitted to the registrar at least *fourteen days* before the commencement of the examination. These examinations may be held not only at the University of London, but also, under special arrangement, in other parts of the United Kingdom, or in the Colonies. Candidates for any degree granted by this University are required to have passed the matriculation examination. This examination is accepted (1) by the College of Surgeons; (2) by the Incorporated Law Society, in lieu of their preliminary examinations. It also exempts candidates for admission to the Royal Military College from the preliminary test, except in geometrical drawing, and it is also among those examinations of which some one must be passed (1) by every medical student on commencing his professional studies ; and (2) by every person entering upon articles of clerkship to an attorney —any such person matriculating in the first division being entitled to exemption from one year's service.

This and all other examinations of the university, together with the prizes, exhibitions, scholarships, and medals depending upon them, are open to women upon exactly the same conditions as to men.

If in the opinion of the examiners any candidates for matriculation in the honours division of not more than 20 years of age at the commencement of the examination shall possess sufficient merit, the first among such candidates shall receive an exhibition of £30 per annum for the next two years; the second shall receive an exhibition of £20 per annum for the next two years; and the third shall receive an exhibition of £15 per annum for the next two years; such exhibitions to be payable in quarterly instalments, provided that on receiving each instalment the exhibitioner shall declare his intention of pre-senting himself either at the two examinations for B.A., or at the two examinations for B.Sc., the intermediate examination in Laws, or at the preliminary scientific M.B. examination and interme-diate examination in Medicine, within 3 academical years from the time of his passing the matri-culation examination. There are also minor prizes.

The Gilchrist Scholarships are awarded as follows :

I.—BRITISH SCHOLARSHIPS, &c.

(a) For Male Candidates.— £50 per annum for three years to the candidate from the Royal Medical College, Epsom, who at the June matriculation examina-tion stands highest among the candidates approved by the head master, and who passes either in honours or in the first division. Particulars may be obtained on application to the secretary of the Royal Medical College, 37, Soho-sq, W. A similar amount to the highest candidate at the same ex-amination from Owen's College, Manchester, provided he pass in honours. Should no candidate so pass, two scholarships of £25 per annum each are awarded to the two candidates from that college who shall stand highest in the first division. Particulars may be ob-tained on application to the principal of Owen's College.

A scholarship of £50 per annum, tenable for three years, is also annually awarded to that candi-date in the honours division at the June matric. exam. who shall stand highest of the candidates previously approved by the Prin-cipal of University College, Bristol; and who intends to study at that college with a view to graduation in one of the Faculties of the University of London. (N.B.—This scholarship is open to women.) Further particulars may be ob-tained on application to the Prin-cipal of University College, Bristol.

(b) For Female Candidates.— An exhibition of £30, and one of £20, tenable for two years, will be awarded to the two female can-didates (of not more than twenty years of age) who pass highest in the honours division ; and two further exhibitions—one of £40 and the other of £30 per annum, tenable for two years—will be awarded to the two female candidates who pass highest at the intermediate examination in arts. A book

prize of the value of £10 will be awarded to the female candidate who passes highest in the B.A. examination, provided she obtain not less than two-thirds of the total number of marks.

See also the Bristol Scholarship under *(a)*.

II. INDIAN SCHOLARSHIP.

A scholarship of the value of £150 per ann., and tenable for four years, is annually awarded to the Native candidate who passes highest in the Jan. matric. exam. carried on at the three presidential capitals and Colombo ; provided that such candidate passes either in the honours or in the first division.

III. COLONIAL SCHOLARSHIPS.

1. A scholarship of £100 per annum, for three years, is annually awarded to the highest among those candidates at the June matric. exam. carried on in the Dom. of Canada, who pass either in honours or in the first division.

2. A similar scholarship, under the same conditions, is annually awarded to the candidate who passes the highest at the Jan. matric. exam. carried on in the West India Colonies.

3. A similar scholarship, under the same conditions, is annually awarded to the candidate who passes highest at the Jan. matric. exam. at Melbourne, Sydney, Adelaide, or Hobart Town.

4. A similar scholarship, under the same conditions, is biennially awarded to the candidate who passes highest at the Jan. matric. exam. in New Zealand. Every candidate for a Colonial scholar-ship must either be a native of the colony in which he presents him-self, or have resided therein for five years preceding. Further information respecting them may be obtained on application to the secretary to the Gilchrist Educa-tional Trust, 4, Broad Sanctuary, Westminster.

The West Scholarship of the value of £30, tenable for one year, is awarded by the Council of University College, London, to that candidate at the June ma-triculation examination who dis-tinguishes himself the most in English. Particulars of the Secre-tary at the College, Gower-st.

Two Tuffnell scholarships of the value of about £100 each, two years, are awarded for distinction in analytical and practical chemis-try and general chemistry alter-nately, to undergraduates of the

University of London of not mor than three years' standing.

A free studentship, at Bedford College, tenable for two years, of the annual value of £31 10s., is offered by Mrs. Reid's trustees to the woman passing highest in the honours of the June matriculation examination. Another scholar-ship of same value, tenable for one year, at Bedford College, is awarded to the woman taking the highest place at the 1st B.A. or 1st B.Sc. examination. Particulars of the trustees, Bedford College, 8, York-pl.

The Gilchrist and other scholar-ships are awarded by the respec-tive educational bodies upon the result of the university examina-tions ; but the university has other-wise no control over, and is not responsible for, such award.

All further information may by obtained from, and all communica-tions should be addressed to, "The Registrar of the University of London, W."

EXAMINATIONS IN 1888.

The following are the dates at which the several examinations in the University of London for the year 1888 will commence.

MATRICULATION.—Mon., Jan-uary 9, and Mon., June 18.

BACHELOR OF ARTS. — Inter-mediate, Mon., July 16 ; B.A., Mon., October 22.

MASTER OF ARTS.—Branch I., Mon., June 4 ; Branch II., Mon., June 11 ; Branch III., Mon., June 18 ; Branch IV., Mon., June 25.

DOCTOR OF LITERATURE.—Tu., December 4.

SCRIPTURAL EXAMINATIONS.—Tu., November 27.

BACHELOR OF SCIENCE.—Inter-mediate, Mon., July 10 ; B.Sc., Mon., October 15.

DOCTOR OF SCIENCE.—Within the first twenty-one days of June.

BACHELOR OF LAWS. — Inter-mediate and LL.B., Mon., Jan. 2.

DOCTOR OF LAWS.—Tu., Jan-uary 17.

BACHELOR OF MEDICINE.—Preliminary Scientific, Mon., Jan 16, and Mon., July 16 ; Interme-diate, Mon., Jan. 16, and July 9 M.B., Mon., October 29.

BACHELOR OF SURGERY.—Tu., December 4.

MASTER IN SURGERY. — Mon., December 3.

DOCTOR OF MEDICINE.—Mon., December 3.

BACHELOR OF MUSIC.—Inter-

mediate, Mon., December 10;
B.Mus., Mon., Dec. 17.

DOCTOR OF MUSIC. — Inter-
mediate, Mon., December 10;
D.Mus., Mon., December 17.

ART, &c., OF TEACHING.—Tu.,
Dec. 11.

The Regulations relating to the
above Examinations and Degrees
may be obtained on application to
"The Registrar of the University
of London, Burlington Gardens
London, W."

**Uruguay, Republic of
Monte Video.**—CONS., 35, New
Broad-st, E.C. NEAREST *Ry.
Stns.*, Broad-st (N.L.) and Moor-
gate-st (Met.); *Omnibus Rtes.*,
Bishopsgate-st and Finsbury-pave-
ment; *Cab Rank*, New Broad-st.

Uxbridge Road, the great
W. road, is certainly the finest approach to London, the road being
everywhere broad and straight.
At Shepherd's Bush London may
be said to begin. Thence a
wide road leads up through
Notting-hill, past the mansions of
Holland-pk, with their line of
poplar trees skirting the road,
through Notting-hill High-st, and
then on past the N. side of Kensington-gdns and Hyde-pk to the
Marble Arch. Upon the N. side
of the road are a succession of handsome terraces, conspicuous among
which are Lancaster-gate and
Hyde-pk-gdns. At the end of
May, when the foliage is at
its brightest and freshest, and the
road is alive with handsome equi-
pages, its beauty is remarkable.
This drive is well worth taking.
Omnibuses run at frequent intervals from Regent's-cir to Shepherd's Bush.

Vaudeville Theatre, 404,
Strand (Map 7).—One of the most
successful little theatres in Lon-
don. Its specialty may be defined
as comedy. NEAREST *Ry. Stns.*,
Charing-✝ (Dis. & S.E.); *Omnibus
Rtes.*, Strand and St. Martin's-la;
Cab Rank, Bedford-st.

Vauxhall Bridge (Map 13)
is an iron structure of the Southwark type, of five spans. It was
built in 1811-16 from the designs
of Mr. J. Walker. NEAREST
Ry. Stns., Vauxhall (S.W.) and
Victoria (Dis., L. & B., and L. C.
& D.) ; *Omnibus Rtes.*, Vauxhall-
br-rd and Albert Embankment;
Cab Rank, Grosvenor-rd.

Vegetarian Restaurants.
—The following is a list of vegetarian dining-rooms in London :

The Alpha Restaurant, 23,
Oxford-st.

The Apple Tree, 34, London-
wall, E.C.

The Apple Tree, 34 and 35,
Poultry, E.C.

The Arcadian, Queen-st, Cheapside.

The Bouverie, 63, Fleet-st.

The Café, 12, Bell-yd, Fleet-
st, E.C.

The Drummond Street Vege-
tarian Restaurant, 81, Drummond-
st, N.

The Eastward Ho ! Sussex-pl,
94, Leadenhall-st, E.C.

The Garden Restaurant, 24,
Jewin-st.

The Garden Restaurant, 155,
Minories.

The Healtheries, 16, Bishopsgate-st-without, E.C.

The Orange Grove, 37, St.
Martin's-la, Charing ✝, W.

The Orchard, 38, Aldersgate-st,
City.

The Porridge Bowl, 278, High
Holborn.

The Queen Victoria, 303,
Strand, W.C.

The Rose, 2A, South-pl, Finsbury-pavement.

The Wheatsheaf, 13, Rathbone-
pl, Oxford-st, W.

**Venezuela, United States
of.**—MINISTRY and CONSULATE,
4, Tokenhouse-buildings, E.C.—
NEAREST *Ry. Stns.*, Moorgate-
st and Broad-st.; *Omnibus Rtes.*,
Moorgate-st and Cornhill ; *Cab
Rank*, Bartholomew-la.

**Vernon Town and River
Club, The,** 5, Park-pl, St.
James's; Riverside House, Thames
Ditton. Established 1885. Annual subscription: town members,
£6 6s.; country members, £4 4s.;
riverside club only, £3 3s.

**Vestries and District
Boards of Works :**—

BERMONDSEY, Spa-rd, Bermond-
sey, S.E.—*Clerk*, J. Harrison ;
Surveyor, George Elkington ;
Analyst. Dr. Muter, 325, Ken-
nington-rd, S.E. ; *Medical
Officer*, J. Dixon.

BETHNAL GREEN, Vestry Hall,
Church-row, Bethnal Green.—
Clerk, Robert Voss, Vestry
Hall ; *Surveyor*, Frederick W.
Barratt, office of Board ;
Analyst, Alfred W. Stokes,
Laboratory, Paddington; *Medi-
cal Officer of Health*, Geo.
P. Bate, M.D., 42, Bethnal
Green-rd

CAMBERWELL, Vestry, Peckham-
rd, S.E.—*Clerk*. G. W. Marsden,
113, The Grove, Camberwell ;
Medical Officer, J. S. Bristow ;
Surveyor, John Cook Reynolds, 43, Vicarage-rd, Camberwell ; *Analyst*, Professor A.
Bernays, St. Thomas's Hospital.

CHELSEA, Vestry Hall, King's-rd,
S.W.—*Clerk*, J. Eisdell Salway ;
Surveyor, G. R. Strachan,
C.E., office of Board ; *Medical
Officer and Analyst*, E. Seaton,
M.D., office of Board.

FULHAM, Walham Green, S.W.—
Clerk, C. J. Foakes ; *Surveyor*,
J. P. Norrington; *Analyst*, C.H.
Piesse, 2, New Bond-st, W.;
Medical Officer of Health, W.
Egan.

GREENWICH, 141, Greenwich-rd,
Greenwich, S.E. — *Clerk*, S.
Spencer ; *Surveyor (Engineer)*,
John Nidd Smith, office of Board;
Road Surveyor, James Richard
Heward, office of Board ; *An-
alyst*, R. H. Harland ; *Me-
dical Officers*, C. H. Hartt and
H. W. Roberts.

HACKNEY, Town Hall, Mare-st,
Hackney. — *Clerk*, Richard
Ellis ; *Surveyor*, James Love-
grove, C.E., 18, Urswick-rd,
Lower Clapton ; *Analyst and
Medical Officer*, John William
Tripe, M.D., L.R.C.P., 232,
Richmond-rd.

HAMLET OF MILE END, OLD
TOWN.—*Clerk*, Millner Jutsum ;
Surveyor, John M. Knight, 50,
Bow-rd, E. ; *Medical Officer*,
Thos. Taylor, 131, Mile End-rd ;
Analyst, R. H. Harland.

HAMMERSMITH, Vestry Hall,
Hammersmith, W.—*Clerk*, W.
P. Cockburn ; *Surveyor*, H. G.
Bean, office of Board ; *Medical
Officer*, N. C. Collier ; *Analyst*,
R. H. Davies.

HOLBORN, Town Hall, Gray's-inn-
rd, W.C.—*Clerk*, Samuel Wey-
mouth Hopwood ; *Medical Officer of Health*, Septimus Gib-
bon, M.D., office of Board; *Surveyor*, Lewis Henry Isaacs, office
of Board ; *Analyst*, Dr. Theophilus Redwood, 17, Bloomsbury-sq.

ISLINGTON, Vestry Hall, Upper-
st, Islington, N.—*Clerk*, Wm.
Francis Dewey; *Medical Officer
of Health*, Charles Meymott
Tidy, M.B., office of Board;
Surveyors, Charles Higgins
and J. P. Barber; *Analyst*,
Charles Meymott Tidy, M.B.

LAMBETH, Vestry Hall, Kennington-green, S.E.—*Clerk*, Henry John Smith ; *Medical Officer of Health*, Walter Verdon ; *Surveyor*, Hugh McIntosh, Lambeth Vestry Hall, Kennington-green ; *Analyst*, Dr. Muter, 397, Kennington-rd, S.E.

LEWISHAM, Rushey-gn, Catford, S.E.—*Clerk*, Templer L. Downe ; *Medical Officer of Health*, Dr. F. E. Wilkinson, Battle Cottage, Sydenham ; *Surveyor*, John Carline, office of Board ; *Analyst*, Charles Heisch, 79, Mark-lane.

LIMEHOUSE, White Horse-st, Commercial-rd, E.—*Clerk*, Thomas Wrake Ratcliff ; *Medical Officer of Health and Analyst*, George Arthur Rogers, 164, High-st, Shadwell ; *Surveyor*, C. Dunch, office of Board.

MILE END.—(*See* HAMLET OF.)

PADDINGTON, Vestry Hall, Harrow-rd, W. — *Clerk*, Frank Dethridge ; *Surveyor*, George Weston, office of Board ; *Medical Officer*, Dr. James Stevenson ; *Analyst*, Alfred W. Stokes, office of Board.

PLUMSTEAD DISTRICT BOARD OF WORKS, Old Charlton, Kent.—*Clerk*, G. Whale ; *Surveyors*, J. Rowland H. Woods, E. L. Rumble, and J. L. Bennett ; *Medical Officers*, W. C. Wise, M.D., J. Burton, D. King, M.D., H. L. Bernays. *Analyst*, H. Smith, M.D., office of Board.

POPLAR, 117, Poplar High-st, E.—*Clerk*, Wm. Henry Farnfield ; *Surveyor*, Robert Parker, 117, Poplar High-st, E. ; *Analyst*, Wm. Charles Young, 22, Windsor-rd, Forest-gate ; *Medical Officers*, F. M. Corner and R. M. Talbot.

ROTHERHITHE, Lower-rd, Rotherhithe, S.E.—*Clerk*, James J. Storkes ; *Surveyors*, George Legg, 61, King William-st, E.C., and Edward Thomas, 234, Deptford Lower-rd, S.E. ; *Analyst*, Dr. John Muter, 325, Kennington-rd, S.E. *Medical Officer*, J. Shaw.

ST. GEORGE'S, HANOVER - SQ Board-room, Mount-st, W.— *Clerk*, J. H. Smith ; *Surveyor*, George Livingstone, 1, Pimlico-rd, S.W.; *Analyst and Medical Officer*, W. H. Corfield, M.A., M.D., F.R.C.P., 19, Savile-row, W.

ST. GEORGE'S-IN-THE-EAST, Vestry Hall, Cable-st, E.—*Clerk*,

H. Thompson ; *Medical Officer*, Dr. Rygate, M.B., office of Board ; *Analyst*, W. C. Young, office of Board ; *Surveyor*, Geo. A. Wilson, office of Board.

ST. GEORGE - THE - MARTYR, Vestry Hall, Borough-rd, S.E. —*Clerk*, A. Millar ; *Surveyor*, Alfred Moser Hiscocks, C.E.; *Analyst*, Dr. J. Muter, F.C.S., 325, Kennington - rd, S.E.; *Medical Officer*, Dr. Waterworth.

ST. GILES'S, 197, High Holborn, W.C. — *Clerk*, H. C. Jones ; *Surveyor*, George Wallace, office of Board ; *Analyst*, Dr. Theophilus Redwood, 17, Bloomsbury-sq ; *Medical Officer of Health*, Dr. S. R. Lovett, 13, Great Russell-street, W.C.

ST. JAMES AND ST. JOHN, CLERKENWELL, 58, Rosoman-st, E.C.—*Clerk*, Robert Paget, office of Board ; *Surveyor*, Wm. Iron, office of Board ; *Medical Officer of Health*, J. W. Griffith, M.D., 50, Camberwell-grove ; *Analyst*, Dr. T. Redwood, 17, Bloomsbury-sq.

ST. JAMES'S, WESTMINSTER, Piccadilly. — *Clerk*, Harry Wilkins ; *Medical Officer of Health and Analyst*, James Edmunds, M.D., office of Board; *Surveyor*, Henry Monson, office of Board.

ST. JOHN, Hampstead.—Vestry Hall, Haverstock-hill, N.W.; *Clerk*, Thos. Bridger; *Medical Officer of Health*, Dr. Edmund Gwynn, 6, Hampstead-hill - gdns ; *Surveyor*, Charles Harlowe Lowe, 18, Fairfax-rd, Hampstead ; *Analyst*, Charles Heisch, 79, Mark-lane.

ST. LEONARD, SHOREDITCH, Town Hall, Old-st, E.C.—*Clerk*, Enoch Walker ; *Medical Officer*, Henry Gawen Sutton, M.D., office of Board ; *Surveyor*, Geo. Charles Perrett, office of Board ; *Analyst*, Thomas Stevenson, M.D., Guy's Hospital.

ST. LUKE'S, Vestry Hall, City-rd, E.C.—*Clerk*, Geo. W. Preston; *Surveyor*, M. C. Meaby, office of Vestry ; *Medical Officer of Health*, G. E. Yarrow, M.D.; *Analyst*, J. W. Stokes.

ST. MARTIN - IN - THE - FIELDS, Vestry Hall, St. Martin's-pl, W.C.—*Clerk*, G. W. Murnane ; *Medical Officer of Health*, J. J. Skegg, L.R.C.P., M.R.C.S., 29, Craven-st, W.C.; *Surveyor*, Henry Jacques, office of Board ;

Analyst, C. W. Heaton, Charing ✚ Hospital.

ST. MARY ABBOTTS, Kensington, Town Hall, Kensington High-street, W. — *Clerk*, Reuben Green ; *Medical Officer of Health*, Dr. Thos. Orme Dudfield, 8, Upper Phillimore-pl ; *Surveyor*, Wm. Weaver, C.E., office, Town Hall ; *Analyst*, C. E. Cassal, office, Town Hall.

ST. MARYLEBONE, Court House, Marylebone-lane, W. — *Clerk and Solicitor*, W. H. Garbutt ; *Surveyor*, H. Tomkins; *Analyst and Medical Officer*, A. Wynter Blyth, M.R.C.S., F.C.S.

ST. MARY, NEWINGTON, Vestry Hall, Walworth, S.E. — *Clerk*, L. J. Dunham, 118, Walworth-rd ; *Medical Officer of Health*, W. T. Iliff, M.D., 37, Kennington-pk-rd ; *Surveyor*, James Gledhill, 172, New Kent-rd ; *Analyst*, Dr. John Muter, F.C.S., 325, Kennington-rd, S.E.

ST. OLAVE, 86, Qn. Elizabeth-st, S.E. — *Clerk*, Edric Bayley ; *Surveyor*, George W. Thompson; *Analyst and Medical Officer*, James Northcote Vinen, M.D., 4, Church-row, S.E.

ST. PANCRAS, Vestry Hall, Pancras-rd, N.W. — *Vestry Clerk*, T. E. Gibb, M.P. ; *Clerk to the Guardians*, Alfred Millward; *Surveyor*, W. B. Scott, C.E.; *Medical Officer of Health*, J. F. J. Sykes, M.B. ; *Analyst*, Dr. Thomas Stevenson, Guy's Hospital.

ST. SAVIOUR'S, 3, Emerson-st, S.E. — *Clerk*, W. H. Atkins ; *Medical Officer of Health*, Robert Bianchi, 8, Blackfriars-rd, S.E. ; *Surveyor*, G. R. Norrish, office of Board ; *Analyst*, Dr. Bernays, St. Thomas's Hospital.

STRAND, 5, Tavistock-st, Covent-gdn.—*Clerk*, Thos. M. Jenkins, office of Board ; *Medical Officer of Health*, Conway Evans, M.D., Garden House, Clement's-inn ; *Surveyor*, Arthur Ventris, office of Board ; *Analyst*, C. H. Cribb, 50, Frith-st, W.

WANDSWORTH, Battersea - rise, Wandsworth, S.W. — *Clerk*, H. G. Hills ; *Medical Officers*, Dr. Kempster, J. Oakman, Dr. Newsholme, W. Young Orr, Dr. Sutton, and Dr. Nicholas ; *Surveyors*, for Battersea, John T. Pilditch ; Clapham, Arthur Southam ; Putney, John Chas.

Radford; Streatham and Tooting, James Barber; Wandsworth, Anthony Dobson; *Analyst*, Dr. John Muter, F.C.S., 325, Kennington-rd, S.E.

WESTMINSTER DISTRICT BOARD OF WORKS, Town Hall, Caxton-st, S.W.—*Clerk*, J. E. Smith; *Surveyor*, G. R. W. Wheeler, office of Board; *Analyst*, A. Dupré, Ph.D., Westminster Hospital, S.W.; *Medical Officer*, B. Holt.

WHITECHAPEL, 15, Great Alie-st, Whitechapel, E.—*Clerk*, Alfred Turner; *Medical Officer of Health*, J. Loane, office of Board; *Surveyor*, William La Riviere, office of Board; *Analyst*, William Chas. Young, Lee-ter, Plaistow, E.

WOOLWICH, Town Hall, Woolwich.—*Clerk*, A. C. Read; *Surveyor*, H. O. Thomas; *Medical Officer*, vacant; *Analyst*, H. Smith.

Veterinary College Museum, Gt. College-st, Camden Tn. (Map 2).—Admission daily from 9 till 5 in winter, and 9 till 6 in summer, on presentation to the curator of visiting card. The Museum contains several thousand specimens of anatomy and diseases of domesticated animals.

Victoria. — AGENCY - GENERAL, 8, Victoria-chambers, Victoria-st.—NEAREST *Ry. Stn.*, St. James's-pk; *Omnibus Rtes.*, Victoria-st and Parliament-st; *Cab Rank*, Victoria-st.

Victoria Club, Wellington-st, Strand.—For the association of gentlemen connected with sport, principally racing. Entrance, £5; subs., £5.—(*See* RACING.)

Victoria Coffee Music Hall (Royal), Waterloo-rd.—Once the Victoria Theatre, now a Temperance Music Hall, with "specially - provided entertainments for the working-classes, free from anything objectionable." Prices 3d. to 3s.; private boxes, 6s. to £1 1s. Commence at 8. NEAREST *Ry. Stns.,* Waterloo (S.W.) and Blackfriars (Dis. and L.C.&D.); *Omnibus Rtes.*, Waterloo-rd and Blackfriars-rd.

Victoria Embankment (Map 7) extends along the left bank of the Thames, from Westminster to Blackfriars, about a mile and a quarter, and was constructed by Sir Joseph Bazalgette, the engineer to the Metropolitan Board of Works. The whole of the space now occupied by the Em-

bankment was covered by water or mud, according to the state of the tide, and few London improvements have been more conducive to health and comfort. The substitution of the beautiful curve of the Embankment, majestic in its simplicity, with its massive granite walls, flourishing trees, and trim gardens, is an unspeakable improvement on the squalid foreshore, and tumble - down wharves, and backs of dingy houses, which formerly abutted on the river. It is to be regretted that difficulties of approach make this noble thoroughfare less useful than it should be. At Westminster and at Charing ✠, both from Northumberland-avenue and from Whitehall-pl, and at Blackfriars, the approaches are all that can be desired, and are worthy of the Embankment itself; but the streets leading from the Strand, such, for instance, as Arundel-st and Norfolk-st, are both steep and inconvenient. The general appearance of the Victoria Embankment is still somewhat marred by the presence here and there of unsightly buildings, which it may be hoped will ere long be removed—and probably not even the designer of the Charing ✠ Ry. Stn. would call that useful building in any way ornamental—but it is nevertheless singularly rich in architectural features. Somerset House, the Temple, the Adelphi-ter, the St. Stephen's Club, the National Liberal Club, the School Board house, the City of London School, and other fine buildings, are either on or visible from the Embankment. It would seem from the numerous pedestals which the architect inserted in his design, that it was in contemplation to place an alarming number of statues along the road. At present the Embankment has fortunately but six statues to offer to the inspection of the critic: those of Sir James Outram, at the foot of Whitehall-pl; Brunel, near Somerset House; John Stuart Mill, near Norfolk - st; William Tyndale, the first English translator of the New Testament; Raikes, the originator of Sunday Schools, a short distance west of Waterloo-br; and Robert Burns, near Charing ✠ Stn. In curious contrast to the modern statues, and to the busy life about it, is Cleopatra's Needle, which, owing to the public spirit and energy of the late Sir (then Mr) Erasmus Wilson

and Mr. John Dixon, is now a conspicuous object on the river-wall at the bottom of Salisbury-st. NEAREST *Ry. Stns.*, Westminster (Dis.), Charing ✠ (Dis. & S.E.), Temple (Dis.), Blackfriars (Dis.), and St Paul's (L.C. & D.); *Omnibus Rtes.*, the Strand and Fleet-st.

Victoria Park (Map. 4), one of the largest and finest in London, lies in what is at present the extreme N.E. corner of the town. It is very prettily laid out with ornamental water, &c., and differs from the West End parks in being supplied with various appliances for amusement, usually on summer evenings very liberally patronised. Victoria-pk is one of the things which no student of London life should miss seeing, and its most characteristic times are Sat. or Sun. evenings—or both, for each has its distinct features—and Bank Holidays. NEAREST *Ry. Stns.*, Victoria - pk (N.L.) and Cambridge-heath (G.E.); *Omnibus Rtes.*, Victoria - pk - rd and Roman-rd.

Victoria Stations, at the west end of Victoria-st, Westminster (Map 6). Here are the West End termini of the L.C. & D.R. and L.B. & S.C.R. Opposite is the Victoria-st Stn. of the District Ry. Adjoining the Brighton Stn. is the large and popular Grosvenor Hotel. *Omnibus Rte.*, Victoria-st; *Cab Fare* to Bank, 2s.; to Charing ✠, 1s.

Vine Club, now the YORK CLUB, 8, St. James's-sq (*which see*).

Vintners' Company (The), 68½, Upper Thames-st, was incorporated by Edward III., in whose days claret was sold in London at 4d. the gallon, and Rhenish at 6d. Charles I. allowed the vintners to raise the price 1d. per quart in return for the duty of £2 per tun. The present hall is not ancient. There is a fine piece of tapestry in excellent preservation representing St. Martin of Tours, the patron saint of the vintners, in one of the ante-chambers; and in the court-room, above the fire-place, there is a painting of St. Martin dividing his cloak with a beggar, which looks like a Rubens. The company possesses a magnificent salt-cellar, silver-gilt, by Cellini. The oak carving in the hall and court-room is remarkably fine.

Volunteers.—(*See* MILITARY HOME DISTRICT.)

War Office, Pall Mall (Map 13).—Hours, 10 to 5. NEAREST *Ry. Stn.*, St. James's-pk; *Omnibus Rtes.*, Piccadilly, Regent-st, and Strand; *Cab Rank*, St. James's-sq. Besides the general clerical staff, the principal sub-divisions are the Commander - in - Chief's Office; the Adjutant-General's Department; the Office of Deputy - Adjutant - General of Artillery; of Inspector-General of Artillery (office, Whitehall, S.W.); of Deputy - Adjutant - General of Engineers; the Quartermaster-General's Office; the Intelligence Branch, 16, Queen Anne's-ga, S.W.; the Army Contract Department; the Director of Works (Horse Guards); the Military Education Department, 21, St. James's-sq, S.W.); the Rl. Army Clothing Depôt (Grosvenor-rd, S.W.); the Rl. Gun Factory, the Rl. Carriage Department, the Chemical Department, and the Rl. Laboratory, at Woolwich; the Small Arms Factories at Enfield and Birmingham; the Rl. Engineers' Office (Horse Guards); and the School of Military Engineering, Chatham.

Water. — The names of the London Water Companies, with the addresses of their chief offices, are as follows:

CHELSEA, 35, Commercial-rd, Pimlico, S.W.

EAST LONDON, 16, St. Helen's-pl, Bishopsgate.

GRAND JUNC., 65, S. Molton-st.

KENT, Mill-la, Deptford, S.E.

LAMBETH, Brixton-hill, S.W.

NEW RIVER COM., Clerkenwell, E.C.

SOUTHWARK AND VAUXHALL, Sumner-st, Southwark, S.E.

WEST MIDDLESEX, 19, Marylebone-rd, W.

All water companies are obliged, when required, to provide and keep throughout their limits a constant supply of pure and wholesome water, sufficient for the domestic purposes of the inhabitants within such district, constantly laid on, and are compelled at all times to keep charged with water under proper pressure all their pipes to which fire-plugs are affixed (unless prevented by frost, unusual drought, accident, or necessary repairs), and are to allow all persons at all times to take and use such water for extinguishing any fires without making any charge for

the same. Companies may supply water by measure, and let meters out for hire, if authorised by special Act of Parliament, for such sum as may be agreed between the parties.

All owners and occupiers of premises are entitled to demand a supply of water for domestic purposes only where they have laid down pipes communicating with the company's pipes, and paid or tendered the water-rate in respect thereof, and any such owner or occupier desiring to make a connection with the company's pipes is allowed to open or break up such part of the pavement and ground between the pipes of the company and his premises, upon giving notice to the local authorities and reinstating the same without delay. Such owner or occupier may lay down any leaden or other service-pipes, which in the absence of special provisions must not have a bore exceeding half an inch unless with the consent of the company, and such pipes must be approved by the company, and fourteen days' notice given before commencing to lay down the same. The connection of the service-pipes to the company's pipes must be made under the supervision of the company's surveyor, and two days' notice of the hour and day fixed for such connection must be given.

The service-pipes are provided by the persons seeking the supply except where such water is supplied to premises under the annual value of £10 in a street where the company's pipes are laid down, in which case the company is compelled, on request of the occupier, with the owner's consent, to lay down service-pipes and keep the same in repair, the company being entitled in addition to the water-rate to charge such a reasonable annual charge as may be agreed upon. Water-rates are paid according to the annual value of the premises supplied, and must be paid in advance. The owner and not the occupier of houses not exceeding the annual value of £10 is liable for the rates, and if any person supplied with water neglect to pay such water-rate, the company may cut off the supply of water to the premises, and recover the rates due from such person if less than £20 by proceedings before the justices, together with the costs of cutting off the supply and recovering the same, and afterwards

by distress and sale of the defaulter's goods: or if the rates amount to more than £20, the company may sue for the same, with expense of cutting off and recovering thereof.

No greater dividend than £10 per cent. per annum on the paid-up capital, unless authorised by a special Act, can be declared, except when a larger dividend shall be necessary to make up a deficiency of any previous dividends which shall have fallen short of such £10 per cent. If the clear profits amount to more than sufficient, after making up any such deficiency, if any, the excess must be invested at compound interest, and forms a reserved fund, which fund shall not exceed, unless a prescribed sum is set out in any special Act of Parliament, one-tenth part of the nominal capital. If any person supplied with water either causes or permits waste, misuse, undue consumption, or contamination, the company may, without prejudice to any remedy they may have against such person, cut off the supply of water to his premises.

The character and qualities of the water supplied to London by the different companies differ considerably. The south-east of London is supplied by the Kent Company, which takes the water from the chalk hills. This water is purer organically than any other supplied to London, but is sometimes objected to on account of its hardness. The New River Company, which supplies the north-east districts and the City, also supplies a water which has the character of being purer than the water taken from the Thames. The other companies, viz., West Middlesex, Grand Junction, Chelsea, Lambeth, Southwark and Vauxhall, take their supplies from the Thames, and filter all the water through large filter-beds. Upon the efficiency of their filtration depends the purity of the water they supply. By efficient filtration there is no doubt that the Thames water can be supplied as pure as water from the deepest and purest spring, the purity of such spring water being simply caused by filtering through the ground. It is, therefore, a question of importance to public health that the companies should be made to filter thoroughly; and if that were done we should hear nothing more of schemes for bringing water from distant lakes. As an extra precaution against contaminated water, householders should always provide themselves with a good filter. The Silicated Carbon Filter has been proved to be wonderfully efficacious in removing organic matter from water, and has been known to remove even vegetable poisons, such as strychnine, immediately. The whole question of the London Water Supply has now been for some time under consideration with a view to the transfer from the various companies to the municipal authorities. Early in 1880 a Bill was brought in by Lord Beaconsfield's Government with this object but the terms proposed to be conceded to the companies were considered too high, and the Bill met with an unfavourable reception.

Water - Colours, Royal Institute of Painters in (Map 6).—The fine new galleries of this society, at 189, Piccadilly, were opened in the spring of 1883. The exhibitions are open to the works of all artists, subject to selection, and members are elected from the works exhibited. The exhibitions are annual, and commence at the end of April, the admission being 1s.; illustrated catalogues, 1s. President, Sir James D. Linton; Vice-President, H. G. Hine; Treasurer, E. M. Wimperis; Secretary, W. T. Blackmore. NEAREST *Ry. Stn.*, Charing ✚ (S.E. & Dis.); *Omnibus Rtes.*, Piccadilly and Waterloo-pl; *Cab Rank*, St. James's-st.

Water - Colours, Royal Society of Painters in. Gallery: 5A, Pall Mall East, S.W. (Map. 6).—The Society (often called "The Old Society") was founded in 1804, and has held annual exhibitions since that year. There are two exhibitions, the summer, and the winter, which is composed of sketches and studies. The former is open to the public towards the end of April, and the opening of the latter is this year fixed for November 29th. The Society exhibitions are confined to the works of the members and associates. The officers are as follows:—President, Sir John Gilbert, R.A.; Treasurer, George H. Andrews, F.R.G.S.; Secretary, Alfred D. Fripp. Council: L. Alma Tadema, R.A., Alfred W. Hunt, Deputy President, Edward F. Brustnall, Edward A. Goodall, Carl Haag, Henry

Wallis, E. K. Johnson, H. Clarence Whaite. Keeper, George L. Ridge. The number of members is forty, and of associated exhibitors at present forty-two (no restriction as to number). In connection with this society is the ROYAL WATER-COLOUR SOCIETY ART CLUB, of which Sir John Gilbert, R.A., is president. Established in 1884, "for the purpose of holding in the gallery of the society an annual series of conversazione, to which members shall be invited to send works of art for exhibition." Election by a committee of twelve, two black balls to exclude. Admission fee, £1 1s., and annual subscription £1 1s., but the entrance fee is not required from members or associates of the Royal Society of Painters in Water-Colours, or of the Royal Academy. NEAREST *Ry. Stns.*, Charing ✚ (S.E. & Dis.); *Omnibus Rtes.*, Cockspur-st and Haymarket; *Cab Rank*, Haymarket.

Waterloo Bridge (Map 7), the earliest of John Rennie's three, is perhaps the handsomest bridge across the Thames; consisting of nine elliptical arches 120 ft. in span and 35 ft. in height, supported on piers 20 ft. wide at the spring of the arches, and surmounted by an open balustrade. It is not so wide as London-br by 11 ft., but is very nearly half as long again—1,380 ft. It was opened on the second anniversary of Waterloo, 18th June, 1817. NEAREST (N. side) *Ry. Stns.*, Temple and Charing ✚ (Dis.); *Omnibus Rte.*, Strand; *Cab Rank*, Wellington-st; (S. side) *Ry. Stn.*, Waterloo (S.W.); *Omnibus Rte.*, Waterloo-rd; *Cab Rank*, York-rd.

Waterloo Station (Map 13), a short distance south of Waterloo-br, was built by the L. & S.W.R. Co. in 1848, after the passenger terminus at Nine Elms, Vauxhall, was abandoned, and long before it had entered into anyone's head to carry a railway across the Thames. The station, which is now a double one, the southern building being principally used for suburban traffic, is large and fairly convenient; but as it is built on the top of a rise, the approaches are very steep and awkward. Travellers by the L.& S.W.R. have only to cross Waterloo-br (about half a mile) to find themselves in the heart of the London hotel district. *Omnibus Rte.* Waterloo-rd.

Weights and Measures (INSPECTORS OF).—Mr. David Faulkner, 116, Bethnal Green-rd, E. (District No. 1); Mr. Samuel Foulsham, 47, Cyrus-st, Clerkenwell, E.C. (District No. 2); Mr. Charles P. Cox, 17, Arthur-st, Oxford-st (District No. 3); Mr. Edwin James Stephens, Brentford, W. (District No. 4).

Wellington Club, 1, Grosvenor-pl, S.W.— Established in 1885, as a social club, to which ladies are admitted as visitors. Full particulars from sec., G. A. Hart-Dyke, Esq. Entrance fee, £21; annual subscription, £10 10s.

Wesleyan Methodists, and Places of Worship.—The Revs. John and Charles Wesley began their great work in London in the year 1739, and in the same year founded "The Society of the People called Methodists." The Rules of this Society, drawn up and signed by the brothers Wesley, bear date May 1st, 1743. In them the Society is described as "no other than a company of men having the form, and seeking the power, of godliness; united in order to pray together, to receive the word of exhortation, and to watch over one another in love, that they may help each other to work out their salvation." The society is divided into small companies called classes, containing about 12 persons in every class, one of whom is styled the leader, whose chief duties are "to see each person in his class once a week, in order to enquire how their souls prosper; to advise, reprove, comfort, or exhort, as occasion may require; to receive what they are willing to give towards the support of the Gospel; and to inform the minister of any that are sick, or of any that walk disorderly and will not be reproved." The condition of membership is thus stated: "There is only one condition previously required in those who desire admission into these societies—viz., "a desire to flee from the wrath to come, and to be saved from their sins." "It is expected of all who continue in these societies that they should continue to evidence their desire of salvation; 1st, by doing no harm, by avoiding evil in every kind, especially that which is most generally practised; 2nd, by doing good, by being in every kind merciful after their power, as they have opportunity, doing good of every possible sort, and as far as possible to all men; 3rd, by attending upon all the ordinances of God: such are, the public worship of God, the ministry of the Word, either read or expounded, the Supper of the Lord, family and private prayer, searching the Scriptures, and fasting or abstinence." Persons, not being members of the society, are admitted to the Lord's Supper on application to the minister. By such rules as the above the Wesleyan Methodists are united in what is often called "The Methodist Connexion." Although the phrase, "The Methodist Church," is now in common use, it was not used by Mr. Wesley and the early Methodists, nor has any definition of a *Church*, as such, been authoritatively made. The central authority of the Methodist Connexion is "The Conference," which, when purely ministerial affairs are considered, is composed of ministers only, of whom 100, chosen according to certain prescribed rules, constitute "The Legal Conference," by whom all acts of the Conference must be ratified. In the year 1877 it was determined that when certain affairs other than what are judged to be purely ministerial are considered, the Conference shall consist of "the president, and of 240 ministers and 240 laymen." The doctrinal views of the Methodists are mainly those of the Church of England. It is stated that the various Methodist organizations throughout the world embrace upwards of 20,000,000 adherents, nearly 5,000,000 of whom are recognised Church members.

The following are the principal buildings in London:

THE CITY-ROAD CHAPEL, built by Mr. Wesley in the year 1777. It is the oldest and most interesting of the Methodist chapels. In it and the surrounding burial-ground are many monuments of the earlier Methodists. At the side of it stood the "Morning Chapel," where Mr. Wesley held his early morning services. It was recently destroyed by fire, and the larger chapel much injured. Both have been restored. Here are also Mr. Wesley's house and other buildings erected for the use of his preachers.

Near to the chapel is THE CONFERENCE OFFICE, or BOOK-ROOM, situated in Castle-st, City-rd. This is the principal publishing house of the Methodists. It was founded by Wesley for the purpose of circulating cheap and useful literature. There is a branch publishing house at 66, Paternoster-row.

THE CENTENARY HALL, or MISSION-HOUSE, in Bishopsgate-st, is used mainly for the transaction of business connected with the Wesleyan Methodist Foreign Missionary Society. The offices of the Home Missionary Society are also in this building, and most of the principal committees hold their meetings here, for which there is ample accommodation.

THE TRAINING COLLEGE for Day Schoolmasters is situated in Horseferry-rd, Westminster. There is a similar college for the training of Day Schoolmistresses, in Battersea. In the former is accommodation for 131 students; and in the latter for 109.

THE THEOLOGICAL COLLEGE for the training of (missionary) ministers, situated at Richmond, was opened in 1843.

THE CHILDREN'S HOME, embracing orphanage, refuge, and training institute. The central building is in Bonner-rd, Victoria-pk, E. This institution exists for the nurture and education of orphans and destitute children. There are branches of the home in Edgworth, Lancashire; Milton next Gravesend; and Hamilton, in Canada. In the London Home are 223 children.

THE WESLEYAN METHODIST SUNDAY SCHOOL UNION has its publishing house and offices at 2, Ludgate-cir-bdgs.

There are several societies in London connected with the Wesleyan Methodists, the principal of which are:

THE LONDON LAY MISSION.

THE SEAMEN'S MISSION.

THE LORD'S DAY OBSERVANCE COMMITTEE.

THE METROPOLITAN CHAPEL BUILDING FUND, established in the year 1862. By its means, in the first ten years of its existence, accommodation was made for 27,000 people, at a cost of nearly £150,000. In the year 1870, a proposal was made to build fifty additional chapels in ten years. This has not been fully accomplished; but upwards of 80,000 additional sittings have been provided since the commencement of the effort.

THE TEMPERANCE COMMITTEE.

THE STRANGERS' FRIEND SOCIETY, established 1785.

THE FUND FOR THE EXTENSION OF METHODISM, by means of which it is proposed to assist in the erection of 1,000 chapels in the country villages and towns.

The following is a list of the principal Wesleyan Methodist chapels in London and the neighbourhood:

Acton Chapel, Gunnersbury.
Alsen Road, Highgate.
Approach Road Chapel, Victoria-pk, E.
Barking Road Chapel, Canning-town, E.
Barrow Hill Road Chapel, St. John's Wood.
Barry Road Chapel, Peckham Rye, S.E.
Bassein Park Chapel, Goldhawk-rd, Starch-gn.
Battersea Chapel, S.W.
Bayswater Chapel, Denbigh-rd, W.
Blackheath Chapel, Bennet's-pk, S.E
Bow Common Chapel, E.
Bow Road Chapel, E.
Brentford Chapel.
Brixton Hill Chapel, S.W.
Brockley Chapel, S.E.
Bromley Chapel, S.E.
Brunswick Chapel, Limehouse, E.
Buckhurst Hill Chapel.
Caledonian Road Chapel, Holloway, N.
Caledonian Road, Twyford Hall, N.
Camden Town Chapel, Camden-st, N.W.
Cassland Road Chapel, Homerton, E.
Charlton Vale Chapel, Woolwich.
Chelsea Chapel, Sloane-ter, S.W.
Chequer Alley Home Mission Station, City-rd, E.C.
Children's Home Chapel, Bonner-rd, E.
Child's Hill Chapel.
Chingford Hatch.
Chislehurst Chapel, Chislehurst.
City Chapel, 35, Aldersgate-st, E.C.
City Road Chapel, City-rd, E.C.
Clapham Chapel, High-st, Clapham, S.W.
Clapton Chapel, Lower Clapton, E.
Clifton Street Chapel, Wandsworth-rd, S.W.
Cubitt Town Chapel.
Dalston Chapel, Mayfield-ter, E.
Deptford Chapel, High-st, S.E.
Ealing Chapel, W.
East Finchley Chapel, N.
East Greenwich Mission Church.
Edmonton Chapel, High-rd, Lower Edmonton, N.

Enfield Chapel, N.

Enfield Highway Chapel, N.

Epping Chapel.

Essex Hall, Essex-rd, Islington.

Feltham Chapel.

Finsbury Park Chapel, Seven Sisters'-rd, N.

Forest Gate Chapel, Stratford.

Forest Hill, S.E.

French's Fields, S.E.

Fulham Road. Salem Chapel.

German Wesleyan Methodist Chapel, Canning Tn., E.

German Wesleyan Methodist Chapel, Commercial-rd, E.

German Wesleyan Methodist Chapel, Frith-st, Soho, W.

German Wesleyan Methodist Chapel, Fulham.

German Wesleyan Methodist Chapel, Hammersmith.

Gillespie Road, N.

Globe Road Chapel, Globe-rd, E.

Great Queen's Street Chapel, Lincoln's Inn Fields, W.C.

Green Lanes Chapel, Highbury, N.

Greenwich Chapel, London-st, Greenwich.

Hackney Road Chapel, Hoxton, E.

Hackney Wick Wesleyan Mission Chapel, Elgin-st, Hackney Wick, E.

Haggerston, Hertford-st, N.

Hammersmith Chapel, W.

Hampstead Chapel, N.W.

Harrow Chapel.

High Barnet Chapel.

High Beech Chapel.

Highbury Chapel, N.

Highgate Chapel, Archway-rd, N.

Hinde Street Chapel, Manchester-sq, W.

Holly Park Chapel, Highgate, N.

Hornsey Chapel, N.

Hornsey Road Chapel, N.

Hounslow Chapel, S.W.

Isleworth Chapel.

Justice Walk Chapel, Chelsea, S.W.

Kensal Town Chapel, W.

Kensington Chapel, Clarence-pl, W.

Kentish Town Chapel, Lady Margaret-rd, N.W.

King's ✠ Chapel, Liverpool-st, W.C.

Lambeth Chapel, Lambeth-rd, S.E.

Lambeth (South) Chapel, Dorset-st, S.W.

Lancaster Road Chapel, Notting-hill, W.

Lewisham Chapel, S.E.

Leyton Chapel, High-st.

Leytonstone Chapel.

Liverpool Road Chapel, Islington, N.

Lockfield's Chapel, S.E.

Loughton Chapel.

Lower Norwood Chapel, S.E.

Lower Road, Deptford, S.E.

Lycett Memorial, Mile End-rd, E.

Matthias Road, Mildmay-pk, N.

Mildmay Park Chapel, Islington, N.

Mile End Chapel, E.

Millwall Chapel, E.

Milton Street Chapel, St. John's Wood, N.W.

Mostyn Road Chapel, S.W.

Munster Park, S.W.

New Barnet Chapel, Station-rd.

New ✠ Chapel.

New North Road Chapel, Hoxton, N.

North Woolwich Chapel.

Oakley Place Chapel, Old Kent-rd, S.E.

Old Ford Road Chapel, Bow, E.

Ordnance Road, Stoke Newington.

Penge Chapel, Penge, S.E.

Pimlico Chapel, Claverton-st, S.W.

Plaistow Chapel.

Plumstead Common Chapel, Woolwich.

Plumstead Village Chapel, Woolwich.

Poplar Chapel, East India-rd, E.

Prince of Wales's Road Chapel, Haverstock-hill, N.W.

Putney Chapel, S.W.

Queensland Road, Highbury, N.

Queen's Road Chapel, Peckham, S.E.

Queen's Road, Wandsworth-rd, S.W.

Quex Road Chapel, Kilburn, N.W.

Radnor Street Chapel, Radnor-st, E.C.

Richmond Road Chapel, Richmond-rd, Hackney, E.

Roupell Park Chapel.

St. George's Chapel, Cable-st, E.

St. John's Chapel, St. John's-sq, Clerkenwell, E.C.

St. Paul's Road, Camden-rd, N.W.

Seamen's Mission Chapel, Commercial-rd-east, E.

Shooter's Hill Chapel, Woolwich.

Silver Street Chapel, Rotherhithe, S.E.

Southall Chapel.

South Street, Walworth, S.E.

Southwark Chapel, Long-lane, S.E.

Southwark Park Chapel, Rotherhithe, S.E.

Spitalfields Chapel, Church-st, E.

Stamford Street Chapel, Blackfriars-rd, S.E.

Stanhope Street Chapel, Hampstead-rd, N.W.

Stoke Newington Chapel, High-st, N.

Stratford Chapel, The Grove, E.

Studley Road Chapel, Stockwell, S.W.

Sutherland Gardens Chapel, Paddington, W.

Sydenham Chapel, Dartmouth-rd, S.E.

Tooting Chapel.

Tottenham Chapel, High-rd, N.

Turnham Green.

Twickenham Chapel.

Upper Norwood, S.W.

Upton Park, S.E.

Vauxhall Chapel, Vauxhall-walk, Lambeth, S.E.

Waltham Abbey Chapel.

Walthamstow Chapel.

Walworth Road Chapel, S.E.

Wandsworth Chapel, St. John's-hill, S.W.

Wanstead Road Chapel.

Warwick Gardens Chapel, Kensington, W.

Welsh Chapel, 186, Aldersgate-st, E.C.

Welsh Wesleyan Methodist Chapel, Portland-st, Oxford-st, Soho.

West Finchley Chapel.

West Kensington Park Chapel, Shepherd's Bush-gn, W.

Westminster Chapel, Horseferry-rd, S.W.

Westow Hill Chapel, Upper Norwood, S.E.

Whetstone Chapel.

Willesden Chapel.

Wilson Street, Finsbury-sq, E.C.

Woodford Chapel.

Wood Green Chapel, N.

Woolwich Chapel, William-st.

Western Australia.

Agency General: Crown Agents for the Colonies, Downing-st, S.W. NEAREST Ry. Stn., St. James-pk (Met.); Omnibus Rte., Whitehall; Cab Rank, Palace-yard.

Westminster Abbey

(Map 13), from its associations the most famous of all English buildings with the exception of the Tower, was originally founded by Edward the Confessor between the years 1055 and 1065. Previously, however, it is believed that Sebart, king of the East Saxons, built a church upon the present site some time during the seventh century. The name Westminster was used to distinguish the abbey from the cathedral church of St. Paul, which was once known as Eastminster. Of the Confessor's work but little remains saving the pyx-house, which lies to the south of the present abbey adjoining the chapter-house, and that part of the cloister which Westminster schoolboys now use as a gymnasium. Henry III., who exhibited a rare taste in building, erected the principal portion of the existing edifice; he pulled down the greater part of Edward the Confessor's work, and built a chapel to the Virgin at the east end. Henry VII. in his turn demolished Henry III.'s work, and immortalised himself by his chapel, which now stands behind the head of the cross in the form of which the abbey has been constructed. With the exception of the two towers, the upper parts of which were built by Wren, at the western entrance—the foot of the cross—which faces the Aquarium and the Hotel, Westminster Abbey as regards its outward aspect is very much what Henry VII. left it. Inside, the abbey is at once imposing and inspiring. The height of the building, the symmetry of its proportions, the solemn grandeur of "the long-drawn aisles," the fact that the sightseer is at every step treading upon the graves of England's wisest and noblest, cannot but render a visit to Westminster Abbey a thing to remember and to respect. An attempt to describe the statues, the bas-reliefs, the busts, and the allegorical illustrations in marble of departed prowess and virtue, would occupy more space than is permitted to us. A few of the most prominent relics we may, however, refer to. The chapel of Edward the Confessor, which lies behind the present altar-screen, contains the shrine of that monarch, beside which devout persons used to sit in order to cure themselves of earthly disorders. The remains of Henry III. are also supposed to rest here; also what is left of Edward I., Edward III., and Henry V., whose saddle and helmet, used at Agincourt, are fixed to a rail over the gallant monarch's tomb. Against the altar-screen stand the coronation chairs; under the seat of the king's chair is the identical stone which Edward I. brought from Scone, and on which the Scottish kings were crowned. The second chair was made for the coronation of Mary, the much beloved consort of William III. Round the Confessor's chapel are a number of smaller chapels, filled with the tombs and emblazoned eulogies of bygone peers and peeresses. Immediately behind the sarcophagus

of Henry V. is the chapel built by Henry VII., intended as a place of sepulture for himself and his successors, as fine a specimen of what is called florid Gothic architecture as exists. The exterior was restored by Wyatt. The gates are brass, cunningly wrought, but are now dingy and look more like iron. Knights of the Bath are installed in this chapel, and at some distance above the stalls hang the tattered banners of many famous members of the order. On the left of the chapel, which contains the tomb of Henry VII. and Edward VI., is the burial place of Qn. Elizabeth; on the right lies Mary Queen of Scots. At the S.E. corner is the slab which rests over the remains of Lady Augusta Stanley, wife of the late Dean of Westminster, and the intimate friend of Qn. Victoria. To the left of Lady Augusta Stanley is the marble tomb of the Duc de Montpensier, brother of Louis Philippe, King of the French. Among the distinguished Britons buried in the abbey is Charles Darwin the naturalist. George Edward Street and Sir Gilbert Scott, the architects, also lie in the abbey, and near the grave of the latter is that of Livingstone. Poet's Corner, which forms the most southern portion of the arm of the cross, is by no means the least imposing portion of the building. Here is the grave of Charles Dickens, by whose side is Cumberland, the dramatist. At his feet is Sheridan, and above is Handel, the composer; close by are Tom Campbell, David Garrick, and Samuel Johnson; marble busts of Thackeray and Macaulay are placed on brackets within a few feet of these illustrious dead. Close to Edward the Confessor's shrine, and up a winding flight of steps, is a collection of waxen effigies to which the general public are not admitted. The figures are life size, and are enclosed in glass cases, on which the vulgar have scratched their names with persistent enthusiasm. They are eleven in number, and are considered remarkable as portraits. Charles II. stands in ordinary costume, with, however, an undignified smut on his nose. Next to his merry majesty is the Duke of Buckingham, lying in state, a coronet upon his head. Queen Anne, looking uncomfortable in her state robes and crown, is sitting on her throne, and holds with some

difficulty her orb and sceptre. The Duchess of Buckingham and her little son, and the Duchess of Richmond (1702), are standing immediately opposite the dead Duke; and the Earl of Chatham, in his robes of office, does not look quite the energetic statesman we would fain regard him. William and Mary are in a glass case together, and by their side is Queen Elizabeth, with a magnificent ruff of real lace, and next to her is a lifelike effigy of Nelson. Permission to see the wax-work may be obtained from the Dean or a member of the chapter.

At the south of the Abbey are the cloisters, which contain some of the oldest graves in the country; one inscribed with the name of Gervasius de Blois, Abbas, 1106, is in excellent preservation. From the cloisters admission is gained to the chapter-house, which was built by Henry III. in 1250, and re stored by Sir Gilbert Scott in 1865. Formerly the chapter-house was used as a council chamber for the monks and the abbot, and we are assured that offending recluses were flogged at the central pillar. The House of Commons subsequently met here until the days of Henry VIII., after which the house was used as a depository for public records. When the documents were removed to Fetter-la, it was considered desirable that the chapter-house should be restored, and accordingly Sir Gilbert Scott was employed, with results which the public may see without charge to-day. The illustrations on the walls were executed by one of the monks attached to the abbey in the fifteenth century. In the vestibule is a Roman sarcophagus, discovered in the North Green some seventeen years ago.

Services are held every day in the abbey, to which the public are admitted free. Admission fee to the smaller chapels, including that of Henry VII., is 6d. NEAREST *Ry. Stns.*, Westminster-br (Dis.) and St. James's-park (Dis.); *Omnibus Rtes.*, Parliament-st and Victoria-st; *Cab Rank*, Palace-yd.

Westminster Bridge

(Map 13) varies very much in appearance with the state of the tide. When the river is full, and the height of the structure reduced as much as possible, there is a certain grace about it. When, however, the water is low, and the flat arches are exposed at the full height of their long lanky piers, the effect is almost mean. Except, however, for the excessive vibration arising from lightness of construction, it is one of the best, from a practical point of view, in London, the roadway being wide and the gradient very slight. NEAREST *Ry. Stn.*, Westminster (Dis.); *Omnibus Rtes.*, Westminster-br-rd and Parliament-st ; *Cab Rank*, Palace-yd.

Westminster Hall.—
(*See* LAW COURTS.)

Westminster School
(Map 13).—The foundation of Qn. Elizabeth consists of 40 Queen's Scholars. The admission is by open competition, which takes place annually in June or July, and scholars enter into residence in the following September. There is no restriction in respect of birthplace. Candidates who have been a year previously in the school must be under the age of 15 on March 25th of the year of admission. If not previously attending the school, they must be under the age of 14 on March 25th of the year. The Queen's Scholars hold their scholarships subject to an annual examination, in which any scholar may forfeit his place on the foundation. The fixed expenses of a Queen's Scholar are £30 annually payable in advance by three equal instalments—viz., £10 at the beginning of each term. This charge includes maintenance, as well as tuition, except certain extras. For boys not on the foundation, the sch. fees are £5 5s. entrance, and £31 10s. annually for tuition, also payable in advance in three equal instalments as above. These fees include all the ordinary instruction. All boys, according to their position, share in the expenses of sch. games. The age of admission is ordinarily from 10 to 14 years. Boys not on the foundation may board, either wholly or partially, at one of the boarding houses, or entirely at home. They may also dine, if desired, in the coll. hall, for which there is a separate charge of £12 yearly. The boarding-house fees are £5 5s. entrance, and £68 5s. yearly for boarders, or £25 4s. for half-boarders, besides tuition fees. Exhibitions, tenable at the sch., are offered annually to competitors (whether previously in the sch. or not) of ages between 12 and 14. The ages are dated fro' . March 25th preceding

the examination. They are of the value some of £30, and some of £20, which may be augmented in the case of boarders. These exhibitions are all tenable for two years, subject always to the result of the annual examination, or until the holder is elected upon the foundation. The examination is held at the same time as that for the scholarships. No entrance fee is charged for exhibitioners. The sch. prizes are numerous and valuable. The Annual Benefactions open to competition, for all boys proceeding to the universities, who shall have been at least three years previously in the sch., are at present : Three Scholarships at Christ Church, Oxford, of the total annual value of about £80 each. These scholarships are tenable for five years, and are augmented, in all cases of merit, by gifts from the Carey Benefaction, the income of which amounts to £600 a year, and is divisible among the Westminster scholars of Christ Church. Three Exhibitions at Christ Church, Oxford, of the annual value of £50, tenable for three years. Three exhibitions at Trinity Coll., Cambridge, of £40 a year, tenable for three years, or until the time for taking the B.A. degree. The Senior Exhibitioner receives also a Samwaies's Exhibition of about £24, tenable for two years at Trinity. The second exhibitioner, a similar exhibition, tenable for one year. Two or more exhibitions from the bequest of Dr. Triplett, tenable for three years at any coll. of Oxford or Cambridge, conditionally on certificates of residence and good conduct from the authorities of the coll. These are not open to students of Christ Church. Westminster Abbey is used as the chapel of the school, and Vincent-sq is the playground. For further information apply to Rev. the Head-master, 19, Dean's-yd.

White Friars Club, Anderton's Hotel, Fleet-st.—Instituted for the association of gentlemen connected with literature, science, and arts. The committee elect candidates. Entrance fee, £2 2s. ; subscription, £2 2s.

Whitehall. —(*See* CHAPELS ROYAL.)

Whitehall Club, 47, Parliament-st.—No special qualification. The committee elect, seven are a quorum, and three black balls exclude. The entrance fee is £21 ;

the subscription for town members, £10 10s. ; for country members, or such as do not habitually reside within 50 miles of London, £7 7s.

White's Club, 37, St. James's-st. — Proprietary. Social. Entrance fee, £19 19s. Subscription, £11 11s.

Wimbledon Common, with its neighbourhood, not only affords some of the most beautiful walks within easy reach of London, but is particularly attractive to visitors during the meeting of the National Rifle Association, which takes place annually in July. The shooting itself, except to experts and the friends of competitors, is not particularly interesting, unless it be on such special occasion as the final hour of the last stage of the Queen's Prize, or on the days when Oxford and Cambridge, the Houses of Parliament, the public schools, or the national teams meet at the ranges. As a matter of sight-seeing, the camp itself is well worthy of a long visit. The remarkably successful sanitary arrangements should by no means be overlooked. Always noticeable are the quarters of the London Scottish and of the Victorias, and any visitor having a friend in either of these cheery settlements is to be congratulated. Those who are not so fortunate as to have friends in camp will find in the refreshment department everything they can reasonably require. The commissariat department is one which has always received particular attention from the executive, and is at present confided to the care of Messrs. Bertram & Roberts. The presentation of prizes, which takes place on the last day of the meeting, was at one time followed by a review. The space at the disposal of the commanding officer was very small, and the evolutions, consequently, were of a somewhat confused and unsatisfactory sort. The stations for Wimbledon Camp are at Wimbledon itself, and at Putney (South-Western line, about twenty minutes from Waterloo), both of which are some distance from the scene of action. Plenty of vehicles are always in waiting at the stations at reasonable fares, but it is well that the price to be paid should be distinctly understood before starting. Wimbledon is the only place near London, with the exception of Blackheath, which affords Scotsmen the opportunity ot practising the national game of golf. A pleasant way of reaching Wimbledon is by steamer from any of the London piers to Putney, and the Putney omnibuses also run along the Strand and Piccadilly route to the Middlesex end of Putney-br. The best route, however, from any internal part of London is by the new Putney-br extension of the District line branching from Earl's Court.

Windham Club, 13, St. James's-sq, S.W.—Has for its object to secure a convenient and agreeable place of meeting for a society of gentlemen, all connected with each other by a common bond of literary or personal acquaintance. The election of members is by ballot; the number being limited to 650. No ballot is valid unless twenty members actually vote; and one black ball in ten excludes. The entrance fee is £31 10s., and £1 1s. to the library fund; subscription, £10. Foreign members, £2.

Woods, Forests, and Land Revenues, 1 and 2, Whitehall-pl, S.W.—Hours 10 to 4. NEAREST *Ry. Stns.,* Charing + (S.E. & Dis.); *Omnibus Rtes.,* Whitehall and Strand; *Cab Rank,* Horse Guards.

Yachting.—The principal London Yacht Clubs having Clubhouses in town are The Royal Thames, The Royal London, and The New Thames, which will be found described under their respective heads. For general information in regard to Thames Yacht Clubs, *see* DICKENS'S DICTIONARY OF THE THAMES.

York Club, 8, St. James's-sq, S.W. Proprietary. Established in 1885 as a first-class social and non-political club, open to the various services and to the professions at home, abroad, and in the colonies. A suite of apartments, with entrance in York-st, and distinct from the club, has been provided for the accommodation of members' wives and lady friends. The proprietor and committee have made an agreement that members can obtain for home consumption, wines, &c., at a rate not exceeding seven-and-a-half per cent. over cost price. Election by committee. Entrance fee suspended for the present; subscription, £8 8s. If introduced by a member the entrance fee is £5 5s. only.

Young Men's Christian Association, The.—Founded in 1844, after the meeting of a dozen friends in the room of Mr. George Williams, then an assistant, and afterwards partner, in the house of Messrs. Hitchcock in St. Paul's-churchyard, this most useful association rapidly grew to such proportions, and threw out so many branches all over the world, 3,766 at the present time, that it has long ceased to be connected with London alone. The London head-quarters are at Exeter Hall, in the Strand, which was purchased for the use of the members in 1880 and opened in 1881, where all information may be obtained by intending members

Young Men's Christian Institute, 309, Regent-st, W., the premises formerly occupied by the Polytechnic Institution. Young men between the ages of 16 and 25 are eligible for membership (present limit to number of members 3,500). In consequence of the large number of applications for admission to the institute, the limited number has long since been attained. Candidates can, however, book their names in the secretary's office, and they will be admitted as vacancies occur. Candidates, on booking their names, are required to pay 1s. registration fee, which will constitute their entrance fee when they become members. As vacancies occur candidates will be communicated with by the secretary, according to the date of their registration. The subscriptions are 10s. 6d. annually, or 3s. per quarter, payable in advance, entitling members, amongst other advantages, to free use of the library, reading, social, chess and draught rooms; admission to the Saturday evening popular concerts, entertainments, lectures, &c., at a nominal fee; and the privilege of joining the classes at greatly reduced rates; also to the use of one of the finest gymnasiums in London, with tuition in boxing, fencing, singlesticks, gymnastics, &c., by a skilled instructor. The institute is open every evening—Sundays and Bank Holidays excepted—from 5.30 to 10.30. A Bible class for members and friends (young men only) is conducted every Sunday afternoon, at 3.15. A class for the

study of the Bible is also held on Thursday evenings at 8.30. Evangelistic services, open to all, are held every Sunday evening at 7. and every Wednesday evening at 8.30. Classes for instruction in many of the most useful branches of a general education, as well as in practical matters, both technical and scientific in their nature, are open to all at extremely moderate fees, and at convenient hours in the evening. There are also certain Saturday afternoon and day classes for both sexes. Besides the classes the institute provides for its members many opportunities of amusement, such, for instance, as are afforded by athletic clubs for the practice of football, cricket, rowing, swimming, bicycling, paper-chasing, and lawn-tennis, while in the same direction are the bands—brass and reed, drum and fife, and orchestral—the chess and draughts club, the Volunteer company, the gymnasium, and the Polytechnic Parliament. There is also a good library, and provident habits are encouraged by an accident insurance agency, a savings bank, and a sick fund. In short, there is scarcely anything good for a young man which he will not find as part of the scheme of the Polytechnic Christian Institute The secretary will be glad to afford full information upon any matter connected with the institute, either personally or otherwise.

Zoological Society of London (Map 2). — Candidates for admission must be proposed by three Fellows of the Society (one of whom is acquainted with the candidate), and elected by ballot. Persons elected Fellows pay an admission fee of £5, and an annual contribution of £3, or a composition of £30 in lieu thereof; the whole payment, including the admission fee, being £35. Fellows elected after the 30th of September are not liable to the subscription for the year in which they are elected. Fellows have personal admission to the gardens with two companions daily, upon signing their names in the book at the entrance gate. Fellows of the Society upon payment of their subscription for the current year receive a book of Sat. and a book of Sun. orders. These orders admit two persons to the gardens on each Sat., and two on each Sun. in the year. But the Sat' orders are not available if the Fellow uses his privilege of personally introducing two companions on the same day. Fellows also receive twenty free tickets, each valid for the admission of one adult, any day of the week including Sun., or forty similar tickets, each valid for the admission of one child (under 12 years of age) any day of the week including Sun. The books of orders and the free tickets are not delivered until applied for, but Fellows who have compounded for their annual subscriptions, or have given a banker's order for its regular payment, may give a general order for the delivery of their tickets on the 1st January in every year. Forms for this purpose may be had on application. The wife of a Fellow can exercise all these privileges in his absence, upon payment of £1 1s. per annum. Fellows are entitled to receive all the Society's publications for the year; they are also entitled to purchase the transactions and

other publications of the Society at 25 per cent. less than the price charged to the public. Fellows may also obtain on payment of £1 1s. annually an ivory ticket, which will admit a named person of their immediate family, resident in the same house with them, to the gardens with one companion daily. They may also obtain a transferable ivory ticket, admitting two persons, available throughout the whole period of Fellowship on payment of £10 in one sum. A second similar ticket may be obtained on payment of a further sum of £20. Fellows intending to be absent from the United Kingdom during the space of one year or more, may, upon giving to the secretary notice in writing, have their names placed on the "dormant list" and will be thereupon exempt from the payment of subscription during such absence. Fellows are entitled to attend the annual, general, and scientific meetings of the Society which are held at the

Society's house in Hanover-sc they are also allowed free acces to the library from 10 till 2 o Sat., and from 10 till 5 on othe days, Sun. excepted. The Societ was instituted in 1826 under th auspices of Sir Humphry Davy Bart., Sir Stamford Raffles, an other eminent individuals, fo the advancement of Zoolog: and Animal Physiology, and fo the introduction, exhibition, an acclimatization of subjects of the animal kingdom. The Society received a Charter of Incorpo ration on March 27th, 1829. The office, 3, Hanover-sq, where al communications should be addressed, is open from 10 till 5 and on Sat. from 10 till 2 o'clock. The Secretary is Dr. Philip Lutley Sclater, M.A., F.R.S. *(For description, &c., of the GARDENS OF THE SOCIETY, see Appendix.)* NEAREST *Ry. Stns.*, Portland-rd (Met.), Chalk Farm (North Lon.), and St. John's Wood-rd (Met.); *Omnibus Routes*, Albany-st and Albert-rd ; *Cab Ranks*, at N. exits.

APPENDIX.

The Anglo-Danish Exhibition, South Kensington, opened by the Princess of
Wales on the 14th of May, was organised for the double purpose of celebrating the
Silver Wedding of the Prince and Princess of Wales and for rebuilding the British
Home for Incurables, and will remain open during the summer months. Some of
the old Exhibition buildings have been utilised for the display of various articles
directly connected with the English and Danish nations. An important and attractive
feature of the show will be the *al fresco* illuminations, always popular, and nowhere
seen to greater advantage than in the grounds of the Royal Horticultural Society.
Among the various out-door attractions will be found a very realistic representation
of a Danish Village, inhabited by Danish Peasants, wearing the picturesque costume
of their country, a Switchback Railway, Tobogganing, and an Exhibition of Stuffed
Animals, flanked by a view of the great icebergs of Greenland. Within the building
an interesting feature will be the series of tableaux illustrating Danish fairy lore ; and
there will also be found a Fine Art Gallery, comprising numerous specimens of
Danish Art, and a most interesting collection of the flora and fauna of Denmark and
her dependencies. The Exhibition promises to be a great success, and to attract a
very large number of sight-seers. NEAREST *Railway Station*, South Kensington ;
Omnibus Route and *Cab Rank*, Kensington Road.

Crystal Palace, Sydenham.—This beautiful building—which was opened by
Her Majesty the Queen in June, 1854, and in the construction of which, as all the
world knows, were used the materials of the Great Exhibition Building of 1851—
contains such an immense variety of objects of interest that it is impossible to attempt
any exhaustive account of them in the limited space at our command. Every information respecting the various Courts and their contents, which make the Crystal Palace
a show quite unique in the world, will be found in the official Guide Books, which
are sold in the building, and which are both useful and interesting.

For intending visitors during the present season, the following sketch of the
arrangements may be useful :

Grand Firework Displays, by the famous firm of C. T. Brock & Co., will commence on Her Majesty's Birthday, Thursday, May 24th, and will be continued on
Thursdays throughout the summer. Dramatic Performances by the best London and
Provincial Companies will take place two or three times a week, Tuesdays and
Thursdays being the regular dramatic days. Popular Evening Concerts and Dramatic Entertainments are also given. Illuminated Garden Fêtes on a grand scale
and with novel effects, will be given every evening during the summer, from June 9th,
fifty acres of the most picturesque parts of the grounds being chosen for the

displays of lighting. An important feature will be the *facsimile* of the new Tower Bridge, now being built across the Thames at a cost of three-quarters of a million sterling. This great model (one-quarter size) is erected over the South Fountain Basin, from designs kindly furnished by the Corporation of the City of London ; when illuminated in all its outlines it forms a realistic and striking adjunct to the scene. A grand Pastoral Ballet, Promenade Music by Military Bands, and other suitable outdoor evening attractions will heighten the enjoyment of these unique *al fresco* entertainments. Horticultural Shows of the flowers in season will be held periodically. Bank Holidays will, as usual, be celebrated by an incessant series of popular indoor and outdoor amusements; and other popular Fêtes will be given on dates to be found in the Season Programme, a pamphlet to be obtained gratuitously at the Palace. The Picture Gallery is under the superintendence of Mr. C. Wentworth Wass ; and in connection therewith a Crystal Palace Art Union has been established, membership of which is open to Guinea Season Ticket-holders, on payment of Half a Guinea in addition to the price of the Season Ticket. Amongst the other standing attractions are the Museum, the Aquarium, the Skating Rink, the Toboggan, the Switchback Railway, the Swimming Bath, and the Panorama of the Defence of Rome by the Garibaldians in the grounds, to which an extra charge for admission is made. The great popular Fêtes and Bank Holiday meetings may be recommended to strangers who are curious to know what a great London crowd is like.

The Company's Orchestral Band (which has attained a world-wide reputation), under the conductorship of Mr. August Manns, daily performs selections of classical and popular music, and the Company's Military Band also plays frequently in the building and in the park. Daily performances are given on the Great Handel Organ by Mr. Alfred J. Eyre.

The great national celebration of 1888 will be the Triennial Handel Festival, to be held at the Crystal Palace on the 22nd, 25th, 27th, and 29th of June. These festivals are national in the truest sense of the word, for there is scarcely a remote corner of the United Kingdom which does not send its contingent to the Festival Choir. The immense audiences which these incomparable and unique performances never fail to call together, represent still more perfectly every class and every county in the British Isles, and nearly every journal of standing in the country sends its representative. The executants number 4,000. The width of the great orchestra is 216 feet, or double the diameter of the dome of St. Paul's ; its sides are 60 feet in height, or about the same as the Birmingham Town Hall. The central point of the arch of the roof is 100 feet in height, and the central depth of the orchestra from back to front is about 100 feet. The area is more than 16,000 square feet, or double that of St. James's Hall in London. Yet this enormous structure, capable of seating far more than the whole area of most of the largest concert halls in the world, has an auditorium so truly proportioned to itself that its vast dimensions only appear as in perfect keeping with all the surroundings. To quote a leading journal's comments of twenty years ago : " Where else are we to seek a concert-room that has an orchestra capable of receiving the entire population of many a famous city, and an auditorium in which all the inhabitants of a kingdom may find 'ample space and verge enough'?" Again : "The vast area mellows both the voices and the band, so that while the audience is conscious of overwhelming power of sound, that sound is, if we may so speak, etherealised—it is the *spirituel* of music in chorus." The soloists of the 1888 Festival will include Madame Albani, Madame Nordica, and Madame Valleria ; Madame Patey and Madame Trebelli ; Mr. Edward Lloyd and Mr. Santley. The "Messiah" will be performed on the first day of the Festival (June 25th), a Selection from Handel's sacred and secular works on the second day (June 27th), and "Israel in Egypt" on the third day (June 29th).

The Educational Institutions of the Crystal Palace are among the most important results of one of its original purposes. In general terms they utilise the vast artistic and other collections for educational work, and use them with enormous advantage as a sort of endowment. The highest class of instruction is afforded by distinguished professors ; and for *Ladies* there is a University more complete in its variety than almost any other. It has thirty-three instructors and five hundred students, affording education of the best character. For young men there are at present developed the School of Practical Engineering (1872), probably the most successful and the most practical in the country ; and the Department for the Artistic and Economic Improvement of Land, and Landscape Gardening.

The very extensive Refreshment Department is in the trustworthy hands of Messrs. Bertram & Co., whose arrangements and catering are always excellent, whether for a *recherché* little private dinner, or for the miscellaneous feeding of a Bank Holiday crowd of sixty or seventy thousand persons.

Sunday Dining.—The Directors of the Crystal Palace have renewed their permission for visitors who come to dine, to be admitted to the Palace during the appointed hours on Sundays, in the months of June and July, on production of their visiting cards. The dinners are served in the Garden Rooms of the Palace, whence not only the Gardens, but the great landscape can be contemplated—an unrivalled scene of beauty. The dinners served are of the highest quality and character. Special trains run on Sundays from Victoria on the L. C. & D. and the L. B. & S. C. Railways, for the convenience of those wishing to dine at the Crystal Palace.

The charge for admission to the Palace is, on ordinary days, 1s. This rate, however, is subject to alteration on Special Fête days, and during a portion of the winter the Saturday charge is 2s. 6d. before 5 o'clock and 1s. after. Particulars of alterations, as well as such general arrangements as may from time to time be made, will always be found advertised in the daily papers. Reductions in the prices of admission are made in favour of schools and large parties, and for information on this head, application should be made to the Manager at the Palace.

The most ordinary mode of transit from London to the Palace is by rail. The principal stations to start from are at London Bridge, Victoria, and Addison Road, Kensington, for the London and Brighton Railway, and at Moorgate Street, Holborn Viaduct, Ludgate Hill, St. Paul's, and Victoria for the High Level Line. These are main routes, and on each of them are Junctions through which the passenger from almost any district can make his way to the Crystal Palace—viz., Clapham Junction, Mitcham Junction, Norwood Junction, or Croydon ; New Cross, from East End ; by Willesden Junction, whence the line comes viâ Kensington and Nunhead on the High Level.

Trains run from all Stations on the North London Railway, viâ Willesden Junction and Kensington ; from all Stations on the Metropolitan and St. John's Wood Railways, viâ Kensington, and thence by Brighton Company's Line, or by changing at Farringdon Street, viâ the London, Chatham, and Dover Railway Company's High Level Line ; and from Stations on the East London Line (Liverpool Street, Shoreditch, Whitechapel, Shadwell, Wapping, Rotherhithe, Deptford), viâ New Cross, on the Brighton Company's Line.

Residents on the Lines of the Great Western and London and North-Western Railways can reach the Palace without passing through London, viâ Kensington, by the Brighton Line, and are thus in direct communication with the Palace.

The Great Northern and Midland Railway Companies' trains run to Farringdon Street and Aldersgate Street in connection with the London, Chatham, and Dover High Level Train Service.

The Stations on the South-Western Line are also put in nearly direct communication, viâ Clapham Junction, as well as Brixton. Trains run from Richmond, Kew, &c., at frequent intervals.

The London, Chatham, and Dover Railway (Main Line) has Stations at Penge and Sydenham Hill, the Brighton Company bringing its passengers from the Stations on the Main Line, viâ Croydon, to the Palace, and also to Anerley, Penge, and Sydenham (all within easy walking distance of the Palace).

Thus it will be seen that every part of London, as well as the suburbs, and the country for miles round, is in more or less direct communication with the Crystal Palace.

Trains run frequently on all the various lines.

When the number of visitors is large, special trains are despatched from the principal London Stations as occasion may require. The ordinary fares (exclusive of admission) from London Bridge and Victoria (London, Brighton, and South Coast Railway), and from Ludgate Hill, Blackfriars, and Victoria (London, Chatham, and Dover Railway) to the High Level Station, are as follows :

	1st C. s. d.	2nd C. s. d.	3rd C. s. d.
Single journey (either way)...	1 3	1 0	0 7
Return journey (ditto)	2 0	1 6	1 0

RAILWAY CONVEYANCE, INCLUDING ADMISSION.

From London Bridge and Victoria, by the London, Brighton, and South Coast Railway.

From Victoria, Moorgate Street, Ludgate Hill, and Holborn, by the London, Chatham, and Dover Railway.

SHILLING DAYS.

1st Class Return.	2nd Class Return.	3rd Class Return.
2s. 6d.	2s.	1s. 6d.

Children under Twelve, on all days, half-price.

N.B.—The above Tickets (which include admission) are available for the return journey by either Line.

Reductions in the price of conveyance are made to schools and large bodies, particulars of which may be obtained on application to the General Managers of the London, Brighton, and South Coast, and the London, Chatham, and Dover Railway Companies. Promoters of excursions from the provinces should address for particulars the manager of the line of railway nearest the starting-point.

The Irish Exhibition in London.—Perhaps no Exhibition of recent years is likely to give results more practically useful than the one which is to be opened early in the coming summer at Olympia. Ireland possesses great natural resources and important industries, and a comprehensive display of what she can produce or manufacture will not only be an object lesson of the greatest interest to the people of Great Britain, but will do much to assist the revival of trade in Ireland. The Exhibition is begun under the happiest auspices. It knows neither politics, religion, nor class, but has for its Executive Council and Patrons the most distinguished representative men. Perhaps for no other purpose could nearly 700 names, representing every phase of political, religious, and social life, be brought together in active union. Its great objects are : (1) To place before the English public a clear view of the predominant industries of Ireland ; (2) To awaken public interest in the efforts being made to revive her trade ; (3) To exhibit to the many thousands of persons in England who have never crossed the Irish Channel somewhat of her deeply interesting historical and antiquarian treasures ; (4) To illustrate the worth and significance of Irish Art ; and, finally, to help to moderate prejudices which, frequently tending to fetter the judgment, are at the very root of misunderstandings between people and people. With a view of giving the humble Irish artisan the same opportunity for exhibiting the product of his skill as the large manufacturer, the Council have wisely determined to make no charge for the space occupied in the Exhibition, except in special cases. The Exhibition will be opened on the 4th of June, and remain open until the end of October, and the whole of the vast space at Olympia will be utilised. Among the special features will be a representation of an Irish village, with the veritable peasants at work upon their cottage industries—the dyeing of yarn, making lace, knitting, etc. *Honorary Secretary*, LORD ARTHUR HILL, M.P.

The arrangements for the Refreshment Department are very complete and perfect, and the catering is in the experienced hands of Messrs. Bertram & Co.

The Italian Exhibition, Earl's Court, West Brompton, which occupies the site of the American Exhibition of last year, will continue open until the end of October. It is under the immediate patronage of the King of Italy, and is certain to prove a most attractive show, and to draw to its doors an enormous number of visitors. It is the first Exhibition ever held in a foreign country of products exclusively Italian, and in it will be found many magnificent specimens of Italian painting and sculpture. In addition to these, the scenes from Italy, comprising Roman Market Place and Forum, view of Vesuvius, the Italian Fleet, and naval exhibits, etc., lace and glass making, Italian illuminations, the Alpine switchback railway, and the Italian restaurant and cookery are sure to be of very great interest to all. The grounds are laid out in the Italian style, with terraces in imitation of those in the Borghese Gardens, and will certainly be one of the chief attractions of an eminently attractive exhibition. The Italian Exhibition in London is very easily reached by omnibus or rail, the West Brompton Station of the District Railway being close to the building.

Olympia stands upon twelve acres of ground immediately adjoining the Addison Road Railway Station, and within as small a number of yards of the Hammersmith Road. If, as has been humorously said, one can get to anywhere from Clapham Junction, so it may with equal truth be said of Addison Road. At Addison Road almost every line in the kingdom has through communication, either directly, like the Great Western, the London and North-Western, the London and South-Western, the Chatham and Dover, the Brighton and South Coast, the North London, and the Metropolitan railways—or indirectly, by means of running powers and working arrangements. To the very doors of Olympia may be brought by an all-rail route visitors from every quarter of the country ; and as for expedition, a few examples from lines on which trains stop every few miles on the road will serve. From the principal stations on the metropolitan systems Olympia can be reached in the following time : *East*, Mansion House, in 29 minutes ; Victoria, 18 minutes. *West*, Willesden Junction, in 10 minutes ; Richmond, 21 minutes. *North*, King's Cross, in 29 minutes ; Westbourne Park, 14 minutes. *South*, Crystal Palace, in 34 minutes ; Clapham Junction, 13 minutes.

Next, let us look at the part-rail and part-road route. To the east is the High Street Station, Kensington, and to the west, Hammersmith Station ; on the south lies West Kensington Station, all but a few minutes' walk from Olympia ; and very little further off is Earl's Court Station, whence it is an easy stroll for any who prefer to alight there instead of going right on to Addison Road. Finally, we have the all-road route, which many will doubtless adopt during hot summer days and balmy evenings, unless haste be necessary. From the far east, from the west and the west central, from the north-west and the north, 226 omnibuses pass every few minutes ; and from every other part of the metropolis the Hall may be reached in like manner by probably not more than one change from 'bus to 'bus.

The visitor having, by one or other of the routes described, arrived at Addison Road Station, catches a first, and a most impressive, view of Olympia. Facing to the east is the imposing, but by no means heavy, front of the building. Stretching right and left is a handsome façade built of red brick, with Portland stone cornices and mouldings. The proportions are fine and striking, in the style of the Italian Renaissance, and there is a sufficient amount of decoration to avoid any possible appearance of sameness, sculptured symbolical groups of figures showing conspicuously over the main entrance. The brick and stone work well deserve examination, but *the* feature which will most quickly absorb the attention of the spectator is the glass roof, which rises in a half-circle from the solid walls to a central height of 100 feet. Firm and massive as it undoubtedly is, this graceful glass roof presents a marvellously light and airy appearance. It is built of glass and iron, but so graceful are the lines, that it is difficult to realise that iron sufficiently strong to ensure safety from the heaviest winds forms an element in the construction. It consists of three spans, the centre one of which is actually 170 feet of clear span, with a height from the floor to the crown of fully 100 feet. The significance of this one fact will perhaps be better appreciated if we state that it is 25 feet higher than the Agricultural Hall, Islington, 30 feet higher than the Victoria Station roof, 40 feet higher than the Paddington Station, and as much higher than the Royal Aquarium, 45 feet above the Albert Palace, and as high as the far-famed roof of St. Pancras Station. Another useful comparison is that this single span of 170 feet is greater by 45 feet than the longest over the Islington Agricultural Hall, while the total width covered by the roof is 240 feet, with a total length of 450 feet.

As a "National Agricultural Hall"—to give its full and official title—Olympia is available for cattle, horse, poultry, dairy, dog, and implement shows, and all and any other displays which will illustrate in an instructive way the agricultural industry of this and other countries. For all-round diversion there are to be national and international exhibitions, military tournaments, hippodrome performances, horse-racing, trotting matches, foot-races, assaults-at-arms, and athletics generally ; theatrical performances, concerts, bazaars, balls, picture galleries, and so on. Science will be illustrated not only in the national exhibitions, but by special displays demonstrating the progress made in inventions, engineering, electric lighting, and other branches of science. Railways, traders and farmers, sportsmen, and other classes will have their own expositions ; circuses will from time to time occupy the building ; youth and beauty will be provided with lawn-tennis and racquets, archery, and other *al fresco* amusements ; public men will find ample facility for holding meetings or banquets ; and the benevolently inclined will be enabled to indulge at all times in that fashionable form of philanthropy—charity fêtes.

There are five and a half acres of gardens for the open-air recreation of the multitudes who will flock to this monster establishment. Connected with the Great Hall by a short subway, these grounds will be laid out in the most pleasant and useful style, with as much open green turf as possible, on which the bandstand, châlets, and refreshment pavilions will be constructed, and many other accessories provided to adapt the gardens to open-air fêtes, concerts, and garden parties. In the summer evenings, with the strains of music wafted through the air, and the lawn and walks thronged with youth and beauty and fashion, the gardens of Olympia will form a paradise of pleasure which Londoners will not be slow to appreciate.

Theatres.—The following is a complete list of the various London Theatres, with the ordinary prices of admission and the separate entrances to the different parts of each house. Covent Garden and Her Majesty's Theatres are omitted, as the prices and arrangements for

	Name.	Private Boxes. Entrance.	Stalls. Entrance.	Balcony. Entrance.	Dress Circle. Entrance.	
1	ADELPHI	411, Strand. £1 1s. to £3 3s.	411, Strand. 10s.	None.	411, Strand. 5s.	1
2	ALHAMBRA (Now a Music Hall.)	Leicester-sq.	Leicester-sq.	Leicester-sq.	Leicester-sq.	2
3	ASTLEY'S	Westminster-br-rd £1 1s. to £5 5s.	Westminster-br-rd 2s. 6d.	Westminster-br-rd. 1s. 6d.	Westminster-br-rd 4s.	3
4	AVENUE	Northumb.-aven. £2 2s. to £4 4s.	Northumb.-aven. 10s. 6d.	Northumb.-aven. 7s. 6d.	Northumb.-aven. 6s.	4
5	BRITANNIA	High-st, Hoxton. £1 1s. or 2s. each.	High-st, Hoxton. 1s.	None.	None.	5
6	COMEDY	Panton-st, Hymkt. £2 2s. and £3 3s.	Panton-st, Hymkt. 10s.	None.	Panton-st, Hymkt. 6s.	6
7	COURT	Corner Sloane-sq.	Corner Sloane-sq.	None.	Corner Sloane-sq.	7
8	CRITERION	Pcadly. £1 11s.6d., £2 2s. and £3 3s.	Piccadilly. 10s. 6d.	None.	Piccadilly. 7s.	8
9	DRURY LANE	Catherine-st. £1 1s. to £5 5s.	Catherine-st. 7s.	Catherine-st. 3s.	Catherine-st. 5s.	9
10	ELEPHANT & CASTLE	New Kent-rd. 10s. 6d. to £2 2s.	New Kent-rd. 1s.	None.	New Kent-rd. 2s.	10
11	EMPIRE (Now a Music Hall.)	Leicester-sq.	Leicester-sq.	Leicester-sq.	None.	11
12	GAIETY	Strand. £1 1s. to £3 3s.	Strand. 10s.	Strand. 5s.	None.	12
13	GARRICK	Leman-st.	Leman-st.	Leman-st.	None.	13
14	GLOBE	Nwcstle-st,Strand. £1 1s. to £3 3s.	Nwcstle-st, Strand 10s. 6d.	Nwcstle-st, Strand 6s.	Nwcstle-st, Strand 4s.	14
15	GRAND	High-st.	High-st.	High-st.	High-st.	15
16	HAYMARKET	Haymarket. £1 1s. to £4 4s.	Haymarket. 10s.	Haymarket. 7s.	Haymarket. 5s. and 4s.	16
17	IMPERIAL (Now part of Royal Aquarium.)					17
18	LYCEUM	Wellington-st. £1 11s.6d. to £4 4s.	Wellington-st.	None.	Wellington-st. 6s.	18
19	MARYLEBONE	Church-st. 10s. 6d. to £1 1s.	Church-st. Reserved Boxes, 2s.	Church-st. 1s.	Church-st. 1s. 6d.	19
20	NOVELTY *					20
21	NEW SADLR'S. WELLS	St. John's-ter. £2 10s.	St. John's-ter. 7s. 6d.	St. John's-ter. 4s.	None.	21
22	OLYMPIC	Drury-la. £1 1s. to £3 3s.	Drury-la. 7s. 6d.	None.	Drury-la. 5s.	22
23	OPERA COMIQUE	Strand. £1 1s. to £3 3s.	Strand. 10s.	Strand. 6s., 5s., and 4s.	None.	23
24	PAVILION	Whitechapel-rd. £1 1s.	Whitechapel-rd. 1s.	None.	Whitechapel-rd. 1s. 6d.	24
25	PRINCESS'S	Oxford-st. £1 1s. to £8 8s.	Oxford-st. 10s.	Oxford-st. Orches. Stalls, 5s.	Oxford-st. 5s.	25
26	PRINCE OF WALES'S	Coventry-st. £2 2s. to £3 3s.	Coventry-st. 10s. 6d.	Coventry-st. 7s. 6d.	Coventry-st. 6s.	26
27	ROYALTY	73, Dean-st, Soho. £2 2s. and £3 3s.	73, Dean-st, Soho. 10s.	None.	73, Dean-st, Soho. 5s.	27
28	ST. JAMES'S	King-st. £1 10s.6d. to £3 3s.	King-st. 10s. 6d.	None.	King-st. 6s.	28
29	SAVOY	Beaufort-bdgs, for foot-passengers Thames Embank. for carriages. £2 2s. and £3 3s.	Beaufort-bdgs, for foot-passengers Thames Embank. for carriages. 10s. 6d.	Beaufort-bdgs, for foot-passengers Thames Embank. for carriages. 6s. and 7s. 6d.	Beaufort-bdgs, for foot-passengers Thames Embank. for carriages. 3s.	29

* Now available for Amateur Performances.

seating the audience vary according to the entertainment to which, for the time being, they may be devoted. The Court, Garrick, and Grand Theatres being closed at the time of going to press, we are unable to include their prices :—

Theatres—Continued.

	Upper Circle. Entrance.	Pit Stalls. Entrance.	Pit. Entrance.	Amphitheatre. Entrance.	Gallery. Entrance.	
1	411, Strand. 3s.	None.	411, Strand. 2s.	None.	Bull Inn-ct. 1s.	1
2	None.	Leicester-sq.	Leicester-sq.	None.	Leicester-sq.	2
3	None.	Westminster-br-rd. 2s.	Westminster-br-rd. 1s.	Westminster-br-rd. 1s. 6d.	Palace-rd. 6d.	3
4	Northumb.-avenue. 4s. and 3s.	None.	Northumb.-avenue 2s.	None.	Northumb.-avenue 1s.	4
5	High-st, Hoxton. 1s.	High-st, Hoxton. 1s.	High-st, Hoxton. 6d.	None.	High-st, Hoxton. 3d.	5
6	Panton-st, Haymkt. 4s.	None.	Oxenden-st. 2s.	Panton-st. 1s. 6d.	Oxenden-st. 1s.	6
7	Corner Sloane-sq.	None.	Corner Sloane-sq.	Corner Sloane-sq.	Corner Sloane-sq.	7
8	None.	None.	Piccadilly.	Jermyn-st. 2s. 6d.	Jermyn-st. 1s.	8
9	Catherine-st. 4s.	None.	Russell-st and Vinegar-yd. 2s.	Russell-st and Vinegar-yd. 1s.	Vinegar-st. 6d.	9
10	New Kent-rd. 1s.	None.	New Kent-rd. 6d.	Caroline-pl. 6d.	Caroline-pl. 3d.	10
11	Leicester-sq.	Leicester-sq.	Leicester-sq.	Leicester-sq.	Lisle-st.	11
12	Strand. 3s.	None.	Catherine-st. 2s.	Catherine-st. 1s.	None.	12
13	None.	Leman-st.	Leman-st. 2s.	None.	Tenter-st-east.	13
14	None.	None.	Wych-st. 2s.	Wych-st. 1s. 6d.	Wych-st.	14
15	None.	High-st.	High-st.	High-st.	High-st.	15
16	Haymarket. 2s. 6d.	None.	None.	None.	Haymarket. 1s.	16
17						17
18	Wellington-st. 3s.	None.	Strand. 2s.	Wellington-st. 2s. 6d.	Exeter-st. 1s.	18
19	Church-st. 1s.	Church-st. 1s.	Church-st. 6d.	None.	Little Church-st. 4d.	19
20						20
21	St. John's-ter. 2s.	Arlington-st. 2s.	Arlington-st. 1s.	Arlington-st. 1s.	Arlington-st. 6d.	21
22	Drury-la. 4s.	None.	Maypole-alley. 2s.	Maypole-alley. 1s. 6d.	Maypole-alley. 1s.	22
23	Holywell-st and Wych-st. 2s. 6d.	None.	Wych-st. 2s.	Holywell-st and Wych-st, 1s. 6d.	Wych-st. 1s.	23
24	None.	None.	Whitechapel-rd. 6d.	None.	Baker's-row. 3d.	24
25	None.	None.	Winsley-st. 2s.	Winsley-st. 1s. 6d.	Winsley-st. 1s.	25
26	None	Oxenden-st. 4s.	Oxenden-st. 2s. 6d.	None.	Oxenden-st. 1s.	26
27	73, Dean-st, Soho. 3s.	None.	73, Dean-st, Soho. 2s.	73, Dean-st, Soho. 1s.	73, Dean-st, Soho. 6d.	27
28	King-st. 4s.	None.	King-st. 2s. 6d.	None.	King-st. 1s.	28
29	None.	None.	Beaufort-bdgs, for foot-passengers. 2s. 6d.	Beaufort-bdgs, for foot-passengers. 2s.	Carting-la, 89, Strand. 1s.	29

	Name.	Private Boxes.	Stalls.	Balcony.	Dress Circle.	
		Entrance.	Entrance.	Entrance.	Entrance.	
30	STANDARD	203, High-st, E. 10s. 6d. to £3 3s.	203, High-st, E. 4s.	203, High-st, E. 3s.	None.	30
31	STRAND............	Strand. £2 2s. and £3 3s.	Strand. 10s.	Strand. 6s.	Strand. 5s.	31
32	SURREY	Blackfriars-rd. £1 1s. to £3 3s.	Blackfriars-rd. 5s.	None.	Blackfriars-rd. 3s.	32
33	TERRY'S............	105. Strand. £1 1s. to £3 3s.	105, Strand. 10s. 6d.	105, Strand. 7s. 6d.	105, Strand. 3s.	33
34	TOOLE'S (*late* FOLLY)	K. Will.-st, Char+ £1 1s. to £3 3s.	K. Will.-st, Char+ 10s.	None.	K. Will.-st, Char+ 6s.	34
35	VAUDEVILLE	404, Strand. £2 2s. to £3 3s. £2 2s.	404, Strand. 10s. and 7s. 6d.	404, Strand. 5s.	404, Strand. 6s. 3s.	35

Moore and Burgess Minstrels.—Originally known as the Christy Minstrels from the fact of the company having been founded by the late E. P. Christy, of New York, in 1842. After making several tours through the United States Christy opened at Palmer's Opera House, New York, in 1846, whence he migrated to the Mechanics' Hall, 472, Broadway, where he remained permanently until 1854. Crowds nightly thronged the hall, and from 1847 to 1854 Christy literally coined money, bought horses, owned Brougham's Lyceum Theatre, speculated largely in stocks, lived in splendour, in fact became the lion of the day. At the time of his death, in 1862, he was worth 200,000 dollars. For some time prior to his death he became the prey of monomania, and fancied that the Confederates would capture the City of New York, and confiscate the whole of his enormous property; thus, in the midst of all his wealth, he thought of nothing but probable penury. The best efforts of his friends failed to eradicate this impression, and he finally committed suicide by jumping from the second storey of his own mansion in East 18th Street, New York.

On Christy's retirement from the management, in 1854, the company was carried on by John Raynor, who conceived the idea of bringing it to England, which he accordingly did in 1857, opening at the St. James's Theatre, where the undertaking was crowned with very great success; from the St. James's Theatre the company went to the Polygraphic Hall, now Toole's Theatre. After a long and prosperous season there this company made a lengthy tour of the provinces, everywhere meeting with success. In 1860 Raynor disposed of his interest to Messrs. Collins and Nash, two members of the company, who continued the undertaking until 1864, when Collins and Nash being desirous of returning to their native country, Mr. George Moore and Mr. J. P. Crocker undertook its future management, and continued the tour until June, 1865. About this period they were induced by Mr. Frederick Burgess to revisit London, the scene of their earliest triumph in this country. They accordingly opened at the St. James's Hall on the 18th of September, 1865, where they have continued to give their entertainment down to the present period. It is worthy of remark that the Moore and Burgess Minstrels have given upwards of 9,000 consecutive performances at St. James's Hall. For many years they have given nine performances in each week throughout the year; while at each succeeding Christmas season they have been compelled to remove from their own Hall into the larger one above, in order to accommodate the great influx of visitors. When the Minstrels originally appeared at the St. James's Theatre in 1857, the company comprised but eight members; at the present time forty-two performers are engaged.

Performances are given every evening at 8, and on Monday, Wednesday, and Saturday afternoons at 3; and the prices of admission are: Fauteuils, 5s.; Stalls, 3s.; Area, 2s.; Gallery, 1s.

Tussaud's Wax Works.—Almost as well known as that of Mrs. Jarley, "the delight of the nobility and gentry," is the name of Madame Tussaud, the founder of the collection of wax-works which has been for considerably more than half a century one of the most deservedly popular of all the London shows. There has been hardly

Theatres—*Continued.*

	Upper Circle.	Pit Stalls.	Pit.	Amphitheatre.	Gallery.	
	Entrance.	Entrance.	Entrance.	Entrance.	Entrance.	
30	203, High st, E. 2s.	204, High-st, E. & Gt. Eastern-st. 1s.	Great Eastern-st. 6d.	204, High-st, E. 1s. 6d.	Great Eastern-st. & Holywell-st, 4d.	30
31	Strand. 3s.	None.	Surrey-st. 6d.	Strand. 1s.	None.	31
32	Blackfriars-rd. 2s.	None.	Blackfriars-rd. 6d.	None.	Blackfriars-rd. 6d.	32
33	105, Strand. 4s.	None.	Savoy-buildings. 2s. 6d.	None.	Savoy-buildings. 1s.	33
34	K.Will.-st,Char ✠ 3s.	None.	K.Will.-st, Char ✠ 2s. 6d.	K.Will.-st,Char ✠ 1s.	None.	34
35	404, Strand. 2s. 6d.	None.	404, Strand. 2s.	None.	Lumley-ct. 1s.	35

a character of modern times who has achieved conspicuous eminence, notoriety, or infamy, without finding a place in the Tussaud collection, and the waning popularity of many a once distinguished name has been oddly emphasised by its disappearance from the catalogue. An excellent collection of the Sovereigns of England in their habits as they lived gives also a certain educational interest to the show, while the undoubtedly genuine relics of Napoleon I. are of very remarkable interest. They comprise the military carriage in which he made the campaign of Russia, and which was captured on the evening of the Battle of Waterloo, the camp bedstead which he used for seven years at St. Helena, a favourite garden-chair, and an infinity of other curious relics.

Indeed, people who like to gaze upon mementoes of celebrated men and places would find themselves quite at home at Madame Tussaud's, where are preserved all sorts of queer odds and ends, such, for instance, as the Coronation Robes of George IV., garments of Lord Nelson, the Duke of Wellington, and Joseph Bonaparte, while among the more doubtful exhibits may be mentioned the Shirt of Henry IV. of France, worn by him when stabbed by Ravaillac, and the knife with which Margaret Nicholson attempted to assassinate George III. ; and, requiring a still larger grain of salt, a " Piece of the Cloth of Gold, from the field of that name, time of Henry VIII.," to quote the catalogue, which seems to have no doubt about it. Very grim and a trifle horrible is the Chamber of Horrors, which contains counterfeit presentments of some of the most desperate criminals of late years, with a gallows to suggest the means by which the world got quit of them. There are also some particularly blood-curdling casts of heads dating from the first French Revolution, and the original Guillotine, bought by Madame Tussaud from Samson, grandson to the "Monsieur de Paris" of the time of the Terror. There is no better place in London for children than Madame Tussaud's, but parents and guardians will do well to remember that the contents of the Chamber of Horrors are somewhat over-strong meat for babes. The Exhibition was for many years situated in Baker-street, over the Bazaar ; but in 1884 it was removed to handsome new rooms, specially built for its reception in the Marylebone-road. The price of admission is One Shilling, with Sixpence extra to the Napoleon Room and the Chamber of Horrors. Children half-price. The nearest Railway Station is that of the Metropolitan Railway, Baker-street, which is also a junction of the St. John's Wood and North of London systems. Omnibuses run along the Marylebone-road, and the "Atlas" and "City Atlas" lines run along Baker-street close by.

Zoological Gardens.— The Gardens of the Zoological Society of London contain the largest and by far the best arranged collection of wild beasts, birds, and reptiles in the world, and, being themselves laid out in the best taste and kept in the most perfect order, afford the best place of open-air amusement to be found in London.

They are situated at the north end of the Regent's Park, and may be approached by the omnibuses which run from Camberwell viâ the Strand and Regent-street to the "York and Albany," at the Gloucester Gate-bridge over the Regent's Canal ; by omnibus running between Camden Town and Westbourne-grove, along the Albert-road ; by railway to the St. John's Wood-road station of the Metropolitan Railway, which is 1460 yards from the main entrance ; the Portland-road station, which is the most convenient for the entrance in the Park ; or to the Chalk Farm Station of the North London Railway, which is 1480 yards from the main entrance. The cab fare from Charing Cross is 1s. 6d.

The Gardens are divided into three portions, of which the largest and most important is that which adjoins the open space and broad walk of the Park, and in which are the main entrance in the Outer Circle and the south entrance in the Broad Walk. Here the principal attraction is the magnificent lion house, two hundred and thirty feet long and seventy feet wide, in which are fourteen capacious dens, and plenty of space for spectators, although at feeding-time on crowded days the resources of even this fine hall are taxed to the uttermost. Close by, and a little to the westward, is the sea-lions' pond, which is always a centre of attraction, and a little further to the north-west is the monkey house, built in 1864, and so arranged that its inmates disport themselves in what is practically a light and elegant conservatory. On the left of the Park entrance is another handsome new building, only completed in the winter of 1883-84, and devoted to the fine collection of reptiles. Also in this division of the Gardens is a conveniently arranged refreshment room, and visitors may be recommended to try the table-d'hôte dinner, which they can have served under the shade of the verandah, a very agreeable institution on a pleasant summer evening. The second division of the Gardens is reached by a tunnel under the drive in the Outer Circle, the principal buildings being those devoted respectively to the parrots, the elephants and rhinoceroses, the hippopotami, and the giraffes. From here by a bridge facing the road which leads from the tunnel is approached what is called the North Garden, containing the tortoise house and the new insectarium. Here also is the north entrance, which is distant only 873 yards from the Chalk Farm Station, and 1494 yards from the St. John's Wood Station.

The Gardens are open daily except Sunday from 9 a.m. to sunset. On Sundays members and ticket-holders only are admitted from 1 p.m., except at the main entrance, which is open at 9 a.m.

The charge for admission is one shilling, except on Mondays and at certain holiday seasons, when it is reduced one-half, the charge for children being always sixpence. A military band plays on Saturdays during the season from 4 to 6 p.m., and this is the time for those visitors who wish to see the Gardens at their best as a promenade. Those who like having plenty of elbow-room, and wish, at their leisure, to study the manners and customs of the inhabitants of the "Zoo," will do well to select the morning.

The feeding times of the animals, when of course they hold their most crowded receptions, are as follows : the pelicans, 2.30 p.m.; the otters, 3 p.m. ; the eagles (except Wednesdays), 3.30 p.m.; the lions and tigers, 4 p.m.; and the sea-lions, 4.30 p.m. In November, December, January, and February, the lions and tigers are fed at 3 p.m., and the sea-lions at 3.30 p.m. For a detailed and interesting account of all objects of interest to be found in the Gardens, see the excellent "Guide" published by Messrs. Bradbury & Agnew, and sold in the Gardens, price sixpence.

NEAREST *Railway Stations*, Portland-road (Met.) ; Chalk Farm (North London) ; and St. John's Wood-road (Met.). *Omnibus Routes*, Albany-street and Albert-road. *Cab Ranks* at main and north entrances, and at the "York and Albany."

Baedeker's London and its Environs 1900

This comprehensive guide takes us on a tour of the world's greatest city at the close of the Victorian era. All major sites are described in detail. There are 33 walking tours including The City, St. Paul's, Regent's Park Zoo and London Docks and a dozen by river steamer and train including The Crystal Palace, Windsor Castle and as far afield as Rochester and St.Albans. Each is packed with directions, historical facts, travel arrangements and prices. The advice on etiquette, security, accommodation, travel to and within Britain and recommended shops paint a fascinating picture of life a century ago. There is a history of London. Over 500 pages, a fold out map, plans of notable buildings and 31 pages of coloured street plans, printed facsimile from the original edition. A source of fascination for anyone wishing to explore London a century ago.

Murray's Handbook of Modern London 1860

Although essentially a guide for visitors, this book is also an excellent read containing well written descriptions of pretty all a tourist might wish to know if he were visiting London a century and a half ago. Packed with well researched facts and statistics we can wander around the streets, markets and fine buildings being told who lived where, what treasures were be found within, the volume of trade conducted in the markets, the number of patients in the hospitals and the courses available at universities and colleges. We also visit prisons, exhibitions, clubs and societies, residences of the famous, sites associated with remarkable events and witness the diverse commodities passing through the docks. Much can also be learned about how daily life then differed from ours today. Some things were better such as the workings of the Post Office 'letters posted before 6 in the evening would be delivered the same evening within 3 miles'. But much was worse such as the appalling sewage arrangements. A jewel of a book for anyone wishing to explore London during the first half of Victoria's reign.

Bacon's up to date map of London, 1902

The reign of no other monarch saw such extensive changes as those which took place when Queen Victoria was on the throne. This street map of London originally published at the end of her long life provides a perfect contrast with our map of London 1843. Gone are the orchards of Chelsea and the marshes of The Isle of Dogs. Earl's Court and other villages lying beyond the built up area at the beginning of her reign have now been swallowed by the expanding conurbation. There is massive development and activity on the lower reaches of the Thames where there is much evidence of the new docks servicing the needs of both the Empire and the mother country. Many of the underground railway lines we know today have already been built. But there was much more to be completed during the coming century and places such as Willesden and Herne Hill were still surrounded by countryside in 1902.

Old House Books, Moretonhampstead, Devon, TQ13 8PA. UK
www.OldHouseBooks.co.uk info@OldHouseBooks.co.uk 01647 440707

London Stories 1910

These stories first appeared as magazine articles before the First World War. During the previous century travel had become the great occupation. Whether a Grand Tour of Europe's finest cities or a mere train journey out of London to the coast of Kent it was now possible for everyone and a plethora of guide books appeared. But they all concentrated on the places and not on the people. John O' London (a pen name which says it all!) recognised that nowhere is anywhere without the people who lived there and the extraordinary happenings, traditions and curiosities that coloured their lives. He introduces us to The Duke of Wellington's outspoken boot maker, the 'apple woman' who annexed Hyde Park and the recluse who weighed the world. We read of the curious wanderings of Cromwell's head, the semaphore system which sent signals from the Admiralty to Deal in less than a minute and a fatal duel fought in Kensington for the most absurd reason. We hear of a fire at Drury Lane Theatre, military executions in Hyde Park, visit Dr Johnson's favourite pub and read a letter to The Times that prompted the building of Nelson's column. London Stories is a cornucopia of anecdotal gems that allow us to wander through the past and meet some of the people who helped define the greatest city the world had ever seen.

Enquire Within upon Everything 1890

In the wake of the Industrial Revolution the population swiftly developed a thirst for knowledge about the myriad of new goods and ideas that were becoming available. But before the days of television, newspaper advertising and junk mail how did people get to know about everything? Over a million people solved the problem by buying a copy of this book which caused a publishing sensation in Victorian Britain. Because it explained so much about so many different aspects of life it continues to provide a very enjoyable and informative peep into the lifestyle of our forebears.

In 2775 entries the enquiring Victorian learns to tell if food is fresh and when it is in season; how to dance; the difference between dialects; correcting grammar and spelling; the rules of games and puzzles; hints on etiquette; kitchen and household hints and recipes; cures for scores of ailments including rheumatism and baldness; the origins of Christian names; first aid; employment and rental regulations; keeping fit; dressmaking and embroidery; births, marriages and deaths; personal conduct as well as scores of others.

We know when and where the Victorians lived. This fascinating book explains much about how they lived.

Old House Books, Moretonhampstead, Devon, TQ13 8PA. UK
www.OldHouseBooks.co.uk info@OldHouseBooks.co.uk 01647 440707